Figure 12.2 The Efficient Sustainable Yield for a Fishery

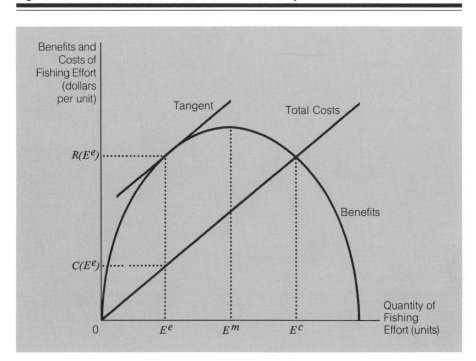

Figure 14.3 Cost-Effective Allocation of a Uniformly Mixed Pollutant

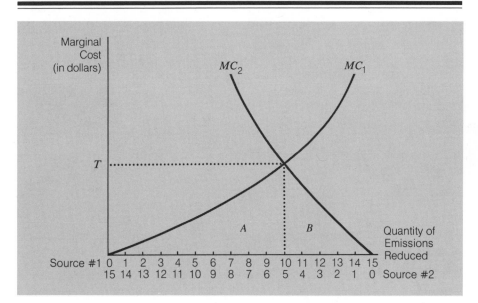

Environmental and Natural Resource Economics

Second Edition

Tom Tietenberg
Colby College

Scott, Foresman and Company
Glenview, Illinois
Boston   London

To Florence M. and Harry H. Tietenberg who provided me with a healthy environment conducive to growth.

Acknowledgments for literary selections and illustrations appear at the back of the book on p. 559, which is an extension of the copyright page.

Library of Congress Cataloging-in-Publication Data
Tietenberg, Thomas H.
  Environmental and natural resource economics.

  Bibliography: p.
  Includes index.
  1. Environmental policy.   2. Natural resources–
Government policy.   3. Raw materials–Government policy.
I. Title.
HC79.E5T525   1988   333.7   87-23250
ISBN 0-673-18945-7

123456-KPF-929190898887

PREFACE

The central concept of *Environmental and Natural Resource Economics* remains unchanged in this new edition. It attempts to bring those who are only beginning the study of environmental and natural resource economics close to the frontiers of knowledge. Although it is designed to be accessible to students who have completed only a two-semester introductory course in economics or a one-semester introductory microeconomics course, it has been successfully used in several institutions in lower-level and upper-level undergraduate courses as well as lower-level graduate courses. Intertemporal optimization is handled within a discrete-time, mathematical programming framework and all mathematics other than simple algebra is relegated to appendices. Graphs and numerical examples are used to provide an intuitive understanding of the principles suggested by the math and the reasons for their validity. The feedback I have received from the first edition suggests that this intuition is firmly grounded and that students are able to apply these principles in contexts other than those specifically covered in the text. In this edition I have tried to retain the strengths that seem particularly valued by users, while expanding the coverage, clarifying some of the more difficult arguments, and updating the material to include the very latest developments.

The structure and topical coverage of this book facilitates its use in a variety of contexts. For a survey course in environmental and natural resource economics, all chapters are appropriate, though many of us have found that there is somewhat more material in the book than can be covered adequately in a quarter or even a semester. This provides some flexibility for the instructor to choose those topics which best fit his or her course design. A one-term course in natural resource economics could be based on Chapters 1–13 and 21–23. A brief introduction to environmental economics could be added by including Chapter 14. A single-term course in environmental economics could be structured around Chapters 1–4 and 14–20. Chapter 6 could be added if a brief introduction to natural economics seemed desirable.

This edition greatly expands the coverage of both environmental and natural resource economics. Three new chapters have been added: Water Scarcity, Forest Resources, and Regional and Global Air Pollutants. Several previously included topics have received more attention, including benefit estimation, substitution and the vulnerability of imports, the economics of enforcement, the economics of nonpoint water pollution control, the emissions trading program, the greenhouse effect, and economic incentives and technological change. New topics covered in this edition include: rent seeking and government failure, estimates of the costs of raising children, conservation and load management by electric utilities, EPA's lead banking program, the efficiency of vehicle inspection programs for reducing mobile emissions, market power in emission permit markets, and the control of hazardous air pollutants. New boxed examples highlight special topics including: nuclear winter, net benefit analysis of the ambient air quality standard for particulates, tropical deforestation, forest death in Germany, damages from acid rain, and the role of ethics and risk-aversion in coping with the greenhouse effect. All data and references to governing legislation have been updated, and the text incorporates references to significant recent environmental and natural resource "events" such as the toxic accidents in Bhopal, India; Sevesco, Italy; and Basel, Switzerland; as well as the Chernobyl nuclear disaster and the most recent developments within OPEC.

The second edition retains the strong policy orientation of the first edition. Though there is a great deal of theory and empirical evidence discussed, both are motivated by the desire to increase understanding of intriguing policy problems and discussed in the context of those problems. This explicit integration of research and policy within each chapter avoids the frequently encountered problem in applied economics textbooks in which the theory developed in earlier chapters is only loosely connected to the rest of the book.

This is an economics book, but it goes beyond economics. Insights from the natural and physical sciences, literature and political science, as well as other disciplines are scattered liberally through the text. In some cases these references raise unresolved issues which economic analysis can help resolve, while in others they affect the structure of the economic analysis or provide a contrasting point of view. They have an important role to play in overcoming the tendency to accept the material uncritically at a superficial level by highlighting those characteristics that make the economics approach unique.

Tom Tietenberg

ACKNOWLEDGMENTS

Perhaps the most rewarding part of writing this textbook has been the fact that it has put me in touch with so many thoughtful people I had not previously met. I very much appreciate the rather large number of users who took the time to write, pointing out areas of particular strength or areas where coverage could be expanded in this edition. I have been overwhelmed by the support that my approach has received from both faculty and students. One can begin to understand the magnitude of my debt to my colleagues by glancing at the several hundred names in the lists of references contained in the Name Index. Because their research contributions make this an exciting field, full of insights worthy of being shared, my task in writing this textbook was made easier and a lot more fun than it might otherwise have been.

I am particularly indebted to the large number of faculty who have made suggestions for improvement. Valuable comments were received during various stages of the writing from:

Maurice Ballabon	Baruch College
Richard V. Butler	Trinity College
Charles J. Chicchetti	University of Wisconsin, Madison
Jon Conrad	Cornell University
Gregory B. Christainsen	California State University, Hayward
Maureen L. Cropper	University of Maryland
John H. Cumberland	University of Maryland
Randall K. Filer	Brandeis University
Anthony C. Fisher	University of California, Berkeley
Marvin Frankel	University of Illinois, Urbana-Champaign
A. Myrick Freeman, III	Bowdoin College
A. R. Gutowsky	California State University, Sacramento
W. Eric Gustafson	University of California, Davis
John J. Hovis	University of Maryland
Craig Infanger	University of Kentucky
James R. Kahn	State University of New York, Binghamton
Dwight Lee	University of Georgia
Randolph M. Lyon	University of Texas, Austin
Giadomenico Majone	Harvard University
David Martin	Davidson College
Nicholas Mercuro	University of New Orleans
David E. Merrifield	Western Washington University
Frederic C. Menz	Clark University
Thomas C. Noser	University of Alabama
Lloyd Orr	Indiana University

J. Barkely Rosser, Jr.	James Madison University
Frederic O. Sargent	University of Vermont
W. Douglas Shaw	Williams College
James S. Shortle	Pennsylvania State University
Leah J. Smith	Swarthmore College
Joe B. Stevens	Oregon State University
Myles Wallace	Clemson University
Anthony Yezer	The George Washington University

I am indebted to them for their close reading and for their willingness to share ideas on how the manuscript could be improved.

I have been fortunate to have been aided by a large number of extremely capable student research-assistants over the years. Judi Greene, Alison Jones, Susan French, Fidel Fajardo, Elaine Johnson, Diane Peterec, Susan Charrette, Vicki Howe, Marc Gordon, Faith Delaney, Tom Menzies, Margaret Wimmer, Jill Stasz Harris and Melissa Raffoni have all helped to shape this book.

A special word of thanks is also due to my editors Carol Leon and George Lobell. Working with them has been a pleasure.

Finally, I would like to say a deeply felt word of thanks to my family for putting up with a father and husband who spent more time writing than they deserve. I couldn't have done it without their support.

CONTENTS

4   *REGULATING THE MARKET: INFORMATION AND UNCERTAINTY*   *64*

5   *THE POPULATION PROBLEM*   *90*

**6   THE ALLOCATION OF DEPLETABLE AND
RENEWABLE RESOURCES: AN OVERVIEW   *113***

**7   DEPLETABLE, NONRECYCLABLE ENERGY
RESOURCES: OIL, GAS, COAL, AND URANIUM   *137***

CHAPTER ONE

Visions of the Future

From the arch of the bridge to which his Guide has carried him, Dante now sees the Diviners . . . coming slowly along the bottom of the Fourth Chasm. By help of their incantations and evil agents, they had endeavoured to pry into the Future which belongs to the Almighty alone, and now their faces are painfully twisted the contrary way; and being unable to look before them, they are forced to walk backwards.
DANTE ALIGHIERI, *Divine Comedy: The Inferno,*
TRANSLATED BY CARLYLE (1867)

INTRODUCTION

The Self-Extinction Premise

About the time the American colonies became independent, Edward Gibbon completed his monumental *The History of the Decline and Fall of the Roman Empire.* In a particularly poignant passage which opens the last chapter of his opus, he recreates a scene in which the learned Poggius, a friend, and two servants ascend the Capitoline Hill after the fall of Rome. They are awed by the contrast between what Rome once was and what Rome had become:

> In the time of the poet it was crowned with the golden roofs of a temple; the temple is overthrown, the gold has been pillaged, the wheel of fortune has accomplished her revolution, and the sacred ground is again disfigured with thorns and brambles. . . . The forum of the Roman people, where they assembled to enact their laws and elect their magistrates, is now enclosed for the cultivation of potherbs, or thrown open for the reception of swine and buffaloes. The public and private edifices, that were founded for eternity lie prostrate, naked, and broken, like the limbs of a mighty giant; and the ruin is the more visible, from the stupendous relics that have survived the injuries of time and fortune. [Vol. 6, pp. 650–51]

What could cause the demise of such a grand and powerful society? Gibbon weaves a complex thesis to answer this question, suggesting ultimately that the seeds for Rome's destruction were sown by the Empire itself.[1] Though Rome finally succumbed to such external forces as fires and invasions, its vulnerability was based upon internal weakness.

The premise that societies germinate the seeds of their own destruction has long fascinated scholars. In one historically significant study in the early nineteenth century, Thomas Malthus foresaw a time when the urge to reproduce would create a situation in which population growth would outstrip the growth of food supply, resulting in starvation and death.

The 1970s and 1980s have ushered in a revival of interest in Malthus' premise, mainly because of the growing number of writers who believe that modern society has embarked on a path that leads to self-destruction. Modern ecologists, for example, have suggested that the environment possesses a unique "carrying capacity" to support humans, and once that capacity is exceeded, widespread ecological disruption occurs with disastrous consequences for humanity.[2] The focus is no longer on individual societies, but rather on the survival of the world economic system. Because of physical interdependencies (such as long-range transport of pollutants) and monetary interdependencies (such as capital flows) among nations, the new concern has become global in scope.

The Malthus theory has influenced many disciplines, including economics.[3] For several decades economists have been concerned with topics such as exhaustible resources and pollution, but during the last decade, the frequency of related books and articles has accelerated rapidly.[4] Consequently, we've come to better understand the relationship between humanity and the environment and how that relationship affects, and is affected by, economic and political institutions.

The Use of Models

In this book you will study the rapidly growing field of environmental and natural resource economics. All of the topics covered will be examined as a part of the general focus on economic growth in the presence of limited environmental and natural resources. Because this subject is so complex, it is better understood when broken into manageable portions. Once we have mastered the components, we can then reassemble them to form a complete picture.

---

[1]Rome does not provide the only historical example of a powerful society which followed a path to self-extinction. It has been suggested, for example, that the classic Maya civilization succumbed when its concentrated population proved too large to be supported by the soils around it. See Jeremy A. Sabloff, "The Collapse of Classic Maya Civilization," in *Patient Earth,* John Harte and Robert H. Socolow, eds. (New York: Holt, Rinehart and Winston, 1971), 16–27; Lester R. Brown, "World Population Growth, Soil Erosion, and Food Security," *Science* 214 (November 27, 1981): 995–1002.

[2]See G. Tyler Miller, Jr., *Living in the Environment: Concepts, Problems and Alternatives* (Belmont, CA: Wadsworth Publishing, 1975), 105–107.

[3]Symptomatic of this impact has been the effect on the field of economics known as economic development. One of the well-known texts in the field, authored by Benjamin Higgins, was originally entitled *Economic Development: Principles, Problems and Policies.* When this book was revised and updated in 1979 with co-author Jean Downing Higgins, it bore the title *Economic Development of a Small Planet.*

[4]One article which is generally credited with sparking a renewed interest in natural resource problems is John Krutilla, "Conservation Reconsidered," *The American Economic Review* 57 (September, 1968): 777–786.

In economics, as in most other disciplines, we use models to illustrate complex subjects, such as relationships between the economy and the environment. In using these models, however, we should also be sensitive to their limitations.

Models are simplified characterizations of reality. For example, although a road-map, by design, leaves a lot out, it is a useful guide to reality. The map shows how various locations relate to each other and gives an overall perspective. It cannot, however, capture the unique details which characterize any particular location. The map highlights only those characteristics crucial for the purpose at hand.

The models in this text are like that. Through simplification, less is held in view so that more can be understood of what is retained. Models allow us to rigorously study issues which are interrelated and global in scale, but, through their selectivity, models may yield conclusions that are dead wrong. What is omitted may turn out, in retrospect, to be crucial in understanding a particular dimension. Models are therefore useful abstractions that should always be viewed with some skepticism.

Most people's views of the world are based on models, though frequently those models are implicit rather than explicit. The assumptions and relationships involved may be hidden, perhaps even subconscious. In economics the models are explicit; objectives, relationships, and assumptions are clearly specified so that the reader understands exactly how the conclusions were derived.

In this chapter we will use two models for thinking systematically about the future. While models can be used successfully to forecast future problems, this has not always been the case. Long-range forecasts may heighten our sensitivity to possible outcomes, but they must never be treated as fact (Example 1.1).

The two visions presented in this chapter (the basic pessimist model and the basic optimist model) demonstrate areas of concern that will be given closer scrutiny later in this text. They also highlight the key relationships that motivate the conclusions drawn by authors of those visions, so that we can assess the adequacy of these relationships as guides to reality.

The pessimist and optimist visions were chosen from the literally hundreds that exist because they define, in some sense, the end points of a spectrum. We shall, of course, want to explore not only these end points, but the vast intervening territory as we proceed through the book.

THE BASIC PESSIMIST MODEL

One end of the spectrum is defined by an ambitious study published in 1972 under the title *The Limits to Growth*.[5] Based on a technique known as *systems dynamics*, developed by Professor Jay Forrester at MIT, a large-scale computer model was constructed to simulate likely future outcomes of the world economy. The most prominent feature of systems dynamics is the use of feedback loops to explain behavior. The *feedback loop* is a closed path that connects an action to its effect on the surrounding conditions

---

[5]The popular version of this study appears as Donella H. Meadows et al., *The Limits to Growth* (New York: Universe Books, 1972).

██
EXAMPLE 1.1
██

The Dangers of Prognostication

One's view of the future can be limited by his or her understanding of the past and present, as well as of the technological possibilities which lie around the corner. Often that understanding is not what it should be and the forecasts based on it, in retrospect, can seem rather absurd.

In 1486, for example, a committee headed by Fray Hernando de Talavera was established by King Ferdinand and Queen Isabella to advise them on the merits of funding Christopher Columbus' plan to sail to the West Indies. Following four years of work, the committee reported its conclusion that a voyage of the type contemplated was impossible because: (1) the Western Ocean was infinite and probably not navigable; (2) even if the Antipodes (the expected landfall) were reached, the return journey would be impossible; and (3) there probably were no Antipodes to be reached because most of the world was presumably covered by water; St. Augustine said so.

In 1835 Thomas Tredgold, a British railroad designer declared, "Any general system of conveying passengers—at a velocity exceeding 10 miles an hour, or thereabouts—is extremely improbable."

The chief geologist of the U.S. Geological Survey reported in 1920 that only seven billion barrels of petroleum remained to be recovered with existing techniques. He predicted that, at the contemporary annual rate of consumption of a half billion barrels, American oil resources would be exhausted in fourteen years— by 1934. However, when that fateful year arrived, twelve, not seven, billion barrels had been produced and there was an additional twelve billion barrels of proved reserves.

Economists are certainly not immune from the dangers of prognostication. In his *The Coal Question: An Inquiry Concerning the Progress of the Nation and the Probable Exhaustion of our Coal Mines* published in 1865, Stanley Jevons concluded that the rapid increase in coal consumption coupled with the finite nature of the supply of coal would cause progress to stop in the near future. In John Maynard Keynes' discussion of Jevon's work, he also notes in passing that Jevons had a similar fear of an increasing scarcity of paper. Jevons apparently acted on those fears for, some fifty years after his death, his children had not used up the stock of paper he had accumulated.

Sources: Glenn Hueckel, "A Historical Approach to Future Economic Growth," *Science* 191 (March 14, 1975): 925–31; Harry U. Spiegel, ed., *The Development of Economic Thought* (New York: John Wiley, 1952): 490–525; Edward Cornish et al., *The Study of the Future* (Washington, D.C.: World Future Society, 1977): 106–08.

██

which, in turn, can influence further action. As the examples presented subsequently in this chapter demonstrate, depending on how the relationships are described, a wide variety of complex behavior can be described by this technique.

Conclusions of Pessimist Model

Three main conclusions were reached by this study. The first suggests that within a time span of less than 100 years with no major change in the physical, economic, or social relationships that have traditionally governed world development, society will run out of the nonrenewable resources on which the industrial base depends. When the resources have been depleted, a precipitous collapse of the economic system will result, manifested in massive unemployment, decreased food production, and a decline in population as the death rate soars. There is no smooth transition, no gradual slowing down of activity; rather, the economic system consumes successively larger amounts of the depletable resources until suddenly they are gone. The characteristic behavior of the system is overshoot and collapse (see Figure 1.1).

The second conclusion of the study is that piecemeal approaches to solving the individual problems will not be successful. To demonstrate this point, the authors arbitrarily double their estimates of the resource base and allow the model to trace out an alternative vision based on this new, higher level of resources. In this alternative vision the collapse still occurs, but this time it is caused by excessive pollution generated by the increased pace of industrialization permitted by the greater availability of resources. The authors then suggest that if the depletable resource and pollution problems were somehow jointly solved, population would grow unabated and the availability of food would become the binding constraint. In this model the removal of one limit merely causes the system to bump subsequently into another one, usually with more dire consequences.

As its third and final conclusion, the study suggests that overshoot and collapse can be avoided only by an immediate limit on population and pollution, as well as a cessation of economic growth. The portrait painted shows only two possible outcomes: the termination of growth by self-restraint and conscious policy—an approach that avoids the collapse—or the termination of growth by a collision with the natural limits, resulting in societal collapse. Thus, according to this study, one way or the other, growth will cease. The only issue is whether the conditions under which it will cease will be congenial or hostile.

The Nature of the Model

Why were these conclusions reached? Clearly they depend on the structure of the model. By identifying the characteristics that yield these conclusions, we can then, in subsequent chapters of this book, examine the realism of those characteristics.

The dominant characteristic of the model is exponential growth coupled with fixed limits. Exponential growth in any variable (for example, 3 percent per year) implies that the absolute increases in that variable will be greater and greater each each.[6] Furthermore, the higher the rate of growth in resource consumption, the faster a fixed stock of it will be exhausted. Suppose, for example, current reserves of a resource

---

[6]Suppose, for example, that in some initial year there are 100 units of a specific variable. If that variable is growing at 10 percent per year then it will grow ten units during the first year and eleven units the second year.

FIGURE 1.1   The Limits-to-Growth Standard Run

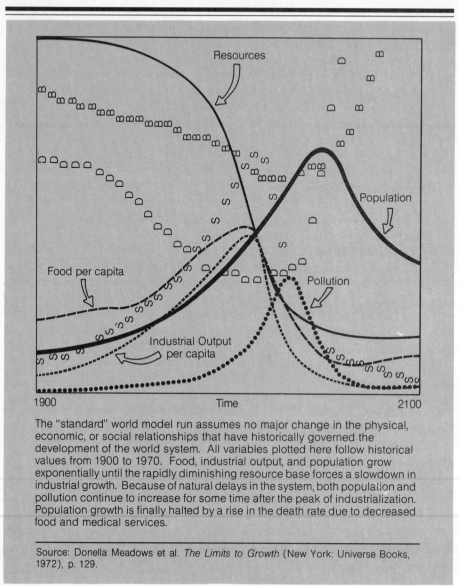

The "standard" world model run assumes no major change in the physical, economic, or social relationships that have historically governed the development of the world system. All variables plotted here follow historical values from 1900 to 1970. Food, industrial output, and population grow exponentially until the rapidly diminishing resource base forces a slowdown in industrial growth. Because of natural delays in the system, both population and pollution continue to increase for some time after the peak of industrialization. Population growth is finally halted by a rise in the death rate due to decreased food and medical services.

Source: Donella Meadows et al. *The Limits to Growth* (New York: Universe Books, 1972), p. 129.

are 100 times current use and the supply of reserves cannot be expanded. If consumption were not growing, this stock would last 100 years. However, if consumption were to grow at 2 percent per year, the reserves would be exhausted in 55 years, and at 10 percent, exhaustion would occur after only 24 years.

Several resources are held in fixed supply be the model. These include the amount of available land and the stock of depletable resources. In addition, the supply of food is fixed relative to the supply of land. The combination of exponential growth in demand, coupled with fixed sources of supply, necessarily implies that, at some point, resource supplies must be exhausted. The extent to which those resources are essential thus creates the conditions for collapse.

This basic structure of the model is in some ways reinforced and in some ways tempered by the presence of a large number of *positive* and *negative feedback loops*. *Positive feedback loops* are those in which secondary effects tend to reinforce the basic trend. An example of a positive feedback loop is the process of capital accumulation. New investment generates greater output, which, when sold, generates profits. These profits, in turn, can be used to fund additional new investments. This example suggests a manner in which the growth process is self-reinforcing.

A *negative feedback loop* is self-limiting rather than self-reinforcing, as illustrated by the role of death rates in limiting population growth in the model. As growth occurs, it causes larger increases in industrial output, which, in turn, cause more pollution. The increase in pollution triggers a rise in death rates, retarding population growth. From this example it can be seen that negative feedback loops can provide a tempering influence on the growth process, though not necessarily a desirable one.

Because of the dominance of positive feedback loops, coupled with fixed limits on essential resources, the structure of the model preordains its conclusion. While the values assumed for various parameters (the size of the stock of depletable resources, for example) affect the timing of the various effects, they do not substantially affect the nature of the outcome.

The dynamics implied by the notion of a feedback loop is helpful in a more general sense than the specific relationships embodied in this model. As we proceed with our investigation, the degree to which our economic and political institutions serve to intensify or to limit emerging environmental problems will be a key concern.

Unfortunately it is not hard to come up with other examples of positive feedback loops. When shortages of a commodity are imminent, for example, consumers typically begin to hoard the commodity. Hoarding intensifies the shortage. Similarly, people faced with shortages of food commonly eat the seed that is the key to more plentiful food in the future. Situations giving rise to this kind of downward spiral are particularly troublesome.

THE BASIC OPTIMIST MODEL

Is the portrait of the fate of the world economy painted by the *Limits to Growth* model an accurate one? Because Herman Kahn and his associates did not think so, they presented an alternative vision in a book titled *The Next 200 Years: A Scenario for America and the World*.[7] This vision is an optimistic one based in large part on the

---

[7]Herman Kahn, William Brown, and Leon Martel, *The Next 200 Years: A Scenario for America and the World* (New York: William Morrow, 1976).

continuing evolution of a form of technological progress that serves to push back the natural limits until they are no longer limiting.

Conclusions of Optimist Model

The basic conclusion reached by this study is stated in the opening pages of the book:

> . . . 200 years ago almost everywhere human beings were comparatively few, poor and at the mercy of the forces of nature, and 200 years from now, we expect, almost everywhere they will be numerous, rich and in control of the forces of nature. [p. 1].

The future path of population growth is expected by Kahn and his associates to approximate an *S*-shaped logistic curve. This image suggests that an omniscient observer during 1976 looking backward through time and then forward into the future would see rather different things. The retrospective glance would reveal a period of exponential population growth, while the glance into the future would reveal continued growth, but with steadily declining growth rates, until, at the end of the next 200-year period, growth would automatically come to a halt. By that time, however, the population would have increased four times its current level and the average person in the world economy would be earning $20,000 a year (in constant dollars) — a far cry from the 1976 average of $1300 (see Figure 1.2).

To Kahn and his associates, interference with this natural evolution of society would not only be unwarranted, it would be unethical. As they see it, tampering with the growth process would consign the residents of the poorest developing countries — and indeed, the poorest residents of the developed countries — to a life of poverty, a life without hope. In contrast, they see continued growth as providing continued betterment for both

FIGURE 1.2   The Kahn Perspective on Prospects for Humanity (in fixed 1975 dollars)

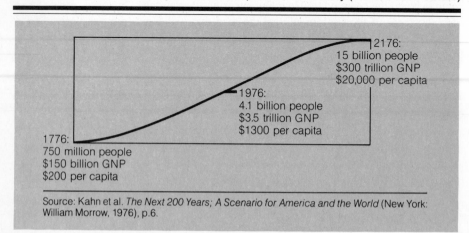

2176:
15 billion people
$300 trillion GNP
$20,000 per capita

1976:
4.1 billion people
$3.5 trillion GNP
$1300 per capita

1776:
750 million people
$150 billion GNP
$200 per capita

Source: Kahn et al. *The Next 200 Years; A Scenario for America and the World* (New York: William Morrow, 1976), p.6.

groups; although, due to an expected decline in the gap between the rich nations and the poor, those in the poorest nations would benefit most from continued growth.

The Nature of the Model

The Kahn model is more qualitative than the *Limits to Growth* model and therefore its structure is less specific. It is not a computer program that simulates the future. Rather, Kahn and his associates devised scenarios they believed to be plausible and then verified that the various components of these scenarios were consistent with each other. The book is filled with reasons why the chosen scenario is reasonable. These lists of reasons frequently include new technologies that, when certain limits are reached, will be introduced. These technologies effectively either remove the limit or buy time until a subsequent technology can remove the limit.

The principles underlying Kahn's work can best be illustrated through the use of two examples: food and energy. One of the sources of collapse in the *Limits to Growth* model was the inability of food supply to keep up with consumption. Kahn, by contrast, sees food production rising so rapidly as to create an eventual abundance of food. This vision, in turn, depends on some specific sources of optimism: (1) physical resources will not effectively limit production during the next 200 years, and (2) substantial increases can be expected in conventional foods produced by conventional means, conventional foods produced by unconventional means, and unconventional foods produced by unconventional means.

All of these sources of optimism are related to technological progress. The availability of physical resources can be expanded through the use of better (solar-powered, for example) irrigation systems. Conventional food production can be increased by the spread of better farming techniques and by the development of new hybrid seeds. If soils become depleted or scarce, then food can be raised with *hydroponics*, a process using no soil.[8] Finally, Kahn points to the development of single-cell protein as a viable means of converting municipal waste into a food supplement.

A similar approach is taken when describing the world energy future. The authors of *The Next 200 Years* construct a list of technologies that can provide the transition to solar energy, making the case that solar energy can ultimately sustain a high level of economic activity. The list includes technologies that use coal, either directly or indirectly, (such as gas produced from coal); those which exploit the vast world reserves of shale oil; nuclear power (fission, in the near term, replaced subsequently by fusion); and new solar technologies including windmills, photovoltaics, and ocean thermal power, to mention only a few.

---

[8]This technique grows plants in recirculating water, complemented by nutrient film. In the advanced versions of this technique, no soil at all is required even for stability. As an interesting aside, the technology is apparently sufficiently advanced that it is currently being used to grow marijuana illegally. See "Pot Growers Turn over New Leaf, Try State-of-the-Art Hydroponics," *Wall Street Journal*, January 15, 1981, p. 25.

When all of these lists are combined, the prevailing message is that currently recognized technologies can overcome the limitations envisioned by the *Limits to Growth* view. *The Next 200 Years* staff, then, believes that the creators of *Limits to Growth* erred in being myopic; they were too tied to conventional technologies. When the need arises, they argue, these new technologies will be developed. The cliché, "Necessity is the mother of invention," captures the flavor of the belief of Kahn and his associates that these technologies will be developed as they are needed.

THE ROAD AHEAD

The two models used in this chapter were developed by people trained primarily in the natural sciences rather than the social sciences. This natural-science orientation gives the models a flavor that contrasts rather markedly with the economic models presented in the rest of the book. The most striking difference is the central role that human behavior plays in the social-science models, while it is relegated to a rather trivial role in natural-science models.

Perhaps this distinction can best be illustrated through an analogy: When a pipe carrying water springs a leak, we plug the hole. The solution is simple, direct, and usually sufficient. However, correcting problems in an economic system with this direct approach not only may be ineffective, but it may be counterproductive.

The manner in which the government chose to regulate the price of natural gas provides a prime example. In its desire to guarantee "just and reasonable" prices for this important fuel, Congress imposed ceilings on the prices. The evidence is now clear that this direct approach created shortages. The price ceiling lowered the quantity of natural gas available by reducing the incentives for suppliers to find new sources.[9] The failure to realize the effect of this policy on the behavior of suppliers led to a situation in which the very people the law tried to protect were, instead, victimized by it. Thus, in order to gain a more complete understanding of what challenges to expect of the future, as well as possible solutions, we must consider the role of human behavior.

The Issues

Obviously these visions of the future present us with rather different conceptions of what the future holds, as well as different views of what policy choices should be made. They also suggest that to act as if one vision is correct, when it is not, could prove to be a costly move. Thus, it is important to determine if one of these two views or, alternatively, some third view, is correct.

In order to assess any model or view, it is necessary to address the basic issues:

1. Is the problem correctly conceptualized as exponential growth with fixed, immutable resource limits?

---

[9]There were other problems caused by the act, as well. See Chapter 7 for a detailed examination of natural gas allocation.

2. If these limits do exist, have they been measured correctly or, as Kahn argues, has the *Limits to Growth* team been rather myopic in the way they treat resources?

3. How does the economic system respond to scarcities? Is the overshoot-and-collapse syndrome an accurate characterization of the process?

4. To what extent does the economic system contain self-correction or self-reinforcing mechanisms that may tend to either ameliorate or intensify the basic problems identified in *Limits to Growth?* If the economic system is capable of either response, depending upon the circumstances, can we identify the circumstances where the normal response may be detrimental to the interests of society?

5. What is the role of the political system in controlling these problems? In what circumstances is government intervention necessary? Is this intervention uniformly benign, or can it make the situation worse? What is an appropriate role for the executive, legislative and judicial branches?

6. Many environmental problems involve a considerable degree of uncertainty about the nature of the problem and possible solutions. Can our economic and political institutions respond to this uncertainty in reasonable ways?

7. Can the economic and political systems work together to produce a "reformed" growth process that retains the benefits of growth while eliminating its excesses, or is it necessary to forcibly move to zero growth in order to insure a congenial future for subsequent generations?

8. Though they differ in how this transition will occur, both studies suggest that somewhere in the next 200 years the economic system will undergo transition to a steady growth process with substantially lower, if not zero, growth rates. What implications does that transition have for the way of life to which we are now accustomed? What are its implications for Third World countries?

The rest of the book uses economic analysis to suggest answers to these questions.

An Overview of the Book

In the following chapters you will study the rich and rewarding field of environmental and natural resource economics. The menu of topics is broad and varied. Economics provides a powerful analytical framework for examining the relationships between the environment, on the one hand, and the economic and political systems, on the other. The study of economics can assist in identifying circumstances that give rise to environmental problems, in discovering causes of these problems, and in searching for solutions. Each chapter is an introduction to a unique topic in environmental and natural resource economics, while our overarching focus on growth in a finite environment weaves these topics together into a single theme.

We begin in Chapter 2 by comparing perspectives being brought to bear on these problems by economists and noneconomists. The manner in which scholars in various disciplines view problems and potential solutions depends on how they organize the available facts, how they interpret those facts, and what kinds of values they apply in translating these interpretations into policy. Before going into a detailed look at environmental problems, we shall compare the ideology of conventional economics to other prevailing ideologies in both the natural and social sciences. This comparison not only explains why reasonable people may, upon examining the same set of facts, reach different conclusions but also conveys some sense of the strengths and weaknesses of economic analysis as it is applied to environmental problems.

Chapters 3 and 4 delve more deeply into the conventional economic approach. Specific evaluation criteria are defined and examples are developed to show how these criteria can be applied to specific environmental problems.

After examining the major perspectives shaping environmental policy, we shall then turn (Chapters 5–13) to the physical limits identified by *Limits to Growth;* to the manner in which the economic and political institutions have dealt with the resulting problems and the potential for improvement in the future. We begin our examination in Chapter 5 with an inquiry into the nature, causes, and consequences of population growth, a major factor in determining how rapidly the limits could be reached.

Chapters 6–13 deal with several topics traditionally falling under the label of natural resource economics. Chapter 6 provides an overview of the models used to portray how natural resources are allocated over time. These models allow us to show how the allocation depends on such factors as the cost of extraction, environmental costs, and the availability of substitutes. Chapter 7 discusses energy as an example of a depletable, nonrecyclable resource, and examines such topics as the role of OPEC, the balance between imports and domestic production, the role of nuclear power, and many aspects of past and present energy policy. Chapter 8 focuses on minerals to illustrate how depletable, recyclable resources are allocated over time, and to define the appropriate role for recycling. The degree to which the current situation approximates this ideal is assessed, with particular attention paid to aspects such as tax policy, disposal costs, and product durability.

Chapters 9, 10, 11, and 12 focus on renewable or replenishable resources. These chapters show that the effectiveness with which current institutions manage renewable resources depends on whether the resources are living or inanimate and whether they are treated as private or common property. In Chapter 9, the focus is on allocating water in arid regions. Water is an example of an inanimate but replenishable resource. Specific examples from the American Southwest illustrate how the political and economic institutions have coped with this particular form of impending scarcity. In Chapter 10, the focus is on cereal grain, an animate, private-property resource, which is the most important source of food in combatting the world hunger problem, and the land on which the grain is grown. Chapter 11 deals with forestry as an example of a renewable and storable private property resource. Managing this resource is somewhat unique in that the amount of time required to produce an efficient harvest is longer than for the other resources considered. In Chapter 12, fisheries are used to illustrate the problems associated with an animate, common-property resource and to explore possible means of solving these problems.

The final chapter concerned with natural resources, Chapter 13, confronts the fear that we are entering an era of generalized resource scarcity. It seeks answers to key questions: Are we in an era of increasing scracity? How can we tell? What indicators can be used and what do they reveal? What responses should be taken given this evidence?

We then move on to an area of public policy — pollution control — which is coming to rely much more heavily on the use of economic incentives to produce the desired response. Chapter 14, an overview chapter, emphasizes not only the nature of the problems, but the policy approaches taken to resolve them. The unique aspects of local air pollution, regional and global air pollution, automobile air pollution, water pollution, and the control of toxic substances are dealt with in five subsequent individual chapters. Special attention is paid in Chapter 20 to the impacts of those policies, not only on the problems they were designed to correct, but also on other important policy concerns, such as the distribution of the benefit and cost burdens among various socioeconomic groups and geographic areas.

Following this examination of the limits to growth and the policies that can be, and have been, used to circumvent the limits, the book turns to the growth process itself. Certain questions must be asked. What are the causes and consequences of economic growth? What role do natural resources and environmental control play in the growth process? What is the likely future for economic growth? Is an immediate transition to a zero-economic-growth path (as suggested by *Limits to Growth*) necessary? Or, if unnecessary, is it desirable?

In Chapter 23 the book closes by assembling the bits and pieces of evidence accumulated in each of the preceding chapters and fusing them into an overall response to the questions posed in this chapter. That chapter also suggests some of the major unresolved issues in environmental policy that are likely to be among those commanding center stage over the next several years or decades.

SUMMARY

Is our society so myopic that it has chosen a path which can only lead to the destruction of society as we now know it? We have examined briefly two studies which provide two different answers to that question. *The Limits to Growth* responds in the affirmative, while Kahn and his associates respond negatively. The pessimistic view is based upon the inevitability of running out of resources when a finite resource base is coupled with exponential growth in demand. The optimistic view sees initial scarcity triggering sufficiently powerful reductions in population growth and increases in technological progress that the future brings abundance, not deepening scarcity.

Our examination of these rather different visions has revealed a number of questions which must be answered if we are to assess what the future holds. Seeking answers to these questions requires that we accumulate a much better understanding about how choices are made in economic and political systems and how those choices affect, and are affected by, the natural environment. We shall begin that process in Chapter 2, where the economic approach is developed in broad terms and is contrasted with other conventional approaches.

FURTHER READING

Beckerman, Wilfred. *Two Cheers for the Affluent Society: A Spirited Defense of Economic Growth* (New York: St. Martin's Press, 1974). As the title suggests, an always spirited, frequently irreverent defense of continued economic growth.

Heilbroner, Robert. *An Inquiry into the Human Prospect.* (New York: W. W. Norton & Company, Inc., 1974). A noted economist finds the outlook rather grim for both socialist and capitalist nations.

Hirsh, Fred. *Social Limits to Growth* (Cambridge, Mass.: Harvard University Press, 1976). An intriguing argument that the true limits to growth are social, not physical.

Kaysen, Carl. "The Computer that Printed Out W*O*L*F." *Foreign Affairs* L (July, 1972): 660–68. An early, ringing indictment of the *Limits to Growth* study.

Leontief, Wassily. *The Future of the World Economy* (New York: Oxford University Press, 1977). A major empirical study led by a Nobel Laureate in economics commissioned by the United Nations to examine the feasibility of closing the per capita income gap between the rich nations and the poor.

Simon, Julian L. *The Ultimate Resource* (Princeton: Princeton University Press, 1981). The tone of this optimistic study is conveyed by the title of his third chapter, "Can the Supply of Natural Resources Really Be Infinite? Yes!" Concludes that the ultimate resource is human imagination and that resource knows no limit.

Weintraub, Andrew, Eli Schwartz, and J. Richard Aronson, eds. *The Economic Growth Controversy* (New York: International Arts and Sciences Press, Inc., 1973). A collection of articles on the inevitability and desirability of continued economic growth.

ADDITIONAL REFERENCES

Cole, H. S. D., ed. *Models of Doom: A Critique of the Limits to Growth* (New York: Universe Books, 1973).

Council on Environmental Quality and Department of State, *The Global 2000 Report to the President of the U.S.: Entering the 21st Century,* Vols. I–III (New York: Pergamon Press, 1980).

Hughes, Barry. *World Futures: A Critical Analysis of Alternatives* (Baltimore: Johns Hopkins University Press, 1985).

Kahn, Herman, William Brown, and Leon Martel. *The Next 200 Years: A Scenario for America and the World* (New York: William Morrow, 1976).

Meadows, Donella H., *et al. The Limits to Growth* (New York: Universe Books, 1972).

Meadows, Dennis L., *et al. Dynamics of Growth in a Finite World* (Cambridge, Mass: Wright-Allen Press, 1974).

Mesarovic, Michaklo and Edward Pestel. *Mankind at the Turning Point: The Second Report to the Club of Rome* (New York: The New American Library, 1974).

Simon, Julian L. and Herman Kahn. *The Resourceful Earth: A Response to Global 2000* (New York: Blackwell, 1984).

DISCUSSION QUESTIONS

1. A central concept in the *Limits to Growth* view of the future is the finiteness of resources. In his book *The Ultimate Resource*, Julian Simon makes the point that calling the resource base "finite" is misleading. To illustrate this point he uses a yardstick, with its one-inch markings, as an analogy. The distance between two markings is finite—one inch—but an uncountably infinite number of points is contained in that finite space. Therefore, in one sense what lies between the markings is finite, while in another, equally meaningful sense, it is infinite. Is the concept of a finite resource base useful or not? Why or why not?

2. This chapter contains two rather different views of the future. Since the validity of these views cannot completely be tested until the time period covered by the forecast has past (so that predictions can be matched against actual events), how can we ever hope to establish whether one is a better view than the other? What criteria might be proposed for evaluating predictions?

CHAPTER TWO

Economics of the Environment: An Overview

*It is hard to explore what happens when people behave with a
purpose without becoming curious, even concerned, about how
well or how badly the outcome serves the purpose. Social
scientists are more like forest rangers than like naturalists. The
naturalist can be interested in what causes a species to become
extinct, without caring whether or not it does become extinct.
(If it has been extinct for a million years his curiosity is surely
without concern.) The ranger will be concerned with whether
or not the buffalo do disappear, and how to keep them in a
healthy balance with their environment.*
THOMAS C. SCHELLING, *Micromotives and Macrobehavior* (1978)

INTRODUCTION

Before examining specific environmental problems and the policy responses to them,
it is important that we develop and clarify the approach to be taken in this study, so
that we will have some sense of the forest before examining each of the trees. By having a feel for the conceptual framework, it becomes easier not only to deal with individual cases, but, perhaps more importantly, to see how they fit together into a
comprehensive approach.

In this chapter we shall develop the general conceptual framework used in economics
to approach environmental problems. We shall begin by examining the relationship
between human actions, as manifested through the economic system, and the environmental consequences of those actions. We can then establish criteria for judging
the desirability of the outcomes of this relationship. These criteria not only provide
a basis for identifying the nature and severity of environmental problems, they also
provide a foundation for designing effective policies to deal with the identified problems.

Throughout this chapter the economic point of view will be contrasted with different
points of view. These contrasts bring the economic approach into sharper focus and
stimulate deeper and more critical thinking about all possible approaches.

THE HUMAN ENVIRONMENT RELATIONSHIP

The Environment as an Asset

In economics the environment is viewed as a composite asset that provides a variety of services. It is a very special asset, to be sure, since it provides the life-support systems that sustain our very existence, but it is an asset nonetheless. As with other assets, we wish to prevent undue depreciation of the value of this asset so it may continue to provide us with aesthetic and life-sustaining services.

The environment provides the economy with both raw materials, which are transformed into consumer products by the production process, and energy, which fuels this transformation. Ultimately these raw materials and energy return to the environment as waste products (see Figure 2.1).

The environment also provides services directly to consumers. The air we breathe, the nourishment we receive from food and drink, and the protection we derive from shelter and clothing are all benefits we receive either directly or indirectly from the

FIGURE 2.1 The Economic System and the Environment

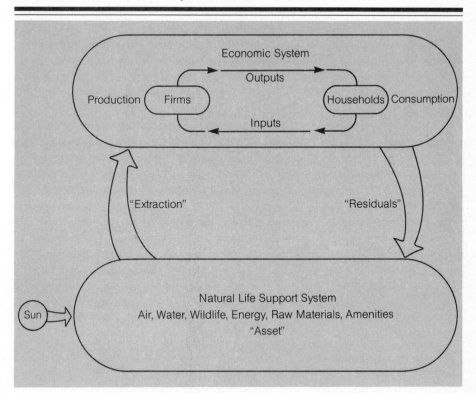

environment. In addition, anyone who has experienced the exhilaration of white-water canoeing, the total serenity of a wilderness trek, or the breathtaking beauty of a sunset will readily recognize that the environment provides us with a variety of amenities for which there is no substitute.

If the environment is defined broadly enough, the relationship between the environment and the economic system can be considered a *closed system.* For our purposes, a closed system is one in which no inputs (energy, matter, and so on) are received from outside the system and no outputs are transferred outside the system. An *open system,* by contrast, is one in which the system imports or exports matter or energy.

If we restrict our conception of the relationship in Figure 2.1 to our planet and the atmosphere around it, then clearly we do not have a closed system. We derive most of our energy from the sun, either directly or indirectly. We have also sent spaceships well beyond the boundaries of our atmosphere. Nonetheless, historically speaking, for *material* inputs and outputs (not including energy), this system can be treated as a closed system because the amount of exports (such as abandoned space vehicles) and imports (moon rocks, for example) are negligible. Whether the system remains closed depends on the degree to which space exploration opens up the rest of our solar system as a source of raw materials.

The treatment of our planet and its immediate environs as a closed system has an important implication, which is summed up in the *first law of thermodynamics* – a law stating that neither energy nor matter can be created or destroyed.[1] The law implies that the mass of materials flowing into the economic system from the environment has to either accumulate in the economic system or return to the environment as waste. To the extent that accumulation does not take place, the mass of materials flowing into the economic system is equal in magnitude to the mass of waste flowing into the environment.

Excessive wastes can, of course, depreciate the asset; when they exceed the absorptive capacity of nature, wastes reduce the services that the asset provides.[2] Examples are easy to find: air pollution can cause respiratory problems; polluted drinking water can cause cancer; smog destroys scenic vistas.

The relationship of people to the environment is also conditioned by another physical law, the *second law of thermodynamics.* Known popularly as the *entropy law,* this law states that entropy increases. *Entropy* is the amount of energy not available for work.[3] Applied to energy processes, this law implies that no conversion from one form of energy to another is completely efficient and that the consumption of energy is an irre-

---

[1]We know, however, from Einstein's famous equation ($E = MC^2$) that matter can be transformed into energy. It is this transformation which is the source of energy in nuclear power.

[2]A detailed economic model, known as the materials balance model, has been constructed to integrate physical mass flows and the economic system. Description of this model is beyond the scope of this chapter, but can be found in Allen V. Kneese, Robert U. Ayers, and Ralph G. d'Arge, *Economics and the Environment: A Materials Balance Approach* (Washington, D.C.: Resources for the Future, 1970).

[3]For a technical description of entropy and its relationship to economics see Stuart Burness et al., "Thermodynamic and Economic Concepts as Related to Resource-Use Policies," *Land Economics* 56 (February, 1980): 1–9.

versible process. Some energy is always lost during conversion, and the rest, once used, is no longer available for further work. This law also implies that in the absence of new energy inputs, any closed system must eventually use up its energy. Since energy is necessary for life, when energy ceases, life ceases.

We should remember that our planet is not even approximately a closed system with respect to energy; we gain energy from the sun. The entropy law does suggest, however, that this flow of solar energy establishes an upper limit on the flow of energy that can be sustained. Once the stocks of stored energy (such as fossil fuels and nuclear energy) are gone, the amount of energy available for useful work will be determined solely by this flow and by the amount that can be stored (dams, trees, and so on). Thus, over the very long run, the growth process will be limited by the availability of solar energy and our ability to put it to work.

Two different types of economic analysis can be applied to increase our understanding of the relationship between the economic system and the environment: *Positive* economics attempts to describe *what is, what was,* or *what will be. Normative* economics, by contrast, deals with *what ought to be.* Disagreements within positive economics can usually be resolved by an appeal to the facts. Normative disagreements, however, involve value judgments.

Both branches are useful. Suppose, for example, we want to be precise about how the economic system treats the environmental asset. Positive economics would be used to describe the service flows and to show how those service flows would be affected by a change in the system (such as the discovery of a new production process). Positive analysis could not, however, be used to provide any guidance on the question of whether these service flows were optimal. That judgment would have to come from normative economics.

The essence of the normative approach in economics is to maximize the value of the asset. As long as humans exist, they cannot avoid affecting the environment. The issue, therefore, cannot be *whether* humans should have any impact on the environment; rather, the issue is to define the optimal level of impact.

Valuation of the Asset

The normative approach attempts to maximize the value of the environmental asset by creating a balance between the preservation and use of that asset. In order to define this balance, it is necessary to place some sort of value on the various service flows received, including the negative effects of using the environment as a receptacle for waste. In the economic point of view, this valuation is decidedly *anthropocentric,* or human-centered. Effects on the ecosphere are valued in terms of their ultimate effects on humanity. As Example 2.1 indicates, this approach is not universally accepted.

We can argue that it is appropriate to assign humans the right to govern this balance without necessarily arguing that the resulting decisions are correct. Decisions are deemed incorrect, for example, if the decision-making process leads to outcomes that are inconsistent with the collectively desired outcomes, which is precisely what the economic approach suggests. According to the economic approach, in many cir-

EXAMPLE 2.1

Nature Knows Best

The view that the environment should be managed by humans has not gone unopposed. In *The Closing Circle,* Barry Commoner poses what he calls the third law of ecology: nature knows best. Commoner elaborates on this view:

> . . . living things accumulate a complex organization of compatible parts; those possible arrangements that are not compatible with the whole are screened out over the long course of evolution. Thus, the structure of a present living thing or the organization of a current natural ecosystem is likely to be "best" in the sense that it has been so heavily screened for disadvantageous components that any new one is very likely to be worse than the present one. [p. 43]

This principle of minimum interference with the ecosphere would, if carried to an extreme, obviate any need to decide what injuries to the ecosphere were justified; none would be.

The conflict between the economic approach and that proposed by Commoner is perhaps best illustrated by the controversy over the Tellico Dam and the snail darter. The Tellico Dam was an ambitious water project on the Little Tennessee River authorized by Congress in 1967. During the summer of 1973, a Tennessee ichthyologist, Dr. David A. Etnier, Jr., discovered a previously unknown species of perch called the snail darter. During 1975, with the dam 75 percent complete, the Secretary of the Interior declared the snail darter an endangered species, which, under the Endangered Species Act of 1973, was sufficient to stop construction of the dam. The Supreme Court in 1978 upheld the act. The final turn of events, however, in this twisted saga came in 1979 when Congress passed, as a rider on an energy and water appropriations bill, an exemption from the Endangered Species Act for the snail darter.

The economic approach stacks up the worth of the project against the worth of the snail darter, both as a species and as a member of the larger ecological system. The principle of minimum interference suggests that regardless of the importance of the snail darter and regardless of the cost, it should be preserved.

Ironically, this clash of principles need not have taken place. An economic analysis showed the dam to be a poor investment and the snail darter was subsequently successfully transplanted to the nearby Hiwasee River. Nonetheless, this issue serves to illustrate that the seemingly abstract conflict between alternative sets of values can have very practical implications.

Sources: "Endangered Species Curbs" *Congressional Quarterly Almanac* Vol. 34 (1978), p. 707; "Public Works Energy Development Funds" *Congressional Quarterly Almanac,* Vol. 35 (1979), p. 223; "Endangered Species Act" *Congressional Quarterly Almanac,* Vol. 35 (1979), p. 661; Barry Commoner, *The Closing Circle* (New York: Alfred A. Knopf, 1972).

cumstances the individually rational choice differs from the collectively rational choice. Thus, the problem is not the *values* that are being applied to those choices but the *process* by which choices are reached.

NORMATIVE CRITERIA FOR DECISION MAKING

Since choices concerning the treatment of the environmental asset are inevitable, there has to be a criterion for judging the desirability of various options. We shall initially consider the criterion typically used to judge resource allocations at a point in time, a useful criterion when choices in various time periods are independent. We shall then expand our horizons and consider criteria for making choices that have effects not only on our generation but on subsequent generations as well.

Static Efficiency

The chief normative criterion for choosing among various allocations occurring at the same point in time is called *static efficiency,* or merely *efficiency.* An allocation of resources is said to satisfy the static-efficiency criterion if the net benefit from the use of those resources is maximized by that allocation. The *net benefit* is simply the excess of benefits over costs resulting from that allocation. But how do we measure benefits and costs?

Measurement of benefits is derived from the demand curve for the resource in question. Demand curves measure the amount of a particular good people would be willing to purchase at various prices. In a typical situation, a person will purchase less of the commodity (or environmental service) the higher is its cost. In Figure 2.2., when the price is p_0, q_0 will be purchased, but if the price rises to p_1, purchases will fall to q_1.

The meaning of these demand curves can be illustrated with this hypothetical experiment: Suppose you were asked, "At a price of X dollars, how much commodity Y would you buy?" Your answer could be recorded as a point on a diagram, such as Figure 2.2. By repeating the question many times for different prices, we could trace out a locus of points. Connecting these points yields an individual *demand curve.* Adding up all of the individual demand curves yields a market demand curve.

For each quantity purchased, the corresponding point on the market demand curve represents the amount of money some person is willing to pay for the last unit of the good. The *total willingness to pay* for some quantity of this good—say, 3 units—is the sum of the willingness to pay for each unit. Thus the total willingess to pay for 3 units would be measured as the sum of the willingness to pay for the first, second, and third units respectively. It is now a simple extension to determine that the total willingness to pay is the area under the continuous market demand curve to the left of the allocation in question. For example, in Figure 2.3 the total willingess to pay for 5 units of

FIGURE 2.2 The Individual Demand Curve

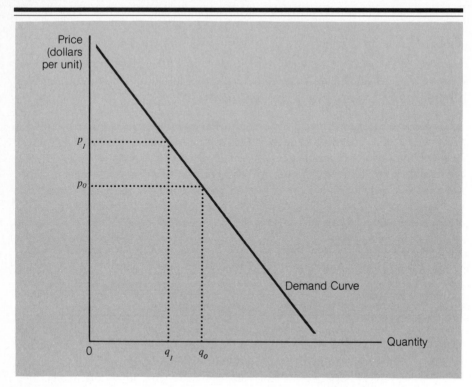

the commodity is the shaded area.[4] Total willingness to pay is the concept we shall use to define total benefits. Thus *total benefits* are equal to the area under the market demand curve from the origin to the allocation of interest.

To measure total costs on the same graph is relatively simple and involves logic similar to measuring total benefits. In measuring costs, however, we use the marginal cost curve rather than the demand curve. You may remember from your introductory economics course that the *marginal cost* curve defines the additional cost of producing the last unit. In purely competitive markets, the marginal cost curve is identical to the supply curve.

Total cost is simply the sum of the marginal costs.[5] The total cost of producing 3 units is equal to the cost of producing the first unit plus the cost of producing the second unit plus the cost of producing the third unit. As with total willingness to pay,

---

[4]From simple geometry it can be noticed that for linear demand curves this area is the sum of the areas of the triangle on top plus the rectangle on the bottom. The area of a right triangle is ½ × base × height. Therefore, in our example this area is (½)($5)(5) + ($5)(5) = $37.50.

[5]Strictly speaking, the sum of the marginal costs is equal to total variable cost. In the short run this is smaller than total cost by the amount of the fixed cost. For our purposes this distinction is not important.

FIGURE 2.3 The Relationship of Demand to Willingness to Pay

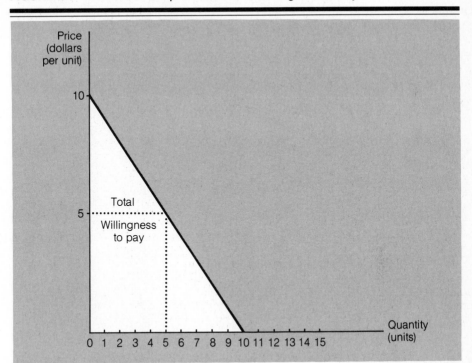

the geometric representation of the sum of the individual elements of a continuous marginal cost curve is the area under the marginal cost curve—as illustrated in Figure 2.4 by the shaded area *FGIJK*.[6]

Some of you, no doubt, have wondered how this concept of cost can be applied to environmental services produced by nature, not humans. Does the fact that they are produced without any input from humans mean that they are costless? In general the answer is no.

The correct way to reflect the cost of these services is to consider their *opportunity cost*—the net benefit forgone because the resources providing the service can no longer be used in their next most beneficial use. The notion that these resources are free is misleading if they can be put to alternative uses. For example, suppose a particular stretch of river can be used either for white-water canoeing or to generate electric power. Since the dam that generates the power would flood the rapids, the two uses are incompatible. The opportunity cost of saving the river for white-water canoeing is the foregone net benefit (after accounting for the cost of generation and distribution) of electricity.

It is now a simple matter to illustrate net benefit graphically. Since net benefit is defined as the excess of benefits over costs, it follows that net benefit is equal to that

---

[6]Notice again that this area is the sum of a right triangle and a rectangle. In Figure 2.4 the total variable cost of producing five units is $18.75. Can you see why?

FIGURE 2.4 The Relationship of Marginal Cost and Total Cost

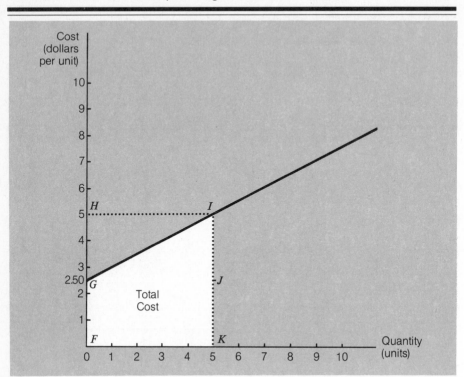

portion of the area under the demand curve which lies above the supply curve. Consider Figure 2.5, which combines the information in Figure 2.3 with that in Figure 2.4.

Our search for the efficient allocation begins by establishing the net benefit for an arbitrary production level—say, 4 units. At 4 units the total benefit is equal to *OLMNS*, while the total cost is equal to *OKNS*. Net benefit is, therefore, depicted by area *KLMN*. Is 4 units an efficient allocation? It is if it maximizes the net benefit. Do 4 units maximize the net benefit?

We can answer that question by establishing whether it is possible to increase the net benefit by producing more or less of the resource. If the net benefit can be increased, clearly the original allocation could not have maximized the net benefit and, therefore, could not have been efficient. Consider what would happen if society were to choose 5 units instead of 4. What happens to the net benefit? It *increases* by area *MNR*. Since we can find another allocation with greater net benefit, 4 units could not have been efficient. Are 5? The answer is yes. Let's see why.

We know that 5 units convey more net benefit than any allocation smaller than 4. If this allocation is efficient, then it must also be true that the net benefit is smaller for levels of production higher than 5. Notice that the additional cost of producing the sixth unit (the area under the marginal cost curve) is *larger* than the additional benefit received from producing it. Therefore, the triangle *RTU* represents the *reduction* in

FIGURE 2.5 The Derivation of Net Benefits

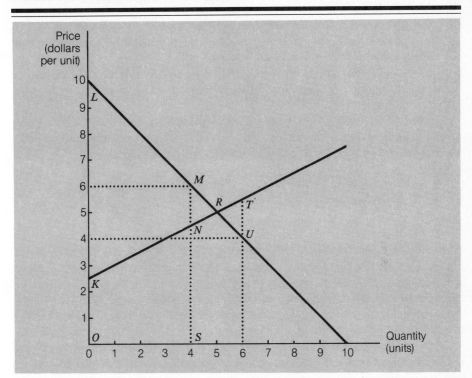

net benefit that occurs if 6 units are produced rather than 5. Production levels greater than 5 are not efficient. Since the net benefit is reduced, both by producing less than 5 and by producing more than 5, we conclude that 5 units is the production level that maximizes net benefit. Therefore, from our definition, a level of 5 units constitutes an efficient allocation.[7]

The ethical basis for this criterion is derived from a concept called *Pareto optimality*, named after the Italian-born, Swiss economist Vilfredo Pareto, who first proposed it around the turn of the twentieth century. Allocations are said to be *Pareto optimal* if there exists no rearrangement of that allocation that would benefit some people without any deleterious effects on someone else. (A rearrangement of a resource allocation could involve changing the level produced or changing the shares received by each of the ultimate users of the resource.)

Allocations that do *not* satisfy this definition are suboptimal in the sense that it is always possible to rearrange these allocations so that some people are better off and no one is hurt by the rearrangement. In this rearrangement from a suboptimal alloca-

---

[7]Can you calculate the monetary worth of the net benefit? It is the sum of two right triangles and it equals (½)($5)(5) + (½)($2.50)(5) or $18.75. Can you see why?

tion to an optimal one, the gainers would gain more than the losers lose. Therefore, the gainers could use a portion of their gains to compensate the losers sufficiently to ensure they were at least as well off as they were prior to the reallocation.

Efficient allocations are Pareto optimal. Since net benefits are maximized by an efficient allocation, it is not possible to increase the net benefit by rearranging the allocation. Without an increase in the net benefit, there is no way the gainers could sufficiently compensate the losers; the gains to the gainers would necessarily be smaller than the losses to the losers.

Inefficient allocations are seen as inferior because they do not maximize the net benefit. By failing to maximize net benefit, they are forgoing an opportunity to make some people better off without harming others.

Dynamic Efficiency

The static-efficiency criterion is very useful for comparing resource allocations when time is not an important factor. Yet many of the decisions made now affect the value of the asset for future generations. Time is a factor. Exhaustible energy resources, once used, are gone. Biological renewable resources (such as fisheries or forests) can be overharvested, leaving smaller and possibly weaker populations for future generations. Persistent pollutants can accumulate over time. How can we make choices when the benefits and costs may occur at different points in time?

The traditional criterion used to address this problem is called *dynamic efficiency*, a generalization of the static-efficiency concept already developed. In this generalization, the criterion provides a way for thinking not only about the magnitude of benefits and costs, but also about timing. In order to do this, the criterion must provide a way to compare the net benefit received in one period with the net benefit received in another. The concept that allows this comparison is called *present value*. Therefore, before defining dynamic efficiency, we must define present value.

Present value explicitly incorporates the time value of money. A dollar today invested at 10 percent interest yields $1.10 a year from now (the return of the $1 principal plus $0.10 interest). The present value of $1.10 received one year from now is, therefore, $1 because, given $1 now, you can turn it into $1.10 a year from now by investing it at 10 percent interest. We can find the present value of any amount of money (X) received one year from now by computing $X/(1 + r)$, where r is the appropriate interest rate (10 percent in the above example).

What could your dollar earn in two years at r percent interest? Because of compound interest, the amount would be $1(1 + r)(1 + r) = $1.00(1 + r)^2$. It follows then that the present value of X received two years from now is $X/(1 + r)^2$.

By now the pattern should be clear. The *present value* of a *one-time* net benefit received n years from now is

$$PV[B_n] = \frac{B_n}{(1 + r)^n}.$$

The present value of a *stream* of net benefits $\{B_0, \ldots, B_n\}$ received over a period of n years is computed as

$$PV[B_0, \ldots, B_n] = \sum_{i=0}^{n} \frac{B_i}{(1 + r)^i},$$

where r is the appropriate interest rate and B_0 is the amount of net benefits received immediately. The process of calculating the present value is called *discounting*, and the rate r is referred to as the discount rate.[8]

The number resulting from a present-value calculation has a straightforward interpretation. Suppose you were investigating an allocation that would yield the following pattern of net benefits on the last day of each of the next five years: $3,000, $5,000, $6,000, $10,000, $12,000. If you use an interest rate of 6 percent ($r = 0.06$) and the above formula, you will discover that this stream has a present value of $29,210.

What does that number mean? If you put $29,210 in a savings account earning 6 percent interest and wrote yourself checks respectively for $3,000, $5,000, $6,000, $10,000, and $12,000 on the last day of each of the next five years, your last check would just restore the account to a zero balance. Thus, you should be indifferent to receiving $29,210 now or the specific five-year stream of benefits totaling $36,000; given one you can get the other. Hence, the method is called present value because it translates everything back to its current worth.

It is now possible to define dynamic efficiency. An allocation of resources across n time periods is dynamically efficient if it maximizes the present value of net benefits that could be received from all the possible ways of allocating those resources over the n periods.

To illustrate, we can use the dynamic-efficiency criterion to define an efficient allocation of a depletable, nonrecyclable resource. Dynamic efficiency assumes that society's objective is to balance the current and subsequent uses of the resources by maximizing the present value of the net benefit derived from the use of the resource. We shall demonstrate by using a very simple model which assumes there are only two time periods in which the resource can be used. In subsequent chapters we shall show how these conclusions generalize to longer times and more complicated situations.

Let's begin with a case in which the marginal cost of extracting the resource is constant, but there is a fixed supply of it to allocate between the two periods. Let's assume that demand is constant in the two periods, the marginal willingness-to-pay is given by the formula $P = 8 - 0.4\,q$, and marginal cost is constant at $2 per unit (see Figure 2.6).

---

[8]The discount rate should equal the social opportunity cost of capital. See Raymond Mikesell, *The Rate of Discount for Evaluating Public Projects* (Washington, DC: American Enterprise Institute for Public Policy Research, 1977) for detailed examination of the reasons for this choice and its implications. We shall examine the question of whether private firms can be expected to use the socially correct discount rate in Chapter 3 and the question of how the discount rate is chosen by the government in Chapter 4.

FIGURE 2.6   The Allocation of an Abundant Depletable Resource

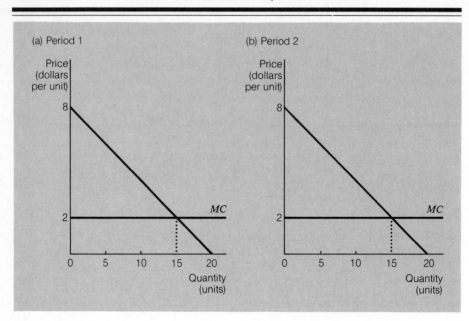

Notice that if the total supply were 30 or greater, and we were only concerned with these two periods, an efficient allocation would produce 15 units in each period, *regardless of the discount rate.* The supply is sufficient to cover the demand in both periods; the production in period 1 does not reduce the production in period 2. In this case the static-efficiency criterion is sufficient, since time is not an important part of the problem.

Examine, however, what happens when the available supply is less than 30. Suppose it is equal to 20. How do we determine the efficient allocation? According to the dynamic-efficiency criterion, the efficient allocation is the one that maximizes the present value of the net benefit. The present value of the net benefit for both years is simply the sum of the present values in each of the two years. To take a concrete example, consider the present value of a particular allocation: 15 units in the first period and 5 in the second. How would we compute the present value of that allocation?

The present value in the first period would be that portion of the geometric area under the demand curve which is over the supply curve—$45.00.[9] The present value in the second period is that portion of the area under the demand curve which is over the supply curve from the origin to the 5 units produced multiplied by $1/(1 + r)$. If

---

[9]The area of a right triangle is equal to ½ of the base times the height of that triangle. In this case the height of the triangle is $6 [$8 − $2] and the base is 15 units. The area is therefore ½ × $6 × 15 = $45.

FIGURE 2.7 The Dynamically Efficient Allocation

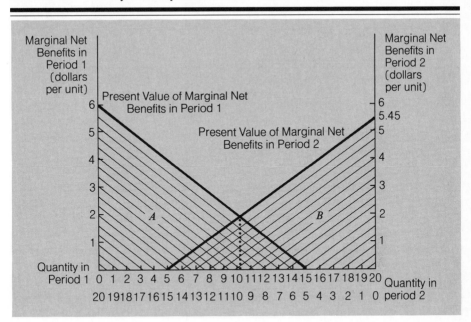

we use $r = 0.10$, then, the present value of the net benefit received in the second period is 22.73,[10] and the present value of net benefits for the two years is $67.73.

We now know how to find the present value of net benefits for any allocation. How does one find the allocation that maximizes present value? One way is simply, with the aid of a computer, to try all possible combinations of q_1 and q_2, which sum to 20. The one yielding the maximum present value of net benefits can then be selected. That is tedious and, for those who have the requisite mathematics, unnecessary.

The dynamically efficient allocation of this resource has to satisfy the condition that the present value of the marginal net benefit from the last unit in period 1 equals the present value of the marginal net benefit in period 2 (see Appendix at the end of this chapter). Even without mathematics, this principle is easy to understand, as can be demonstrated with the use of a simple graphical representation of the two-period allocation problem.[11]

Figure 2.7 depicts the present value of the marginal net benefit for each of the two periods. The net-benefit curve for period 1 is to be read from left to right. The

---

[10]The undiscounted net benefit is $25.00. (Can you see why?) The discounted net benefit is therefore 25/1.10 = 22.73.

[11]This type of analysis first appeared in James M. Griffin and Henry B. Steele, *Energy Economics and Policy* (New York: Academic Press, 1980), 70.

net-benefit curve intersects the vertical axis at $6; demand would be zero at $8 and the marginal cost is $2, so the difference (marginal net benefit) is $6. The marginal net benefit for the first period goes to zero at 15 units because, at that quantity, the willingness to pay for that unit exactly equals its cost.

The only tricky aspect of drawing the graph involves constructing the curve for the present value of net benefits in period 2. There are two aspects worth noting. First, the zero axis for the period 2 net benefits is on the right rather than the left side. Therefore, increases in period 2 are recorded from right to left. This way, any point along the horizontal axis yields a total of 20 units allocated among the two periods. Any particular point on that axis picks a unique allocation between the two periods.[12]

Second, the present value of the marginal benefit curve for period 2 intersects the vertical axis at a different point than does the comparable curve in period 1. Why? This intersection is lower because the marginal benefits in the second period are discounted. Thus with the 10 percent discount rate we are using, the marginal net benefit is $6 and the present value is $6/$1.10 = $5.45. The message worth carrying away from this discussion of the curve for period 2 is that larger discount rates rotate the marginal benefit curve around the point of zero net benefit ($q_1 = 5$, $q_2 = 15$) toward the right-hand axis. We shall use this fact in a moment.

The efficient allocation is now readily identifiable as the point where the present value of marginal net benefit curves cross. The total present value of net benefits, then, is the area under the marginal net-benefit curve for period 1 up to the efficient allocation (labeled area *A*), plus the areas under the present value of marginal net-benefit curve for period 2 from the right-hand axis up to its efficient allocation (labeled area *B*). The fact that we have an efficient allocation means that the sum of these two areas is maximized.[13]

Because we have developed our efficiency criteria independent of an institutional context, these criteria are equally appropriate for evaluating resource allocations generated by markets, government rationing or even the whims of a dictator. One of the messages of this analysis is that *any* efficient allocation method must take scarcity into account. The details of precisely how that is done depends on the context (we shall elaborate on this point in Chapter 6), but we can develop the general concept here and use our numerical example to illustrate how scarcity should be taken into account in this type of two-period model.

Scarcity imposes an opportunity cost that we shall henceforth refer to as the *marginal user cost*. When resources are scarce, greater current use diminishes future opportunities. The marginal user cost is the present value of these foregone opportunities at the margin. To be more specific, uses of those resources which would have been appropriate in the absence of scarcity may no longer be appropriate once scarcity is

---

[12]Note that the sum of the two allocations on Figure 2.7 is always 20. The left-hand axis represents an allocation of all 20 units to period 2 while the right-hand axis represents an allocation entirely to period 1.

[13]Demonstrate by first allocating slightly more to period 2 (and therefore less to period 1) and showing that the total area decreases. Conclude by allocating slightly less to period 2 and showing that, in this case as well, total area declines.

present. Using lots of water to keep lawns lush and green may be wholly appropriate for an area with sufficiently large replenishable water supplies, but quite inappropriate when it denies drinking water to future generations. Failure to take the higher scarcity value of water into account in the present will lead to an inefficiency or an extra cost to society due to the extra scarcity imposed on the future. This additional marginal value that scarcity creates is the marginal user cost.

We can illustrate how this concept is used by returning to our numerical example. If there were 30 or more units, each period would be allocated 15 and the type of scarcity which gives rise to the marginal user cost would not exist. With 30 or more units, therefore, the marginal user cost would be zero.

With 20 units, however, scarcity does exist. No longer can 15 units be allocated to each period; each period will have to be allocated less than would be the case without scarcity. The marginal user cost for this case is not zero. As can be seen from Figure 2.7 the present value of the marginal user cost, the additional value created by scarcity, is graphically represented by the vertical distance between the quantity axis and the intersection of the two present value curves. It is identical to the present value of the marginal net benefit in each of the periods. This value can either be read off the graph or determined more precisely to be $1.905 from the Appendix to this chapter.

We can make this concept even more concrete by considering its use in a market context. An efficient market would have to consider not only the marginal cost of extraction for this resource, but the marginal user cost as well. Whereas in the absence of scarcity the price would equal the marginal cost of extraction, with scarcity the price would equal the sum of marginal extraction cost and marginal user cost.

This can be seen in our numerical example by solving for the prices that would prevail in an efficient market facing scarcity over time. Inserting the efficient quantities (10.238 and 9.762 respectively) into the willingness-to-pay function ($P = 8 - 0.4q$) yields $P_1 = 3.905$ and $P_2 = 4.095$. The corresponding supply and demand diagrams are given in Figure 2.8.

The marginal user cost for each period is the difference between the price and the marginal cost of extraction. Notice that it takes on the value $1.905 in the first period and $2.095 in the second. In both years the *present value of the marginal user cost* is $1.905. In the second year the actual marginal user cost is $1.905* (1 + r)$. Since $r = 0.10$ in this example, the marginal user cost for the second period is $2.095.[14] Thus, while the present value of marginal user cost is equal in both periods, the actual marginal user cost rises over time.

Both the size of the marginal user cost and the allocation of the resource between the two periods is affected by the discount rate. In Figure 2.7 because of discounting the efficient allocation allocates somewhat more to period 1 than to period 2. Using a discount rate larger than 0.10 would be incorporated in this diagram by rotating the period 2 curve an appropriate amount toward the right-hand axis, holding the point at which it intersects the horizontal axis fixed. The larger the discount rate is, the greater the amount of rotation required. The amount allocated to the second period would be

---

[14]You can verify this by taking the present value of $2.095 and showing it to be equal to $1.905.

FIGURE 2.8   The Efficient Market Allocation of a Depletable Resource:
The Constant-Marginal-Cost Case

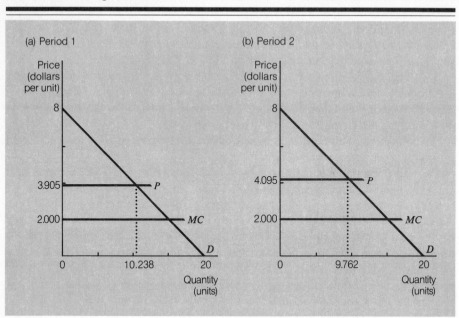

necessarily smaller with larger discount rates. The general conclusion, which shall hold
for all of the models we shall consider, is that higher discount rates tend to skew the
allocation toward the present, because they give the future less weight in balancing
the relative value of present and future resource use.

Sustainability

While no generally accepted standards of fairness or justice exist, some have more prominent support than others. One such standard concerns the treatment of future generations.

What legacy should earlier generations leave to later ones? This is a particularly
difficult issue because, in contrast to other groups for which we may want to insure
fair treatment, future generations cannot articulate their wishes, much less negotiate
with current generations ("We'll take your radioactive wastes, if you leave us plentiful
supplies of titanium.")

One starting point for intergenerational equity is provided by philosopher John Rawls
in his monumental work, *A Theory of Justice.* Rawls suggests one way to derive general
principles of justice is to place, hypothetically, every person in an original position
behind a "veil of ignorance." This veil of ignorance would prevent them from knowing
their eventual position in society. Once behind this veil, people would decide on rules
to govern the society that they would, after the decision, be forced to live in.

In our context this approach would suggest a hypothetical meeting of all members of present and future generations to decide on rules for allocating resources among generations. Because these members are prevented by the veil of ignorance from knowing the generation to which the will belong, they will not be excessively conservationist (lest they turn out to be a member of an earlier generation) or excessively exploitative (lest they become a member of a later generation).

What kind of rule would emerge from such a meeting? Perhaps the most common answer is known as the sustainability criterion. The *sustainability criterion* suggests that, at a minimum, future generations should be left no worse off than current generations. Allocations that impoverish future generations, in order to enrich current generations, are, according to this criterion, patently unfair.

It is also important to understand what this criterion does *not* specify. It does not say, for example, that it is unfair for current generations to enrich themselves at the expense of future generations *as long as future generations remain at least as well off as current generations.*

This distinction is important. It is sometimes argued, for example, that currently we should be depending solely on renewable resources. This argument suggests that since every unit of a depletable resource now in use is a unit unavailable for future generations, the use of depletable resources is unfair. It is not valid to conclude from the sustainability criterion that relying on depletable resources is unfair *unless the consumption of these resources causes future generations to be worse off than we are.*

In future chapters we will apply the sustainability criterion, giving particular attention to whether intertemporally efficient allocations are always sustainable or whether they are unfair to future generations. Furthermore, we shall investigate whether market allocations are efficient and/or sustainable.

SUMMARY

The relationship between humanity and the environment requires many choices. Some basis for making rational choices is absolutely necessary. If not made by design, decisions will be made by default.

The economics approach views the environment as a composite asset, supplying a variety of services to humanity. The intensity and composition of those services depends on the actions of humans as constrained by physical laws, such as the first and second laws of thermodynamics.

Economics has two rather different means of enhancing understanding of environmental and natural resource economics. Positive economics is useful in describing the actions of people and the impact of those actions on the environmental asset. Normative economics can provide guidance on how optimal service flows can be defined and achieved.

Normative economics suggests two precise criteria for judging the optimal level and composition of services: efficiency and sustainability. The former suggests maximizing the present value of net benefits to society. When the use of a natural resource in one period introduces scarcity or increases the degree of scarcity of that resource in subsequent periods, the efficient allocation must take the marginal user cost into account. Failure to take marginal user cost into account would cause a smaller than efficient amount of the resource to be conserved. The sustainability criterion allows us to judge the fairness rather than the efficiency of these intertemporal allocations. Future chapters will determine the degree to which our social institutions yield allocations that conform to these criteria.

FURTHER READING

Arrow, Kenneth J. *The Limits of Organization* (New York: W. W. Norton, 1974). In this short, but pithy book, Nobel Laureate Kenneth Arrow analyzes why – and how – human beings organize their common lives to overcome the basic economic problem of allocating scarce resources. Alternative models of achieving efficient allocations are explored, including markets and governments.

Fisher, Anthony C., and Frederick M. Peterson. "The Environment in Economics: A Survey." *Journal of Economic Literature* XIV (March, 1976): 1–33. A technical, but thorough, review of the literature in environmental economics prior to the mid-1970s. An extensive bibliography.

Peterson, Frederick M., and Anthony C. Fisher. "The Exploitation of Extractive Resources: A Survey." *Economic Journal* LXXXVII (December, 1977): 681–721. A companion piece to the A. C. Fisher and F. M. Peterson (1976) listing above which surveys the field of natural resource economics. Also has an extensive bibliography.

Schelling, Thomas C. *Micromotives and Macrobehavior* (New York: W. W. Norton, 1978). Through familiar and readily grasped examples, Professor Schelling demonstrates how members of a society tend to be blind to the collective consequences of their separate decisions.

ADDITIONAL REFERENCES

Burness, Stuart, Ronald Cummings, Glenn Morris, and Inga Paik. "Thermodynamic and Economic Concepts as Related to Resource-Use Policies," *Land Economics,* 56 (February, 1980): 1–9.

Butlin, J. A., ed. *The Economics of Environmental and Natural Resource Policy* (Boulder, Colo.: Westview Press, 1981).

Dorfman, Robert, and Nancy S. Dorfman, eds. *Economics of the Environment: Selected Readings,* 2nd ed. (New York: W. W. Norton, 1977).

Fisher, Anthony C., *Resource and Environmental Economics* (Cambridge, England: Cambridge University Press, 1981).

Kneese, Allen V., Robert U. Ayers, and Ralph C. d'Arge. *Economics and the Environment: A Materials Balance Approach* (Washington: Resources for the Future, 1970).

Kneese, Allen V. *Economics and the Environment* (New York: Penguin Books, 1977).

Krutilla, John. "Conservation Reconsidered," *The American Economic Review,* 57 (September, 1968): 777–786.

Rawls, John. *A Theory of Justice* (Cambridge, Mass.: The Belknap Press of Harvard University Press, 1971).

Siebert, Horst. *Economics of the Environment* (Lexington, Mass.: Lexington Books, 1981).

DISCUSSION QUESTIONS

1. It has been suggested that we should use the "net energy" criterion to make choices among various types of energy. Net energy is defined as the total energy content in the energy source minus the energy required to extract, process, and deliver it to consumers. According to this criterion, we should use those sources with the highest net energy content first.

   Would the dynamic efficiency criterion and the net energy criterion be expected to yield the same choice? Why or why not?

2. The notion of sustainability is not the same in the natural sciences as in economics. In the natural sciences, sustainability frequently means maintaining a constant *physical* flow of each and every resource (e.g., fish or wood from the forest), while in economics it means maintaining the *value* of those service flows. When might the two criteria lead to different choices? Why?

PROBLEMS

1. One convenient way to express the willingness-to-pay relationship between price and quantity is to use the inverse demand function. In an inverse demand function, the price consumers are willing to pay is expressed as a function of the quantity available for sale. Suppose the inverse demand function (expressed in dollars) for a product is $P = 80 - q$, and the marginal cost (in dollars) of producing it is $MC = 1q$, where P is the price of the product and q is the quantity demanded and/or supplied. (a) How much would be supplied in a static efficient allocation? (b) What would be the magnitude of the net benefits (in dollars)?

2. In the numerical example given in the text the inverse demand function for the depletable resource is $P = 8 - 0.4q$ and the marginal cost of supplying it is $2.00. (a) If 20 units are to be allocated between two periods, in a dynamically efficient allocation how much would be allocated to the first period and how much to the second period when the discount rate is zero? (b) What would the efficient price be in the two periods? (c) What would the marginal user cost in each period be?

3. Assume the same demand conditions as stated in question 2 above, but for this question let the discount rate be 0.10 and the marginal cost of extraction be $4.00 instead of $2.00. How much would be produced in each period in an efficient allocation? What would the marginal user cost be in each period? Would the static and dynamic efficiency criteria yield the same answers for this problem or would they yield different answers? Why?

APPENDIX

The Simple Mathematics
of Dynamic Efficiency*

Assume that the demand curve for a depletable resource is linear and stable over time. Thus the inverse demand curve in year t can be written as

$$P_t = a - bq_t. \tag{1}$$

The total benefits from extracting an amount q_t in year t is then the integral of this function (= the area under the inverse demand curve):

$$\text{Total benefits}_t = \int_0^{q_t} a - bq \; dq$$
$$= aq_t - \frac{b}{2} q_t^2. \tag{2}$$

Further assume that the marginal cost of extracting that resource is a constant c and therefore the total cost of extracting any amount q_t in year t can be given by

$$TC_t = cq_t. \tag{3}$$

If the total available amount of this resource is equal to $\bar{Q}$, then the dynamic allocation of a resource over n years is the one which fulfills the following maximization problem:

$$\underset{q_t}{\text{Max}} \sum_{i=1}^{n} \frac{\left(aq_i - \frac{b}{2} q_i^2 - cq_i\right)}{(1 + r)^{i-1}} + \lambda\left[\bar{Q} - \sum_{i=1}^{n} q_i\right]. \tag{4}$$

---

*Greater detail on the mathematics of constrained optimization can be found in any standard mathematical economics text such as Alpha Chiang, *Fundamental Methods of Mathematical Economics*, 2nd ed. (New York: McGraw-Hill, 1974).

Assuming that $\bar{Q}$ is less than would normally be demanded, the dynamically efficient allocation must satisfy

$$\frac{a - bq_i - c}{(1 + r)^{i-1}} - \lambda = 0 \qquad i = 1, \ldots, n \tag{5}$$

$$\sum_{i=1}^{n} q_i - \bar{Q} = 0 \tag{6}$$

We can illustrate the use of these equations with the two-period example dealt with in the text. The following parameter values are assumed in that problem:

$$a = 8 \qquad c = \$2$$
$$b = .4 \qquad \bar{Q} = 20$$
$$r = .10.$$

Using these, we obtain

$$8 - 0.4\, q_1 - 2 - \lambda = 0 \tag{7}$$

$$\frac{8 - 0.4\, q_2 - 2}{(1.10)} - \lambda = 0 \tag{8}$$

$$q_1 + q_2 = 20.$$

It is now readily verified that the solution (accurate to the third decimal place) is

$$q_1 = 10.238 \qquad \lambda = \$1.905$$
$$q_2 = 9.762$$

We can now demonstrate the propositions discussed in the text.

1. Verbally, equation (7) states that in a dynamic efficient allocation, the present value of the marginal net benefit in period 1 ($8 - .4q_1 - 2$) has to equal λ. Equation (8) states that the present value of the marginal net benefit in period 2 should also equal λ. Therefore, they must be equal to each other. This demonstrates the proposition shown graphically in Figure 2.7.

2. The present value of marginal user cost is represented by λ. Thus equation (7) states that price in the first period ($8 - .4q_1$) should be equal to the sum of marginal extraction cost ($\$2$) and marginal user cost ($\$1.905$). Multiplying (8) by $(1 + r)$, it becomes clear that price in the second period ($8 - .4q_2$) is equal to the marginal extraction cost ($\$2$) plus the higher marginal user cost [$\lambda(1 + r) = (1.905) \times (1.10) = \$2.095$] in period 2. These results show why the graphs in Figure 2.8 have the properties they do. They also illustrate the point that, in this case, marginal user cost rises over time.

CHAPTER THREE

Property Rights, Externalities, and Environmental Problems

> *The charming landscape which I saw this morning, is indubitably made up of some twenty or thirty farms. Miller owns this field, Locke that, and Manning the woodland beyond. But none of them owns the landscape. There is a property in the horizon which no man has but he whose eye can integrate all the parts, that is, the poet. This is the best part of these men's farms, yet to this their land deeds give them no title.*
> RALPH WALDO EMERSON, *NATURE* (1836)

INTRODUCTION

In the last chapter we developed specific normative criteria for making rational choices about the relationship between the economic system and the environment. According to those criteria, an environmental problem exists when resource allocations are either inefficient or expected to leave future generations worse off than we are. We also suggested that these breaches of efficiency or sustainability could occur when our economic and/or political institutions make decisions resulting in allocations which are quite different from those collectively desired.

Why would this happen? Why would individual or group interests diverge from those of society at large? What circumstances give rise to this division of interests, and what can be done about it? The answers to these questions are based on the concept known as a *property right*. In this chapter we will explore this concept and how it can be used to understand why the environmental asset can be undervalued by both the market and governmental policy. We will also discuss how the government and the market can, on occasion, use knowledge of property rights and their effects on incentives to orchestrate a coordinated approach to resolving these difficulties.

ROLE OF PROPERTY RIGHTS

Property Rights and Efficient Market Allocations

The manner in which producers and consumers use environmental resources depends on the property rights governing those resources. In economics *property right* refers to a bundle of entitlements defining the owner's rights, privileges, and limitations for use of the resource. By examining such entitlements and how they are used, we will better understand how environmental problems arise from government and market allocations.

These property rights can be vested either with individuals, as in a capitalist economy, or with the state, as in a centrally planned socialist economy. It is not uncommon to hear that the source of environmental problems in a capitalist economy is the market system itself, or, more specifically, the pursuit of profits. You may have heard this point of view expressed as, "Corporations are more interested in profits than they are in the needs of people." Those who espouse this view look longingly at centrally planned economies as a means of avoiding these problems.

There are two problems with this viewpoint. Centrally planned economies, such as the Soviet Union, have not historically avoided pollution excesses (Example 3.1). On the other hand, the pursuit of profits is not inevitably inconsistent with fulfilling the needs of the people. Though the pursuit of profits may sometimes be inconsistent with fulfilling these needs, it is not always inconsistent. In fact, this pursuit is often the essential ingredient in meeting people's needs. How can we tell when the pursuit of profits is consistent with societal objectives, such as efficiency and sustainability, and when it is not?

Efficient Property Right Structures

Let's begin by describing the structure of property rights that could produce efficient allocations in a well-functioning market economy. An efficient structure has four main characteristics:

1. *Universality*   All resources are privately owned and all entitlements completely specified.
2. *Exclusivity*   All benefits and costs accrued as a result of owning and using the resources should accrue to the owner, and only to the owner, either directly or indirectly by sale to others.
3. *Transferability*   All property rights should be transferable from one owner to another in a voluntary exchange.
4. *Enforceability*   Property rights should be secure from involuntary seizure or encroachment by others.

EXAMPLE 3.1

Pollution in Centrally Planned Economies: The Soviet Union

Since environmental problems are thought to be caused by a divergence between individual incentives and collective incentives, it is not uncommon to hear that centrally planned economies avoid environmental problems. This argument suggests that the centralization of decision making—by putting it in the hands of the state, as occurs in a centrally planned economy—allows collective decisions to be made at the outset.

A study by economist Marshall Goldman shows that this expectation is not borne out by facts. His extensive study of air and water pollution in the Soviet Union suggests that the problems found in market economies occur with equal intensity in the Soviet Union.

How can this be? Goldman suggests that the centralized planning system in the Soviet Union creates different, but no less potent, divergences between individual and collective incentives. For example, as of 1970, 65 percent of all factories in the largest Soviet republic, the Russian Soviet Federated Socialist Republic, discharged their waste into the water without any attempt to clean it up. They did this because the managers were being judged solely in terms of output, not in terms of the harm they caused to the environment. The central plans which set the priorities to be followed by the managers very simply emphasized economic growth over the environment.

In his summary Goldman states:

> . . . If the study of environmental disruption in the Soviet Union demonstrates anything, it shows that not private enterprise but industrialization is the primary cause of environmental disruption. This suggests that state ownership of all the productive resources is no cure-all.

Source: Marshall I. Goldman, "The Convergence of Environmental Disruption," in *Ecology and Economics: Controlling Pollution in the 70's,* Marshall I. Goldman, ed. (Englewood Cliffs: Prentice-Hall, 1972): 211–224; D. Powell, "The Social Costs of Modernization: Ecological Problems in the USSR," *World Politics* 22 (1971):327–334, and Marshall I. Goldman, "Economics of Environmental and Renewable Resources in Socialist Systems," in Allen V. Kneese and James L. Sweeney, eds. *Handbook of Natural Resource and Energy Economics: Vol. II* (Amsterdam: North-Holland, 1985): 725–45.

An owner of a resource with a well-defined property right (one exhibiting these four characteristics) has a powerful incentive to use that resource efficiently because a decline in the value of that resource represents a personal loss. Take the case of a ˙ for example. The farmer has an incentive to fertilize and irrigate his land because ˙ increased production raises his income level. Similarly, he has an incen- ˙ when that raises the productivity of his land.

When well-defined property rights are exchanged, as in a market economy, this exchange facilitates efficiency. We can illustrate this point by examining the incentives consumers and producers face when a well-defined system of property rights is in place. Because the seller has the right to prevent the consumer from consuming the product in the absence of payment, the consumer must pay to receive the product. Given a market price, the consumer decides how much to purchase by choosing that amount which maximizes his or her individual net benefit (Figure 3.1).

The consumer's net benefit is the area under the demand curve minus the area representing cost. The cost to the consumer is the area under the price line, since that area represents the expenditure on the commodity. Obviously, for a given price P^*, consumer net benefit is maximized by choosing to purchase Q_d units. Area A is then the geometric representation of the net benefit received, known as *consumer surplus*. It is the area under the demand curve that lies above the price, bounded from the left by the vertical axis and from the right by the quantity of the good being considered.

Meanwhile, sellers face a similar choice (Figure 3.2). Given price P^*, the seller maximizes his own net benefits by choosing to sell Q_s units. The net benefit received (Area B) by the seller is called *producer surplus*. It is the area under the price line that lies over the marginal cost curve, bounded from the left by the vertical axis and the right by the quantity of the good being considered.

The price level which producers and consumers face will adjust until supply equals demand, as depicted in Figure 3.3. Given that price, consumers maximize their surplus, producers maximize their surplus, and the market clears.

FIGURE 3.1 The Consumer's Choice

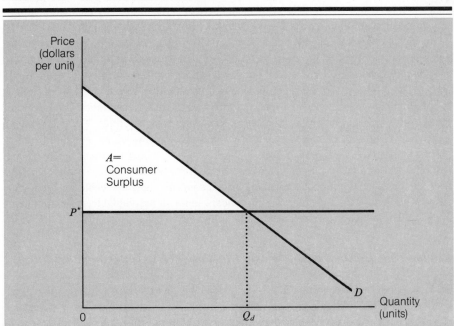

FIGURE 3.2   The Producer's Choice

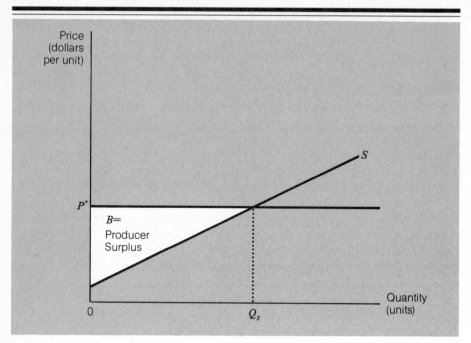

Is this allocation efficient? Using our definition of static efficiency from the previous chapter, it is clear the answer is yes. The net benefit is maximized by the market allocation and, as seen in Figure 3.3., it is equal to the sum of consumer and producer surplus. Thus we have not only established a way to measure the net benefit, but a way to talk about how it is distributed between consumers as a group and producers as a group.

This distribution is crucially significant. Efficiency is *not* achieved because consumers and producers are seeking efficiency. They aren't! In a system with well-defined property rights and competitive markets in which to sell those rights, producers try to maximize their surplus and consumers try to maximize their surplus. The price system, then, induces those self-interested parties to make choices which are efficient from the point of view of society as a whole.

Though familiarity may have dulled our appreciation for it, it is noteworthy that a system designed to produce a harmonious and congenial outcome could function effectively while allowing consumers and producers so much individual freedom in making choices. This is truly a remarkable accomplishment.

Producer's Surplus, Scarcity Rent, and Long-Run Competitive Equilibrium

Since the area under the price line is total revenue, and the area under the marginal-cost curve is total variable cost, producer's surplus is related to profits. (In the long run when all costs are variable, they are identical. In the short run when some costs

FIGURE 3.3 Market Equilibrium

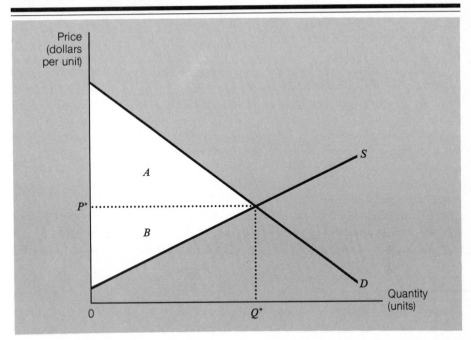

are fixed, producer's surplus is equal to profits plus fixed cost.) As long as new firms can enter into an industry where positive profits are earned without raising the prices of inputs, long-run profits (and producer's surplus) will equal zero.

Essentially, the long-run marginal cost curve in this kind of industry (known as a *constant-cost industry*) is a horizontal line which coincides with the price line. In this case, the net benefit for society as a whole is equal to consumer's surplus. Competition eliminates the producer's surplus. The notion of profits being driven to zero in a long-run competitive equilibrium is probably familiar from an earlier course in microeconomics.

Scarcity Rent

Most natural-resource industries, however, are not constant-cost industries and, therefore, producer's surplus is not eliminated by competition, even with free entry. This producer's surplus which persists in long-run competitive equilibrium is called *scarcity rent*.

David Ricardo was the first economist to recognize the existence of scarcity rent. Ricardo suggested that the price of land was determined by the marginal unit of land which was the least fertile. [The price had to be sufficiently high to allow the poorer land to be brought into production.] Meanwhile, other, more fertile land could be farmed at a positive economic profit at that price. Competition could not erode that profit because the amount of land was limited and lower prices would serve only to reduce the supply of land below the demand for it. In an increasing-cost industry, the only way to expand production is to bring additional, less fertile land (more costly to farm) into production; consequently, additional production does not lower price, as it does in a constant-cost industry.

There are other sources of scarcity rent for natural resources. We have already shown how the allocation of depletable resources gives rise to a positive marginal user cost. The existence of this marginal user cost implies that the efficient price will exceed the marginal cost of extraction, creating a scarcity rent for those resources as well. The first-period scarcity rent, which was computed in our two-period numerical example in the last chapter, is depicted graphically in Figure 3.4.

In this graph the marginal extraction cost is designated as *MEC* and the marginal user cost as *MUC*. A similar graph could be drawn for the second period in which the scarcity rent would be equal to the area under the price line and above the marginal cost of extraction. This scarcity rent is appropriated by the owner of the resource and becomes part of his or her producer surplus as long as property rights are correctly defined. A similar scarcity rent would exist for scarce renewable resources.

It is important to clear up one possible source of confusion. Why is user cost included as part of producer surplus when other costs, such as extraction costs, are not? The distinction between these costs lies in whether or not they are actually paid. The

FIGURE 3.4 Scarcity Rent for a Constant-Extraction-Cost Depletable Resource

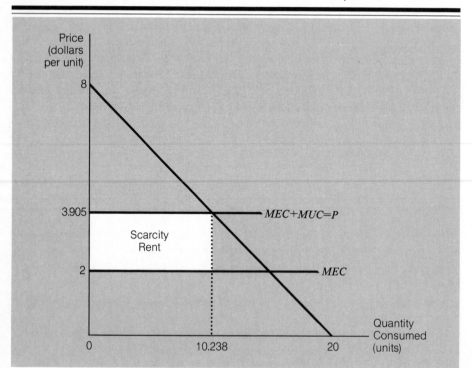

marginal extraction cost is actually paid; it consumes resources. The marginal user cost, in contrast, is an opportunity cost, a cost that would be paid in the form of reduced profits or a reduced net benefit only if the owner of the resource would deviate from the profit-maximizing allocation of the resource over time. When the profit-maximizing allocation is chosen, this cost is not actually borne and, therefore, the owner of the resource appropriates it as scarcity rent. This source of producer surplus is not eliminated by competition and, therefore, even when time is an important consideration, in the presence of well-defined property rights, market allocations and efficient allocations coincide.

The economic system does not always sustain efficient allocations, however, and environmental problems represent one important class of circumstances when it doesn't. If cases of inefficient depreciation of the environment are to be rectified, we must understand the circumstances which lead to inefficiency and what can be done about them.

EXTERNALITIES AS A SOURCE OF MARKET FAILURE

The Concept Introduced

One of the characteristics of an efficient property-rights structure is exclusivity. There are many circumstances when this characteristic is violated in practice. One broad class of violations occurs when an agent making a decision does not bear all of the consequences of his or her action.

Suppose two firms are located by a river. The first produces steel, while the second, somewhat downstream, operates a resort hotel. Both use the river, though in different ways. The steel firm uses it as a receptacle for its waste, while the second uses it to attract customers seeking water recreation—swimming, sailing, and water skiing. If these two facilities are owned by different owners, an efficient use of the water is not likely to result. Because the steel plant does not bear the cost of reduced business at the resort resulting from waste being dumped into the river, it is not sensitive to that cost in its decision making. As a result, it dumps too much waste into the river and an efficient allocation of the river is not attained.

This situation is referred to as an externality. An *externality* exists whenever the welfare of some agent, either a firm or household, depends directly, not only on his or her activities, but also on activities under the control of some other agent as well. In the example, the increased waste in the river imposed an external cost on the resort, a cost the steel firm could not be counted upon to consider appropriately in deciding the amount of waste to dump.

The effects of this external cost on the steel industry can be seen in Figure 3.5, in which the market for steel is depicted. Steel production inevitably involves producing pollution as well. The demand for steel is shown by the demand curve D and the private marginal cost of producing the steel (exclusive of pollution control and damage) is depicted as MC_p. Because society considers both the cost of pollution and the cost of producing the steel, the social marginal cost function (MC_s) includes both of these costs as well.

FIGURE 3.5 Market Allocation With Pollution

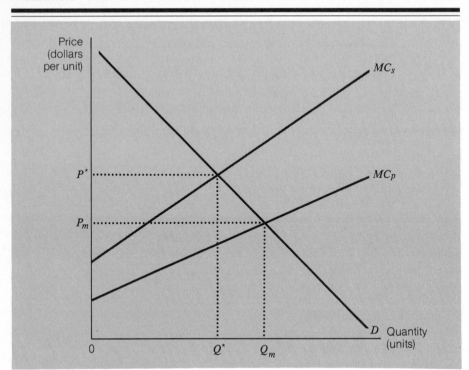

If the steel industry faced no outside control on its emission levels, it would seek to produce Q_m. That choice, in a competitive setting, would maximize their private producer surplus. But that is clearly not efficient, since the net benefit is maximized at Q^* not Q_m.

With the assistance of Figure 3.5, we can draw a number of conclusions about market allocations of commodities causing pollution externalities:

1. The output of the commodity is too large.
2. Too much pollution is produced.
3. The prices of products responsible for pollution are too low.
4. There are no incentives to search for ways to yield less pollution per unit of output.
5. Recycling and reuse of the polluting substances are discouraged since release into the environment is so inefficiently cheap.

The effects of a market imperfection for one commodity end up affecting the demands for raw materials, labor, and so on. The ultimate effects are felt through the entire economy.

Types of Externalities

External effects can be either positive or negative. Historically, the terms *external diseconomy* and *external economy* have been used to refer, respectively, to circumstances in which the affected party is damaged or benefited by the externality. Clearly, the water-pollution example represents an external diseconomy. External economies are not hard to find, however. Someone who purchases a particularly scenic area provides an external economy to all who pass. Generally, when external economies are present, the market will undersupply the resources.

One other distinction is important. One class of externalities, known as *pecuniary externalities,* do not present the same kinds of problems as pollution does. Pecuniary externalities arise when the external effect is transmitted through higher prices. Suppose that a new firm moves into an area and drives up the rental price of land. That increase creates a negative effect on all those paying rent and, therefore, is an external diseconomy.

This pecuniary diseconomy, however, does not cause a market failure, because the resulting higher rents are reflecting the higher costs to all parties. The land market provides a mechanism by which the parties can bid for land; the prices that result reflect the value of the land in its various uses. Without pecuniary externalities the price signals would fail to sustain an efficient allocation.

The pollution example is *not* a pecuniary externality because the effect is not transmitted through prices. In this example, prices do not adjust to reflect the increasing waste load. The scarcity of the water resource is not signaled to the steel firm. An essential feedback mechanism that is present for pecuniary externalities is not present for the pollution case.

The externalities concept is a broad one covering a multitude of sources of market failure. It is clear that externalities occur when the exclusivity of property rights is violated. The next step is to investigate some specific circumstances which can give rise to externalities.

IMPROPERLY DESIGNED PROPERTY RIGHTS SYSTEMS

Common Property Resources

The first class of problems with market allocations occurs when the property rights to the resource lack one or more of the four characteristics described earlier. Perhaps the largest category of resources for which this is true is called common property resources. *Common property resources* are those that are not exclusively controlled by a single agent or source. Access to these resources is not restricted, and therefore, the resources can be exploited on a first-come, first-served basis.

It is not difficult to derive a host of examples. Two of our important life-sustaining resources, air and water, are treated by our legal system as common property resources.

Other examples are migratory wild birds, and fish and animal populations. Even oil can, under certain circumstances, become a common property resource; if there is a large subsurface "pool" of oil, and the individual property rights controlling drilling and extraction are defined in terms of a surface area which is small in comparison to the geographic coverage of the pool, then by owning these rights, several different companies could tap the same source of oil. Since none of these has exclusive control over extraction from this field, the oil in this field becomes a common property resource.

Animal populations, such as the American bison, have also been treated as common property. In the early history of our country bison were plentiful; that they were common property was not a problem. Frontier people who needed hides or meat could easily get whatever they needed; the aggressiveness of any one hunter did not affect the time and effort expended by other hunters. In the absence of scarcity, efficiency was not threatened by treating the herd as a common property resource.

As the years slipped by, however, the demand for bison increased and scarcity became a factor. As the number of hunters increased, the time came when every additional unit of hunting activity increased the amount of time and effort required to produce a given yield of bison.

In Figure 3.6, we depict a constant marginal cost of hunting activity by portraying marginal and average cost as a horizontal line. The benefits derived from this hunting activity are reflected in the *AP* (for average product) curve. This curve represents the average value of bison harvested as a function of the amount of hunting activity expended. It is calculated by multiplying, for each level of hunting activity, the (assumed)

FIGURE 3.6   Exploitation of a Common-Property Resource

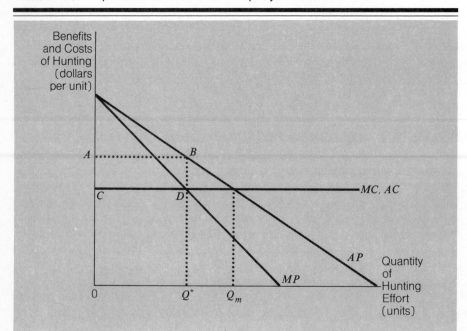

constant price of bison by the amount harvested and dividing this revenue by the number of units of hunting activity. It is downward-sloping because the greater the amount of hunting effort expended, the smaller is the resulting population size. Smaller populations support smaller harvests per unit of effort expended.

The efficient level of hunting activity in this model (Q^*) is the level where the marginal product (or equivalently, marginal benefit) curve crosses the marginal cost curve. At this level of activity the marginal benefit would be just equal to the marginal cost, implying that net benefits are maximized. This allocation would yield society a scarcity rent equal to area *ABCD*.

If there were several hunters and the property rights to the buffaloes were nonexclusive, the resulting allocation would not be efficient. No individual hunter would have an incentive to protect that scarcity rent by restricting the hunting effort. Individual hunters, without exclusive rights, would exploit the resource until their average benefit equalled average cost. This is represented by a level of effort equal to Q_m. This inefficient allocation results because individual hunters cannot appropriate the scarcity rent; therefore, they ignore it. One of the losses from further exploitation which would be recognized with exclusive ownership—the opportunity cost of overexploitation—is not part of their decision-making process when the resource is treated as common property.

Two characteristics of the common-property allocation are worth noting: (1) in the presence of sufficient demand, common property resources are overexploited, and (2) the scarcity rent is dissipated; no one appropriates the rent, so it is lost.

Why does this happen? The unlimited access destroys the incentive to conserve. An individual hunter who can preclude others from hunting this stock has an incentive to keep the herd at an efficient level. This restraint results in lower costs in the form of less time and effort expended to produce a given yield of bison. On the other hand, an individual hunter exploiting a common property resource would not have any incentive to conserve because the benefits derived from restraint would, to some extent, be captured by other hunters. Thus common property resources are not likely to be exploited in an efficient manner because the property-rights system which governs them allows unrestricted access to those resources.

Public Goods

Resources known as *public goods* present a particularly difficult category of environmental problems: These resources exhibit consumption indivisibilities and, additionally, are fully accessible to all.

Consumption is said to be *indivisible* when one person's consumption of a good does not diminish the amount available for others. Several common environmental resources are public goods, such as the "charming landscape" referred to in the chapter-opening quote by Emerson, clean air, clean water, and biological diversity.[1]

---

[1]Notice that public "bads" such as dirty air and dirty water are also possible.

Biological diversity includes two related concepts: genetic diversity and ecological diversity. *Genetic diversity* refers to the amount of genetic variability among individuals within a single species. *Ecological diversity* refers to the number of species within a community of organisms.

Genetic diversity, critical to species survival in the natural world, has also proved to be important in the development of new crops and livestock.[2] Genetic diversity enhances the opportunities for crossbreeding and thus the development of new and better strains. The availability of different strains was the key, for example, in developing a new disease-resistant barley.

While genetic diversity is important to humans, ecological diversity has even greater potential for impact. Because of the interdependence of species within ecological communities, any particular species may have a value to the community far beyond its intrinsic value. Certain species contribute balance and stability to their ecological communities by providing food sources or holding the population of other species in check.

The richness of diversity within and among species has provided new sources of food, energy, industrial chemicals, raw materials, and medicines. Yet there is considerable evidence that biological diversity is decreasing. Of the five to ten million species currently in existence worldwide, at least one million are likely to be lost within your lifetime.[3]

Can we rely on the private sector to produce the efficient amount of public goods such as biological diversity? Unfortunately, the answer is no! Suppose that in response to diminishing ecological diversity we decide to take up a collection to provide some means of preserving endangered species. Would the collection yield sufficient revenue to pay for an efficient level of ecological diversity? The general answer is no. Let's see why.

In Figure 3.7 we represented the demand curves for ecological diversity as determined by the preferences of two consumers, *A* and *B*. Person *A* values diversity more, in that her demand curve is further to the right. Now, because of consumption indivisibility, the market demand curve is represented by the *vertical* summation of the individual demand curve.[4] This is in contrast to a market demand curve for a divisible good, which is constructed by a *horizontal* summation of the individual demand curves. The (constant) marginal cost of providing clean-up services is represented by the *MC* curve.

What is the efficient level of diversity? It can be determined by a direct application of our definition of efficiency. The efficient allocation maximizes net benefits. Net benefits, in turn, are represented geometrically by the portion of the area under the

---

[2]For an example of the argument that genetic diversity is important see Norman Myers, *The Sinking Ark* (New York, NY: Pergamon Press, 1979).

[3]Council on Environmental Quality, *Environmental Quality—1980* (Washington, D.C.: U.S. Government Printing Office, 1980), pp. 31–38.

[4]A vertical summation is necessary because everyone can simultaneously consume the same amount of ecological diversity. We are, therefore, able to add the amounts of money they would be willing to pay for that level of diversity.

FIGURE 3.7   Public Goods and Inefficiency

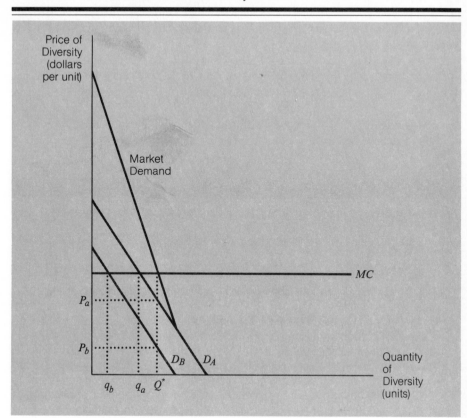

market demand curve which lies above the marginal cost curve. The allocation which maximizes net benefits is Q^*, the allocation where the demand curve crosses the marginal cost curve.

Will our collection box yield enough revenues to supply this level of diversity? The answer is no. Consider the following sequence of events: person B comes to the collection box first and notices there is nothing in it. Therefore he chooses to contribute. How much? He contributes until his net benefits are maximized, at q_b. Now person A comes along. She notices that person B has already purchased q_b. How much more will she purchase? The answer is $q_a - q_b$, because this maximizes her net benefits, given that q_b had already been purchased. The total collection, therefore, is sufficient to defray the cost of q_a units of diversity. Notice that this is less than the efficient amount.

Why does this happen? It happens because each person is able to become a *free rider* on the other's contribution. Because of the consumption indivisibility and nonexcludability properties of the public good, consumers receive the benefits of any diversity which results from the money contributed by other people. When this happens, it tends to diminish each person's incentive to contribute and the final outcome is not efficient.

Notice, however, that the amount privately supplied is not zero. There will be some diversity privately supplied. Indeed, as suggested by Example 3.2, the amount privately supplied may be considerable. The point is that the amount privately supplied is likely to be less than would be efficient.

One further insight can be gained from Figure 3.7 and it is this insight which led to characterizing public-good problems as "particularly difficult" in the opening sentence of this section. The efficient market equilibrium for a public good would require different prices for each consumer. In Figure 3.7 if consumer A is charged P_a and consumer B is charged P_b then both consumers will be satisfied with the efficient allocation (the efficient allocation will have maximized their net benefits given the prices).

EXAMPLE 3.2

Public Goods Privately Provided: The Nature Conservancy

Sometimes there is skepticism about whether there is really any demand for a public good such as biological diversity or whether, if there were, the market would respond at all to that demand. The existence of an organization called The Nature Conservancy suggests that this skepticism is misplaced.

The Nature Conservancy was born of an older organization called the Ecologist Union on September 11, 1950, for the purpose of establishing natural area reserves to preserve or aid in the preservation of areas, objects, and fauna and flora which have scientific, educational, or aesthetic significance. This organization purchases, or accepts as donations, land which has some unique ecological or aesthetic significance to keep it from being used for other purposes. In so doing they preserve many species by preserving the habitat.

From humble beginnings, The Nature Conservancy has, as of 1981, been responsible for the preservation of 1,802,062 acres of forests, marshes, prairies, mounds, and islands. These areas serve as home to rare and endangered species of wildlife and plants. Some 2,743 projects have been completed since the first preserve was acquired in 1954. The preserves, once acquired, are either donated to appropriate government agencies or maintained by the Nature Conservancy and managed by volunteers.

There is considerable merit to this approach. A private organization can move more rapidly than the public sector. Because it has a limited budget, the Nature Conservancy sets priorities and concentrates on acquiring the most ecologically unique areas. Yet the theory of public goods reminds us that if this were to be the sole approach to the preservation of biological diversity, it would preserve a smaller than efficient amount.

Source: *The Nature Conservancy Annual Report,* 1981.

Furthermore, the revenue collected will be sufficient to finance the supply of the public good (since $P_b \times Q^* + P_a \times Q^* = MC \times Q^*$). Thus, while an efficient pricing system exists, it is very difficult to implement. The efficient pricing system requires charging a different price to each consumer and, in the absence of excludability, consumers may not choose to reveal exactly how intensive their preference for this commodity is. Therefore, it would be impossible for the producer to know what prices to charge.

IMPERFECT MARKET STRUCTURES

Environmental problems also occur when one of the participants in an exchange of property rights is able to exercise an inordinate amount of power over the outcome of the transaction. This can occur, for example, when a product is sold by a single seller, or *monopoly*.

It is easy to show that monopolies violate our definition of efficiency (Figure 3.8). According to our definition of static efficiency (Chapter 2), the efficient allocation would

FIGURE 3.8 Monopoly and Inefficiency

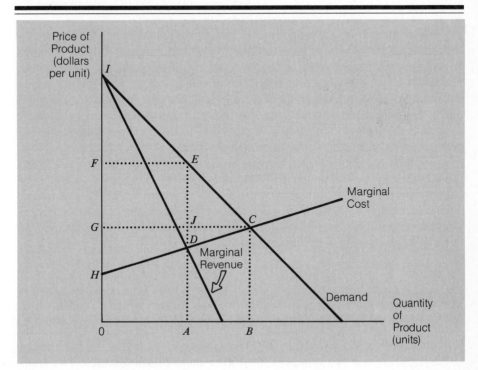

result when *B* is supplied. This would yield net benefits of *HIC*. The monopoly, however, would produce and sell *OA*, where marginal revenue equals marginal cost, and would charge price *OF*. At this point, producer's surplus is maximized, yet it is clearly inefficient because this choice causes society to lose net benefits equal to *EDC*.[5]

Imperfect markets clearly play some role in environmental problems. For example, the major oil-exporting countries have formed a cartel resulting in higher than normal prices and lower than normal production. A *cartel* is a collusive agreement among producers to restrict production and raise prices. This collusive agreement allows the group to act like a monopolist.

DIVERGENCE OF SOCIAL AND PRIVATE DISCOUNT RATES

We concluded above that producers, in their attempt to maximize producer surplus, also maximize the present value of net benefits under the "right" conditions, such as the absence of externalities, the presence of properly defined property rights, and the presence of competitive markets within which the property rights can be exchanged.

Now let's consider one more condition. If resources are to be allocated efficiently, firms must use the same rate to discount future net benefits as is appropriate for society at large. If firms were to use a higher rate, they would extract and sell resources faster than would be efficient. Conversely, if firms were to use a lower-than-appropriate discount rate, they would be excessively conservative.

Why might private and social rates differ? As stated in the previous chapter, the social discount rate is equal to the social opportunity cost of capital. This cost of capital can be separated into two components: risk-free cost of capital and the risk premium.[6] The *risk-free cost of capital* is the rate of return earned when there is absolutely no risk of earning more or less than the expected return. The *risk premium* is an additional cost of capital required to compensate the owners of this capital when the expected and actual returns may differ. Therefore, because of the risk premium, the cost of capital is higher in risky industries than in no-risk industries.

One difference between private and social discount rates may stem from a difference in social and private risk premiums. If the risk of certain decisions is different from the risks faced by society as a whole, then the social and private risk premiums may differ. One obvious example is the risk *caused* by the government. If the firm is afraid its assets will be taken over by the government, it may choose a higher discount rate to make its profits before nationalization occurs.[7]

---

[5]Producers would lose *JDC* compared to the efficient allocation but they would gain area *FEJG*, which is much larger. Meanwhile, consumers would be worse off, since they lose the area *FECJG*. Of these, *FEJG* is merely a transfer to the monopoly while *EJC* is a pure loss to society. The total pure loss *(EDC)* is called a *deadweight* loss.

[6]This point is discussed in more detail in most principles of economics texts.

[7]This case is described in James M. Griffin and Henry B. Steele, *Energy Economics and Policy* (New York: Academic Press, 1980), 85–86.

From the point of view of society—as represented by government—this is not a risk and, therefore, a lower discount rate is appropriate. When private rates exceed social rates, current production is higher than is desirable to maximize the net benefits to society.[8] The result is misallocation.

Though there is no general presumption that private and social discount rates diverge, there are circumstances when they may. When those circumstances arise, market decisions are not efficient.

GOVERNMENT FAILURE

Market processes are not the only source of inefficiency. Political processes are fully as culpable. As will become clear in the chapters which follow, some of the environmental problems we shall encounter arise from a failure of political rather than economic institutions. To complete our study of the ability of institutions to allocate environmental resources, we must understand this source of inefficiency as well.

Government failure shares with market failure the characteristic that improper incentives are the root of the problem. Special interest groups use the political process to engage in what has become known as *rent-seeking*. Rent-seeking is the use of resources in lobbying and other activities directed at securing protective legislation.[9] Successful rent-seeking activity will increase the net benefits going to the special interest group, but it will also frequently lower net benefits to society as a whole. In these instances it is a classic case of the aggressive pursuit of a larger slice of the pie leading to a smaller pie.

Why don't the losers rise up to protect their interest? One main reason is voter ignorance. It is economically rational for voters to remain ignorant on many issues simply because of the high cost of keeping informed and the low probability that any single vote will be decisive. In addition, it is difficult for diffuse groups of individuals, each of whom is affected only to a small degree, to get together to form a coherent, unified opposition. Successful opposition is, in a sense, a public good, so there is a tendency for free-riding on the opposition of others. This implies that the opposition to special interests will be underfunded.

Rent-seeking can take many forms. Producers can seek protection from competitive pressures brought by imports or can seek price floors to hold prices above their efficient levels. Consumer groups can seek price ceilings or special subsidies to transfer part of their costs to the general body of taxpayers. Whatever form it takes, the existence of rent-seeking provides a direct challenge to the presumption that more direct intervention by the government automatically leads to greater efficiency.

---

[8]In this case, the use of a different discount rate by the private sector results from misspecified property rights. The property rights did not have the enforceability characteristic.

[9]See Richard B. McKenzie and Gordon Tullock, "Rent Seeking," *The New World of Economics: Explorations into the Human Experience,* 3rd ed. (Homewood, IL: Richard D. Irwin, 1981), Chapter 15.

These cases illustrate the general economic premise that environmental problems arise because of a divergence between individual and collective objectives. This is a powerful explanatory device because, not only does it suggest why these problems arise, but it also suggests how they might be resolved—by realigning individual incentives to make them compatible with collective objectives.

As self-evident as this approach may be, it is controversial (see Example 3.3). The issue is whether the problem is our improper values or the improper translation of our quite proper values into action.

Economists have always been reluctant to argue that values of consumers are warped because that would necessitate dictating the "correct" set of values. Both capitalism and democracy are based on the presumption that the majority knows what it is doing, whether it is casting ballots for representatives or dollar votes for goods and services. That presumption may be wrong, but over two hundred years of history suggest it isn't.

THE PURSUIT OF EFFICIENCY

We have seen that environmental problems arise when property rights are ill defined, when these rights are exchanged under something other than competitive conditions, and when social and private discount rates diverge. We can now use our definition of efficiency to explore possible remedies, such as private negotiation, judicial determinations, and regulation by the legislative and executive branches of government.

Private Resolution through Negotiation

The simplest means to restore efficiency occurs when the number of affected parties is small, making negotiation feasible. Suppose, for example, the noise of a stereo system shatters the tranquility of an evening. This situation is an environmental problem because the stereo owner does not exclusively bear all the costs of his or her actions. Because of the externality, an inefficiency occurs (Figure 3.9). Without considering the neighbor's welfare, the stereo owner chooses q_m decibels, a choice dictated solely by the owner's enjoyment of loud music. Meanwhile the efficient level q^* is the level which maximizes the net benefit.

How can efficiency be restored in this nonmarket relationship? The first possibility is individual negotiation. The neighbor could bribe the stereo owner. Suppose, for example, the neighbor offered to pay P^* for each decibel reduced. The owner should, in that case, be willing to reduce the level to q^* decibels because of the advantages. The owner loses benefits Cq_mq^* but gains revenue equal to the rectangle CBq_mq^*, which is larger. Meanwhile, the neighbor is also better off than before. Though he or she had to pay the bribe (CBq_mq^*), the neighbor no longer bears the cost of the loud noise (ACq^*q_m), which is greater. Notice that in equilibrium it does not pay the neighbor to offer a per unit bribe either greater than P^* or less than P^*, because those bribes would, respectively, yield too much, or too little, reduction in noise level.

FIGURE 3.9   Noise Pollution: An Example of External Cost

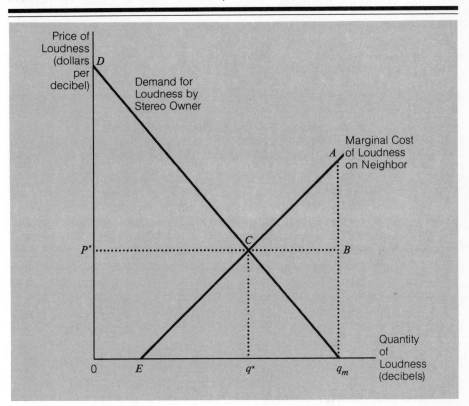

Our discussion of individual negotiations raises two particular questions: (1) Should the property right always belong to the person who gained or seized it first? (2) How can accidents be handled where prior negotiation is clearly impractical? These are questions routinely handled by the court system.

The Courts: Property Rules and Liability Rules

The court system can respond to environmental conflicts by imposing either property rules or liability rules. *Property rules* specify the initial allocation of the entitlement. The entitlements at conflict in our example are, on the one hand, the right to play a stereo loudly and, on the other, the right to peace and quiet. In applying property rules, the court merely decides which right is pre-eminent and places an injunction against violating that right. The injunction is removed only upon obtaining the consent of the party whose right was violated. Consent is usually obtained in return for an out-of-court monetary settlement.

Notice that in the absence of a court decision there is a natural allocation of the entitlement to the party which can most easily seize it. In our example the natural allocation would give the entitlement to the party who likes to play loud music. The courts have to decide whether to overturn this natural allocation.

How would they make that decision? Could the courts allocate the entitlement in such a manner as to restore efficiency? In a classic article, economist Ronald Coase [1960] held that as long as negotiation costs are negligible and affected consumers can

EXAMPLE 3.3

Religion as the Source of Environmental Problems

One of the many alternative explanations of the source of environmental problems was advanced by historian Lynn White, Jr. His thesis, simply put, is that the environmental crisis is due to the teachings of Judaism and Christianity which in Western culture have created a warped view of the proper relationship between humans and their environment.

The basis for this thesis is to be found in the first book of the Old Testament:

Then God said, "Let us make man in our image, after our likeness; and let them have dominion over the fish of the sea, and over the birds of the air, and over the cattle, and over all the earth, and over every creeping thing that creeps upon the earth." [Gen. 1:26]

There are two aspects of this passage which are crucial to his argument: (1) God created man in His own image and (2) man was given dominion over the other forms of life. Both of these aspects make man the dominant force on earth and, according to White, suggest that "it is God's will that man exploit nature for his proper ends." White also make the point that, among the world's religions, this is a rather unique view of the human/environment relationship.

His policy solution follows directly:

More science and more technology are not going to get us out of the present ecological crisis until we find a new religion, or rethink our old one. [p. 1205]

White believes that we must adopt new values which reject the primacy of humans and elevate the stature of nature.

This view provides a stark contrast to the economics approach, which suggests that the problem is neither the primacy of humans nor warped values but rather an imperfect translation of those values into practice.

Sources: Lynn White, Jr., "The Historical Roots of Ecologic Crisis," *Science* 155 (March 10, 1967): 1203–1207; E. F. Schumacher, "Buddhist Economics" in *Small is Beautiful* (New York: Harper Colphon Books, 1973): 50–58; Keith Thomas, *Man and the Natural World* (New York: Knopf, 1983): 17–25.

negotiate freely with each other (when the number of affected parties is small), the court can allocate the entitlement to *either* party and an efficient allocation will result. The only effect of the court's decision is to change the distribution of costs and benefits among the affected parties. This remarkable conclusion has come to be known as the *Coase Theorem*.

We have already shown (in Figure 3.9) that if the stereo owner has the property right, it is in the neighbor's interest to offer a bribe of P^* per decibel of noise reduction resulting in the desired level of q^*. Suppose, now, the neighbor had the property right instead. To play the stereo loudly, the owner must bribe the neighbor. It would be advantageous to offer the neighbor P^* per decibel allowed, and upon receiving this offer, the neighbor would maximize personal net benefit by accepting q^* decibels.

The difference between these two allocations lies in how the cost of obtaining the efficient decibel level is shared between the parties. When the property right is assigned to the owner of the stereo, the cost is borne by the neighbor. When the property right is assigned to the neighbor, the cost is borne by the owner. In either case the efficient decibel level results. The Coase Theorem shows that the very existence of an inefficiency means there are pressures for improvements. Furthermore, the existence of this pressure does not depend on the assignment of property rights.

Yet the importance of this theorem should not be overstated. Both theoretical and practical objections can be raised. The chief theoretical qualification concerns the implicit assumption of zero wealth effects. The decision to confer the property right on a particular party results in a transfer of wealth to that party. This transfer might shift the demand curve out, as long as the income elasticity of demand is not zero. Thus, giving the property right to the stereo owner in Figure 3.9 would shift the demand curve to the right, while giving it to the neighbor would shift the cost curve to the left. As long as there are wealth effects, the type of property rule affects the outcome.

Wealth effects normally are small, so the zero wealth effect assumption is probably not a serious flaw. There are, however, some serious practical flaws. The first involves the incentives for noisemaking that result when the property right is assigned to the stero owner. Since with this assignment noise production would be a profitable activity, this might stimulate other neighbors to turn their stereos up in order to earn the bribes. That certainly would not be efficient.

This solution is also difficult to apply when the number of people affected by the noise is large. You may have already noticed that in the presence of several affected parties noise reduction is a public good.[10] The free-rider problem will make it difficult for the group as a whole to offer an efficient bribe.

When individual negotiation is not practical, for one reason or another, the courts can turn to *liability rules*. These are rules which award monetary damages, after the fact, to the injured party. The amount of the award is designed to correspond to the amount of damage inflicted. Thus, returning to Figure 3.9, an efficient liability rule would impose damages equal to the area under *ECA* from *E* to the chosen decibel level.

---

[10]In this case our graph would reflect the situation by vertically summing the individual marginal cost curves to obtain a curve which reflected the total damage to all parties.

Suppose, for example, the stereo owner persisted in transmitting q_m decibels. If the court decided that damages were appropriate, it would award an amount equal to EAq_m.

The interesting characteristic of liability rules, from an economics point of view, is their application to potential future cases. Examine, for example, what the incentives are for a stereo owner deciding how loud to play the stereo if the person knows that damages will have to be paid to affected parties.

The owner might initially be tempted now to play the music louder than OE, but, upon reflection, he would certainly resist that temptation. The owner would derive additional benefits beyond OE that would be greater than the costs of the damages. Knowing the damages to be paid (equal to the area formed under the line ECA from E to the chosen decibel level), the owner would choose $q*$. For further reductions more benefits would be lost than would be gained in reduced damages paid. (Why doesn't he decide to increase the decibel level beyond $q*$?) Thus, appropriately designed liability rules can also correct inefficiencies by forcing those who cause damage to bear the cost of that damage.

This approach, however, also has its limitations. It relies on a case-by-case determination based on the unique circumstances for each case. Administratively, such a determination is very expensive. Expenses, such as court time, lawyers' fees, and so on, fall into a category called *transaction costs* by economists. In the present context, these are the administrative costs incurred in attempting to correct the inefficiency. When the number of parties involved in a dispute is large and the circumstances are common, we are tempted to correct the inefficiency by statutes or regulations rather than court decisions.

Legislative and Executive Regulation

These remedies can take several forms. The legislature could dictate that no one should play their stereo louder than $q*$. This dictum might then be backed up with sufficiently large jail sentences or fines to deter potential violators. Alternatively, the legislature could impose a tax on decibels. A per unit decibel tax of $P*$, for example, would induce the stereo owner to reduce the noise to $q*$ (Figure 3.9).

Legislatures could also establish rules to permit greater flexibility and yet reduce damage. For example, some apartment buildings for young singles might allow louder stereos while others, catering to older folks or couples with young children needing large amounts of sleep, could have stricter silence standards. With this approach, those who like loud music could pick the former building and those who do not, the latter.

AN EFFICIENT ROLE FOR GOVERNMENT

While the economic approach suggests that government action can well be used to restore efficiency, it also suggests that an inefficiency is not a sufficient condition to call for government intervention. Any corrective mechanism involves transaction costs. If these transaction costs are high enough, and the benefit to be derived from correcting the inefficiency small enough, then it is best simply to live with the inefficiency.

Consider, for example, the pollution problem. The campfires used by the cowboys in the wild West were sources of pollution, but because the capacity of the air to absorb the emissions was sufficient, no problem resulted. As society has evolved, however, the scale of economic activity (and emissions) has expanded. Cities are experiencing severe problems because of the clustering of activities. Both the expansion and the clustering have increased the amount of emissions per unit volume of air. As a result, pollutant concentrations have caused perceptible problems with human health, vegetation growth, and aesthetics.

Historically, as incomes have risen, the demand for leisure activities has also risen. Many of these leisure activities, such as canoeing and backpacking, take place in unique, pristine environmental areas. With the number of these areas declining, due to development for other purposes, the value of remaining areas has increased. Thus, the benefits from protecting some areas have risen over time until they have exceeded the transaction costs of protecting them from pollution and/or development.

The level and concentration of economic activity, having increased pollution problems and driven up the demand for clean air and pristine areas, have created the preconditions for government action. Can government respond or will rent-seeking prevent efficient political solutions? We shall devote a good deal of the rest of this book to a search for the answer to that question.

SUMMARY

How producers and consumers use the resources making up the environmental asset depends on the nature of the property rights governing their use of the resources. When property-right systems are universal, exclusive, transferable, and enforceable, the owner of a resource has a powerful incentive to use that resource efficiently, since the failure to do so results in a personal loss.

For scarce natural resources, the owners derive a scarcity rent. In properly specified property-right systems, this rent is not dissipated by competition. It allows owners to efficiently balance their extraction and conservation decisions.

The economic system will not always sustain efficient allocations, however. Specific circumstances which could lead to inefficient allocations include externalities; improperly defined property-right systems (such as common property resources and public goods); imperfect markets for trading the property rights to the resources (monopoly); and the divergence of social and private discount rates (under the threat of nationalization). When these circumstances arise, market allocations do not maximize the present value of the net benefit.

Due to rent-seeking behavior by special interest groups or the less-than-perfect implementation of efficient plans, the political system can produce inefficiencies as well. Voter ignorance on many issues coupled with the public good nature of any results of political activity tend to create an environment in which private, but not social, net benefits are maximized.

The efficiency criterion can be used to assist in the identification of circumstances in which our political and economic institutions lead us astray. It can also assist in the search for remedies by facilitating the design of regulatory, judicial or legislative solutions.

FURTHER READING

Anderson, Terry L., and P. J. Hill. "The Evolution of Property Rights: A Study of the American West," *The Journal of Law and Economics,* XVIII (April, 1975): 163–79. An interesting test of the proposition that as the efficiency losses from common-property resources in the West rose, individuals increased the amount of time and resources devoted to definition and enforcement of rights to land, water, and livestock.

Bromley, Daniel W. "Property Rules, Liability Rules and Environmental Economics," *Journal of Economic Issues,* XII (March, 1978): 43–60. An elaboration of the role of property rules and liability rules in solving environmental problems.

"Coase Theorem Symposium: Part I." *Natural Resources Journal,* XIII (October, 1973): 557–716; and "Coase Theorem Symposium: Part II." *Natural Resources Journal,* XIV (January, 1974): 1–54. A wide ranging, penetrating series of essays on the limits and implications of the Coase Theorem.

Furubotn, Eirik G., and Svetozar Pejovich. "Property Rights and Economic Theory: A Survey of the Recent Literature," *Journal of Economic Literature,* X (December, 1972): 1137–62. A somewhat dated, nonmathematical survey of the property-rights literature in economics. Contains a bibliography of 124 sources.

ADDITIONAL REFERENCES

Coase, Ronald. "The Problem of Social Cost," *The Journal of Law and Economics,* Vol. 3 (October, 1960): 1–44.

Mercuro, Nicholas, and Warren J. Samuels. "The Role and Resolution of the Compensation Principle in Society, I" *Research in Law and Economics* Vol. 1 (Greenwich, Conn.: JAI Press, 1979): 157–94 and "The Role and Resolution of the Compensation Principle, II" *Research in Law and Economics* Vol. 2. (Greenwich, Conn.: JAI Press, 1980): 103–28.

Powell, D. "The Social Costs of Modernization: Ecological Problems in the USSR," *World Politics,* Vol. 22 (1971): 327–334.

Pryde, Philip R. "The 'Decade of the Environment' in the U.S.S.R., *Science,* Vol. 220 (15 April 1983): 274–279.

DISCUSSION QUESTIONS

1. In a well-known legal case, *Miller* v. *Schoene* (287 U.S. 272), a classic conflict of property rights was featured. Red cedar trees, used only for ornamental purposes, carried a disease that could destroy apple orchards within a radius of two miles. There was no known way of curing the disease except by destroying the cedar trees

or by ensuring that apple orchards were at least two miles away from the cedar trees. Apply the Coase Theorem to this situation. Does it make any difference to the outcome whether the cedar tree owners are entitled to retain their trees or the apple growers are entitled to be free of them? Why or why not?

2. In primitive societies the entitlements to use land were frequently possessory rights rather than ownership rights. Those on the land could use it as they wished but they could not transfer it to anyone else. One could acquire a new plot by simply occupying and using it, leaving the old plot available for someone else. Would this type of entitlement system cause more or less incentive to conserve the land than an ownership entitlement? Why? Would a possessory entitlement system be more efficient in a modern society or a primitive society? Why?

PROBLEMS

1. Suppose the state is trying to decide how many miles of a very scenic river it should preserve. There are 100 people in the community, each of whom has an identical inverse demand function given by $P = 10 - 1.0q$, where q is the number of miles preserved and P is the per-mile price he or she is willing to pay for q miles of preserved river. (a) If the marginal cost of preservation is $500 per mile, how many miles would be preserved in an efficient allocation? (b) How large are the net benefits?

2. (a) Compute the consumer surplus and producer surplus if the product described by the first problem in Chapter 2 were supplied by a competitive industry. Show that their sum is equal to the efficient net benefits.
   (b) Compute the consumer surplus and the producer surplus assuming this same product was supplied by a monopoly. (Hint: The marginal revenue curve has twice the slope of the demand curve.)
   (c) Show that when this market is controlled by a monopoly, producer surplus is larger, consumer surplus is smaller, and net benefits are smaller than when it is controlled by competitive industry.

CHAPTER FOUR

Regulating the Market: Information and Uncertainty

Cost-benefit analysis is valuable in regulatory decision making, but unless we recognize its shortcomings we are likely to force a superficial quantification of issues that cannot wholly be grasped by the reassuringly precise embrace of numbers. [If this technique is used inappropriately] we shall be guided by a bright light in the wrong place, and the result will be not only bad cost-benefit analysis, but bad decisions.

DOUGLAS M. COSTLE (1981),
EPA ADMINISTRATOR DURING CARTER ADMINISTRATION

INTRODUCTION

The last chapter discussed circumstances in which markets cannot, by themselves, achieve an efficient allocation of resources. We also explored possible ways to correct this problem by realigning individual incentives through the judicial and/or legislative process. In order for this realignment to take place, however, the judges or legislators need a great deal of information on the costs and benefits of various choices they might make. This information is crucial in determining whether additional policies are needed and, if so, the types of policies which would be most efficient.

The process of regulating the market has its own transaction costs. The regulatory staffs have to be hired to draw up the regulations and administer them. An additional staff must be hired to enforce the regulations and to handle the inevitable exceptions and appeals. The firms being regulated must hire larger staffs to comply with the regulations and to fill out the reports which inevitably accompany regulation. The regulations themselves may be imperfectly designed and the resulting loss of net benefits is a further cost society must bear. In light of this fact, it is important to quantify the potential gains to be captured from regulation so that these may be weighed against the costs.

Quantification is not a trivial exercise. Information must be identified and structured in such a way as to allow rational decisions to be made. If this quantification is to prove useful, it must be reliable and must deal realistically with circumstances in which information is not available.

On February 17, 1981, President Reagan issued Executive Order 12291, which requires executive agencies to make more extensive use of benefit/cost analysis in defining and defending proposed regulatory changes. This decision was roundly applauded by some and, as the Costle quote at the beginning of this chapter suggests, severely criticized by others. In order to understand this controversy, we must delve into the procedures used to perform benefit/cost analysis and investigate what alternative forms of analysis are available to policy makers when the available information is not sufficient to allow the efficient allocation to be defined with precision.

This chapter examines the various techniques, starting with benefit/cost analysis, which seek to provide quantitative guidance to decision makers. We will be concerned specifically with the availability and reliability of information to implement these techniques; their usefulness when information is scarce or relatively untrustworthy; and the manner in which these techniques deal with uncertainty about the future. Brief summaries of case studies are presented to illustrate the principles and their applicability to actual policy situations.

BENEFIT/COST ANALYSIS

The most ambitious of the techniques is benefit/cost analysis. Though it makes the most precise statements about which policy choices are efficient, it also imposes the largest requirement for information in order to provide those statements. It is fairly easy for most people to accept the general premise that benefits and costs of actions should be weighed prior to deciding on a particular policy choice. The technique becomes more controversial, however, when specific numbers are attached to the anticipated benefits and costs and specific decision rules for translating these numbers into a decision are followed.

The Decision Rules

We start our investigation by discussing how the benefit and cost information is used once it is available. Three main decision rules are commonly used and they are *not* equivalent.

The *Maximum Net-Present Value Criterion* is the empirical counterpart to the present value of net-benefits criterion used to define dynamic efficiency. This criterion suggests that resources should be commited to those uses maximizing the present value of net benefits received. If accomplished properly, this analysis will correctly identify an efficient allocation.

In practice, however, two other related criteria are frequently used which do not guarantee that the efficient allocation will be identified. These are the *Benefit/Cost Ratio Criterion* and the *Positive Net-Present Value Criterion*. The decision rule for the former criterion implies that an activity should be undertaken if the ratio of the present value of benefits to the present value of costs exceeds 1.0. The decision rule for the second criterion implies that an activity should be undertaken whenever the present value of net benefits is greater than zero. While both of these techniques guarantee that no ac-

FIGURE 4.1   Benefit/Cost Analysis and Efficiency

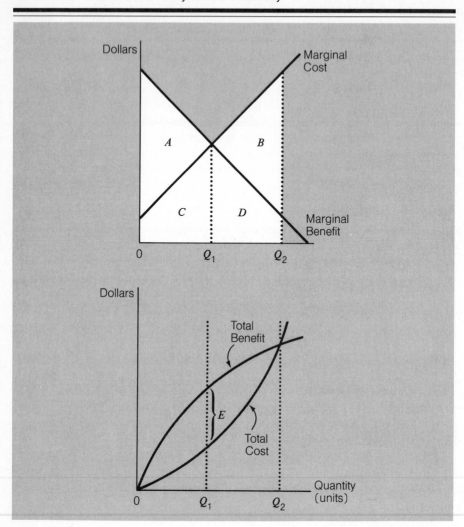

tivity which confers more costs on society than benefits will be undertaken, they do not guarantee efficiency. The point can be illustrated most easily using our definition of static efficiency.

Recall from Chapter 2 that efficiency is attained when the *marginal* benefit equals the *marginal* cost. Neither a benefit/cost ratio greater than 1.0 nor a positive net benefit insures that these marginal conditions will hold. In fact, when the benefit/cost ratio is equal to 1.0 (or, equivalently, the net benefit is equal to 0.0), this ensures that total benefit equals total cost (Figure 4.1).

The net benefit is maximized when Q_1 is supplied. At this point the marginal benefit is equal to the marginal cost, so that total benefits exceed total costs by the largest possible amount. In fact, the net benefit is equal to E which is considerably greater than zero.[1]

At what allocation would net benefit equal zero? In Figure 4.1 the answer is Q_2. The figure is drawn such that area A equals area B. Since area B represents net cost (or, equivalently, negative net benefit) and area A represents positive net benefit, the net benefit from allocation Q_2 is zero. This implies that *average* benefits equal *average* costs, *total* benefits equal *total* costs, and the benefit/cost ratio equals 1.0.[2]

This result suggests that whenever the benefit/cost ratio or positive net present value criteria are used, the government may choose inefficient activities. Only the maximum net-present value approach is compatible with efficiency.

Measuring Benefits

For many resource problems, measurement of benefits is relatively uncomplicated because the resource in question is a marketed commodity and information on prices and quantities consumed can be used to derive the demand curve. Once the demand curve is defined, it can be used to quantify the willingness to pay, the concept used to measure benefits.

Greater difficulties are encountered when the resource in question is not handled through normal markets. One classic example arises when we compare the value of preserving an environmental resource, such as a unique canyon, with that of developing a resource, such as hydroelectric power. We must compare the recreational benefits without development to the power benefits with development.

Recreation Benefits. Recreation benefits could be estimated from the recreational demand curve for that resource, if it were known. However, it is difficult to know what the true demand is, since visitors normally are not charged anything but nominal fees for using publicly owned recreation areas. Market prices do not prevail and demands are not revealed.

To get around this problem, a technique called the *Clawson-Knetsch method* was developed for estimating the recreational demand for a particular site when market prices are not available.[3] This technique uses travel costs to measure how much people would be willing to pay to come to the area.

The simplest version of the procedure is as follows:[4]

---

[1]Total benefits are $A + C$ while total costs are equal to C.

[2]Average benefits are equal to $A + C + D \div Q$ and average costs are equal to $B + C + D \div Q$. Therefore, as long as $A = B$, average benefits equal average costs.

[3]This is described in detail in Marion Clawson and Jack Knetsch, *Economics of Outdoor Recreation* (Baltimore, Md.: Johns Hopkins University Press for Resources for the Future, 1966); Jack L. Knetsch, "Economics of Including Recreation as a Purpose of Eastern Water Projects," *Journal of Farm Economics* 46 (December 1964): 1148–1157.

[4]This description is taken from A. Myrick Freeman, III, *The Benefits of Environmental Improvement: Theory and Practice* (Baltimore, MD: The Johns Hopkins Press for Resources for the Future, Inc. 1979), pp. 201–209. Some newer approaches are discussed in R. Mendelsohn and G. M. Brown, Jr., "Revealed Preference Approaches to Valuing Outdoor Recreation," *Natural Resources Journal*, vol. 23, no. 3 (July, 1983): 607–618.

1. For a given recreation site, the surrounding area is divided into concentric circular zones for the purpose of measuring the travel cost from each zone to the site and return.

2. Visitors at the site are sampled to determine their zones of origin.

3. Visitation rates defined as visitor days per capita are calculated for each zone of origin.

4. A travel-cost measure is constructed to indicate the cost of travel from the origin zone to the recreation site and return.

5. Using a statistical technique known as regression analysis, visitation rates are then related to travel costs and socioeconomic variables such as average income, median educational attainment, and the like.

6. The observed total visitation for the site from all travel-cost zones represents one point on the demand curve for that site; that is, the intersection of the present horizontal price line (either at a zero price or the typical nominal fee) with the true economic demand curve.

7. Other points on the demand curve are found by assuming that visitors will respond to a $1 increase in admission price in the same way that they would respond to a $1 increase in computed travel cost. To find the point on the demand curve for the site where the admission price rises by $1, the estimated visitation-rate equation is used to compute visitation rates and total visits for all travel-cost zones with the existing travel cost plus $1. Visits are summed across travel-cost zones to determine the predicted total visitation at the higher price. These calculations are repeated for higher and higher hypothetical admission prices and the full demand curve is traced out.

This technique is valid as long as there is no congestion at the site when the visitation rates are derived. Congestion serves to reduce demand artificially and, hence, the use of the Clawson-Knetsch method to estimate the demand for a particular congested site would lead to an underestimate of the recreation benefits at that site.

The next difficulty in comparing preservation and development involves forecasting how the benefits from these alternative uses will change over time. The demand for recreational activity has a positive income elasticity, which implies that the demand curve will shift out over time as income increases. Necessarily, the benefits of the preservation alternative will increase over time as well. If benefits of preservation increase faster than costs, then the net benefits of preservation increase over time. As demonstrated by Example 4.1, preservation may be the preferred alternative, even if the benefits from preservation in the current year are lower than the benefits from development. Furthermore, as is clear from Example 4.1, the dominance of the preservation alternative may turn out to be not very sensitive to the specific estimate of recreational benefits, a comforting finding in light of the difficulty of obtaining precise estimates.

Pollution Control Benefits.   Some of the most difficult problems of benefit estimation are raised by the search for an efficient level of pollution control. The benefits derived from pollution control are the damages prevented. The benefit derived from

EXAMPLE 4.1

Preservation versus Development: The Hell's Canyon Case

Hell's Canyon, on the Snake River separating Oregon from Idaho, is the deepest canyon on the North American continent. It affords a visitor some of the most spectacular vistas in the country as well as providing a natural habitat for a variety of wildlife. It also offers one of the best remaining sites for the development of hydroelectric power.

During the 1970s a major controversy developed concerning whether a portion of this canyon should be dedicated to the production of hydroelectric power through the construction of the High Mountain Sheep Dam or preserved in its natural state. If the dam were developed, a large lake would be formed behind the dam, changing the character of the canyon.

During this controversy several economists from an organization called Resources for the Future, Inc., a respected Washington think tank, performed a benefit/cost analysis on the choice. The issues were relatively clear. As an environmental resource supporting recreational activities, this canyon was unique in the area. The demand for those activities was increasing at a very rapid rate, but the construction of the dam would diminish the value of the site for those purposes. On the other hand, the electricity produced by the dam would also be valuable.

In contrast to the use of the resource as a natural area, which, due to its uniqueness has very few substitutes, electricity could be produced by other methods. Unfortunately, these other methods would be more expensive. The benefit of the dam, then, would be the costs saved by generating electricity in this manner rather than by the next cheapest source (nuclear), while the cost would include the opportunity cost of the recreational activities forgone.

What did the analysis suggest? The authors concluded that the net benefits from preservation were rising rapidly over time and, therefore, even though current benefits from preservation were less than the current benefits from producing electricity, in present value terms the preservation option yielded higher net benefits. The analysis indicated that if the current annual value of recreational activities exceeded $80,000, then the efficient decision would be to preserve the site. Their estimate of the current annual value of recreational activities at that site was approximately $900,000. Even though the data on which this latter estimate was based were not very solid, $900,000 is more than ten times higher than needed to justify preservation. The likelihood that the "true" estimate would be less than $80,000, if it were known, is very low. Therefore they recommended preservation. On the basis of this recommendation and other considerations, Congress voted to prohibit further development of this section of the river.

Source: Anthony C. Fisher, John V. Krutilla, and Charles J. Chicchetti, "Alternative Uses of Natural Environments: The Economics of Environmental Modification," in *Natural Environments: Studies in Theoretical and Applied Analysis,* John V. Krutilla, ed. (Washington, D.C.: Johns Hopkins University Press for Resources for the Future, 1972): 18–53.

more control over pollution is the difference between the level of damage when emissions are controlled at one level and the lower level of damage which would result from greater control. Our measurement of benefits, then, depends upon our ability to estimate the damage that results from various levels of pollution.

The damage caused by pollution can take many different forms. The first, and probably most obvious, is the effect on the health of humans. Polluted air and water can cause disease when ingested. Other forms of damage include loss of enjoyment from outdoor activities and damage to vegetation, animals, and materials.

Assessing the magnitude of this damage requires: (1) identification of the affected categories; (2) estimation of the physical relationship between the pollutant emissions (including natural sources) and the damage caused to the affected categories; (3) estimation of responses by the affected parties toward averting or mitigating some portion of the damage; and (4) placing a monetary value on the physical damages. Each of these steps is typically difficult to accomplish.

Because the experiments used to track down causal relationships are uncontrolled, identifying the affected categories is a complicated matter. Obviously we cannot run large numbers of people through controlled experiments. If people were subjected to different levels of some pollutant, such as carbon monoxide, so that we could study the short-term and long-term effects, some might become ill and even die. Ethical concern precludes human experimentation of this type.

This leaves us essentially two choices—we can either try to infer the impact on humans from controlled laboratory experiments on animals,[5] or we can do an after-the-fact statistical analysis of differences in mortality or disease rates for various human populations living in polluted environments to see the extent to which they are correlated with pollution concentrations. Neither approach is completely acceptable.

Animal experiments are expensive and, even when they are accomplished, the extrapolation from effects on animals to effects on humans is tenuous at best. Many of the significant effects, about which we might properly be concerned if we knew more about them, do not appear for a long time. To determine these effects in a reasonable period of time, we must subject test animals to large doses for a relatively short period of time. The researcher then extrapolates from the results of these high-dosage, short-duration experiments to estimate the effects of lower doses over a longer period of time on a human population. Since these extrapolations move well beyond the range of experimental experience, many scientists disagree on how the extrapolations should be accomplished.

Statistical studies, on the other hand, deal with human populations subjected to low doses for long periods but, unfortunately, have another set of problems—mainly that correlation does not imply causation. To illustrate, the fact that death rates are higher in cities with higher pollution levels does not mean that the higher pollution *caused* the higher death rates. Perhaps those same cities averaged older populations, which would tend to lead to higher death rates. Or perhaps they had more smokers. The studies which have been accomplished have been sophisticated enough to account

---

[5]Extrapolation from animal studies is used mainly in determining the toxicity of chemicals and has not been used to any appreciable degree in determining the effects of "conventional" pollutants.

for many of these other possible influences, but, because of the relative paucity of data, they have not been able to cover them all.

The problems discussed so far arise when identifying *whether* or not a particular effect results from pollution. The next step is to estimate *how strong* the relationship is between the effect and the pollution concentrations. In other words, it is necessary not only to discover whether pollution causes an increased incidence of respiratory disease, but also to estimate how much reduction in respiratory illness could be expected from a given reduction in pollution.

The nonexperimental nature of the data makes this a difficult task. It is not uncommon for researchers analyzing the same data to come to remarkably different conclusions.[6] Diagnostic problems are compounded when the effects are *synergistic*, that is, when the effect depends in a nonadditive way on what other elements are in the surrounding air or water at the time of the analysis.

Once physical damages have been identified, the next step is to place a monetary value on them. It is not difficult to see how complex an undertaking this is. Consider, for example, the difficulties in assigning a value to extending a human life by several years or to the pain, suffering, and grief borne by a cancer victim and his or her family.

Economists have used several different approaches to place a value on reductions in physical damages.

The first method, the *contingent valuation* approach, relies on surveys to ascertain how much respondents would be willing to pay to preserve the environment, to reduce the amount of man-made injury to it, or to lower the various types of environmental risk posed by modern industrial society. To name but a few of the large numbers of existing studies, this approach has been used to value air quality improvements in the Los Angeles area[7], the recreational use of two rivers in Maine[8], reductions in nuclear plant injuries[9], and migratory waterfowl in the Pacific flyway[10].

The major concern with the use of the contingent valuation method has been the potential for survey respondents to give biased answers. Four types of potential bias

[6]For example, economists Lester B. Lave and Eugene P. Seskin, *Air Pollution and Human Health* (Baltimore, Md: Johns Hopkins University Press, 1977), in their often-cited study based on a large volume of data, concluded that a 50-percent reduction in air pollution nationally would lead to a 4.7 percent reduction in mortality. Working with the same data, a pair of mathematicians with General Motors Research Corporation came to the conclusion that a 50-percent reduction in air pollution would drop mortality by only 0.43 percent. This controversy is described in "New Perspective on Air Pollution," *Science News* CXIX: 152.

[7]David S. Brookshire, *et al*, *Experiments in Valuing Nonmarket Goods: A Case Study of Alternative Benefit Measures of Air Pollution Control in the South Coast Air Basin, Vol. 2 of Methods Development for Assessing Air Pollution Control Benefits* (Washington, DC: U.S. Environmental Protection Agency, 1978).

[8]William O'Neil and Kristin Hallberg, *Estimating the Value of River-Related Recreational Activities: A Comparison of Two Approaches Based on Case Studies of the West Branch of the Penobscot River and the Saco River* (Orono, ME: Maine Land and Water Resources Center, 1985).

[9]Patricia J. Mulligan, "Willingness-to-Pay for Decreased Risks of Nuclear Accidents", Working Paper Number 3, Energy Extension Programs, Pennsylvania State University, 1977.

[10]Gardener Mallard Brown, Jr. and Judd Hammock, "A Preliminary Investigation of the Economics of Migratory Waterfowl," in John V. Krutilla, ed. *Natural Environments: Studies in Theoretical and Applied Analysis* (Baltimore: Johns Hopkins University Press for Resources for the Future, Inc., 1972).

have been the focus of a large amount of research: (1) *strategic bias,* (2) *information bias,* (3) *starting point bias,* and (4) *hypothetical bias.*

Strategic bias arises when the respondent provides a biased answer in order to influence a particular outcome. If a decision to preserve a stretch of river for fishing, for example, depends on whether or not the survey produces a sufficiently large value for fishing, the respondents who enjoy fishing may be tempted to provide an answer that assures a high value, rather than a lower value that reflects their true valuation.

Information bias may arise whenever respondents are forced to value attributes with which they have little or no experience. For example, the valuation by a recreationist of a loss in water quality in one body of water may be based on the ease of substituting recreation on another body of water. If the respondent has no experience using the second body of water, the valuation will be based on an entirely false perception.

Starting point bias may arise in those survey instruments in which a respondent is asked to check off his or her answers from a predefined range of possibilities. How that range is defined by the designer of the survey may affect the resulting answers. A range of $0 to $100 may produce a different valuation by respondents, for example, than a range of $10 to $100, even if no bids are in the $0 to $10 range.

The final source of bias, hypothetical bias, can enter the picture because the respondent is being confronted by a contrived, rather than an actual, set of choices. Since he or she will not have to actually pay the estimated value, the respondent may treat the survey casually, providing ill-considered answers.

A large amount of experimental work has now been done on contingent valuation to determine how serious a problem these biases may present.[11] In general the results seem to suggest that while these biases certainly exist, they can be kept acceptably small with suitably designed survey instruments.

A quite different approach involves inferring the valuation of an environmental attribute which is not directly observable from related markets where values are directly observable. Common examples include the housing and labor markets.

Housing market studies, also called property value studies, start from the presumption that the purchaser's willingness to pay for property takes the quality of the local environment into account. All other things being equal, for example, one would expect houses in neighborhoods with clean air to command higher prices than houses in neighborhoods with polluted air. By statistically comparing the market values of similar houses in neighborhoods with different levels of air quality, these studies attempt to decompose the value of housing into its component parts. Since one of those component parts is a premium paid for clean air, this premium can serve as a measure of the value of clean air.

For labor markets the presumption is that workers facing higher levels of environmental risk (such as an exposure to a potentially hazardous substance) have to

---

[11]For a comprehensive survey of the state of the art see Ronald G. Cummings, David S. Brookshire, and William D. Schulze, eds., *Valuing Environmental Goods: An Assessment of the Contingent Value Method* (Totowa, NJ: Rowman and Littlefield, 1986).

be compensated in order to accept that risk. By decomposing wages into their component parts and isolating the environmental risk premium, this premium can be used to value the benefits that would be conferred by a reduction in this risk.

In general the statistical studies support the basic common premise behind these two approaches — property values and wages do indeed reflect the existence of pollution as well as other forms of environmental risk, but they have also indicated that we still have a lot to learn about risk valuation. In particular it now seems clear that environmental risk valuations are sensitive to the context in which they arise; valuations derived in one context (such as the risk of contracting lung cancer from smoking) cannot automatically be transferred to another context (such as the risk of contracting lung cancer though exposure to a radioactive substance). Furthermore, the type of risk, such as whether the exposure is voluntary or involuntary, seems to make quite a difference in the value placed on reducing that risk.[12]

Perhaps surprisingly, these rather different approaches yield quite similar valuations, as can be illustrated by an explicit comparison of the property value and contingent valuation methods for providing a measure of the benefits derived from reducing pollution in the Los Angeles area.[13] Based on the statistical analysis, the property value approach found that the average household would be willing to pay $42 to achieve a 30 percent improvement in its air quality. According to the mean bid in the contingent valuation survey, the average household should be willing to pay $29 for that improvement. Considering the very different bases for deriving these numbers, they are rather close.

One fascinating public policy area where these various approaches have been applied is in the valuation of human life. Many government programs from those controlling hazardous pollutants in the workplace or drinking water to those improving nuclear power plant safety are designed to save human life as well as to reduce illness. How resources should be allocated among these programs depends crucially on the value of human life. How is life to be valued?

The simple answer, of course, is that life is priceless, but that turns out not to be very helpful. Since the resources used to prevent loss of life are scarce, choices must be made. The economic approach to valuing life-saving reductions in environmental risk is to calculate the change in the probability of death resulting from the reduction in environmental risk and to place a value on the change. Thus it is not life itself that is being valued, but rather a reduction in the probability that some segment of the population could be expected to die earlier than otherwise.

It is possible to translate the value derived from this procedure in an "implied value of human life." This is accomplished by dividing the amount each individual is willing to pay for a specific reduction in the probability of death by the probability reduction. Suppose, for example, that a particular environmental policy could be expected to re-

---

[12]See the discussion of context in environmental risk valuation in V. Kerry Smith, "The Valuation of Environmental Risks Using Hedonic Wage Models" in Martin David and Timothy Smeeding, eds., *Horizontal Equity, Uncertainty, and Economic Well-Being* (Chicago: University of Chicago Press, 1985).

[13]Brookshire, et al. [1978, Table 6.1, p. 198].

duce the average concentration of a toxic substance to which one million people are exposed. Suppose further that this reduction in exposure could be expected to reduce the risk of death from 1 out of 100,000 to 1 out of 150,000. This implies that the number of expected deaths would fall from 10 to 6.67 in the exposed population as a result of this policy. If each of the one million persons exposed is willing to pay $5 for this risk reduction (for a total of $5 million), then the implied value of a life is approximately $1.5 million ($5 million divided by 3.33).

What actual values have been derived from these methods? A recent survey of a large number of studies examining reductions in a number of life-threatening risks found that most implied values for human life clustered within one of two common ranges. The low range placed the implied value of human life between $300,000 and $600,000 (in 1981 dollars), while the high range placed it between $1,000,000 and $7,000,000.[14]

This same survey went on to suggest that the lower range should be treated as a lower bound on the value of human life. In other words all government programs resulting in risk reductions costing less than $300,000 to $600,000 would be justified in benefit/cost terms.[15] Those costing more might or might not be justified, depending on the appropriate value of a life saved in the particular risk context being examined.

Issues in Benefit Estimation[16]

The analyst charged with the responsibility for performing a benefit/cost analysis encounters many decision points requiring judgment. If we are to understand benefit/cost analysis, the nature of these judgments must be clear in our minds.

Primary Versus Secondary Effects.   Environmental projects usually trigger both primary and secondary consequences. For example, the primary effect of cleaning a lake will be an increase in recreational uses of the lake. This primary effect will cause a further ripple effect on services provided to the increased number of users of the lake. Are these secondary benefits to be counted?

The answer depends upon the employment conditions in the surrounding area. If this increase in demand results in employment of previously unused resources, such as labor, the value of the increased employment should be counted. If, on the other hand, the increase in demand is met by a shift in previously employed resources, from one use to another, this is a different story. In general, secondary employment benefits should be counted in high-unemployment areas or when the particular skills demanded

[14]Energy and Resource Consultants, Inc., *Valuing Reductions in Risks: A Review of the Empirical Estimates* (Washington, DC: U.S. Environmental Protection Agency, 1983), p. 6–2.

[15]This is a controversial point. Martin Bailey (1984) argues that the lower range is the only reasonable range, not merely a lower bound.

[16]This section relies heavily on Henry M. Peskin and Eugene P. Seskin, *Cost-Benefit Analysis and Water Pollution Control Policy* (Washington, D.C.: The Urban Institute, 1975).

are underemployed at the time the project is commenced. They should not be counted when the project simply results in a rearrangement of productively employed resources.

Tangible Versus Intangible Benefits.   Tangible benefits are those which can reasonably be assigned a monetary value. *Intangible* benefits are those which cannot be assigned a monetary value, either because data are not available or reliable enough, or because it is not clear how to measure the value even with data.

How are intangible benefits to be handled? One answer is perfectly clear: they should not be ignored. To ignore intangible benefits is to bias the results. The fact that benefits are intangible does not mean they are unimportant.

Intangible benefits should be quantified to the extent possible. One frequently used technique is to conduct a sensitivity analysis of the estimated benefit values derived from less than perfectly reliable data. We can determine, for example, whether or not the outcome is sensitive, within wide ranges, to the value of this benefit. If not, then not much time has to be spent on the problem. If the outcome is sensitive, the person or persons making the decision bear the ultimate responsibility for weighing the importance of that benefit.

Approaches to Cost Estimation

Estimating costs is easier, in general, than estimating benefits, but it is not easy. One major problem for both derives from the fact that benefit/cost analysis is forward looking and thus requires an estimate of what a particular strategy *will* cost, which is much more difficult than tracking down what an existing strategy *does* cost.

Another frequent problem is posed by collecting cost information when availability of that information is controlled by a firm having an interest in the outcome. Pollution control is an obvious example. Two rather different approaches have been used to deal with this problem.

The Survey Approach.   One way to discover the costs associated with a policy is to ask those who bear the costs, and presumably know the most about them, to reveal the magnitude of the costs to policy makers. Polluters, for example, could be asked to provide control-cost estimates to regulatory bodies.

The problem with this approach is the strong incentive not to be truthful. An overestimate of the costs can trigger less-stringent regulation; therefore, it is financially advantageous to provide overinflated estimates.

The Engineering Approach.   The engineering approach bypasses the source being regulated by using general engineering information to catalogue the possible technologies which could be used to meet the objective and to estimate the costs of purchasing and using those technologies. The final step in the engineering approach is to assume that the sources would use technologies which minimize cost. This produces a cost estimate for a "typical," well-informed firm.

This approach has its own problems. The expertise needed to develop these estimates is limited. Furthermore, there is no guarantee that these estimates approximate the actual cost of any particular firm. There may be unique circumstances which cause the costs of that firm to be higher, or lower, than estimated; the firm, in short, may not be typical.

The Combined Approach.   To circumvent these problems, analysts frequently use a combination of survey and engineering approaches. The survey approach collects information on possible technologies, as well as special circumstances facing the firm. Engineering approaches are used to derive the actual costs of those technologies, given the special circumstances. This combined approach attempts to balance information best supplied by the source with that best derived independently.

In the cases described so far, the costs are relatively easy to quantify and the problem is simply finding a way to acquire the best information. This is not always the case, however. Some costs are not easy to quantify, though economists have developed some ingenious ways to secure monetary estimates even for those costs.

Take, for example, a policy designed to conserve energy by forcing more people to carpool. If the effect of this is simply to increase the average time of travel, how is this cost to be measured?

Transportation analysts have, for some time, recognized that people do value their time, and quite a literature has now grown up to provide estimates of this valuation. The basis for this valuation is opportunity cost—how the time might be used if it weren't being consumed in travel. Although the results of these studies depend on the amount of time involved, individuals seem to value their time at a rate not more than half their wage rates.[17]

The Treatment of Risk

For many environmental problems, it is not possible to state with certainty what consequences a particular policy will have, because scientific estimates, themselves, often are imprecise. Determining the efficient exposure to potentially toxic substances requires obtaining results at high doses and extrapolating to low doses, as well as extrapolating from animal studies to humans. It also requires relying upon epidemiological studies which infer a pollution-induced adverse human-health impact from correlations between indicators of health in human populations and recorded pollution levels.

Another illustration of the significance of scientific uncertainty is afforded by the chlorofluorocarbon pollution problem. Chlorofluorocarbons, when emitted into the atmosphere, are suspected of depleting the ozone level in the upper atmosphere. If this suspicion is correct, it could have very serious implications. The ozone layer buffers harmful rays from the sun; as it is depleted, more of these rays reach the earth and increase the incidence of skin cancer. The conjecture that chlorofluorocarbons are, in

---

[17]See M. E. Beesley, *Urban Transport: Studies in Economic Policy* (London: Butterworth, 1973): pp. 160, 179.

fact, depleting the ozone in the upper atmosphere is based upon a computer model and has only partially been validated. This is a prototypical example of a problem which is poorly understood, but, if the conjectures are true, could pose significant problems in the future.

There are two major dimensions of the treatment of risk in the policy process: (1) identifying and quantifying the risks; and (2) deciding how much risk is acceptable. The former is primarily scientific and descriptive, while the latter task is more evaluative or normative.

Benefit/cost analysis grapples with the evaluation of risk in several ways. Suppose, for example, that we have a range of policy options *A, B, C, D* and a range of possible outcomes *E, F, G* for each of these policies depending on how the economy evolves over the future. These outcomes, for example, might depend on whether the demand growth for the resource is low, medium, or high. Thus, if we choose policy *A*, we might end up with outcomes *AE, AF,* or *AG*. Each of the other policies has three possible outcomes as well, yielding a total of twelve possible outcomes.

We could conduct a separate benefit/cost analysis for each of the twelve possible outcomes. Unfortunately, the policy which maximizes net benefits for *E* may be different from that which maximizes net benefits for *F* or *G*. Thus if we only knew which outcome would prevail, we could select the policy which maximized net benefits; the problem is that we don't. Furthermore, choosing the policy which is best if outcome *E* prevails may be disastrous if *G* results instead.

When a dominant policy emerges, this problem is avoided. A *dominant policy* is one which confers higher net benefits for every outcome. In this case, the existence of risk concerning the future is not relevant for the policy choice. Though this fortuitous circumstance is exceptional rather than common, it can occur (Example 4.2).

Other options exist even when dominant solutions do not emerge. Suppose, for example, that we were able to assess the likelihood that each of the three possible outcomes would occur. Thus we might expect outcome *E* to occur with probability 0.5, *F* with probability 0.3, and *G* with probability 0.2. Armed with this information, we can estimate the expected present value of net benefits. The *expected present value of net benefits* for a particular policy is defined as the sum over outcomes of the present value of net benefits for that policy where each outcome is weighted by its probability of occurrence. Symbolically this is expressed as:

$$EPVNB_j = \sum_{i=1}^{I} P_i \cdot PVNB_{ij} \qquad j = 1, \ldots J \qquad (4.1)$$

when

$EPVNB_j$ = the expected value of net benefits for policy j,

P_i = the probability of the ith outcome occurring,

$PVNB_{ij}$ = is the present value of net benefits for policy j, if outcome i prevails,

J = the number of policies being considered, and

I = the number of outcomes being considered.

EXAMPLE 4.2

The Helium Problem: An Application of Benefit/Cost Analysis

Helium is an exceptional substance. It is seven times lighter than air, nonflammable, and it will not combine with other substances. It has the lowest boiling point of any known substance. This combination of unique properties makes helium relatively indispensable in many uses.

Although helium is abundantly available in the atmosphere, it would be very expensive to recover because it is available only in very low concentrations. Currently, large amounts of helium are being extracted as a by-product of the extraction of natural gas. Since more helium is being found than is needed for current use, it can either be stored for future use or vented (dispersed into the atmosphere). Once vented, this low-cost source of helium would be lost to future generations, but storage also imposes costs. What should the government do?

Two economists, Dennis Epple and Lester Lave, subjected this problem to a formal benefit/cost analysis. They examined two projected demand patterns for helium out to the year 2122, providing the basis for the benefits. Then they estimated the various expected sources of helium which would be available in the future and their associated cost. Then, using precisely the same concepts as we developed in Chapter 2, they found the production and storage plan which would maximize the present value of net benefits under each of the demand scenarios and a variety of interest rates.

Because the future is uncertain and no one can be sure which of the scenarios will most closely approximate the actual future as it unfolds, Epple and Lave choose to examine various policy strategies for the next 15 years to see how well or how badly they fared under each of the scenarios. They considered a total of six pricing and storage strategies ranging from holding the price at current levels for the next fifteen-year period, while storing helium that is currently being separated, to more aggressive strategies involving higher prices (to curtail demand) and more sources of helium separated and stored. Interestingly enough, they found that the least aggressive of these policies (holding prices constant and storing what helium is currently being separated) tended to dominate the more aggressive pricing and storage strategies for all scenarios examined.

Dominant solutions, as in this problem, do not always occur, but when they do, it is comforting in the face of so many uncertainties about the future. Benefit/cost analysis can assist in the detection of those strategies.

Source: Dennis Epple and Lester Lave, "Helium: Investments in the Future," *The Bell Journal of Economics* 11 (Autumn, 1980): 617–630.

Having accomplished this calculation, the final step is to select the policy with the highest expected present value of net benefits.

This approach has the substantial virtue that it weighs higher probability outcomes more heavily. It also, however, makes a specific assumption about society's preference for risk. This approach is appropriate if society is risk neutral. *Risk neutrality* can be defined most easily by the use of an example. Suppose you were allowed to choose between being given a definite $50 or entering a lottery in which you had a 50 percent chance of winning $100 and a 50 percent chance of winning nothing. (Notice that the expected value of this lottery is $50 = 0.5 ($100) + 0.5($0).) You would be said to be risk neutral if you would be indifferent between these two choices. If you view the lottery as more attractive, you would be exhibiting *risk loving* behavior, while a preference for the definite $50 would suggest *risk averse* behavior. Using the expected present value of net benefits approach implies that society is risk neutral.

Is that a valid assumption? The evidence is mixed. The existence of gambling suggests that at least some members of society are risk lovers while the existence of insurance suggests that others are risk averse. Since the same people may gamble and own insurance policies, it's possible that the type of risk may be important.

There is a movement in national policy in both the courts[18] and the legislature[19] to search for imaginative ways to define acceptable risk. In general the policy approaches reflect a case-by-case approach. As we shall see in subsequent chapters, current policy reflects a high degree of risk aversion toward a number of enviornmental problems.

Choosing the Discount Rate

In the previous chapter we discussed how the discount rate could be defined conceptually as the social opportunity cost of capital. This cost of capital can be divided further into two components: (1) the riskless cost of capital and (2) the risk premium. The question we now face is how the social opportunity cost of capital can be measured.

As Example 4.3 indicates, this has been, and continues to be, an important issue. When the public sector uses a discount rate lower than that in the private sector, the public sector will find more projects with longer payoff periods worthy of authorization. And as we have already seen, the discount rate is a major determinant of the allocation of resources among generations, as well.

Traditionally, economists have used long-term interest rates on government bonds as one measure of the cost of capital, adjusted by a risk premium which would depend on the riskiness of the project considered. Unfortunately, the choice of how large an adjustment to make has been left to the discretion of the analysts. This ability to affect the desirability of a particular project or policy by the choice of discount rate led to

[18]For an example of court action, see the review article by Paolo F. Ricci and Lawrence S. Molton, "Risk and Benefit in Environmental Law," *Science* 214 (December 4, 1981): 1096–1100.

[19]Risk-benefit analysis in the legislative process is explored in U.S. Congress, *Risk/Benefit Analysis in the Legislative Process.* Joint Hearing before the Subcommittee on Science, Research, and Technology of the Committee on Science and Technology, U.S. House of Representatives and the Subcommittee on Science, Technology, and Space of the Committee on Commerce, Science, and Transportation. United States Senate, 96th Congress, First Session, July 24–25, 1979.

a situation in which government agencies were using a variety of discount rates to justify programs or projects they supported. One set of hearings conducted by Congress during the 1960s discovered that, at that time, agencies were using discount rates ranging from zero percent to 20 percent.[20]

During the early 1970s the Office of Management and Budget came out with a circular which required, with some exceptions,[21] all government agencies to use a discount rate of 10 percent in their benefit/cost analysis.[22] This standardization reduces biases by eliminating the agency's ability to choose a discount rate which justifies a predetermined conclusion. It also allows a project to be considered independently of fluctuations in the true social cost of capital due to cycles in the behavior of the economy. On the other hand, when the social opportunity cost of capital differs from this administratively determined level, the benefit/cost analysis will not, in general, define the efficient allocation.

A Critical Appraisal

The approaches to benefit estimation are sophisticated, but most observers feel that the resulting estimates are not yet sufficiently reliable that they could be used to fine-tune policy. One well-known survey of the field, commissioned by the Council on Environmental Quality, a government body, concluded:

> This report makes two points quite clear. First, in spite of recent advances, the estimation of certain kinds of environmental benefits is still in need of much additional refinement. . . . Second, where state-of-the-art analyses of environmental benefits have been undertaken — as exemplified by the studies in this report — they strongly suggest that environmental protection is good economics. (Freeman, 1979; xi–xii)

While the estimates are certainly good enough to tell us that the benefits from environmental control are large and worth pursuing, they are not reliable enough to use in picking a single pollution level as the efficient one.

Similar concerns can be raised about costs. The Environmental Protection Agency (EPA) commissioned a study to examine just how accurate cost forecasts were. The study compared actual capital outlays by firms responding to the pollution-control laws

---

[20]Senator William Proxmire, "PPB, The Agencies and the Congress," in *The Analysis and Evaluation of Public Expenditures: The PPB System*, U.S. Congress, Joint Economic Committee, Subcommittee on Economy in Government (Washington, D.C.: Government Printing Office, 1969), p. xiii.

[21]The main exception involves water resources projects. The discount rates used for these projects are computed once each year by the U.S. Treasury Department and transmitted to the Water Resources Council, an independent, executive coordinating agency. See Charles W. Howe, *Natural Resources Economics: Issues, Analysis, and Policy* (New York: John Wiley, 1979), 158.

[22]Circular No. A-94, as revised March 27, 1972.

EXAMPLE 4.3

The Importance of the Discount Rate

For years the United States and Canada had been discussing the possibility of constructing a tidal-power project in the Passamaquoddy Bay between Maine and New Brunswick. This project would have heavy initial capital costs, but low operating costs which presumably would hold for a long time into the future. As part of their analysis of the situation, a complete inventory of costs and benefits was completed in 1959.

Using the same benefit and cost figures, Canada concluded that the project should not be built, while the United States concluded that it should. Because these conclusions were based on the same benefit/cost data, the differences can be attributed solely to the use of different discount rates. The United States used 2.5 percent while their Canadian counterparts used 4.125 percent. The higher discount rate makes the initial cost weigh much more heavily in the calculation, leading to the Canadian conclusion that the project yields a negative net benefit. Since the lower discount rate weights the lower future operating costs relatively more heavily, the Americans saw the net benefit as positive.

There are a number of other examples, as well. During 1962, Congress authorized a number of water projects which had been justified by benefit/cost analysis using a discount rate of 2.63 percent. Upon examining these projects, economists Fox and Herfindahl [1964, p. 202] found that, at an 8 percent rate of discount, only 20 percent of the projects would have had favorable benefit/cost ratios.

The choice of the discount rate even played a major role during a highly publicized dispute between President Jimmy Carter and Congress. President Carter wanted to rescind authorization from many previously approved water projects that he viewed as wasteful. The President based his conclusions on a discount rate of 6.38 percent while Congress was using a lower one.

Far from being an esoteric subject, the choice of the discount rate is fundamentally important in defining the role of the public sector, the types of projects undertaken, and the allocation of resources across generations.

Sources: Edith Stokey and Richard Zeckhauser, *A Primer for Policy Analysis* (New York: W. W. Norton, 1978): 164–5; Raymond Mikesell, *The Rate of Discount for Evaluating Public Projects* (Washington, D.C.: The American Enterprise Institute for Public Policy Research, 1977): 3–5; Irving K. Fox and Orris C. Herfindahl, "Attainment of Efficiency in Satisfying Demands for Water Resources," *American Economic Review* 54 (May 1964): 202.

to the forecasts of those same costs made earlier by both the EPA and by affected industries. When issued in June, 1980, the report found that "both EPA and industry forecasts tend to overestimate compliance costs more often than they underestimate these costs.[23] Further, the report found that some of these overestimates were substantial. For the oil-refining industry, for example, both EPA and the industry projected capital costs of $1.4 billion. The actual costs were around $590 million, less than half of the projected total.

We have seen that it is sometimes, though not always, difficult to estimate benefits and costs. When this estimation is difficult or unreliable, it limits the value of a benefit/cost analysis. This problem would be particularly disturbing if biases tended to systematically increase or decrease net benefits. Do such biases exist?

In the early 1970s, economist Robert Haveman did a major study which sheds some light on this question. Focusing on Army Corps of Engineers water projects, such as flood control, navigation, and hydroelectric power generation, Haveman compared the *ex ante* (before the fact) estimates of benefits and costs with their *ex post* (after the fact) counterparts. Thus he was able to address the issues of accuracy and bias. His conclusions were:

> In the empirical case studies presented, *ex post* estimates of benefits often showed little relationship to their *ex ante* counterparts. On the basis of the few cases and the *a priori* analysis presented here, one could conclude that there is a serious bias incorporated into agency *ex ante* evaluation procedures, resulting in persistent overstatement of expected benefits. Similarly in the analysis of project construction costs, enormous variance was found among projects in the relationship between estimated and realized costs. Although no persistent bias in estimation was apparent, nearly 50 percent of the projects displayed realized costs that deviated by more than plus or minus 20 percent from *ex ante* projected costs. [Haveman, 1972, p. 111].

In the cases examined by Haveman, at least, the notion that benefit/cost analysis is purely a scientific exercise was clearly not consistent with the evidence; the biases of the analysts were merely translated into numbers.

Another shortcoming of benefit/cost analysis is that it does not really address the question of who reaps the benefits and who pays the cost. It is quite possible for a particular course of action to yield high net benefits, but to have the benefits borne by one group of society and the costs borne by another. This admittedly extreme case does serve to illustrate a basic principle—insuring that a particular policy is efficient provides an important, but not always the sole, basis for public policy. Other aspects, such as who reaps the benefit or bears the burden, are also important.

In summary, on the positive side, benefit/cost analysis is frequently a very useful part of the policy process. Even when the underlying data are not strictly reliable, the outcomes may not be sensitive to that unreliability. In other circumstances, the data may be reliable enough to give indications of the consequences of broad policy directions, even when they are not reliable enough to "fine-tune" those policies. Benefit/cost analysis, when done correctly, can provide a useful complement to the other influences on the political process by clarifying what choices yield the highest net benefits to society.

---

[23]Cited in "Antipollution Costs Were Overestimated by Government and Industry, Study Says," *Wall Street Journal,* 19 June 1980, p. 7.

On the negative side, benefit/cost analysis has been attacked as seeming to promise more than can actually be delivered, particularly in the absence of solid benefit information. There have been two responses to this kind of concern. First, regulatory processes have been developed which can be implemented with very little information and yet have desirable economic properties. The recent reforms in air-pollution control provides a powerful example, which we shall cover in Chapter 15.

The second approach involves techniques which supply useful information to the policy process without relying on controversial techniques to monetize environmental services which are difficult to value. The rest of this chapter deals with the two most prominent of these—cost-effectiveness analysis and impact analysis.

Even when benefits are difficult or impossible to quantify, economic analysis has much to offer. Policy makers should know, for example, how much various policy actions will cost and what their impacts on society will be, even if the efficient policy choice cannot be identified with any certainty. Cost-effectiveness analysis and impact analysis both respond to this need, albeit in different ways.

COST-EFFECTIVENESS ANALYSIS

The point of departure for a cost-effectiveness analysis is the realization that, without a good measure of benefits, the efficient allocation cannot be determined by the analysis. Therefore the policy objective (for example, nitrogen oxide concentrations should not exceed 100 micrograms per cubic meter in the ambient air) must be determined on some other basis.[24] Once that objective is specified, however, the analysis can have a great deal to say about the cost consequences of choosing a means of achieving that objective.

Typically there are several means of achieving the specified objective; some will be relatively inexpensive, while others will turn out to be very expensive. The problems are frequently complicated enough that identifying the cheapest manner of achieving an objective cannot be accomplished without analyzing the situation.

Cost effectiveness analysis frequently involves an *optimization procedure*. An optimization procedure, in this context, is merely a systematic method for finding the lowest cost means of accomplishing the objective. This procedure does not, in general, produce an efficient allocation because the predetermined objective may not be efficient. All efficient policies are cost effective, but all cost-effective policies are not necessarily efficient.[25]

---

[24]This objective is usually specified by the political process. A survey of evidence on the physical consequences of alternatives is used to judge the "appropriate" level.

[25]You may recognize an analogy from your introductory economics course. A firm which uses the cheapest possible method for producing a given output will not be maximizing profits unless the chosen output level is the one which maximizes profits. Thus profit maximization implies cost minimization, but the converse is not necessarily true.

These principles can be illustrated by defining a desirable pollution-control policy. Cost-effectiveness analysis can be used to find the least-cost means of meeting a particular standard and its associated cost. Using this cost as a benchmark case, we can estimate how much costs can be expected to increase from this minimum level if policies which are not cost effective are implemented. Cost-effectiveness analysis can also be used to determine how much compliance costs can be expected to change if the EPA chooses a more-stringent or less-stringent standard. The case study presented in Example 4.4 not only illustrates the use of cost-effectiveness analysis, it also shows that costs can be very sensitive to the approach chosen by the EPA.

IMPACT ANALYSIS

What can be done when the information needed to perform a benefit/cost analysis or a cost-effectiveness analysis is not available? The analytical technique designed to deal with this problem is called impact analysis. An *impact analysis,* regardless of whether it focuses on economic impact or environmental impact or both, attempts to quantify the consequences of various actions.

In contrast to benefit/cost analysis, a pure impact analysis makes no attempt to convert all these consequences into a one-dimensional measure, such as dollars, to ensure comparability. In contrast to both benefit/cost analysis and cost-effectiveness analysis, impact analysis does not necessarily attempt to optimize. Impact analysis places a large amount of relatively undigested information at the disposal of the policy maker. It is up to the policy maker to assess the importance of the various consequences and act accordingly.

On January 1, 1970, President Nixon signed the National Environmental Policy Act of 1969. This act, among other things, directed all agencies of the Federal Government to:

> include in every recommendation or report on proposals for legislation and other major Federal actions significantly affecting the quality of the human environment, a detailed statement by the responsible official on—
> (i) the environmental impact of the proposed action,
> (ii) any adverse environmental effects which cannot be avoided should the proposal be implemented,
> (iii) alternatives to the proposed action,
> (iv) the relationship between local short-term uses of man's environment and the maintenance and enhancement of long-term productivity, and
> (v) any irreversible and irretrievable commitments of resources which would be involved in the proposed action should it be implemented.[26]

This was the beginning of the environmental-impact statement, which is now a familiar, if controversial, part of environmental policy making.

---

[26]83 STAT 853.

EXAMPLE 4.4

NO₂ Control in Chicago: An Example of Cost-Effectiveness Analysis

As part of its mandate to implement and enforce the Clean Air Act, the Environmental Protection Agency, a part of the executive branch of the federal government, commissioned a study to examine, among other things, the cost consequences of implementing two different air quality standards by a variety of regulatory approaches. The final report, issued on September 17, 1979, shows just how sensitive costs in this area are to the regulatory approach.

The authors of the report used information on the cost of control for each of 797 stationary sources of nitrogen-oxide emissions in the city of Chicago for various degrees of control. A total of 100 receptors measured the air quality at 100 different locations within the city. The relationship between ambient air quality at those receptors and emissions from the 797 sources was then modeled using mathematical equations. Once these equations were estimated, the model was calibrated to insure that it was capable of recreating the actual situation in Chicago. Following successful calibration, this model was used to simulate what would happen if EPA were to take various regulatory actions.

The first issue addressed was, "How much would costs increase, in the least cost solution, if the ambient air quality standard were changed from 500 micrograms to 250 micrograms per cubic meter?" Note that the latter implies much cleaner air than the former. The analysis indicated that the least-cost means of meeting the more stringent standard would cost about $24 million a year, while the cost of meeting the 500 microgram per cubic meter standard would be only $1 million. In other words, the stricter standard implies an annual cost some 24 times as high. Note that this analysis does not give any hint as to whether the additional expenditure is efficient. One would need the benefit estimates to decide that.

The second issue addressed was the sensitivity of control costs for meeting the more stringent 250-microgram per-cubic-meter standard to the regulatory approach chosen by EPA. The study considered several possibilities, two of which were: (1) equal percentage reductions in all sources and (2) the least-cost solution. The results were striking. In order to insure that the standard was met by all receptors under the equal-percentage reduction approach, all sources were required to cut back their emissions by 90 percent at an annual cost of $254 million. The least-cost solution, which targets the greatest reductions at those firms capable of achieving them most cheaply, was estimated to cost only $24 million per year.

Conclusions such as these have triggered a series of major reforms in air-pollution control which are designed to reduce costs without sacrificing air quality. These reforms have the potential to reduce some of the conflict between environmentalists and industrialists. We shall cover these in some detail in Chapter 15.

Source: Robert J. Anderson, Jr., Robert O. Reid, Eugene P. Seskin, *An Analysis of Alternative Policies for Attaining and Maintaining a Short-Term NO₂ Standard* (Princeton, NJ: MATHTECH, Inc., 1979).

Current environmental-impact statements are more sophisticated than their early predecessors and may contain a benefit/cost analysis or a cost-effectiveness analysis in addition to other more traditional impact measurements. Historically, however, the tendency had been to issue huge environmental impact statements which are virtually impossible to comprehend in their entirety.

In response, the Council on Environmental Quality, which, by law, administers the environmental-impact statement process, has set content standards that are now resulting in shorter, more concise statements. To the extent that they merely quantify consequences, statements can avoid the problem of "hidden value judgments" that sometimes plague benefit/cost analysis, but they do so only by bombarding the policy makers with masses of noncomparable information. All three of the techniques discussed in this chapter are useful, but none of them can stake a claim as being universally the "best" approach. The nature of the information which is available and its reliability make a difference.

SUMMARY

In this chapter, we have examined the most prominent, but certainly not the only, techniques available to supply policy makers with the information needed to implement efficient policy. We have seen that benefit/cost analysis offers the most concrete guidance and is often very useful. For some functions, such as choosing the efficient level of pollution control, it is difficult to implement. Even when difficult to implement, the exercise of identifying the costs and benefits, as well as assessing their importance, is an extremely valuable part of the policy process. Unless one policy tends to so dominate the others that the outcome is not sensitive to uncertainty about possible outcomes or to a lack of reliability in the underlying data, however, we certainly have grounds to suspect any specific number or numbers which come out of that process.

Even when benefits are difficult to calculate, however, economic analysis in the form of cost effectiveness can be valuable. This technique can establish the least expensive ways to accomplish predetermined policy goals and to assess the extra costs involved when policies other than the least-cost policy are chosen. What it cannot do is answer the question of whether those predetermined policy goals are efficient.

At the end of the spectrum is impact analysis which merely identifies and quantifies the impacts of particular policies without any pretense of optimality or even comparability of the information generated. For a government policy based on impact analysis to result in an efficient allocation would represent a pure coincidence; the analysis itself does not guarantee that outcome.

This chapter has examined a major issue which will reoccur throughout the book—the role of information in structuring an appropriate relationship between humankind and the environment. We have seen information problems at many levels—the absence of knowledge about the consequences of various courses of action; inability to compare different types of information in an uncontroversial way, even when we can identify impacts; and possible biases in the structuring of information, as well as in the process transmitting it to policy makers. We must remain cognizant of these issues as we examine specific environmental problems. We begin that investigation in the next chapter with population growth, which is a major influence on both the timing and the intensity of many other environmental problems.

FURTHER READING

Ackerman, Bruce, *et al. The Uncertain Search for Environmental Quality* (New York: Free Press, 1974). An interdisciplinary team critically examines the pitfalls of incorporating complex economic analysis in the policy process using, as a case study, water pollution control in the Delaware Estuary.

Cummings, Ronald G., David S. Brookshire, and William D. Schulze, *Valuing Environmental Goods: An Assessment of the Contingent Valuation Method* (Totowa, NJ: Rowman and Littlefield, 1986). A critical evaluation of the contingent valuation method by both practitioners and impartial reviewers.

Kelman, Steven. "Cost-Benefit Analysis—An Ethical Critique." *Regulation* (January/February, 1981), 33–40. Kelman suggests that attempts to expand the use of benefit/cost analysis in the areas of environmental, health, and safety regulation raise troubling ethical questions.

Kneese, Allen V., *Measuring the Benefits of Clean Air and Water* (Washington, D.C.: Resources for the Future, Inc., 1984). An accessible introduction to a large number of studies attempting to quantify the benefits of cleaner air and water.

Lave, Lester B., ed. *Quantitative Risk Assessment in Regulation* (Washington, D.C.: The Brookings Institution, 1982). This book examines the requirements for quantitative risk assessment and the role it has played in the recent decisions of several regulatory agencies. The authors of the essays see a much larger possible role for quantitative risk assessment.

Mishan, E. J. *Cost-Benefit Analysis.* (New York: Praeger Special Studies, 1976). A standard, comprehensive textbook treatment of cost/benefit analysis by a noted economist. Some use of examples.

Pearce, David W., ed. *The Valuation of Social Cost* (London: Allen and Unwin, 1978). A number of leading experts explore the theoretical and practical attempts to place a monetary value on items which cannot be bought or sold.

Peskin, Henry M., and Eugene P. Seskin. *Cost-Benefit Analysis and Water Pollution Control Policy* (Washington: The Urban Institute, 1975). A collection of essays by some of the foremost scholars in the field concerning the problems with and prospects for using cost/benefit analysis to guide water pollution control policy.

Smith, V. Kerry, ed., *Environmental Policy under Reagan's Executive Order: The Role of Benefit-Cost Analysis* (Chapel Hill: The University of North Carolina Press, 1984). Written by leading practitioners, this collection of essays takes stock of how President Reagan's Executive Order No. 12291 has affected the making of policy.

Swartzman, Daniel, Richard A. Liroff, and Kevin G. Croke, eds. *Cost-Benefit Analysis and Environmental Regulation: Politics, Ethics, and Methods.* (Washington, D.C.: The Conservation Foundation, 1982). The proceedings of a conference which critically examined President Reagan's executive order requiring benefit-cost analysis by federal agencies. Discussions include the historical experience with benefit-cost analysis as used to analyze natural resource problems at state and national levels, an analysis of the strengths and weaknesses of the techniques, and an overview of the ethical issues raised.

ADDITIONAL REFERENCES

Bailey, Martin J., *Reducing Risks to Life: Measurement of the Benefits* (Washington, D.C.: American Enterprise Institute for Public Policy Research, 1980).

Brookshire, D. S., M. A. Thayer, W. D. Schulze, and R. C. d'Arge. "Valuing Public Goods: A Comparison of Survey and Hedonic Approaches," *The American Economic Review,* Vol. 72 (March, 1982): 165–177.

Clawson, Marion, and Jack Knetsch. *Economics of Outdoor Recreation* (Baltimore: Johns Hopkins University Press, for Resources for the Future, 1966).

Fisher, Anthony C., John V. Krutilla, and Charles J. Chicchetti, "Alternative Uses of Natural Environments: The Economics of Environmental Modification," in John V. Krutilla, ed., *Natural Environments: Studies in Theoretical and Applied Analysis* (Washington: Johns Hopkins University Press, for Resources for the Future, 1972): 18–53.

Freeman, A. Myrick, III, *The Benefits of Environmental Improvement: Theory and Practice* (Baltimore: The Johns Hopkins University Press, for Resources for the Future, 1979).

Freeman, A. Myrick, III, *Air and Water Pollution Control: A Benefit-Cost Assessment* (New York: John Wiley & Sons, 1982).

Freeman, A. Myrick, III, *The Benefits of Air and Water Pollution Control: A Review and Synthesis of Recent Estimates,* a report prepared for the Council on Environmental Quality (December, 1979).

Haveman, Robert H., *The Economic Performance of Public Investments: An* Ex Post *Evaluation of Water Resource Investments* (Baltimore: Johns Hopkins University Press, for Resources for the Future, Inc., 1972).

Lave, Lester B., and Eugene P. Seskin. *Air Pollution and Human Health* (Baltimore: Johns Hopkins University Press, 1977).

Lave, Lester B., ed., *Quantitative Risk Assessment in Regulation* (Washington, D.C.: The Brookings Institution, 1982).

Mikesell, Raymond, *The Rate of Discount for Evaluating Public Projects* (Washington D.C.: The American Enterprise Institute for Public Policy Research, 1977).

Rowe, R. D., R. d'Arge, and D. S. Brookshire, "An Experiment on the Economic Value of Visibility," *Journal of Environmental Economics and Management,* Vol. 7 (March, 1980): 1–19.

DISCUSSION QUESTIONS

1. Is risk neutrality an appropriate assumption for cost/benefit analysis? Why or why not? Does it seem more appropriate for some environmental problems than others? If so which ones? Why?

2. Was the executive order issued by President Reagan mandating a heavier use of cost/benefit analysis in regulatory rulemaking a step toward establishing a more rational regulatory structure or was it a subversion of the environmental policy process? Why?

PROBLEMS

1. In Mark A. Cohen, "The Costs and Benefits of Oil Spill Prevention and Enforcement", *Journal of Environmental Economics and Management,* Vol. 13, no. 2 (June, 1986) an attempt was made to quantify the marginal benefits and marginal costs of U.S. Coast Guard enforcement activity in the area of oil spill prevention. His analysis suggests (p. 185) that the marginal per gallon benefit from the current level of enforcement activity is $7.50 while the marginal per gallon cost is $5.50. Assuming these numbers are correct, would you recommend that the Coast Guard increase, decrease or hold at the current level their enforcement activity? Why?

2. In his book *Reducing Risks to Life: Measuring the Benefits,* Martin Bailey estimates that the cost per life saved of current government programs ranges from $72,000 for kidney transplants to $624,976,000 for a proposed standard to reduce occupational exposure to acrylonitrile.

(a) Assuming these values to be correct, how might efficiency be enhanced in these two programs?

(b) Should the government strive to equalize the marginal costs per life saved across all life-saving programs?

CHAPTER FIVE

The Population Problem

One of the most serious challenges to destiny in the last third of this century will be the growth of the population. Whether man's response to that challenge will be a cause for pride or for despair in the year 2000 will depend very much on what we do today.

PRESIDENT RICHARD M. NIXON (1969)

INTRODUCTION

In the first chapter of this book we examined two strikingly different views of what the future holds for the world economic system. At the heart of those differences lie rather divergent views of the world population problem. Meadows and his team see population growth as continuing relentlessly, putting enormous pressure on food and environmental resources. Kahn, on the other hand, sees the world as being in a period of transition from high rates of natural increase to strikingly lower ones, culminating eventually in zero population growth. Because of abundant technological possibilities for satisfying the temporarily increasing, but eventually stable, population, Kahn's optimistic outlook is maintained.

These views are symptomatic of a larger debate. Paul Ehrlich [1969] in his provocatively titled book, *The Population Bomb,* argued that population is not merely *an* important problem but is *the* problem in ensuring long-term survival of the species. Contrasting views are held by representatives of third-world countries and some prominent population economists, such as Julian Simon [1977] who maintains that not only has Ehrlich overstated the case of the seriousness of the problem in many cases, but also that he fails to recognize that population growth in many of the developing countries is desirable. It should be clear from this brief review that there is no consensus on the seriousness of the problem or, indeed, whether the problem exists at all.

In this chapter we shall examine the macroeconomic issues relating to population and economic growth, as well as the microeconomic issues dealing with economic determinants of fertility. We shall briefly examine the effects that population growth and

TABLE 5.1 Annual Average Rate of World Population Growth 1950–85 (percent)

	1950–55	*1955–60*	*1960–65*	*1965–70*	*1970–75*	*1975–80*	*1980–85*	*Forecast 1985–90*
World	1.8	1.9	1.8	2.1	2.0	1.7	1.7	1.6
More Developed*	1.3	1.3	1.2	0.9	0.9	0.7	0.6	0.4
United States	1.7	1.7	1.5	1.1	1.1	1.1	0.9	0.9
Less Developed**	2.1	2.2	2.1	2.5	2.4	2.1	2.1	1.8
Africa	2.2	2.3	2.5	2.6	2.7	2.8	3.0	3.0

*Includes North America, Europe, the Soviet Union, Australia and New Zealand.

**Includes all countries of the world except those listed above.

Sources: 1950–1985 data: U.S. Department of Commerce, Bureau of the Census, *World Population: 1983* (Washington, DC: 1983), Pages 29 and 448. 1985–90 data: U.S. Department of Commerce, Bureau of the Census, *World Population: 1984* (Washington, DC: 1984), pages 2 and 6.

economic growth each have on the other. We shall then focus on a conceptual approach for understanding the demand for children, the empirical evidence which assesses the validity of this framework, and finally, the possibilities for controlling population.

HISTORICAL PERSPECTIVE

World Population Growth

It has been estimated that at the beginning of the Christian era, AD 1, world population stood at about 250,000,000 people and was growing at 0.04 percent per year (not 4 percent!). Not long ago, the world's population passed 4,000,000,000 and was growing at an annual rate around 2.0 percent per year. If that 2.0 percent growth rate were to continue unabated, the world's population would double in only 35 years. Since the beginning of time, the population has grown to 4 billion people; at a 2.0 percent growth rate, the next 4 billion could take only 35 years.

In recent years, with the notable exception of Africa, the average rate of population growth has declined (Table 5.1). This slowdown has been experienced in both developed and less-developed countries, although rates remain higher in the less-developed countries.

The World Fertility Survey, a multinational survey of some 400,000 women in 61 countries, revealed a significant downward trend in fertility and birth rates over the last decade.[1] This tendency appears in both developing and developed nations, with

[1]For an analysis of recent trends, see W. Parker Maudlin, "Patterns of Fertility Decline in Developing Countries, 1970–5" in *Fertility Decline in the Less Developed Countries*, Nick Eberstadt, ed. (New York: Praeger, 1981): 72–96.

only African nations bucking the trend.[2] The survey found several apparent causes, including increased use of contraception, a growing preference for fewer children, and couples marrying later.

Although the trend toward falling birth rates is very pervasive, the fact remains that most developing countries still have, and can be expected to have in the future, substantial increases in their populations. Some 90 percent of the population growth between 1980 and 2000 is expected to occur in the poorer countries.

For example, in 1973–83, Honduras, Kenya, Liberia, Zimbabwe, and Nicaragua all had annual average growth rates in excess of 3.0 percent. During the same period, Austria, the United Kingdom, Finland, Belgium, Denmark and Sweden all experienced annual average growth rates of less than 0.5 percent. East and West Germany both currently have declining populations.[3]

Population Growth in the United States

As seen in Table 5.1, population growth in the United States has followed the general declining pattern of most of the developed world, although in most periods American growth rates have exceeded the average for all developed countries. These large reductions in population growth rates have been due primarily to declines in the birth rate, which fell from a high of 55.2 live births per thousand population in 1820 to only 14.6 live births per thousand in 1975, the lowest recorded birth rate in the period covered by the data. By 1984 the birth rate had climbed back to 15.7 (Figure 5.1).

Birth rates, however, provide a rather crude measure of the underlying population trends, primarily because they do not account for age structure. To understand the effect of age structure, let's separate the birth-rate experience into two components: (1) the number of persons in the childbearing years, and (2) the number of children those persons are bearing.

To quantify the second of these components, the Census Bureau uses a concept known as the *total fertility rate,* which is the number of live births an average woman has in her lifetime if, at each year of age, she experiences the average birth rates occurring in the general population of similarly aged women. This concept can be used to determine what level of fertility would, if continued, lead to a stationary population. A *stationary population* is one in which age- and sex-specific fertility rates yield a birth rate which is constant and equal to the death rate, so the growth rate is zero. The level of the total fertility rate which is compatible with a stationary population is called the *replacement rate.* Rates higher than the replacement rate would lead to population growth, while rates lower would lead to population declines. Once the replacement fertility rate is reached, the World Bank estimates that it takes approximately 25 years

[2]For an analysis of the factors underlying the tendency of African nations to be experiencing increases in fertility rates, see John C. Caldwell, "Fertility in Africa," in *Fertility Decline in the Less Developed Countries,* Nick Eberstadt, ed. (New York: Praeger, 1981): 97–118.

[3]The comparative population growth-rate figures can be found in World Bank, *World Development Report: 1985* (Washington, DC: International Bank for Reconstruction and Development, 1985): 210–211.

FIGURE 5.1 U.S. Birth Rates From 1880–1984

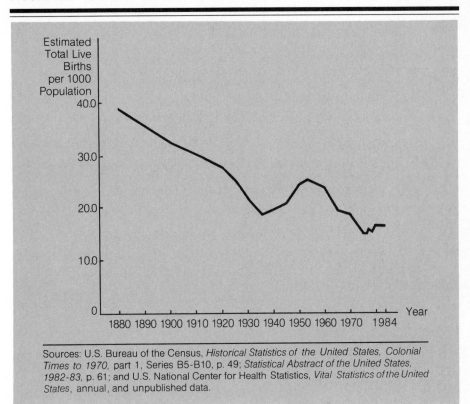

Sources: U.S. Bureau of the Census, *Historical Statistics of the United States, Colonial Times to 1970*, part 1, Series B5-B10, p. 49; *Statistical Abstract of the United States, 1982-83*, p. 61; and U.S. National Center for Health Statistics, *Vital Statistics of the United States*, annual, and unpublished data.

before the population stabilizes, due to the large numbers of families in the childbearing years. As the age structure reaches it older equilibrium, the growth rate declines until a stationary population is attained.

In the United States, the replacement rate is 2.11. The two children replace the mother and her mate, while the extra 0.11 is to compensate for those women who do not survive the childbearing years and for the fact that slightly more than 50 percent of births are males. The United States total fertility rate dropped below the replacement rate in 1972 and has remained below it ever since (Figure 5.2). In 1982 (the latest year for which data were available) the rate stood at 1.83. If it were to remain at this level for 25 years, the U.S. population could be expected to decline at a rate of 5.2 percent per year.

This introduction to the population situation serves to raise two questions: (1) What is the relationship between population growth and economic growth? and (2) How can the rate of population growth be altered when alteration is appropriate? The first question lays the groundwork for considering the effect of population growth on quality of life, including the effects of a stationary population. The second allows us to consider public policies geared toward manipulating the rate of population growth when desirable.

FIGURE 5.2   Total U.S. Fertility Rate, 1940–1984

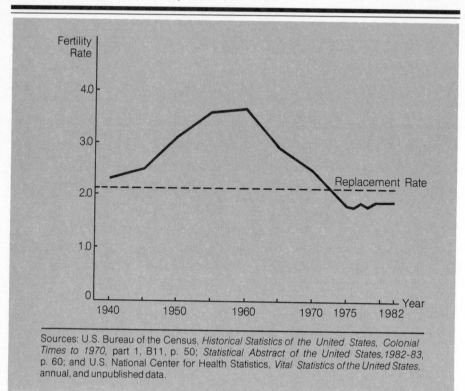

Sources: U.S. Bureau of the Census, *Historical Statistics of the United States, Colonial Times to 1970,* part 1, B11, p. 50; *Statistical Abstract of the United States,1982-83,* p. 60; and U.S. National Center for Health Statistics, *Vital Statistics of the United States,* annual, and unpublished data.

EFFECTS OF POPULATION GROWTH ON ECONOMIC GROWTH

A number of questions guide our inquiry. Does population growth enhance or inhibit the opportunities of a country's citizens? Does the answer depend on the stage of development? Given that several countries are now entering a period of declining population growth, what are the possible effects of this decline on economic growth?

Population growth affects economic growth and, as long as each person contributes something, those effects generally are positively correlated. As long as their marginal product is positive, additional people mean additional output. Since this is not a very restrictive condition, it should usually hold true.

However, the existence of a positive marginal product is not a very appropriate test of the desirability of population growth! Perhaps a better one is to ask whether population growth positively affects the average citizen. Whenever the marginal product of an additional person is lower than the average product, adding more persons simply reduces the welfare of the average citizen. Can you see why?

There is a range of marginal productivities, between zero and the average product, where economic growth measured in aggregate terms would increase but measured in per-capita terms would decrease. Similarly, there is a range of marginal productivities—those greater than the average product—where economic growth increases regardless of whether it is measured in aggregate or per-capita terms. Whether or not the material status of the average citizen is improved by population growth becomes a question of whether the marginal product of additional people is higher or lower than the average product.

To facilitate our examination of the population-related determinants of economic growth let's examine a rather simple definition of output:

$$O = L \cdot X,$$

where O is the output level, X is the output per worker, and L is the number of workers. This equation can be expressed in per-capita terms by dividing both sides by population, denoted as P:

$$\frac{O}{P} = \frac{L}{P} \cdot X.$$

This equation now states that output per capita is determined by the product of two factors: the share of the population which is in the labor force and the output per worker. Each of these two factors provides a channel through which population growth affects economic growth.

The most direct effect of population growth on the percentage of the population employed, the *age structure effect*, results from induced changes in the age distribution. Suppose that we were to compare two populations—one rapidly growing and one slowly growing. The one with the rapid growth would contain a much larger percentage of younger persons (Figure 5.3).

Due to its slow growth, the U.S. population is in general older. While approximately 45 percent of Mexico's population is 14 years of age or younger, the comparable figure for the United States is 23 percent. This is reinforced at the other end of the age structure, where some 10.9 percent of the U.S. population is 65 or older as compared to only 3.4 percent in Mexico.

These differences in the age structure have mixed effects on the percentage of the labor force available to be employed. The abundance of youth in a rapidly growing population creates a large supply of people too young to work, a situation referred to as the *youth effect*. On the other hand, a country characterized by slow population growth has a rather larger percentage of persons who have reached, or are past, the traditional retirement age of 65, a situation referred to as the *retirement effect*. Some developing countries are experiencing both effects simultaneously as better public-health policies reduce death rates while birth rates remain high. How do the youth and retirement effects interact to determine the percentage of the population in the labor force? Does the youth effect dominate the retirement effect?

FIGURE 5.3 Age Structure of Two Populations

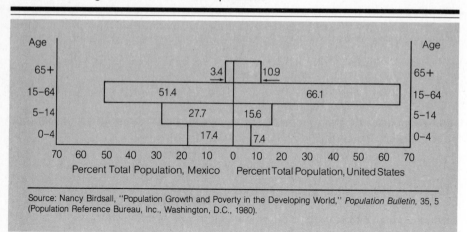

Source: Nancy Birdsall, "Population Growth and Poverty in the Developing World," *Population Bulletin,* 35, 5 (Population Reference Bureau, Inc., Washington, D.C., 1980).

Examine the percentage of population in the prime working ages, 15–64. As Figure 5.3 shows, this percentage is much higher for the United States. A larger percentage of the population is in the working force in the United States than in Mexico. For Mexico the youth effect dominates.

This dominance of the youth effect generalizes to other countries. For example, in 1978 the 38 lowest income countries had an average 55 percent of the population in the prime working age while the 18 most industrialized countries averaged 65 percent.[4] Thus, high population growth retards per-capita economic growth by decreasing the percentage of the population in the labor force.

Rapid growth also affects the percentage available to be employed through the *female availability effect.* With a slower growth rate and fewer children to care for, more women are available to join the labor force. Both the dominance of the youth effect (over the retirement effect) and the female availability effect suggest that rapid population growth reduces the percentage of the population in the labor force which, in turn, has a depressing effect on economic growth per capita.

How about possible relationships between population growth and the second factor, the amount of output produced by the average worker? The most common way to enhance productivity is through the accumulation of capital. As the capital stock is augmented (for example, through the introduction of assembly lines or production machinery), workers become more productive. Is there any connection between population growth and capital accumulation?[5]

---

[4]World Bank, *World Development Report, 1980* (Washington, D.C.: International Bank for Reconstruction and Development, 1980): 146–47.

[5]This connection is clearly articulated in Ansley J. Coale and Edgar M. Hoover, *Population Growth and Economic Development in Low Income Countries* (Princeton, N.J.: Princeton University Press, 1958).

The main connection examined by researchers has been between savings and capital accumulation. The availability of savings determines the level of additions to the capital stock. Availability of savings, in turn, is affected in part by the age structure of the population. Older populations are presumed to save more because less is spent directly on the care and nurturing of children. Therefore, all other things being equal, societies with rapidly growing populations could be expected to save proportionately less. This lowered availability of savings would lead to lower amounts of capital stock augmentation and lower productivity per worker.

Many economists have also suggested that population growth not only adversely affects the *level* of saving, it also affects the *composition* of saving. Savings that do occur are channeled to less productive types of investments, causing a larger augmentation of consumer durables, such as housing and automobiles, rather than producer durables. Because production-enhancing goods are the only goods capable of stimulating greater productivity, rapid population growth serves not only to reduce capital accumulation, but also to reduce the productivity of that which has been accumulated.

A final model suggesting a negative effect of population growth on economic growth involves the presence of some fixed essential factor for which limited substitution possibilities exist (land, raw materials, and so on). In this case, the *law of diminishing marginal productivity* applies. This law states that in the presence of a fixed factor (land), successively larger additions of a variable factor (labor) will eventually lead to a decline in the marginal productivity of the variable factor. It suggests that in the presence of fixed factors successive increases in labor will drive the marginal product down. When it falls below the average product, per capita income will decline with further increases in the population.

Not all of the arguments suggest that growth in output per capita will be restrained by population growth. Perhaps the most compelling arguments for the view that population growth enhances per capita growth are those involving technological progress and *economies of scale* (Figure 5.4).

The vertical axis shows marginal productivity measured in units of output. The horizontal axis describes various levels of labor employed on a fixed amount of land. Population growth implies an increase in the labor force, which is recorded on the graph as a movement to the right on the horizontal axis.

The curve labeled $P(t_1)$ shows the functional relationship between the marginal product of labor and the amount of labor employed on a fixed plot of land at a particular point in time (t_1). Different curves represent different points in time because in each period of time there exists a unique state-of-the-art in the knowledge of how to use the labor most effectively. Thus, as time passes, technological progress occurs, advancing the state-of-the-art and shifting the productivity curves outward, as demonstrated by $P(t_2)$ and $P(t_3)$.

Three particular situations are demonstrated by Figure 5.4. At time t_1, an application of $L(t_1)$ yields a marginal product of $M(t_1)$. At times t_2 and t_3, the application of $L(t_2)$ and $L(t_3)$ units of labor respectively yield $M(t_2)$ and $M(t_3)$ marginal units of output. Marginal products have increased as larger amounts of labor were added.

FIGURE 5.4   Technological Progress and the Law of Diminishing Returns

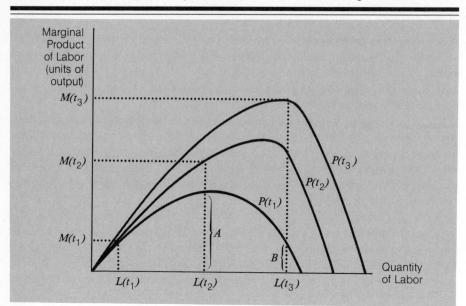

Consider what would have happened, however, if the state of technical knowledge had not increased. The increase in labor from $L(t_2)$ to $L(t_3)$ would have been governed by the $P(t_1)$ curve, and the marginal product would have declined from A to B. This is precisely the result anticipated by the law of diminishing marginal productivity. Technological progress provides one means of escaping the law of diminishing marginal productivity.

The second source of increase in output per worker is economies of scale. Economies of scale occur when increases in inputs lead to a more than proportionate increase in output. Population growth, by increasing demand for output, allows these economies of scale to be exploited. In the United States, at least, this has been a potent source of growth. Edward Dennison [1974], in a major study of U.S. economic growth, concluded that economies of scale accounted for slightly over 10 percent of growth in total potential national income per unit input in the 1929–69 period. While it seems clear that the population level in the United States is already sufficient to exploit economies of scale, the same is not necessarily true for all developing countries.

Because these *a priori* arguments suggest that population growth could either enhance or retard economic growth, it is necessary to rely on empirical studies to sort out the relative importance of these effects. Several researchers have attempted to validate the premise that population growth inhibits per capita economic growth. Their attempts were based on the notion that if the premise were true, one should be able to observe lower growth in per capita income in countries with higher population growth rates, all other things being equal.

To date, the empirical work has not yielded conclusive results.[6] Therefore, we must conclude that the premise is wrong, empirically insignificant, or that we have not yet been clever enough to account for the other factors which obviously affect growth in order to allow the relationship to emerge.[7]

Even when rapid population growth does not adversely affect output per capita, it may increase the inequality of income. Perhaps the clearest statement of this argument comes from Peter Lindert [1978]. He believes that high population growth increases the degree of inequality for a variety of reasons, but the most important involve a depressing effect on the earning capacity of children and on wages.

The ability to provide for the education and training of children, given fixed budgets of time and money, is a function of the number of children in the family—the fewer the children, the higher the proportion of income (and wealth, such as land) available to develop each child's earning capacity. Since low-income families tend to have larger families than high-income families do, the offspring from low-income families are usually more disadvantaged. The result is a growing gap between the rich and the poor.

Espenshade [1984, pp. 2–4] has provided some revealing estimates of parental expenditures on childrearing in the United States that tend to confirm certain key aspects of this argument. The average expenditure to raise a child to age 18 depends crucially on income level and the size of the family, ranging from an expenditure of $135,700 (in constant 1981 dollars) for high-income couples including a working wife and only one child, to $58,300 spent on the average child by a lower-income couple including a wife who does not work and three children. Adding in college expenditures where appropriate would boost these figures considerably.

Espenshade also examines the proportion of the typical family's income spent on childrearing as well as the sensitivity of this proportion to the number of children in the family. According to his analysis, families with only one child will commit about 30 percent of total family expenditures to their child. This percentage rises to between 40 and 45 percent for two-child families and nearly 50 percent in three-child families. The detailed data in this study make clear that average expenditures per child consistently decline as the number of children in a family increases.

Another link between population growth and income inequality results from the effect of population growth on the labor supply. High population growth could increase the supply of labor faster than otherwise, depressing wage rates *vis a vis* profit rates. Since low-income groups have a higher relative reliance on wages for their income than do the rich, this effect would also increase the degree of inequality.

---

[6]See, for example, Simon Kuznets, *Population, Capital, and Growth: Selected Essays* (New York, NY: W. W. Norton, 1973); Richard A. Easterlin, "Population," in *Contemporary Economic Issues*, Neil Chanberlin, ed. (Homewood, Ill.: Richard Irwin, 1972): 301–352; Nancy Birdsall, "Population Growth and Poverty in the Developing World," *Population Bulletin* 35 (December 1980): 1–46.

[7]Even if technological progress and economies of scale have ameliorated the harmful effects of population growth historically, they may be less helpful in the future. Are there diminishing returns to technological progress? Though we cannot yet answer this question, we shall investigate it further in Chapter 21.

After an extensive review of the historical record for the United States, Lindert concludes:

> There seems to be good reason for believing that extra fertility affects the size and "quality" of the labor force in ways that raise income inequalities. Fertility, like immigration, tends to reduce the average "quality" of the labor force, by reducing the amounts of family and public school resources devoted to each child. The retardation in the historic improvement in labor force quality has in turn held back the rise in the incomes of the unskilled relative to those enjoyed by skilled labor and wealth-holders. [p. 258]

If Lindert's interpretation of the American historical record is valid for developing countries, it provides an additional powerful motivation for controlling population. Slower population growth reduces income inequality.

EFFECTS OF ECONOMIC GROWTH ON POPULATION GROWTH

Up to this point, we have considered the effect of population growth on economic growth. We have now to examine the converse relationship. Does economic growth affect population growth? Table 5.1 suggests that it may, since the higher-income countries are characterized by lower population growth rates.

This suspicion is reinforced by some further evidence. Most of the industrialized countries have passed through three stages of population growth. The conceptual framework which organizes this evidence is called the *theory of demographic transition*. This theory suggests that as nations develop they eventually reach a point where birth rates fall (Figure 5.5).

During Stage 1, the period immediately prior to industrialization, birth rates are stable and slightly higher than death rates, ensuring population growth. During Stage 2, the period immediately following the initiation of industrialization, death rates fall dramatically with no accompanying change in birth rates. This decline in mortality results in a marked increase in life expectancy and a rise in the population-growth rate. In Western Europe, Stage 2 is estimated to have lasted somewhere around fifty years.

Stage 3, the period of demographic transition, involves large declines in the birth rate which exceed the continued declines in the death rate. Thus, the period of demographic transition involves further increases in life expectancy, but rather smaller population growth rates than characterized the second stage. The Chilean experience with the demographic transition is illustrated in Figure 5.6. Can you identify the stages?

The theory of demographic transition is useful because it suggests that reductions in population growth might accompany industrialization, at least in the long run. However, it also leaves many questions unanswered. Why does the fall in birth rates occur? Can the process by speeded up? Will lower-income countries automatically experience demographic transition as they industrialize? Is industrialization a possible solution to "the population problem"?

FIGURE 5.5 The Demographic Transition

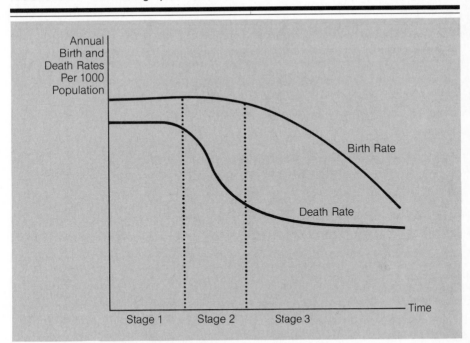

Thomas Malthus, a late eighteenth-century and early nineteenty-century classical economist, concluded that population growth posed a trap for countries seeking development. His model, with some modern elaboration, has become known as the *Malthusian population trap model.*[8]

This model implies that low-income countries are caught in a trap which condemns them to perpetual poverty. Their current per-capita income level is stable; any movement away from this equilibrium is seen by the model as calling forth changes in population that restore the equilibrium. Temporary increases in income, for example, are assumed to increase population growth to such an extent that population growth outstrips economic growth, driving per-capita income back to the subsistence level. Conditions reducing per-capita income eventually result in higher death rates until the equilibrium is once again restored. This model, if correct, implies that less-developed countries would never reach the point where birth rates would fall.

Is this an accurate model for modern times? Recent econometric work by Julian Simon [1980] suggests it is not. He finds the long-run elasticity of fertility with respect to income to be negative. In other words, as income rises, fertility eventually falls.

---

[8]For a more detailed examination of this model see Michael P. Todaro, *Economic Development in the Third World,* 2nd ed. (New York: Longman, 1981): 183–87.

FIGURE 5.6   Annual Birth Rates, Death Rates, and Rates of Natural Population Increase in Chile, 1929–1970

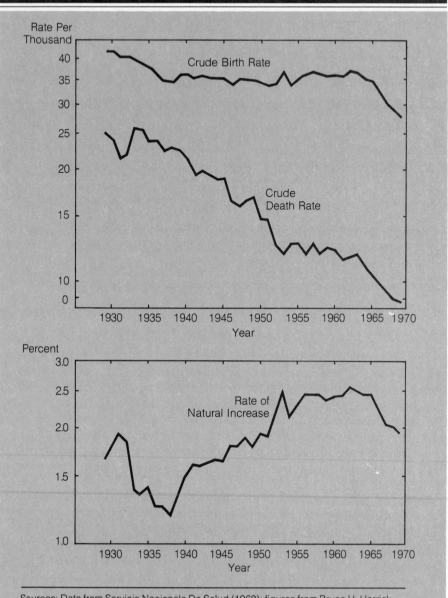

Sources: Data from Servicio Nacionale De Salud (1969); figures from Bruce H. Herrick, "Economic Effects of Chilean Fertility Decline, " in Michael C. Keeley, ed. *Population, Public Policy and Economic Development* (New York: Praeger Publishers, 1976): Figure 2.1, p. 52.

Due to better health conditions as income rises, the short-run elasticity may be positive, indicating the immediate response may be for fertility to increase, but it is too weak to counterbalance the long-run negative elasticity. When we consider this evidence on the existence and strength of the ultimate decline in birth rates which accompanies rises in per-capita income, the Malthusian population trap model emerges as an excessively harsh characterization of the nonetheless real difficulties experienced by the less-developed countries.

THE ECONOMIC APPROACH TO POPULATION CONTROL

Is the current rate of population growth efficient? There are two ways to attack this question. The first is to conduct a benefit/cost analysis of population control to see whether some government control would maximize efficiency. Such a study was conducted by Enke and Zind (Example 5.1).

This study focused purely on the effects of additional population on output per capita. Though the study found that increased population control was necessary to increase the net benefit, the presumption on which it is based (population growth retards economic growth) has not yet been shown to be universally valid.

The demonstration that population growth reduces per-capita income, however, is not sufficient to prove that an inefficiency exists. If the reduced output is borne entirely by the families of the children, this reduction may represent a conscious choice by parents to sacrifice production in order to have more children. The net benefit gained from having more children (not measured by Enke and Zind) would exceed the net benefit lost as output per person declined.

To establish whether or not population control is efficient, we must establish whether or not there are potential behavioral biases toward overpopulation. Will parents always make efficient childbearing decisions?

There are several reasons why a negative response seems appropriate. The first is derived from the previously discussed evidence that high population growth may exacerbate income inequality. Income equality is a public good. The population as a whole cannot be excluded from the degree of income equality which exists. Furthermore, it is an indivisible good because, in a given society, the prevailing income distribution is the same for all the citizens of that society.

Why should individuals care about inequality *per se* as opposed to simply caring about their own income? Aside from a pure humane concern for others, particularly the poor, people care about inequality because it can create social tensions. When these social tensions exist, society is a less-pleasant place to live.

The demand to reduce income inequality clearly exists in modern society, as evidenced by the large number of private charitable organizations created to fulfill this demand. Yet because the reduction of income inequality is a public good we also know that these organizations cannot be relied upon to reduce inequality to its efficient level.

Similarly, for the same reason we know that parents will not take it sufficiently into account when they make their childbearing decisions. They will have too many children and will exacerbate income inequality in the process.

There are two other externalities as well: (1) the cost of food and (2) the cost of education. It is common for developing countries to subsidize food by holding prices below market levels. Lower-than-normal food prices artificially lower the cost of children

---

EXAMPLE 5.1

The Value of an Averted Birth

If population growth tends to reduce average income, then the nation experiencing this population growth would have an incentive to spend money on population control. The determination of how much money should be spent depends upon a comparison of the costs of the population control program with the value of an averted birth.

Enke and Zind developed a simulation model to assess the value of an averted birth. The model allowed for substitution among capital and labor, the restraining effect of the dependency ratio, and the effect of an age structure and income on saving. To obtain the value of averted births, they compared a scenario with no birth control to one in which a reduction in fertility over a 30-year period was compatible with 50 percent of all women in each age group practicing contraception. The implied terminal fertility rate was approximately 23 per 1,000.

On the basis of this simulation they concluded:

> A modest birth control programme, costing perhaps 30 cents a year per head of national population, can raise average income over only 15 years by almost twice the percentage that it would rise without birth control. . . . The value of permanently preventing the birth of a marginal infant is about twice an LDC's annual income per head. [p. 41]

This is a controversial finding because there is not uniform agreement that the simulated mechanisms approximate those which would actually prevail in developing countries, particularly if the population growth is moderate rather than rapid.* Nonetheless, for those countries which are experiencing very rapid population growth it does suggest that the potential payoff to instituting means of controlling that population growth could be substantial.

*See, for example, Simon [1977] who argues that moderate growth (as opposed to either zero or rapid growth) may increase, not decrease, average incomes.

Sources: S. Enke and R. Zind, "Effect of Fewer Births on Average Income," *Journal of Biosocial Science* 1 (1969): 41–55; Julian L. Simon, *The Economics of Population Growth* (Princeton: Princeton University Press, 1977).

as long as the quantities of food available are maintained by government subsidy (we will discuss this further in Chapter 10).[9]

The second area in which the costs of children are not fully borne by the parents is education. Primary education is usually state financed with the funds collected by taxes. The point is *not* that parents do not pay these costs; in part they do. The point is rather that their level of contribution is not usually sensitive to the number of children they have. The school taxes one pays are generally the same whether parents have two children, ten children or even no children. Thus the marginal educational expenditure for a parent – the additional cost of education due to the birth of a child – is certainly lower than the true social cost of educating that child.

Unfortunately, there seems to have been very little accomplished on assessing the empirical significance of these externalities. Despite this lack of evidence, there is considerable interest in controlling population – a difficult task. The right to bear children is considered in many countries, if not most, as an inalienable right immune to influences outside the family. Indira Gandhi, the Prime Minister of India, lost an election in the late 1970s due principally to her aggressive and direct approach to population control.[10] Though she subsequently regained her position, it is unlikely political figures in other democratic countries would miss the message. Dictating that no family can have more than two children is not politically palatable at this time. Such a dictum is seen as an unethical infringement on the rights of those who are mentally, physically, and monetarily equipped to care for larger families.

What, then, is a democratic country to do? How can it gain control over population growth while allowing individual families considerable flexibility in choosing their family size? The answer may lie in a more careful examination of fertility decline during the demographic transition. By uncovering the sources of fertility decline, we might use them to manipulate population growth. This approach *indirectly* controls population by controlling the environment in which family decisions on childbearing are made. In order to use it, we need to know how fertility decision making is affected by the economic environment experienced by the family.

The major model attempting to assess the determinants of childbirth decision making from an economic viewpoint is called the *microeconomic theory of fertility*.[11] The point of departure for this theory is viewing children as consumer durables. The key insight is that the demand for children will, as with more conventional commodities, be downward sloping. All other things being equal, the more expensive children become, the fewer will be demanded.

---

[9]Notice, however, that if the food is domestically produced and the effect of price controls is to lower the prices farmers receive for their crops, the effect is to lower the demand for children in the agricultural sector. Can you see why?

[10]See, for example, Myron Weiner, *India at the Polls* (Washington, D.C.: American Enterprise Institute for Public Policy Research, 1978).

[11]The major works in the development of this framework were developed by Becker [1960] and Easterlin [1968]. Also, the *Journal of Political Economy: Special Supplement* published March/April, 1973, is dedicated to the economics of fertility. A critical review of the area can be found in Leibenstein [1974]. See references at end of chapter for full source citations.

With this point of departure, childbearing decisions can be modeled within a traditional demand-and-supply framework (Figure 5.7). We shall designate the initial situation, prior to the imposition of any controls, as the point where demand, designated by D_1, and marginal cost, designated by MC_1, are equal. The desired number of children at this point is given as q_1. Notice that, according to the analysis, the desired number of children can be reduced either by an inward shift of the demand curve to D_2, or an upward shift in the marginal cost of children to MC_2, or both. What would cause these to shift?

Let's consider the demand curve. Why might it have shifted inward during the demographic transition? There are several reasons:

1. The shift from an agricultural to an industrial economy reduces the productivity of children. In an agricultural economy, extra hands are useful, but in an industrial economy, child labor laws result in children contributing substantially less to the family. Therefore the investment demand for children is reduced.[12]

2. In countries with primitive savings systems, one of the very few ways a person can provide for old-age security is to have plenty of children to provide for him or her in the twilight years. One would not, at first glance, think of children as social security systems, but, in many societies, they are precisely that. When alternative means of providing for old-age security are developed, the demand for children decreases.

3. A decrease in infant mortality can also cause the demand curve to shift inward. When infant mortality is high, it takes a large number of births to produce the desired number of children at the ages when they are needed. Support for this argument was obtained recently during an attempt to reduce infant mortality in one of the Southern states of India. Apparently, this program did have the side effect of reducing the birth rate [Kaufman, 1980].

4. There is also some evidence that the amount the demand curve shifts inward as a result of economic growth depends on the manner in which the increased employment associated with development is shared among the members of society. It has been pointed out [Repetto, 1981] that those countries which have typically entered into a phase of sustained fertility decline in spite of low levels of average per capita income levels are usually characterized by a relatively equal distribution of income and a relatively widespread participation in the benefits of growth.

The desired number of children is also affected by changes in the cost of children. There are many ways in which the costs of children have been, and could be, changed as a means of controlling population.

---

[12]A detailed exploration of the relationship between fertility and urbanization can be found in David Goldberg, "Residential Location and Fertility," in Ronald Ridker, ed. *Population and Development: The Search for Selective Intervention* (Baltimore: Johns Hopkins University Press, 1976): 387–428. Urban fertility rates generally are lower.

FIGURE 5.7   The Demand for Children

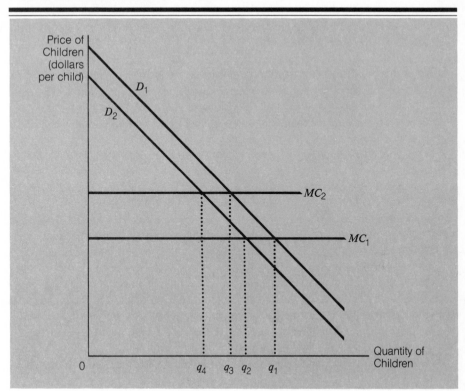

1. One of the main components of the cost of children is the opportunity cost of the mother's time. By increasing the labor market opportunities for women, the opportunity cost of raising children is increased. This can affect the observed fertility rate both by deferring the time of marriage and by causing a reduction in the desired number of children, once married.

2. As societies urbanize and industrialize, housing space becomes more expensive due to the concentrated demands in specific locations. Thus while the cost of extra space for children may be low in rural settings it is much higher in urban settings.

3. The cost of children is also affected to a large extent by the cost of education. As nations struggle to improve their literacy rates by universal compulsory education, they simultaneously raise the cost of children. These costs rise not only because of the increased expenditures on education but also because of the earnings which are forgone when the children are in school rather than working. This source can be a potent one. It has been estimated [Caldwell and Ruzicka, 1978] that the increasing cost of educating children was the most important factor in the dramatic decline in fertility in Australia during the last quarter of the nineteenth century.

4. As development occurs, generally the returns to education increase, creating a larger demand for education of their children by parents. The effect of this increased demand for education is to raise the cost of every child even if the cost of education is not rising.

All of this provides a menu of opportunities for population control. The reasons listed above represent potent forces for change. Korea provides one example (Example 5.2). Yet these methods should be used with care. Inducing a family to have fewer children without assisting the family in satisfying the basic need the children were fulfilling (such as old-age security) would be inequitable.

Many countries are using economic incentives to alter population growth. Some, such as the Soviet Union, are using economic incentives to increase growth. Traditionally, the Soviet Union has granted medals and glorified "hero mothers," those who bear and raise ten children or more. Seeing little success with these programs, in 1981 government officials announced they would set aside the equivalent of some $12.1 billion to be given out as payments to childbearing families as cash bonuses and salary supplements. The 1981 allocation is expected to fund the program until 1985.[13]

In what seems to Western eyes a clear step backward, they have also taken steps to ban women from some 460 occupations in which they had previously been permitted to participate. Apparently, the negative effects on birth rates from these expanded opportunities were larger than desired so that equal opportunity goals were dropped.[14]

Policies in China illustrate just how far economic incentives can be carried.[15] In announced regulations, one-child parents receive subsidized health expenditures, priority in education, health care and housing, and additional subsidized food. Meanwhile, parents who have more than two children will receive a reduction of 5 percent in the total income for the third child (6 percent for the fourth, and so on). Also, their families will be denied access to further subsidized grain beyond that which they would already receive for their two previous children.

There are a host of other measures available to any country seeking to reduce fertility. These include enhancing the status of women, providing alternative sources of old-age security, and equalizing the income distributions. There is no shortage of opportunities.

SUMMARY

World population growth has slowed considerably in recent years with only African nations resisting the trend. Population declines are already occurring in East Germany and are expected in the near future in a number of Northern European countries. The United States' total fertility rate is now below the replacement level. If maintained for

[13]"Soviets Offer Bonuses for Births," *Central Maine Morning Sentinel (4 June 1981)*: 11.

[14]"In the Interest of Women," *Wall Street Journal* (13 January 1981), 32.

[15]John S. Aird, "Fertility Decline in China," in *Fertility Decline in the Less Developed Countries,* Nick Eberstadt, ed. (New York: Praeger, 1981): 119–227.

EXAMPLE 5.2

Fertility Decline in Korea: A Case Study

The dramatic fertility decline in the Republic of Korea which occurred during the period from 1960–1974 has been one of the fastest ever recorded. Therefore, it provides a unique opportunity to study the forces which led to this decline and the extent to which they might be applicable to other countries.

The period prior to the dramatic decline contained a series of shattering events, including the Korean War. Culturally homogeneous to start with, Korea emerged from this period as a relatively egalitarian society. During the fertility decline, Korea experienced very rapid economic growth stimulated to a large extent by imported capital and technology. Because the development approach focused on labor-intensive technologies, the fruits of this development were spread rather uniformly throughout the economy. Rising real wages and an expanded demand for labor served to preserve the relatively equal-income distribution which had been inherited from the 1950s.

This combination of rapid economic growth and widespread participation in that growth among various sectors of the economy produced a dramatic fertility decline in almost all groups of society. Birth rates started to decline simultaneously in all regions, classes, and categories of households.

The changes in economic institutions which accompanied economic growth reinforced the tendency toward declining fertility rates. This period saw the rise, for example, of savings institutions, the widespread ownership of property (which permitted the accumulation of some wealth), and social insurance. These tended to provide alternative mechanisms for assuring old-age security.

There was also a substantial increase in the percentage of females in the labor force, resulting in an increase in the age of marriage and a reduction in the fertility rate of married women. At the same time, education levels of women rose, which also contributed to the decline.

Though the degree of income and cultural equality in Korea was unusual, many of the other factors contributing to fertility decline, such as pursuing a development plan which reduced income inequality as the nation grew, providing alternative social security systems, and assuring expanding labor-market opportunities for women, are available to other nations.

Source: Robert Repetto, *Economic Equality and Fertility in Developing Countries* (Baltimore, Md: The Johns Hopkins University Press, 1979), pp. 69–120.

a number of years, this fertility behavior would usher in an era of zero or negative population growth for the United States as well.

Those countries experiencing declines in their population growth will also experience a rise in the average age of their population. This transition to an older population should boost income per capita growth by increasing the share of the population in the labor force and by stimulating a higher rate of savings available to finance capital accumulation.

Slower population growth should also help to reduce income inequality. A reduction in family size allows more money to be spent on each child, raising his or her earning capacity. Since they typically have larger families, on average this effect will be felt most strongly in lower-income families. This tendency for incomes of lower-income families to increase faster than those of higher-income families should be reinforced by the effects on labor supply. By preventing an excess supply of labor which holds wages down, slower population growth benefits wage earners. Wages are a particularly important source of income for lower-income families.

Contrary to the views of some, developing countries do not seem to be caught in a population trap. With development can come a demographic transition in which birth rates fall. The speed of this transition can be increased using a number of economic incentive systems such as expanding opportunities for women, providing a social security system for the elderly, and ensuring that the fruits from development are shared among the population as equally as possible.

While it may well be premature to proclaim, as some have, an end to the population explosion,[16] it is similarly premature to label population growth as an insoluable problem. The evidence of the last few years suggests that steps to defuse *the population bomb* have been undertaken and are meeting with success.

FURTHER READING

Berelson, Bernard, ed. *Population Policy in Developed Countries* (New York: McGraw Hill, 1974). A country-by-country analysis of population policies in 24 developed nations.

Commission on Population Growth and the American Future, *Research Reports.* Edited by Elliot R. Morss and Richie H. Reed (Washington, D.C.: Government Printing Office, 1972).

Vol. I	Demographic and Social Aspects of Population Growth
Vol. II	Economic Aspects of Population Change
Vol. III	Population Resources and the Environment
Vol. IV	Governance and Population: The Governmental Implications of Population Change
Vol. V	Population Distribution
Vol. VI	Aspects of Population Growth Policy
Vol. VII	Statements at Public Hearings

An excellent survey of population issues as they relate to the American future. Volumes II and III are particularly relevant to the theme of this book.

Easterlin, Richard A. "The Economics and Sociology of Fertility: A Synthesis." In *Historical Studies of Changing Fertility,* edited by Charles Tilly (Princeton: Princeton University Press, 1978): 57–133. One of the very few comprehensive surveys of the literature accessible to readers who are not mathematically adept.

---

[16]For an articulation of this position, see Donald J. Bogue, "The End of the Population Explosion," *Public Interest* (Spring 1967): 11–20. For a critical appraisal, see Paul Demeny, "On the End of the Population Explosion," *Population and Development Review* 5 (March 1979): 141–162.

Easterlin, Richard A., ed. *Population and Economic Change in Developing Countries* (Chicago: The University of Chicago Press, 1980). An excellent collection of essays on subjects ranging from child costs and economic development to an examination of the population explosion in preindustrial England.

King, Timothy *et al. Population Policies and Economic Development* (Baltimore: Johns Hopkins University Press, 1974). Contains a good summary of population policies in developing countries.

"New Economic Approaches to Fertility," a special supplement of the *Journal of Political Economy* 81 (2) (March/April, 1973). A highly technical collection of essays that refine and test the economic theory of fertility. An excellent bibliography is included.

Schultz, T. Paul. *Economics of Population* (Reading, Mass.: Addison-Wesley, 1981). A useful intensive introduction to the field that is intended for undergraduates. Gives a sense of the controversies existing in the field.

Simon, Julian L. *The Economics of Population Growth* (Princeton: Princeton University Press, 1977). A comprehensive survey of the literature plus original work; proposes the idea that moderate population growth (as opposed to zero or high) may be helpful to developing countries.

ADDITIONAL REFERENCES

Becker, Gary. "An Economic Analysis of Fertility" in *Demographic and Economic Changes in Developed Countries* (Princeton: Princeton University Press, 1960): 209–31.

Caldwell, John C. and Lado T. Ruzicka, "The Australian Fertility Transition: An Analysis," *Population and Development Review* 4 (March 1978): 81–104.

Coale, Ansley J. and Edgar M. Hoover. *Population Growth and Economic Development in Low Income Countries* (Princeton: Princeton University Press, 1958).

Dennison, Edward. *Accounting for United States Economic Growth, 1929–1969* (Washington, D.C.: The Brookings Institution, 1974), p. 128–30.

Easterlin, Richard A. *Population, Labor Force and Long Swings in Economic Growth* (New York: Columbia University Press, 1968).

Eberstadt, Nick. *Fertility Decline in the Less Developed Countries* (New York: Praeger Publishers, 1981).

Enke, S. and R. Zind, "Effect of Fewer Births on Average Income," *Journal of Biosocial Science* 1 (1969): 41–55.

Espenshade, Thomas J. *Investing in Children: New Estimates of Parental Expenditures* (Washington, DC: The Urban Institute Press, 1984).

Kaufman, Michael T. "South India Success Story: Small Families the Norm," *The New York Times* (6 March 1980): 2.

Kuznets, Simon. *Population, Capital, and Growth: Selected Essays* (New York: W. W. Norton, 1973).

Leibenstein, Harvey. "An Interpretation of the Economic Theory of Fertility: Promising Path or Blind Alley?" *Journal of Economic Literature,* Vol. 22 (June, 1974): 457–79.

Lindert, Peter. *Fertility and Scarcity in America* (Princeton: Princeton University Press, 1978).

Repetto, Robert. *Economic Equality and Fertility in Developing Countries* (Baltimore: The Johns Hopkins University Press, 1979).

Repetto, Robert. "The Effects of Income Distribution on Fertility in Developing Countries" in Nick Eberstadt, ed. *Fertility Decline in the Less Developed Countries* (New York: Praeger Publishers, 1981): 254–73.

Ridker, Ronald, ed., *Population and Development: The Search for Selective Interventions* (Baltimore: The Johns Hopkins University Press, 1976).

Simon, Julian L., "There Is No Low-Level-Fertility-and-Development Trap," *Population Studies,* Vol. 34 (November, 1980): 476–86.

DISCUSSION QUESTIONS

1. Fertility rates vary widely among various ethnic groups in the United States. Black and Spanish-speaking Americans have above-average rates, for example, while Jews have below-average fertility rates. This may be due to different ethnic beliefs, but it may also be due to economic factors. How could you use economics to explain these fertility rate differences? What tests could you devise to see whether this explanation has validity?

2. The microeconomic theory of fertility provides an opportunity to determine how public policies which were designed for quite different purposes could affect fertility rates. Identify some public policies (e.g., subsidies to people who own their own home, or subsidized day care) which could have an effect on fertility rates, and describe the relationship.

PROBLEMS

1. Some education is funded by property taxes while other forms of education are funded by charging each student tuition. Suppose that within a community, more money is needed for education. Assuming that they raise the same amount of revenue, would the rising cost of education have the same effect on the desired number of children regardless of whether the system was funded by property taxes or tuition? Using the microeconomic theory of fertility, trace out the expected impacts.

2. Using the terminology presented in Chapter 1, is the relationship between population growth and the gap between the rich and the poor in a particular country a positive or negative feedback loop? Why?

CHAPTER SIX

The Allocation of Depletable and Renewable Resources: An Overview

> *The whole machinery of our intelligence, our general ideas and laws, fixed and external objects, principles, persons, and gods, are so many symbolic, algebraic expressions. They stand for experience; experience which we are incapable of retaining and surveying in its multitudinous immediacy. We should flounder hopelessly, like the animals, did we not keep ourselves afloat and direct our course by these intellectual devices. Theory helps us to bear our ignorance of fact.*
> SANTAYANA *The Sense of Beauty* [1896]

INTRODUCTION

In the *Limits to Growth* vision of the future, society's demand for resources suddenly exceeds their availability. Rather than anticipating a smooth transition to a steady state, this vision estimates that the system will overshoot the resource base, precipitating a collapse. Is this realistic? Is profit maximization inconsistent with smooth adjustments to increasing scarcity?

We shall approach these questions in several steps, first by defining and discussing a simple but useful *resource taxonomy* (classification system), as well as explaining the dangers of ignoring the distinctions of this taxonomy. We can then specifically define an efficient allocation of an exhaustible resource over time, exploring the conditions any efficient allocation must satisfy and using numerical examples to illustrate the meaning of these conditions.

In a subsequent discussion of whether or not the market is capable of yielding a dynamically efficient allocation in the presence or absence of a renewable substitute, we shall examine the effects of extraction and environmental costs on this capability. Succeeding chapters will use these principles to examine the efficiency of market allocations of energy, mineral, water, fishery, and food resources.

A RESOURCE TAXONOMY

There are three separate concepts used to classify the stock of depletable resources: (1) *current reserves,* (2) *potential reserves,* and (3) *resource endowment.* The United States Geological Survey (USGS) has the official responsibility for keeping records of the U.S. resource base, and they have developed the classification system described in Figure 6.1.

Notice the two dimensions—one economic and one geological. A movement from top to bottom represents movement from cheaply extractable resources to those extracted at substantially higher prices. By contrast, a movement from left to right represents increasing geological uncertainty about the size of the resource base.

Current reserves (white area in Figure 6.1) are defined as known resources that can profitably be extracted at current prices. The magnitude of these current reserves can be expressed as a number.

Potential reserves, on the other hand, are most accurately defined as a function rather than a number. The amount of reserves potentially available depends upon the price people are willing to pay for those resources—the higher the price, the larger the potential reserves. For example, Congress conducted a study on the amount of additional oil that could be recovered from existing oil fields using enhanced recovery techniques, such as injecting solvents or steam into the well to lower the density of the oil. These techniques, more expensive than conventional ones, allow greater amounts of oil to be recovered. As price is increased, the amount of oil that can be economically recovered also increases (Table 6.1).

The *resource endowment* represents the natural occurrence of resources in the earth's crust. Since prices have nothing to do with the size of the resource endowment, it is a geological rather than economic concept. This concept is important because it represents an upper limit on the availability of terrestrial resources.

TABLE 6.1   Estimates of Ultimately Recoverable Oil from Enhanced Oil Recovery with 10 Percent Minimum Rate of Return (price in constant 1976 dollars)

Price per Barrel	Ultimate Recovery (10^9 barrels)
$11.62	21.2
$13.75	29.4
$22.00	41.6
$30.00	49.2
More than $30.00	51.1

Source: U.S. Congress, Office of Technology Assessment, *Enhanced Oil Recovery Potential in the United States* (Washington, D.C.: OTA, 1978), p. 7.

FIGURE 6.1 A Categorization of Resources

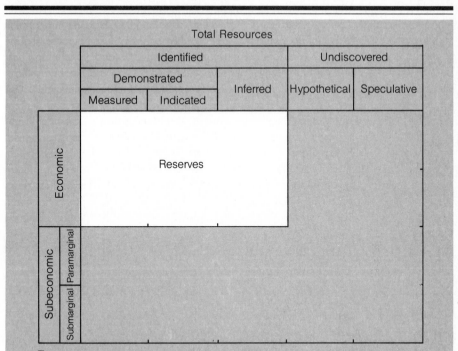

Terms

Identified resources: specific bodies of mineral-bearing material whose location, quality, and quantity are known from geological evidence, supported by engineering measurements.

Measured resources: material for which quantity and quality estimates are within a margin of error of less than 20 percent, from geologically well-known sample sites.

Indicated resources: material which quantity and quality have been estimated partly from sample analyses and partly from reasonable geological projections.

Inferred resources: material in unexplored extensions of demonstrated resources based on geological projections.

Undiscovered resources: unspecified bodies of mineral-bearing material surmised to exist on the basis of broad geological knowledge and theory.

Hypothetical resources: undiscovered materials reasonably expected to exist in a known mining district under known geological conditions.

Speculative resources: undiscovered materials that may occur either known types of deposits in favorable geological settings where no discoveries have been made, or in yet unknown types of deposits that remain to be recognized.

SOURCE: U.S. Bureau of Mines and the U.S. Geological Survey. "Principle of the Mineral Resource Classification System of the U.S. Bureau of Mines and the U.S. Geological Survey," *Geological Survey Bulletin* 1450-A, 1976.

The distinctions among these three concepts are significant. One common mistake in failing to respect these distinctions is using data on current reserves synonymously with potential reserves. As Example 6.1 indicates, this fundamental error can lead to conclusions wide of the mark.

A second common mistake is to assume that the entire resource endowment can be made available as potential reserves at some price people would be willing to pay. Clearly, if an infinite price were possible, then the entire resource endowment could be exploited. However, an infinite price is not likely.

For reasons explained in Chapter 13 there exist mineral sources so costly to extract that it is inconceivable any current or future society would be willing to pay the price necessary to extract them. Thus, it seems likely that the maximum feasible size of the potential reserves is smaller than the resource endowment. Exactly how much smaller cannot yet be determined with any degree of certainty, though Chapter 13 surveys the available evidence.

EXAMPLE 6.1

The Pitfalls in Misusing Reserve Data

It is relatively common practice to estimate the number of years a given resource will last by computing what is known as the *static reserve index,* the ratio of current reserves to current consumption. The result of the calculation is supposed to be interpreted as the number of years remaining until the resource is exhausted. This is a correct calculation of the time to exhaustion *if and only if:* (1) the consumption of the resource remains at current levels until the time of exhaustion (it can neither increase nor decrease); and (2) no additions to the reserves occur in the intervening period (current reserves and potential reserves are equal for the prices which can be expected to prevail in the intervening period).

These assumptions generally are not even approximately accurate. For example, in 1934 the static index for copper was 40, indicating the reserves would be exhausted in 40 years. In 1974, 40 years later, this index stood at 57. A similar calculation for crude oil, iron oil, and lead would reveal the same pattern; the static index tends to underestimate the time until exhaustion.

The *Limits to Growth* study used an index called the *exponential reserve index,* which tends to underestimate the time to exhaustion by an even greater amount than the static index. This index assumes that consumption will grow over time at a constant rate of growth. No correction is made for additions to reserves or for the effects of higher prices on demand. It is therefore neither very surprising, nor very interesting, that their time of exhaustion estimates are so proximate.

Sources: Paul R. Ehrlich and Anne H. Ehrlich, *Population Resources Environment,* 2nd ed. (San Francisco: W. H. Freeman, 1972): 70–72; Earl Cook, "Limits to Exploitation of Nonrenewable Resources," *Science* 191 (20 February 1976): 667–82.

Other distinctions among resource categories are also useful. The first category includes all depletable, recyclable resources, such as copper. A *depletable resource* is one for which the natural-replenishment feedback loop can safely be ignored. The rate of replenishment for these resources is so low that it does not offer a potential for augmenting the stock in any reasonable time frame.

A *recyclable resource* is one which, although currently being used for some particular purpose, exists in a form allowing its mass to be recovered once that purpose is no longer necessary or desirable. For example, copper wiring from an automobile can be recovered after the car has been shipped to the junk yard. The degree to which a resource is recycled is determined by economic conditions, a subject covered in Chapter 8.

The current reserves of a depletable, recyclable resource can be augmented by economic replenishment, as well as by recycling. There are many sources of economic replenishment, all sharing the characteristic that they turn previously unrecoverable resources into recoverable ones. One obvious stimulant for this replenishment is price. As price rises, producers find it profitable to explore more widely, dig more deeply, use lower-concentration ores, and so on.

Higher prices also stimulate technological progress. Technological progress simply means an advancement in the state of knowledge which allows us to do things we were not able to do before. One profound, if controversial, example can be found in the successful harnessing of nuclear power.

The other side of the coin for depletable, recyclable resources is that their potential reserves can be exhausted. The depletion rate is affected by the demand for and the durability of the products built with the resource, and the ability to reuse the products. Except where demand is totally price inelastic (that is, insensitive to price) higher prices tend to reduce the quantity demanded. Durable products last longer, reducing the need for newer ones. Reusable products provide a substitute for new products. In the commercial sector, reusable soft-drink bottles provide one example, while flea markets (where secondhand items are sold) provide another for the household sector.

For some resources, the size of the potential reserves depends explicitly on our ability to store the resource. For example, as pointed out in Chapter 4, helium generally is found commingled with natural gas in common fields. As the natural gas is extracted and stored, unless the helium is simultaneously captured and stored, it diffuses into the atmosphere. This results in such low concentrations that extraction of helium from the air is not economical at current or even likely future prices. Thus, the useful stock of helium depends crucially on how much we decide to store.

Not all depletable resources permit recycling or reuse. Depletable energy resources such as coal, oil, and gas are consumed as they are used. Once combusted and turned into heat energy, the heat dissipates into the atmosphere and becomes nonrecoverable.

The endowment of depletable resources is of finite size. Current use of depletable, nonrecyclable resources precludes future use; hence, the issue of how they should be shared among generations is raised in the starkest, least forgiving, form.

Depletable, recyclable resources raise this same issue, though somewhat less starkly. Recycling and reuse make the useful stock last longer, all other things being equal. It is tempting to suggest that depletable recyclable resources could last forever with 100 percent recycling, but unfortunately the physical theoretical upper limit on recycling is less than 100 percent—an implication of a version of the entropy law defined in Chapter 2. Some of the mass is always lost during recycling.

For example, copper pennies can be melted down to recover the copper, but the amount rubbed off during circulation would never be recovered. As long as less than 100 percent of the mass is recycled, the useful stock must eventually decline to zero. Even for recyclable depletable resources, the cumulative useful stock is finite, and current consumption patterns still have an effect on future generations.

Renewable resources are differentiated from depletable resources primarily by the fact that natural replenishment augments the flow of renewable resources at a nonnegligible rate. Solar energy, water, cereal grains, fish, forests, and animals are all examples of renewable resources. Thus it is possible, though not inexorable, that a flow of these resources could be maintained perpetually.[1]

For some renewable resources, the continuation and volume of their flow depend crucially on humans. Soil erosion and nutrient depletion reduce the flow of food. Excessive fishing reduces the stock of fish, which in turn reduces the rate of natural increase of the fish population. Other examples abound. For other renewable resources, such as solar energy, the flow is independent of humans. The amount consumed by one generation does not reduce the amount that can be consumed by subsequent generations.

Some renewable resources can be stored; others cannot. For those that can, storage provides a valuable way to manage the allocation of the resource over time. We are not left simply at the mercy of natural ebbs and flows of the source. Food, without proper care, perishes rapidly, but, with storage, can be used to feed the hungry in times of famine. Unstored solar energy radiates off the earth's surface and dissipates into the atmosphere. While solar energy can be stored in many forms, the most common natural form of storage occurs when it is converted to biomass by photosynthesis.

Storage of renewable resources usually performs a different service than storage of depletable resources. Storing depletable resources extends their economic life; we store renewable resources, on the other hand, to smooth out the cyclical imbalances of supply and demand. Surpluses are stored for later time periods when deficits may occur. Food stockpiles and the use of dams to store hydropower are two familiar examples.

Managing renewable resources presents a different challenge than managing depletable resources, though an equally significant one. The challenge for depletable resources involves allocating dwindling stocks among generations while meeting the ultimate transition to renewable resources. In contrast, the challenge for managing renewable resources involves the maintenance of an efficient substainable flow. The next six chapters deal with how the economic and political sectors have responded to these challenges for particularly significant types of resources.

---

[1]Even renewable resources are ultimately finite, because their renewability is dependent on energy from the sun and the sun is expected to serve as an energy source for only the next five or six billion years. That fact does not eliminate the need to manage resources effectively until that time. Furthermore, the finiteness of renewable resources is sufficiently far into the future to make the distinction useful.

EFFICIENT INTERTEMPORAL ALLOCATIONS

If we are to judge the adequacy of market allocations, we must define what is meant by efficiency in relation to the management of depletable and renewable-resource allocations. Because the allocation over time is the crucial issue, we must rely on our definition of dynamic efficiency.

The dynamic-efficiency criterion assumes that society's objective is to maximize the present value of net benefits coming from the resource. For a depletable, nonrecyclable resource, this requires a balancing of the current and subsequent uses of the resource. In order to recall how the dynamic-efficiency criterion defines this balance, we shall begin with an elaboration of the very simple, two-period model developed in Chapter 2. In subsequent sections we shall show how these conclusions generalize to longer planning horizons and more complicated situations.

The Two-Period Model Revisited

In Chapter 2 we defined a situation involving the allocation over two periods of a finite resource which could be extracted at constant marginal cost. With a stable demand curve for the resource, an efficient allocation meant that more than half of the resource was allocated to the first period and less than half to the second period. This allocation was affected both by the marginal cost of extraction and by the marginal user cost.

Because there are fixed and finite supplies of depletable resources, production of a unit today precludes production of that unit tomorrow. Therefore, production decisions today must take foregone future net benefits into account. Marginal user cost is the opportunity cost measure that allows balancing to take place.

The marginal cost of extraction is assumed to be constant, but the current value of the marginal user cost rises over time. In fact, as was demonstrated mathematically in in the appendix at the end of Chapter 2, when the demand curve is stable over time and the marginal cost of extraction is constant, the rate of increase in the current value of the marginal user cost is equal to r, the discount rate. Thus, in period two, the marginal user cost would be $1 + r$ times as large as it was in period one.[2] Marginal user cost rises at rate r in an efficient allocation in order to preserve the balance between present-versus-future production.

In summary, our two-period example suggests that an efficient allocation of a finite resource with a constant marginal cost of extraction involves rising marginal user cost and falling quantities consumed. We can now generalize to longer time periods and different extraction circumstances.

---

[2]The condition that marginal user cost rises at rate r is true only when the marginal cost of extraction is constant. Later in this chapter, we shall show how the marginal user cost is affected when marginal extraction cost is not constant.

FIGURE 6.2a Constant Marginal Extraction Cost with No Substitute Resource: Quantity Profile

FIGURE 6.2b Constant Marginal Extraction Cost with No Substitute Resource: Marginal-Cost Profile

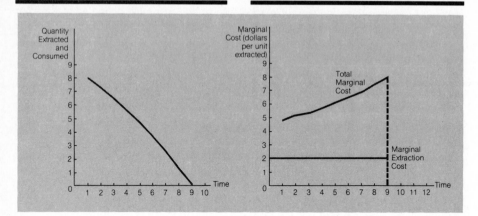

The N-Period Constant-Cost Case

We begin this generalization by retaining the constant-marginal-extraction-cost assumption, while extending the time horizon within which the resource is allocated. In the numerical example shown in Figure 6.2a and 6.2b, the demand curves and the marginal-cost curve from the two-period case are retained. The only changes in this numerical example from the two-period case involve spreading the allocation over a large number of years and an increase in the total recoverable supply from 20 to 40. (For those who are interested, the mathematics behind this and subsequent examples is presented in the Appendix to this chapter).

Figure 6.2a demonstrates how the efficient quantity extracted varies over time, while Figure 6.2b shows the behavior of the marginal user cost and the marginal cost of extraction. Total marginal cost refers to the sum of the two. The marginal cost of extraction is represented by the lower line while the marginal user cost is depicted as the vertical distance between the marginal cost of extraction and the total marginal cost. To avoid confusion, you should note that the horizontal axis is defined in terms of time.

There are several trends worth noting. First of all, in this case as in the two-period case, the efficient marginal user cost rises steadily in spite of the fact that the marginal cost of extraction remains constant. This rise in the efficient marginal user cost reflects increasing scarcity and the accompanying rise in the opportunity cost of current consumption.

In response to these rising costs over time the quantity extracted falls over time until it finally goes to zero, which occurs precisely at the moment when the total marginal cost becomes $8. At this point total marginal cost is equal to the highest price anyone is willing to pay, so demand and supply simultaneously equal zero. Thus, even in this difficult case involving no increase in the cost of extraction, an efficient allocation envisions a smooth transition to the exhaustion of a resource. There is no sense in which a resource "suddenly" runs out, although in this case it does run out.

Transition to a Substitute

So far we have discussed the allocation of a depletable resource when there is no substitute available to take its place. Suppose, however, we consider the nature of an efficient allocation when there is a substitute renewable resource available at constant marginal cost. This case, for example, could describe the efficient allocation of oil or natural gas when solar energy is available as a substitute. How could we define an efficient allocation in this circumstance?

This problem is very similar to the one already discussed. We will still run out of the depletable resource, but that will be less of a problem, since we'll merely switch to the renewable one at the appropriate time. For the purpose of our numerical example, assume that there exists a perfect substitute for the depletable resource which is infinitely available at a cost of $6 per unit. The transition from the depletable resource to this renewable resource would ultimately take place because its marginal cost ($6) is less than the maximum willingness to pay ($8). (Can you figure out what the efficient allocation would be if the marginal cost of this substitute resource was $9 instead of $6?)

The total marginal cost for the depletable resource in the presence of a $6 perfect substitute would never exceed $6, because society could always use the renewable resource instead, whenever it was cheaper. Thus, while the maximum willingness to pay (the *choke price*) sets the upper limit on total marginal cost when no substitute is available, the marginal cost of extraction of the substitute sets the upper limit when one is available at a marginal cost lower than the choke price. The efficient path for this situation is given in Figures 6.3a and 6.3b on the next page.

In this efficient allocation, the transition is once again smooth. Quantity extracted is gradually reduced as the marginal use cost rises until the switch is made to the substitute. There is no abrupt change in either marginal cost or quantity profiles.

Because the renewable resource is available, more of the depletable resource is extracted in the earlier periods than was the case in our previous numerical example when there was no renewable resource. As a result, the depletable resource would be exhausted sooner than it would have been without the renewable resource substitute. In this example the switch is made during the sixth period, whereas in the last example, the last units were exhausted at the end of the eighth period.

At that point, called the *switch point,* consumption of the renewable resource begins. Prior to the switch point, only the depletable resource is consumed, while after the switch point only the renewable resource is consumed. This sequencing of the consumption pattern results from the cost patterns. Prior to the switch point, the depletable resource is cheaper. At the switch point, the marginal cost of the depletable resource (including marginal user cost) rises to meet the marginal cost of the substitute, and the transition occurs. Due to the availability of the substitute resource, consumption never drops below five units in any time period. This level is maintained because five

FIGURE 6.3a   Constant Marginal Extraction Cost with Substitute Resource: Quantity Profile

FIGURE 6.3b   Constant Marginal Extraction Cost with Substitute Resource: Marginal-Cost Profile

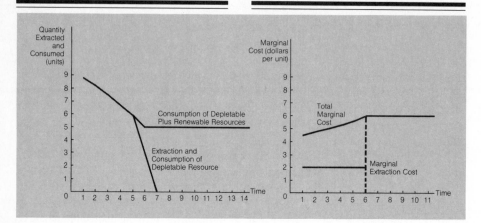

is the amount which maximizes the net benefit when the marginal cost equals $6 (the price of the substitute).

Though we shall not show the numerical example here, it is not difficult to see how an efficient allocation would be defined when the transition is from one constant marginal-cost depletable resource to another depletable resource with a constant, but higher, marginal cost (Figure 6.4). The total marginal cost of the first resource would rise over time until it equalled that of the second resource at the time of transition. In the period of time prior to transition (T^*), only the cheapest resource would be consumed; all of it would have been consumed by T^*.

A close examination of the total marginal-cost path reveals two interesting characteristics worthy of our attention. First, even in this case, the transition is a smooth one; there is never a jump in total marginal cost. Second, the rate of increase in total marginal cost slows down after the time of transition.

The first characteristic is easy to explain. The total marginal costs of the two resources have to be equal at the time of transition. If they weren't equal, the net benefit could be increased by switching to the lower-cost resource from the more expensive resource. Total marginal costs are not equal in the other periods. In the period before transition, the first resource is cheaper and therefore used exclusively, while after transition, the first resource is exhausted, leaving only the second resource.

The rate of increase in marginal cost is slower after transition simply because the component of total marginal cost that is growing (the marginal user cost) represents a smaller portion of the total marginal cost of the second resource than the first. The total marginal cost of each resource is determined by the marginal extraction cost plus the marginal user cost. In both cases the marginal user cost is increasing at rate r and the marginal cost of extraction is constant. As seen in Figure 6.4, at the time of transition the marginal cost of extraction, which is constant, comprises a much larger pro-

FIGURE 6.4 The Transition from One Constant-Cost Depletable Resource to Another

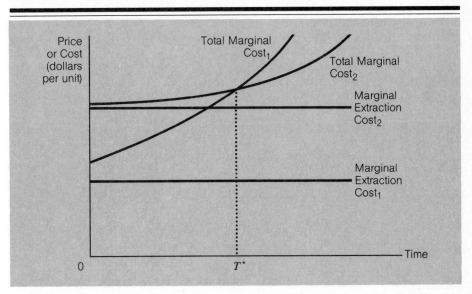

portion of total marginal cost for the second resource than for the first. Hence, total marginal cost rises more slowly for the second resource, at least initially.

Increasing Marginal Extraction Cost

We have now expanded our examination of the efficient allocation of depletable resources to include longer time horizons and the availability of other depletable or renewable resources which could serve as prefect substitutes. As part of our trek toward increasing realism, we will next consider a situation in which the marginal cost of extracting the depletable resource rises with the cumulative amount extracted. This is commonly the case, for example, with minerals, where the higher-grade ores are extracted first, followed by an increasing reliance on lower-grade ones, which are more costly to extract.

Analytically, this case is handled in the same manner as the previous case except that the function describing the marginal cost of extraction is slightly more complicated.[3] It increases with the cumulative amount extracted. The dynamic efficient allocation of this resource is found by maximizing the present value of the net benefits using this modified cost of extraction function. The results of that maximization are portrayed below in Figure 6.5a and 6.5b.

The most significant difference between this case and the others lies in the behavior of marginal user cost. In the previous case we said that marginal user cost *rose* over time at rate r. When the marginal cost of extraction increases with the cumulative amount

---

[3]The marginal cost of extraction is $MC_t = \$2 + 0.1Q_t$ where Q_t is cumulative extraction to date.

FIGURE 6.5a   Increasing Marginal
Extraction Cost with Substitute
Resource: Quantity Profile

FIGURE 6.5b   Increasing Marginal
Extraction Cost with Substitute
Resource: Marginal-Cost Profile

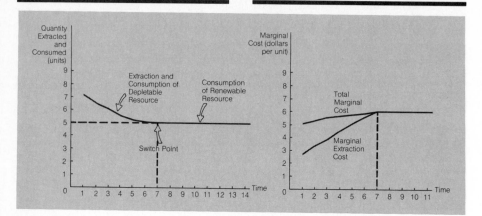

extracted, marginal user cost *declines* over time until, at the time of transition to the renewable resource, it goes to zero. Why is that?

Remember that marginal user cost is an opportunity cost reflecting forgone future net benefits. In contrast to the constant marginal cost case, in the increasing cost case every unit extracted raises the cost of extraction. Therefore, as the current marginal cost rises over time, the sacrifice made by future generations diminishes; the net benefit that would be received by a future generation if a unit of the resource were saved for them gets smaller and smaller as the marginal extraction cost of that resource gets larger and larger. By the last period the marginal extraction cost is so high there is virtually no sacrifice at all. The opportunity cost of current extraction drops to zero and total marginal cost equals the marginal extraction cost at the switch point.[4]

There is another important way in which the increasing cost case differs from the constant cost case. In the constant cost case, the depletable resource reserve is completely exhausted. In the increasing cost case, however, the reserve is not exhausted; some if left in the ground because it is too expensive to take out.

Up to this point in our analysis, we have examined how an efficient allocation would be defined in a number of circumstances. First we examined a situation in which a finite amount of a resource was to be extracted at constant marginal cost. Despite the absence of increasing extraction cost, an efficient allocation involves a smooth transi-

---

[4]Total marginal cost cannot be greater than the marginal cost of the substitute. Yet, in the increasing marginal extraction cost case, at the time of transition the marginal extraction cost also must equal the marginal cost of the substitute. If that weren't true, it would imply that some of the resource which was available at a marginal cost lower than the substitute was not used. This would clearly be inefficient, since net benefits could be increased by simply using less of the more expensive substitute. Hence, at the switch point, in the rising marginal cost case, the marginal extraction cost has to equal total marginal cost, implying a zero marginal user cost.

tion to a substitute, when one is available, or to abstinence, when one is not. The complication of increasing marginal cost changes the time profile of the marginal user cost, but it does not alter the basic finding of declining consumption of depletable resources coupled with rising total marginal cost.

As a look at the historical record reveals, the consumption patterns of most depletable resources have involved increases, not decreases, in consumption over time. Is this *prima facia* evidence that the resources are not being allocated efficiently?

Exploration and Technological Progress

Using the historical patterns of increasing consumption to conclude that depletable resources are not being allocated efficiently would not represent a valid use of the theory of depletable resources. The models considered to this point have not yet included a consideration of the role of exploration for new resources or the role of technological progress, historically two significant factors in the determination of actual consumption paths.

The search for new resources costs money. As easily discovered resources are exhausted, we must search in less-rewarding environments, such as the bottom of the ocean or locations deep in the earth. This suggests the *marginal cost of exploration,* which is the marginal cost of finding additional units of the resource, should be expected to rise over time, just as the marginal cost of extraction does.

As the total marginal cost for a resource rises over time, society should actively explore possible new sources of that resource. The higher the marginal cost of extraction for known sources is expected to rise, the larger is the potential increase in net benefits from exploration.

Some of this exploration would be successful; new sources of the resource would be discovered. If the marginal extraction cost of the newly discovered resources is low enough, these discoveries could lower, or at least retard, the increase in the total marginal cost of production. As a result, the new finds would tend to encourage more consumption. Compared to a situation with no exploration possible, the model with exploration would show a smaller and slower decline in consumption, while the rise in total marginal cost would be dampened.

It is also not difficult to expand our concept of efficient resource allocations to include technological progress, the general term economists give to advances in the state of knowledge. In the present context, technological progress would be manifested as reductions in the cost of extraction. For a resource which can be extracted at constant marginal cost, a one-time breakthrough lowering the marginal cost of extraction would move the time of transition further into the future. Furthermore, for an increasing-cost resource, more of the total available resource would be recovered in the presence of technological progress than would be recovered without it. (Can you see why?)

The most pervasive effects of technological progress are felt when it results in continuous downward shifts in the cost of extraction over a time period. The total marginal cost of the resource could actually fall over time if technological progress became so potent that, in spite of increasing reliance on inferior ore, the marginal cost of extraction decreased (Example 6.2). With a finite amount of this resource, the fall in total marginal cost would be transitory, since ultimately it would have to rise, but, as we shall see in the next few chapters, this period of transition can last quite a long time.

MARKET ALLOCATIONS

In the preceding sections we have examined in detail the question of how an efficient allocation of a depletable resource over time would be defined in a variety of circumstances. We must now address the question of whether actual markets can be expected to produce an efficient allocation. Can the private market involving millions of consumers and producers each reacting to his or her own unique preferences *ever* result in a dynamically efficient allocation? Is profit maximization compatible with dynamic efficiency?

Appropriate Property-Right Structures

The most common misconception of those who believe that even a perfect market could never achieve an efficient allocation is a belief that producers want to extract and sell the resources as fast as possible, since that is how they derive the value from the resource. This misconception makes people see markets as myopic, and be unconcerned about the future.

As long as the property rights governing natural resources have the characteristics of exclusivity, universality, transferability, and enforceability (Chapter 3), the markets in which those resources are bought and sold will not necessarily lead to myopic choices. When bearing the marginal user cost, the producer acts in an efficient manner. A resource in the ground has two potential sources of value to its owner: (1) a use value when it is sold; and (2) an asset value when it remains in the ground. As long as the price of a resource continues to rise, the resource in the ground is becoming more valuable. The owner of this resource accrues this capital gain, however, only if the resource is conserved. A producer who sells all resources in the earlier periods loses the chance to take advantage of higher prices in the future.

A prescient, profit-maximizing producer attempts to balance present and future production in order to maximize the value of the resource. Since higher prices in the futue provide an incentive to conserve, a producer who ignores this incentive would not be maximizing the value of the resource. We would expect the resource to then be bought by someone willing to conserve and prepared to maximize its value. As long as social and private discount rates coincide, in the presence of well-defined property-right structures and reliable information about future prices, a producer who selfishly pursues maximum profits simultaneously provides the maximum present value of net benefits for society.

EXAMPLE 6.2

Technological Progress in the Iron Ore Industry

The term "technological progress" plays an important role in the economic analysis of mineral resources. Yet, at times, it can appear abstract, even mystical. It shouldn't! Far from being a blind faith detached from reality, technological progress refers to a host of ingenious ways in which people have reacted to impending shortages with sufficient imagination that the available supply of resources has been expanded by an order of magnitude and at reasonable cost. To illustrate how concrete a notion technological progress is, let's discuss one example of how it has worked in the past.

In 1947 the president of Republic Steel, C. M. White, calculated the expected life of the Mesabi range of northern Minnesota (the source of some 60 percent of iron ore consumed during World War II) as being in the range from five to seven years. By 1955, only eight years later, *U.S. News and World Report* was able to conclude that worry over the scarcity of iron ore could be forgotten. The source of this remarkable transformation of a problem of scarcity into one of abundance was the discovery of a new technique, called *pelletization,* of preparing iron ore.

Prior to pelletization, the standard ores from which iron was derived contained from 50 to more than 65 percent iron in crude form. There was a significant percentage of taconite ore available containing less than 30 percent iron in crude form, but no one knew how to produce it at reasonable cost. Pelletization is a process by which these ores are processed and concentrated at the mine sight prior to shipment to the blast furnaces. The advent of pelletization allowed the profitable use of the taconite ores.

While expanding the supply of iron ore, pelletization reduced the cost of iron ore in spite of the inferior grade being used. There were several sources of the cost reduction. First there was substantially *less* energy used; the shift in ore technology toward pelletization produced net energy savings of 17 percent in spite of the fact that the pelletization process itself required more energy. The reduction came from the discovery that the blast furnaces could be operated much more efficiently using pelletization inputs. The process also reduced labor requirements per ton by some 8.2 percent while increasing the output of the blast furnaces. A blast furnace owned by Armco Steel in Middleton, Ohio, which had a rated capacity of approximately 1500 tons of molten iron per day, was able by 1960 to achieve production levels of 2700 and 2800 tons per day when fired with 90 percent pellets. Pellets nearly doubled the blast furnace productivity!

Sources: Peter J. Kakela. "Iron Ore: Energy Labor and Capital Changes with Technology," *Science* 202 (15 December 1978): 1151–1157; Peter J. Kakela. "Iron Ore: From Depletion to Abundance," *Science* 212 (10 April 1981): 132–136.

The implication of this analysis is that, in prescient competitive resource markets, the price of the resource equals the total marginal cost of extracting and using the resource. Thus, Figures 6.2a through 6.5b can illustrate not only an efficient allocation but also the allocation produced by an efficient market. When used to describe an efficient market, the total marginal cost curve describes the time path that prices could be expected to follow.

Environmental Costs

One of the most important situations in which property-right structures may not be well defined is that in which the extraction of a natural resource imposes an environmental cost on society not internalized by the producers. The aesthetic costs of strip mining, the health risks associated with uranium tailings and the acids leached into streams from mine operations are all examples of associated environmental costs. Not only is the presence of environmental costs empirically important, it is also conceptually important, since it forms one of the bridges between the traditionally separate fields of environmental economics and natural-resource economics.

Suppose, for example, that the extraction of a resource caused some damage to the environment not adequately reflected in the costs faced by the extracting firms. This would be, in the language of Chapter 3, an external cost. The cost of getting the resource out of the ground, as well as processing and shipping it, is borne by the resource owner and considered in the calculation of how much of the resource to extract. The environmental damage, however, is not borne by the owner and, in the absence of any outside attempt to internalize that cost, will not be part of the extraction decision. How would the market allocation, based on only the former cost, differ from the efficient allocation, which is based on both?

We can examine this issue by modifying the numerical example used earlier in

FIGURE 6.6a Increasing Marginal Extraction Cost with Substitute Resource in the Presence of Environmental Costs: Quantity Profile

FIGURE 6.6b Increasing Marginal Extraction Cost with Substitute Resource in the Presence of Environmental Costs: Price Profile

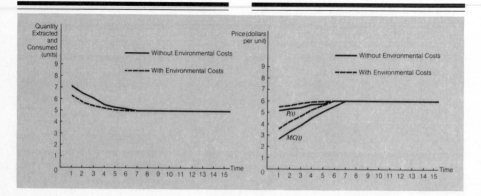

this chapter. Suppose the environmental damage can be included by increasing the marginal cost by $1.00.[5] The additional dollar reflects the cost of the environmental damage caused by producing another unit of the resource. What effect do you think this would have on the efficient time profile for quantities extracted?

The answers are given in Figures 6.6a and 6.6b. The result of including environmental cost on the timing of the switch point is interesting because it involves two different effects that work in opposite directions. On the demand side, the inclusion of environmental costs results in higher prices, which tend to dampen demand. This lowers the rate of consumption of the resource, which, all other things being equal, would make it last longer.

All other things are not equal, however. The higher marginal cost also means that a smaller cumulative amount of the resource would be extracted in an efficient allocation. (Can you figure out why?) In our example depicted in Figures 6.6a and 6.6b, the efficient cumulative amount extracted would be 30 units instead of the 40 units extracted in the case where environmental costs were not included. This supply-side effect tends to hasten the time when a switch to the renewable resource is made, all other things being equal.

Which effect dominates? In our numerical example the supply-side effect dominates and, as a result, the time of transition for an efficient allocation is sooner than for the market allocation. In general, the answer depends on the shape of the marginal-extraction-cost function. With constant marginal cost, for example, there would be no supply-side effect and the market would transition later. If the environmental costs were associated with the cost of the substitute resource rather than the depletable resource, the time of transition for the efficient allocation would have been later than the market allocation.

What can we learn from these graphs about the allocation of depletable resources over time when there are environmental side effects not borne by the agent determining the extraction rate? The price of the depletable resource would be too low and too much of the resource would be extracted. This once again shows the interdependencies among the various decisions we have to make about the future. Environmental and natural resource decisions are intimately linked.

SUMMARY

The efficient allocation of a depletable resource depends on the circumstances. When the resource can be extracted at a constant marginal cost, the efficient quantity extracted declines over time. If no substitute is available, the quantity declines smoothly to zero. If a renewable constant-cost substitute is available, the quantity of the depletable resource extracted will decline smoothly to the quantity available from the renewable

---

[5]Including environmental damage, the marginal cost function would be raised to $3 + 0.1Q$ instead of $2 + 0.1Q$.

resource. In both cases, all of the available depletable resource would be eventually used up and marginal user cost would rise over time, reaching a maximum when the last unit of depletable resource was extracted.

The efficient allocation of an increasing marginal cost resource is similar in that the quantity extracted declines over time, but differs with respect to the behavior of marginal user cost and the cumulative amount extracted. Whereas marginal user cost typically rises over time when the marginal cost of extraction is constant, it declines over time when the marginal cost of extraction rises. Furthermore, in the constant cost case the cumulative amount extracted is equal to the available supply; in the increasing cost case it is less.

Introducing technological progress and exploration activity into the model tends to delay the transition to renewable resources. Exploration expands the size of current reserves while technological progress keeps marginal extraction cost from rising as much as it otherwise would. If these effects are sufficiently potent, marginal cost could actually decline for some period of time, causing the quantity extracted to rise.

Market allocations of depletable resources can, when property right structures are properly defined, be efficient. There is no necessary conflict between self-interest and community interest.

When the extraction of resources imposes an external environmental cost, however, market allocations will not generally be efficient. The market price of the depletable resource would be too low and too much of the resource would be extracted.

In an efficient market allocation, the transition is smooth and exhibits none of the overshoot and collapse characteristics of the *Limits to Growth* view of the world. Whether the actual market allocations of these various types of resources are efficient remains to be seen. To the extent they are, a laissez-faire policy would represent an appropriate response by the government. On the other hand, if the market is not capable of yielding an efficient allocation, then some form of government intervention may be necessary.

In the next few chapters we shall examine these questions for a number of different resource types. We shall then return to the issue of aggregate scarcity and a survey of the empirical evidence on whether or not resource scarcity in a general sense is increasing.

FURTHER READING

Bohi, Douglas R. and Michael A. Toman. *Analyzing Nonrenewable Resource Supply* (Washington, DC: Resources for the Future, Inc., 1984). A reinterpretation and evaluation of existing research which attempts to weave together theoretical, empirical, and practical insights concerning the management of depletable resources.

Fisher, Anthony C. *Resource and Environmental Economics* (Cambridge: Cambridge University Press, 1981). This volume presents a careful heuristic development of the major mathematical results in optimal resource use for depletable and renewable resources. It also has chapters on preserving natural environments and on pollution. This text is written for graduate students or upper-level undergraduates.

Howe, Charles W. *Natural Resource Economics: Issues, Analysis and Policy* (New York: John Wiley, 1979). A textbook intended for upper-division undergraduates and graduate students taking their first course in natural-resource economics. Chapters vary considerably in the mathematical and economic sophistication required of the student. Several chapters would be accessible to the typical reader of this textbook.

Toman, Michael A., " 'Depletion Effects' and Nonrenewable Resource Supply," *Land Economics,* Vol. 62 (November, 1986):341–53. An excellent, non-technical discussion of the increasing cost case with and without exploration and additions to reserves.

Williams, Stephen F. "Running Out: The Problem of Exhaustible Resources," *The Journal of Legal Studies:* VII (January, 1978), 165–99. An excellent, nontechnical introduction to the basic ideas contained in this chapter written by a natural-resource lawyer.

ADDITIONAL REFERENCES

Anders, Gerhard, W. Philip Gramm, S. Charles Maurice, and Charles W. Smithson. *The Economics of Mineral Extraction* (New York: Praeger Publishers, 1980).

Dasgupta, P.S. and G. M. Heal. *Economic Theory and Exhaustible Resources* (Cambridge, England: Cambridge University Press, 1979).

Dasgupta, Partha. *The Control of Resources* (Cambridge, Mass.: Harvard University Press, 1982).

Kneese, Allen V. and James L. Sweeney, eds. *Handbook of Natural Resource and Energy Economics: Vol. III* (Amsterdam: North-Holland, 1986).

Peterson, Frederick M., and Anthony C. Fisher. "The Exploitation of Extractive Resources: A Survey," *Economic Journal,* LXXXVIII (December, 1977): 681–721.

Scott, Anthony, ed. *Progress in Natural Resource Economics* (Oxford: Clarendon Press, 1985).

PROBLEMS

1. Consider an increasing marginal cost depletable resource with no effective substitute. (a) Describe in general terms how the user cost for this resource in the earlier time periods would depend on whether the demand curve for that resource was stable or shifting outward over time. (b) How would the allocation of that resource over time be affected?

2. Many states are now imposing severance taxes on resources being extracted in their states. In order to understand the effect of these on the allocation of the mineral over time, assume a stable demand curve. (a) How would the competitive allocation of an increasing marginal cost depletable resource be affected by the imposition of a per unit tax (e.g., $4.00 per ton) if there exists a constant marginal cost substitute? (b) Comparing the allocation without a tax to one with a tax, in general terms what are the differences in cumulative amounts extracted and the price paths?

Extensions of the
Basic Depletable Resource Model

In the Appendix to Chapter 2 we derived a simple model to describe the efficient allocation of a constant marginal-cost depletable resource over time and presented the
numerical solution for a two-period version of that model. In this Appendix, the
mathematical derivations for the Chapter 6 extensions to that basic model will be
documented and the resulting numerical solutions for these more complicated cases
will be explained.

The N-Period, Constant-Cost, No Substitute Case

The first extension involves calculating the efficient allocation of the depletable resource
over time when the number of time periods for extraction is unlimited. This is a more
difficult calculation because how long the resource will last is no longer predetermined;
the time of exhaustion must be derived as well as the extraction path prior to exhaustion of the resource.

The equations describing the allocation net which maximizes the present value of
benefits derived in the Appendix to Chapter 2 are:

$$\frac{a - bq_t - c}{(1 + r)^{t-1}} - \lambda = 0 \qquad t = 1, \ldots, n \qquad (1)$$

$$\sum_{i=1}^{n} q_i - \bar{Q} = 0 \qquad (2)$$

The parameter values assumed for the numerical example presented in the text are:

$$a = \$8 \qquad c = \$2$$
$$b = 0.4 \qquad \bar{Q} = 40$$
$$r = 0.10$$

The allocation which satisfies these conditions is:

$q_1 = 8.004$	$q_4 = 5.689$	$q_7 = 2.607$	$n = 9$
$q_2 = 7.305$	$q_5 = 4.758$	$q_8 = 1.368$	$\lambda = 2.7983$
$q_3 = 6.535$	$q_6 = 3.733$	$q_9 = 0.000$	

The optimality of this allocation can be verified by substituting these values into the above equations. (Due to rounding, these add to 39.999, rather than 40.000.)

Practically speaking, solving these equations to find the optimal solution is not a trivial matter, but neither is it very difficult. One method of finding the solution involves developing a computer algorithm (computation procedure) which converges on the correct answer. One such algorithm for this example can be constructed as follows: *(1)* assume a value for λ, *(2)* using equation set *(1)* solve for all q's based upon this λ, *(3)* if the sum of the calculated q's exceeds $\bar{Q}$, adjust λ upward or if the sum of the calculated q's is less than $\bar{Q}$, adjust λ downward (the adjustment should use information gained in previous steps to ensure that the new trial will be closer to the solution value), *(4)* repeat steps *(2)* through *(3)* using the new λ, *(5)* when the sum of the q's is sufficiently close to $\bar{Q}$, stop the calculations. As an exercise, those interested in computer programming might construct a program to reproduce these results.

Constant Marginal Cost with an Abundant Substitute

The next extension assumes the existence of an abundant perfect substitute, available in unlimited quantities at a cost of $6 per unit. To derive the dynamically efficient allocation of both the depletable resource and its substitute, let q_t be the amount of a constant marginal cost depletable resource extracted in year t and q_{st} the amount used of a constant marginal cost substitute resource that is perfectly substitutable for the depletable resource. The marginal cost of the substitute is assumed to be $\$d$.

With this change the total benefit and cost formulae would take on the following form:

$$\text{Total Benefit} = \sum_{t=1}^{T} a(q_t + q_{st}) - \frac{b}{2}(q_t + q_{st})^2 \tag{3}$$

$$\text{Total Cost} = \sum_{t=1}^{T} cq_t + dq_{st} \tag{4}$$

The objective function is thus:

$$PVNB = \sum_{t=1}^{T} \frac{a(q_t + q_{st}) - \frac{b}{2}(q_t^2 + q_{st}^2 + 2q_t q_{st}) - cq_t - dq_{st}}{(1 + r)^{t-1}} \tag{5}$$

subject to the constraint on the total availability of the depletable resource:

$$\bar{Q} - \sum_{t=1}^{T} q_t \geq 0 \tag{6}$$

Necessary and sufficient conditions for an allocation maximizing this function are expressed in equation sets (7), (8) and equation (9).

$$\frac{a - b(q_t + q_{st}) - c}{(1 + r)^{t-1}} - \leq 0 \qquad t = 1, \ldots n \tag{7}$$

[Any member of equation set (7) will hold as an equality when $q_t > 0$ and will be negative when $q_t = 0$.]

$$a - b(q_t + q_{st}) - d \leq 0 \qquad t = 1, \ldots n \tag{8}$$

[Any member of equation set (8) will hold as an equality when $q_{st} > 0$ and will be negative when $q_{st} = 0$].

$$\bar{Q} - \sum_{i=1}^{t} q_t \geq 0. \tag{9}$$

For the numerical example used in the text the following parameter values were assumed:

$$a = \$8 \qquad c = \$2$$
$$b = 0.4 \qquad d = \$6$$
$$\bar{Q} = 40 \qquad r = 0.10$$

It can be readily verified that the optimum conditions are satisfied by:

$q_1 = 8.798$	$q_3 = 7.495$	$q_5 = 5.919$
$q_2 = 8.177$	$q_4 = 6.744$	$q_6 = 2.863$
$q_{s6} = 2.137$	$q_{st} = 5.000$ for $n > 6$ and $q_{st} = 0$ for $n < 6$	
	$\lambda = 2.481$	

The depletable resource is used up before the end of the sixth period and the switch is made to the substitute resource at that time. From equation set (8) in competitive markets, the switch occurs precisely at the moment when the resource price rises to meet the marginal cost of the substitute.

The switch point in this example is earlier than in the previous example (the sixth period rather than the ninth period). Since all characteristics of the problem except for the availability of the substitute are the same in the two numerical examples, the difference can be attributed to the availability of the substitute.

Increasing Marginal Cost Case

In this case the cost function for the depletable resource differs from the previous case. Specifically instead of $TC_t = cq_t$ the function is $TC_t = cq_t + (f/2)(\sum_{i=1}^{t} q_i)^2$ prior to the switch point and $TC_1 = dq_{st}$ after. In addition there is no availability constraint; availability in this case is determined by cost, not by a finite limit on the amount available. With this change the objective function is:

$$PVNB = \sum_{t=1}^{n} \frac{a(q_t + q_{st}) - \frac{b}{2}(q_t^2 + q_{st}^2 + 2q_t q_{st}) - cq_t - dq_{st}}{(1 + r)^{t-1}} \qquad (10)$$

$$- f \sum_{t=1}^{n} \frac{\left(\sum_{t=1}^{t} q_t\right)^2}{2(1 + r)^{t-1}}$$

Necessary and sufficient conditions for any allocation satisfying this function are:

$$\frac{a - b(q_t - q_{st}) - c - f\left(\sum_{i=1}^{t} q_i\right)}{(1 + r)^{t-1}} - \sum_{i=t+1}^{n} \frac{fq_i}{(1 + r)^{i-1}} \le 0 \quad t = 1, \ldots n \quad (11)$$

[Any member of equation set (11) will hold as an equality when $q_t > 0$ and will be negative when $q_t = 0$.]

$$a - b(q_t + q_{st}) - d \le 0 \qquad (12)$$

[Any member of equation set (12) will hold as an equality when $q_{st} > 0$ and will be negative when $q_{st} = 0$.]

In equation set (11) the term immediately before the $\le$ sign is the marginal user cost. Note that it diminishes over time as t approaches the switch point.

For the increasing cost numerical example which ignores environmental costs the assumed parameter values were:

$$a = \$8 \qquad c = \$2$$
$$b = 0.4 \qquad d = \$6$$
$$r = 0.10 \qquad f = 0.10$$

It is easily verified that the following solution satisfies the optimum conditions:

$q_1 = 7.132$ $q_3 = 6.017$ $q_5 = 5.304$ $q_7 = 4.316$

$q_2 = 6.523$ $q_4 = 5.610$ $q_6 = 5.099$ $n = 7$

$q_{st} = 0$ for $t < 7$; $q_{st} = 0.684$ for $t = 7$; and $q_{st} = 5.000$ for $t > 7$

All of the depletable resource that is available at a cost lower than the substitute is used up prior to the switch point.

Including Environmental Cost

For the case with environmental costs all formulas are the same and only one parameter value is changed. Specifically the environmental cost simulation assumes $c = \$3$ rather than $c = \$2$ as had been true in the previous simulation. The difference is presumed to reflect the environmental costs associated with extracting this resource.

With this parameter change, the new solutions become:

$q_1 = 6.297$	$q_3 = 5.470$	$q_5 = 5.048$	
$q_2 = 5.834$	$q_4 = 5.207$	$q_6 = 2.144$	for $n > 6$, $q_{st} = 5.00$
$n = 6$	$Q = 30$	$q_{s6} = 2.856$	for $n < 6$, $q_{st} = 0.00$

CHAPTER SEVEN

Depletable, Nonrecyclable Energy Resources: Oil, Gas, Coal, and Uranium

If it ain't broke, don't fix it!
OLD MAINE PROVERB

INTRODUCTION

Energy deserves its reputation as one of the most critical resources; without it, life would cease. We derive energy from the food we eat. Through photosynthesis, the plant life we consume—both directly and indirectly when we eat meat—depends on energy from the sun. The materials we use to build our houses and produce the goods we consume are extracted from the earth's crust, then transformed into finished products with expenditures of energy.

Currently, most industrialized countries depend on oil and natural gas for most of their energy needs. In the United States, for example, these two resources together supply 67 percent of all energy consumed. Both are depletable, nonrecyclable sources of energy. Their proven reserves peaked during the 1970s in the United States, and since that time, the amount extracted has exceeded additions to reserves.

According to the models in Chapter 6, oil and natural gas would be transition fuels in an efficient allocation. They would be used until the marginal cost of further use exceeded the marginal cost of substitute resources—either more abundant depletable resources, such as coal, or renewable sources, such as solar energy.[1] In an efficient market path, the transition to these alternative sources would be smooth and harmonious.

---

[1]When used for other purposes, oil can be recyclable. Waste lubricating oil is now routinely recycled.

Have the allocations of the last several decades been efficient or not? In a 1977 speech to the nation, President Jimmy Carter suggested that the resolve needed to solve our energy problems was "the moral equivalent of war." The existence of a crisis atmosphere suggests that the allocations have not been efficient. Why not? Is the market mechanism flawed in its allocation of depletable recyclable resources? If so, is the flaw fatal? If not, what caused the inefficient allocations? Is the problem correctable?

These are the questions we shall examine. Because energy is too complex a subject to treat comprehensively in one chapter, additional references are provided at the end of the chapter. This text will examine some of the major issues associated with the allocation of energy resources and how economic analysis can clarify our understanding of both the sources of the problems and their solution.

NATURAL GAS: PRICE CONTROLS

During the winter of late 1974 and early 1975, there were serious shortages of natural gas. Customers who had contracted and were willing to pay for natural gas were unable to get as much as they wanted. The shortage (or curtailments as the Federal Energy Regulatory Commission calls them) amounted to 2.0 trillion cubic feet of natural gas in 1974–75 which represented roughly 10 percent of the marketed production in 1975.[2] In an efficient allocation, shortages of that magnitude would never have happened. Why did they?

The source of the problem can be traced directly to government controls over natural-gas prices. This story begins, oddly enough, with the rise of the automobile, which does not even use natural gas as a fuel. The increasing importance of the automobile for transportation created a rising demand for gasoline, which in turn stimulated a search for new sources of crude oil. This exploration activity uncovered large quantities of natural gas (known as associated gas) in addition to large quantities of crude oil, which was the object of the search.

As natural gas was discovered, it replaced manufactured gas—and some coal—in the geographic areas where it was found. Then, as a geographically dispersed demand developed for this increasingly available gas, a long-distance system of gas pipelines was designed and constructed. In the period following World War II, natural gas became an important source of energy for the United States.

The regulation of natural gas began in 1938 with the passage of the Natural Gas Act. This act transformed the Federal Power Commission (FPC) into a federal regulatory agency charged with maintaining "just" prices. In 1954, a Supreme Court decision in *Phillips Petroleum Co.* v. *Wisconsin* forced the FPC to extend their price control regulations to the producer. Prior to that time, they had merely limited their regulation to pipeline companies.

---

[2]The curtailment figure comes from Federal Energy Administration, *National Energy Outlook* (Washington, D.C., 1976): 121., and the marketed figure is from U.S. Department of Energy, *Monthly Energy Review: April, 1978* (Washington, D.C.: Government Printing Office, 1978): 24.

FIGURE 7.1a Increasing Marginal Extraction Cost with Substitute Resource in the Presence of Price Controls: Quantity Profile

FIGURE 7.1b Increasing Marginal Extraction Cost with Substitute Resource in the Presence of Price Controls: Price Profile

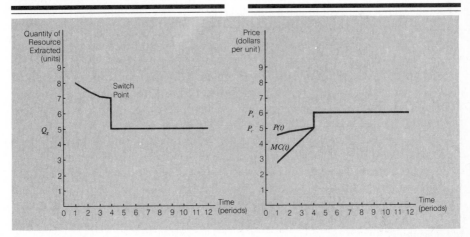

Because the process of setting price ceilings proved cumbersome, the hastily conceived initial "interim" ceilings remained in effect for almost a decade before the Commission was able to impose more carefully considered ceilings.[3] What was the effect of this regulation?

By returning to our models in the previous section, we can see the havoc this would raise. The ceiling would prevent prices from reaching their normal levels. Since price increases are the source of the incentive to conserve, the lower prices would cause more of the resource to be used in earlier years. Consumption levels in those years would be higher under price controls than without them.

Importantly, however, there are also effects on the supply side. Producers would only produce the resource when they could do so profitably. Once the marginal cost rose to meet the price ceiling, no more would be produced, in spite of the large demand for the resource at that price. Thus, as long as price controls are permanent, less of the resource would be produced with controls than without. Furthermore, more of what would be produced would be used in the earlier years.

The combined impact of these demand and supply effects would be to distort the allocation significantly (Figures 7.1a and 7.1b). While there are a number of differences between this allocation and an efficient one, two are of particular importance: (1) the time of transition is earlier under price controls, and (2) the transition is abrupt, with prices suddenly jumping to new higher levels. Both are detrimental. The first effect means we would not be using all of the natural gas available at prices consumers were

---

[3]For an excellent discussion of this period, see Stephen G. Breyer and Paul W. MacAvoy, *Energy Regulation by the Federal Power Commission* (Washington, D.C.: The Brookings Institution, 1974).

willing to pay. Among other things, this could cause a transition to the substitute before the technologies to use it were adequately developed.

The discontinuous jump to a new technology, which results from price controls, can place quite a burden on consumers. Attracted by artificially low prices, consumers would invest in equipment to use natural gas, only to discover — after the transition — that natural gas was no longer available.

One interesting characteristic of price ceilings is that they affect behavior even when they are not binding (when the market price is lower than the price ceiling, for example).[4] This effect is clearly illustrated in Figures 7.1a and 7.1b in the earlier years. Even though the price in the first year is lower than the price ceiling, it is not equal to the efficient price. This is because the price ceiling causes a reallocation of resources toward the present, which, in turn, affects prices in the earlier years.

Price controls may cause other problems as well. Up to this point, we have discussed permanent controls. Not all price controls are permanent; they can change at the whim of the political process in unpredictable ways. The fact that prices could suddenly rise when the ceiling is lifted also creates unfortunate incentives. If producers expect a large price increase in the near future, they have an incentive to stop production and wait for the higher prices. Needless to say, this circumstance could cause severe problems for consumers.

For legal reasons the price controls on natural gas were placed solely on gas shipped across state lines. Gas consumed within the states where it was produced could be priced at what the market would bear. As a result, gas produced and sold within the state received a higher price than that sold in other states. Consequently, the share of gas in the interstate market fell over time as producers found it more profitable to commit reserve additions to the *intrastate,* rather than the *interstate,* market. In the 1964–69 period, about 33 percent of the average annual reserve additions were committed to the interstate market. By 1970–74, this commitment had fallen to a little less than 5 percent.

The practical effect of charging less for gas destined for the interstate market was to cause the shortages to be concentrated in states served by pipeline and dependent on the interstate shipment of gas. As a result, the damage caused was greater than it would have been if all consuming areas had shared somewhat more equitably in the shortfall. The price-control system not only caused the damage, it intensified it!

Our description of how price controls affected natural-gas allocations over time suggested that one effect would be to hasten the time of transition to a substitute resource. The controls had the additional effect of causing a transition to an inefficient substitute. The reason for this substitution bias and its implications are explored in Example 7.1.

It seems fair to conclude that, by sapping the economic system of its ability to respond to changing conditions, price controls on natural gas created a significant amount of turmoil. If this kind of political control is likely to recur with some regularity, perhaps some of the *Limits to Growth* concerns may be valid, though for different reasons.

---

[4]For a complete analysis of this point see Dwight R. Lee, "Price Controls, Binding Constraints, and Intertemporal Economic Decision Making", *Journal of Political Economy,* Vol. 86, no.2 (1978): 293–301.

The overshoot and collapse syndrome in this case would be caused by government interference rather than any pure market behavior. If so, the proverb which opens this chapter becomes particularly relevant!

Why did Congress embark on such a counterproductive policy? The answer is found in rent-seeking behavior which can be explained through the use of our consumer- and producer-surplus model. Let's examine the political incentives in a simple model.

EXAMPLE 7.1

Price Controls and Substitution Bias

Faced with shortages, pipeline companies looked for alternative sources of supply. Two that they discovered were liquid natural gas (LNG), shipped from abroad in pressurized ships, and synthetic natural gas (SNG), manufactured from various petroleum products. These sources were both very expensive.

Pipeline companies induced consumers to use these substitutes by using average cost pricing. The artificially cheap natural gas was blended with the synthetic gas and sold at the average cost of the two depending on the proportions. Thus, if they used 90 percent natural gas at $1 per unit and 10 percent other sources at $5 per unit, the cost of the combined gas is $1.40 per unit (0.90 × $1 + 0.10 × $5.). Thus, instead of paying the high marginal cost of the substitute for additional units consumed, as efficiency would dictate, consumers paid the much lower average cost. The pricing system sent them the wrong signal.

This system of pricing created a bias toward substitutes which could be blended with natural gas and away from substitutes which could not. In this case the bias was particularly unfortunate; not only did it create additional demand for imported energy sources (LNG) at a time when the official policy was to discourage such imports, but it also encouraged lower levels of thermodynamic efficiency in the use of our diminishing oil resources. The conversion to gas caused some of the potential energy to be lost. Substitutes rendered noneconomic in certain parts of the country by this pricing system included heat pumps and residential solar space heating.

Because this system of average cost pricing encouraged pipeline companies to accept high cost sources of imported or synthetic gas that could be commingled with the artificially cheap natural gas during the 1970's, when natural gas prices began to be decontrolled in the early 1980's, the price rise was especially rapid and sharp. The large base of artificially low-cost natural gas was no longer there to counterbalance the very high cost of the new sources. Average residential prices for natural gas rose from $2.98 per thousand cubic feet in 1979 to $6.06 in 1983. Since that time they have stabilized with the 1986 price being $6.13; the excess demand in the natural gas market had been eliminated by higher prices.

Sources: Thomas H. Tietenberg, "Substitution Bias in a Depletable Resource Model with Administered Prices," in *Erschopfbare Ressourcen* (Berlin: Duncker and Humblot, 1980): 529–552 and Energy Information Administration, *Monthly Energy Review* (January, 1986): 99.

Consider Figure 7.2. An efficient market allocation would result in Q^* supplied at price P^*. The net benefits received by the country would be represented by the total geometric area encompassed by the areas denoted as A and B. Of these net benefits, area A would be received by consumers as consumer surplus and B would be received by producers as a producer surplus.

Suppose now that a price ceiling were established. From the above discussion we know that this ceiling would reduce the marginal user cost because higher future prices would no longer be possible. In Figure 7.2, this has the effect for current producers of lowering the perceived supply curve, due to the lower marginal user cost. As a result of this shift in the perceived supply curve, current production would expand to Q_c and price would fall to P_c. Current consumers would unambiguously be better off, since consumer surplus would be area $A + B + C$ instead of area A. They would have gained a net benefit equal to $B + C$.

It may appear that producers could also gain if $D > B$, but that is not correct. Because producers would be overproducing, they would be giving up the scarcity rent they could have gotten without price controls, Area D measures only current profits without considering scarcity rent. When the loss in scarcity rent is considered, producers unambiguously lose net benefits.

Future consumers, meanwhile, are also worse off. Since the supplies are exhausted more rapidly, eventually the point will be reached when the price to consumers is higher

FIGURE 7.2   The Effect of Price Controls

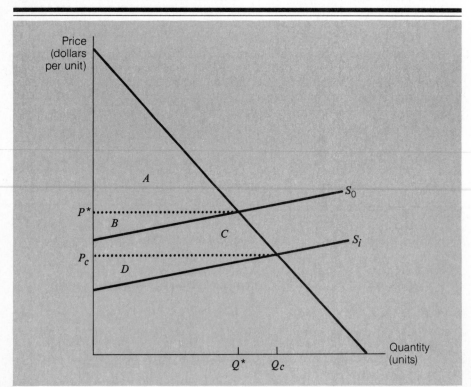

than it would otherwise be. This occurs because the switch to the more expensive substitute is made prematurely. Future consumers who might have used natural gas had the controls not been in effect, would be forced to use the more expensive substitute. The higher price implies lower consumer surplus.

Congress may view scarcity rent as a possible source of revenue to transfer from producers to consumers. As we have seen, however, scarcity rent is an opportunity cost which serves a distinct purpose—the protection of future consumers. When government attempts to reduce this scarcity rent through price controls, the result is an overallocation to current consumers and an underallocation to future consumers. Thus, what appears to be a transfer from producers to consumers is, in large part, also a transfer from future consumers to present consumers. Since current consumers mean current votes and future consumers may not know whom to blame when the time shortages appear, price controls are politically attractive. Unfortunately, they are also inefficient; the losses to future consumers and producers are greater than the gains to current consumers and because they distort the allocation toward the present, controls are unfair. Thus, markets in the presence of price controls are indeed myopic, but the problem lies with the controls, not the markets themselves.

Over the long run, price controls end up harming consumers rather than helping them. Scarcity rent plays an important role in the allocation process, and attempts to eliminate it can create more problems than are solved. After long debating the price-control issue, Congress passed the Natural Gas Policy Act on November 9, 1978.[5] This act calls for the eventual phased decontrol of natural-gas prices. Included among its other provisions are a movement away from the average-cost pricing of substitute gas for industrial customers and the imposition of price controls for the first time on intrastate gas, until such time as all prices are decontrolled. Furthermore, this movement toward decontrol was not merely an isolated case; price controls on oil have been phased out as well.

OIL: THE CARTEL PROBLEM

Since we have considered similar effects on natural gas, we shall merely note that price controls have been responsible for much mischief in the oil market as well.[6] There is a second source of misallocation in the oil market, however, not yet discussed. Most of the world's oil is produced by a cartel called the Organization of Petroleum Exporting Countries (OPEC). The members of this organization collude to exercise power over oil production and prices. As established in Chapter 2, seller power over resources due to a lack of effective competition leads to an inefficient allocation. When they have

---

[5]For an excellent discussion of this complex act, see Walter J. Mead, "The Natural Gas Policy Act of 1978: An Economic Evaluation," in *Contemporary Economic Problems 1979,* William Fellner, ed. (Washington, D.C.: American Enterprise Institute, 1979): 325–355.

[6]The price controls on oil were similar to, but not the same as, price controls on natural gas. For a discussion of the effects of those controls, see Kenneth J. Arrow and Joseph P. Kalt, *Petroleum Price Regulation: Should we Decontrol?* (Washington, D.C.: American Enterprise Institute, 1979).

market power, sellers can restrict supply and thus force prices higher than they would otherwise be.

Though these conclusions were derived in Chapter 2 for nondepletable resources, they are valid for depletable resources as well. A monopolist can extract more scarcity rent from a depletable resource base than competitive suppliers can, simply by restricting supply. The monopolist allocation results in slower production and higher prices.[7] The monopolistic transition to a substitute, therefore, occurs later than a competitive transition. It also reduces the net benefit society receives from these resources.

The process of how OPEC was able to form an effective cartel is informative, both because it suggests how we got in this situation and because it offers a view of how many other resources may be subject to similar problems in the future.

The conscious policy of encouraging energy investment abroad was facilitated in the early 1900s when major United States oil companies worked in conjunction with the State Department[8] to establish concessions in countries having what were later discovered to be very large oil reserves. These concessions gave the major oil companies access to large geographic areas of potentially productive, oil-bearing, geological formations for a large number of years.

The companies were granted almost total control over production and pricing. In return, the host governments (or rulers) received fixed production royalties, loans against future royalties, and rental payments on the land until royalties began to flow in.[9] Initially the arrangements satisfied both parties. The host countries needed revenue and had neither the financial capital nor the technical expertise to develop their own resources. The benefits to the oil companies of gaining access to these large new fields was obvious.[10]

These arrangements lasted without significant modification until the 1940s. By then, pressures for change were growing in the host countries for several reasons. The fixed royalty payments provided no hedge against inflation. The host countries were selling their resources at a fixed price, while the costs of the goods they were buying were rising. Nationalism was growing stronger in the host countries, and this led to resentment about the degree of control exercised by foreign oil companies. Finally, since

---

[7]The conclusion that a monopoly would extract a resource more slowly than a competitive mining industry is not perfectly general. It is possible to construct demand curves such that the extraction rate of the monopolist is greater than or equal to that of a competitive industry. As a practical matter, these conditions seem unlikely. That a monopoly would restrict output, while not inevitable, is the most likely conclusion to draw. See the discussion in Anthony C. Fisher, *Resource and Environmental Economics* (Cambridge, England: Cambridge University Press, 1981): 37–39.

[8]Harold F. Williamson, et al., *The American Petroleum Industry, 1899–1959: The Age of Energy, Vol. 2* (Evanston, Illinois: Northwestern University Press, 1963): 517–519.

[9]The ARAMCO concession agreement in Saudi Arabia was fairly typical. See Donald A. Wells, "ARAMCO: The Evolution of an Oil Concession," in *Foreign Investment in the Petroleum and Mineral Industries*, Raymong F. Mikesell *et al.*, ed. (Baltimore, Md.: Johns Hopkins Press for Resources for the Future, 1971): 216–236.

[10]The American companies were, however, accepting some risk. For example, although the first test drilling occurred in Saudi Arabia in 1934, the first successful wells were not located until 1938. It was not until after World War II that the size of the Saudi Arabian reserve was fully appreciated. See Neil H. Jacoby, *Multinational Oil: A Study in Industrial Dynamics* (New York: MacMillan, 1974): 36.

the oil companies had done their job well, substantial reserves were uncovererd. It was becoming increasingly clear to the host countries just how valuable these reserves were.

The initial change occurred in 1943, when Venezuela passed a law altering the relationship of the concessionaire to the mineral deposits in the host country.[11] Among other innovations, the law, as amended in 1945, 1947, and 1948, established the principle that profits earned on the crude production were to be shared between the multinational oil companies and the host countries. The inclusion of this principle into concession agreements soon spread to the Middle Eastern countries as well. By 1950, for example, the ARAMCO–Saudi Arabian agreement had been modified to include this provision.[12]

The device used to operationalize this concept was the "posted price," which was administratively determined. Although the posted price could and did change periodically, it changed less frequently than a market-determined price would have and therefore offered more price stability. This stability was valued by the multinational oil companies as a means of limiting serious competition and by the countries as protection against price declines.

In 1957, crude oil posted prices were raised. M. A. Adelman [1972, p. 161] attributed this not to scarcity, but rather to an attempt by the American oil companies to thwart the rapid growth of imports into the United States by American independent refiners. This rise in posted prices was supported by the producing nations because it increased their tax revenue per barrel sold. The industry, however, subsequently changed its mind about the efficacy of higher prices; it discovered that it was not able to translate these higher crude prices into higher product prices because of the introduction of wide-scale discounting.

Therefore, in 1959, the oil companies asserted their power to reduce posted prices and this became a major source of irritation to the governments of the producing states. In response, OPEC was formed in 1960 for the purpose of developing a coordinated, unified position for the producing nations. While the balance of power between the host countries and the oil companies had shifted substantially toward the host countries since the original concession agreements, the oil companies still maintained an upper hand. They had the technical expertise and, more importantly, they controlled the distribution and marketing channels. Unlike the host countries, the multinational oil companies had demonstrated an ability to act in concert.[13]

A necessary condition for transforming OPEC into a power was the dilution of power of the integrated oil companies. This dilution was actively sought, particularly by Algeria and Libya, by bringing more independent oil companies into the world petroleum market. As Adelman puts it, "The old internationals were perhaps reluctant

---

[11]Fuad, Rauhani, *A History of O.P.E.C.* (New York, NY: Praeger Publishers, 1971), pp. 45–46.

[12]Donald A. Wells, "ARAMCO: The Evolution of an Oil Concession," in *Foreign Investment in the Petroleum and Mineral Industries,* Raymond F. Mikesell *et al.* (Baltimore, Md: Johns Hopkins Press for Resources for the Future, 1971), p. 220.

[13]In the Achnaccary Agreement of 1928, Shell, British Petroleum, and Exxon reportedly had entered into an agreement to share markets outside the United States and to coordinate facilities to stabilize prices. See Neil H. Jacoby, *Multinational Oil: A Study in Industrial Dynamics* (New York: MacMillan, 1974): 36.

rivals; but competition kept breaking or creeping in and long before the end of the decade they had lost control of the market."

Also, during this period, an Arab-Israeli war closed the Suez Canal. This increased the attractiveness of Libyan oil for Europe, and by 1969, about 30 percent of Europe's needs were coming from that source. In May 1970, the Trans-Arabian pipeline was blocked by Syria, and the Libyan government began production cutbacks to force an agreement on higher taxes. The result was an increase in the delivered price in Rotterdam of about 50 percent. Since demand growth had now eliminated any excess production capacity,[14] the Libyan companies capitulated and agreed to higher prices. This action was soon followed in other countries by similar agreements. The price increases were followed in the next two years by nationalization of certain companies in Iraq and increased participation in others by Libya and Saudi Arabia.

During the early 1970s, the balance of power had fully swung to the host nations, now the chief oil-exporting nations. Oil was vitally important to the consuming nations. In the short run, good substitutes were not available. The power of the major international oil companies had been diluted. By 1973 the oil exporting nations possessed both the ability and the motivation to impose their will upon the world petroleum market.

Two main actions taken in October 1973 asserted this power. On October 16, the decision was taken by the Persian Gulf members of OPEC to raise prices unilaterally by 70 percent. On the following day this action was ratified by OPEC as a whole. In addition, the Arab states undertook a series of production cutbacks and attempted to target the shortfalls by a complete embargo of all exports to the United States, Canada, the Netherlands, the Bahamas, Trinidad, the Netherlands Antilles, Puerto Rico, and Guam. Other nations did not totally escape. Some "most favored" nations received approximately their September 1973 levels while other "neutral" nations were allocated the remaining oil, prorated on their September 1973 import levels.

The Arab nations made clear that a nation's position on the Arab-Israeli dispute would influence its classification within these categories. In addition, following a November summit meeting in Algiers, the Saudi Arabian and Algerian oil ministers toured Europe, explicitly linking the restoration of production to a pullback by Israel from the occupied territories. On December 22, 1973, posted prices were again raised, this time by 130 percent. The embargo against the United States was lifted by most Arab states, as abruptly as it had begun, on March 18, 1974. The price hikes remained in force.

As illustrated in Example 7.2, the cartelization of the oil suppliers was very effective. Why? Were the conditions which made it profitable unique to oil or are there significant possibilities for cartelizing other resources? To answer these questions, we must isolate those factors which make cartelization possible. Though there are others, four stand out: (1) the price elasticity of demand for OPEC oil in both the long run and the short run; (2) the income elasticity of demand for oil; (3) the supply responsiveness of the oil producers who are not OPEC members; and (4) the compatibility of interests among members of OPEC.

---

[14]James W. McKie, "The Political Economy of World Petroleum," *The American Economic Review: Papers and Proceedings* LVIX (May 1974): 51–57.

Price Elasticity of Demand

The elasticity of demand is an important ingredient because it determines how responsive demand is to price. When demand elasticities are less than 1.0, price increases lead to increased revenue. Exactly how much revenue would increase when prices increase depends on the price elasticity of demand. In general, the lower the price elasticity of demand the larger the gains to be derived from forming a cartel.

The price elasticity of demand for oil depends on the opportunities for conservation, as well as on the availability of substitutes. As storm windows cut heat losses, the same temperature can be maintained with less heating oil. Smaller automobiles reduce the amount of gasoline needed to travel a given distance. The larger the set of these opportunities and the smaller the cash outlays required to exploit them, the more price elastic the demand. This suggests that the price elasticity of demand in the long run (when sufficient time has passed to allow adjustments) will be greater, perhaps significantly, than in the short run.

The availability of substitutes is important because it limits the degree to which prices can be raised by a producer cartel. When there are larger quantities of substitutes available at prices not far above competitive oil prices, these act as an upper limit. Unless OPEC controls those sources as well—and it doesn't—any attempts to raise prices above those limits would cause the consuming nations to simply switch to these alternative sources; OPEC would have priced itself out of the market.

Alternative sources clearly exist, although they are expensive and the time of transition is long. One extensive survey of world energy resources, for example, concluded that about as much petroleum could be extracted from unconventional sources—such as deep offshore wells, wells in the polar seas, heavy oils, enhanced recovery techniques, oil shales, tar sands, and synthetic oils—as is currently available from conventional petroleum reserves. It further concludes, however, that those sources wouldn't make much of a dent in the oil market until the end of the twentieth century and then only at very high cost. This report conjectured that the high cost of these sources would confine their use to transportation and chemicals.[15]

Coal is clearly a substitute for some uses and is available in large supplies. As we shall see in the next section, however, coal has large environmental costs associated with its use.

Clearly, the ultimate substitute is solar energy and it is the cost of solar energy that will set the long-run upper limit on the ability of OPEC to raise its prices. Since in many parts of the United States solar energy is currently cost competitive for space and hot-water heating, that limit is probably not substantially higher than recent OPEC prices. Although it will take a significant amount of time for these new technologies to get all the bugs worked out and begin to penetrate the market on a massive scale, the transition seems to be proceeding smoothly. As Example 7.3 indicates, this transition has extended to electricity production as well, which some observers felt would resist that change.

---

[15]World Energy Conference, *World Energy Resources: 1985–2020* (New York, NY: IPC Science and Technology Press, 1978): 2–3.

EXAMPLE 7.2

Optimal OPEC Pricing

In 1978 Robert Pindyck, an economist on the faculty at the Massachusetts Institute of Technology, published a study of optimal OPEC pricing. His model was quite similar to that used in this book with two exceptions: (1) he chose his parameters to be consistent with current demand and reserve patterns (whereas our model is explicitly hypothetical), and (2) he incorporates into his model the fact that demand responds to higher prices slowly rather than immediately.

In this study he calculates optimal price trajectories for OPEC if it were to act competitively and if it were to act as a cartel. Each of these trajectories is calculated using two discount rates [5 percent and 10 percent]. From this calculation it is possible to derive the additional gains to producers from establishing a cartel. The results are presented in the accompanying figure. As expected the monopoly prices are higher, at least in the earlier years. In the later years when the competitive allocation begins to experience more severe scarcity, competitive prices would rise above the monopoly prices. The initial dip in monopoly prices is due to the lagged response in demand. In the initial years when demand responds rather sluggishly, the price can be held high, but as demand becomes more responsive, prices have to drop to prevent too severe reductions in demand.

Using a 10 percent discount rate, Pindyck calculates that compared to a competitive allocation, the present value of producers' profits would be 1.94 times higher if the producers acted as a cartel. Most of the advantages of cartelization are ac-

Income Elasticity of Demand

The income elasticity of oil demand is important because it relates how sensitive oil demand is to growth in the world economy. At constant prices, as income grows, oil demand should grow. This continual increase in demand fortifies the ability of OPEC to raise its prices. High income elasticities of demand support the cartelization of oil. All other things being equal, the higher the income elasticity of demand, the higher the price would have to rise to bring demand to zero (in the absence of substitutes) or the more rapidly it would rise to the level of the substitute resource when one is available.

The income elasticity of demand is also important because it registers how sensitive demand is to the business cycle. The higher the income elasticity of demand, the more sensitive demand is. This is a major source of the weakening of the caretel which occurred during 1983. A recession caused a large reduction in the demand for oil, putting new pressure on the cartel to absorb these demand reductions.

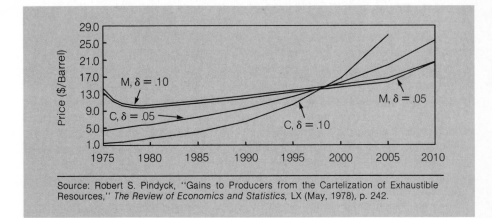

Source: Robert S. Pindyck, "Gains to Producers from the Cartelization of Exhaustible Resources," *The Review of Economics and Statistics,* LX (May, 1978), p. 242.

crued in the first few years. Pindyck calculates that the present value of profits accrued during the first five years in the monopoly case is 5.78 times as large as those in the competitive case. There seems little doubt that in the case of oil, cartelization has been extremely profitable to the producers as well as inefficient for the world economy.

Source: Robert Pindyck, "Gains to Producers from Cartelization of Exhaustible Resources," *Review of Economics and Statistics* 60 (May, 1978): 238–51.

Non-OPEC Suppliers

Another key factor in the ability of producer nations to exercise power over a natural-resource market is their ability to prevent new suppliers, not part of the cartel, from entering the market and undercutting the price. Currently OPEC produces about two-thirds of the world's oil. If the remaining producers were able, in the face of higher prices, to expand their supply dramatically, they would increase the amount of oil supplied and cause the prices to fall, decreasing OPEC's market share. If this response were large enough, the allocation of oil would approach the competitive allocation.

Currently only Mexico appears to have large enough reserves to make an individual difference in the world oil market. Since both size of its reserve and its production profile are uncertain, it is difficult to assess Mexico's ultimate impact on the future world market.

This does not mean, however, that non-OPEC members collectively do not have an impact on price. They do. The cartel must take the nonmembers into account when

EXAMPLE 7.3

Are Soft Energy Paths Doomed?

In 1976 a young physicist named Amory Lovins published an article in *Foreign Affairs* which built an immediate following for him and his ideas. His thesis, boldly stated, was that there were two paths to our energy future. One, dubbed by Lovins as the "hard path," consisted of an increasing reliance on large-scale, centralized technologies, while the second, the "soft path," relied more on smaller, decentralized technologies. The former is epitomized by nuclear-power plants, while solar home heating, windmills, and small dams provide examples of the latter. Furthermore, Lovins argued, these paths are mutually exclusive and the existing system is biased toward the former. If valid, this argument would cast a dark shadow over any expectation that the transition to the soft path would be efficient and smooth.

Lovins suggests that the current system of relying upon centralized power has allowed the build-up of vested interests having a stake in maintaining the status quo. One way this dominance could be perpetuated is for the utilities to refuse to purchase excess power from the soft-path producers. With no market or distribution system, producers would have less incentive to produce power by these means.

Whatever validity that argument may have had at the time it was made, it seems to have been weakened by congressional action. In 1978 Congress passed the Public Utility Regulatory Policies Act to encourage the production of electricity from renewable resources and from cogeneration systems. *Cogeneration* is the combined production of electricity and useful thermal energy. Among other provisions, this act: (1) requires utilities to purchase excess power at a price equal to what it would have cost the utilities to generate the power themselves; (2) requires utilities to provide backup power to those producers at average cost (usually lower than the price utilities pay the producers for excess power); and finally (3) stipulates that the qualifying small-production units cannot be owned by utilities. Though this is a controversial piece of legislation, there is little doubt it is spurring the development of renewable, small energy sources for producing electricity.

Source: Amory B. Lovins, "Energy Strategy: The Road Not Taken?" *Foreign Affairs* LV (October 1976): 65–96. The importance of this act to potential investors in renewable resources is described in Colin Norman, "Renewable Power Sparks Financial Interest," *Science* CCXII (26 June 1981): 1479–1481.

setting prices. Salant [1976] has put forth an interesting model of monopoly pricing in the presence of a fringe of smaller nonmember producers that serves as a basis for exploring this issue. In his model there are a number of suppliers. Some form a cartel. Others, a smaller number, form a "competitive fringe." The cartel is assumed to set the price of oil to maximize its collective profits by restricting production, taking the competitive fringe production into account. The competitive fringe cannot directly set the price, but since it is free to choose the level of production which maximizes its own profits, its output does affect the cartel's pricing strategy.

What conclusions does this model yield? The model concludes, first of all, that a resource cartel would set different prices when faced with a competitive fringe than when it is not. With a competitive fringe, it would set the initial price somewhat lower and allow price to rise more rapidly than would otherwise be the case. This strategy maximizes cartel profits by forcing the competitive fringe to produce more in the earlier periods (in response to higher demand) and eventually to exhaust their supplies. After the competitive fringe has depleted its reserves, the cartel would raise the price and thereafter prices would increase much more slowly.

Thus, the optimal strategy, from the point of view of the cartel, is to hold back on its own sales during the initial period, letting the other suppliers exhaust their supplies. Sales and profits of the competitive fringe, in this optimal cartel strategy, decline over time, while sales and profits of the cartel increase over time as prices rise and the cartel captures a larger share of the market.

One fascinating implication of this model is that the formation of the cartel raises the present value of profits of the competitive fringe by an even greater percentage than the present value of profits for the cartel. Those without the power gain more in percentage terms than those with the power!

Though this may seem counterintuitive, it is actually easily explained. The cartel, in order to keep the price up, must cut back on its own production level. The competitive fringe, however, is under no such constraint and is free to take advantage of the high prices without cutting back its own production. Thus, the profits of the competitive fringe are higher in the earlier period. All the cartel can do is wait until the competitive suppliers become less of a force in the market. The implication of this model is that the competitive fringe is a collective force in the oil market, even if they control as little as one-third of the production.

The impact of this competitive fringe on OPEC behavior was dramatically illustrated by events in the 1985–86 period. In 1979, OPEC accounted for approximately 50 percent of world oil production, while in 1986 this had fallen to approximately 30 percent. Taking account of the fact that total world oil production was down during this period over 10 percent for all producers, the pressures on the cartel mounted and prices ultimately fell. The average cost of crude oil imports in the United States fell from $36.52 per barrel in 1981 to $25.94 in January, 1986. OPEC simply was not able to hold the line on prices because the necessary reductions in production were too large for the individual cartel members to sustain.

Compatibility of Member Interests

The final factor we shall consider in determining the potential for cartelization of natural-resource markets is the internal cohesion of the cartel. When there is only one seller, the objective of that seller can be pursued without worrying about alienating others who could undermine the profitability of the enterprise. In a cartel composed of many sellers, that freedom is no longer as wide ranging. The incentives of each member and the incentives of the group as a whole may diverge.

There is an incentive for cartel members to cheat. A cheater, if undetected by the other members, could surreptitiously lower its price and steal part of the market away from the others. Formally, the price elasticity of demand facing an individual member is substantially higher than that for the group as a whole, because some of the increase in individual sales at a lower price represents sales reductions for other members. With a higher price elasticity, lower prices maximize profits. Thus, successful cartelization presupposes a means for detecting cheating and enforcing the collusive agreement.[16]

In addition to cheating, however, there is another threat to the stability of cartels – the degree to which members fail to agree on pricing and output decisions. Oil provides an excellent example of how these dissensions can arise. Since the 1974 rise of OPEC as a world power, Saudi Arabia has exercised a moderating influence on the pricing decisions of OPEC. Why?

Though there may be other reasons as well, certainly a main reason is the size of Saudi Arabia's oil reserves. Saudi Arabia holds approximately 33 percent of the OPEC proved reserves; its reserves are larger than those of any other member. Because of this, Saudi Arabia has an incentive to preserve the value of those resources. It is worried about setting prices so high as to undercut the future demand for its oil. As was stated above, the demand for oil in the long run is more price elastic than in the short run. The countries with smaller reserves, meanwhile, know that in the long run their reserves will be gone and are more concerned about the near future. Since alternative sources of supply are not much of a threat in the near future because of long development times, other countries want to extract as much rent as possible now.

The size of Saudi Arabia's production also gives it the potential to make its influence felt. Its capacity to produce is so large that it can unilaterally affect world prices. In January of 1981, for example, it was producing approximately 10.3 million barrels of crude oil a day – representing about 41 percent of all OPEC production.[17]

Cartelization is not an easy path to pursue for producers, but when possible, it can be very profitable. When the resource is a strategic and pervasive raw material, cartelization can be very costly for consuming nations.

Strategic-material cartelization also confers on the members political, as well as economic, power. Economic power can become political power when the revenue is used to purchase weapons or the capacity to produce weapons. The producer nations can also use an embargo of the material as a lever to cajole reluctant adversaries into foreign policy concessions. When the material is of strategic importance, the potential for embargoes casts a pall over the normally clear and convincing case for free trade of raw materials among nations. What is an efficient resolution of this problem?

---

[16]During February, 1985, OPEC hired a large Dutch accounting firm to help it detect cheating among its members. See "Dutch Accountants Take on a Formidable Task: Ferreting Out 'Cheaters' in the Ranks of OPEC," *Wall Street Journal*, February 26, 1982, p. 39.

[17]Energy Information Administration, U.S. Department of Energy, *Monthly Energy Review: May 1981* (Washington, D.C.: U.S. Government Printing Office, 1981): 92–93.

OIL: NATIONAL SECURITY PROBLEM

As early as 1933, the United States placed controls on imported oil to reduce dependence on foreign suppliers. Abandoned in 1935 after the Supreme Court ruled that the National Industrial Recovery Act—the legislative basis for import controls—was unconstitutional, the controls were resurrected again on a voluntary basis during 1957, and on a mandatory basis during 1959.

From an economic point of view, vulnerable strategic imports have an added cost which is not reflected in the marketplace. National security is a classic public good. No individual importer correctly represents our collective national security interests in making a decision on how much to import. Thus, leaving the determination of the appropriate balance between imports and domestic production to the market generally results in an excessive dependence on imports (Figure 7.3).

There are three relevant supply curves. The first, S_d, is the long-run domestic supply curve. Its upward slope reflects increasing availability of domestic oil at higher prices, given sufficient time to develop those resources. There are two supply curves for imported foreign oil: S_{f0} reflects the world price and S_{f1} includes a "vulnerability premium" in addition to the world price. This premium reflects the additional national security

FIGURE 7.3 The National Security Problem

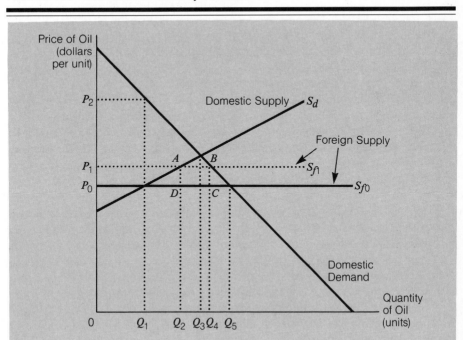

costs caused by imports. Both curves are drawn horizontally to the axis to reflect the assumption that U.S. action on imports is unlikely to affect the world price for oil.

In Figure 7.3 the market would generally demand and receive Q_5 units of oil. Of this total amount, Q_1 would be domestically produced and $Q_5 - Q_1$ would be imported. Can you see why?

However, in an efficient allocation incorporating the national security costs, only Q_4 units would be consumed. Of these, Q_2 would be domestically produced and $Q_4 - Q_2$ would be imported. Notice that when national security is an issue, the market in general tends to consume too much oil and domestic production is too small. Both of these factors raise vulnerable strategic imports above their efficient level.

What would happen during an embargo? Be careful! At first glance you would guess that we would consume Q_3 relying solely on domestic production. We may well rely solely on domestic production; yet, the amount consumed would be Q_1 and the price, P_2. Why?

Remember that S_d is the domestic supply curve, *given enough time to develop the resources.* If an embargo hits, there is not enough time to develop additional resources (six-year time lags are common). Therefore, in the short run, the supply curve becomes perfectly inelastic (vertical) at Q_1. The price will rise to P_2 to equate supply and demand. As the graph indicates, the loss in consumer surplus during an embargo can be very large indeed.

How can the country react to this inefficiency? On November 7, 1973, shortly after the embargo had been initiated, President Richard Nixon, in a nationwide address, announced Project Independence, a massive effort comparable to the Manhattan Project, designed to achieve energy self-sufficiency by the 1980s. If imports were reduced to zero, as President Nixon suggested, the vulnerability problem would disappear. Is self-sufficiency the answer?

If the situation is adequately represented by Figure 7.3, then the answer is clearly no. The net benefit from self-sufficiency (the allocation in which consumption is Q_3 and imports are zero) is clearly lower than the net benefits from the efficient allocation (Q_4). The size of the efficiency loss is indicated by the shaded area in Figure 7.3.

Why, you might ask, is self-sufficiency so inefficient when embargoes obviously impose so much damage and self-sufficiency can make us immune? Another way to rephrase the question is to ask why we would want any imports at all when national security is at stake.

The simple answer is that the vulnerability premium is lower than the cost of becoming self-sufficient, but that response merely begs the question. Why is the vulnerability premium lower? It is lower for three primary reasons: (1) embargoes are not certain events—they may never occur; (2) there are domestic steps we can take to reduce vulnerability of the remaining imports; and (3) to accelerate domestic production would incur a user cost by lowering the amounts available to future users.

The expected damage caused by one or more embargoes depends on the likelihood of occurrence, as well as the intensity and duration. This means that the S_{fl} curve will be lower for imports having a lower likelihood of being embargoed. Imports from countries less hostile to our interests are more secure and the vulnerability premium on those imports is smaller.[18]

For vulnerable imports, we can adopt certain contingency programs to reduce the damage an embargo would cause. The most obvious measure is to develop a domestic stockpile of oil to be used during an embargo. The United States has taken this route. The stockpile, called the *strategic petroleum reserve,* was designed to contain one billion barrels of oil. It would replace three million barrels a day for slightly less than one year or a larger number of barrels per day for a shorter period of time. This reserve would serve as an alternative source of supply, which, unlike our other oil resources, could be rapidly deployed on short notice. It is, in short, a form of insurance protection. The less expensive this protection is, the lower S_{fl} is and the more attractive imports are.[19]

To understand the third and final reason that paying the vulnerability premium would be less costly than self-sufficiency, we must consider vulnerability in a dynamic, rather than static, framework. Because oil is a depletable resource, there is a user cost associated with its efficient use. To reorient the extraction of that resource toward the present, as a self-sufficiency strategy would do, reduces future net benefits. Thus the self-sufficiency strategy tends to be myopic, in that it solves the short-term vulnerability problem by creating a more serious one in the future. Paying the vulnerability premium creates a more efficient balance between the present and future, as well as between current imports and domestic production.

We have established the fact that government can reduce our vulnerability to imports, which tends to keep the risk premium as low as possible. Certainly for oil, however, even after the stockpile has been established, the risk premium is not zero, S_{fo} and S_{fl} will not coincide.[20] Consequently, the government must also concern itself with

---

[18]It is this fact which explains the tremendous U.S. interest in Mexican oil, in spite of the fact that, historically, it has not been cheaper.

[19]Economic analysis can also be used to derive the optimal sized stockpile. The optimal stockpile is the one which minimizes the sum of expected damages plus the costs of stockpiling. This stockpile will be the one where the expected damage from not storing the last barrel of oil is equal to the cost of storing it. Larger stockpiles would cost more to establish than they would save in reduced damages. Examples of this analysis can be found in Thomas Teisberg, "A Dynamic Programming Model of the U.S. Strategic Petroleum Reserve," *The Bell Journal of Economics* 12 (Autumn 1981): 526–546; A. L. Nichols and R. J. Zeckhauser, "Stockpiling Strategies and Cartel Prices," *Bell Journal of Economics 7 (Spring 1976): 66–96.*

[20]Those who have examined the question of the premium are uniform in their agreement that it exists, but the estimates of how large it is vary from two times the current price to something less than the current price. See Robert Stobaugh and Daniel Yergin, eds. *Energy Future: Report of the Energy Project at the Harvard Business School* (New York: Random House, 1979): 227; Hans H. Landsberg, *Energy: The Next Twenty Years* (Cambridge, Mass.: Ballinger Publishing Company, 1979): 221; Energy Modeling Forum, *World Oil: Summary Report,* Report 6 of the Energy Modeling Forum, Stanford University (February 1982), pp. 67–75; and E. Folkerts-Landau, "The Social Cost of Imported Oil," *Energy Journal,* Vol. 5, no. 3, (July, 1984): 41–58.

achieving both the efficient level of consumption and the efficient share of that consumption borne by imports. Let's examine some of the policy choices.

Energy conservation is one popular approach to the problem. One way to accomplish additional conservation is by means of a tax on energy consumption, such as the widely used gasoline tax. Graphically, this approach would be reflected as a shift inward of the after-tax demand curve. Such a tax would reduce consumption (an efficient result) but would not achieve the efficient share of imports (an inefficient result). An energy tax falls on *all* energy consumption, whereas the problem involves only imports. While energy conservation may increase the net benefit, it cannot ever be the sole policy instrument used or an efficient allocation will not be attained.

Another possible strategy employs the subsidization of domestic supply. This approach was taken by Congress in establishing the Synthetic Fuel Corporation in 1980 to stimulate and subsidize the development of synthetic fuels.[21] Diagramatically, this would be portrayed in Figure 7.3 as a shift of the domestic supply curve to the right. Notice that the effect would be to reduce the share of imports in total consumption (a desired effect) but not reduce consumption (an inefficient result). While subsidies may be better than nothing, they cannot be the sole solution to the problem, either.

A final approach would tailor the response more closely to the problem. One could use either a tariff on imports equal to the vertical distance between S_{f0} and S_{f1} or a quota on imports equal to $Q_4 - Q_2$. With either of these approaches, the price to consumers would rise to P_1, total consumption would fall to Q_4 and imports would be $Q_4 - Q_2$. In short, when either tariffs or quotas are used correctly with the contingency programs discussed earlier, an efficient allocation may be attained. As Example 7.4 makes clear, however, if these instruments are not used correctly they can cause more harm than good.[22]

There are also some redistributive consequences of the use of tariffs or quotas. Suppose a tariff were imposed in imports equal to $P_1 - P_0$. The area *ABCD* would then represent tariff revenue collected by the government.

If a quota system were used instead of a tariff and the quotas were simply given to importers, area *ABCD* in Figure 7.3 would represent the value of those quotas to the importers, the difference between the cost of the oil and the price at which it can be sold. This explains why importers prefer this system to a tariff system.

The effect of either system on domestic producer surplus should also be noticed. Producers of domestic oil would be better off with a tariff or quota on imported oil than without it. Each raises the cost or reduces the availability of the foreign substitute, which results in higher domestic prices for the product. This result induces producers to produce more, but it also means that they earn higher profits on the oil which would have been produced anyway, echoing the premise that public policies may restore efficiency but also tend to redistribute wealth.

---

[21]During January, 1986, President Reagan signed a bill abolishing the U.S. Synthetic Fuels Corporation, ending its short but turbulent history.

[22]Tariffs could also be used as a weapon to slow down OPEC price increases. See, for example, the provocative proposals in A. P. Lerner, "OPEC—A Plan—If you Can't Beat Them Join Them," *Atlantic Economic Journal* 8 (September 1980): 1–3.

TRANSITION FUELS: ENVIRONMENTAL PROBLEMS

Currently we depend on oil and gas for most of our energy. In the distant future we shall make a transition to renewable sources of energy. How about the intermediate time period?

Though some observers believe the transition to renewable sources will proceed so rapidly that no transition fuels will be necessary, most believe that transition fuels will probably play a significant role. Though there are other contenders, such as natural gas from deep wells, the fuels receiving the most attention as transition fuels are coal and uranium.

Domestic coal is abundantly available. Coal resources are approximately 22 times as large as oil and gas resources combined on a heat-equivalent basis. Neither availability nor dependency on foreign countries is an issue with coal.

Resource availability is a problem with uranium as long as we depend on conventional reactors. However, if the United States moves to the new generation of breeder reactors, which can use a wider range of fuel, availability will cease to be an important issue. On a heat-equivalent basis, domestic uranium resources are 4.2 times as great as domestic oil and gas resources if they are used in conventional reactors. With breeder reactors, the United States uranium resource base is 252 times the size of its oil and gas base.

The main issue defining the role for these two fuels involves their environmental impact. The main drawback from coal is its contribution to air pollution. Its high sulfur content makes it a potentially large source of sulfur dioxide emissions, one of the chief culprits in the acid-rain problem. It is also a source of particulate emissions. Since both of these will be covered later, we shall not consider them any further here except to note that, if those who burn coal fail to consider the costs, the market will foster an excessive reliance on coal.

Coal also shares with the other fossil fuels some responsibility for increasing the amount of carbon dioxide in the air. The balance of carbon dioxide and other gases in the air has traditionally been maintained by complex chemical and physical forces. Over the last two decades or so, an increase in the concentrations of carbon dioxide in the air has occurred. One source of that increase has been the carbon dioxide generated by the combustion of fossil fuels.

One effect on an increased carbon dioxide concentration is an increased temperature on the earth's surface. Labelled the "greenhouse effect," this occurs because the carbon dioxide contains the sun's rays that have been reradiated from the earth's surface, much the same function performed by glass in a greenhouse. The National Research Council, a committee of the prestigious National Academy of Science (NAS), concluded that a fivefold increase in the annual amount of fossil carbon fuels burned over the next 100 years could produce an increase of about 2° to 3° C in mean surface temperature and perhaps 5° to 10° at higher latitudes.[23]

---

[23]National Research Council, *Energy and Climate* (Washington, D.C.: National Academy of Science, 1977).

EXAMPLE 7.4

The Inefficiency of the Mandatory Oil Import Program

In 1959 the Mandatory Oil Import Program was established to protect the United States from what was seen as an increasingly dangerous dependence on foreign oil. This program relied on import quotas as the sole policy measure. We know from the discussion in this chapter that this is an inefficient approach. An exclusive reliance on import quotas fails to take advantage of opportunities to import from more secure sources and it fails to use a stockpile to reduce the vulnerability of remaining imports. Import quotas leave the risk premium of imports too high. Therefore in order to produce the desired amount of safety in the absence of these complementary policies, import quotas must be more stringent (allowing fewer imports) than would normally be the case.

This is illustrated in the accompanying figure, where S_1 is the market supply curve; S_2 is the societal supply curve, which includes the risk premium after accounting for the contingency programs; and S_3 is the societal supply curve which includes the risk premium when no contingency programs are considered. Notice that the "best" quota without the contingency programs $(Q_3 - Q_1)$ implies fewer imports and a smaller net benefit than the quota combined with other measurements $(Q_4 - Q_1)$. The white area represents the loss in net benefits from relying exclusively on import controls.

The demonstration that such losses exist does not establish that they are empirically significant. If they are not, they could be safely ignored. One set of estimates of the size of this inefficiency for the 1960–70 period is provided by Bohi

---

This warming would have both beneficial and detrimental effects. Some increase in agricultural potential would, most certainly, result in relatively northern latitudes with traditionally short growing seasons. On the other hand, increased temperatures could cause major expansions of deserts in normally arid regions.

Many uncertainties are associated with the carbon dioxide problem. Dust and moisture, for example, may mitigate the effects. The NAS report also emphasizes our lack of knowledge about the sources and "sinks" for carbon dioxide. For example, only about half of the current carbon dioxide created by combustion can be accounted for by increases in the atmosphere. Where is the rest going? Neither of the traditional sinks, oceans and plant life, can account for the difference.

Our depletable-resource model suggests what the efficient market response to the carbon dioxide problem would be, if it turns out to be a real problem. The true cost of using coal, as well as oil and gas, would rise, less coal would be used each year, and less would be used cumulatively. Fossil fuels would play a less important role in the transition period. However, NAS found that, since the effects will certainly be small,

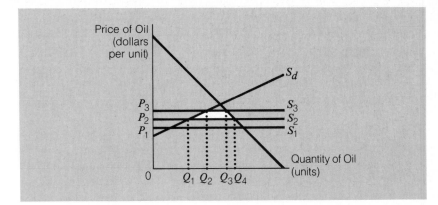

and Russell [1978]. Their conclusion was that the quota was effective in reducing imports, but it accomplished this goal while wasting a significant amount of resources. Specifically, their estimated annual resource cost of the oil import program was $2.3 billion, while a combination of storage policies (sufficient to cover three-fourths of insecure imports for one year) and a tariff yielding comparable security would have cost about $965 million per year, a substantial difference.

Source: Douglas Bohi and Milton Russell, *Limiting Oil Imports: An Economic History and Analysis* (Baltimore: Johns Hopkins University Press for Resources for the Future, 1978).

gradual, and reversible, over the next several decades, most observers believe that coal use should not be discouraged while the problem is further studied.[24]

The other main transition fuel, uranium, used in nuclear electrical generation stations, has its own limitations, principally safety. There are many sources of concern, but two stand out: (1) nuclear accidents, and (2) the storage of radioactive waste. Is the market likely to make the correct decisions on these questions? In both cases the answer is no, given the current decision-making environment. Let's consider these issues one by one.

The production of electricity by nuclear reactors requires radioactive elements. If these elements escape into the atmosphere and come in contact with humans in sufficient concentrations, they produce birth defects, cancer, or death. Some radioactive

---

[24]See, for example, Hans H. Landsberg, ed., *Energy: The Next Twenty Years* (Cambridge, Mass.: Ballinger Publishing Company, 1979): 334. This will be covered in more detail in a later chapter.

elements may also escape during the normal operation of a plant, but the greatest risk of nuclear power is still the threat of nuclear accidents.

Nuclear accidents may inject large doses of radioactivity into the environment. The most dangerous of these possibilities is the core meltdown. Unlike other types of electrical-generation, nuclear processes continue to generate heat even after the reactor is turned off. This means that the nuclear fuel must be continuously cooled or the heat levels will escalate beyond the design capacity of the reactor shield. If, in this case, the reactor vessel should fracture, clouds of radioactive gases and particulates would be released into the atmosphere.

For some time conventional wisdom had held that nuclear accidents involving a core meltdown were a remote possibility. On April 25, 1986, however, a serious core meltdown occurred at the Chernobyl nuclear plant in the Soviet Union. Though safety standards are generally conceded to be much higher in the western developed world than in the Soviet Union, this incident has added yet another burden for an already troubled industry to bear.

Nuclear power has been beset by economic as well as political forces. New nuclear power plant construction has become much more expensive, in part due to the increasing regulatory requirements designed to provide a safer system. Its economic advantage over coal has dissipated and the demand for new nuclear plants has been eliminated. In the United States, for example, in 1973, 219 nuclear power plants were either planned or in operation. By the end of 1986 that number had fallen to 130, the difference being explained by cancellations.[25] No new applications for nuclear plants are pending.

An additional concern relates to storing nuclear wastes. The waste-storage issue relates to both ends of the nuclear-fuel cycle—the disposal of uranium tailings from the mining process and spent fuel from the reactors, though the latter receives most of the publicity. Uranium tailings contain several elements, the most prominent being thorium-230, which decays with a half-life of 78,000 years to a radioactive, chemically inert gas, radon-222. Once formed, this gas has a very short half-life (38 days).

The spent fuel from nuclear reactors contains a variety of radioactive elements with quite different half-lives. In the first few centuries, the dominant contributors to radioactivity are fission products, principally strontium-90 and cesium-137. After approximately 1000 years, most of these elements will have decayed, leaving the transuranic elements having substantially longer half-lives. These remaining elements would remain a risk for up to 250,000 years. Thus, decisions made today affect not only the level of risk borne by the current generation—in the form of nuclear accidents—but also that borne by a host of succeeding generations (due to the longevity of radioactive risk from the disposal of spent fuel).

Can we expect the market to make the correct choice with respect to nuclear power? We might expect the answer for the problem of nuclear accidents to be no, because this seems to be a clear case of externalities. Third parties, those living near the reac-

---

[25]Energy Information Administration, *Monthly Energy Review*, (January, 1986): 84.

FIGURE 7.4   The Efficient Level of Precaution

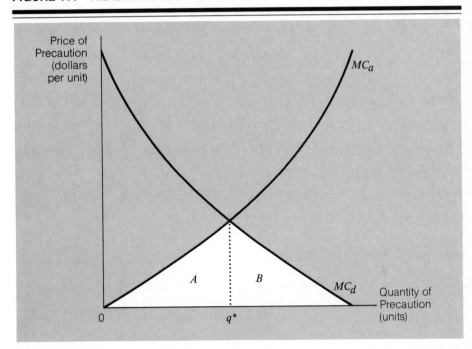

tor, would receive the brunt of the damage from a nuclear accident. Would the utility have an incentive to choose the efficient level of precaution?

If the utility had to compensate fully for all the damages caused, then the answer would be yes. To see why, consider Figure 7.4. The curve labeled MC_a is the marginal cost of damage avoidance. The more precautions that are taken, the higher is the cost of additional measures. The curve labeled MC_d is the marginal cost of damage, suggesting that as more precautionary measures are taken, the additional reduction in damages obtained from those measures declines.

The efficient level of precaution is the one minimizing the sum of the costs of precaution and the costs of the unabated damage. In Figure 7.4 that point is given as point $q*$ and the total cost to society from that choice is represented by the sum of area A and area B.

Will a private utility choose $q*$? Presumably it would, if the curves it actually faces are MC_a and MC_d. The utility would be responsible for the costs of precautionary behavior, so it would face MC_a. How about MC_d? We might guess that the utility would face MC_d because people incurring damages could, through the judicial system, sue for damages. That guess is not correct for two reasons: (1) the role of the government in sharing the risk, and (2) the role of insurance.

When the government first allowed private industry to use atomic power to generate electricity, there were no takers. No utility could afford the damages if an accident occurred. No insurance company would underwrite the risk. Then in 1957, with the passage of the Price-Anderson Act, the government underwrote the liability. That act provided for a liability ceiling of $560 million (once that amount had been paid out no more claims would be honored), of which the government would bear $500 million. The industry would pick up the remaining $60 million. The Act was originally designed to expire in ten years, at which time the industry would assume full responsibility for the liability.

The Act didn't expire, though over time there has been a steady diminution of the government's share of the liability. Currently the liability ceiling still exists, albeit at a higher level; the amount of private insurance has increased; and a system has been set up to assess all utilities by retrospective premium, in the event an accident occurs.

The effect of the Price-Anderson Act is to shift inward the marginal damage curve that any utility faces. Both the liability ceiling and the portion of the liability borne by government reduce the potential compensation the utility would have to pay. As the industry assumes an increasing portion of the liability burden, the risk sharing embodied in the retrospective premium system (the means by which it assumes that burden) breaks the link between precautionary behavior by the individual utility and the compensation it might have to pay. Under this system, increased safety by the utility does not reduce its premiums.

The individual utilities pay into a fund that compensates victims. The important point is that the actual cost of an accident to the utility is not sensitive to the level of precautions it takes. The cost to all utilities, whether they have accidents or not, is the premium paid both before and after any accident. These premiums do not reflect the amount of precautionary measures taken by an individual plant; therefore, there is little incentive for individual utilities to purchase an efficient amount of safety.

In recognition of the utilities' lower-than-efficient concern for safety, the federal government has established the Nuclear Regulatory Commission to oversee the safety of nuclear reactors, among its other responsibilities. In the aftermath of the nuclear accident at Three Mile Island on March 28, 1979, a Presidential Commission was established to provide an independent evaluation of this system of safety regulation. Their final report,[26] issued on October 30, 1979, was highly critical of the existing system and made a series of recommendations to improve it. While the problem of nuclear accidents is manageable in principle, it may or may not be manageable in practice.

Both the operating safety and the nuclear-waste storage issue can be viewed as a problem of determining appropriate compensation. Those who gain from nuclear power should be forced to compensate those who lose. If they can't, in the absence of externalities, the net benefits from adopting nuclear power are not positive. If nuclear power is efficient, by definition the gains to the gainers will exceed the losses to the losers. Nonetheless, it is important that this compensation actually be paid because without compensation, the losers can block the efficient allocation.

A compensation approach is already being taken in other countries. The French government, for example, has announced a policy of reducing electricity rates by roughly

---

[26]The President's Commission on the Accident at Three Mile Island, *The Need for Change: The Legacy of TMI* (New York: Pergamon Press, 1979).

15 percent for those living near nuclear stations. And in Japan during 1980, the Tohoku Electric Power Company paid the equivalent of $4.3 million to residents of Ojika, in northern Japan, to get them to withdraw their opposition to a nuclear power plant being built there.

This approach could also help resolve the current political controversy over the location of nuclear-waste disposal sites. Most plans currently focus on burying the waste in some geologically stable formation. Current and future generations of people living near the chosen sight would have a tendency to oppose nuclear power, since the costs to them appear to outweigh the benefits. To others, however, who may enjoy nuclear-produced electricity and may live far from the sites, the benefits might exceed the costs. This rationale prompted a number of states to pass laws permitting nuclear power but prohibiting the permanent storage of waste in their state.

Under a compensation scheme, those consuming nuclear power should be taxed to compensate those who live in the areas of the disposal site. If the compensation is adequate to induce them to accept the site, then nuclear power is a viable option and the costs of disposal are ultimately borne by the consumers. There are towns such as Naturita, Colorado, which are actively seeking to become disposal sites. If taxes to obtain a sufficient number of disposal sites are so high that nuclear energy becomes noncompetitive, then nuclear energy is not an efficient source.

Are future generations adequately represented in this transaction? The quick answer is no, but that answer is not correct. Those living around the sites will experience declines in the market value of land reflecting the increased risk of living or working there. The payment system is designed to compensate those who experience the reduction, the current generation. Future generations, should they decide to live near a disposal site, would be compensated by lower land values. If the land values were not cheap enough to compensate them, they would not have to live there. Those who do bear the cost by locating near the sites do so only if they are willing to accept the risk in return for lower land values.

At this stage there seems no inclination on the part of our federal government to move to this kind of system. The failure to do so, however, may be quite detrimental. Should the government force the sites on local residents without adequate compensation for the surrounding land, nuclear energy will be underpriced and overused.

CONSERVATION AND LOAD MANAGEMENT

As the previous discussion indicated, there are problems associated with the transition fuels which present particular difficulties for generating electrical power. While alternative fuels and solar power will eventually play an increasing role, most experts seem to feel that they will penetrate the market slowly as they become more familiar and accessible. How then is the transition to these long-term solutions to be managed by the electrical utilities sector in light of the problems associated with the transition fuels?

For a number of utilities, conservation has assumed an increasing role. To a major extent conservation has already been stimulated by market forces. High oil and natural gas prices, coupled with the rapidly increasing cost of both nuclear and coal-fired generating stations, have reduced electrical demand significantly. Yet many Public Utilities Commissions, the state bodies charged with regulating the production, transmission, and sale of electricity, are coming to the conclusion that more conservation is needed.

Perhaps the most significant role for conservation is its ability to defer capacity expansion. Each new electrical generating plant tends to cost more than the last and frequently the cost increase is substantial. When the new plants come on line, rate increases to finance the new plant are necessary. By reducing the demand for electricity, conservation delays the date when new capacity is needed to satisfy the higher demand, which delays the rate increases as well.

The dominant electricity pricing system is ill-designed to stimulate the efficient amount of conservation. Average-cost pricing is common. This pricing system implies that the new higher-cost sources are averaged in with the lower-cost sources, yielding a rate which is substantially lower than the true marginal cost of the power being generated. Thus the consumer considering investing in conservation will save less money by conserving with average cost pricing than would be the case if the energy saved were priced at its true marginal cost. Less than an efficient amount of conservation would be the expected outcome.

Utilities are reacting to this situation in a number of ways. One is to consider investing in conservation, rather than in new plants, when conservation is the cheaper alternative. The thrust of these programs can be illustrated by referring to a few of the programs instituted by the Pacific Gas and Electric Company (P, G & E), a leader in the field. P, G and E has established a system of rebates for residential customers to install conservation measures in their homes, has provided free home weatherization to qualified low-income homeowners, has offered owners of multi-family residential buildings incentives for installing solar water heating systems, and has provided subsidized energy audits to inform customers about money-saving conservation opportunities. Similar incentives have been provided to the commercial, agricultural, and industrial sectors. P, G & E reports that the savings have been dramatic and customer satisfaction has been high.[27]

The total amount of electrical energy demanded in a given year is not the only concern utilities have. They are also concerned with how that energy demand is spread out over the year. The capacity of the system must be high enough to satisfy the demand even during the periods when the energy demand is highest (called peak periods). During the other periods, much of the capacity remains underutilized.

Demand during the peak period imposes two rather special costs on utilities. First, the peaking units, those generating facilities fired up only during the peak periods, produce electricity at a much higher marginal cost than do base load plants, those fired up virtually all the time. Typically peaking units are cheaper to build than base-load plants, but they have higher operating costs. Second, it is the growth in peak demand

---

[27]Pacific Gas and Electric Company, *Report on 1984 Energy Management and Conservation Activities* (San Francisco, CA: 1985).

that frequently triggers the need for capacity expansion. By slowing down the growth in peak demand, the need for new expensive capacity expansion may be delayed.

Utilities are also responding to this problem by adopting load-management techniques to produce a more balanced use of this capacity over the year. One economic load-management technique is called *peak-load pricing*. Peak-load pricing attempts to impose the full (higher) marginal cost of supplying peak power on those consuming peak power by charging higher prices during the peak period.

While many utilities have now begun to use simple versions of this approach, some are experimenting with very innovative ways of implementing a rather refined version of this system. In Brighton, England, for example, a system is being tested which transmits electricity prices every five minutes over regular power lines. In a customer's household the lines attached to one or more appliances can be controlled by switches which turn the power off any time the prevailing price exceeded a limit established by the customer. Other less-sophisticated pricing systems simply inform consumers in advance the prices that will prevail in predetermined peak periods.

A recent study by economists at the Rand Corporation in California indicates that even the rudimentary versions of peak-load pricing work.[28] Based on the actual experience with time-of-day rates by more than 6,000 commercial and industrial customers, they found that business customers saved themselves and utilities on average $1,000 per year for an added metering cost of only $50. Working with an additional sample of over 3000, the authors found residential customers also saved by shifting some of their demand to less expensive periods. The greatest shifts were registered by the largest residential customers and those with several electrical appliances.

Interestingly, this study found the gains from peak-load pricing in the United States to be somewhat lower than those reported for European customers, who have been exposed to peak-load pricing for a longer period of time. Attributing the larger European response in part to the longer time Europeans have had to adapt to this system, the authors speculate that the longer-term response by U.S. customers could turn out to be quite a bit greater than already recorded.

SUMMARY

We have seen that the relationship between government and the market is not always positive. In the past, price controls have tended to reduce energy conservation; to discourage exploration and supply; to cause biases in the substitution among fuel types to penalize future consumers; and to create the potential for abrupt, discontinuous tran-

---

[28]Jan Paul Acton, *et.al.*, *Time-of-day electricity Rates for the United States* (Santa Monica, CA: Rand Corporation Report #R-3086-HF, 1983) and Rolla Edward Park and Jan Paul Acton, *Response to Time-of-Day Electricity Rates by Large Business Customers: Initial Analysis of Data from Ten U.S. Utilities* (Santa Monica, CA: Rand Corporation Report #R-3080-HF/MD/RC, 1983).

sitions to renewable sources. In this important area there seems a clear case for less, not more, regulation.

That is not universally true, however, Other dimensions of the energy problem suggest the need for some government role. In particular, insecure foreign sources require tariffs and stockpiles to reduce vulnerability and to balance the true costs of imported and domestic sources. In addition, government should ensure that the costs of energy fully reflect the potentially large environmental costs. Government should also oversee nuclear reactor safety and should ensure that communities forced to accept nuclear waste disposal sites are fully compensated. Given the environmental difficulties with both of the traditional transition fuels (coal and uranium), conservation and load-management techniques are now playing and will continue to play a larger role in the electric utilities sector. Subsidizing conservation where it is cheaper for the utility than capacity expansion, and peak-load pricing are two economic measures that have been instrumental in ushering in this greater role. The potential for an efficient allocation of energy resources by the economic and political institutions clearly exists, even if historically it has not always occurred.

FURTHER READING

Duchesneau, Thomas D. *Competition in the U.S. Energy Industry*. (Cambridge, Massachusetts: Ballinger Publishing Company, 1975). Funded as part of a major Ford Foundation study of energy, this study examines how competitive the U.S. energy industry is. Concludes that "concentration levels have not reached a level where one would feel certain that market forces, if allowed to operate without government interference, are incapable of allocating resources efficiently. Present market structures are not monopolistic."

Griffin, James M., and Henry B. Steele, *Energy Economics and Policy*. 2nd ed. (New York: Academic Press, 1986). A very readable textbook on energy economics aimed at undergraduates with one course in the principles of economics. Covers OPEC, environmental issues, national security, conservation, price controls, and market structure regulations, as well as energy research and development.

Landsberg, Hans H., ed. *Energy: The Next Twenty Years* (Cambridge, Mass.: Ballinger Publishing Company, 1979). A comprehensive report combining the effort of 19 experts across the country funded by the Ford Foundation. Contains nine recommendations including decontrol of oil and natural-gas prices, development of an effective oil stockpile program, improving the acceptability of coal, vigorous pursuit of conservation, and removal of impediments to the use of solar power.

Schurr, Sam H. *et al. Energy in America's Future: The Choice before Us*. (Baltimore: Johns Hopkins Press for Resources for the Future, 1979). A monumental, twenty-chapter book attempting to synthesize what is known and not known about energy demand, supply, health, safety, and environmental issues and the process of making energy choices. Concludes "it will be possible to fulfill the expansionist requirement that enough energy will be available to support economic growth while meeting the conservationist demand that energy use be lessened substantially from what previously was thought to be the necessary minimum."

Stobaugh, Robert, and Daniel Yergin, eds. *Energy Future: Report of the Energy Project at the Harvard Business School.* (New York: Random House, 1979). A nontechnical, almost chatty collection of essays concerning the near term energy choices for America written by persons associated with the Harvard Business School as students or faculty. Concludes the only viable program that would politically reduce dependence on foreign oil is for the government to give financial incentives to encourage conservation and the use of solar energy.

Walton, A. L., and E. H. Warren, Jr. *The Solar Alternative: An Economic Perspective* (Englewood Cliffs: Prentice-Hall, Inc., 1982). A short, uncomplicated introduction to the economics of solar energy including chapters on market distortions and the equity issues associated with a transition to solar power.

Webb, Michael G., and Martin J. Ricketts, *The Economics of Energy* (New York: John Wiley and Sons, Inc., 1980). Written by two British economists and aimed at undergraduates who have had intermediate microeconomic theory. This textbook is particularly rich in examples drawn from the British experience.

ADDITIONAL REFERENCES

Adelman, M. A. *The World Petroleum Market* (Baltimore: Johns Hopkins Press for Resources for the Future, 1972).

Arrow, Kenneth J. and Joseph P. Kalt, *Petroleum Price Regulation: Should We Decontrol?* (Washington, D.C.: American Enterprise Institute, 1979).

Bohi, Douglas R. and Milton Russell. *Limiting Oil Imports: An Economic History and Analysis* (Baltimore: Johns Hopkins University Press for Resources for the Future, 1978).

Cropper, M. L. "Pollution Aspects of Nuclear Energy Use," *Journal of Environmental Economics and Management,* Vol. 7 (December, 1980): 334–52.

Griffin, James M., "OPEC Behavior: A Test of Alternative Hypotheses", *The American Economic Review,* Vol. 75, No. 5 (December, 1985): 954–963.

Lerner, A. P. "OPEC – A Plan – If You Can't Beat Them, Join Them." *Atlantic Economic Journal,* Vol. 8 (September, 1980): 1–3.

Lind, Robert C., *et al. Discounting for Time and Risk in Energy Policy* (Washington, D.C.: Resources for the Future, Inc., 1982).

Nichols, A. L. and R. J. Zeckhauser. "Stockpiling Strategies and Cartel Prices," *Bell Journal of Economics,* Vol. 7 (Spring, 1976): 66–96.

The President's Commission on the Accident at Three Mile Island, *The Need for Change: The Legacy of TMI* (New York: Pergamon Press, 1979).

Salant, S. W. "Exhaustible Resources and Industrial Structure: A Nash-Cournot Approach to the World Oil Market," *Journal of Political Economy,* 84 (1976): 1079–93.

Teisberg, Thomas. "A Dynamic Programming Model of the U.S. Strategic Petroleum Reserve," *The Bell Journal of Economics,* Vol. 12 (Autumn, 1981): 526–46.

World Energy Conference, *World Energy Resources: 1985–2020* (New York: IPC Science and Technology Press, 1978).

DISCUSSION QUESTIONS

1. Should benefit/cost analysis play the dominant role in deciding the proportion of American electrical energy to be supplied by nuclear power? Why or why not?

2. One economist (Lerner [1980]) proposed that the United States impose a tariff on oil imports equal to 100 percent of the import price. This tariff is designed to reduce dependence on foreign sources as well as to discourage OPEC from raising prices (since, due to the tariff, the delivered price would rise twice as much as the OPEC increase, causing a large subsequent reduction in consumption). Should this proposal become public policy? Why or why not?

PROBLEMS

1. During a worldwide recession in 1983 the oil cartel began to lower prices. Why would a recession make the cartel more vulnerable to price cutting? How would the reduced demand be shared between the competitive fringe and the cartel members in the absence of this price cutting?

2. Assume the demand and marginal cost conditions given in the first problem in Chapter 2 as well as a competitive market to allocate the product. In addition assume that the government imposes a price control at $P = \$80/3$. (a) Find the consumer and producer surplus associated with the resulting allocation. (b) Compare this allocation to the monopoly allocation in the second problem in Chapter 3.

3. Recently a conflict between a paper company and a coalition of environmental groups arose over the potential use of a Maine river for hydroelectric power generation. As one aspect of its case for developing the dam, the paper company argued that without hydroelectric power the energy cost of operating five particular paper machines would be so high that they would have to be shut down. Environmental groups countered that the energy cost was estimated to be too high by the paper company only because it was assigning all of the high cost (oil-fired) power to these particular machines. That was seen as inappropriate because all machines were connected to the same electrical grid and therefore drew power from all sources, not merely the high-cost sources. They suggested, therefore, that the appropriate cost to assign to the machines was the much lower average cost. Revenue from these machines was expected to be sufficient to cover this average cost. Who was right?

4. In the section of this chapter dealing with load management by the utilities, it was mentioned that peaking plants are typically cheap to build (compared to base-load plants), but that they have relatively high operating costs. Explain why it makes sense for utilities to use this low capital, but high operating cost type of plant for peaking and the high capital, but low operating cost type of plant for base-load.

CHAPTER EIGHT

Depletable, Recyclable Resources: Minerals

*The Nation is in the position of a man, who, bequeathed a
fortune, has gone on spending it recklessly, never taking the
trouble to ask the amount of his inheritance, or how long it is
likely to last.*

NATIONAL CONSERVATION COMMISSION (1908)

INTRODUCTION

Once used, energy resources dissipate into heat energy. They cannot be recycled. Mineral resources, in contrast, retain their basic physical and chemical properties during use and under the proper conditions can be recycled or reused. They therefore represent a separate category for us to examine.

What is an efficient amount of recycling? Will the market automatically generate this amount in the absence of government intervention? How does the efficient allocation over time differ between recyclable and nonrecyclable resources? The phrase *planned obsolescence* is sometimes used to suggest that industries have an incentive to produce products with a short life span. Does the market produce an efficient level of product durability? What impact does product durability have on the allocation of virgin and recycled materials?

We shall begin our investigation by describing how an efficient market in recyclable, depletable resources would work. We then use this as a benchmark to examine specific ways in which the actual allocation may diverge from this ideal. We close by relating our findings back to the central question of growth in a finite environment.

AN EFFICIENT ALLOCATION OF RECYCLABLE RESOURCES

Extraction and Disposal Cost

How would an efficient market, one devoid of any imperfections, allocate recyclable mineral resources? The models developed in Chapter 6 provide a point of departure for answering this question. In the earliest periods, reliance would generally be exclusively on the virgin ore, because it is cheapest. As more concentrated ores are extracted, the mining industry would turn to the lower-grade ores and to foreign sources for higher-grade ores.

In the presence of technological progress, the increasing reliance on the lower-grade ores would not necessarily precipitate an increase in cost (as shown in Example 6.2), at least initially. Eventually, however, as the sources became increasingly difficult to extract, a point would be reached when the costs of extraction and prices of the virgin material would begin to rise.

At the same time, the costs of disposing of the products, once the consumer is done with them, would probably rise. For example, over the last two centuries the United States has experienced a large increase in the geographic concentrations of people. The attraction of cities and exodus from farms led an increasingly large number of Americans to live in urban or near-urban environments.

This concentration creates waste-disposal problems. Historically, when land was plentiful, waste could be buried. But as land became scarce and expensive, burial was no longer economically viable, particularly in cities. In addition, concerns over environmental effects have made buried waste less attractive.

The rising costs of virgin materials and of waste disposal have increased the attractiveness of recycling. By recovering and reintroducing materials into the system, recycling provides an alternative to virgin ores, and also reduces the waste-disposal load.

Consumers, as well as manufacturers, play a role on both the demand and supply side of the market. On the demand side, consumers would find that products depending exclusively on virgin raw materials are subject to higher prices than those relying on recycled materials. Consequently, consumers would have a tendency to switch to products made with the cheaper, recycled raw materials, as long as quality is not adversely affected. This powerful incentive is called the *composition of demand effect*.

As long as consumers bear the cost of disposal, they have the additional incentive to return their used recyclable products to collection centers. By doing so they avoid disposal costs, while at the same time reaping financial rewards for supplying a product someone wants.

For some materials it is more costly for consumers to do the separation and recovery of materials and thus more efficient for municipal agencies to accomplish recycling. One example is currently operating in Saugus, Massachusetts, a North Shore suburb of Boston, processing up to 1500 tons of Boston refuse per day. From this waste, the facility annually recovers some 25,000 tons of ferrous metals and 40,000 tons of other materials suitable for use in construction. In addition, the plant is capable of producing two billion pounds of steam annually, which it sells to a nearby General Electric plant.[1]

Recycling: A Closer Look

The model in the preceding section would lead us to expect that recycling would increase over time as virgin ore and disposal costs rose. This seems to be the case. Take copper, for example. During 1910, recycled copper accounted for about 18 percent of the total production of refined copper in the U.S. By 1977 this percentage had risen to 49 percent.

Though these percentages may seem low, in most cases recycling is not cheap. Transport and processing costs are usually significant. The sources of scrap are usually concentrated around cities, where the products are used, while for historical reasons the producing facilities are concentrated near the sources of the virgin materials. Scrap materials must first be transported to the production facility; then there are additional expenses in collecting, separating, and processing them. Even when there is acute scarcity, nowhere near 100 percent of the materials are recycled; costs don't permit it!

As recycling becomes cost competitive, rather dramatic changes occur in the manufacturing process. Not only do manufacturers rely more heavily on recycled inputs, they also begin to design their products to facilitate recycling. Facilitating recycling through product design is already important in industries where the connection between the manufacturer and disposal agent is particularly close. Telephone companies, for example, are responsible for cleaning up after installations; to avoid disposal costs, the companies have designed products and procedures that facilitate the recycling of the scrap copper wire. Special recycling bags are used to separate the waste and hence to lower collection costs. In addition, the manufacturing process avoids insulating materials difficult to separate from copper. Aircraft manufacturers, which often are asked to scrap old aircraft, may stamp the alloy composition on parts during manufacturing to facilitate recycling.[2]

Recycling and Virgin Ore Depletion

How does the efficient allocation of a recyclable resource over time compare with that of a nonrecyclable resource? Thinking back to the models in Chapter 6, perhaps the most important difference occurs in the timing of the switch point. As long as the resource can be recycled at a marginal cost lower than that of the substitute, the market tends to rely on the recyclable resource longer than it does on a nonrecyclable resource with an identical extraction cost curve. This should not be surprising, since the effect of recycling is simply to add more of the resource.

---

[1] Example taken from "RESCO's Saugus Plant Pioneers Solid Waste-to-Steam Approach," *Solid Waste Magazine* (October, 1978).

[2] Council on Environmental Quality, *Environmental Quality—1980* (Washington, D.C.: U.S. Government Printing Office, 1980), p. 221.

This point can be illustrated using a simple numerical example. Suppose there exist 100 units of a resource in a product with a useful life of one year. Suppose further that 90 percent of the resource could be recovered and reused after one year. During the first year, the full 100 units could be used. At the end of the first year, 90 percent could be recovered, leaving 90 units for the second year. At the end of the second year, 90 percent of the remaining 90 units could once again be recovered, leaving 81 units for the third year, and so on.

How much more of this resource was made available by recycling? Algebraically, if we let the original stock be A, and the recovery rate be r, then the total amount used would be an infinite sum of the form $A + Ar + Ar^2 + Ar^3$. It turns out that the sum of this series as time becomes infinitely long is $A/(1 - r)$. Notice that nonrecyclable resources are represented by the special case where $r = 0$. In this case the sum of resource use equals the available stock. Whenever $r > 0.0$, however, as it would be when any of the resource was recycled, the sum of the resource flows exceeds the size of the stock. The closer to 1.0 r is, the larger the sum of the resource flows. For example if $r = 0.9$, as it was in our example, the sum of the flows is ten times the size of the stock. The effect of recycling is to increase the size of the available resources by a factor of ten.

This formulation also points out another feature of recycling. Unless the recycling rate is 100 percent ($r = 1.0$) the sum of the resource flows is finite. This means that while some recycled materials can be recycled forever, the amount will become infinitesimally small as time goes on.

An efficient economic system will orchestrate a balance between the consumption of depletable and recycled materials, between disposing of used products and recycling, and between imports and domestic production. Example 8.1 provides an example of how an efficient market can work. Mercury is an appropriate example because, according to the static reserve index, it is very scarce.

How close are we to efficiency? Have we achieved an efficient balance between imports and domestic production? Is the common pejorative notion that we are a "throwaway society" an accurate one? If so, is the market behaving efficiently — in the sense that the time for recycling has not yet come — or are there clearly identified sources of market failure, implying that the wrong price signals are being sent? The next few sections investigate these issues. Let's begin by examining the balance between domestic and foreign sources.

THE STRATEGIC-MATERIAL PROBLEM REVISITED

General Principles

Oil is not the only substance for which the United States demand has outpaced domestic supply, necessitating an increased importation. When these imports are of strategic importance in wartime situations and/or are supplied by a relatively few foreign producers, they require special treatment. As we saw in the last chapter, this situation implies that

EXAMPLE 8.1

Mercury Prices and Recycling

Mercury provides an interesting example of how a depletable recyclable resource can be allocated over time in a manner consistent with the principles discussed earlier in this chapter. It is a resource where the ratio of proved reserves to current consumption is quite low, suggesting that scarcity could be a factor. The historical experience with mercury prices and production is presented in the accompanying figure. In the early 1850s price did not rise very much as production rose. After the peak production in the 1870s, however, prices began to rise and production began to fall.

Very little mercury was recycled initially, but the importance of recycling rose with prices. By 1979, a year in which prices were higher after several years of depressed prices and production, the domestic production of mercury was 29,519 flasks, while 4,287 flasks came from recycling. Even with higher prices, recycling accounted for only about 14 percent of the total amount consumed during that year. The costs of recycling prevented a larger contribution, even in the face of scarcity. Major sources of recycled mercury were industrial and control instruments, batteries, sludges, and dental amalgams.

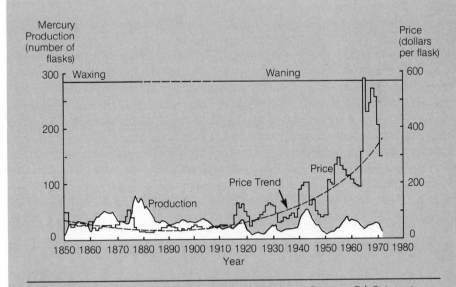

Source: E.H. Bailey, A.L. Clark, and R.M. Smith, in *United States Minerals Resources*, D.A. Brobst and W.P. Pratt, eds. (U.S. Geological Survey, Washington D.C., 1973), figure 46, p. 404.

FIGURE 8.1   Net Import Reliance As a Percent of Consumption, 1982

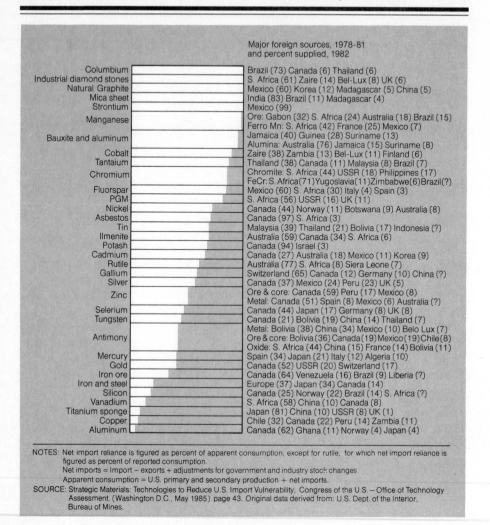

Major foreign sources, 1978-81 and percent supplied, 1982

Mineral	Major foreign sources
Columbium	Brazil (73) Canada (6) Thailand (6)
Industrial diamond stones	S. Africa (61) Zaire (14) Bel-Lux (8) UK (6)
Natural Graphite	Mexico (60) Korea (12) Madagascar (5) China (5)
Mica sheet	India (83) Brazil (11) Madagascar (4)
Strontium	Mexico (99)
Manganese	Ore: Gabon (32) S. Africa (24) Australia (18) Brazil (15)
	Ferro Mn: S. Africa (42) France (25) Mexico (7)
Bauxite and aluminum	Jamaica (40) Guinea (28) Suriname (13)
	Alumina: Australia (76) Jamaica (15) Suriname (8)
Cobalt	Zaire (38) Zambia (13) Bel-Lux (11) Finland (6)
Tantaium	Thailand (38) Canada (11) Malaysia (8) Brazil (7)
Chromium	Chromite: S. Africa (44) USSR (18) Philippines (17)
	FeCr: S. Africa (71) Yugoslavia (11) Zimbabwe (6) Brazil (?)
Fluorspar	Mexico (60) S. Africa (30) Italy (4) Spain (3)
PGM	S. Africa (56) USSR (16) UK (11)
Nickel	Canada (44) Norway (11) Botswana (9) Australia (8)
Asbestos	Canada (97) S. Africa (3)
Tin	Malaysia (39) Thailand (21) Bolivia (17) Indonesia (?)
Ilmenite	Australia (59) Canada (34) S. Africa (6)
Potash	Canada (94) Israel (3)
Cadmium	Canada (27) Australia (18) Mexico (11) Korea (9)
Rutile	Australia (77) S. Africa (8) Siera Leone (7)
Gallium	Switzerland (65) Canada (12) Germany (10) China (?)
Silver	Canada (37) Mexico (24) Peru (23) UK (5)
Zinc	Ore & core: Canada (59) Peru (17) Mexico (8)
	Metal: Canada (51) Spain (8) Mexico (6) Australia (?)
Selerium	Canada (44) Japan (17) Germany (8) UK (8)
Tungsten	Canada (21) Bolivia (19) China (14) Thailand (7)
	Metal: Bolivia (38) China (34) Mexico (10) Belo Lux (7)
Antimony	Ore & core: Bolivia (36) Canada (19) Mexico (19) Chile (8)
	Oxide: S. Africa (44) China (15) France (14) Bolivia (11)
Mercury	Spain (34) Japan (21) Italy (12) Algeria (10)
Gold	Canada (52) USSR (20) Switzerland (17)
Iron ore	Canada (64) Venezuela (16) Brazil (9) Liberia (?)
Iron and steel	Europe (37) Japan (34) Canada (14)
Silicon	Canada (25) Norway (22) Brazil (14) S. Africa (?)
Vanadium	S. Africa (58) China (10) Canada (8)
Titanium sponge	Japan (81) China (10) USSR (8) UK (1)
Copper	Chile (32) Canada (22) Peru (14) Zambia (11)
Aluminum	Canada (62) Ghana (11) Norway (4) Japan (4)

NOTES: Net import reliance is figured as percent of apparent consumption, except for rutile, for which net import reliance is figured as percent of reported consumption.
Net imports = Import − exports + adjustments for government and industry stock changes
Apparent consumption = U.S. primary and secondary production + net imports.
SOURCE: Strategic Materials: Technologies to Reduce U.S. Import Vulnerability, Congress of the U.S. − Office of Technology Assessment, (Washington D.C., May 1985) page 43. Original data derived from: U.S. Dept. of the Interior, Bureau of Mines.

the true social cost of these resources is higher than their market price. If this divergence is large enough, some government corrective action may be appropriate.

The appropriate policy response would be to establish a tariff on imports of the strategic material and use the proceeds to finance a stockpile. This stockpile would provide a form of insurance against supply disruptions by providing a rapid-response alternative source of supply. The tariff would signal the social cost of the resources and thereby encourage domestic production and a search for substitutes. By using the tariff revenues to finance the stockpile, those who are creating the vulnerability, by demanding the resource, would pay the cost of protecting against it.

The first step in defining a list of vulnerable strategic minerals is to identify those for which foreign sources of supply are particularly important. Figure 8.1 lists many

YOUR PREMIER PUBLISHER IN ECONOMICS & FINANCE

ADDISON WESLEY LONGMAN

Request your complimentary examination copy today! E-mail information below to exam@awl.com, fax to 1.800.284.8292, or mail this card.

AWL book title _____ Book author _____

Book ISBN _____ Edition _____

Course title _____ Course number _____

Name _____ Department _____

Text in use (author/title) _____ School _____

Estimated annual enrollment _____ Address _____

Adoption decision date (month/year) ❑ Individual ❑ Committee   City/State/Zip _____

e-mail address _____ Phone _____

P718/9/98

SAMP.#	STATE	COLL.NO.

BUSINESS REPLY MAIL

FIRST CLASS   PERMIT NO. 11   READING, MA

Postage Will Be Paid By Addressee

Addison Wesley Longman
Attn: Jennifer Thalmann
One Jacob Way
Reading, MA 01867-9903

common minerals and the level of imports as a percentage of apparent consumption, as well as the major foreign sources of these imports.

For the 42 most critical minerals—as defined by the government—the United States is dependent on foreign sources for more than 50 percent of 24 of them. Four of these—cobalt, chromium, manganese, platinum—receive the lion's share of attention. South Africa, a country with which the United States has had turbulent relations over their racial policy of apartheid, is a major supplier of three of the four minerals. The fourth, cobalt, comes primarily from the African nations of Zambia and Zaire. Clearly the strategic-minerals problem is not a trivial one.

Government Response

The Strategic and Critical Materials Stockpiling Act of 1946 initiated the first major government program to protect defense needs during a wartime. Since that time the program has had a checkered history. In 1954, for example, the Agricultural Trade Development and Assistance Act authorized the acquisition of strategic materials with the foreign currencies obtained from the sale of surplus agricultural commodities. This authority was subsequently revoked in 1966 by the Food for Peace Act.

The two main laws currently guiding materials policy are the Strategic and Critical Materials Stockpiling Revision Act of 1979, and National Materials and Minerals Policy, Research and Development Act of 1980. These laws consolidated a number of separately mandated stockpiles into a single program and provided specific guidance to the President on determining the materials to be included in the stockpile and the quantities of each to be stockpiled.

The 1979 Act also created a National Defense Stockpile Transaction Fund to receive funds from sales of resources in the stockpile and to support purchases of resources for the stockpiles when actual levels fell below desired levels. Currently the national defense stockpile goals require a reserve adequate to supply the material requirements of the first three years of a conventional war, after subtracting the amounts available from domestic sources and secure foreign sources.[3]

Cobalt: A Case Study

To apply these principles, we must consider a particular mineral. Cobalt provides a particularly interesting example because it is generally considered to be one of the most strategic and vulnerable of our imported minerals.[4]

Cobalt alloys are important to a number of American industries, especially aerospace

---

[3]For more on these policies, see U.S. General Accounting Office, *Actions Needed to Promote a Stable Supply of Strategic and Critical Minerals and Materials,* Report #GAO/EMD-82-69 (3 June 1982).

[4]This section was based upon Richard J. Barbera, *Cobalt: Policy Options for a Strategic Mineral* (Washington, D.C.: Congressional Budget Office, 1982); Daniel Fine, "A Cobalt War May Endanger U.S. Security," *Business Week* (8 November 1982); 58, 63; Cheryl Simon, "Cobalt Crusts: Deep Deposits," *Science News* 122 (30 October 1982); 283, and "Cobalt" in Bureau of Mines, *Mineral Commodities Summaries: 1984* (Washington, D.C.: U.S. Department of the Interior, 1984).

and defense. Its properties make it particularly useful in high-temperature settings such as jet engines. Short-term substitution possibilities are limited.

At present the United States produces none of its own cobalt. Therefore, all supplies come from reduction in stockpiles, recycling, or foreign producers. Currently about 7 percent of American consumption comes from recycling.

The supply situation has been volatile. During the 1970s, cobalt prices rose from $5.50 per pound to $25 per pound; spot prices went as high as $50 at one point. As of May 1982, the price had fallen to $12.40 and during October 1982, Zaire offered some 2000 tons at only $5.80 a pound.

The American government responded erratically; although a cobalt stockpile has existed for some time, the appropriateness of its size has been the subject of much debate. Major purchases occurred throughout the 1950s, but in 1973, during the Nixon Administration, millions of pounds of cobalt were sold from the stockpile. In late 1976 the Ford Administration effectively reversed that decision and a new goal of 85.4 million pounds was established. As of 1983 about 54 percent of that target level had been reached.

Subsequently, President Reagan issued a report calling for subsidies to domestic producers as another means of coping with cobalt vulnerability. Officials of the Anschutz Mining Corporation were reportedly seeking a federally guaranteed price of $28.50 per pound to open their Fredericktown, Missouri, mine while Noranda Mining sought $25 per pound to open its mine in Blackbird, Idaho. If the federal government were to purchase the approximately 40 million pounds needed to bring the stockpile up to its target level from these domestic producers at $25 a pound rather than from Zaire at $10 a pound, the additional cost would be $600 million.

The fact that the stockpile is not yet at the target level is not the only problem with current policy. As of January 1, 1984, all cobalt ores and concentrates could enter the country free of tariffs.[5] Since a tariff is an important part of an efficient policy package, we have not yet achieved an efficient allocation of this resource.

Substitution and Vulnerability

The vulnerability of a nation importing a strategic mineral depends not only on the severity of the shortfall it could experience, but also on its ability to cope with the shortfall. Coping in this context may be accomplished either by substituting other materials for the one in short supply or suffering the resulting reduction in output. In assessing vulnerability, therefore, it is important to take the costs of both substitution and abstinence into account.

Some recent work by Hazilla and Kopp (1984) attempts to accomplish this difficult task within the context of a detailed econometric model of the production process. The various production processes involving five specific strategic minerals—titanium, vanadium, cobalt, columbium, and cadmium—were modeled. These models included

---

[5]"Cobalt" in Bureau of Mines, *Mineral Commodities Summaries: 1984* (Washington, D.C.: U.S. Department of the Interior, 1984): 36–37.

not only substitution possibilities and their associated costs, but the costs to society from any resulting reduced output as well. To quantify the degree of vulnerability the authors estimated the total cost to the U.S. economy that would be expected to result from various levels of shortfalls of these strategic materials (Table 8.1).

Two interesting insights emerge from this information. First small disruptions, loosely defined as those involving 35 percent or less of the available supply, could be handled without serious impact on the economy, but disruptions larger than that could be quite serious. Second, the vulnerability ranking depends on the size of the shortfall. For small shortfalls the scarcity of titanium imposes the largest cost on society. Notice, however, that when the shortage is in the range of 50 percent, cobalt presents a more serious problem. For shortfalls of 85 percent, the largest costs are imposed by shortages of vanadium. No one mineral imposes the highest cost in all shortfall scenarios.

This econometric approach has the substantial virtue that it allows the analyst to ask the kind of "what if" questions that give rise to the estimates in Table 8.1. It also has the disadvantage, however, that it is so general that the particular details of substitution are buried in the mathematics. Other authors therefore have attempted to learn more of the details by doing case studies of particular minerals.

One such study by Tilton (1983) examined the substitution effects resulting from the rapid rise of tin prices during the 1970's. Three particular uses of tin were selected for study—beverage containers, solder, and tin-based chemicals used in manufacturing plastic pipe.

Substantial substitution was uncovered. The tinplate beverage can, for example, after years of increasing its share of the market, began in the 1960s to lose market share, first to aluminum cans and ultimately to plastic bottles. As this was going on new technologies reduced the amount of tin in the average tinplate beverage can by over 93 percent between 1950 and 1977. Even the use of solder, thought by many to be impervious to substitution, was reduced as the introduction of low-tin alloys reduced the need for high-tin-content solder in automobile bodies. Similarly, in the plastic pipe industry, the introduction of new second- and third generation stabilizers reduced the tin content by over 50 percent.

Based on this analysis, the Tilton study concluded that changes in material prices seem to have had little effect on materials usage in the short run, because producers

TABLE 8.1 Mineral Supply Disruption Scenarios (Cost in Millions of 1974 Dollars)

Shortfall	Titanium	Vanadium	Cobalt	Columbium	Cadmium
5%	23	19	6	6	—
15%	69	38	12	11	—
25%	140	98	30	35	—
35%	198	159	49	46	1
50%	340	21532	25667	17136	2
85%	33475	80752	74976	78800	4

Source: Data extracted from Michael Hazilla and Raymond J. Kopp, "Assessing U.S. Vulnerability to Raw Material Supply Disruptions: An Application to Nonfuel Minerals," *Southern Economic Journal*, Vol. 52, No. 2 (October, 1984): Table IV., p. 351.

are constrained by existing technologies and equipment. Over the long run, however, they can have a significant effect.

WASTE DISPOSAL AND POLLUTION DAMAGE

The stratetic mineral problem suggests that an imperfection may arise in the way the market reacts to imports *vis a vis* domestically produced minerals. When the imports are critically important and come from risky sources, the market perceives a price ratio which fails to incorporate some of these social costs of imports. The result would be an inefficient and excessive reliance on imports.

There are other market imperfections as well. The treatment of waste by producers and consumers can lead to biases in the market balance between recycling and the use of virgin ores. Since disposal cost is a key ingredient in determining the efficient amount of recycling, the failure of an economic agent to bear the full cost of disposal implies a bias toward virgin materials and away from recycling. We begin by considering the disposal of potentially recyclable waste.

The Disposal Decision

There are two types of scrap: old scrap and new scrap. *New scrap* is composed of the residual materials generated during production. For example, as steel beams are formed, the small remnants of steel left over are new scrap. *Old scrap* is recovered from products used by consumers.

To illustrate the relative importance of new scrap and old scrap, consider the aluminum industry. In 1979, a total of 1.7 million short tons of aluminum were recovered from scrap of both kinds. Of this, 1.2 million short tons came from new scrap while 0.6 million short tons came from old, including the recycling of some 8.3 billion aluminum cans.[6] About 23 percent of the aluminum ingots used to make aluminum products are currently being derived from scrap.

The difficulties in recycling new scrap are significantly less than those in recycling old scrap. New scrap is already at the place of production and with most processes, it can simply be reentered into the input stream without transportation costs. Transport costs tend to be an important part of the cost of using old scrap.

Equally important are the incentives involved. Since new scrap never leaves the factory, it remains under the complete control of the manufacturer. Having the joint responsibility of creating a product and dealing with the scrap, the manufacturer now has an incentive to design the product with the use of the scrap in mind. It would be advantageous to establish procedures guaranteeing the homogeneity of the scrap and

---

[6]Aluminum Association, Inc., *Aluminum Statistical Review 1979* (Washington, D.C.: Aluminum Association Inc., 1980), p. 41.

minimizing the amount of processing necessary to recycle it. For all these reasons, it is likely the market for new scrap will work efficiently and effectively.

Unfortunately, the same is not true for old scrap. The market works inefficiently because the product users do not bear the full marginal social costs of disposing of their product. As a result, there is a bias away from recycling and toward the use of virgin materials.

The key to understanding why these costs are not internalized lies in the incentives facing individual product users. Suppose you had some small aluminum products which were no longer useful to you. You could either recycle them, which usually means driving to a recycling center, or you could toss them into your trash. In comparing these two alternatives, notice that recycling imposes one cost on you (transport cost) while the second imposes another (disposal cost).

It is difficult for consumers to make this comparison accurately because of the way trash collection is financed. Urban areas generally finance trash collection with taxes, if publicly provided, or user fees, if privately provided. In neither of these approaches is the size of an individual's payment directly related to the amount of waste to be disposed of. The *marginal* cost to the homeowner of throwing out one more unit of trash is negligible, even when the cost to society is not. There is a divergence between the marginal private-disposal cost and the cost to society as a whole (Figure 8.1).[7]

When the private marginal cost of disposal (MC_P) is lower than the marginal social cost of disposal (MC_S), the market level of recycling (where the marginal cost of recycling (MC_R) is equal to the marginal private disposal cost) is inefficient. Only if all social costs are included in the marginal cost of disposal will the efficient amount of recycling (Q_S) be attained.

This point can be reinforced by a numerical example. Suppose your city provides trash pickup for which you pay $150 a year in taxes. Your cost will be $150 regardless (within reasonable limits) of how much you throw out. In that year your additional (marginal) cost from throwing out these items is *zero*. Certainly the marginal cost to society is *not* zero and, therefore, the balance between these alternatives as seen by the individual homeowner is biased in favor of throwing things out.[8]

Littering is an extreme example of what we have been talking about. The cost to society of littering is the aesthetic loss plus the risk of damage to automobile tires and pedestrians caused by sharp edges of discarded cans or glass. Tossing used containers outside the car is relatively costless for the individual, but costly for society.[9]

---

[7]Why don't we use a pricing system that more accurately reflects marginal cost? Though there are several reasons, the most important is the difficulty of implementing a true marginal-cost pricing system for trash disposal. The available research, however, suggests that the net benefits of a change from tax-financed disposal to marginal cost pricing are positive and appreciable. See Haynes C. Goddard, "The Net Benefits of User Charges for Solid Waste Management: The Issues and Evidence," a paper presented at the December, 1985 meetings of the Association of Environmental and Resource Economists in New York City.

[8]The problem is *not* that $150 is too low; indeed it may be too high! The point is that the cost of waste disposal does not increase with the amount of waste to be disposed.

[9]Using economic analysis, would you expect transients or residents to have a higher propensity to litter? Why?

FIGURE 8.2 The Efficient Level of Recycling

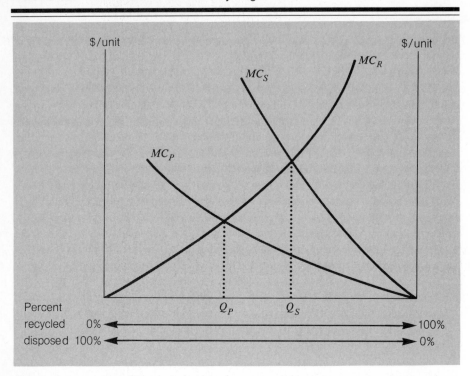

Disposal Costs and the Scrap Market

How would the market respond to a policy forcing product users to bear the true marginal disposal cost? The major effect would be on the supply of materials to be recycled. Consumers would now be able to avoid disposal costs, and might even be paid for discarded products. This would cause the diversion of some materials to recycling centers where they could be reintegrated into the materials process. If this expanded supply allows dealers to take advantage of previously unexploited economies of scale, this expansion could well result in a lower average cost of processing, as well as more recycled materials.

Such a development would affect the old scrap market (Figure 8.3). S_r, S_d, and S_t represent, respectively, the supply curves for recycled old scrap, domestically supplied virgin ores, and the total supply curve (the horizontal summation of the other two) when disposal costs are *not* considered. S'_r and S'_t represent, respectively, the supply curves for recycled old scrap and the total supply curve when disposal costs are considered. The graph demonstrates what we stated in the previous paragraph—when disposal costs are included, the supply of recycled scrap increases. More is available at lower cost.

The effect on the market is now clearly evident. The total consumption of inputs increases from q_t to q'_t because the price falls from P to P'. The use of recycled materials increases from q_r to q'_r. The amount of virgin ore falls. Thus the correct inclusion of

FIGURE 8.3   The Market Response to Increased Disposal Costs

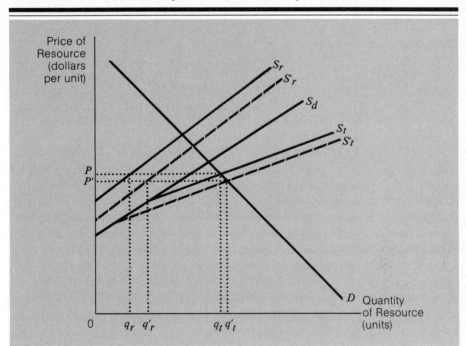

disposal cost would tend to increase the amount of recycling and reduce the demand for depletable, recyclable resources.

Can this misallocation resulting from the problem of inefficiently low disposal cost be corrected? There have been several suggested remedies. One would be to impose user charges reflecting the true social cost of disposal.[10] The problem with this approach is that it requires a fairly complicated pricing schedule and attendant billing procedure. The efficient price depends not only on weight and volume of the item but also on its chemical composition.

Another suggestion now being applied in many areas is the refundable deposit. Already widely accepted for beverage containers, such deposits could become a remedy for such divergent waste products as oil[11] and chlorofluoromethanes used as coolants in refrigerators.[12]

---

[10]The advantages and disadvantages of this approach are explored in Judith M. Guiron, "Economics of Solid Waste Handling and Government Intervention," in *Public Prices for Public Products.* Selma Mushkin, ed. (Washington, D.C.: The Urban Institute, 1972), pp. 173–215.

[11]A system similar to this is currently being used in Germany for waste oil. The system is described in Talbot Page, *Conservation and Economic Efficiency: An Approach to Materials Policy* (Baltimore, Md: Johns Hopkins University Press for Resources for the Future, Inc., 1977), p. 98.

[12]See Peter Bohm, *Deposit-Refund System: Theory and Application to Environmental, Conservation, and Consumer Policy* (Baltimore, Md: Johns Hopkins University Press for Resources for the Future, Inc., 1981), pp. 130–154.

A refund system is designed to accomplish two purposes: (1) the initial charge reflects the cost of disposal and produces the desired composition of demand effect, and (2) the refund, attainable upon turning the product in for recycling, helps conserve virgin materials. Such a system already is employed in Sweden to counter the problem of abandoned automobiles (Example 8.2).

As attractive as they may be for some waste-disposal problems, deposit-refund schemes are not universally applicable. Because of high administrative costs, this system must be used selectively. Only in selected applications do the benefits gained by society clearly exceed the costs of implementation. We must be wary of "solutions" that end up costing more than the problem!

It may be possible to develop policy approaches that can be administered easily enough to increase the net benefit, even if they are not capable of sustaining an efficient allocation. One such approach involves product charges, which differ from deposits in that there is no refund involved.

There have been two types of product charges seriously considered. The first, *product-disposal charges,* was the subject of a Senate hearing in 1976, while the second, a *recycling-incentive tax,* was proposed by New York City in 1971 but was never fully implemented due to a legal challenge.[13]

Product-disposal charges would be based directly on disposal costs. The rate considered in 1976 was $26 per ton of packaging material—the estimated national average cost of disposal. The charges would be levied on bulk producers or importers of packaging materials. The proposed legislation envisioned changes in the tax rate every two or three years to reflect changes in disposal cost.

The recycling-incentive tax was a more finely tuned program designed to create price differentials favorable to containers that did not create serious solid-waste problems. The suggested rates differed among container types and were higher for containers which neither held recycled materials nor were particularly easy to recycle. For example, plastic bottles—the least degradable and most resistant to compaction—were to be charged the highest rate.

Both systems were expected to generate revenue well in excess of the cost of administering the system,[14] though the revenue would be used differently. A small part of the revenue from the product-disposal tax was earmarked to subsidize those packaging companies using recycled materials with the rest accruing to the municipality. The subsidy would be phased out over a ten-year period. The revenue from the recycling incentive tax was intended to go directly into general municipal funds.

Product charges are not a complete, efficient means for controlling solid waste problems. When levied at the national level at a uniform rate, they are unable to take into

---

[13]These programs are discussed in Frederick P. Anderson, et. al., *Environmental Improvement Through Economic Incentives* (Baltimore, Md: Johns Hopkins University Press for Resources for the Future, Inc., 1977), pp. 71–73.

[14]One estimate places the administrative cost burden at 2 to 5 percent of the revenue collected. See John A. Butlin, "The Contribution of Economic Instruments to Solid Waste Management," in *The Economics of Environmental and Natural Resources Policy.* John A. Butlin, ed. (Boulder, Colo.: Westview Press, 1981), p. 149.

EXAMPLE 8.2

Deposits as a Solution to Abandoned Automobiles

In many countries abandoned automobiles are the source of a significant visual externality. When the prices offered by junk dealers are low, for whatever reasons, discarded cars begin appearing in parking lots, meadows, forests, and even in lakes and rivers. Generally it is difficult to trace the ownership of these vehicles, so penalties are not the answer.

In Sweden a deposit-refund system was introduced in 1976 to remedy this problem. Swedish car owners who turn over their hulks to authorized junk dealers get a bonus of about $60 per car over and above whatever arrangements they could make with the junk dealer. Buyers of new cars pay a fee in the same amount. Since total deposits exceed total refunds, a surplus has accumulated. Part of this surplus has been used to finance local efforts to clean up wrecks that were abandoned before the program began.

The success of this program suggests that such an approach can work. It also suggests some pitfalls to be avoided. During the first year, a reduction in abandoned vehicles occurred. After that initial period, however, the program seemed less effective. There were two main reasons: (1) the bonus payment was eroded by high inflation and therefore provided less incentive, and (2) the bottom dropped out of the market for scrapped automobiles, so dealers began charging customers to take their hulks, rather than paying them. In some areas, even with the bonus payment, the act of turning the car in may have cost the donor additional money.

The Swedish experience suggests that a deposit system can work, providing it is flexible enough. The deposits and refunds should be indexed for inflation and, unless the refund is high enough to cover the estimated social damage caused by abandoned car wrecks, refund rates must vary inversely with the net scrap value of automobiles.

Source: Peter Bohm, *Deposit-Refund System: Theory and Application to Environmental, Conservation, and Consumer Policy* (Baltimore, Md: Johns Hopkins University Press for Resources for the Future, 1981): 120–124.

account the differences in waste disposal cost that characterize local areas. Even when levied at the local level, these charges have weaknesses because locally produced products are not necessarily disposed of locally. When the products are marketed regionally or nationally, they are most likely to be disposed of at the location where they were used, not at the location where they were produced.

Thus while it is possible to design economic-incentive strategies to eliminate the disposal cost bias, those strategies are not yet in widespread use. Future use depends upon a compromise between fine tuning the incentive structures and keeping administrative and enforcement costs as low as possible.

Pollution Damage

There is another situation influencing the use of recycled and virgin ores. When environmental damage results from extracting and using virgin materials and not from the use of recycled materials, the market allocation will be biased away from recycling. This damage might be experienced at the mine, such as the erosion and aesthetic costs of strip mining, or at the point of processing, where the ore is processed into a usable resource.

Suppose that the mining industry was forced to bear the cost of this environmental damage. What difference would the inclusion of this cost have on the scrap market? The internalizing of this cost results in a leftward shift in the supply curve for the virgin ore (S_d) in Figure 8.3. This would, in turn, cause a leftward shift in the total-supply curve. The market would be using less of the resource—due to higher price—while recycling more. Thus the correct treatment of these environmental costs would share with disposal costs a tendency to increase the role for recycling.

One study by Spofford [1971] examines the significance of this cost in the context of the paper industry which, in spite of the fact it is based on a renewable resource, does rely on the recycling of used paper. In his study (summarized in Figure 8.4), Spofford considers four costs: acquiring and processing virgin pulp; using scrap paper; treatment and disposal of resulting pollutants; and the external damage caused by untreated pollutants. These are graphed as a function of the reuse ratio. The external damages and treatment costs are much higher with lower reuse ratios, since the use of virgin materials generates most of these costs.

Spofford also differentiates the costs to society as a whole from the costs to the paper-making firm. These differ because society bears all the costs while the firm bears only the costs of acquiring and processing virgin pulp and the costs of using scrap paper. The private costs do not include either the treatment costs (in the absence of government control the firm would not choose to treat the pollutants) or the external damages. The major conclusion to be drawn is that the efficient reuse ratio (0.8) is significantly higher than what the market would automatically provide (0.55) due to the undervaluation of environmental damage by the market.

TAX TREATMENT OF MINERALS

Built into the United States tax code is a series of special provisions for selected extractive industries. These provisions were designed to avoid taxing, as profits, the returns which really represented a liquidation of assets. The assets in this case are the reserves of natural resources being depleted. Thus these provisions, chiefly that known as the depletion allowance, expand the conventional treatment of capital assets to include depletable resources. They stimulate the extraction of targeted minerals and fuels by providing implicit tax-reduction subsidies to extractive industries. It has been estimated that this subsidy amounted to over $3.5 billion dollars during 1972.[15]

---

[15]Talbot Page, *Conservation and Economic Efficiency: An Approach to Materials Policy* (Baltimore, Md: Johns Hopkins University Press for Resources for the Future, Inc., 1977), p. 109.

FIGURE 8.4 Optimal Reuse Ratio for Paper Residuals in the Production of Newsprint

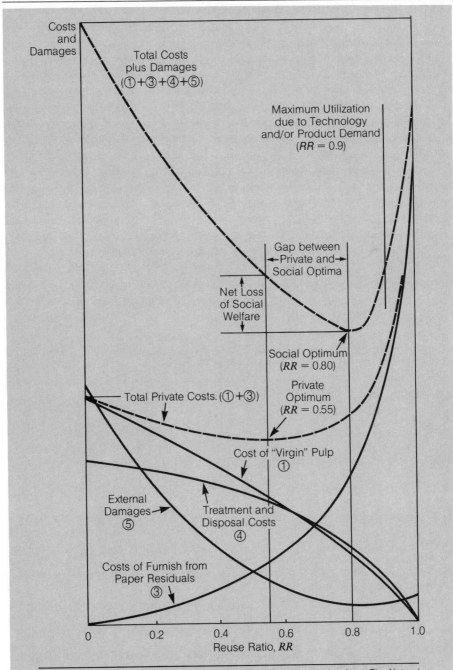

Source: Walter O. Spofford, Jr., Figure 4, Reprinted with permission from *The Natural Resources Journal*, 585 (1971), published by the University of New Mexico School of Law, Albuquerque, N.M.

While the subsidy has taken several forms, the overall effect is to lower the after-tax cost of extraction for virgin ores. According to our models, this should have the effect of increasing the amount of virgin ore mined.

There are other effects as well. Because these tax breaks are accrued by some but not all minerals, they create a bias in favor of those minerals whose lobbying groups were sufficiently strong that they were able to get favorable tax treatment. They also create a bias against recycling, since recycled materials are not eligible for the special tax treatment. [16]

Not all tax treatment, however, is favorable to the virgin ores. One in particular, the *severance tax,* tends to counteract these biases induced by other portions of the tax code. This is a tax levied on minerals as they are extracted. The states having severance taxes argue that the revenues compensate current citizens for localized environmental damage caused by extraction and compensate future generations for the loss of the resource by financing public investments. [17] Others suspect that states also use severance taxes to export their tax liability to consumers in other states. [18] Regardless of the reason for implementation, the rates were not designed to eliminate a bias against recycling. It is not surprising they don't do a very good job of it.

In general, severance taxes are not high—except for coal, which as an energy source is not recyclable, anyway. [19] They are not levied on all minerals, nor are they levied by all states; the coverage is limited and uneven. Furthermore, there is some evidence that, even for those minerals and states where the severence tax is levied, this tax has only from one-third to one-tenth the impact on market price that the depletion allowance has. [20]

While severance taxes may be useful in raising revenue for whatever purpose, they do little to correct the lack of balance between environmental and virgin resources. Furthermore, they may well make the strategic-mineral problem worse. Only domestic ore suppliers are taxed; foreign ore suppliers can avoid the tax.

---

[16]One provision, the foreign tax credit, which stipulates favorable tax treatment of foreign sources of minerals produced by U.S. corporations, may exacerbate the strategic mineral problem. This subsidy which applies to all corporations, not merely those in the extractive industries, was estimated to be $3.7 billion dollars in 1968. About one half went to oil and gas companies. See Gerard M. Brannon, *Energy Taxes and Subsidies* (Cambridge, Mass.: Ballinger Publishing Company, 1974), p. 38.

[17]For an example, see Arthur A. Link, "Political Constraint and North Dakota's Coal Severance Tax," *National Tax Journal* 31 (September 1978): 263–268. Link was the Governor of North Dakota when this severance tax was imposed.

[18]The extent to which this can be done is questionable. See, for example, the discussion of the Texas severance tax in Charles McLure, Jr., "Economic Constraint on State and Local Taxation of Energy Resources," *National Tax Journal* 31 (September 1978): 257–262.

[19]On July 2, 1981, the Supreme Court ruled Montana's 30 percent severance tax on coal constitutional. The highest severance tax in the country, Montana's tax had been attacked as being "confiscatory." It remains to be seen whether this decision will usher in a wave of new and higher severance taxes.

[20]Robert C. Anderson, "Evaluation of Economic Benefits of Resource Conservation," U.S. Environmental Protection Agency Report EPA-60015-78-015 (September 1978), p. 23.

DISCRIMINATION IN TRANSPORT COST

Earlier in this chapter we raised the point that old scrap prices were generally more sensitive to transportation costs than new scrap or virgin ores. For that reason, the economic viability of old scrap is rather sensitive to the cost of transporting it.

For years the scrap industry has argued that the structure of transport costs discriminates unfairly against the shipments of old scrap. There are two major strands in the argument. Not only are scrap shippers believed to pay higher rates on average for a comparable shipment, but also for them freight rates constitute a larger fraction of the total value of old scrap than for virgin materials. This latter argument implies that when the rates are changed over time by equal percentage increases (historically, a common practice) it causes old scrap to become increasingly disadvantaged.

Railroad freight rates are not market determined. Rather they are established by a regulatory body known as the Interstate Commerce Commission (ICC). The railroads must submit any proposed rate schedules and changes in those schedules to the ICC. The ICC then holds hearings in which the affected industries participate as witnesses. At the conclusion of these hearings, the ICC renders its decision.

Are the arguments put forward by the scrap industry correct? Talbot Page, [1977] an economist with Resources for the Future, a Washington think tank, has examined this issue closely. He concludes:

> . . . as one of the groups of commodities paying part of the cost of shipment of virgin materials, scrap material is paying a disproportionate share. . . . [p. 76]

He also suggests, however, that the current decisions of the ICC are moving in the direction of correcting this bias. In addition in the current deregulation environment the ICC is leaving more and more rates to the market.[21] While a bias does seem to exist, there are good reasons for believing it will diminish over time.

PRODUCT DURABILITY

In a memorable passage from *Death of a Salesman,* Willy Loman, the title character, laments:

> Once in my life I would like to own something outright before it's broken! I'm always in a race with the junkyard! I just finish paying for the car and it's on its last legs. The refrigerator

---

[21]For a description of this trend see Thomas Gale Moore, "Rail and Trucking Deregulation" in Leonard W. Weiss and Michael W. Klass, editors, *Regulatory Reform: What Actually Happened?* (Boston: Little, Brown and Company, 1986): 14–39.

consumes belts like a goddam maniac. They time those things. They time them so when you've finally paid for them, they're used up.

Willy is not alone in his anguish. In the early 1960s popular author Vance Packard came out with a book called *The Waste Makers* which suggested that Willy's plight was the product of a conscious marketing strategy by corporations. If products wear out faster, the argument goes, consumers have to buy them more often and sales are increased. Is this a valid argument? If it is, the drain on the resource base is artificially high and we have another reason for corrective measures.

Packard identifies three possible types of product obsolescence. *Functional obsolescence* occurs when a new product can perform the function in a superior manner to an older product. The vacuum tube became functionally obsolescent when it was replaced by the transistor. *Fashion obsolescence* occurs when consumers prefer a new product for reasons of taste. Wide ties and short skirts become obsolete when tastes shift to narrow ties and long skirts. *Durability obsolescence* occurs when the product can no longer perform its function because of wear and tear. A refrigerator becomes obsolete when it can no longer keep its inside temperature stable and cool. The economic implications of these three types of obsolescence are quite different.

Functional Obsolescence

Because functional obsolescence is not really a problem, we will spend little time on it. A vigorous amount of inventive activity is a natural and desirable consequence of a market economy. Those who find better ways of doing things can become wealthy from the sales of their product, whether it be a tastier way to fry chicken or a cheaper, higher quality method of copying documents. Far from representing a problem, functional obsolescence is the natural consequence of the successful search for better products.

Fashion Obsolescence

Fashion obsolescence is trickier. On the one hand, if fashion is a valued characteristic for consumers, then it is possible to conceive fashion obsolescence as merely a special case of functional obsolescence. New fashions replace old because they are more satisfying to the consumer. In this view there is no problem with fashion obsolescence because it is merely the result of the market continually doing a superior job of satisfying consumer preference.

The opposite point of view starts from the premise that those consumer preferences being satisfied by the market are, in fact, *created* by the market.[22] If consumer

---

[22]For an articulation of this position, see John Kenneth Galbraith, *The Affluent Society* (New York,: Houghton Mifflin Company, 1958). For an opposite point of view, see F. A. Hayek, "The Non Sequitur of 'Dependence Effect'," *Southern Economic Journal* 27 (April 1961): 346–352.

preferences are created by producers, then it is appropriate to question whether consumers are legitimately being made better off or are merely being manipulated into believing they are better off.

The apparel industry is certainly one where fashion obsolescence plays a strong role. However, it is not clear that fashion obsolescence is as important for other products. The automobile has certainly had its share of fashion obsolescence, perhaps best epitomized by the era in the 1950s when pronounced tailfins were in vogue. Yet, clearly the auto industry can go only so far. It would be very difficult, for example, to explain the shift in consumer buying toward small imported automobiles in the late 1970s and early 1980s as reflecting a shift in what was fashionable.

Indeed, some observers believe that a significant portion of the malaise of the domestic auto industry in the 1980s was caused by its inability to anticipate and respond to consumer preferences. That is important because the automobile market is one in which consumer preferences are thought to be dominated by the big three automakers.[23]

Even when fashion influences consumer preferences, it is not clear that taste is dictated by the manufacturer or that it relates solely to new products. Antique furniture and antique cars are fashionable, but these fashions certainly are not created by manufacturers and do not help sell new cars or new furniture.

In looking at the totality of consumer decisions, we cannot conclude that consumer tastes are systematically manipulated by industry. Markets do exist for which a strong case can be made, but they seem to be isolated examples, rather than typical.

Durability Obsolescence

We come then to the final category, the one which triggered Willy Loman's lament. We must, for this category, begin to answer two questions: (1) what is an efficient level of durability? and (2) will the market supply that level?

The *efficient level of durability* is the one which maximizes the net benefit from the product. Products that last longer confer more benefits on society, but they also cost more. Therefore, it is not obvious that the most durable product is also the most efficient one. Can we trust the market to find the efficient level of durability? To examine that issue, let's look at both the demand and supply sides of the market.

On the demand side, the consumer makes his or her choices by discounting benefits and costs. The capital costs of consumer durables are borne immediately (although payments can be spread out by borrowing money), while the benefits (flow of services), as well as operating and maintenance costs, are accrued as a flow over time. He or she will purchase the commodity only if the net benefit is maximized by that level of durability (the additional cost of making a more durable commodity is justified by the additional benefit received). In performing this balancing between cost and durability,

---

[23]See, for example, Vance Packard, *The Waste Makers* (New York, NY: David McKay Company, 1960), "How to Outmode a $4,000 Vehicle in Two Years."

will the consumer make efficient choices or, because of lack of information or some other market imperfection, will durability be undervalued or overvalued?

One way to test this is to examine a case in which the benefits and costs are relatively easy to quantify, thereby allowing a comparison of the discount rates implied by consumer purchases of durable goods with market rates. If their individual discount rates are higher than the social opportunity cost of capital (as measured by interest rates), consumers are undervaluing durability. If they use lower discount rates, they are overvaluing it.

Jerry Hausman [1979] of MIT conducted a fascinating study which relates to this issue. He was able to acquire data on individual purchases of energy-using consumer durables (room air conditioners). For each of these purchases he could calculate the benefits (longer life plus energy savings resulting from higher energy efficiency) and cost (purchase price as well as expected operating and maintenance costs). From this information he could calculate the discount rates implied by the purchase made by the average consumer. High discount rates indicate a special sensitivity to the initial cost.

Interestingly, in his sample, the implied discount rates were higher than the market rates. Furthermore, Hausman found that discount rates were highest for the lowest income people, while they approximated the efficient rates for higher income classes. This suggests that consumers—particularly low-income consumers—purchase less durability and less energy efficiency than is dictated by the dynamic-efficiency criterion. Whether or not these results generalize to other products is unclear; if they do, there might be some role for government intervention.

To be able to structure the appropriate policy response, however, the government would have to know more about the reasons for the higher implied discount rates. If the reason is inadequate consumer information, then the appropriate policy might well be increasing the flow of reliable information through testing, labeling requirements, and so on. If it is purely that the market rate of interest is higher for low-income consumers because they have a higher probability of defaulting on loan repayments, then some means of providing easier access to capital markets might be called for. In other cases, measures such as tax subsidies or enforced standards might be appropriate.

We must also consider the supply side of the market. If they can get away with it, producers as a group have an incentive to reduce product durability below the efficient level. By doing so, they reduce their cost per unit and sell many more units over time. For example, a household could satisfy its demand over a ten-year period with one appliance lasting ten years, but would have to purchase two if the appliance only lasted five years. As long as the profit were higher on the sale of two, rather than one (the presumption), firms would be better off with planned obsolescence.

But the key question is whether or not they can get away with it. As long as there are competitive suppliers, or even potential competitive suppliers, which could enter the market to supply more durable goods, the consumer could turn to these alternative suppliers instead. In a normal market process, competition prevents individual firms from producing insufficiently durable products. Those who sell products which don't last find their markets drying up.

There seem to be two cases where this market process may not work efficiently. The first case occurs when consumers are not well informed about the differences in durability so they do not have enough information to make efficient choices. This, remember, was one possible interpretation of the Hausman study. To the extent they face ignorant consumers, producers would have an incentive to position themselves in the lower initial price portion of the market by lowering the durability of their products.

In recognition of the importance of this information, organizations have been set up to supply it. Consumers' Union, the publisher of *Consumer Reports,* is one such organization. It performs its own independent testing and evaluating, a service which can rectify this lack of information at reasonable cost. Its chief limitation probably relates to products undergoing rapid technological change.

For rapidly changing products, by the time the testing lab acquires the product, tests it, and reports the results, other untested but potentially superior products are already on the market. This flaw, however, is not fatal; it merely means the rate of adoption would be rather more sluggish than would be dictated by efficiency.

The second case where a firm could profit by producing a good with an inefficiently low durability is when it does not face competition. This would require either a monopoly—which is, of course, very rare—or explicit collusion to cut corners by all the members of the industry. Since competition comes from foreign, as well as domestic, firms and from potential entrants, as well as existing firms, this must be a relatively rare circumstance.

SUMMARY

Market mechanisms automatically create pressures for recycling and reuse which are generally in the right direction, though not always of the correct intensity. Higher disposal costs and increasing mineral scarcity do create a larger demand for recycling. This is already evident for a number of products, such as those containing copper or aluminum.

Yet, there are also a number of imperfections in the market which tend to suggest the degree of recycling we are currently experiencing is less than the efficient amount. There are several sources of this imperfection. The absence of sufficient stockpiles and the absence of tariffs means that our national security interests are not being adequately considered in market decisions involving strategic minerals. From the perspective of efficiency, the reliance on vulnerable imports is excessive.

Artificially low disposal costs, tax breaks for virgin sources, and discriminatory pricing practices by the Interstate Commerce Commission all combine to depress the role which old scrap can, and should, play. Severance taxes provide a limited, if poorly targeted, redress for some minerals.

One imperfection, the supposed tendency of American manufacturers to produce products less durable than efficient, seems overstated. Although the Hausman study indicates that lower-income people purchase products less durable than efficient, other income groups do not. This is a more limited view of product durability problems than is usually espoused by writers such as Vance Packard.

One cannot help but notice that many of these problems—such as pricing, municipal disposal services, tax breaks for virgin ores, and pricing decisions of the ICC—result from government actions. It therefore appears in this area that the appropriate role for government is selective disengagement complemented by some fine-tuning adjustments.

This is not true, however, for a final source of imperfection—environmental damage due to littering, air and water pollution, and strip mining. When a product is produced from virgin materials, rather than recycled or reusable materials, and the cost of any associated environmental damage is not internalized, some government action may be called for.

The selective disengagement of government in some areas must be complemented by the enforcement of programs to internalize the costs of environmental damage. The commonly heard ideological prescriptions suggesting that environmental problems can be solved either by ending government interference or by increasing the amount of government control are both inaccurate. The efficient role for government in achieving a balance between the economic and environmental systems requires less control in some areas and more in others.

FURTHER READING

Bohm, Peter. *Deposit-Refund System: Theory and Application to Environmental, Conservation, and Consumer Policy* (Baltimore: Johns Hopkins University Press for Resources for the Future, Inc., 1981). A highly readable and analytically sound exploration of the experience with and potential applications for deposit-refund systems.

Manthy, Robert S. *Natural Resource Commodities—A Century of Statistics* (Baltimore: Johns Hopkins University Press for Resources for the Future, 1978). A basic reference source on natural-resource prices, output, consumption, foreign trade and employment in the United States, 1870–1973. It draws no conclusions.

Page, Talbot. *Conservation and Economic Efficiency: An Approach to Materials Policy* (Baltimore: Johns Hopkins University Press for Resources for the Future, Inc., 1977). An accessible, scholarly, and in parts, innovative treatment of many of the issues covered in this chapter.

Roxburgh, Nigel. *Policy Responses to Resource Depletion: The Case of Mercury* (Greenwich: JAI Press, Inc., 1980). An intensive examination of the depletion experience with one particular material—mercury. Includes chapters on the resource base, extractive and scrap-metal industries, and various industries which are heavy users of mercury.

ADDITIONAL REFERENCES

Banks, Ferdinand E. *Bauxite & Aluminum: An Introduction to the Economics of Non-Fuel Minerals* (Lexington, Mass.: Lexington Books, 1979).

Foley, Patricia T. and Joel P. Clark. "The Effects of State Taxation on United States Copper Supply," *Land Economics,* Vol. 58 (May, 1982): 153–180.

Gulley, D. A. "Severance Taxes and Market Failure," *Natural Resources Journal,* Vol. 22 (July, 1982): 597–617.

Hausman, Jerry. "Individual Discount Rates and the Purchase and Utilization of Energy-using Durables." *Bell Journal of Economics* 10 (Spring, 1979): 33–54.

Hazilla, Michael and Raymond J. Kopp, "Assessing U. S. Vulnerability to Raw Material Supply Disruptions: An Application to Nonfuel Minerals", *Southern Economic Journal*, Vol. 51, No. 2 (October, 1984): 341–355.

Kakela, Peter J. "Iron Ore: Energy, Labor and Capital Changes with Technology," *Science*, Vol. 202 (15 December 1978): 1151–1157.

Kakela, Peter J. "Iron Ore: From Depletion to Abundance," *Science*, Vol. 212 (10 April 1981): 132–136.

Smith, Vernon L. "Dynamics of Waste Accumulation versus Recycling" *Quarterly Journal of Economics*, Vol. LXXXV (November, 1972): 600–616.

Spofford, W. O. "Solid Residual Management: Some Economic Considerations," *Natural Resource Journal* 11 (July 1971): 561–89.

Stollery, Kenneth R. "Mineral Depletion with Cost as the Extraction Limit: A Model Applied to the Behavior of Prices in the Nickel Industry," *Journal of Environmental Economics and Management*, Vol. 10 (June, 1983): 151–165.

Tilton, John E., ed. *Material Substitution: Lessons from Tin-Using Industries* (Washington, DC: Resources for the Future, Inc., 1985).

DISCUSSION QUESTIONS

1. Glass bottles can either be recycled (crushed and remelted) or reused. The market will tend to choose the cheapest path. What factors will tend to affect the relative costs of these options? Is the market likely to make the efficient choice? Are the "bottle bills" passed by many of the states requiring deposits on bottles a move toward efficiency or not? Why?

2. Many areas have attempted to increase the amount of recycled waste lubricating oil by requiring service stations to serve as collection centers or by instituting deposit refund systems. On what grounds, if any, is government intervention called for? In terms of the effects on the waste lubrication oil market what differences should be noticed among those states which do nothing, those which require all service stations to serve as collection centers, and those implementing deposit-refund systems? Why?

PROBLEMS

1. Suppose a product can be produced using virgin ores at a marginal cost given by $MC_1 = .5q_1$ and with recycled materials at a marginal cost given by $MC_2 = 5 + .1q_2$. (a) If the inverse demand curve were given by $P = 10 - .5(q_1 + q_2)$, how many units of the product would be produced with virgin ores and how many units with recycled materials? (b) If the inverse demand curve was $P = 20 - .5(q_1 + q_2)$, what would your answer be?

2. When the government allows private firms to extract minerals offshore or on public lands, two common means of sharing in the profits are bonus bidding and production royalties. The former awards the right to extract to the highest bidder, while the second charges a per-ton royalty on each ton extracted. Bonus bids involve a single, upfront payment, while royalties are paid as long as minerals are being extracted.

(a) If the two approaches are designed to yield the same amount of revenue, will they have the same effect on the allocation of the mine over time? Why or why not?

(b) Would either or both be consistent with an efficient allocation? Why or why not?

(c) Suppose the size of the mineral deposit and the future path of prices are unknown. How do these two approaches allocate the risk between the mining company and the government?

CHAPTER NINE

Replenishable but Depletable Resources: Water

You'll never miss the water
Till your well runs dry.
WILLIAM CHRISTOPHER HANDY
Joe Turner's Blues (1915)

INTRODUCTION

"To the red country and part of the gray country of Oklahoma, the last rains came gently, and they did not cut the scarred earth. . . . The sun flared down on the growing corn day after day until a line of brown spread along the edge of each green bayonet. The clouds appeared and went away, and in awhile they did not try anymore."[1]

With these words John Steinbeck sets the scene for his powerful novel *The Grapes of Wrath*. Drought and poor soil conservation practices combined to destroy the agricultural institutions which had provided nourishment and livelihood to Oklahoma residents since settlement in that area had begun. In desperation, those who had worked that land were forced to abandon not only their possessions, but their past. Moving to California to seek employment, they were uprooted only to be caught up in a web of exploitation and hopelessness.

Based on an actual situation, the novel demonstrates how the social fabric can tear when subject to tremendous stress, such as an inadequate availability of water, and how painful those tears can be. Clearly problems such as these should be anticipated and prevented as much as possible.

Water is one of the essential elements of life. We humans depend not only on an

---

[1]John Steinbeck, *The Grapes of Wrath* (New York: The Viking Press, 1939), p. 3.

intake of water to replace the continual loss of body fluids, but also on food sources which themselves need water to survive. This is a resource that deserves special attention.

In this chapter we shall examine this resource in detail. The overarching question regards how our economic and political institutions have allocated this important resource in the past and how they might improve on its allocation in the future. We initiate our inquiry by examining the likelihood and severity of water scarcity. Turning to the management of our water resources, we will define the efficient allocation of ground and surface water over time and compare these allocations to current practice, particularly in the United States. Finally, we will examine the menu of opportunities for meaningful institutional reform.

THE POTENTIAL FOR WATER SCARCITY

The earth's renewable supply of water is governed by the hydrologic cycle, a system of continuous water circulation (Figure 9-1). Enormous quantities of water are cycled each year through this system, though only a fraction of circulated water is available each year for human use.

Available supplies are derived from two rather different sources—surface water and ground water. As the name implies, *surface water* consists of the fresh water in rivers, lakes, or reservoirs that collects and flows on the earth's surface. *Ground water* by contrast collects in porous layers of underground rock known as aquifers. Though some ground water is renewed by percolation of rain or melted snow, most was accumulated over geologic time and, because of its location, cannot be recharged once it is depleted. Of the 16,000 trillion gallons of ground water estimated to be available for extraction in the United States, only about 400 trillion gallons are available on a renewable basis. The rest is a finite, depletable resource.[2]

If we were simply to add up the available supply of fresh water (total runoff) on a global scale and compare it with the demand for it, we would discover that the supply is currently about 10 times demand. Though comforting, that statistic is also misleading because it masks the impact of growing demand and the rather severe excess demand situations that already exist in certain parts of the world. Taken together, these insights suggest that in many parts of the world water scarcity is already upon us, and other areas, including several parts of the United States, can be expected to experience water scarcity in the next few decades.

The Global 2000 Report estimates that by the year 2000, worldwide available water supplies will be only 3.5 times demand because of population growth.[3] Due to the temporal and geographic variation in both water available and population growth, some

---

[2]Council on Environmental Quality, *Environmental Trends* (Washington, D.C.: Government Printing Office, 1978), p. 213.

[3]Gerald O. Barney, *The Global 2000 Report to the President of the U.S.: Entering the 21st Century, Volume 1: The Summary Report* (New York: Pergamon Press, 1980), p. 155.

FIGURE 9.1   The Hydrologic Cycle

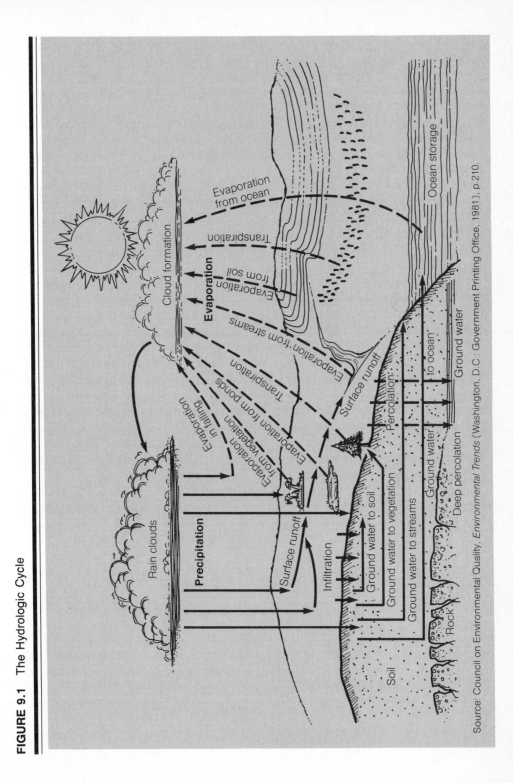

Source: Council on Environmental Quality, *Environmental Trends* (Washington, D.C.: Government Printing Office, 1981), p.210.

parts of the world are expected to be particularly vulnerable. Areas noted as being especially susceptible to water shortages include parts of Africa, North America, the Middle East, Latin America, and South Asia.

The United States is not expected to escape water scarcity problems. The Water Resources Council estimates that "The problem of inadequate surface water supply is or will be severe by the year 2000 in 17 subregions located mainly in the Midwest and Southwest."[4] The problem with ground water is even more severe. Ground water levels have been declining recently in some areas of the country as a result of intensive pumping. Regionally, significant depletion of ground water supplies has occurred in three major areas—southern Arizona, the High Plains (from Nebraska to Texas), and California.[5] Kenneth Frederick of Resources for the Future, Inc. has estimated that annual withdrawals exceed recharge in Western aquifers by more than 22 million acre feet.[6] The number is even larger in particularly dry years.

The city of Tucson, Arizona provides one concrete example of the problem. Tucson, which averages about 11 inches of rain a year, is the largest city in the United States to rely entirely on ground water. There are wells in the Tucson area where the water level has dropped 110 feet in 10 years. Tucson annually pumps five times as much water out of the ground as nature puts back in. It is expected that at *current* consumption rates the aquifers supplying Tucson would be exhausted in less than 100 years.[7] Despite the rate at which its water supplies are being depleted, Tucson continues to grow at a rapid rate. To solve the problem a giant network of dams, pipelines, tunnels, and canals known as the central Arizona Project is being constructed to transfer water from the Colorado River to Tucson. The expected completion date is 1991.

Though the discussion this far has focused on the quantity of water, that is not the only problem. Quality is also a problem. Much of the available water is polluted with chemicals, radioactive materials, or bacteria. Though we shall reserve for Chapter 16 a detailed look at the water pollution problem, it is important to keep in mind that water scarcity has a qualitative as well as quantitative dimension.

What this brief survey of the evidence suggests is that in certain parts of the world ground water supplies are being depleted to the potential detriment of future users. Supplies, which for all practical purposes will never be replenished, are being used now to satisfy current needs. Once used, they are goine. Is this allocation efficient or are there demonstrable sources of inefficiency? Answering this question requires us to be quite clear about what is meant by an efficient allocation of surface and ground water.

---

[4]U.S. Water Resources Council, *The Nation's Water Resources, 1975-2000, Volume 1* (Washington, D.C.: Government Printing Office, 1978), p. 56.

[5]Council on Environmental Quality, *Environmental Quality 1983: The 14th Annual Report of the Council on Environmental Quality* (Washington, D.C.: Council on Environmental Quality, 1984), p. 86.

[6]Kenneth D. Frederick, "Water Supplies" in Paul Portney, ed., *Current Issues in Natural Resources Policy* (Washington, D.C.: Resources for the Future, Inc., 1982): 227.

[7]David Sheridan for the Council on Environmental Quality, *Desertification of the United States* (Washington, D.C.: Government Printing Office, 1981), p. 66.

THE EFFICIENT ALLOCATION OF SCARCE WATER

What efficiency means for the allocation of water depends crucially on whether surface water or ground water is being tapped. In the absence of storage, the problem with surface water is to allocate a renewable supply among competing users. Intergenerational effects are not important as future supplies depend on natural phenomena (such as precipitation) rather than on current withdrawal practices. For ground water, on the other hand, withdrawing water now does affect the resources available to future generations. In this case, the allocaiton over time is a crucial aspect of the analysis. Because it represents a somewhat simpler analytical case, we shall consider the efficient allocation of surface water first.

Surface Water

An efficient allocation of surface water must achieve two objectives: (1) it must strike a balance among a host of competing users, and (2) it must supply an acceptable means of handling the year-to-year variability in surface water flow. The former issue is an acute one because there are so many different potential users, ranging from those who withdraw the water for consumptive use (such as muncipal drinking water suppliers or farmers) to those who use but do not consume the water (such as swimmers or boaters). All have legitimate competing claims. The latter challenge arises from the fact that surface water supplies are not constant from year to year. Since precipitation, runoff, and evaporation all change from year to year, in some years there will be less water to be allocated than in others. It is therefore important not only to provide a system for allocating the average amount of water, but also to anticipate and to deal with above-average and below-average years.

    With respect to the first problem, the dictates of efficiency are quite clear—the water should be allocated so that the marginal net benefit is equalized for all uses. To demonstrate why this is so, consider a situation in which the marginal net benefits are *not* equal. We shall show that in this situation it is always possible to increase net benefits by reallocating the water. Since net benefits can be increased by this reallocation, the initial allocation could not have maximized net benefits. Since an efficient allocation maximizes net benefits, the allcoation through which net benefits are not equalized could not have been efficient.

    If marginal net benefits are not equalized, it is possible to increase net benefits by transfering water from those uses with low net marginal benefits to those with higher net marginal benefits. By transferring the water to the users who value the marginal water most, the net benefits of the water use are increased; those losing water are giving up less than those receiving the additional water are gaining. When the marginal net benefits are equalized, no such transfer is possible. This can be seen in Figure 9.2.

    Two individual demand curves (labeled *A* & *B*) are depicted along with the market demand curve that portrays the aggregate willingness to pay. For supply situation S_o, the amount of water available is Q_T^0. An efficient allocation would give Q_B to use *B*

FIGURE 9.2   The Efficient Allocation of Surface Water

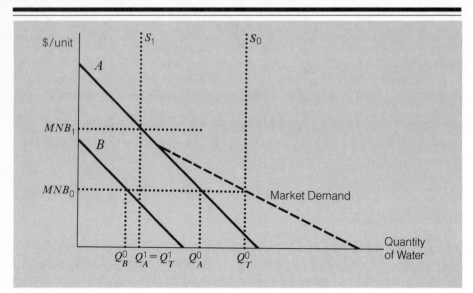

and Q_A to use A. (By construction $Q_A^0 + Q_B^0 = Q_T^0$.) For this allocation, notice that the marginal net benefit (MNB_0) is equal for the two uses.

Now let's consider the second problem—dealing with fluctuations in supply. As long as the supply level can be anticipated, the equal marginal net benefit rule still applies, but different supply levels may imply very different allocations among users. This is an important attribute of the problem because it implies that simple allocation rules, such as each user receiving a proportion of the available flow, are not likely to be efficient.

Consider Figure 9.2 again, but this time focus on the water supply labelled S_1. Less water is available in this situation than when supply equals S_0 than it did in the previous discussion of this figure. With S_1, a very different efficient allocation prevails; specifically, use B receives no water while use A receives it all. Why does the efficient allocation change so radically between S_0 and S_1? The answer lies in the shape of the two demand curves for water.

The demand curve for water in use A lies above that for B, implying that the cost (the foregone net benefits) of doing without water as supplies diminish is much higher for A than for B. To minimize this cost, more of the burden of the shortfall is allocated to B than A. What this suggests is that users who can most easily find substitutes or conserve on the use of water receive proportionately smaller allocations when supplies are diminished, while those who have few alternatives receive proportionately more.

Ground Water

The extension of this analysis to cover ground water requires that the depletable nature of ground water supplies be explicitly taken into account. When the withdrawals exceed recharge from a particular aquifer, the resource will be mined over time until either the supplies are exhausted or the marginal cost of pumping additional water becomes prohibitive. The similarity of this case to the increasing-cost, depletable-resource model discussed in Chapter 6 allows us to exploit that similarity to learn something about the efficient allocation of ground water over time.

The first transferable implication is that there is a user cost associated with mining ground water, reflecting the opportunity cost associated with the unavailability in the future of any unit of water used in the present. An efficient allocation considers this user cost.

The efficient extraction path for constant demand involves declining use of ground water over time. The marginal extraction cost (the cost of pumping the last unit to the surface) would rise over time as the water table fell. Pumping would stop either when (1) the water table ran dry or (2) when the marginal cost of pumping was either greater than the marginal benefit of the water or greater than the marginal cost of acquiring water from some other source.

If there is abundant surface water in proximity to the location of the ground water, then this could serve as a substitute, effectively setting an upper bound on the marginal cost of extraction. The user would not pay more to extract a unit of ground water than it would cost to acquire surface water. Unfortunately in many parts of the country where ground water overdrafts are particularly severe, the competition for surface water is already keen; a cheap source of surface water doesn't exist.

In efficient ground water markets, the price would rise over time until it equalled the marginal pumping cost. Depending on the situation, this would occur at the point of exhaustion, the point at which the marginal pumping cost becomes prohibitive or when the marginal cost of pumping becomes equal to the next least-expensive source of water. In all three cases the net price, the difference between the price of the water and the marginal extraction cost, would decline over time, reaching zero at the switch point (if a substitute were available) or the point of exhaustion (if it were not).

THE CURRENT ALLOCATION SYSTEM

Riparian and Prior Appropriation Doctrines

Within the United States the means of allocating water differ from one geographic area to the next, particularly with respect to the legal doctrines that govern conflicts. In this section we shall focus on the allocation systems that prevail in the arid Southwest, which must cope with the most potentially serious and imminent scarcity of water.

In the earliest days of settlement in the American Southwest and West, the government had a minimal presence. Residents were pretty much on their own in creating a sense of order. Property rights played a very important role in reducing conflicts in this potentially volatile situation.

As water was always a significant factor in the development of an area, the first settlements were usually oriented near bodies of water. The property rights that evolved, called *riparian rights,* allocated the right to use the water to the owner of the land adjacent to the water. This was a practical solution because by virtue of their location, these owners had easy access to the water. Furthermore, there were enough sites with access to water that virtually all who sought water could be accommodated.

With population growth and the consequent rise in the demand for land, this allocation system became less appropriate. As demand increased, the amount of land adjacent to water became scarce, forcing some spillover onto land which was not adjacent to water. The owners of this land began to seek means of acquiring water to make their land more productive.

About this time, with the discovery of gold in California, mining became an important source of employment. With the advent of mining came a need to divert water away from streams to other sites. Unfortunately, riparian property rights made no provision for water to be diverted to other locations. The rights to the water were tied to the land and could not be separately transferred.

As economic theory would predict, this situation created a demand for a change in the property right structure from riparian rights to one which was more congenial to the need for transferability. The waste resulting from the lack of transferability became so great that it outweighed any transition costs of changing the system of property rights. The evolution that took place in the mining camps became the forerunner of what has become known as the *prior appropriation* doctrine.

The miners established the custom that the first person to arrive had the superior claim on the water.[8] In practice, this severed the relationship which had existed under the riparian doctrine between the rights to land and the rights to water. As this new doctrine became adopted in legislation, court rulings, and even state constitutions, widespread diversion of water based on prior appropriation became possible. Stimulated by the profits that could be made in shifting water to more valuable uses, private companies were formed to construct irrigation systems, and to transport water from surplus to deficit areas. Agriculture flourished.[9]

Although prior to 1860 the role of the government was rather minimal, after 1860 that began to change—slowly at first, but picking up momentum as the Twentieth Century began. The earliest incursions involved establishing the principle that the ownership of water properly belonged to the state. Claimants were accorded only the right to use, known as a *usufructory right,* rather than an ownership right. The establishment of this principle of public ownership was followed in short order by the establishment of state control over the rates charged by the private irrigation companies, imposing restrictions on the ability to transfer water out of the district, and creating a centralized bureaucracy to administer the process.

This was only the beginning. The demand for land in the arid West and Southwest was still growing, creating a complementary demand for water to make the desert bloom.

---

[8]For a detailed treatment of this evolution see Charles W. McCurdy, "Stephen J. Field and Public Land Law Development in California, 1850–1866: A Case Study of Judicial Resource Allocation in Nineteenth Century America," *Law and Society* (Winter, 1976): 235–266.

[9]The powerful impact of this evolution on agriculture in the West is described in Alfred G. Cuzan, "Appropriators versus Expropriators: The Political Economy of Water in the West," in Terry L. Anderson, ed. *Water Rights: Scarce Resource Allocation, Bureaucracy, and the Environment* (Cambridge, MA: Ballinger Publishing Company, 1983): 19–20.

The tremendous profits to be made from large-scale water diversions created the political climate necessary for the federal government to get involved. Using land reclamation and improved navigation as a rationale, Congress passed the Newlands Reclamation Act of 1902, which allowed water project developers access to federally subsidized, interest-free loans to finance construction costs. Because the periods of time for repayment were very flexible, and the interest costs so low, the resulting subsidies for water projects were very large.

This, in a nutshell, is the current situation for water. Both the state and federal governments play a large role. Though the prior appropriation doctrine stands as the foundation of this allocation system, it is heavily circumscribed by government regulations and direct government appropriation of a substantial amount of water.

Sources of Inefficiency

The current system is not efficient. The prime source of inefficiency involves restrictions that have been placed on water transfers, preventing their gravitation to the highest valued use, though other sources, such as charging inefficiently low prices, must bear some of the responsibility.

Restrictions on Transfers.[10]   One of the characteristics an efficient allocation of water should exhibit is for the marginal net benefits to be equalized across all consumptive uses of the water. With a well-structured system of water property rights this equalization would be a direct result of the transferability of the rights. Users receiving low marginal net benefits would trade their rights to those who would receive higher net benefits from the water. Both parties would be better off. The payment received by the seller would exceed the net benefits foregone, while the payment made by the buyer would be less than the value of the water acquired.

Unfortunately, the existing mixed system of prior appropriation rights coupled with quite restrictive regulations has diminished the degree of transferability that can take place. Diminished transferability in turn reduces the market pressures which cause equalization of the marginal net benefits. By itself this indictment is not sufficient to demonstrate that the existing system is inefficient. If it could be shown that this regulatory system was able to substitute some bureaucratic process for finding and maintaining this equalization, efficiency would still be possible. Unfortunately, that has not been the case, as can be seen by examining in more detail the specific nature of these restrictions. The allocation is inefficient.

---

[10]More information of the details of these restrictions can be found in Micha Gisser and Ronald N. Johnson, "Institutional Restrictions on the Transfer of Water Rights and the Survival of an Agency," in Terry L. Anderson, ed. *Water Rights: Scarce Resource Allocation, Bureaucracy and the Environment* (Cambridge, MA: Ballinger Publishing Company, 1983); 137–165 and Terry L. Anderson, *Water Crisis: Ending the Policy Drought* (Washington, D.C.: Cato Institute, 1983): 56–62.

One of the earliest restrictions required that users put their water to "beneficial use" or lose their rights to it. It is not difficult to see what this "use it or lose it" principle does to the incentive to conserve. Particularly careful users who, at their own expense, find ways to use less water would find their allocation reduced accordingly.

A second restriction, known as "preferential use" attempts to establish bureaucratically a value hierarchy of uses. With this doctrine, the government attempts to establish allocation priorities across categories of water. Within categories (irrigation for agriculture, for example) the priority is determined by prior appropriation ("first in time—first in right"), but among categories the preferential use doctrine governs.

The preferential use doctrine supports three rather different kinds of inefficiencies. First, it substitutes a bureaucratically determined set of priorities for market priorities, resulting in a lower likelihood that marginal net benefits would be equalized. Second, it reduces the incentive to make investments which complement water use in lower preference categories for the simple reason that their water could be withdrawn as the needs in higher level categories grow. Finally, it allocates the risk of shortfalls in an inefficient way.

Although the first two inefficiencies are rather self-evident, the third merits further explanation. Because water supplies fluctuate over time, unusual scarcities can occur in any particular year. With a well-specified system of property rights, damage caused by this risk would be minimized by allowing those most damaged by a shortfall to purchase a larger share of the diminished amount of water available during a drought from those suffering the increased shortfall with smaller consequences.

By diminishing, and in some cases eliminating, the ability to transfer rights from so called "high preferential use" categories to "lower preferential use" categories during times of acute need, the damage caused by shortfalls is higher than necessary. In essence, the preferential use doctrine fails to adequately consider the marginal damage caused by temporary shortfalls, something a well-structured system of property rights would do automatically.

Federal Reclamation Projects.   Federal reclamation projects have also introduced two direct sources of inefficiency. First, by providing subsidies to approved projects, water was diverted to these projects even when the net benefits in the absence of subsidies would have been low. Since the subsidies were substantial,[11] this is in all probability a considerable source of inefficiency. Second, transfers of water from these projects must be approved by the Bureau of Reclamation. According to Meyers and Posner (1971, p. 20), precise criteria determining when approval should be granted have not been developed, so, at the very least, this process creates uncertainty about the possibility of transfer and probably raises the cost of any transfers that occur.

---

[11]For evidence on this point see Randal R. Rucker and Price V. Fishback, "The Federal Reclamation Program: An Analysis of Rent-Seeking Behavior," in Terry Anderson, ed. *Water Rights: Scarce Resource Allocation, Bureaucracy and the Environment* (Cambridge, MA: Ballinger Publishing Company, 1983): pp. 53 and 62.

Water Pricing. Restrictions on transfers are not the only source of inefficiency in the current allocation system. Much of the water is sold by public utilities and the prices charged by those utilities do not promote efficiency of use.

Both the level of prices and the rate structure are at fault. In general the price level is too low and the rate structure does not adequately reflect the costs of providing service to different types of customers.

In part, perhaps because it is considered an essential commodity that everyone should have access to, the prices charged by public water companies are too low. For surface water the rates are sometimes too low because they fail to cover costs. This can only happen with public companies since they have access to tax funds to make up the difference. The result is excessive water use and too little conservation. When relying on ground water, these companies frequently fail to include a user cost to reflect the depletion of the stocks in the calculation of prices. One study by Martin, et. al., (1984) found that due to a failure to include a user cost, rates in Tucson, Arizona are about 58 percent too low despite some recent increases. This too encourages an excessive rate of depletion.

Including this user cost in water prices is rather more difficult than it may first appear. Water utilities are typically regulated because they have a monopoly in the local area. One typical requirement for the rate structure of a regulated monopoly is that it earn only a "fair" rate of return. Excess profits are not permitted. Charging a uniform price for water to all users where the price includes a user cost would generate profits for the seller. (Remember the discussion of scarcity rent in Chapter 3?) The scarcity rent accruing to the seller as a result of incorporating the user cost would represent revenue in excess of operating and capital costs.

One way that water utilities are attempting to respect the rate of return requirement while promoting water conservation is through the use of an increasing block rate. Under this system the price per unit of water consumed rises as the amount consumed rises (Figure 9.3).

In this example the first ten ccf of water cost .70 per ccf.[12] The next 10 ccf cost .80 per ccf while the third costs .90 per ccf. A customer using 26 ccf would pay a bill for the month of $20.40 (10 × .70 + 10 × .80 + 6 × .90).

This type of structure encourages conservation by ensuring that the marginal cost of consuming additional water is high. At the margin where the consumer makes the decision of how much extra water to be used, quite a bit of money can be saved by being frugal with water use. It also, however, holds revenue down by charging a lower price for the first units consumed. This has the added virtue that those who need some water, but cannot afford the marginal price paid by more extravagant users, can have access to water without placing their budget in as much jeopardy as would be the case with a uniform price.

Other aspects of the rate structure are important as well. Efficiency dictates that prices equal the marginal cost of provision (including marginal user cost when ap-

---

[12]A ccf is one hundred cubic feet. One hundred cubic feet corresponds to 748 gallons.

FIGURE 9.3   Increasing Block Rate Structure

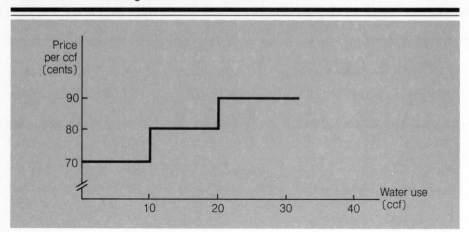

propriate). Several practical correlaries follow from this theorem. First, prices during peak demand periods should exceed prices during off-peak periods. It is peak use which strains the capacity of the system and therefore triggers the need for expansion. Therefore, peak users should pay the extra costs associated with system expansion by being charged higher rates. Few current water pricing systems satisfy this condition in practice.

Another correlary of the marginal cost pricing theorem is that when it costs a water utility more to serve one class of customers than another, each class of customers should bear the costs associated with its service. Typically this implies, for example, that those farther away from the source or at higher elevations (requiring more pumping) should pay higher rates. In practice utility water rates make fewer distinctions among customer classes than would be efficient. As a result, higher-cost water users are in effect subsidized; they receive too little incentive to conserve and too little incentive to locate in parts of the city that can be served at lower cost.

A somewhat more subtle, but no less important, violation of this rule occurs in rapidly expanding areas where population growth necessitates system expansion. Let's suppose, for example, that due to rapid population growth a particular city has to build a rather large water project to import water from another area. Efficiency dictates that these new users should pay higher rates to cover the additional costs of expanding the system; since, in the absence of population growth, the expansion would not be needed, existing residents should not have to foot the bill.

This efficiency condition is typically violated in practice in two different ways. First, the federal or state governments can usually be counted on to pick up a portion of the tab, so state or federal taxpayers end up paying one of the costs that should be borne by new residents. Second, local areas often attempt to mitigate the adverse effects on growth that this system would trigger by prorating the expansion costs over all residents—existing and new. In essence, all customers pay an average cost rather than the marginal cost of supplying their water.[13]

Average cost pricing in this context means an excessive demand for water. New residents moving into the area are not forced to bear the full cost of their move. As a result, this location appears more attractive than it should and one automatic dampening mechanism that the market provides to prevent excessive population growth in water scarcity areas is thwarted.

Common Property Problems.   For ground water there is one more problem. When many users tap the same aquifer, that acquifer becomes a common property resource. Tapping a common property resource will tend to deplete it too rapidly; users lose the incentive to conserve.

The incentive to conserve a ground water resource in an efficient market is created by the desire to prevent pumping costs from rising too rapidly and the desire to capitalize on the higher prices that could reasonably be expected in the future. With common property resources, neither of these desires translates into conservation for the simple reason that water conserved by one party may simply be used by another party because the conserver has no exclusive right to the water that is saved. Water saved by one party to take advantage of higher prices can easily be pumped out by another user before the higher prices ever materialize.

For common property resources, economic theory suggests several direct consequences. Pumping costs would rise too rapidly, initial prices would be too low, and too much water would be consumed by the earliest users. The burden of this waste would not be shared uniformly. Because the typical aquifer is bowl-shaped, users on the periphery of the aquifer would be particularly hard hit. When the water level declines, the edges go dry first, while the center can continue to supply water for substantially longer periods. Future users would also be hard hit relative to current users.

POTENTIAL REMEDIES

Economic analysis points the way to a number of possible means of remedying the current water situation in the Southwestern United States. These reforms would promote efficiency of water use while affording more protection to the interests of future generations of water users.

The first reform would reduce the number of restrictions on water transfers. The "use it or lose it" component of the beneficial use doctrine can promote the extravagant use of water. Allowing users to capture the value of water saved by permitting them to sell it would stimulate water conservation. As Exmaple 9–1 indicates, allowing sales

---

[13]Notice the parallel between this water price problem and the synfuels price problem discussed in Example 7–1.

EXAMPLE 9.1

**Using Economic Principles to Save Water
and Curb Agricultural Pollution in California**

How are California problems of water scarcity for irrigation and agricultural water pollution to be solved in the face of the financial plight for farmers? The answer, according to the Environmental Defense Fund (EDF), lies in the application of economic principles.

Agriculture discharges a variety of water pollutants—salts, suspended solids, pesticides, nutrients, and trace elements—that can harm human health and biological populations. To control these pollutants in California, the U.S. Bureau of Reclamation has long advocated the San Luis Drain, a plan that would dump the pollutants in the San Francisco Bay and Delta, financed largely from taxes.

EDF has suggested an alternative approach that would save water, protect the Bay and Delta, and reduce, if not eliminate, any financial contribution by taxpayers. For farmers, this proposal envisions more efficient irrigation, growth of low-water and salt-tolerant crops, and removing poor soil from irrigation. Economic incentives would be created by allowing farmers to sell the water saved. Off-the-farm reverse osmosis treatment plants would claim up to 90 percent of the remaining water for reuse, while generating saleable electricity and isolating certain saleable chemical constituents of the pollutants.

EDF analysis of these proposals suggests that as long as the water saved and electricity generated are valued at the marginal cost of new supplies from other sources, both the farmer's actions and the treatment plants could pay for themselves. Innovative applications of economic principles such as these could provide the basis for a new approach to sound management of water resources.

Source: W. R. Z. Willey, "The Agriculture and Water Pollution Crisis—Can Government and Private Sector Meet the Challenge?" *EDF Letter* (New York: Environmental Defense Fund, July, 1985) p. 2.

of excess water by conservers may be the foundation for achieving other social objectives as well.

One of the problems with the current water use doctrine in the Western and Southwestern United States is that it fails to provide adequate protection for the instream uses of water, such as fishing or boating. As long as use requires diversion, as it does typically in the beneficial use doctrine, water left for fish habitat or recreation is undervalued.

This undervaluation of instream uses is not inevitable, however, as some enterprising fishermen have discovered.[14] In the Yellowstone River Valley in Montana,

---

[14]These examples were drawn from Terry L. Anderson, *Water Crisis: Ending the Policy Drought* (Washington, D.C.: Cato Institute, 1983): 81–85.

several spring creeks are wholly contained with the boundaries of property owned by a single landowner. Since these creeks are not subject to the same legal restrictions as waterways crossing property boundaries, landowners can sell the daily fishing rights. The revenues from these sales provide owners with an incentive to develop spawning beds, protect the fish habitat, and in general make the fishing experience as desirable as possible. By limiting the number of fishermen, the owners prevent overexploitation of the resource.

In England and Scotland, markets are relied upon to protect instream uses more than they are in the United States. Private angling associations have been formed to purchase fishing rights from landowners. Once these rights have been acquired, the associations charge for fishing, using some of the revenues to preserve and to improve the fish habitat. Since fishing rights in England sell for as much as $220,000, the holders of these rights have a substantial incentive to protect their investments. One of the forms this protection takes is illustrated by the Angelers Cooperative Association, which has taken on the responsibility of monitoring the streams for pollution and alerting the authorities to any potential problems.

Another set of changes that would enchance efficiency involves reforming the water pricing policies followed by public water distribution utilities. The traditional practice of charging only for the costs of distributing water and treating the water itself as a free good should be abandoned in favor of a system that includes a scarcity value for water in the price. Since scarce water is not in any meaningful sense a free good, the user cost of that water must be imposed on current users. Only in this way will the proper incentive for conservation be created and the interests of future generations of water users be preserved.

One market-oriented way of determining and incorporating this scarcity value has been proposed by Professor Vernon L. Smith of the University of Arizona.[15] Specifically, he suggests that a new system of water deeds be created to complement the system of land deeds which already exists. The two types of deeds he envisions would convey to users the rights to use predefined proportions of the available annual flow of water and the available stock of ground water, respectively.

Professor Smith uses a case study of Tucson, Arizona in 1976 to illustrate how his proposal would work. The first step is to select a base year (1975, in his example). During this base year each individual property deed holder i, used some amount of water X_i. The sum of the X_i's in 1975 was 224.6 thousand acre-feet.

The first type deed conveys to the ith deedholder the right to consume r_i acre-feet of water per year in perpetuity where:

$$r_i = \frac{74.6\ X_i}{224.6}.$$

The 74.6 figure represents the annual flow of renewable water available (in thousands of acre-feet) to Tucson users. This deed then allocates this renewable water among all users on the basis of their 1975 consumption of all water.

---

[15]Vernon L. Smith, "Water Deeds: A Proposed Solution to the Water Valuation Problem" *Arizona Review,* Vol. 26 (January, 1977): 7–10.

The second deed conveys the rights to use the 30 million acre-feet of nonrenewable ground water that are estimated to be available in the area. The ith property owner is allocated the same proportion of this water as surface water:

$$R_i = \frac{30\ X_i}{224.6}.$$

As long as actual consumption is less than or equal to r_i (meaning that only renewable water is consumed) the property owner does not use up any of his allocation of the nonrenewable ground water. For every acre-foot of ground water he uses, however, he must surrender the equivalent amount from his second water deed. In other words if he originally was allocated 100 acre-feet and he used 3 acre-feet, he would have 97 acre-feet left. Since both types of deeds would be fully transferable, they could flow to the highest valued users. Conservation would be rewarded because excess rights could be sold. New users would have to buy the rights to water use from existing users; the impact of increased development on water scarcity would be reflected in the market price. The existence of these deeds would guarantee that the scarcity value of water would be considered. They would transform water from a free good to a valuable commodity.

Since the adoption of this type of system would represent quite a change from the existing approach, it is probably worth exploring less radical (and ultimately less efficient) alternatives. One of these would involve more widespread adoption of the principles of marginal cost pricing. More-expensive-to-serve users should pay higher prices for their water than their cheaper-to-serve counterparts. Similarly, when new, much higher cost sources of water are introduced into a water system to serve the needs of a particular category of users, those users should pay the marginal cost of that water, rather than the lower average cost of all water supplied. Finally, when a rise in the peak demand triggers a need for expanding either the water supplies or the distribution system, the peak demanders should pay the higher costs associated with the expansion.

These principles suggest a much more complicated rate structure for water than merely charging everyone the same price. As Example 9.2 demonstrates, the political consequences of introducing these changes may be rather drastic.

SUMMARY

Though on a global scale the amount of available water exceeds the demand, at particular times and in particular locations water scarcity is already a serious problem. In a number of locations, the current use of water exceeds replenishable supplies, implying that aquifers are being drained.

Efficiency dictates that replenishable water be allocated so as to equalize the marginal net benefits of water use even when supplies are higher or lower than normal. The efficient allocation of ground water requires that the user cost of that depletable resource be considered. When it is considered, water conservation creates a balance between present and future users. Typically, the marginal pumping cost would rise over time until either it exceeded the marginal benefit received from that water or the reservoir runs dry.

In earlier times, markets played the major role in allocating water. Governments have begun to play a much larger role in allocating this crucial resource.

There are several sources of inefficiency in the current system of water allocation in the Southwestern United States. The transfers of water among various users are restricted. The prices charged for water by public suppliers typically do not cover costs. For ground water, user cost is rarely included and for all sources of water, the rate structure does not usually reflect the costs of services. These deficiencies combine to discourage conservation of water to the detriment of potential future users.

Reforms are possible. Allowing conservers to capture the value of water saved by selling it would stimulate conservation. Creating separate fishing rights that can be

---

EXAMPLE 9.2

Politics and the Pricing of Scarce Water

As economics can make specific recommendations about the level and structure of water prices, politics can provide insights on the implementation of those recommendations. The implementation process is not always smooth or predictable, as the people of Tucson, Arizona found out.

In 1976, the city of Tucson faced what it perceived as a water crisis. The development of its service capacity had not kept pace with rapid population growth, and artificially low prices reduced the incentive to conserve. The ground water supplies on which the city depended were being depleted.

The utility, assisted by a newly elected City Council, instituted a new rate structure involving higher water prices overall and more attention to the cost of service in determining the rate structure. An unexpectedly dry year (creating an abnormally high demand), coupled with a newly implemented increasing block rate structure, conspired to insure that water bills increased tremendously soon after the change. The resulting anger of the residents spawned a recall campaign in which the councillors responsible for the rate increase were retired from office.

Are major changes in prices politically infeasible? The authors of the Tucson study believe not, though they do believe that feasible increases also have to be implemented with great care. In particular, they believe that local politicians must be willing to take risks, that the local residents must be convinced that a real problem exists and the burden of the increases must be distributed so no one group is asked to bear too large a share.

Source: William E. Martin, Helen M. Ingram, Nancy K. Laney, and Adrian H. Griffin, *Saving Water in a Desert City* (Washington, D.C.: Resources for the Future, 1984).

sold would provide some incentive to protect streams as fish habitats. Pricing systems can be changed to better reflect costs. To the extent that more fundamental change is politically possible, a set of transferable water deeds can be instituted to provide for more efficiency in the consumptive uses of water.

Water scarcity is already a serious problem and unless preventive measures are taken, it will get worse. The problem is not insoluble, though to date the steps necessary to solve it have not been taken.

FURTHER READING

Anderson, Terry L. *Water Crisis: Ending the Policy Drought* (Washington, D.C.: The Cato Institute, 1983). An excellent survey of the political economy of water, concluding that we have to rely more on the market to solve the crisis.

Anderson, Terry L., ed., *Water Rights: Scarce Resource Allocation, Bureaucracy, and the Environment* (Cambridge, MA: Ballinger Publishing Company, 1983). Nine essays examining the causes, consequences, and possible solutions to water scarcity in the Southwestern United States from a property rights point of view.

Martin, William E., Helen M. Ingram, Nancy K. Laney, and Adrian H. Griffin, *Saving Water in a Desert City* (Washington, D.C.: Resources for the Future, Inc., 1984). A detailed look at the political and economic ramifications of an attempt by Tucson, Arizona to improve the pricing of its diminishing supply of water.

Rucker, Randal R., and Price V. Fishback, "The Federal Reclamation Program: An Analysis of Rent-Seeking Behavior, in Terry Anderson, ed. *Water Rights: Scarce Resource Allocation, Bureaucracy and the Environment* (Cambridge, MA: Ballinger Publishing Company, 1983): 45–81.

Meyers, Charles J., and Richard A. Posner, *Market Transfers of Water Rights,* Legal Study No. 4 (Washington, D.C.: National Water Commission, 1971).

Willey, W. R. Z. "The Agriculture and Water Pollution Crisis – Can Government and Private Sector Meet the Challenge?" *EDF Letter* (New York: Environmental Defense Fund, 1985): 2.

Smith, Vernon L. "Water Deeds: A Proposed Solution to the Water Valuation Problem," *Arizona Review* Vol. 26 (January, 1977): 7–10.

U.S. Water Resources Council, *The Nation's Water Resources 1975–2000* (Washington, D.C.: Government Printing Office, 1978). A multi-volume series examining on a location-by-location basis the present and future supply of and demand for water.

ADDITIONAL REFERENCES

Barney, Gerald O. *The Global 2000 Report to the President of the U.S.: Entering the 21st Century* (New York: Pergamon Press, 1980).

Council on Environmental Quality, *Environmental Quality 1983: The 14th Annual Report of the Council on Environmental Quality* (Washington, D.C.: Council on Environmental Quality, 1984).

Council on Environmental Quality, *Environmental Trends* (Washington, D.C.: Government Printing Office, 1978).

Cuzan, Alfred G. "Appropriators versus Expropriators: The Political Economy of Water in the West," in Terry L. Anderson, ed. *Water Rights: Scarce Resource Allocation, Bureaucracy and the Environment* (Cambridge, MA: Ballinger Publishering Company, 1983): 13–43.

Frederick, Kenneth D. "Water Supplies" in Paul R. Portney, ed. *Current Issues in Natural Resource Policy* (Washington, D.C.: Resources for the Future, Inc., 1982): 216–252.

Gisser, Micha, and Ronald N. Johnson, "Institutional Restriction on the Transfer of Water Rights and the Survival of an Agency" in Terry L. Anderson, ed., *Water Rights: Scarce Resource Allocation, Bureaucracy and the Environment* (Cambridge, MA: Ballinger Publishing Company 1983): 137–165.

McCurdy, Charles W. "Stephen J. Field and Public Land Law Development in California, 1850–1866: A Case Study in Judicial Resource Allocation in Nineteenth Century America," *Law and Society* (Winter, 1976): 235–266.

Sheridan, David for the Council on Environmental Quality, *Desertification of the United States* (Washington, D.C.: Government Printing Office, 1981).

DISCUSSION QUESTIONS

1. Who stands to gain and lose compared to the current system if the Smith system of water deeds were to be instituted? Politically, where might the support for or opposition to such a proposal come from?

PROBLEM

1. Suppose that in a particular area the consumption of water varies tremendously throughout the year with average household summer use exceeding winter use by a great deal. What effect would this have on an efficient rate structure for water?

CHAPTER TEN

Reproducible Private-Property Resources: Food

The Commission's assessment of the future prospects for over-coming world hunger has led to one conclusion . . . the out-come of the war on hunger, by the year 2000 and beyond, will not be determined by forces beyond human control, but, rather, by decisions and actions well within the capability of nations working individually and together.

PRESIDENTIAL COMMISSION ON WORLD HUNGER,
Overcoming World Hunger: The Challenge Ahead (1980)

INTRODUCTION

In Chapter 1, food was a point of contention between Kahn and the *Limits to Growth* team. The *Limits to Growth* team foresaw the demand for food (driven by population growth) outstripping the supply (primarily due to a decline in the remaining availability of arable land), suggesting a resulting famine as one source of societal collaspe. Kahn, on the other hand, foresaw population growth as diminishing, and a tremendous expansion in food supplies forthcoming from the applications of new technologies. Which vision seems more accurate?

Not long ago the World Bank concluded that somewhere in the neighborhood of one-half billion persons were subsisting on a diet not sufficient to provide adequate nutrition. Though there may be some quarrel with this specific number, there exists a wide recognition that a substantial proportion of the world's population is currently malnourished.

In its report, *Overcoming World Hunger: The Challenge Ahead,* the Presidential Commission on World Hunger suggests that world hunger has been transformed by inaction from a low-profile moral concern to a decisive and explosive factor in international relations. During the 1970s the rise in mutual suspicion among developed countries of the "North" and less-developed countries of the "South" made itself felt in international conferences addressing global problems. One source of apparent hostility is the fact that instead of being a problem which is faced by the citizens of all nations, malnutrition is heavily concentrated in nations of the South. Thus allocating food is a task which will test the resilience of our political and economic systems.

Why has this situation arisen? Cereal grain, the world's chief supply of food, is a renewable private-property resource which, if maanged effectively, could be sustained as long as we receive energy from the sun. Because land is typically not a common-property resource, farmers have an incentive to invest in irrigation and other means of increasing yield because they can appropriate the additional revenues generated. On the surface, a flaw in the market process is not apparent. We must dig deeper to uncover the sources of the problem.

In this chapter we shall explore the validity of three common hypotheses used to explain widespread malnourishment: (1) a persistent global scarcity of food; (2) a maldistribution of that food both among nations and within nations; and (3) temporary shortages caused by weather or other natural causes. These hypotheses are not mutually exclusive; they could all be valid sources of a portion of the problem. As we shall see later in the chapter, it is important to distinguish among these sources and assess their relative importance because each implies a different policy approach.

GLOBAL SCARCITY

A number of commentators see the problem as an absolute global scarcity—a case of too many people chasing too little food. An example of this point of view is presented by William and Paul Paddock [1967] in their provocatively titled book *Famine—1975!* Written by an agronomist and an experienced foreign-service officer, this book suggested that widespread famine would occur in 1975 causing a worldwide catastrophe of unprecedented proportions. They were not alone in their general assessment of the situation, although there was no consensus about the timing of the anticipated widespread famines.[1]

To some, this onset of a food crisis suggests a need for dramatic changes in the relationship between the agricultural surplus nations and other nations. Garrett Hardin, a human ecologist, has suggested the situation is so desperate that our conventional ethics, which involve sharing the available resources, are not only insufficient but are also counterproductive. He argues we must replace these dated notions of sharing wealth with more stern "lifeboat ethics."[2]

The allegory he invokes involves a lifeboat adrift in the sea which can safely hold 50 or, at most, 60 persons. Hundreds of other persons are swimming about, clamoring to get into the lifeboat, their only chance for survival. Hardin suggests that if passengers

---

[1]See, for example, Lester R. Brown, *In the Human Interest* (New York: W. W. Norton & Company, Inc., 1974).

[2]Garrett Harden, "Living on a Lifeboat," *Bioscience* XXIV (October 1974): 561–568.

in the boat were to follow conventional ethics and allow swimmers into the boat, it would eventually sink, taking everyone to the bottom of the sea. In contrast, he argues, lifeboat ethics would suggest a better resolution of the dilemma; the 50 or 60 should row away, leaving the others to certain death, but saving those fortunate enough to gain entry to the lifeboat. The implication is that food sharing is counterproductive. It would encourage more population growth and ultimately would cause inevitable and even more serious shortages in the future.

The premise for this allegory is that there is a global scarcity of food; famine is inevitable and sharing is counterproductive. If there is no global scarcity (the lifeboat has a large enough capacity for all), then a worldwide famine can be avoided by a sharing of resources. How accurate is the global scarcity premise?

Formulating the Global Scarcity Hypothesis

Most authorities seem to agree that there is currently an adequate amount of food. Studies made by the Food and Agricultural Organization of the United Nations, which report that the available supplies of food are more than adequate to supply the nutritional needs of all the world, are typical.[3]

Because this evidence is limited to a single point in time, however, it gives us no sense of whether scarcity is decreasing or increasing. If we are to identify and evaluate trends, we must develop more precise, measurable notions of how the market allocates food.

As a renewable resource, cereal grains could be produced indefinitely, if managed correctly. Yet there are a couple of facets of the world hunger problem that have to be taken into account. First, while population growth has slowed down, it has not stopped. Therefore, it is reasonable to expect the rising demand for food to continue. Second, the primary input for growing food is land, and land is ultimately fixed in supply. Thus, our analysis must explain how a market reacts in the presence of rising demand for a renewable resource which is produced using a fixed factor of production!

A substantial and dominant proportion of the Western world's arable land is privately owned. Access to this land is restricted; the owners have the right to exclude others and can reap what they sow. The typical owner of farm land has sufficient control over the resource to prevent undue depreciation, but not enough control over the market as a whole to raise the specter of monopoly profits.

What kind of outcome could we expect from this market in the face of rising demand and a fixed supply of land? What do we mean by scarcity and how could we perceive its existence? The answer depends crucially on the nature of the supply curve (Figure 10.1).

Suppose the market is initially in equilibrium with quantity Q_0 supplied at price P_0. Let the passage of time be recorded as shifts outward in the demand curve. Consider what would happen in the fifth time period. If the supply curve were S_a, the quan-

---

[3]The data on which this conclusion is based can be found in Table 10.1 which appears subsequently in this chapter.

FIGURE 10.1 The Market for Food

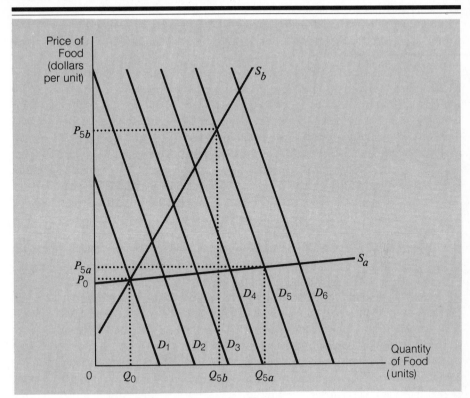

tity would rise to Q_{5a}. However, if the supply curve were S_b, the quantity supplied would only rise to Q_{5b}, but price would rise to P_{5b}.

This analysis sheds light on what is meant by scarcity in the world food market. It does not mean a shortage. Even under relatively adverse supply circumstances pictured by the supply curve S_b, the amount of food supplied would equal the amount demanded. As prices rose, potential demand would be choked off and additional supplies would be called forth.

Some critics argue that the demand for food is not price sensitive. Since food is a necessary commodity for survival, they say, its demand is inflexible and doesn't respond to prices. While food is a necessary commodity, not all food fits that category. We don't have to gaze very long at an average vending machine in a developed country to conclude that some food is far from a necessity.

There are many examples of food purchases being price responsive. One occurred during the 1960s when the price of meat skyrocketed for what turned out to be a relatively short period. It wasn't long before a hamburger substitute appeared in supermarkets made entirely out of soybean meal. The result was a striking reduction in meat consumption. This is a particularly important example because the raising of livestock for meat in Western countries consumes an enormous amount of grain. This evidence suggests that the balance between the direct consumption of cereal grains and the indirect consumption through meat is affected by prices.

But enough about the demand side; what do we know of the supply side? What factors would determine whether S_a or S_b is a more adequate representation of the past and the future?

Rising prices do stimulate supply response. The question is, how much? Land is an increasing-cost, fixed-supply resource that need not be depleted. As the demand for food rises, the supply can be increased either by expanding the amount of land under cultivation, or by increasing the yields on the land already under cultivation, or some combination of the two. Historically, both sources have been important.

Typically, the most fertile land is cultivated first. That land is then farmed more and more intensively until it is cheaper, at the margin, to bring additional, less fertile, land into production. Because it is less fertile, the additional land is brought into production only if the prices rise high enough to make farming it profitable. Thus, the supply curve for arable land (and hence for food, as long as land remains an important factor of productin) can be expected to slope upward.

We can now define two forms of the global scarcity hypothesis that can be tested against the available evidence. The *strong form* suggests that per capita food production is declining. In terms of Figure 10.1, the strong form of the hypothesis would imply that the slope of the supply curve is sufficiently steep that production does not keep pace with population increases in demand brought about by population growth. If the strong form is valid, we should witness declining per capita food consumption. This form triggers the push for lifeboat ethics.

The *weak form* of the global scarcity hypothesis can hold even if per capita consumption is increasing over time. It suggests that the supply curve is sufficiently steeply sloped that food prices are increasing more rapidly than other prices in general; the relative price of food is rising over time. If the weak form is valid, per capita welfare is declining, even if consumption is rising. The problem is related more to the cost of food than the availability of food; as supplies of food increase the cost of food rises relative to the cost of other goods.

Testing the Hypothesis

Now that we have a testable hypothesis, we can assess the degree to which the historical record supports the existence of increasing global scarcity. The evidence for per capita production is clear (Figure 10.2). Food production has increased faster than population in both the developed and developing countries. Per capita production has increased, although the increase has been small. Thus, at least for the recent past, we can rule out the strong form of the global-scarcity hypothesis.

How about the weak form? Have relative agricultural prices risen? Harold Barnett [1979], a noted resource economist, published the results of a preliminary study on trends in resource prices, including agricultural prices. Specifically, he examined the ratio of an index of agricultural prices to the general wholesale price index for a variety of countries over two different time periods (1950–62 and 1961–72). A total of 53 cases were examined. He discovered that for 23 of those cases agriculture prices

FIGURE 10.2 Index of Per Capita Food Production for Developed and Developing Countries (1976–83)

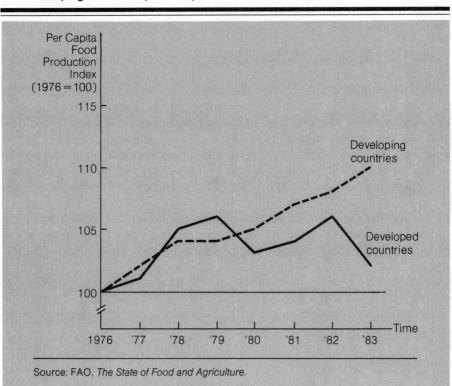

Source: FAO, *The State of Food and Agriculture.*

rose at a statistically significant higher rate than wholesale prices in general. Using only the later time period (involving 31 countries), some 15 countries experienced rises in agricultural prices which significantly exceeded rises in wholesale prices.

This evidence suggests that in about half the countries the supply curve for agricultural products is more steeply sloped than the supply curve for products in general. In those countries, at least, there is support for the weak form of the global-scarcity hypothesis. Since not all market prices are efficient, as we shall see later in this chapter, we must not place too much emphasis on these numbers. Even so, the evidence suggests that agricultural supplies have increased faster than population but at an increasingly relative cost.

Outlook for the Future

What factors will influence the future relative costs of food? Future supplies depend on the abilities of developing nations to supply an increasing share of world food production to meet their increasing shares of population and also on the ability of the United

States to continue its role as a major food exporter. The ability of developing nations to expand their role is considered in the next section as a part of the food-distribution problem. In this section, therefore, we shall deal with forces affecting productivity in the United States.

Technological Progress.   One of the chief historical sources of productivity growth has been technological progress. Increases in crop productivity were stimulated by improvements in machinery; increased utilization of commercial fertilizers, pesticides and herbicides; developments in plant and animal breeding; expanding use of irrigation water; and adjustments in location of crop production. Their combined effect doubled average yield per acre from 1910–1977.[4]

There are reasons for being optimistic about the continuation of technological progress in agriculture. Three techniques appear particularly promising: (1) recombinant DNA, which permits recombining genes from one species with those of another; (2) tissue culture, which allows whole plants to be grown from single cells; and (3) cell fusion, which involves uniting the cells of species that wouldn't normally mate to create new types of plants different from "parent" cells. One knowledgeable reviewer in the field suggested several applications for these generic engineering techniques, including:

1. Making food crops more resistant to diseases and insect pests.
2. Creating hardy new crop plants capable of surviving in marginal soils.
3. Giving staple food crops such as corn, wheat, and rice the ability to make their own nitrogen-rich fertilizers by using solar energy to make ammonia from nitrogen in the air.
4. Increasing crop yields by improving the way plants use the sun's energy during photosynthesis.[5]

The World Bank (1982) has estimated that these techniques could increase yields at least 30 percent beyond those achieved with the best previously available seeds.

The outlook is not uniformly bright, however. Three concerns have arisen regarding the ability of the United States to achieve further productivity gains: the declining share of land allocated to agricultural use, the rising cost of energy, and the rising environmental cost of traditional forms of agriculture.[6]

---

[4]Melvin L. Cotner, Nelson L. Bills, and Robert F. Boxley, "An Economic Perspective of Land Use," in *Economics, Ethics, Ecology: Roots of Productive Conservation,* Walter E. Jeske, ed. (Ankeny, Iowa: Soil Conservation Society of America, 1981), p. 31.

[5]Robert Cooke, "Engineering a New Agriculture," *Technology Review* 85 (May/June 1982): 24–25.

[6]See, for example, Lester R. Brown, "World Population Growth, Soil Erosion, and Food Security." *Science* 214 (27 November 1981): 995–1002.

Allocation of Agricultural Land.   During 1920 in the United States, 958 million acres were used for farming. By 1974 the comparable figure was 465 million acres.[7] Some 50 percent of the agricultural land in 1920 had been converted to nonagricultural purposes by 1974. A simple extrapolation of this trend would certainly raise questions about our ability to increase productivity at historical rates. Is a simple extrapolation reasonable? What determines the allocation of land between agricultural and nonagricultural uses?

Agricultural land will be converted to nonagricultural land when its profitability in nonagricultural uses is higher. If we are to explain the historical experience, we must be able to explain why the relative value of land in agriculture has declined.

Two factors stand out. First, an increasing urbanization and industrialization of society rapidly raised the value of nonagricultural land. Second, rising productivity of the remaining land allowed the smaller amount of land to produce a lot more food. Less land was needed in agriculture to meet the demand for food.

In some cases, the market did not strike the correct balance between agricultural and nonagricultural uses, although the fault seems to be more with public policy than with the market. Government policies created a bias that undervalued the agricultural use of land.

The first of these policies was the use of the property tax, which is based on the value of land and improvements rather than wealth in general, to raise revenue. Thus, activities using much land are hit relatively hard by this tax, compared to activities using less land per dollar of output. Because agriculture is a land-intensive industry, farmers who are land-rich but income-poor find the returns to agriculture lower with a property tax than they would with an income tax.

A second source of imperfect price signals was the subsidization of nonagricultural uses of land. One significant source of the decline in rural land near metropolitan areas, for example, was its conversion to residential use as the suburbs spread outward. This movement was certainly stimulated by the large tax subsidies given to homeowners. By lowering the after-tax cost of owner-occupied residential space, these tax subsidies encouraged the movement from high-density, low-space, urban rental units to low-density, large-lot, single-family detached units. Land became more profitable in suburban residential development than in agriculture.

It seems unlikely that a simple extrapolation of the decline in agricultural land of the magnitude since 1920 would be accurate. Since the middle of the 1970s, the urbanization process has diminished to the point that many urban areas are experiencing declining population. This shift is not merely explained by suburbia spilling beyond the boundaries of what was formerly considered urban. For the first time in our history, a significant amount of population has moved from urban to rural areas.

---

[7]See Melvin L. Cotner, Nelson L. Bills, and Robert F. Boxley, "An Economic Perspective of Land Use," in *Economics, Ethics, Ecology: Roots of Productive Conservation,* Walter E. Jeske, ed. (Ankeny, Iowa: Soil Conservation Society of America, 1981), p. 31.

Furthermore, as increases in food demand are accompanied by rises in prices of food, the value of agricultural land will increase. This will tend to slow conversion and possibly even reverse the trend. To make this impact even greater, several states have now allowed agricultural land to either escape the property tax (until it is sold for some nonagricultural purpose) or to pay lower rates. Confirming evidence for this generally optimistic assessment can be found in the fact that most of the conversion to nonagricultural uses actually occurred prior to World War II.[8]

Energy Costs.   A second area of concern centers around the manner in which the United States has achieved its gains in productivity in the past. Some major portion of those gains resulted from mechanization and the increased use of pesticides and fertilizers. A number of traditional pesticides and most fertilizers are derived from petroleum feedstocks. As we saw in Chapter 7, the cost of petroleum has risen substantially and probably can be expected to continue to rise in real terms. To the extent that the United States cannot develop cheaper substitutes, the supply curve must shift to the left to reflect the increasing costs of doing business.

Ralph d'Arge [1981], an economist investigating this question, sees energy and capital as complements in agriculture. Due to this complementary relationship energy price rises could be expected to trigger some reduction in capital, as well as some reduction in energy on American farms, reducing their productivity. Furthermore, since d'Arge found that farm-wage rates have risen less rapidly than either energy costs or the costs of borrowing (as reflected by interest rates), he concluded there will be a readjustment of American agriculture in the future as labor is substituted for capital. This he expects will cause a shift toward smaller, family-operated units with a consequent reduction in the growth rate in agricultural productivity. So far the evidence does not seem to support this prophesy.

Environmental Costs.   At least some of past productivity gains have come by depreciating the asset. Soil erosion provides a case in point. Some soil erosion is natural, of course, and within certain tolerance limits does not harm productivity. The concern arises because some farm practices partially responsible for increasing productivity (continuous cropping rather than rotations with pasture or other soil-retaining crops) have tended to exacerbate soil erosion. The fears are further intensified by the belief that these losses are irreversible within one generation.

If increased soil erosion is taking place, why would a private property owner allow this depletion? In the past soil conservation simply didn't pay. The techniques to avoid it were expensive and the ready availability of cheap fertilizer to replace lost nutrients meant that the cost of soil depletion was low. Further, the damage caused to rivers and streams by this eroding soil was not borne by the farmers who could best control it.

---

[8]The decline in crop land since 1949 has involved only 13 of more than 400 million acres converted since 1920. For more details on this, see Melvin L. Cotner, Nelson L. Bills, and Robert F. Boxley, "An Economic Perspective of Land Use," in *Economics, Ethics, Ecology: Roots of Productive Conservation*, Walter E. Jeske, ed. (Ankeny, Iowa: Soil Conservation Society of America, 1981), pp. 31–36.

The barriers that prevented erosion from being checked are now disappearing. As the level of topsoil reaches lower tolerance limits, the fertility of the land is affected. Rising cost is making fertilizers a less desirable substitute for soil erosion. In the near future we may see more soil conservation techniques practiced because they are becoming profitable for American farms.[9]

There are other cases in which past agricultural practices have caused environmental damage and the continuation of these would cause rising environmental costs. A great deal of pest control in the past has relied upon pesticides. Many of these persist in the environment, and there is an increasing recognition that some toxicity extends to species other than the target population. In addition, many current pesticides are derived from petroleum, so as the cost of petroleum increases, the cost of these pesticides increases as well.

Irrigation, a traditional source of productivity growth, is running into limits as well, particularly in the western United States. Some traditionally important underground sources used to supply water are not being replenished at a rate sufficient to offset the withdrawals. Therefore, these water supplies are being exhausted.

Salination (rising amounts of salt) in irrigation water is becoming more common. In some cases, this results when an overuse of fresh water reduces the pressure, allowing the intrusion of nearby coastal sea water. In other areas having a natural salinity, irrigation causes the salt to leach into the streams. This salty water becomes less useful for irrigation and, in extreme cases, kills the crops.

A final environmental cost associated with agriculture results from the fertilizers, pesticides, and herbicides used to enhance productivity. Some of the nutrients from fertilizers leak into lakes and stimulate the excessive growth of algae. Aside from the aesthetic cost of a body of water choked with plant life, this nutrient excess can deprive other aquatic life forms of the oxygen they need to survive. The herbicides and pesticides can contaminate water supplies, rendering them unfit for drinking and for supporting normal populations of fish.

Because these environmental costs were not large in the past, they have not dampened agricultural productivity greatly. In the future, however, their role promises to be much larger. Though these adverse environmental effects can be controlled, resources which in the past would have gone to enhance agricultural yields must now be committed to this purpose.

In summing up our findings, it appears that agricultural productivity in the United States will rise in the future, but at lower rates. Also, energy and environmental costs will offset to some extent the expected gains from technological progress. Thus, global scarcity in its strongest form does not now exist, and in light of the declining population-growth rate, is not likely to exist in the near future. Most observers would probably

---

[9]Some interesting confirming evidence is supplied in a speech by the President of Oklahoma State University. L. L. Bolger, "Fitting Conservation into Economic Realities," in *Economics, Ethics, Ecology: Roots of Productive Conservation,* Walter E. Jeske, ed. (Ankeny, Iowa: Soil Conservation Society of America, 1981), pp. 3–11. He notes that Oklahoma farmers planted more than one-half million trees for windbreaks in 1978, twice the number planted five years before.

agree with the thrust, if not the specific numbers, of the forecast of *The Global 2000 Report,* a joint research report issued by the Council of Environmental Quality and the Department of State [1980]:

> On the average, world food production is projected to increase more rapidly than world population, with average per capita consumption increasing about 15 percent between 1970 and 2000. [Vol. 1, p. 17]

This evidence does not support the abandonment of conventional ethics. Humane approaches remain possible and desirable.

DISTRIBUTION OF FOOD RESOURCES

The second view holds that the malnourishment problem may stem more from food distribution than from global availability. According to this outlook, the basic problem is poverty. We would expect, therefore, that the poorest segments of society would be the most malnourished and the poorest countries would contain the largest number of malnourished people.

If accurate, this representation suggests a very different policy orientation than that suggested by global scarcity. If the problem is maldistribution, rather than shortage, the issue is how to get the food to the poorest people. The alleviation of poverty, increasing the ability to pay for food, is a strategy which could alleviate the problem. If the problem were a lack of food, this strategy would be totally ineffectual.

Defining the Problem

There is considerable and persuasive evidence that the problem is a distribution one (Table 10.1). The information in this table is constructed by the Food and Agriculture Organization (FAO) in several steps. First, they calculate a minimum number of calories that will allow normal activity and good health in adults and will permit children to reach normal body weight and intelligence in the absence of disease. Though these vary by country, they are generally in the neighborhood of 2400 kilocalories per day.

In the second step the FAO calculates the number of kilocalories the average citizen of that country receives from his or her food intake. The final step involves calculating the ratio of actual intake to minimum desired intake and multiplying that ratio by 100. The results are portrayed in Table 10.1. An index equal to 100 means that the caloric intake is just sufficient for the average citizen to avoid nutritional deficiency. A number lower than 100 means the average citizen of that country is subject to nutritional deficiencies.

TABLE 10.1 Daily Per Capita Calorie Supply As Percent of Requirements

	1969–71	*1974–76*	*1978–80*	*1977*	*1978*	*1979*	*1980*
				%			
Developing market economies	95.5	95.5	99.2	96.3	99.2	99.8	98.6
Africa	93.5	93.1	93.7	94.3	93.9	93.3	94.0
Far East	92.8	90.8	95.7	91.1	96.0	96.9	94.1
Latin America	105.8	106.7	108.9	107.5	108.4	108.7	109.4
Near East	97.2	106.2	111.0	108.5	109.7	111.3	112.1
Other developing market economies	100.0	101.5	105.7	102.8	105.7	106.3	105.3
Asian centrally planned economies	90.7	97.7	104.3	99.1	101.3	105.0	106.6
Total developing countries	93.9	96.3	100.9	97.2	99.9	101.5	101.2
Least developed countries	88.3	84.1	84.1	82.9	84.3	83.1	85.0
Total developed countries	128.4	130.8	133.1	131.2	132.2	133.7	133.4
World	104.8	106.5	109.8	107.0	109.1	110.4	110.0

Source: Food and Agricultural Organization, *The State of Food and Agriculture: 1982* (Rome: United Nations, 1983), Table 1-1, p. 5.

Though the data are far from perfect,[10] a number of interesting conclusions can be drawn. Looking at the bottom line first, we find that the average member of the world population has a sufficient caloric intake. This reinforces our conclusion that the problem is not one of global scarcity. It is also clear, however, that the food is not uniformly distributed among the world's peoples. During 1979, for example, the diet of the average citizen in developing countries was barely adequate. The average diet in Africa was nutritionally deficient in every year covered by the table. For the least developed countries, the average diet contained fewer calories than the nutritional deficiency threshold. Meanwhile, nutritional levels in developed countries on average were well in excess of the minimum.

Equally interesting, however, is the trend. Clear progress is being made in the developing countries as a whole. The change from the 1966–68 period to the 1975–77 period is strikingly positive. These very positive results, however, are tempered considerably by the results for the least developed nations. For those countries, the average diet was woefully inadequate at the beginning of the period and the situation has deteriorated during the intervening ten years.

Those countries which seem the most resistant to improvement in their nutritional situation seem to share two characteristics: (1) high population growth and (2) low per-capita income. Of the 46 countries included in the FAO most seriously affected group, all but four have population growth rates in excess of 2.0 percent.[11] All but four of

---

[10]Dealing only with calories, these data ignore other kinds of nutritional deficiencies, such as insufficient vitamin or protein intake. By concentrating solely on the average, it ignores the nutritional problems of the very poorest citizens. Considerable hunger can exist in a country where the average citizen is well fed.

[11]Food and Agriculture Organization, *The State of Food and Agriculture: 1979* (Rome: Food and Agriculture Organization of the United Nations, 1980), pp. 1–15.

them had GNP per capita ratios of less than $500 per year. Theses figures compare with an average population growth rate of 0.7 percent and an average GNP per capita of $8070 in the industrialized countries.[12]

As we stated in the chapter on population growth, these characteristics may well be related. High poverty levels are generally conducive to high population growth, and high population growth rates may increase the degree of income inequality. Thus extreme poverty may perpetuate itself. Since we have examined population-control strategies in Chapter 5, we shall now focus on stratgies to increase the amount of food available to the poorest people. What can be done?

Domestic Production in LDCs

The first issue to be addressed concerns the relative merits of increasing domestic production in the less developed countries (LDCs) as opposed to importing more from abroad. There are several reasons for believing that many developing countries can profitably increase the percentage of their consumption domestically produced. One of the most important is that food imports use up precious foreign exchange.

Most developing countries cannot pay for imports with their own currencies. They must pay in an internationally accepted currency, such as the American dollar, earned through the sale of exports. As more foreign exchange is used for agricultural imports, less is available for imports such as capital goods, which could raise the productivity (and hence incomes) of local workers.

The lack of foreign exchange has been exacerbated by the rapid rise in oil prices. Many developing nations must spend a large portion of export earnings merely to import energy. In 1977 the average low-income country spent 16 percent of its export earnings on energy. This is up from 9 percent in 1960. For some countries the situation is even more dismal. Pakistan, for example, spent 43 percent of its export earnings for energy imports.[13] That leaves little for capital goods or agricultural imports.

While this pressure on foreign exchange suggests a need for greater reliance on domestic agricultural production, it would be incorrect to carry that argument to its logical extreme by suggesting that all nations should become self-sufficient in food. The reason why self-sufficiency is not always efficient is suggested by *the law of comparative advantage.*

Nations are better off specializing in those products for which they have a comparative advantage. If its comparative advantage is not in food but in textiles, for example, the country would be better off by producing and exporting textiles, using the

---

[12]The World Bank, *World Development Report, 1980* (Washington, D.C.: International Bank for Reconstruction and Development, 1980), pp. 110, 111 and 142.

[13]The World Bank, *World Development Report, 1980* (Washington, D.C.: International Bank for Reconstruction and Development, 1980), pp. 122.

TABLE 10.2 A Hypothetical Example of the Law of Comparative Advantage

	Hours to Produce One Unit of Textiles	*Hours to Produce One Unit of Wheat*
Less Developed Country	1	3
Developed Country	1	1

earnings to purchase food (Table 10.2). The opportunity costs of producing textiles and wheat (measured in hours of labor per unit output) are given for a hypothetical less developed country (LDC) and a developed country (DC). Suppose we are considering an eight-hour day in each country. If the average worker in each country were to spend four hours of each day on each activity, then eight units of textile (four by the LDC and four by the DC) and five-and one-third units of wheat (one- and one-third by the LDC and four by the DC) would be produced by the two countries each day. (Be sure you can see how these numbers can be derived from the table).

Suppose, however, that the LDC in this case were to specialize in textiles (by allocating all eight hours to textile production) while the DC specialized in wheat. It is easy to verify that the total world production would now be eight units of textiles and eight units of wheat. *When countries specialize in those products in which they have a comparative advantage, total production can increase!*

Why did this happen in our example? It happened because the opportunity cost of making textiles in LDC (in terms of forgone wheat) was lower than in DC, while the opportunity cost of growing wheat in DC (in terms of forgone textile production) was lower than that in LDC. By freeing labor in DC from making textiles, LDC would be able to reap some of the benefits of the increased wheat production.

Although this example is hypothetical, the principle it conveys is real. Total self-sufficiency in food for all nations is not an appropriate goal. Those nations with a comparative advantage in agriculture due to climate, soil type, available land, and so on, such as the United States, should be net exporters, while those nations, such as Japan, with comparative advantage in other commodities should remain net food importers. This balance should not be allowed to get out of line, however, by creating an excessive reliance on either domestic production or imports.

Have the low-income countries as a group been reducing the share of their food consumption which comes from imports? Historically the answer was no. The World Bank [1980] computed an index of food production per capita by country. The index was constructed in such a manner that it took on the value 100 for a domestic production per capita level equal to that achieved by the country on average during the 1969–71 period. Therefore, values of less than 100 indicated a fall in food production per capita. The average value for low-income countries for the 1976–78 period was 97, while it was 108 for industrialized market economies.

The obvious implication was that low-income countries as a group were not even keeping up with population growth, much less making headway in reducing imports.

In the absence of major efforts by these countries to buck the trend, this increasing reliance on imports is expected by some to continue into the twenty-first century.[14] Notice, however, that the most recent optimistic evidence shown in Figure 10.2 conflicts with these earlier views.

The Undervaluation Bias

Why did food production lag population growth for so many years? There is accumulating evidence that the limits to further production are primarily economic and political, not physical or biological.[15] Agriculture in the low-income countries has been undervalued, implying that the rate of return on investment in agriculture is well below what it would be if agricultural output were allowed to receive its full social value. As a result, investments in agriculture were lower than they would otherwise have been and productivity has suffered.

Before investigating the sources and consequences of this problem, let's discuss a myth that periodically appears. According to the myth, peasant farmers do not respond to prices for cash crops because they are too ignorant, and they don't respond to prices for subsistence crops because they eat them rather than market them. Therefore, the myth concludes, there is no price elasticity of supply in peasant economies. Population induced increases in demand would cause higher prices but not increased supplies. As one of many studies, Example 10.1 indicates this argument has one fatal flaw. It is not true!

Governments have used many mechanisms having the undesirable side effect of undervaluing agriculture and destroying incentives in the process. Two stand out — marketing boards and export taxes.

National marketing boards have been established in many developing countries for stabilizing agricultural prices and holding food prices down to protect the poor from malnutrition. Typically, a marketing board sells food at subsidized prices. As the subsidy grows, the board looks around for ways to reduce the amount of subsidy.

Two strategies regularly employed by marketing boards are the wholesale importation of artificially cheap food from the United States (available under the food aid program originally designed to get rid of wheat surpluses) and holding down prices paid to domestic farmers. Both, of course, have the long-term effect of disrupting local production. The perniciousness of this process is shown in Example 10.2

Many developing countries depend on export taxes, levied on all goods shipped abroad, as a principal source of revenue. Some of these taxes fall on cash-crop food exports (bananas, cocoa beans, coffee, and so on). The impact of export taxes is to raise the cost to foreign purchasers, reducing the amount of demand. A reduction in

---

[14]One such forecast is found in Council on Environmental Quality and Department of State, *The Global 2000 Report to the President of the U.S.: Entering the 21st Century Vol. 1: The Summary Report* (New York, NY: Pergamon Press, 1980), pp. 17–18.

[15]For a summary of the evidence, see Sir Charles Pereira, "The Changing Patterns of Constraints on Food Production in the Third World," in *Distortions of Agricultural Incentives*, Theodore W. Schultz, ed. (Bloomington: Indiana University Press, 1978), pp. 24–34.

EXAMPLE 10.1

The Price Responsiveness of Supply: Thailand

The market response to an increasing demand for food resulting from population growth is rising prices. This increase in prices is then presumed to call for further increases in supply. The more price responsive the supply, the less serious effect price rises will have. Therefore, the question of agricultural production responsiveness to prices is of major importance.

There is considerable debate about whether we should expect farmers to respond to prices. Those who believe that prices are important see farmers as rational, calculating individuals seizing the opportunities presented to them in the form of higher prices. The other camp generally believes that small farmers are ignorant and so set in their ways as to be oblivious to what happens in the markets for their products.

Jere Behrman, and economist on the faculty of the University of Pennsylvania, has investigated this question. He published a major empirical study assessing the price responsiveness of four major annual crop supplies in Thailand over the period 1937–63. Three (cassava, corn and *kenaf*)* were cash crops while the fourth (rice) was a subsistence crop where only the surplus was marketed.

Using sophisticated econometric models, he found a substantial amount of price responsiveness in the supply of all four commodities. He notes that the substantial price responses found for kenaf are particularly noteworthy because this crop had been adopted by near-subsistence farmers who previously were, at most, marginal participants in the national market. Behrman also discovered that Thai farmers were quite risk averse; production could be increased by lowering the risk even if the expected price remained the same. In Thailand, at least, policies allowing prices to rise and reducing the risk have had a substantial impact. We shouldn't sell small-scale peasant farmers short!

Kenaf is a fiber used to manufacture gunny sacks, and, to a lesser extent, rope and paper.

Source: Jere Behrman, *Supply Response in Underdeveloped Agriculture* (Amsterdam: North Holland Publishing, 1968).

demand generally means lower prices and lower incomes for the farmers. Thus this strategy also impairs food production incentives.

Feeding the Poor

The undervaluation bias was caused by a misguided attempt to use price controls as the way to provide the poor with access to an adequate diet. It backfired because the price controls served to reduce the availability of food. Is there a way to reduce the nutritional gap among the poor while maintaining adequate supplies of food?

EXAMPLE 10.2

Perverse Government Intervention: The Case of Colombia

The failure of the market to increase productivity in the agricultural sector, or to reduce the incidence of poverty, sometimes has been due to government policies. The experience in Colombia is relatively typical.

Marketing of wheat in Colombia is controlled by the huge Colombian Institute for Agricultural Marketing, operated by the government. In 1951–54 wheat production averaged 140,000 metric tons a year. By 1971, this production level had fallen to 49,000 tons. During this same period, consumption of wheat in Colombia rose from 179,000 tons to 434,000 tons. The difference, of course, had to be made up by imports.

Why did this happen? There seemed to be two reasons, both of which had the effect of lowering the real price of wheat received by Colombian farmers, who, as expected, reacted by cutting production. The first reason was a massive inflow of surplus grain from the United States which was subsidized by the United States government as part of our food aid program. This artificially cheap wheat simply stole much of the market normally supplied by domestic producers.

The second cause was a decision by the marketing institute to hold wheat prices constant in the 1968–71 period in spite of an annual inflation rate approaching 10 percent. The intended purpose, of course, was to hold prices down for consumers, which it temporarily did. The unintended side effect was to discourage domestic production and to increase the losses of the marketing institute which had to pay the difference between what the imported wheat cost and the lower price offered to consumers.

Is there a moral to the story? Possibly. The supply side has to be kept continually in mind as governments attempt to raise the nutrition levels of its citizens.

Sources: Reed Hertford, "Government Price Policies for Wheat, Rice, and Tractors in Colombia," in *Distortions of Agricultural Incentives,* Theodore W. Schultz, ec. (Bloomington, Indiana University Press, 1978), pp. 121–139; World Bank, *World Development Report, 1980* (Washington, D.C.: International Bank for Reconstruction and Development, 1980), p. 87.

Some countries such as Sri Lanka, Colombia, and the United States are using food stamp programs to subsidize food purchases by the poor. Currently, in Colombia, this is being accomplished by issuing food coupons to low-income women and children who are particularly vulnerable to nutritional deficiency. The coupons can be used by recipients to purchase a number of high-nutrition, low-cost foods. About 200,000 households were reached in 1980. By boosting the purchasing power of those with the greatest need, these programs provide access to food while protecting the incentives of farmers. Those countries lowering food prices to everyone necessitate substantially higher payments by the government to finance them. When governments look around for ways to finance these subsidies, they are tempted to try to reduce the subsidy by paying below-market prices to farmers or relying more heavily on artificially low-cost imported food aid. In the long run, either of these strategies can be self-defeating.

Targeting the assistance to those who need it is one strategy that works. Another approach to feeding the poor is to attempt to ensure that the income distribution effects of agricultural policies do not benefit the rich at the expense of the poor. If the major productivity gains can only come from large-scale enterprises, the income distribution effects of increasing productivity will be perverse. In this circumstance, higher farm incomes would be received by the really well-to-do owners of the large enterprises, while the small-scale farmer would remain mired in poverty.

The problem is intensified when large-scale enterprises and small-scale enterprises are located in different parts of the country so that a policy of favoring large-scale enterprise also turns out to favor a particular region. When such favoritism occurs, the consequences can be drastic. Formerly a part of Pakistan, the nation of Bangladesh owes its separate existence to a revolution triggered in no small part by hostilities toward a development plan causing unbalanced regional development. Though the trade-off between increased productivity and an equitable distribution of the gains need not always produce a dire conflict, it can be a difficult issue for most nations. Example 10.3 provides a case study of how this issue arose in India.

It is important to distinguish among the various sources of the problem. Part of the problem is geographic. Certain portions of the country are more fertile because of climate, type of soil, and so on. These differences are natural and not amenable to manipulation by policy. The other portion, however, deals with scale economies per se, regardless of where these economies arise. The question is whether or not economies of scale in agriculture are sufficiently large to create conflict between increased productivity and the alleviation of poverty for the smallest farmers.

According to a major cross-country study for the World Bank and the International Labor Organization by Berry and Cline [1979], except for the very smallest farms, small farms generate higher land productivity specifically and higher productivity for all factors combined. The study goes on to suggest

> it follows that agricultural strategies focusing on small farms start with a major advantage: the demonstrated capacity to achieve high productivity of what is usually the scarcest resource, land (especially in Asia), largely through greater application of the abundant resource, labor. [p. 128]

With respect to scale, there need not be a trade-off between productivity and equity. Small farms can produce as large or larger yields-per-acre providing that mechanisms are established for improving the access of small farms to credit and appropriately scaled new technology.

We are now in a position to define the role for aid from the developed nations. Temporary food aid is helpful when traditional sources are completely inadequate (natural disasters) or when the food aid does not interfere with the earnings of domestic pro-

EXAMPLE 10.3

The Distribution Dilemma: India's Green Revolution

India illustrates the trade-off between efficiency and equity sometimes faced by developing countries. India achieved substantial increases in its production of wheat (and, subsequently, rice) through the introduction of new hybrid seed. Distributed through a limited budget, the new seed could either be given to small farmers in the poorer regions or to the richer Punjab area where the preconditions for rapid-yield expansion were present. India chose the latter strategy.

Several barriers existed to substantially increased yields among the poorer farmers. The smaller farmers did not have the savings or the access to capital markets to put in the complementary inputs (principally irrigation) required to gain the maximum productivity increase from the new seed. In addition, their land holdings were not typically large enough to utilize the optimum scale of these complementary inputs.

Two main developments resulted. Food products did increase substantially, but the gains were captured by larger farmers. Francine Frankel estimates the majority of Indian farmers experienced a relative decline in their economic position (small rice farmers received 75 to 80 percent of the gains received by the larger farmers), while some smaller percentage of them actually experienced an absolute decline. For this latter category the effect of the green revolution was to make them worse off, not better off.

Source: Francine Frankel, *India's Green Revolution: Economic Gains and Political Costs* (Princeton: Princeton University Press, 1971).

ducers. In the long run, developed nations could provide both appropriate technologies (such as solar-powered irrigation systems) and the financial capital to get farmer-owned local cooperatives off the ground. These cooperatives would then provide some of the advantages of scale (such as risk sharing and distribution), while maintaining the existing structure of small-scale farms. Coupled with a balanced development program designed to raise the general standard of living and effective population-control efforts, this approach could provide a solution to the distributional portion of the world food problem.

FEAST AND FAMINE CYCLES

The remaining dimension of the world food problem concerns the year-to-year fluctuations in food availability caused by vagaries of weather and planting decisions. Even if the average level of food availability were appropriate, the fact that the average consists of a sequence of overproduction and underproduction years means that society as a whole can benefit from smoothing out the fluctuations.

The point is vividly depicted by an analogy. If a person were standing in two buckets of water – the first containing boiling hot water, the second, ice cold water – his misery would not be assuaged in the least by a friend telling him that on average the temperature was perfect. The average does not tell the whole story.

The fluctuations of supplies for food seem to be rather large and the swings in prices even larger. Why? One characteristic of the farming sector suggests that farmers' production decisions may actually make the fluctuations worse or at least prolong them. This tendency is explored via the *cobweb model* (Figure 10.3). The source of the name is obvious, though no spider would own up to having created such a pathetic specimen.

Suppose, due to a weather-induced shortage, Q_0 is supplied, driving the price up to P_0. For the next growing season, farmers have to plant well in advance of harvest time. Their decisions about how much to plant will depend on the price they expect to receive. Let's suppose they use this year's price as their guess of what next year's price will be.

They will plan to supply (and in the absence of further weather aberrations *will* supply) Q_1. At price P_0 the market cannot absorb that much of the commodity so the price falls to P_1. If farmers use that price to plan the following year's crop, they will produce Q_3. This will cause the price to rise to P_3 and so on.

What is occurring is a *damped oscillation.* In the absence of further supply shocks, the amplitude of price and quantity fluctuations decreases over time until the equilibrium price and quantity are obtained.[16]

The demand for food tends to be price inelastic, particularly in developing countries. This has some important implications. The more price inelastic the demand curve, the higher the price has to go in order to bring the demand into line with supply when a weather-induced shortage occurs (Figure 10.4).

Figure 10.4 records an initial equilibrium situation where demand D_1 and supply S_0 are equal at point A. A supply shortfall is registered as a shift in the supply curve from S_0 to S_1. In the two demand curves shown, D_1 is the most price elastic. Notice that the more inelastic the demand curve, such as D_2, the higher the price has to go to clear the market.

Figure 10.4 also shows the effects of price shifts on producer revenues. How do supply shocks affect the incomes of farmers? At first glance the result seems ambiguous, since during shortages they get higher prices (a plus!) but have also less to sell (a minus!). Which effect dominates?

Since producer revenue is price times quantity, it is represented as a rectangle. The size of the rectangle depends on the circumstances. Before the supply shift, revenues received are depicted by the rectangle OP_0AS_0. After the supply shift, the revenues with the elastic demand curve (D_1) are OP_1CS_1 and for the inelastic demand curve are OP_2BS_1.

Have revenues increased with the supply shift? To answer the question, we have to compare areas P_0P_1CD (the net amount gained with the elastic demand curve) or

---

[16]Theoretically speaking, undamped oscillations which increase in amplitude over time are possible under certain conditions, but this pattern does not seem to characterize existing food markets.

FIGURE 10.3   The Cobweb Model

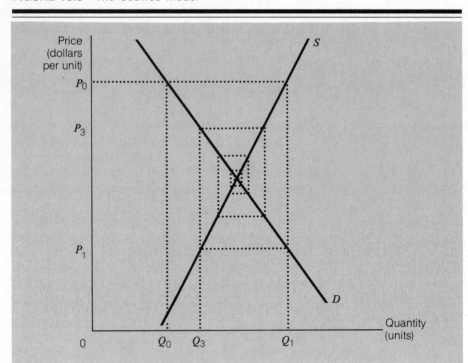

P_0P_2BD (the net amount gained with the inelastic demand curve) to DAS_0S_1 (the revenue lost due to the lower production levels).

One conclusion is immediately obvious—the more inelastic the demand curve, the more likely farmers as a group are to gain from the shortfall. As long as the demand curve is price inelastic in the relevant range (a condition commonly satisfied in the short run by food products), farmers as a group will be better off by supply shortfalls.[17] Conversely, farmers are hurt by periods of excess supply.

On the consumer side of this issue, a quite different picture emerges. Consumers are unambiguously hurt by shortfalls and helped by situations with excess supply. The more price inelastic the demand curve, the greater the loss is in consumer surplus from shortfalls and the greater the gain in consumer surplus from excess supply.

This creates some interesting (and from the policy point of view, difficult) incentives. Producers as a group don't have any particular interest in protecting against supply shortfalls, but they have a substantial interest in protecting against excess supply. Con-

---

[17]This is not necessarily true for every farmer, of course. If the supply reduction is concentrated on a few, they will unambiguously be worse off while the remaining farmers will be better off. The point is that the revenue gains received by the latter group will exceed the losses suffered by the former group.

FIGURE 10.4 Price Elasticity of Demand and the Size of Price Fluctuations

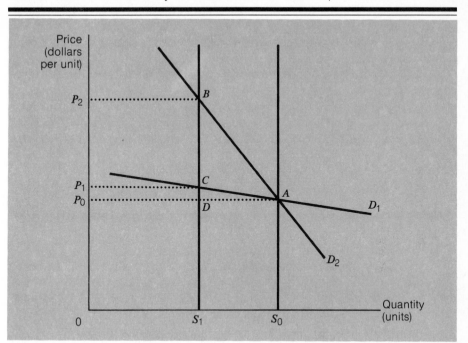

sumers, on the other hand, have no quarrel with excess supply, but want to guard against supply shortfalls.

While society as a whole would gain from the stabilization of prices and quantities, the different segments of society have rather different views of how that stabilization should come about. Farmers would be delighted with price stabilization as long as the average price is high, while consumers would be delighted if the average price is kept low.

The main means of attempting to stabilize prices and quantities is by creating stockpiles. These can be drawn down during periods of scarcity and built up during periods of excess supply. Currently, two different types of food stockpiles exist. The first is a special internationally held emergency stockpile that would be used to alleviate the hunger caused by natural disasters (such as drought). Established in 1975 by the Seventh Special Session of the United Nations General Assembly, with an annual target of 500,000 tons, the World Emergency Stockpile has the potential to greatly reduce suffering without having any noticeable disruptive effect on the world grain market (involving some 70 million tons traded). Unfortunately, its full potential has not yet been reached. Contributions in 1979, for example, totaled 314,000 tons, considerably short of the annual target. The bulk of the accumulated reserves was distributed to needy nations in that same year, leaving little in reserve.

The second kind of stockpile represents the stocks held individually by the various countries. It was hoped that these stockpiles would be internationally coordinated. Despite intensive negotiations, by 1979, the mechanism for coordinating these stocks had not yet been agreed upon, much less implemented. However, the level of the stocks was adequate. The FAO Secretariat estimates the minimum safe level of world carryover stocks for cereals to be between 17 and 18 percent of world consumption. After a rather precipitious decline in 1973, by 1977 the stocks had been rebuilt to the minimum safe levels (Figure 10.5). Almost two-thirds of the stockpile is controlled by the exporting countries.

The process has started to increase food security on a worldwide basis but has not yet reached the point of solving the problem. Significant difficult political decisions on stockpile management, such as timing purchases and sales, have yet to be agreed upon. Until that time, because the interests of producers and consumer nations are so different, it is unlikely that any uncoordinated system will be fully effective.

SUMMARY

The world hunger program is upon us and it is real. Serious malnutrition is currently being experienced in many parts of the world. The root of the chronic problem is poverty – an inability to afford the rising costs of food. The harm caused by poverty is intensified by fluctuations in the availability of food.

These problems are not unsolvable and do not call for a massive retrenchment by the developed world. The main barriers to a solution are political and economic, rather than physical.

The FAO has concluded that developing countries *could* increase their food production by around 4 percent per year through the 1990s, well in excess of population growth. They conclude, however, that this will occur only if the developed nations share technology and provide the developing countries access to their markets and if the developing countries show a willingness to adopt pricing policies which do not restrict output. This can be accomplished without jeopardizing the poor by using direct food purchase subsidies (such as a food-stamp program) rather than price controls.

Because a major part of the world hunger problem is poverty, it is not enough to simply produce more food. The ability of the poor to afford food has also to be improved. This is particularly important in light of the rapidly rising cost of agricultural inputs such as fertilizer. Reducing poverty can be accomplished by bolstering nonfarm employment opportunities, as well as by enhancing the returns of smaller scale farmers.

Since the available evidence suggests that, with respect to scale economies, there does not seem to be a trade-off between efficiency and equity; small-scale farming can compete effectively, given access to credit markets and new improved technologies.

Food stockpiles – the key element in a program to provide food security – exist but are not yet fully effective. The emergency stockpile has not achieved its designed capacity and the system of national stockpiles is large but not effectively managed. The light is at the end of the tunnel and the train is moving, but the journey is distressingly slow.

FIGURE 10.5 Stocks of Cereals, 1971–83

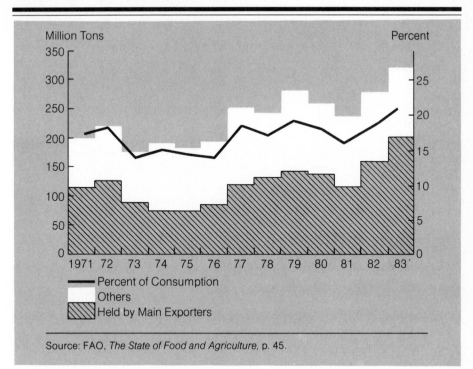

Source: FAO, *The State of Food and Agriculture*, p. 45.

FURTHER READING

Conference on Food and Agricultural Policy. *Food and Agricultural Policy* (Washington, D.C.: American Enterprise Institute for Public Policy Research, 1977). Essays focusing on agriculture in the United States. Aside from interesting surveys of agricultural economies and policies, it also contains sections on food production, processing, and distribution; food and foreign affairs; and future directions for policy.

Crosson, Pierre R., and Sterling Brubaker. *Resource and Environmental Effects of U.S. Agriculture* (Baltimore: Johns Hopkins University Press for Resources for the Future, Inc., 1982). This book identifies the environmental costs associated with future increases in production and suggests measures to deal with them.

Heady, Earl O., and Lary R. Whiting, eds. *Externalities in the Transformation of Agriculture: Distribution of the Benefits and Costs from Development* (Ames, Iowa: The Iowa State University Press, 1975). Contains fourteen essays generally concerned with the relationship between efficiency and equity in agricultural development. Geographic coverage includes the United States, Europe, India, Latin America, and Africa.

Meier, Gerald M. *Leading Issues in Economic Development.* 3rd ed. (New York: Oxford University Press, 1976). A highly regarded extensive collection of integrated short articles on various aspects of the development process. Contains an excellent section of agricultural development with an extensive bibliography.

Presidential Commission on World Hunger. *Overcoming World Hunger: The Challenge Ahead* (Washington, D.C.: U.S. Government Printing Office, 1980).

ADDITIONAL REFERENCES

Barnett, Harold J. "Scarcity and Growth Revisited," in *Scarcity and Growth Reconsidered,* V. Kerry Smith, ed. (Baltimore, Md., Johns Hopkins Press for Resources for the Future, 1979): 163–217.

Behrman, J. R. *Supply Response in Underdeveloped Agriculture* (Amsterdam: North-Holland Publishing Company, 1968).

Berry, R. Albert, and William R. Cline, *Agrarian Structure and Productivity in Developing Countries* (Baltimore: Johns Hopkins University Press, 1979).

Brown, Lester R. "World Population Growth, Soil Erosion, and Food Security," *Science,* Vol. 214 (27 November 1981): 995–1002.

Collins, Robert A., and J. C. Headley. "Optimal Investment to Reduce the Decay of an Income Stream: The Case of Soil Conservation," *Journal of Environmental Economics and Management,* Vol. 10 (March, 1983): 60–71.

d'Arge, Ralph C. "The Energy Squeeze and Agricultural Growth," in *Economics, Ethics, Ecology: The Roots of Productive Conservation,* Walter E. Jeske (Ankeny, Iowa: Soil Conservation Society of America, 1981): 99–105.

Frankel, Francine R. *India's Green Revolution: Economic Gains and Political Costs* (Princeton: Princeton University Press, 1971).

Paddock, William, and Paul Paddock, *Famine – 1975!* (Boston: Little, Brown and Company, 1967).

Regev, Uri, Haim Shalit, and A. P. Guttierrez. "On the Optimal Allocation of Pesticides with Increasing Resistance: The Case of Alfalfa Weevil," *Journal of Environmental Economics and Management,* Vol. 10 (March, 1983): 86–100.

The World Bank, *World Development Report, 1980* (Washington, D.C.: International Bank for Reconstruction and Development, 1980); *World Development Report, 1982.*

DISCUSSION QUESTIONS

1. "By applying modern technology to agriculture the United States has become the most productive food-producing nation in the world. The secret to solving the world food problem lies in transfering this technology to developing countries." Discuss.

2. Under Public Law 480 the United States sells surplus grains to developing countries which pay in local currencies. Since the United States rarely spends all of these

currencies, much of this grain transfer is *de facto* an outright gift. Is this an equitable and efficient way for the U.S. to dispose of surplus grain? Why or why not?

PROBLEMS

1. The two countries Norland and Souland can produce commodities A and B per hour of labor expended according to the following table:

	Amount of A Produced in One Hour	Amount of B Produced in One Hour
Norland	4	8
Souland	2	6

   Which country, if either, has the comparative advantage in producing A? Why?

2. "Food stamp programs only serve to drive food prices higher, not increase the quantity of food available to the poor." What would the elasticity of supply have to be for this statement to be true? What would the elasticity of supply have to be for a food stamp program to increase the availability of food to the poor with no price increase?

CHAPTER ELEVEN

Storable, Renewable Resources: Forests

*Too much light often blinds gentlemen of this sort. They cannot
see the forest for the trees.*
CHRISTOPHER MARTIN WIELAND
Musarion (1786)

INTRODUCTION

Forests provide a variety of services. They provide the raw materials for housing and many products made out of wood. In many parts of the world wood is an important fuel. Paper products are derived from wood fiber. Trees cleanse the air by absorbing carbon dioxide and adding oxygen. Forests provide shelter and sanctuary for wildlife and they play an important role in the ecology of watersheds that supply much of our drinking water. Recreation is another major contribution made by forests.

Although the contributions that trees make to our everyday life are easy to overlook, even the most rudimentary calculations indicate their significance. Slightly less than one-third of the land in the United States is covered by forests, the largest category of land use with the exception of pasture and grazing land. For Maine, an example of a heavily forested state, 85 percent of the land area is covered by forest. In 1980, the comparable figure for the world was 31.3 percent.[1]

As our study of property rights has made clear, ownership patterns can have a profound influence on how resources are managed. Ownership patterns for forest resources vary widely from country to country. While about 72 percent of the world's forests are publicly owned, in the United States only 28 percent are publicly owned.[2]

---

[1]OECD, *OECD Enviromental Data: Compendium 1985* (Paris: Organization for European Co-operation and Development, 1985), p. 103.

[2]Ibid., p. 117.

The vast majority of forested lands in the U.S. are directly controlled by the private market rather than by the government.

Managing forests is no easy task. In contrast to cereal grains, which are planted and harvested on an annual cycle, trees take a long time to mature. The manager must decide not only how to maximize yields on a given amount of land, but also when to harvest and replant. A delicate balance must be established among the various possible uses of forests. Since some of these uses involve harvesting the resource (such as producing lumber), while others involve preserving the stock (such as protecting the aesthetic value of forested vistas), establishing the proper balance requires some means of comparing the value of these potentially conflicting uses. The efficiency criterion is one obvious method.

In the remainder of this chapter we shall explore how economics can be combined with forest ecology to assist in efficiently managing this important resource. We begin by characterizing what is meant by an efficient allocation of the forest resource when the value of the harvested timber is the only concern. Starting simply, we first model the efficient decision to cut a single stand or cluster of trees with a common age by superimposing economic considerations on a biological model of tree growth. This model is then expanded to demonstrate how the multiple values of the forest resource should influence the harvesting decision and how the problem is altered if planning takes place over an infinite horizon, with forests being harvested and replanted in a continual sequence. Turning to matters of institutional adequacy, we shall then examine the allocations that have resulted or can be expected to result from both public and private management decisions.

DEFINING EFFICIENT MANAGEMENT

Special Attributes of the Timber Resource

While timber shares many characteristics with other living resources, it also has some aspects that make it unique. Timber shares with many other animate resources the characteristic that it is both an output and a capital good. Trees, when harvested, provide a saleable commodity, but left standing they are a capital good, providing for increased growth the following year. Each year, the forest manager must decide whether to harvest a particular stand of trees or to wait for the additional growth. In contrast to many other living resources, however, the time period between initial investment (planting) and recovery of that investment (harvesting) is especially long in forestry. Intervals of 25 years or more are common in forestry, but not in many other industries. Finally, forestry is unusually subject to a large variety of externalities. These may be associated with either the standing timber or the act of harvesting timber. These externalities not only make it difficult to define the efficient allocation, they play havoc with incentives, reducing the ability of institutions to manage efficiently.

The Biological Dimension

Tree growth is measured on a volume basis, typically by cubic feet on a particular site. This measurement is taken of the stems, exclusive of bark and limbs, between the stump and a 4-inch top. For larger trees, the stump is 24 inches from the ground. Only standing trees are measured; those toppled by wind or age are not included. In this sense the volume is measured in net rather than gross terms.

Based on this measurement of volume, the data reveal that tree stands go through distinct growth phases. Initially, when the trees are very young, growth is rather slow in volume terms, though the tree may experience a considerable increase in height. A period of sustained, rapid growth follows with volume increasing considerably. Finally, slower growth sets in as the stand fully matures, until growth stops or even reverses.

The actual growth of a stand of trees depends on many factors, including the weather, the fertility of the soil, susceptibility to insects or disease, the type of tree, the amount of care devoted to the trees, and vulnerability to forest fires or air pollution. Thus, there is a tremendous amount of variability of tree growth from stand to stand. Some of these growth-enhancing or growth-retarding factors are under the influence of foresters; others aren't.

Abstracting from these differences, it is possible to develop a hypothetical but realistic, biological model of the growth of a stand of trees. In this case our model (Figure 11.1) is based on the growth of a stand of Douglas fir trees in the Pacific Northwest.[3]

Notice that the figure is consistent with the growth phases mentioned above. Following an early period of limited growth, the stand experiences rapid growth in the middle ages with growth ceasing after 135 years.

When should this stand be harvested? Foresters have come up with a calculation called the *mean annual increment* (MAI) which provides the basis for a biological approach to answering this question. Developing this concept provides a useful contrast to the economic approach which is presented in subsequent sections.

The MAI is calculated by dividing the cumulative volume of the stand at the end of each decade by the cumulative number of years the stand has been growing up to that decade. For tree growth patterns like the ones represented by Figure 11.1, the MAI rises during the early ages and then falls during the later ages (Table 11.1).

According to the biological decision rule, the forest should be harvested at the age when the MAI is maximized. According to our Douglas fir example, this occurs when the stand is 100 years old. Column 4 in Table 11.1 helps us to understand what is special

---

[3]The numerical model in the text is based loosely on the data presented in Marion Clawson, "Decision Making in Timber Production, Harvest, and Marketing," Resources for the Future, Inc. Research Paper R-4, Washington, D.C., 1977, Table 1, p. 13. The mathematical function relating volume to age of the stand in Figure 11.1 is a third degree polynomial of the form $v = a + bt + ct^2 + dt^3$, where v = volume in cubic feet, t = the age of the stand in years and $a, b, c,$ and d are parameters which take on the values 0, 40, 3.1, and -0.016 respectively.

FIGURE 11.1   Model of Tree Growth in a Stand of Douglas Fir

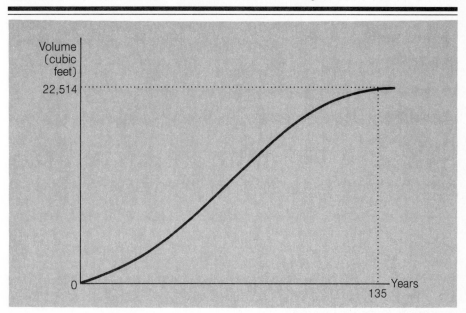

TABLE 11.1   The Biological Harvesting Decision: Douglas Fir

Age (Years) (1)	Volume[1] (Cubic Feet) (2)	MAI[2] (Cubic Feet) (3)	Annual Incremental Growth[3] (Cubic Feet) (4)
10	694	6.9	6.9
20	1,912	95.6	121.8
30	3,558	118.6	164.6
40	5,536	138.4	198.8
50	7,750	155.0	221.4
60	10,104	168.0	235.4
70	12,502	178.6	239.8
80	14,848	185.6	234.6
90	17,046	189.4	219.8
100	19,000	190.0	195.4
110	20,614	187.4	161.4
120	21,792	181.6	117.8
130	22,438	172.6	64.6
135	22,514	166.8	11.6

NOTES: [1]Calculated from the formula used to produce Figure 11.1. See footnote 3.
  [2]Column [2] divided by Column [1].
  [3]Change over intervening period in Column [1] divided by change in number of years in Column [1].

about this age. Annual incremental growth rises until the trees are about 70 years old, declining thereafter. The MAI rises for the first 100 years because the annual incremental growth is above the MAI during that period; it falls in the following years because the annual incremental growth is below the MAI.

The Economics of Forest Harvesting

To an economist, this biological criterion seems rather arbitrary; it fails to consider any of the factors such as the value of the timber, the time value of money, or costs associated with planting and harvesting which would play a central role in an efficient harvesting decision. It is possible, however, to use the basic biological model of growth portrayed in Figure 11.1 as the basis for an economic model of the harvesting decision.

From the definition of efficiency, the optimal time to harvest this stand would be that time which maximizes the present value of the net benefits from the wood. The size of the net benefits from the wood depend on whether the land will be perpetually committed to forestry or left to natural processes after harvest. For our first model we will assume that the stand will be harvested once and the land will be left as is following the harvest. This model will serve to illustrate how the economic principles of forestry can be applied to the simplest case, while providing the background necessary to move to more complicated and more realistic examples.

To derive the benefits from harvesting at various ages in this first case, it is necessary to convert the physical data on volume into value terms by multiplying each cubic foot of wood times the price it could command. Suppose that each cubic foot of wood could bring $1.00; in essence we are assuming that this particular decision will not appreciably affect the price of wood, since the amount supplied by this stand would be small in comparison to the total market.

Two costs are presumed to be important in this decision—planting costs and harvesting costs. Apart from their magnitudes, these costs differ in one significant characteristic—the time at which they are borne. Planting costs are borne immediately, while harvesting costs are borne at the time of harvest. In a present-value calculation harvesting costs are discounted (as is the value of the wood) because they are paid (received) in the future, whereas planting costs are not discounted because they are paid immediately. For the sake of our example, assume that planting this stand costs $1,000 and harvesting costs $0.30 per cubic foot of wood harvested.

With these additions to the model, it is now possible to calculate the present value of net benefits that would be derived from harvesting this stand at various ages (Table 11.2). The net benefits are calculated by subtracting the present value of costs from the value of the timber at that age. Two different discount rates are used to illustrate the influence of discounting on the harvesting decision. The undiscounted calculations ($r = 0.0$) simply indicate the actual values that would prevail at each age, while the positive discount rate takes the time value of money into account.

Two interesting conclusions can be gleaned from Table 11.2. First discounting shortens the time until the stand is harvested. Whereas the maximum undiscounted net benefits occur at 135 years, when a discount rate of only .02 is used, the maximum occurs at 68 years, roughly half the time of the undiscounted case. Higher discount rates would yield even shorter harvesting times. Second, the magnitude of the planting and harvesting costs do not change the optimal harvesting point. Notice that the maximum of the value of timber column and the net benefit column occur in precisely the same year for each of the discount rates. In other words, even if costs were zero, the

TABLE 11.2   Economic Harvesting Decision: Douglas Fir

		Undiscounted (r = 0.0)			Discounted (r = 0.02)		
Age (Years)	Volume (Cu. Ft.)	Value of Timber ($)	Cost ($)	Net Benefits ($)	Value of Timber ($)	Cost ($)	Net Benefits ($)
10	694	694	1,208	−514	567	1,171	−604
20	1,912	1,912	1,574	338	1,288	1,386	−98
30	3,558	3,558	2,067	1,491	1,964	1,589	375
40	5,536	5,536	2,661	2,875	2,507	1.752	755
50	7,750	7,750	3,325	4,425	2,879	1,864	1,015
60	10,104	10,104	4,031	6,073	3,080	1,924	1,156
68	12,023	12,023	4,607	7,416	3,128	1,938	1,190
70	12,502	12,502	4,751	7,751	3,126	1,938	1,118
80	14,848	14,848	5,454	9,394	3,046	1,914	1,132
90	17,046	17,046	6,114	10,932	2,868	1,860	1,008
100	19,000	19,000	6,700	12,300	2,623	1,787	836
110	20,614	20,614	7,184	13,430	2,334	1,700	634
120	21,792	21,792	7,538	14,254	2,024	1,607	417
130	22,438	22,438	7,731	14,707	1,710	1,513	197
135	22,514	22,514	7,754	14,760	1,449	1,466	−17

Notes: Volume of Timber from Table 11.1.
   Value of Timber = Price*Volume/$(1 + r)^t$
   Cost = $1,000 + $0.30*Volume/$(1 + r)^t$
   Net Benefits = Value of Timber − Cost

harvesting decision would occur at the same point. Since the reasons for these conclusions are not immediately apparent, we must look deeper.

Higher discount rates imply shorter harvesting periods because they are less tolerant of the slow timber growth that occurs as the stand reaches maturity. The use of a positive discount rate implies a direct comparison between the increase in the value of the timber that occurs prior to harvesting and the increase in value that would occur if the forest were harvested and the money from the sale invested at rate *r*. In the undiscounted case, there is no opportunity cost of capital, so it pays to leave the money invested in trees as long as some growth is occuring. As long as *r* is positive, however, the trees will be harvested as soon as the growth rate is low enough that more will be earned from financial investments.

The fact that neither harvesting nor planting costs affect the harvesting period results from the form of costs that we have used in the model. Because they are paid immediately, the present value of planting costs is equal to the actual expenditure; it does not vary with the age at which the stand is harvested. Essentially, a constant is being subtracted from the value of timber at any age. The age of the stand that maximizes the value of the timber necessarily maximizes the difference between the present value of the timber and the (constant) present value of the planting cost.

This does not imply, however, that planting costs are irrelevant to the harvesting decision. If planting costs are sufficiently high, they can exceed the maximum value of the timber. In this case, the net benefits would be negative for all possible ages and it would not be efficient to plant this type of tree for commercial harvest.

Harvesting costs are a different matter. They differ from planting costs in two respects. Not only are they borne at the time of harvest, but total harvesting costs are also proportional to the amount of timber harvested ($0.30 for each cubic foot). The present value of total harvesting cost changes with the harvesting period both because they are discounted an amount determined by the harvesting date and because they rise as the volume of wood to be harvested rises.

The impact of this type of cost on the harvesting decision can most easily be seen by realizing that the net benefits of a cubic foot of wood harvested at any given age is the price of that wood minus the marginal cost of harvesting that cubic foot, appropriately discounted. By assumption, both the price and the marginal cost of a cubic foot of wood do not vary with age; they are constants. In the case of our numerical example this constant net value before discounting is $0.70 (the $1.00 price minus the $0.30 marginal harvest cost). If the marginal cost of harvesting were zero, this value would be $1.00. Regardless what the marginal cost of harvesting is, this net value before discounting is a constant that is multiplied times the volume of timber at each age divided by $(1 + r)^t$. Its role is merely to raise or lower the net benefits curve; it does not change its shape. Therefore the net benefits curve will reach its maximum at the same age of the stand regardless of the value of the marginal cost curve, as long as the marginal cost is less than the price received.

What would be the effect of a $0.20 tax levied on each cubic foot of wood harvested in this simple model? In essence this type of tax would serve to raise the marginal cost of harvesting from $0.30 per cubic foot to $0.50 per cubic foot. The $0.30 would reflect the cost of the manpower and the equipment to get the timber out of the forest and to the market. The remaining $0.20 would go to the government as tax revenue.

As indicated by the analysis in the preceeding sections, increasing the marginal harvesting cost in this model would not have any affect on the harvesting period. Since levying a per-unit tax has the effect of increasing marginal harvesting cost, it would have no effect on the harvesting period either.

Extending the Basic Model

Our basic model is somewhat unrealistic in several respects. Perhaps most importantly, it considers the harvest as a single event, rather than a part of an infinite sequence of harvesting and replanting. Typically in the forest industry, harvested lands are restocked and the sequence starts over again in a never-ending cycle.

At first glance it may appear that this is really no different than the case just considered. After all, can't one merely use this model to characterize the efficient interval between planting and harvest for each of the periods? The mathematics tells us that this is not the correct way to think about the problem, and with a bit of reflection it is not difficult to see why.

The single-period model we developed would be appropriate for an infinite planning period if and only if all periods were independent. If interdependencies exist among time periods, the harvesting decision must reflect those interdependencies.

Interdependencies do exist. The decision to delay a harvest imposes an additional cost on an infinite planning model that has no counterpart in our single-harvest model—the cost of delaying the onset of the next planting and harvesting cycle. In our single-harvest model the optimum time to harvest occurs when the marginal benefit of an additional year's growth equals the marginal opportunity cost of capital. When the capital gains from letting the trees grow another year become equal to the return that could be obtained from harvesting the trees and investing the gains, the stand was harvested. In the infinite planning-horizon case the opportunity cost of delaying the next cycle must be covered by the gain in tree growth as well as the other costs which it has in common with the single-period model.

The effect of including this new cost can be rather profound. Assuming that all other aspects of the problem (such as planting and harvesting costs, discount rate, growth function, and price) are the same, the optimal time to harvest (called the *optimal rotation* in the infinite-planning case) is shorter in the infinite-planning case than in the single-harvest case. This follows directly from the fact that the marginal cost of a delay is higher due to the existence of the opportunity cost of starting the cycle later. The efficient forester will harvest a stand sooner when he or she is planning to replant the same area than when the plot will be left inactive after the harvest.

This more complicated model also yields some rather different conclusions than our original model, a valuable reminder of a point made in the first chapter—that conclusions flow from a specific view of the world and are valid only to the extent that view captures the essence of a problem. Consider, for example, the effect of a rise in planting costs. In our single-harvest model they had no effect on the optimal time to harvest. In the infinite-planning case the optimal rotation is affected. Specifically, higher planting costs reduce the marginal opportunity cost of delaying the cycle. By doing so they allow positive net benefits to accrue from delaying the cycle, compared to the case with lower planting costs. As a result the optimal rotation (the time between planting and harvest) would increase as planting costs increase. A similar result would be obtained when harvesting costs are increased.[4] The optimal rotation period would be lengthened.

The fact that in the infinite-horizon model increased harvesting costs lengthen the optimal rotation period immediately implies that a per unit tax on harvested timber will lengthen the optimal rotation period in this model as well. Furthermore lengthening the rotation period implies that the harvested trees would be somewhat older and therefore each harvest would involve a somewhat larger volume of wood.

The vision of a fully regulated forest that emerges from these models involves having a series of forest plots, each with trees of a different age. A sufficient number of plots would be available to provide trees at every age up to the age at which they are harvested. When the trees on a particular plot reach the age stipulated by the optimal rotation, they are harvested and the plot is restocked. The following year a different plot is harvested as its trees reach economic maturity. In this way harvesting activity can take place every year without endangering the sustainability of the forest.

---

[4]For a discussion of the results in this section and the mathematics that lies behind them, see Michael D. Bowles and John V. Krutilla, "Multiple Use Management of Public Forestlands," in Allen V. Kneese and James L. Sweeney, eds., *Handbook of Natural Resource and Energy Economics, Vol. II* (Amsterdam: North-Holland, 1985): 534–537.

Another limitation of our basic model lies in its assumption of a constant relative price for the wood over time. In fact the relative prices of timber have been rising over time. By introducing relative prices for timber that rise at a constant rate in the infinite-horizon model, it is possible to establish that the optimal rotation period would increase.[5] In essence prices which are rising at a fixed rate act to offset the effect of discounting. Since we have already established that lower discount rates imply longer rotation periods, it immediately follows that rising prices also lead to longer efficient rotation periods.

A final concern with the models as elaborated so far is that they all are concerned solely with the sale of timber as a product. In fact, forests serve several other purposes as well, such as providing habitat for wildlife, supplying recreational opportunities and stabilizing watersheds. For these uses additional benefits accrue to the standing timber which are lost or diminished when the stand is harvested.

It is possible to incorporate these benefits into our model to demonstrate the effect they would have on the efficient rotation.[6] Suppose that the amenity benefits conveyed by a standing forest are positively related to the age of the forest. In this case the optimal rotation would once again occur when the marginal benefit of delay equalled the marginal cost of delay. In the case being considered, the marginal benefit of delay would be higher than in the models considered above because of the additional amenity benefit. For this reason the optimal rotation would be lengthened when amenity benefits are considered. If the amenity benefits are sufficiently large, it may be efficient to delay harvest forever, leaving the forest as a wilderness area.

IMPLEMENTING EFFICIENT MANAGEMENT

The Private Sector

Privately owned forests are a significant force all over the world, but in some countries, such as the United States, they are the dominant force. In the United States some 72 percent of forested land is privately owned. Some 15 percent of this forested land is owned by the forest industry, while the remaining privately-owned 57 percent is held by farmers or other landowners. These latter parcels tend to be small in size.

Can prescient private owners be counted upon to manage efficiently? For forests dedicated to timber harvesting, profit maximization can be compatible with efficient

---

[5]See the discussion in Charles W. Howe, *Natural Resource Economics: Issues, Analysis, Policy* (New York: John Wiley & Sons, 1979): 238–9. If prices are rising at a rate g, then the effective discount rate becomes $r - g$.

[6]The mathematics for this section of the model can be seen in R. Hartman, "The Harvesting Decision When a Standing Forest Has Value," *Economic Inquiry*, Vol. 14 (1976): 52–58.

management. As long as social and private discount rates are the same and price expectations are accurate, the rotation which maximizes profits will also maximize net benefits. Both shorter-than-efficient rotations and longer-than-efficient rotations would result in lower profits, so it is in the self-interest of the private owner to act efficiently.

Perhaps even more important are the incentives created by private ownership to increase the yield of forested lands. Since more timber means more profits, efficient techniques to boost yield become very attractive to private forest owners. A great deal of progress has been made in this area since World War II when scientific forestry began to have an impact. New strains of trees have been developed which grow faster and are more disease-resistant. Restocking, pest control, and general management techniques have improved. In principle, markets provide a simple means to achieve efficient forest management.

In practice, however, market allocations are less than perfect, even when the sale of timber is the only objective. An analysis by Marion Clawson (1972 and 1975) indicates that scale is an important element of achieving efficient forest management. On very small holdings it does not pay for the owner to invest the time or money to become informed about good forestry practices, much less implement them. Harvesting equipment is large and expensive. Small owners may have poor access to markets due in part to their infrequent use of them. Furthermore, for many of these holdings the ownership of forest land is incidental to some other activity, so the owner has no intention of maximizing profit from timber harvest. It is therefore not surprising that the evidence suggests that these lands are not efficiently managed.

In the United States, plots of under 100 acres comprise about one-third of all private forests. Another third is held in plots containing from 100 to 5000 acres, considered by Clawson to have no better than fair economic prospects. Despite the amount of forested land tied up in these relatively small holdings, collectively they yield relatively little harvested timber.

In addition, the price expectations which motivate private harvesting behavior may not be accurate. To the extent that forest owners incorrectly anticipate future prices, their decisions will not be accurate.

Bearing external costs is another problem faced by private managers. Private forest decisions are plagued by externally generated costs of various types. Yields are adversely affected by externally imposed costs, such as air pollution (Example 11.1). When heavy investments in forested lands can be wiped out by factors totally out of the control of the owners, the incentive to invest is undermined.

Pest control is another area where externalities are an important factor. Controlling highly mobile pests on one plot of land will have virtually no effect if neighboring lands don't control the pests as well. The supply of pests will simply be restocked naturally from the neighboring lands.

Outbreaks of forest destruction can have rather long-term effects. In Maine, for example, an infestation by the spruce budworm during the 1970s and 1980s killed significant quantities of vulnerable spruce-fir trees. As a result, the outlook is for a severe supply crunch in these trees in the early part of the next century. Although there will still be a considerable volume of spruce-fir wood available in Maine forests, for the

EXAMPLE 11.1

Externalities in Forest Management: *Waldsterben*

When the first signs of forest death began to show up in the forests of West Germany, it was widely assumed that it was the spreading of a white fir decline that had been periodically decimating fir forests in Central Europe for the past 250 years. By the late 1970s, however, when Norway spruce began dying as well, it became apparent to scientists that they were being faced with an unprecedented situation of mass devastation, a situation known in German as *Waldsterben.*

It is spreading rapidly. In 1982, the government of the Federal Republic of Germany estimated that about 8 percent of its forests were damaged. By 1985, a repeat survey discovered that some 52 percent of the stands were affected. Among white firs more than 60 years old, some 95 percent exhibit visible symptoms of decline. The damage is particularly accute in the Black and Bavarian Forests. In 1985, the Union of German Forest Owners estimated the annual costs of *Waldsterben* at some $1 billion a year if present trends continue as expected.

Based on the perplexing array of symptoms, as well as the rapidity with which it is moving through forests, scientists now believe that multiple causes are involved. Early speculation that it was acid rain now seems too simple to explain the magnitude of the destruction. Most current scientific hypotheses about the causes involve the interactions of several pollutants, including nitrogen and sulfur compounds, ozone, aluminum, and a variety of organic chemicals such as ethylene or aniline.

Waldsterben is a good example of the policymaker's dilemma. The destruction is widespread and increasing rapidly, but considerable scientific uncertainty exists about the specific causes. Although the costs of inaction are apparently very high, with so many suspects to choose from, it is hard to formulate an effective control strategy. Meanwhile foresters helplessly watch as their resource bases dwindle due to factors entirely beyond their control.

Source: Don Hinrichsen, "Waldsterben: Forest Death Syndrome," *The Amicus Journal* (Spring, 1986): 23–27.

most part the trees will be too small for current commercial use. By altering the age structure of the forest, these external costs can cause a significant disruption in the even flow of harvesting activity.

Externalities can be conferred by forest owners as well as borne by them. Many of the amenity services provided by forests do not result in an equivalent monetary gain to the owner. As a result owners may not pay sufficient attention to these services as they manage the resource; they may be undervalued and as a result, undersupplied. In some cases this undervaluation may take on a global significance (Example 11.2).

The Public Sector

Since some of the problems having to do with private management of forests arise either because the private plots are too small or because they are plagued by externalities, the public sector appears to provide an answer. With the large amount of resources at its disposal, plus the ability to acquire land through eminent domain proceedings, the government can achieve the efficient scale rather easily. Furthermore, since it is not obligated to maximize profits, it can more easily take external effects on wildlife or recreation into account. Unfortunately, if the U.S. experience is typical, the potential to solve these problems has not yet been completely exploited.

Public ownership of lands in the United States started even before the fledgling nation had a constitution. The first public land, much of it forest land, was accepted as a donation by the Confederation of Congress on October 29, 1782. Though these lands were owned by the government, they were not managed by the government until more than a century later. The forest was treated as common property.

By the second half of the nineteenth century, a number of voices began to decry the apparent wanton destruction of the forests and to call for more enlightened use of the resource. The first piece of legislation designed to respond to this outcry was the Forest Reserve Act of 1891, which authorized the first permanent system of forest reserves. This act made no provision for private harvesting of trees on the forest reserves. It wasn't until 1897, with the passage of a general administration bill, that Congress provided the funds and a process to manage this system. This act authorized private harvesting on forest reserves under rather restrictive conditions.

The management for these reserves was transferred in 1905 to the U.S. Department of Agriculture's Forest Service. The Weeks Act, passed in 1911, enabled the Forest Service to acquire new forest land, which ultimately became a major part of the national forests in the Eastern part of the United States.

The ambitious chief of the USDA Forest Service at that time, Gifford Pinchot, was to have an enormous influence over Forest Service management for several decades. Unlike other contemporaries such as John Muir, who wanted to withdraw these lands from use, Pinchot vigorously pursued a philosophy that they should be used. Focusing first on timber production, his goal was the promotion of a sustainable level of harvest from the national forests. Concern over wildlife and recreation would come much later.

The desire for the maintenance of a sustained level of harvest gave rise to the acceptance of a number of operating procedures by the Forest Service which were explicitly biologically based. Chief among these were the maximum average annual increment described above and the requirement to keep the allowable cut on the national forests steady through time to reduce the potential instability faced by private forest owners caused by flooding the market with timber from the public lands.

Although the Forest Service had to some extent followed a multiple-use philosophy since its inception, in the period following World War II public interest in nontimber uses grew sufficiently that the rather *ad hoc* methods of the Forest Service for achieving a balance were no longer deemed sufficient. During the 1960s and 1970s, a significant amount of new legislation was passed (Table 11.2).

EXAMPLE 11.2

Public Good Aspects of Forest Management: Tropical Deforestation

Tropical rainforests are a very special ecological resource. Covering just 7 percent of the earth's land area, rainforests are estimated to harbor some 40 percent of all living plants and animals. As such they constitute an enormous source of genetic diversity. Genetic diversity has historically been a very important raw material for the development of new plants with yield-increasing characteristics.

As pointed out in Chapter 3 the genetic diversity provided by the tropical rainforest is a public good. It is characterized by both the consumption indivisibility and nonexcludability properties. Who would eventually benefit from the existence of more genetic diversity can't be known with any certainty at this point in time.

The current owners of tropical rainforests cannot be expected to efficiently protect genetic diversity because they do not receive a commensurate flow of benefits from this protection. Since the benefits flow to others in rather ill-defined ways, the standing forest is undervalued relative to the harvested forest.

As might be expected, deforestation of these areas is occuring at a rapid rate. Brazil, for example, which has over 1.3 million square miles of forest (half the Amazon Basin) is losing trees at a rate of approximately 5,000 square miles a year, an area roughly the size of Connecticut. These areas are being deforested with the aid of large government subsidies to provide settlement space for the poor squatters currently flocking to Brazilian cities.

TABLE 11.2 Major U.S. Forest Legislation

Date and Citation	Popular Name	Major Provisions
March 3, 1891 26 Stat. 1095	Forest Reserve Act of 1891	Authorized first system of national permanent forest reserves.
June 12, 1960 74 Stat. 215	Multiple Use–Sustained Yield Act	Provided legislative mandate for multiple use of forestlands. No guidance on policy issues or management strategies.
Sept. 3, 1964 78 Stat. 890	The Wilderness Act of 1964	Designated initial areas to be included as wilderness areas and set stringent rules governing use.
Aug. 17, 1974 88 Stat. 476	Forest and Rangeland Renewable Resources Planning Act	A planning act, requiring an assessment of all renewable resources every ten years and a program for the national forests every five years.

Nutrients released into the soil from the ashes of burned trees support marketable harvests only for a year or so before the pounding rains leach them out. Falling production then forces the settlers to abandon the land or to sell it to large ranchers. What this cycle suggests is that tropical deforestation is not producing the benefits it was designed to produce, but it is producing less genetic diversity. It must be possible to make better provision for the poor of these Third World countries while affording genetic diversity adequate protection.

Since the benefits of preservation are global, a number of observers have begun to suggest that the costs of preservation should be globally shared as well. Two recent proposals for cost-sharing have been offered. Ira Rubinoff (1982) has proposed financing a system of tropical forest preserves financed by a voluntarily assumed progressive tax on the 43 countries with the highest per capita incomes. Nicholas Guppy (1984) suggests that major gains could be made if only tropical timber would no longer be underpriced. Recommending the establishment of an Organization of Timber Exporting Countries to raise prices, Guppy estimates that the higher prices would reduce demand while providing a significant amount of revenue to cover the annual costs of human settlement.

Sources: Ira Rubinoff, "Tropical Forests: Can We Afford Not to Give Them a Future?" *The Ecologist* (November/December, 1982); Nicholas Guppy, "Tropical Deforestation: A Global View" *Foreign Affairs* (Spring, 1984); Edward C. Wolf, "Conserving Biological Diversity," in Lester R. Brown, et al., *State of the World 1985* (New York: W. W. Norton & Co., 1985); and Lansing R. Shepard, "Vanishing Rain Forest" *The Christian Science Monitor* (April 2, 1986).

The Multiple Use–Sustained Yield Act mandated a multiple-use philosophy, without giving a lot of guidance on how to implement that philosophy. In part, this act had been sought by the Forest Service to protect its multiple-use philosophy from attack by those seeking Congressional or judicial support for single interests. Subsequent legislation, however, would force the Forest Service to be much more systematic in how it sought to define and implement a multiple-use philosophy.

The Wilderness Act set aside specific forest areas to be preserved as pristine. No roads were permitted and timber harvests were prohibited. Although initially limited to designating specific areas that had by tradition not been harvested, the act has in fact been the basis of a significant amount of judicial and agency interpretation with the ultimate effect that it has ushered in much more wilderness land than was envisioned by those discussing it in Congress at the time the bill was passed.

Finally the Forest and Rangeland Renewable Resources Planning Act, passed in

1974, and amended by the National Forest Management Act of 1976, resulted from a Congressional sense that the Forest Service lacked an adequate comprehensive planning process. These acts have not only prodded the Service into improving its planning process, but it has also served to increase the role that economic analysis is playing in the planning. Explicit economic models have been developed to provide information useful in balancing the various multiple uses. Harvest rates on national forests have risen closer to efficient levels. Public sector forest management is coming of age.

SUMMARY

Forests represent an example of a storable, renewable source. Typically tree stands go through three distinct growth phases—slow growth in volume in the early stage, followed by rapid growth in the middle years and slower growth as the stand reaches full maturity. The owner who harvests the timber receives the income from its sale, but the owner who delays harvest will receive additional growth. The amount of growth depends on the part of the growth cycle the stand is in.

From an economic point of view the efficient time to harvest a stand of timber is when the net benefits are maximized. The net benefits are maximized when the marginal gain from delaying the harvest one more year is equal to the marginal cost of the delay. For longer-than-efficient delays the additional costs outweight the increased benefits, while for earlier-than-efficient harvests more benefits (in terms of the increased value of the timber) are given up than costs saved. Typically the efficient age at harvest is 25 years or older. Intervals are common.

The efficient harvest age usually depends on the circumstances the owner faces. When the plot is to be left fallow after the harvest, the efficient harvest occurs later than when the land is immediately replanted to initiate another cycle. With immediate replanting, delaying the harvest imposes an additional cost—the cost of delaying the next harvest—which, when factored into the analysis, makes it more desirable to harvest earlier.

A number of other factors affect the size of the efficient rotation as well. In general the larger the discount rate the earlier the harvest. With an infinite-planning horizon model increases in planting and harvesting costs tend to lengthen the optimal rotation, while in a single-harvest model they have no affect on the length of the efficient rotation. If the price of timber grows at a constant rate over time, the efficient rotation is longer than if prices remain constant over time. Finally if standing timber provides amenity services (such as for recreation or wildlife management) in proportion to the volume of the standing timber, the efficient rotation will be longer than it would in the absence of any amenity services.

Profit maximization can be compatible with efficient forest management under the right circumstances. In particular, profit-maximizing private owners have an incentive to adopt the efficient rotation when amenity services are small and to undertake investments which increase the yield of the forest.

In reality, not all private firms will follow efficient forest management practices because they may choose not to maximize profits, they may be operating at too small a scale of operation, or externalities may create inefficient incentives. Many forest owners own very small plots, purchased for some reason other than harvesting timber and they are simply not acting like profit maximizers. Even if they were, small scale plots cannot normally be operated efficiently because of the importance of economies of scale both in learning about scientific forestry and in implementing it. The costs of acquiring this knowledge and putting it into practice may be so large as to eliminate any potential benefits. Finally, when amenity values are large and not captured by the forest owner, the private rotation period may fail to consider these values, leading to an inefficiently short rotation period.

The public sector in the United States has historically not managed the public forests efficiently. In the earlier years the harvests were governed strictly by biological criteria which failed to take all of the costs into consideration. The trend seems to be toward more efficient management as legislatively mandated planning processes formalize multiple-use management through the use of more explicit economic analysis.

FURTHER READING

Bowes, Michael D. and John V. Krutilla, "Multiple Use Management of Public Forestlands" in Allen V. Kneese and James L. Sweeney, eds. *Handbook of Natural Resource and Energy Economics, Vol. II* (Amsterdam: North-Holland, 1985). Excellent analytical treatment of the multiple-use strategy as it applies to U.S. forest policy. Somewhat mathematical.

Clawson, Marion, *The Federal Lands Revisited* (Washington; Resources for the Future, Inc., 1983) A comprehensive overview of current policy issues related to federally owned lands in the United States, including, but not limited to, national forests.

Clawson, Marion, "Private Forests" in Paul R. Portney, ed., *Current Issues in Natural Resource Policy* (Washington: Resources for the Future, Inc., 1982): 283–292. A short summary of the problems of and the prospects for U.S. private forests.

Deacon, R. T., "The Simple Analytics of Forest Economics," in R. T. Deacon and M. B. Johnson, eds. *Forestlands: Public and Private* (San Francisco: Pacific Institute for Public Policy Research, 1985). An especially accessible treatment of forestry economics.

Irland, Lloyd C., *Wilderness Economics and Policy* (Lexington, MA: Lexington Books, 1979). An overview of wilderness policy in the United States and how economic analysis can contribute to a clearer understanding of the issues.

ADDITIONAL REFERENCES

Berck, P., "Optimal Management of Renewable Resources with Growing Demand and Stock Externalities" *Journal of Environmental Economics and Management,* Vol. 8 (1981): 105–117.

Clawson, Marion, *America's Land and Its Uses* (Washington: Resources for the Future, Inc., 1972).

Clawson, Marion, "Decision Making in Timber Production, Harvest, and Marketing," Resources for the Future, Inc., Research Paper R-4, (Washington: 1977).

Clawson, Marion, *Forests For Whom and For What?* (Washington: Resources for the Future, Inc., 1975).

Hartman, R., "The Harvesting Decision When a Standing Forest Has Value," *Economic Inquiry* Vol. 14 (1976): 52–58.

Merrifield, David E. and Richard W. Hayes, "The Adjustment of Product and Factor Markets: An Application to the Pacific Northwest Forest Products Industry," *American Journal of Agricultural Economics,* Vol. 66, no. 1 (February, 1984): 79–87.

Samuelson, Paul A., "Economics of Forestry in an Evolving Society" *Economic Inquiry,* Vol. 14 (1976): 466–492.

DISCUSSION QUESTIONS

1. Should the U.S. national forests become "privatized" (sold to private owners)? Why or why not?

2. In his book *The Federal Lands Revisited,* Marion Clawson proposes what he calls the "pullback concept."

> "Under the pullback concept any person or group could apply, under applicable law, for a tract of federal land, for any use they chose; but any other person or group would have a limited time between the filing of the initial application and granting of the lease or the making of the sale in which to "pull back" a part of the area applied for . . . The user of the pullback provision would become the applicant for the area pulled back, required to meet the same terms applicable to the original application, . . . but the use could be what the applicant chose, not necessarily the use proposed by the original applicant." (p. 216)

Evaluate the "pullback concept" as a means for conservationists to prevent some mineral extraction or timber harvesting on federal lands.

PROBLEMS

1. Suppose there are two forest plots which are identical except that one will be harvested and left while the second will be cleared after the harvest and turned into a housing development. In terms of efficiency, which should have the oldest harvest age? Why?

2. In Table 11.2 when $r = 0.02$, the present value of the cost rises for 68 years and then subsequently declines. Why?

CHAPTER TWELVE

Renewable Common-Property Resources: Fisheries

> *This island is almost made of coal and surrounded by fish.*
> *Only an organizing genius could produce a shortage of coal*
> *and fish in Great Britain at the same time.*
> ANEURIN BEVAN, BRITISH LABOR POLITICIAN (1945)

INTRODUCTION

Renewable resources are those for which the stock of resources can be continually replenished. It is easy to think of renewable resources as perpetual. If this were automatically the case, we could merely assure ourselves that the market would ultimately make a smooth transition from depletable to renewable resources. But that is an overly simple view! Some renewable resources—living populations, such as plants and animals—are also exhaustible if not managed effectively. The growth or decline of these populations in general depends on the size of the population. If, through people's activities, the population is drawn down beyond a critical threshold, the species can become extinct.

Extinction, though important, is not the only critical renewable resource-management issue. If it were, public policy could concentrate on avoiding extinction and not concern itself with any other outcome. Fisheries belong to a class of renewable resources we will call *interactive resources,* wherein the size of the resource stock (population) is determined jointly by biological considerations and by actions taken by society. The size of the population, in turn, determines the availability of the resources for the future. Thus humanity's actions determine the flow of these resources over time. Since this flow is not purely a natural phenomenon, a second crucial dimension is the optimum rate of use across time and across generations. What is the efficient rate of use of interactive renewable resources? In the absence of outside influences, can the market be relied upon to achieve and sustain this rate?

These are particularly pertinent questions in light of the recent history with the world fish catch. In an often-cited book published during the early 1970s, Lester Brown [1974] caught the world's attention with his statement that the world's fish catch had started to decline, thus ushering in a new age of scarcity. Although this decline in total catch turned out to be temporary, during the 1970s the fish catch did not keep pace with population growth. The continuation of this trend depends on whether or not fisheries will be more effectively managed in the future (Table 12.3).

Let's examine these questions by taking a close look at fisheries. The same analysis is sometimes used to study the management of other wildlife. Fisheries are interesting not only because they are an important source of protein,[1] but also because they provide a rich and varied introduction to the problems of managing common-property resources.

Let's begin by defining what is meant by an efficient allocation of the catch from a fishery; we can then examine how the market allocates this common-property resource and which public policies could be applied as solutions.

EFFICIENT ALLOCATIONS

The Biological Dimension

Like many other studies, our characterization of the fishery rests on a biological model originally proposed by Schaefer [1957]. The Schaefer model posits a particular average relationship between the growth of the fish population and the size of the fish population. This is an average relationship in the sense that it abstracts from such influences as water temperature and the age structure of the population. The model therefore does not attempt to characterize the fishery on a day-to-day basis, but rather in terms of some long-term average in which these various random influences tend to counterbalance each other (Figure 12.1).

The size of the population is represented on the horizontal axis and the growth of the population on the vertical axis. The graph suggests that there is a range of population sizes ($\underline{S}$ to $S^\star$) where population growth increases as the population increases and a range ($S^\star$ to $\bar{S}$) where initial increases in population lead to eventual declines in growth.

We can shed further light on this relationship by examining more closely the two points ($\underline{S}$ and $\bar{S}$) where the function intersects the horizontal axis and therefore growth in the stock is zero. $\bar{S}$ is known as the *natural equilibrium,* since this is population size which would persist in the absence of outside influences. Reductions in the stock due to mortality or out-migration would be exactly offset by increases in the stock to births, growth of the fish in the remaining stock, and in-migration.

This natural equilibrium would persist because it is stable. A *stable equilibrium*

---

[1]Some countries, such as Japan and Portugal, obtain more than half of their animal protein from fish.

TABLE 12.1   Total World Fish Catch and Per Capita Fish Catch 1950–83

	Fish Catch[a] (million metric tons)	Fish Catch per Capita[b] (lbs.)
1950	21.1	18.51
1955	28.9	23.21
1960	40.2	29.28
1965	53.2	35.07
1970	65.6	39.32
1975	69.5	36.35
1980	72.0	34.47
1981	74.8	35.38
1982	76.5	35.40
1983	76.5	34.81

Sources: [a]*Environmental Quality 1981* (Washington, D.C.: U.S. Government Printing Office, 1981), p. 254 and OECD Environmental Data Compendium: 1985 (Paris, 1985), p. 74.

[b]Calculated by author using population figures from the *Demographic Yearbook* (New York: Publishing Service, United Nations), various years.

is one in which movements away from this population level set forces in motion to restore it. If, for example, the stock temporarily exceeded $\bar{S}$, it would be exceeding the capacity of its habitat (called carrying capacity). As a result, mortality rates or out-migration would increase until the stock was once again within the confines of the carrying capacity of its habitat at $\bar{S}$.

This tendency for the population size to return to $\bar{S}$ works in the other direction as well. Suppose the population is temporarily reduced below $\bar{S}$. Because the stock is now smaller, growth would be positive and would increase the size of the stock. Over time, the fishery would move along the curve to the right until $\bar{S}$ is reached again.

FIGURE 12.1   The Relationship Between the Fish Population and Growth

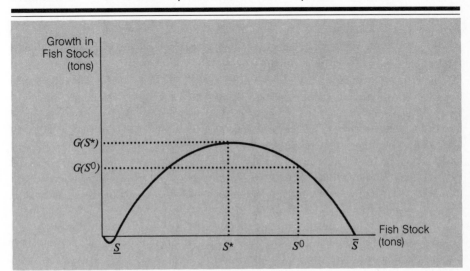

What about the other points on the curve? $\underline{S}$, known as the *minimum viable population,* represents the level of population below which growth in population is negative (deaths and out-migration exceed births and in-migration). In contrast to $\bar{S}$, this equilibrium is unstable. Population sizes to the right of $\underline{S}$ lead to positive growth and a movement along the curve to $\bar{S}$ and away from $\underline{S}$. When the population moves to the left of $\underline{S}$, the population declines until it eventually becomes extinct. In this region there are no forces acting to return the population to a viable level.

A catch level is said to represent a *sustainable yield* whenever it equals the growth rate of the population since it can be maintained forever. As long as the population size remains constant, the growth rate (and, hence, the catch) will remain constant as well.

$S^\star$ is what is known in biology as the *maximum sustainable yield* population, defined as that population size which yields the maximum growth; hence, the maximum sustainable yield is equal to this maximum growth and it represents the largest catch that can be perpetually sustained. If the catch is equal to the growth, the sustainable yield for any population size (between $\underline{S}$ and $\bar{S}$) can be determined by drawing a vertical line from the stock size of interest on the horizontal axis to the point where it intersects the function and then drawing a horizontal line over to the vertical axis. The sustainable yield is the growth in the biomass defined by the intersection of this line with the vertical axis. Thus in terms of Figure 12.1, $G(S^o)$ is the sustainable yield for population size S^o. Since the catch is equal to the growth, population size (and next year's growth) remains the same.

It should now be clear why $G\ (S^\star)$ is the maximum sustainable yield. Larger catches would be possible in the short run, but these could not be sustained; they would lead to reduced population sizes and eventually, if the population were drawn down to a level smaller than $\underline{S}$, to the extinction of the species.

Static-Efficient Sustained Yield

Is the maximum sustainable yield synonymous with efficiency? The answer is no. Efficiency, it may be remembered, is associated with maximizing the net benefit from the use of the resource. If we are to define the efficient allocation, we must include the costs of harvesting as well as the benefits.

Let's begin by defining the efficient sustainable yield without worrying about discounting. The static-efficient sustainable yield is the catch level which, if maintained perpetually, would produce the largest annual net benefit. We shall refer to this as the *static-efficient* sustainable yield to distinguish it from the *dynamic-efficient* sustainable yield, which incorporates discounting. The initial use of this static concept enables us to fix the necessary relationships firmly in mind before dealing with the more difficult role discounting plays. Subsequently, we shall raise the question of whether or not efficiency always dictates the choice of a sustainable yield as opposed to a catch that changes over time.

We shall condition our analysis on three assumptions that simplify the analysis without sacrificing too much realism: (1) the price of fish is constant and does not depend on the amount sold; (2) the marginal cost of a unit of fishing effort is constant;

and (3) the amount of fish caught per unit of effort expended is proportional to the size of fish population (the smaller the population, the fewer fish caught per unit of effort).

In any sustainable yield, catches, population, effort levels, and net benefits remain constant over time. The static-efficient sustainable yield allocation maximizes the constant net benefit.

In Figure 12.2 the benefits (revenues) and costs are portrayed as a function of fishing effort and can be measured in vessel years, hours of fishing, or some other convenient metric. The shape of the revenue function is dictated by the shape of the function in Figure 12.1, since the price of fish is assumed constant. To avoid confusion, notice that increasing fishing effort in Figure 12.1 would result in smaller population sizes and would be recorded as a movement from right to left. Because the variable on the horizontal axis in Figure 12.2 is effort, and not population, an increase in fishing effort is recorded as a movement from left to right.

As sustained levels of effort are increased, eventually a point is reached (E^m) where further effort reduces the sustainable catch and revenue for all years. That point, of course, corresponds to the maximum sustainable yield on Figure 12.2, which involves identical population and growth levels. For every effort level portrayed in Figure 12.2, there is a corresponding population level in Figure 12.2.

The net benefit is presented in the diagram as the difference (vertical distance) between benefits (price times the quantity caught) and costs (the constant marginal cost

FIGURE 12.2 The Efficient Sustainable Yield for a Fishery

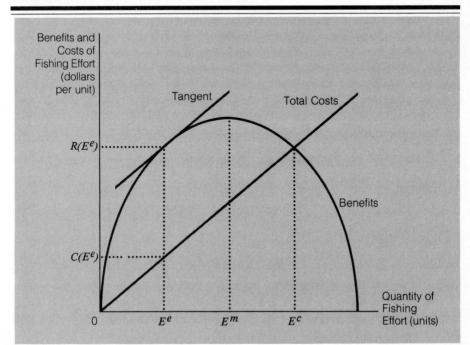

of effort times the units of effort expended). The efficient level of effort is E^e, that point in Figure 12.2 where the vertical distance between benefits and costs is maximized.

E^e is the efficient level of effort because it is where marginal benefit (which graphically is the slope of the total-benefit curve) is equal to marginal cost (the *constant* slope of the total cost curve). Levels of effort higher than E^e are inefficient because the additional cost associated with them exceeds the value of the fish obtained. Can you see why lower levels of effort are inefficient?

Now we are armed with sufficient information to determine whether or not the maximum sustainable yield is efficient. The answer is clearly no. The maximum sustainable yield is efficient only if the marginal cost of additional effort is zero. Can you see why? (Hint: What is the marginal benefit at the maximum sustainable yield?) Since this is not the case, the efficient level of effort is *less* than that necessary to harvest the maximum sustainable yield. Thus the static efficient level of effort leads to a *larger* fish population than the maximum sustainable yield level of effort.

To fix these concepts firmly in mind, consider what would happend to the static efficient sustainable yield if a technological change were to occur (e.g., sonar detection) lowering the marginal cost of fishing. The lower marginal cost would result in a rotation of the total cost curve to the right. With this new cost structure, the old level of effort is no longer efficient. The marginal cost of fishing (slope of the total-cost curve) is now lower than the marginal benefit (slope of the total-benefit curve). Since the marginal cost is constant, the equality of marginal cost and marginal benefit can only result from a decline in marginal benefits. This implies an increase in effort. The new static-efficient sustainable-yield equilibrium implies more effort, a lower population level, a larger catch, and a higher net benefit for the fishery.

Dynamic-Efficient Sustainable Yield

The static-efficient sustainable yield turns out to be the special case of the dynamic-efficient sustained yield where the discount rate is zero. It is not difficult to understand why; the static-efficient sustained yield is the allocation which maximizes the (identical) net benefit in every period. Any higher effort levels than this would yield temporarily larger catches (and net benefit) but this would be more than offset by a reduced net benefit in the future as the stock reached its new lower level. Thus, the undiscounted net benefits would be reduced.

The effect of a positive discount rate for the management of a fishery is similar to its influence on the allocation of depletable resources—the higher the discount rate, the higher the cost (in terms of forgone current income) to the resource owner of maintaining any given resource stock. When positive discount rates are introduced, the efficient level of effort would be increased beyond that suggested by the static-efficient sustained yield with a corresponding decrease in the equilibrium population level.

The increase in the yearly effort beyond the efficient sustained yield level would *initially* result in an increased net benefit from the increased catch. (Remember that the amount of fish caught per unit effort expended is proportional to the size of the population.) However, since this catch exceeds the sustained yield for that population size, the population of fish would be reduced and future population and catch levels would be lower. Eventually, as that level of effort is maintained, a new lower equilibrium level would be attained where the size of the catch once again equals the growth of the population. Colin Clark [1976, pp. 42–44] has shown mathematically that in terms of Figure 12.2, as the discount rate is increased, the dynamic efficient level of effort is increased until, with an infinite discount rate, it becomes equal to E^c, the point at which net benefits go to zero.

It is easy to see why the use of an infinite discount rate to define the dynamic-efficient sustained yield results in allocation E^c. We have seen that interdependent allocations over time give rise to a marginal user cost measuring the opportunity cost of increasing current effort. This opportunity cost reflects the foregone future net benefits when more resources are extracted in the present. For efficient interdependent allocations, the marginal willingness to pay is equal to the marginal user cost plus the marginal cost of extraction.

With an infinite discount rate this marginal-user cost is zero, because no value is received from future allocations. This implies: (1) the marginal cost of extraction equals the marginal willingness to pay, which equals the constant price, and (2) total benefits equal total costs.[2] Earlier we demonstrated that the static-efficient sustained yield implies a larger fish population than the maximum sustained yield. Once discounting is introduced, it is inevitable that the dynamic-efficient sustained yield would imply a smaller fish population than the static-efficient sustained yield and it is possible, though not inevitable, that the sustained catch would be smaller. Do you see why? In Figure 12.2 the sustained catch clearly is lower for an infinite discount rate.

The likelihood of the population being reduced below the level supplying the maximum sustainable yield depends on the discount rate. In general, the lower the extraction costs and the higher the discount rate, the more likely it is that the dynamic-efficient level of effort will exceed the level of effort associated with the maximum sustainable yield. This is not difficult to see if we remember the limiting case discussed earlier. When the marginal extraction cost is zero, the static-efficient sustainable yield and the maximum sustainable yield are equal.

Thus, with zero marginal extraction costs and a positive discount rate, the dynamic-efficient level of effort necessarily exceeds the static-efficient level of effort and the level of effort associated with the maximum sustainable yield. Higher extraction costs reduce the static-efficient sustainable yield but not the maximum sustainable yield. Higher extraction costs reduce the likelihood that discounting would cause the population to be drawn below the maximum sustainable yield level.

Would a dynamically-efficient management scheme lead to extinction of the fishery?

---

[2]This is not difficult to demonstrate mathematically. In our model, the yield (y) can be expressed as $y = qxe$ where q is the proportion of the population harvested with one unit of effort, x is the size of the population and e is the level of effort. One of the conditions a dynamic efficient allocation has to satisfy with an infinite discount rate is $P = c/qx$, where P is the constant price and c is the constant marginal cost per unit of effort and qx is the number of fish harvested per unit of effort. By multiplying both sides of this equation by y and collecting terms, we obtain $Py = ce$. The left-hand side is total benefits while the right is total cost, implying net benefits are zero.

As Figure 12.2 shows, it would not be possible under the circumstances described here, because E^c is the highest dynamically efficient level possible in this model, and that level falls well short of the level needed to drive the population to extinction. It is possible under other circumstances, however.[3]

For extinction to occur under a dynamic-efficient management scheme, the benefit from extracting the very last unit would have to exceed the cost of extracting that unit (including the costs on future generations). As long as the population growth rate exceeds the discount rate, this will not be the case. If, however, the growth rate is lower than the discount rate, extinction can occur in an efficient management scheme if the costs of extracting the last unit are sufficiently low.

Why does the rate of growth have anything to do with whether or not an efficient catch profile leads to extinction? Rate of growth determines the productivity of conservation efforts. With high rates of growth, future generations can be easily satisfied. On the other hand, when the rate of growth is very low, it takes a large sacrifice by current generations to produce more fish for future generations. In the limiting case, where the rate of growth is zero, we have a resource fixed in supply and therefore no different from an exhaustible resource. Total depletion would occur whenever the price commanded by the resource is high enough to cover the marginal cost of extracting the last unit.

We have shown that the dynamic-efficiency criterion is not automatically consistent with sustaining constant yields perpetually for an interactive renewable resource, since it is mathematically possible for an efficient allocation of a fishery to lead to extinction of the resource. How likely are these criteria to conflict in practice?

Although the information is sketchy, most empirical studies suggest that because of the importance of extraction costs, the dynamic-efficient catch rate is usually smaller than the maximum sustainable yield and extinction is rarely, if ever, efficient.[4] The cost of catching the last few fish is usually well in excess of the price received for them. The two criteria are usually completely compatible, although we must bear in mind that they are not inevitably compatible.

APPROPRIABILITY AND MARKET SOLUTIONS

We have now defined an efficient allocation of the fishery over time. The next step is to characterize the normal market allocation and to contrast these two allocations. Where they differ we can entertain the possibility of various public-policy corrective means.

Let's first consider the allocation resulting from a fishery managed by a competitive sole owner. A sole owner would have a well-defined property right to the fish. We can establish the behavior of a sole owner by elaborating on Figure 12.2, as is done

---

[3]See, for example, Kuo-Shung Cheng, et al., "Analysis of Modified Model for Commercial Fishing with Possible Extinctive Fishery Resources," *Journal of Environmental Economics and Management* VIII (June 1981): 151–155, for a mathematical description of sufficient conditions for extinction to occur.

[4]See, for example, the discussion in Colin W. Clark, *Mathematical Bioeconomics: The Optimal Management of Renewable Resources* (New York, NY: Wiley Interscience, 1976), pp. 18–21.

FIGURE 12.3   Market Allocation in a Common-Property Fishery

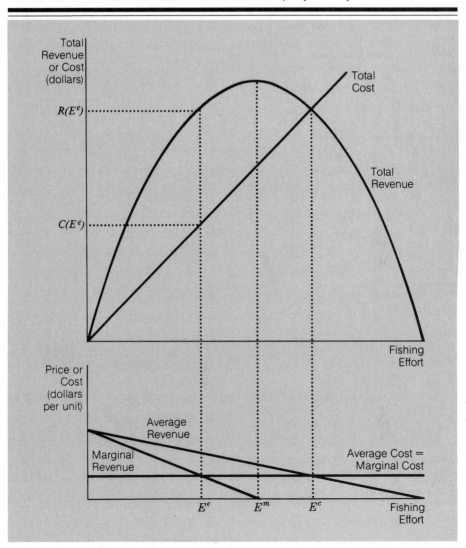

in Figure 12.3. Notice that the two panels share a common horizontal axis which allows us to examine the effect of various fishing-effort levels on both graphs.

A sole owner would want to maximize his or her profits. Ignoring discounting for the moment, the owner can increase profits by increasing fishing effort until marginal revenue equals marginal cost. Clearly this is effort level E^e, the static efficient sustainable yield. This will yield positive profits equal to the difference between $R(E^e)$ and $C(E^e)$.

In ocean fisheries, however, sole owners are not common. Normally ocean fisheries are common property resources — no one exercises complete control over them. Since the property rights to the fishery are not conveyed to any single owner, no single fisherman can exclude others from exploiting the fishery. Sometimes common property resources can coexist in the same market as private property fisheries (Example 12.1).

What problems arise when the fishery is treated as a common-property resource rather than a private-property resource? Common-property resources create two kinds of externalities: a *contemporaneous externality* and an *intergenerational externality*. The contemporaneous externality, which is borne by the current generation, involves the over-commitment of resources to fishing—too many boats, too many fishermen, too much effort. As a result, current fishermen earn a substantially lower rate of return on their efforts. The intergenerational externality, borne by future generations, occurs because overfishing reduces the stock which, in turn, lowers future profits from fishing.[5]

We can use Figure 12.3 to see how these externalities arise. Once there are many fishermen exploiting the same common-property fishery, the property rights to the fish are no longer efficiently defined. At the efficient level, each boat would receive a profit equal to its share of the scarcity rent. This rent, however, serves as a stimulus for new fishermen to enter, drawing up costs and eliminating the rent. Open access results in overexploitation.

The sole owner chooses not to expend more effort than E^e because to do so would reduce the profits of the fishery, resulting in a personal loss to him. When the fishery is common property, a decision to expend efforts beyond E^e reduces profits to the fishery as a whole but not to that individual fisherman. Most of the decline in profits falls on the other fishermen.

In a common-property resource, the individual fisherman has an incentive to expend further effort until profits are zero. In Figure 12.3 that point is at effort level E^c, where average benefit and average cost are equal. It is now easy to see the contemporaneous externality—too much effort is being expended to catch too few fish, and the cost is substantially higher than it would be in an efficient allocation. An intergenerational externality occurs because the size of the population is reduced, causing future profits to be lower than would otherwise be the case. As the existing population is overexploited, the common-property catch initially would be higher, but as growth rates are affected, the steady-state profit level, once attained, would be lower.

We stated in Chapter 6 that the resource owner with exclusive property rights balances the use value against the asset value. When access to the resource is unrestricted, exclusivity is lost. As a result it is rational for the individual fisherman to ignore the asset value, since he can never appropriate it, and simply maximize the use value. In the process all the scarcity rent is dissipated. The allocation that results from treating the fishery as common property is identical to that resulting from a dynamic-efficient sustainable yield when an infinite discount rate is used.

Common-property resources do not automatically lead to a stock lower than that maximizing the sustained yield. We can draw a cost function with a slope sufficiently steep that it intersects the benefit curve at a point to the left of E^m. Nonetheless, it is not unusual for mature common-property fisheries to be exploited well beyond the point of maximum sustainable yield.

---

[5]This will result in fewer fish for future generations as well as smaller profits if the resulting effort level exceeds that associated with the maximum sustainable yield. If the common-property effort level is lower than the maximum sustainable yield effort level (when extraction costs are very high), then reductions in stock would *increase* the growth in the stock, thus supplying more fish (albeit lower net benefits) to future generations.

EXAMPLE 12.1

Property Rights and Fisheries: Oysters

The oyster industry provides a unique opportunity to study the effect of property-right structures on incentives because it contains both private-property and common-property oyster beds. In some cases these private-property and common-property beds compete with each other in the same market. This allows us to compare the price and quantity behavior of markets supplied by fishermen operating under both property-right systems to markets which depend solely on one or the other.

What would we expect to find?

1. Common-property resources should be harvested earlier in the season because there is less incentive to conserve common-property resources.
2. Common-property fishermen should earn lower average incomes because the economic rent is dissipated.
3. The markets served purely by private-property fisheries should have higher prices, since private-property fishermen can respond to market conditions whereas common-property fishermen are driven to catch and sell as many fish as early as possible.

What was revealed by examining data from Maryland, Virginia, Louisiana, and Mississippi?

1. From 1945 to 1970 the ratio of the harvest in the earlier part of the harvesting season to the later part was 1.35 for the common-property resource state (Maryland) and 1.01 for the contiguous private-property state (Virginia).
2. The average annual incomes over the period 1950–69 of fishermen in Virginia was $2,453 while that for Maryland was $1,606. Another comparison revealed that fishermen in the private-property state of Louisiana earned $3,207, while their counterparts in the contiguous common-property state of Mississippi was $870.
3. Over the period 1966–69, the mean price per pound of oysters in markets served purely by private oyster beds was $.94 while the mean price per pound for oysters from the common-property resource averaged only $.73 per pound. In addition, in a comparison of contiguous private- and common-property states, the private-property states all experienced higher prices.

Though these results do not come from carefully controlled experiments and therefore cannot be regarded as definitive, they are completely compatible with our understanding of the way in which property-right structures influence decisions.

Source: Richard J. Agnello and Lawrence P. Donnelley, "Prices and Property Rights in the Fisheries," *Southern Economic Journal* XLII (October 1979): 253–262.

Thus, common-property resources generally violate both the efficiency and sustainability criteria. If these criteria are to be fulfilled, there must be some restructuring of the decision-making environment. How that can be done is the subject of the next section.

PUBLIC POLICY TOWARD FISHERIES

What can be done? There can be a variety of public-policy responses. Perhaps it is appropriate to start with allowing the market to work.

Aquaculture

Having demonstrated that inefficient management of the fishery results from treating it as common, rather than private, property we have one obvious solution—allowing some fisheries to be privately, rather than commonly, held. This approach can work when the fish are not very mobile, such as lobsters, when they can be confined by artificial barriers, or when they instinctively return to their place of birth to spawn.

The advantages of such a move go well beyond the ability to preclude overfishing. The owner is encouraged to invest in the resource and undertake measures that will increase the productivity (yield) of the fishery.[6] This movement toward controlled raising and harvesting of fish is called *aquaculture* and there are some noteworthy examples of success.[7] Probably the highest yields ever attained through aquaculture resulted from using rafts to raise mussels. Some 300,000 kg/hectare of mussels, for example, have been raised in this manner in the Galician bays of Spain.[8] This productivity level approximates those achieved in poultry farming, widely regarded as one of the most successful attempts to increase the productivity of farm-produced animal protein.

In the United States aquaculture has been thwarted by treating bodies of water as common property. This need not be the case, of course. In Example 12.1 we saw that some oysters are raised in the United States in common-property beds and others are raised in private beds. As fish in the common-property resource become more scarce, triggering price increases, aquaculture probably would become more profitable and prevalent.

In some ways, Japan, as a densely populated country depending heavily on fish for protein, has reached the point where merely harvesting what the sea offers is no longer sufficient to satisfy the market at low cost. Consequently, Japan has become

---

[6] For example adding certain nutrients to the water or controlling the temperature can markedly increase the yields of some species.

[7] The examples of aquaculture in this chapter are drawn from John E. Bardach, John H. Ryther, and William O. McClarney, *Aquaculture: The Farming and Husbandry of Freshwater and Marine Organisms* (New York: Wiley Interscience, 1972).

[8] A hectare is a measure of surface area equal to 10,000 square meters. It is equal to 2.471 acres.

a leader in aquaculture, undertaking some of the most advanced and the greatest variety of aquaculture ventures in the world. The government there has been supportive, mainly by creating private-property rights for waters formerly held commonly. The prefecture governments (comparable to states in the United States) initiate the process by designating the areas to be used for aquaculture. The local fisherman's cooperative associations then partition these areas and allocate the sub-areas to individual fishermen for exclusive use. This exclusive control allows the owner to invest in the resource and to manage it effectively and efficiently.

Another market approach to aquaculture involves fish ranching rather than fish farming.[9] Whereas fish farming involves cultivating fish over their lifetime in a controlled environment, fish ranching involves holding them in captivity only for the first few years of their lives.

Fish ranching relies on the strong homing instincts in certain fish such as Pacific Salmon or ocean trout to permit their ultimate capture. The young salmon or ocean trout are hatched and confined in a convenient catch area for approximately two years. When released they migrate to the ocean. Upon reaching maturity, they return by instinct to the place of their births where they are harvested. Brown (1985, p. 90) estimates that 193,000 metric tons of salmon were harvested by the United States, the Soviet Union, and Japan in 1984.

Aquaculture is certainly not the answer for all fish. Although it works well for shellfish, catfish, salmon, and some other species, some fish, such as tuna, will probably never be harvested domestically at a profit. Nonetheless, it is comforting to note that aquaculture can provide a solution in some regions and for some fish. The market can provide a safety valve if allowed to work.

Raising the Real Cost of Fishing

Perhaps one of the best ways to illustrate the virtues of using economic analysis to help design policies is to show the harsh effects of policy approaches that ignore it. Because the earliest approaches to fishery management had a single-minded focus on attaining the maximum sustainable yield with little or no thought given to maximizing the net benefit, they provide a useful contrast.

Perhaps the best concrete example is the set of policies originally designed to deal with overexploitation of the Pacific salmon fishery in the United States.[10] The Pacific salmon is particularly vulnerable to overexploitation, and even extinction, because of its migration patterns. Pacific salmon are spawned in the gravel beds of rivers. As juvenile fish they migrate to the ocean only to return, as adults, to spawn in the rivers

---

[9]See Robert L. Stokes, "The Economics of Salmon Ranching", *Land Economics,* Vol. 58, No. 4 (November, 1982): 464–477.

[10]An excellent, detailed analysis of these policies can be found in J. A. Crutchfield and G. Pontecovo, *The Pacific Salmon Fisheries: A Study of Irrational Conservation* (Baltimore: Johns Hopkins Press for Resources for the Future, Inc., 1969).

of their birth. After spawning, they die. When the adults swim upstream with a instinctual need to return to their native streams, they can easily be captured by traps, nets, or other catching devices.

Recognizing the urgency of the problem, the government took action. To reduce the catch, they raised the cost of fishing. Initially this was accomplished by preventing the use of any barricades on the rivers, and by prohibiting the use of traps (the most efficient catching devices) in the most productive areas. These measures proved insufficient, since mobile techniques (trolling, nets, and so on) proved quite capable, by themselves, of overexploiting the resource. Officials then began to close designated fishing areas and suspend fishing in other areas for certain periods of time. In Figure 12.3 these measures would be reflected as a rotation of the cost curve to the left until it intersected the benefits curve at a level of effort equal to E^e. The aggregate of all these regulations had the desired effect of curtailing the yield of salmon.

Were these policies efficient? They were not and would not have been even had they resulted in the efficient catch! This statement may seem inconsistent, but it is not. Efficiency implies not only that the catch must be at the efficient level, but it must also be extracted at the lowest possible cost. This latter condition was violated by these policies (Figure 12.4).

In Figure 12.4 are reflected the total cost in an efficient allocation (TC_1) and the total cost after these policies were imposed (TC_2). The net benefit received from an efficient policy is shown graphically as the vertical distance between total cost and total benefit. After the policy, however, the net benefit was reduced to zero; the net benefit (represented by vertical distance) was lost to society. Why?

The net benefit was wasted due to the use of excessively expensive means to catch the desired yield of fish. Rather than use traps to reduce the cost of catching the desired number of fish, traps were prohibited. Larger expenditures on capital and labor were required to catch the same number of fish. This additional capital and labor represents one source of the waste.

The limitations on fishing times and fishing areas had a similar effect on cost. Rather than allowing fishermen to fish those areas and times where capital and labor would be most productively applied (while insuring that the target yields were not exceeded), fishermen were forced to use less productive areas and times. The additional time, energy, and equipment were also wasted resources.

These were not the only costs imposed by regulation. It was soon discovered that while the above regulations were adequate to protect the depletion of the fish population, they had no effect on the incentive for individual fishermen to increase their shares of the remaining take. Even though the profits would be small because of high costs, new technological change would allow adopters to increase their shares of the market and put others out of business. To protect themselves, the fishermen were successful in introducing bans on new technology. These restrictions took various forms, but two seem particularly noteworthy. The first was the banning of the use of thin-stranded, monofilament net. The course-stranded net it would have replaced was visible to the salmon in the daytime and therefore could be avoided by them. As a result, it was useful only at night. By contrast, the thinner monofilament nets could be successfully used

FIGURE 12.4   The Effect of Regulation

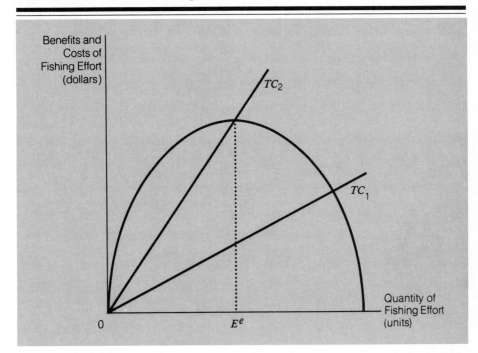

during the daylight hours, as well as night. The monofilament nets were banned in both Canada and the United States soon after they appeared.

The most flagrantly inefficient regulation was one in Alaska which barred gill net-ters in Bristol Bay from using engines to propel their boats. This regulation lasted until the 1950s and heightened the public's awareness of the anachronistic nature of this regulatory approach. The world's most technologically advanced nation was reaping its harvest from the Bering Sea in sailboats, while the rest of the world – particularly Japan and the Soviet Union – was modernizing its fishing fleets at a torrid pace!

Guided by a narrow focus on the maximum sustainable yield which ignored costs, these policies led to a substantial loss in the net benefit received from the fishery. Costs are an important dimension of the problem and, when they are ignored, the consequences can be significant.

Taxes

Is it possible to provide incentives for cost reduction while assuring that the yield is reduced to the efficient level? Can a more efficient policy be devised? Economists who have studied the question believe that more efficient policies are possible.

Consider a tax on effort. In Figure 12.4 taxes on effort would also be represented as a rotation of the *TC* line, and the after-tax cost to the fishermen would be adequately represented by line TC_2. Since the after-tax curve coincides with TC_2, the cost curve for all those inefficient regulations, doesn't this imply that the tax system is just as inefficient? No! The key to understanding the difference is the distinction between *transfer costs* and *real-resource costs*.

Under a regulation system of the type described earlier in this chapter, all of the costs included in TC_2 are real-resource costs, which involve utilization of resources. Transfer costs, by contrast, involve transfers of resources from one part of society to another rather than their use. Transfer costs apply to that part of society bearing them, but are exactly offset by the gain received by the recipients. Resources are not used up; they are merely transferred. Thus the calculation of the size of the net benefit should subtract real-resource costs but not transfer costs from benefits. For society as a whole, transfer costs are retained as part of the net benefit.

In Figure 12.3 the net benefit under a tax system is identical to that under an efficient allocation. The net benefit represents a transfer cost to the fisherman that is exactly offset by the revenues, received by the tax collector. This discussion should not obscure the fact that, as far as the individual fisherman is concerned, these are very real costs. Rent normally received by a sole owner is now received by the government. Since the tax revenues involved can be substantial (Example 12.1), fishermen wishing to have the fishery efficiently managed may object to this particular way of doing it. They would prefer a policy that restricts catches while allowing them to keep the rents. Is that possible?

Quotas

One policy making it possible is a properly designed quota on the number of fish that can be taken from the fishery. The "properly designed" caveat is important because there are many different types of quota schemes and not all are of equal merit. An efficient quota system has several identifiable characteristics:

1. The quotas entitle the holder to catch a specified weight of fish;
2. The total amount of fish authorized by the quotas held by all fishermen should be equal to the efficient catch for the fishery; and
3. The quotas should be freely transferable among fishermen.

Each plays an important role in obtaining an efficient allocation. Suppose, for example, the quotas were defined in terms of the right to own and use a fishing boat rather than in terms of catch—not an uncommon type of quota. Such a quota is not efficient, because under this type of quota an inefficient incentive still remains for each boat owner to build larger boats, to place extra equipment on them, and to spend more time fishing. These actions would expand the capacity of each boat and cause the actual catch to exceed the target (efficient) catch. In a nutshell, the boat quota limits the number of boats fishing but does not limit the amount of fish caught by each boat. If we are to reach and sustain an efficient allocation, it is the catch which must ultimately be limited.

While the purpose of the second condition is obvious, the role of transferability deserves more consideration. With transferability, the entitlement to fish flows naturally to those gaining the most benefit from it because their costs are lower. Because

EXAMPLE 12.2

Efficient versus Market Exploitation of Lobsters

Two economists, Henderson and Tugwell [1979], set out to quantify the degree of overexploitation characterizing these two particular Maritime Canadian common-property lobster fishing ports: Port Maitland and Miminegash. They estimated the relationship between effort and sustainable catch for each of the two fishing grounds and also the costs of various levels of fishing effort. Using these functions, they derived both the optimal and free-market solutions, which could then be compared to each other and to the maximum sustainable yield. These calculations could also be used to derive the tax required to force the market solution to converge to the efficient solution.

	PORT MAITLAND			MIMINEGASH		
Maximum sustainable yield stock	1,766			1,629		
Lobster price/thousand pounds	$485			$370		
Opportunity cost/hundred traps	$1,421			$950		
	Optimal Solution	Free Entry	Actual Average 1959–63	Optimal Solution	Free Entry	Actual Average 1959–63
Lobster stock (thous. lbs.)	3,050	2,490	2,467	2,450	1,125	1,273
Lobster catch (thous. lbs.)	745	1,330	1,183	801	936	1,094
Effort (100s traps)	112	454	—	122	365	—
Ratio: catch/stock	0.25	0.53	0.48	0.33	0.83	0.86
Optimal tax/thousand pounds catch	270	NA	NA	255	NA	NA
Annual resource savings: Value of trap savings less value of reduced catch	$202,173	NA	NA	$180,470	NA	NA

There are several noteworthy features of this table. The "free entry" or market solutions for catch are remarkably close to the actual averages in spite of the uncertainty of estimating the underlying equations. The "free-entry" catch levels are substantially greater than the optimal levels due to an inefficiently high level of effort (traps). The last entries in the table indicate that the welfare losses (compared to the optimum level) run about $202,000 in Port Maitland and $180,000 in Miminegash *each year.* For Port Maitland this represents a loss of some 62 percent of the net benefits obtainable under an efficient program!

The table also presents the optimum tax level which would cause the free access and optimum to converge. For Port Maitland this amounts to $270 per thousand pounds of lobster, approximately 56 percent of the current price ($485). If this tax were levied, some fishermen would exit and the catch would rise, but the remaining fishermen would not have received higher profits. The increased net benefits would be appropriated by the government. It is not difficult to understand why fishermen don't generally support tax policies, even though these policies could prevent overexploitation.

Source: J. V. Henderson and M. Tugwell, "Exploitation of the Lobster Fishery: Some Empirical Results," *Journal of Environmental Economics and Management,* VI (Dec. 1979): 287–96.

it is valuable, the transferable quota commands a positive price. Those who have quotas but also have high costs find they make more money selling the quotas than using them. Meanwhile, those who have lower costs find they can purchase more quotas and still make money.

Transferable quotas also encourge technological progress. Adopters of new cost-reducing technologies can make more money on their existing quotas and make it profitable to purchase new quotas from others who have not adopted the technology. Therefore, in marked contrast to the earlier regulatory methods used to raise costs, both the tax system and the transferable quota system encourage low extraction costs.

How about the distribution of the rent? In a quota system the distribution of the rent depends crucially on how the quotas are initially allocated. There are many possibilities with different outcomes. The first possibility is for the government to auction these quotas off. But the government would then appropriate all the rent and the outcome would be very similar to the outcome of the tax system. If the fishermen do not like the tax system, they would not like the auction system either.

In an alternative approach, the government could give the quotas to the fishermen, say in proportion to their historical catch. The fishermen could then trade among themselves until a market equilibrium is reached. All the rent would be retained only by the *current* generation of fishermen. Fishermen who might want to enter the market would have to purchase the quotas from existing fishermen. Competition among the potential purchasers would drive up the price of the transferable quotas until it reflected the market value of future rents, appropriately discounted.[11]

Thus this type of quota system allows the rent to remain with the fishermen, but only the current generation of fishermen. Future generations see little difference between this quota system and a tax system; in either case they have to pay to enter the industry, whether it be through the tax system or by purchasing the quotas.

There is a further, more difficult, problem that must be addressed by any public-policy program to rectify the overexploitation of the fishery. When a fishery has been exploited as a common property resource for a number of years and the costs of extraction are low, it is likely that the size of the fish population will be substantially lower than efficient. If efficiency is to be achieved, therefore, it would be necessary to build the stock up for a period of time, until the stock reaches the efficient level. Because this is accomplished by allowing the growth of the fish population to exceed the catch, current generations who are already experiencing excessively low-catch levels due to overexploitation must experience *even lower* catches if the population is to be replenished.[12]

---

[11]This occurs because the maximum bid any potential entrant would make is the value to be derived from owning that permit. This value is equal to the present value of future rents (the difference between price and marginal cost for each unit of fish sold). Competition will force the purchaser to bid near that maximum value, lest he or she lose the quota.

[12]It can be shown that frequently the most efficient catch adjustment process involves the so-called "bang-bang" strategy in which there is a total abstinence from fishing until the stock is replenished. Fishing is then resumed at the steady efficient level. There seems little likelihood that current fishermen would accept this strategy without compensation. See P. S. Dasgupta and G. M. Heal, *Economic Theory and Exhaustible Resources* (Cambridge, England: Cambridge University Press, 1979), pp. 128–141.

Is it possible to reduce the catch in a manner that seems fair to the current generation of fishermen? An affirmative answer is suggested by the fact that with the transferable quota system suggested above the current generation of fishermen would be enriched by receiving a valuable quota. If this quota could be used to reduce the current catch, and the rent is large enough, the current generation of fishermen might be better off (because of owning the valuable transferable quota), even with substantially reduced catches.

An interesting program that takes advantage of this possibility was started in the Pacific salmon fishery of Canada in 1968 and similar plans have been appearing in the states of Alaska and Washington since that time.[13] The program essentially induced some fishermen to leave the industry by paying them compensation. The compensation was financed by a relatively small (in proportion to the total rent) tax on the catch of those fishermen remaining in the industry.

The program was both self-financing and self-terminating. It was self-financed from taxes levied on those who remained. Because those remaining benefited from the reduced catch and the value of their entitlement to fish, they were better off even with the tax. Those who left did so voluntarily, preferring to accept the compensation, rather than continue fishing. The program was self-terminating in that, after a few years, enough fishermen had been induced to leave the industry that further inducements were unnecesary. By that time, the rents were beginning to materialize, and the costs of further inducements would have meant larger, politically unpopular taxes on the existing fishermen.

This system is not perfect by any means. For example, the entitlements are boat quotas rather than catch quotas. As we saw above, that does not guarantee an efficient allocation. It does, however, serve to illustrate that economic incentives can be used to structure feasible policies that will improve the situation, if not attain perfection.

The 200-Mile Limit

The final policy dimension concerns the international aspects of the fishery problem. Obviously the various policy approaches to effective management of fisheries requires some governing body to have jurisdiction over a fishery so that it can enforce its regulations.

This is not currently the case for many of the ocean fisheries. Much of the open water of the oceans is a common-property resource to governments, as well as to individual fishermen. Therefore, no single body can exercise control over it. As long as that continues to be the case, corrective action will be difficult to implement. In recognition of this fact there is an evolving law of the sea defined by international treaties. One of the concrete results of this law, for example, has been some limited restrictions on whaling. Whether or not this process ultimately yields a consistent and comprehensive system of management remains to be seen.

---

[13]A description of this program can be found in Peter H. Pearse, "Rationalization of Canada's West Coast Salmon Fishery: An Economic Evaluation," *Economic Aspects of Fish Production* (Paris: Organization of Economic Cooperation and Development, 1972): 172–202.

Countries bordering the sea have declared that their ownership rights extend some 200 miles out to sea. Within these areas, the countries have exclusive jurisdiction and can proceed to implement effective management policies. These declarations have been upheld and are now firmly entrenched in international law. Thus, very rich fisheries in coastal waters can be protected, while those in the open waters await the outcome of an international negotiations process.

The Economics of Enforcement

An area which traditionally has not received much analytical treatment, but is gradually becoming recognized as a key aspect of fisheries management, is enforcement. Policies can be designed to be perfectly efficient as long as everyone voluntarily follows them, but these same policies may look rather tragic in the harsh realities of costly and imperfect enforcement.

Fisheries policies are difficult to enforce. Coastlines are typically long and rugged; it is not difficult for fishermen to avoid detection if they are exceeding their limits or catching species illegally.

Recognizing these realities immediately suggests two implications. First, policy design should take enforcement into consideration and second, what is efficient when enforcement is ignored may not be efficient once enforcement is considered.

Policies should be designed to make compliance as inexpensive as possible. Regulations which impose very high costs are more likely to be disobeyed than regulations that impose costs in proportion to the purpose. Regulations should also contain provisions for dealing with noncompliance. A common approach is to levy monetary sanctions against those failing to comply. The sanctions should be set at a high enough level as to bring the costs of noncompliance (including the sanction) into balance with the costs of compliance.

The enforcement issue points out another advantage of private-property approaches to fisheries management—they are self-enforcing. Fish farmers or fish ranchers have no incentive to deviate from the efficient scheme because they would only be hurting themselves. There is no need for any enforcement activity. Noncompliance with some kind of regulatory constraint, on the other hand, could, in the absence of effective enforcement, be beneficial to those fishing in common property resources. Mounting this enforcement effort is yet another cost associated with the public management of fisheries.

Since enforcement activity is costly, it follows that it should be figured into our definition of efficiency. How would our analysis be changed by incorporating enforcement costs? A recent study by Sutinen and Anderson (1985) suggests that the incorporation of realistic enforcement cost considerations tends to reduce the efficient population below the level declared efficient in the presence of perfect, costless enforcement.

The rationale is not difficult to follow. Assume that there is some kind of quota system in effect to ration access. Enforcement activity would involve monitoring compliance with these quotas and assigning penalties on those found in noncompliance.[14] If the quotas are so large as to be consistent with the common property equilibrium, enforcement cost would be zero because no enforcement is necessary to ensure compliance. Moving the fishery away from the common property equilibrium increases both net benefits and enforcement costs. For this model, as the steady state population size is increased, marginal enforcement costs increase and marginal net benefits decrease. At the efficient population size (considering enforcement cost) the marginal net benefit equals the marginal enforcement cost. This necessarily involves a smaller population size than the efficient population size ignoring enforcement costs because the latter occurs when the marginal net benefit is zero.

SUMMARY

We have seen that common-property fisheries will not automatically be efficiently managed by markets. In general, they are overexploited and, in the case of fisheries characterized by particularly low extraction costs (the Pacific-salmon fishery), extinction is a definite possibility in the absence of outside control. Where extraction costs are higher, extinction is unlikely even with unrestricted access.

There is some reassuring evidence that both the private and public sectors have moved to ameliorate the problems associated with past mismanagement. The reassertion of private-property rights in Japan and other countries has stimulated the development of aquaculture. Governments in Canada and the United States have moved to limit overexploitation of the Pacific salmon. International agreements have been reached to place limits on whaling. It is doubtful that these programs fully satisfy the efficiency criterion, although it does seem clear that sustainable catches will result.

It would be folly to ignore barriers to further action, such as the reluctance of individual fishermen to submit to many forms of regulation, the lack of a firm policy governing open ocean waters, and the difficulties of enforcing various approaches. Whether these barriers will fall before the pressing need for effective management remains to be seen.

FURTHER READING

Anderson, Lee G. *The Economics of Fisheries Management*. Baltimore: Johns Hopkins Press, 1977. A highly recommended text for those wishing to go into the material in this chapter in greater depth.

---

[14]In theory it would be possible to set the penalty so high that only a limited amount of enforcement activity would be necessary. Since very large penalties are rarely imposed in practice, the model rules these out and assumes that increasing enforcement expenditures are necessary to enforce increasingly stringent quotas.

Bell, Frederick W. *Food from the Sea: The Economics and Politics of Ocean Fisheries.* Boulder: Westview Press, 1978. A comprehensive and comprehensible treatment of the actual and potential management of fisheries by an academic economist who was previously chief of economic research for the National Marine Fisheries Service, U.S. Department of Commerce. Full of examples of actual regulation.

Clark, Colin. *Mathematical Bioeconomics: The Optimal Management of Renewable Resources.* New York: Wiley-Interscience, 1976. Accessible only to those with strong undergraduate backgrounds in math, this is an excellent introduction to the use of mathematics to formulate optimal management policies. Focused almost entirely on fisheries.

ADDITIONAL REFERENCES

Agnellos, Richard J. and Lawrence P. Donnelly. "Prices and Property Rights in the Fisheries," *Southern Economic Journal,* XLII (October, 1979): 253–262.

Brown, Lester R., "Maintaining World Fisheries" in Lester R. Brown, et. al. *State of the World: 1985* (New York: W. W. Norton and Company, 1985): 73–96.

Clark, C. W. "Profit Maximization and the Extinction of Animal Species," *Journal of Political Economy,* Vol. 81 (August, 1973): 950–960.

Crutchfield, J. A. and G. Pontecovo. *The Pacific Salmon Fisheries: A Study of Irrational Conservation* (Baltimore: John Hopkins Press for Resources for the Future, Inc., 1969).

Gallastegui, Carmen, "An Economic Analysis of Sardine Fishing in the Gulf of Valencia (Spain), *Journal of Environmental Economics and Management,* Vol. 10 (June, 1983): 138–150.

Henderson, J. V. and M. Tugwell. "Exploitation of the Lobster Fishery: Some Empirical Results," *Journal of Environmental Economics and Management,* VI (December, 1979): 287–296.

Munro, G. R. "Fisheries, Extended Jurisdiction, and the Economics of Common Property Resources," *Canadian Journal of Economics,* Vol. 15 (August, 1982): 405–25.

Schaefer, M. B. "Some Considerations of Population Dynamics and Economics in Relation to the Management of Marine Fisheries," *Journal of the Fisheries Research Board of Canada* XIV (1957): 669–81.

Stokes, R. L. "The Economics of Salmon Ranching," *Land Economics,* Vol. 58 (November, 1982): 464–77.

Sutinen, Jon G. and Peder Anderson, "The Economics of Fisheries Law Enforcement" *Land Economics,* Vol. 61, No. 4 (November, 1985): 387–397.

DISCUSSION QUESTIONS

1. Is the establishment of the 200-mile limit a sufficient form of government intervention to ensure that the tragedy of the commons does not occur for fisheries within the 200-mile limit? Why or why not?

2. With discounting it is possible for the efficient fish population to fall below the level required to produce the maximum sustained yield. Does this violate the sustainability criterion? Why or why not?

PROBLEMS

1. Assume that the relationship between the growth of a fish population and the population size can be expressed as $g = 4P - .1P^2$, where g is the growth in tons and P is the size of the population (in thousands of tons). Given a price of $100 a ton, the marginal benefit of smaller population sizes (and, hence, larger catches) can be computed as $20P - 400$. (a) Compute the population size that is compatible with the maximum sustainable yield. What would be the size of the annual catch if the population were to be sustained at this level? (b) If the marginal cost of additional catches (expressed in terms of the population size) is $MC = 2(160 - P)$, what is the population size which is compatible with the efficient sustainable yield?

2. Assume that a local fisheries council imposes an enforceable quota of 100 tons of fish on a particular fishing ground for one year. Assume further that 100 tons per year is the efficient sustained yield. Once the 100th ton has been caught, the fishery would be closed for the remainder of the year.

   (a) Is this an efficient solution to the common property problem? Why or why not?
   (b) Would your answer be different if the 100 ton quota were divided up into 100 transferable quotas, each entitling the holder to catch one ton of fish, and distributed among the fishermen in proportion to their historical catch? Why or why not?

CHAPTER THIRTEEN

Generalized Resource Scarcity

As a nation, we have always faced choices and always will.
What matters is the range of choice we have and the urgency
with which the need to choose is thrust upon us.
COMMISSION ON POPULATION GROWTH
AND THE AMERICAN FUTURE (1972)

INTRODUCTION

Public concern over natural-resource scarcity is not new. The National Conservation Commission, formed during the Theodore Roosevelt Administration and headed by noted conservationist Gifford Pinchot, conducted the first national inventory of natural resources in 1908. This commission was established in response to a growing concern for natural-resource scarcity. Its mandate was to provide data so that the situation could be assessed and appropriate public policies could be charted. This initial inquiry has been followed by a number of others with a similar focus.[1]

There are a number of sources for this concern that suggest the need for continued vigilance. We have seen, for example, that even though world fertility rates are now falling, the current age structure of the population creates an inertia for population growth which will not, even in the most optimistic projections, allow for a stable world population in the immediate future. These increases in the population will cause the demand for resources to increase faster than it would if the population were stable. The implications of this increasing growth on the demand for resources can be profound, par-

---

[1]A detailed description of the various commissions, boards, and committees set up to advise the executive and legislative branches on resource policies can be found in Robert Cahn and Patricia L. Cahn, "Lessons from the Past," in *The Global 2000 Report to the President of the U.S. Entering the 21st Century, Vol. 1: Summary Report*, Council on Environmental Quality and Department of State (New York: Pergamon Press, 1980): 321–348.

ticularly in the industrial countries such as the United States, where per capita consumption levels are high (Example 13.1).

Previous chapters have demonstrated that while markets automatically provide some corrective responses to scarcity, market and public-policy imperfections have reduced the efficiency of these responses. These imperfections include price controls, common-property resources, externalities, and the tax treatment of resources. We were able to suggest a public-policy response to the particular resource problem under investigation. In some cases the appropriate response was to remove restrictions previously placed on the market.

There seems little doubt that individual mines or wells will be exhausted in the face of this rising demand. But will these remain isolated incidents or will they add up to a pattern of generalized resource scarcity? Generalized scarcity, were it to occur, would be a serious matter having a detrimental impact on the quality of life for this and succeeding generations.

Our search for evidence of generalized scarcity begins with a review and elaboration of the manner in which a market economy copes with increasing scarcity, particularly the roles of exploration and discovery, technological progress, and the substitution of abundant resources for scarce ones. We shall then examine how resource scarcity can be detected. What indicators can be used? What are their strengths and weaknesses? Once we have gained an appreciation for avenues of detection, we shall turn to the evidence revealed by these indicators and discuss how this evidence may be interpreted.

This chapter serves two purposes: an end in itself and a means to understanding more global concerns. It is an end in that the existence or nonexistence of a generalized resource scarcity is inherently important. It also, however, represents a point of departure in the larger debate about the desirability and inevitability of future economic growth. We shall pursue this latter concern further in Chapter 21, when we explore the process of economic growth in the context of limited environmental and natural resources.

FACTORS MITIGATING RESOURCE SCARCITY

The ability of a market economy to cope with pressures on the environmental asset caused by population and income growth depends on alternatives for diffusing these pressures. Three alternatives have been particularly important: (1) exploration and discovery, (2) technological process, and (3) substitution.

Exploration and Discovery

Devarajan and Fisher (1982) have shown that a profit-maximizing firm will undertake exploration activity until the marginal discovery cost equals the marginal scarcity rent

EXAMPLE 13.1

Population Growth and the Demand for Resources

The demand for resources is functionally related to the level of population and per capita consumption by the identity:

$$C = C_P \times P,$$

where C is the consumption of resources, P is the population and C_P is the per capita level of resource consumption. Both population and per capita consumption have increased the demand for resources in the past. The multiplicative nature of the formula causes demand to rise quite rapidly. For example, if population and per captia consumption were both to double, the demand for resources would be four times as high.

The Commission on Population Growth and the American Future [1972] conducted a major study to define the relationship between population growth and the demand for resources in the United States. Specifically they analyzed the effect of two possible population-growth scenarios. These scenarios differ in the number of children the average American family is assumed to contain. The first scenario assumes an average of two children per family and implies that the population would reach 300 million in the year 2015. The population in the second scenario, with its assumed three-child average family, would reach somewhat over 400 million by that same date.

The study concluded that population growth is one of the major factors affect-

received from a unit of the resource sold.[2] Since the marginal scarcity rent—the difference between the price received and the marginal cost of extraction—is the marginal benefit received by the firm engaging in exploration activity, to maximize profits the level of activity should be increased until this marginal benefit is equal to the marginal cost.

An understanding of this relationship between scarcity rent and marginal discovery cost allows us to think about how exploration activity would respond to population and income growth. Since both of these factors contribute to rising demand over time, they raise the marginal user cost and the scarcity rent, stimulating producers to undertake larger marginal discovery costs.

---

[2]This is strictly true only when there is no uncertainty associated with exploration. Even with uncertainty, however, marginal discovery cost is highly related to scarcity rent. See Shantayanan Devarajan and Anthony C. Fisher, "Measures of Resource Scarcity Under Uncertainty," in *Explorations in Natural Resource Economics*, V. Kerry Smith and John V. Krutilla, eds. (Baltimore: Johns Hopkins University Press for Resources for the Future, 1982): 332–342.

ing the demand for resources and the deterioration of the environment and that we would be considerably better off over the next 30 to 50 years if there were a prompt reduction in our population-growth rate. These conclusions were drawn from a number of specific findings including:

1. The *annual* consumption of minerals in the three-child scenario would be 17 percent higher by 2020 than in the two-child scenario.
2. The three-child scenario causes higher pressure on energy demand and results in more imports and higher prices.
3. Water shortages in the Southwest would occur under either scenario but would occur sooner (and would affect a wider geographic area) under the three-child scenario.
4. The demand for recreational facilities would be some 30 percent less under the two-child scenario, leading to lower levels of congestion.
5. Fifty years from now, the population resulting from the three-child average would have to pay food prices some 40 to 50 percent higher than the two-child average population would pay.

Because per capita consumption levels in the United States are so high, reductions in population growth have a disproportionately large impact on the global demand for resources. We would have more time to act and could reduce the strain on our institutions, as well as our resources, by holding population growth permanently in check.

Source: Commission on Population Growth and the American Future, *Population and the American Future* (New York: The American Library, 1972).

How much this demand pressure is relieved depends upon the amount of exploration activity and the amount of resources discovered per unit of exploration activity undertaken. If the marginal-discovery cost curve is flat (implying a large number of relatively available sources), increases in scarcity rent can stimulate large amounts of successful exploration activity. If the marginal-discovery cost curve is steeply sloped (as would be the case when exploration had to take place in increasingly hostile and unproductive environments), increases in scarcity rent stimulate less successful exploration activity.

Technological Progress

Technological progress reduces the cost of ore by discovering new ways to extract, process, and use the ore. In Chapter 6, for example, we showed the significant impact of pelletization on the cost of producing steel from iron ore. The effect was so dramatic that production costs actually fell over time in spite of the need to use a lower grade ore.

It is important to realize that the rate and type of technological progress is influenced by the degree of resource scarcity. Rising extraction costs create new profit opportunities for the development of new technologies. These profit opportunities are largest for technologies that economize on scarce resources and utilize abundant ones. In periods when labor is scarce and capital abundant, new technologies tend to use capital and save labor. If population growth were to reverse the relative scarcity, subsequent technological progress would concentrate on using labor and saving capital. In the past when fossil-fuel energy was abundant and cheap, newly discovered technologies relied heavily on this energy source. As fossil fuel supplies decline, technological progress could be expected to economize by increasing the amount of useful energy received per unit of fossil-fuel input and by replacing fossil-fuel energy with forms of solar energy.

Substitution

The final way in which adverse consequences of resource scarcity can be mitigated is by substituting abundant resources for scarce ones. The easier the substitution of abundant depletable or renewable resources, the smaller will be the impact of declining availability and rising costs (Figure 13.1).

FIGURE 13.1 Output Levels and the Possibilities for Input Substitution

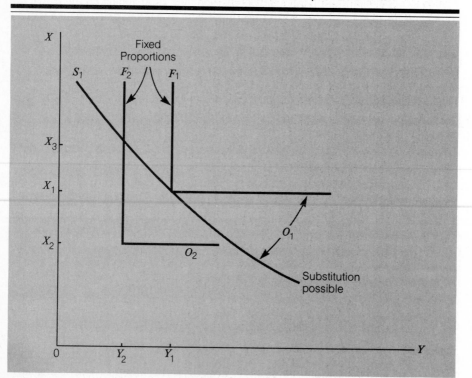

In the graph three isoquants (S_1, F_1, F_2) are pictured. An *isoquant* portrays all the possible combinations of inputs that can produce a given level of output. The two right-angled isoquants (F_1 and F_2) depict the fixed-proportions case, the case in which no input substitution is possible. The fixed-proportions isoquant nearer the origin (F_2) refers to a lower output level than the other fixed-proportion isoquant (F_1). The third isoquant (S_1) does admit of some possibility for input substitution and is drawn in such a way as to produce the same output level (O_1) as F_1. Naturally it implies a different production technology or set of technologies than F_1.

We can illustrate the significance of input substitution on output using Figure 13.1. Assume that the amount of some input Y (a depletable resource) is reduced from Y_1 to Y_2. If the technology involved is characterized by S_1, the constant output level (O_1) can be maintained by increasing the amount of the other resource used from X_1 to X_3. This increase in X compensates for the reduction in Y, leaving output unaffected.

Notice what happens, however, when the production process is characterized by F_1 instead of S_1. A reduction in the availability of Y from Y_1 to Y_2 necessitates a reduction in output from O_1 to O_2. No substitution of X for Y is possible. In addition, because inputs must be used in fixed proportions, the amount of X would be reduced from X_1 to X_2. Any more X would be redundant; it would not result in any additional output.

These examples serve to illustrate a basic premise—the wider the array of substitution possibilities, the smaller the impact of resource scarcity on output. Timber scarcity illustrates an important historical example (Example 13.2) which serves to remind us that our review of the evidence must be sensitive to mitigating circumstances such as substitution possibilities and technological progress.

This short review suggests that factors exist (rising population and incomes) which increase the likelihood of resource scarcity, in addition to other factors (exploration and discovery, technological progress, and input substitution) which mitigate the seriousness of scarcity. To determine which set of factors dominates, we must examine the evidence.

DETECTING RESOURCE SCARCITY

The first step in assessing the seriousness of resource scarcity is to select a means for detecting scarcity. While this may sound like a straightforward exercise, it is not. We shall begin by considering what properties the ideal indicators should have and the degree to which commonly used indicators live up to these standards.

Criteria for An Ideal Scarcity Indicator

An ideal indicator would have at least the three following properties:

1. *Foresight.* The ideal indicator should be forward looking. It should anticipate scarcity and not merely record the scarcity once it has occurred. Thus the ideal

EXAMPLE 13.2

Resource Scarcity in Historical Perspective: Timber

Early in our history timber was very abundant. For those who wanted to farm and had to clear the land, it was too abundant! As a result of low timber prices, Americans began to develop new technologies that relied more heavily on this abundant resource. These included a whole range of woodworking machines for sawing, planing, shaping, and boring, as well as design improvements in the ax.

The use of these machines economized on labor—at that time a scarce commodity—at the cost of much wood. The saws of that period were easy to use, but they made such a wide swath that much of the log ended up as sawdust. It is interesting to note that in England, where labor was abundant and wood was scarce, the production process relied more heavily on labor and used a greater amount of the log.

When rising demand put pressure on the American forest resource base and prices began to rise, the incentive to economize on wood was created. Wood stoves became increasingly popular for increasing the thermal efficiency of wood burning. Substitutes (some of superior quality) came into use. Coal replaced wood for energy. Steel began to replace wood in bridges. Concrete began to replace wood in buildings. Plastics began to replace wood in packaging and toys. New products such as particle board were created to profitably use previously wasted wood by-products.

Meanwhile, other technological changes served to increase the size of the forest resource base. Forest scientists discoverd a number of ways to increase the growth of trees, and the lumber industry found better ways to use what was available. One example of this latter change is provided by improvements in the process of making paper during the 1920s. This process modification made possible the use of a fast-growing southern pine that previously had been unusable.

The moral of the story seems to be that technological progress has opened new avenues which previously were only dimly perceived. The development of these avenues, as well as their exploitation, was triggered by rising prices. Increasing scarcity automatically creates incentives to increase inventive activity and innovation. Whether these incentives are sufficient to call forth such timely and beneficial responses in the future remains an open question.

Source: Nathan Rosenberg, "Innovative Responses to Materials Shortages," *American Economic Review* 63 (May 1973): 111–125.

indicator should incorporate such things as future demand patterns, alternative sources of the resource, changes in extraction cost, and so on.
2. *Comparability.* The ideal indicator should allow direct comparisons to be made among resources for the purpose of identifying the most serious problems. This comparison should facilitate an assessment not only of the degree of scarcity, but also of its seriousness. Thus, the indicator should be able to incorporate

such differences as the importance of the resource and the availability of substitutes.

3. *Computability.* The ideal indicator should be readily calculated from reliable, published sources of information or should depend on information that could be readily collected.

Applying the Criteria

The Physical Indicators. Before moving on to the four types of economic indicators, let's use these criteria to evaluate the physical indices discussed previously in Example 6.1. Both the static and exponential versions of the reserve-to-use ratios result in a number that can be conveniently interpreted as the time until exhaustion. On the surface, this indicator appears to satisfy all three of our criteria. It is forward looking, it allows comparisons to be made, and it is readily calculable.

This surface appearance, however, is deceiving. While reserve-to-use ratios are forward looking, their view of the future is a narrow one on several counts. Their derivation makes no provision for stock augmentation. As a result, when past predictions using these indicators are compared with the actual experience, these predictions have been uniformly and excessively pessimistic. As the little boy tending the flocks discovered, if you cry "wolf!" often when the wolf is not there, people stop listening. When the wolf actually appears, no one reacts. Thus, reserve-to-use ratios satisfy the foresight criterion only in a very limited way.

In a similar vein reserve-to-use ratios do allow comparisons to be made, but the resulting rankings provide no guide to the seriousness of the problems. These ratios not only yield an inaccurate estimated time to exhaustion, but they also provide no estimate of how serious a matter exhaustion would be. For example, running out of an ingredient that is used solely in cosmetics and has an available substitute is less serious than running out of a substance such as helium, which is used for important scientific research and has no known substitute for that use. Reserve-to-use ratios are powerless to make this kind of crucial distinction. Therefore, the comparability which is achieved is not a very useful one for setting resource management priorities.

Reserve-to-use ratios are also powerless to draw conclusions about the seriousness of *renewable* resource scarcity. They focus on a fixed resource reserve, a concept of limited validity when applied to depletable resources that is meaningless when applied to renewable resources. As we have seen in the preceding two chapters, the problem of scarcity with renewable resources can be even more serious than that with depletable resources. Thus, the fact that this indicator allows us to draw no conclusions about scarcity in this important class of resource problems—much less integrate them into a comparable, comprehensive scheme to evaluate all resources—is a serious deficiency.

The outstanding virtue of the reserve-to-use ratio is that it is readily calculated from published data. That fact, along with its easy (but mistaken) interpretation by the general public as "time until exhaustion," probably accounts for its success.

The fact that standard physical indicators are not ideal is interesting and important, but it does not totally discredit their use unless we can show that something better exists. Does it?

Four candidate economic indicators have been suggested by the analysis in this and preceding chapters: (1) resource price; (2) user cost; (3) marginal extraction cost; and (4) marginal discovery cost. In order to determine whether or not these are superior indicators, we must consider their properties in a variety of circumstances.

Resource Prices. In previous chapters we found it useful to distinguish between efficient resource prices, which maximize the net benefits to society, and market prices, which may or may not be efficient. We shall retain that distinction here.

Efficient resource prices satisfy both the foresight and comparability criteria. Current prices are forward looking. They are affected by such factors as rising demand, the possibilities for stock augmentation and substitution, and changes in the cost of extraction. Relative prices are also affected by the price elasticity of demand—the greater the difficulty of doing without the resource, the higher the price. Therefore, price levels and relative price changes allow us to make direct comparisons of depletable and renewable resources which reflect the seriousness of the problem.

The problem with using current efficient resource prices as the sole indicator is that in certain markets they are not directly observable or calculable. This occurs whenever the readily available indicator, the market price, is not equal to the efficient price. In preceding chapters we discussed cases in which these two prices might not be equal—common-property resource markets, markets with government price controls or artificial subsidies, and markets with significant externalities (such as pollution) which have not been internalized.

In these cases the market price may not even be a valid approximation of the efficient price. For example, take the situation with common-property resources. The problem with these resources is overexploitation in the earlier periods, followed (because the stock is so diminished) by underexploitation in the latter years. Thus, the problem is not that price won't rise to reflect scarcity. It will, eventually. The problem is that the lower earlier prices (due to the glut on the market) send a false signal of abundance. In markets where resources are treated as common property, market prices fail to exhibit the foresight property.

A similar problem occurs with uninternalized externalities. We have already seen that when the market fails to recognize these externalities, the market resource price is too low. And in contrast to the common-property resource problem, there is no automatic adjustment mechanism to *ever* cause market prices to reflect this increasing scarcity. Since scarcity in this case (indicated by the rising cost of extraction and reflected in the increasing damage caused by pollution) affects commodities (clean air and water) that are not marketed, there is no market price to signal the problem.

There is one further concern about the role of market prices. The ability of resource markets to exhibit foresight depends, in turn, on the ability of suppliers to assess the future. If they can not correctly anticipate future substitution possibilities, technological changes, demand patterns, and so on, then market prices will fail to reflect these considerations. The information content of prices is only as rich as the information available to those who, by their collective actions, determine prices.

In conclusion, for those resources traded in efficient or nearly efficient markets, the resource price serves as a superior indicator. When markets are not efficient, the dominance of this indicator is no longer obvious. Other indicators become useful either to complement or replace resource prices in those markets.

Scarcity Rent. A second economic indicator is the *scarcity rent*, the payment accruing to a resource owner when the user cost is positive. The efficient scarcity rent is forward looking; indeed, if the future did not matter, there would be no scarcity rent! Use of scarcity rent should anticipate future increases in demand as well as changes in extraction cost as the resource is used up. Scarcity rent can be used as an indicator for both renewable and depletable resource scarcity.

As you can see, up to this point, scarcity rent sounds roughly comparable to resource price as an indicator. For certain types of resources, however, scarcity rent may be superior to the price of the extracted product, the most readily available price. A forestry economist, L.C. Irland [1974], provides a case in point:

> From the Civil War to about 1900, lumber prices were stable while timber prices rose. Prominent forces were the decline in transport costs and improvements in milling.

The use of *lumber* prices as a measure of timber scarcity would lead to an erroneous conclusion. The scarcity reflected in the rising price of timber was camouflaged by declining transportation and milling costs. Only the scarcity rent of the timber (called *stumpage* in the industry) correctly detected the scarcity.[3]

With respect to other resources, however, scarcity rent may well represent a less than adequate measure. As shown earlier, the scarcity rent for common-property resources is zero for all time periods. In that case it is a deficient indicator of scarcity.

Even for efficient markets the relationship between scarcity rent and the degree of resource depletion is not always well defined. For depletable resources having a constant marginal cost of extraction, we expect scarcity rent to *rise* with the depletion. On the other hand, when extraction costs rise with the amount extracted, scarcity rent should *decline* with increasing scarcity. In order to interpret the behavior of scarcity rent, we need to know the underlying structure of extraction costs.

As a result, interpretation becomes an important problem. Declining scarcity rent could represent either increasing availability of the resource, which is desirable, or rising extraction cost, which is undesirable. Since it makes a difference which interpretation is correct, it is risky to base conclusions on this one indicator.

Marginal Discovery Cost. Scarcity rent is not always directly observable, even in those circumstances where it might prove to be a useful indicator. Earlier we derived a relationship capable of resolving this dilemma. We noted that marginal discovery cost, which can be observed, should be equal to marginal scarcity rent. Therefore, marginal discovery cost can be used as a proxy for marginal scarcity rent when information on discovery cost is available and information on scarcity rent is not.

---

[3]Stumpage is the price an extractor pays to the owner of forest land for the privilege of cutting and taking the timber.

Marginal Extraction Cost. The final indicator of resource scarcity suggested by conventional analysis is the marginal cost of extraction. For a given technology of extraction, as lower-grade ores are extracted, we normally expect the marginal cost of extraction to rise. Rising marginal extraction cost should, therefore, serve as a signal of the amount of sacrifice needed to procure each unit of the resource. It is noteworthy that the usefulness of this indicator of scarcity is not undermined when the resources are treated as common property. Thus, it is perhaps the best indicator to be used for common-property resources, such as fish and whales.

Extraction cost, however, is far from a flawless indicator. Of the three economic indicators we have considered so far, extraction cost is the only one which does not fulfill the foresight criterion. Since it is based on the current cost of extraction, it provides no indication of future problems, such as rapidly rising demand or future increases in extraction cost, which may be just around the corner.[4] Business or government leaders wishing to anticipate scarcity, rather than merely react to it once it occurs, do not get much help from this indicator.

Unit extraction cost is also a difficult concept to measure precisely with published information. As a result, analysts have developed means of approximating it with available information. Perhaps the most widely cited example is the unit extraction-cost measure developed by Harold Barnett and Chandler Morse [1963]:

$$C_i = (\alpha_i L_i + \beta_i K_i)/Q_i$$

where C_i = the unit extraction cost for resource i,

L_i = labor in industry i, as measured by employment,

K_i = reproducible capital (equipment and structures),

Q_i = the net amount of the ith resource extracted, and

α_i = and β_i = weights used to aggregate the dissimilar capital and labor inputs.

The logic behind this formulation suggests that capital and labor are primary inputs to the extraction of resources; as society begins the transition to increasingly inferior sources, larger inputs of capital and labor are required per unit of resource extracted. This is recorded as a rise in the index. Conversely, a fall over time in this index suggests either that new, low-cost sources have continually been discovered, or that technological progress has reduced the amount of capital and labor required to extract a unit of the resource to the extent of counteracting the increasing inferiority of the grades used.

There are problems with this particular specification that would not arise if the true extraction cost data were available. One of the most blatant is the omission of factors other than capital and labor that would be involved in the extraction of resources.

---

[4]Unless all environmental costs of extraction are internalized, measured extraction cost will understate the actual cost of extraction.

Energy is one obvious example. If capital equipment consumed more energy over time — which is the expected response to the falling energy prices that occurred until 1974 — then the Barnett-Morse measure would fail to pick one possible source of rising extraction cost, the cost of energy.[5]

The size of distortion caused by this omission is not clear. Combining this omission with the failure of this measure to include (presumably rising) environmental costs, it is, therefore, difficult to put our complete faith in this approximation until we know just how good an approximation it is.

In conclusion, it appears that no indicator of resource scarcity dominates the others in all cases. Real resource prices probably dominate in efficient markets. Scarcity rents probably dominate in those markets, such as timber, where the common-property problem does not exist and where the values of the *in situ* resources are routinely collected. Marginal discovery cost may usefully approximate marginal scarcity rent when it is not directly observable. The cost of extraction is superior for those resources treated as common property. The moral seems to be that we cannot trust any single indicator to provide the desired information. Judgments have to be made on a case-by-case basis using a variety of indicators.

EVIDENCE ON RESOURCE SCARCITY

There have been a number of attempts to assess the degree of scarcity now facing us. Since these have relied on quite different approaches, it is not surprising to discover that they come to rather different conclusions. Our review of these studies begins with those relying mainly on the physical indicators and closes with those using economic indicators.

Physical Indicators

To open our discussion of physical indicators, let's return to the analysis conducted by the *Limits to Growth* team, which demonstrates a typical use of physical indicators. The physical indicators computed as of 1970 are presented as Table 13.1. Of the nineteen depletable resources listed, only one (coal) could be expected to last as long as 100 years according to the exponential index. Resources that would be exhausted by the year 2000 (that is, have an exponential index of less than 30 years) include copper, gold, lead, mercury, natural gas, petroleum, silver, tin, and zinc. During the 1980s we should have already run out of gold, mercury, silver, tin, and zinc. This is a formidable list!

We know from previous discussions that there is a considerable degree of conservatism built into this approach. One way to assess the depth of this conservatism is

---

[5]It would not be difficult to modify the Barnett-Morse measure to incorporate energy. The point is that they did not perform this modification, so their results must be interepreted accordingly.

TABLE 13.1 Static and Exponential Depletion Indices (1970)

Resource	Known Global Reserves[a]	Static Index (years)[b]	Average Projected Rate of Growth (% per Year)[c]	Exponential Index (years)[d]
Aluminum	1.17×10^9 tons	100	6.4	31
Chromium	7.75×10^8 tons	420	2.6	95
Coal	5×10^{12} tons	2300	4.1	111
Cobalt	4.8×10^9 tons	110	1.5	60
Copper	308×10^6 tons	36	4.6	21
Gold	353×10^6 troy oz.	11	4.1	9
Iron	1×10^{11} tons	240	1.8	93
Lead	91×10^6 tons	26	2.0	21
Manganese	8×10^8 tons	97	2.9	46
Mercury	3.34×10^6 flasks	13	2.6	13
Molybdenum	10.8×10^9 lbs.	79	4.5	34
Natural Gas	1.14×10^{15} cu. ft.	38	4.7	22
Nickel	147×10^9 lbs.	150	3.4	53
Petroleum	455×10^9 bbls	31	3.9	20
Platinum Group[e]	429×10^6 troy oz.	130	3.8	47
Silver	5.5×10^9 troy oz.	16	2.7	13
Tin	4.3×10^6 lg tons	17	1.1	15
Tungsten	2.9×10^9 lbs.	40	2.5	28
Zinc	123×10^6 tons	23	2.9	18

Notes: [a]U.S. Bureau of Mines, *Mineral Facts and Problems*, 1970 (Washington, D.C.: Government Printing Office, 1970).

[b]The number of years known global reserves will last at current global consumption. Calculated by dividing known reserves (column 2) by the current annual consumption (U.S. Bureau of Mines, *Mineral Facts and Problems*, 1970).

[c]U.S. Bureau of Mines, *Mineral Facts and Problems*, 1970.

[d]The number of years known global reserves will last with consumption growing exponentially at the average annual rate of growth. Calculated by the formula

$$\text{exponential index} = \frac{\ln\left((r * s) + 1\right)}{r},$$

where r = average rate of growth from column 4

s = static index from column 3.

[e]The platinum group metals are platinum, palladium, iridium, osmium, rhodium, and ruthenium.

Source: Donella H. Meadows et al., *The Limits to Growth* (New York: Universe Books, 1972), Table 4, pp. 56–60.

to relax some of the assumptions that went into the derivation of those numbers. One study allowing us to do this was accomplished for the United Nations by Wassily Leontief [1977].

As part of his analysis, Leontief assumed (as did the *Limits to Growth* team) that proved reserves did not change over time (no stock augmentation). In contrast to the *Limits to Growth* approach, however, his forecast of demand was sensitive to rising prices. In other words, rather than forecast a level of demand that grows at a constant exponential rate and is impervious to outside influences (as is assumed in the exponential index), Leontief calculated the effects of increasing extraction costs on resource prices and estimated the degree to which demand would respond to those higher prices. Thus, the Leontief study retains an intentionally pessimistic approach on the supply side, but allows a bit more reasonable forecast on the demand side.

After incorporating this change, the Leontief forecast finds only two minerals— lead and zinc—for which cumulated expected demand by the year 2000 is expected to exceed current proven reserves. Compare this forecast to the nine minerals listed in Table 13.1 and anticipated by the *Limits to Growth* team to run out by that year. The inclusion of the demand-dampening characteristics of prices reduces the degree of expected scarcity below what the use of the pure exponential index would lead one to expect.

The key on the demand side lies in the ability to substitute renewable for depletable natural resources. One way we can assess the potential degree of substitutability between natural resources and other commodities is to estimate a construct known as the *elasticity of substitution*. The elasticity of substitution (σ) is a measure of the degree to which two factor inputs complement or substitute for each other in the production process.[6]

When σ is positive, the factors are substitutes and when σ is negative they are complements.[7] The larger the positive number, the easier and more complete the substitution will be. Generally an elasticity of substitution greater than 1 indicates considerable ease in substitution. The elasticity of substitution is zero for the fixed-proportions isoquant in Figure 13.1. Though a thorough review of the voluminous literature on input substitution would carry us too far afield, a few representative studies can convey the flavor of that literature.[8]

---

[6]The elasticity of substitution between two factors of production (say, X and Y) is defined as the ratio of the percentage change in the factor ratio to the percentage change in their relative prices (P_x and P_y). Thus

$$\sigma = \frac{\Delta\dfrac{X}{Y} \cdot \Delta\dfrac{P_y}{P_x}}{\dfrac{X}{Y} \cdot \dfrac{P_y}{P_x}}$$

[7]Two factors are said to be complements if an increase in one leads to an increase in the other. If an increase in the first factor leads to a decrease in the second, then those factors are said to be substitutes.

[8]Anyone interested in a thorough review of the state of the art in estimating input substitutability should consult Ernst R. Berndt and Barry C. Field, eds., *Modeling and Measuring natural Resource Substitution* (Cambridge, Mass.: The MIT Press, 1981).

Brown and Field [1979], for example, have estimated elasticities of substitution for some key industries (pulp and paper, steel, aluminum, and copper) between capital and resources, as well as labor and resources. They found both the capital-resource and labor-resource elasticities of substitution to be greater than 1 in all four industries. Studies by other economists, however, have not found elasticities this high. Humphrey and Moroney [1975] found for industries producing food and beverages; textiles and apparels; and stone, clay, and glass, both the capital-resource and labor-resource elasticities were less than 1.0.[9]

One key resource deserving special attention is energy. A number of studies examining the substitutability of energy, with resources and with labor, have been accomplished for the United States and other countries.[10] Generally, the results are mixed. Energy and labor appear uniformly to be substitutes, with the size of elasticities ranging from 0.48 to 3.80, depending on the industry and country. The story about energy and capital is more complicated. Studies based on data for a single country usually find capital and energy to be complements, rather than substitutes. This is relatively easy to understand. Historically when relative energy prices were falling, the natural response by the economic system was to construct and use energy-using capital. This does not necessarily mean that capital and energy remain complements in a period when relative energy prices are rising. We shall have more to say about this in Chapter 21.

What can be said about substitution possibilities? In general they seem quite good, though in particular industries problems may erupt. Both capital and labor are able to serve as substitutes within reasonable limits. The complementarity of capital and energy would be troubling if it were to persist, but there are reasons for believing that in the future capital may substitute for energy as well.[11]

How about the supply side and the longer term? It isn't really a very damning criticism of the *Limits to Growth* to suggest that their estimates were off by 50 or more years. Massive resource scarcity in 50 years would be as deserving of our attention as that occurring sooner.

---

[9]For stone, clay, and glass, Humphrey and Moroney found the elasticity of substitution between capital and resources to be negative, indicating a complementary relationship. See David B. Humphrey and J. R. Moroney, "Substitution Among Capital, Labor and Natural Resource Products in American Manufacturing," *Journal of Political Economy* 83 (February 1975): 57–82.

[10]See, for example, E. R. Berndt and D. Wood, "Technology, Prices and the Derived Demand for Energy," *Review of Economics and Statistics* 57 (August 1975): 259–268; R. Halvorsen and J. Ford, "Substitution Among Energy, Capital and Labor Inputs in U.S. Manufacturing," in *Advances in the Economics of Energy and Resources*, Vol. 1, R. S. Pindyck, ed. (Greenwich, Conn.: JAI Press, 1978); M. Fuss, "The Demand for Energy in Canadian Manufacturing: An Example of the Estimation of Production Structures with Many Inputs," *Journal of Econometrics* 5 (January 1977): 89–116; S. E. Atkinson and R. E. Halvorsen, "Interfuel Substitution in Steam Electric Power Generation," *Journal of Political Economy* 84 (October 1976): 959–978; J. M. Griffen and P. R. Gregory, "An Intercounty Translog Model of Energy Substitution Process," *American Economic Review* 66 (December 1976): 845–857; Anthony C. Fisher, *Resource and Environmental Economics* (Cambridge, England: Cambridge University Press, 1981).

[11]Consider, for example, the use of computers to control heating systems more efficiently allowing substantial savings in energy.

Perhaps the most searching assessment of the future long-term availability of resources was conducted by two physical scientists, Goeller and Weinberg [1976]. These authors went through the entire periodic table of elements and some of the more important compounds to derive estimates of current use and future availability. Their definition of future availability was expansive, including all potential sources of supply from the atmosphere, the ocean, and the crust of the earth down to a depth of one kilometer. Essentially, their estimate of supply corresponds to what we called resource endowment in Chapter 6.

Using the resource endowment as their definition of reserves, Goeller and Weinberg computed static reserve indices for each substance. The resource we would run out of first, phosphorus, according to their calculation would last another 1300 years. For most other resources their indices suggest exhaustion horizons in the millions of years. On the basis of this and a complementary analysis, Goller and Weinberg draw two main conclusions:

1. With three exceptions—phosphorus, a few trace elements for agriculture, and energy fossil fuels—there is virtually an unlimited supply of resources.

2. The transition away from these truly limited resources can be accomplished with relatively little, if any, loss in living standards. In most cases it can be accomplished with real resource prices no more than double current levels.

If we were somehow able to peer into the future with a crystal ball, we would probably find that the actual situation would lie somewhere between the Meadows forecast and the Goeller and Weinberg forecast. The conservatism of the Meadows analysis is now obvious. The optimism of the Goeller and Weinberg analysis rests in part on an assumption that all of the resource endowment they identify could, in fact, be recovered and could be used without causing other environmental problems, such as changes in the climate. This expectation is fully compatible with a traditional geological view of the manner in which resources are distributed within the earth's crust. This view suggests that the lower the grade, the larger is the supply of the resource available. It posits a rather smooth supply curve, devoid of any sharp discontinuities.

Recently, however, Skinner [1976] suggested that a rather different distribution may underlie certain geochemically scarce elements in the earth's crust. This analysis suggests that minerals can be classified into three groups. For the first group—iron, aluminum, titanium, magnesium, and silicon—the distribution of ores results in an inverse relationship between grade and tonnage of the ores. As grade is reduced by depleting the higher-grade ores, even larger tonnages of the lower-grade ores become available.

For the second group of resources—manganese, barium, vanadium, zirconium, sulfur, phosphorus, fluorine, and chlorine—limits to this inverse grade-tonnage relationship are present, but the supplies of ores are so great as to suggest that these limits do not constrain resource availability for the foreseeable future.

For all other metals—which Skinner calls the geochemically scarce metals, such as copper, lead, zinc, molybdenum, and gold—the distribution of ores is quite different.

FIGURE 13.2 Alternative Views of Ore Distribution

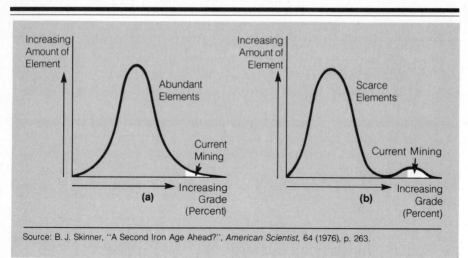

Source: B. J. Skinner, "A Second Iron Age Ahead?", *American Scientist,* 64 (1976), p. 263.

A comparison of the traditional view with that of Skinner is presented as Figure 13.2. The left panel presents the traditional unimodal (single-peaked) function generally found for the more abundant resources. The bimodal function which Skinner posits is presented in the right panel.

The implication of the Skinner hypothesis is that as we mine lower grades of geochemically scarce resources, we shall find less, not more, of that lower-grade ore available over some considerable range of grades. Skinner further suggests the existence of a *mineralogical threshold* between the two peaks. This mineralogical threshold occurs when there is a sharp discontinuity in the manner by which minerals are extracted to the left and to the right of this threshold. His characterization of this threshold is presented as Figure 13.3.

With abundant elements, the energy used per unit output rises smoothly as the grade of the ore is decreased. For the geochemically scarce resources, Skinner posits a sharp discontinuity in energy use when the supply of separate minerals (as represented by the smaller peak of Figure 13.2 above) is exhausted and the remaining sources are trapped as atomic substitutes for more abundant metals in the crystal structure of minerals.

Traditional mineral concentration processes could no longer be used to separate these minerals. The host ores would have to be broken down in order to release the tightly bound metals. Some estimates have suggested that the successful negotiation of this transition would require energy use per unit output some 100 to 1000 times higher than current use.[12] Table 13.2 demonstrates this relationship for copper.

---

[12]See, for example, Donald A. Brobst, "Fundamental Concepts for Analysis of Resource Availability," in *Scarcity and Growth Reconsidered*, V. Kerry Smith, ed. (Baltimore: Johns Hopkins Press for Resources for the Future, 1979): 128.

FIGURE 13.3 The Nature of the Mineralogical Threshold

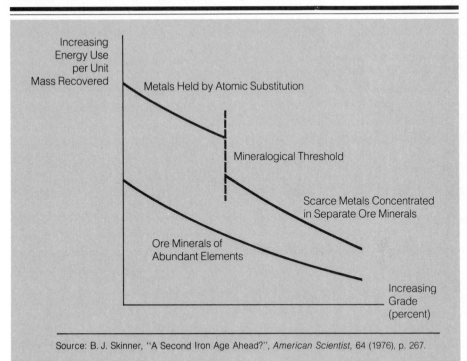

Source: B. J. Skinner, "A Second Iron Age Ahead?", *American Scientist,* 64 (1976), p. 267.

To the extent that the Skinner hypothesis is valid, barring the arrival of unlimited cheap energy, the Goeller and Weinberg analysis will be excessively optimistic, particularly for the geochemically scarce metals. While the resources may indeed be there, we may not be prepared to pay the very high prices necessary to get them.

TABLE 13.2 Energy Used to Mine and Process a Copper Ore in Which All Copper Is Present in Biotite

	Energy Used (BTU/lb. of Copper)		
Grade, percent Cu	0.7	0.1	0.01
Mining plus concentration	19,300	135,000	1,250,000
Preparation of a copper salt	326,858	2,288,010	22,880,100
Smelting	20,000	20,000	20,000
Total	366,158	2,443,010	24,250,100
Equivalent thermal energy in bituminous coal, in pounds of coal	28	188	1,866

Source: D. P. Harris and B. J. Skinner, "The Assessment of Long-term Supplies of Minerals," in *Explorations in Natural Resource Economics,* V. K. Smith and J. V. Krutilla, eds. (Baltimore: Johns Hopkins University Press, 1982), p. 263, Table 8.3.

Economic Indicators

Extraction Cost. The original work that spawned the serious investigation of natural-resource scarcity was published by Barnett and Morse in 1963 under the title *Scarcity and Growth: The Economics of Natural Resource Availability*. This pioneering work is noteworthy both for the methodology it developed and for the conclusions it derived.

The Barnett-Morse empirical evaluations concentrated on two measures constructed using data from 1870 to 1957. The first, called the unit-cost measure, was an attempt to capture any increases in effort required to extract an output of a given quality. This measure was described in the preceding section of this chapter. The second measure recorded the trends in natural-resource prices relative to an index of prices for nonextractive resources. The authors made it clear that they preferred the former measure.

After examining the trends of these two indicators, Barnett and Morse conclude that, with the exception of the forestry sector, no evidence of increasing scarcity was apparent. Furthermore, they found that this conclusion was insensitive to the various subjective judgments they had been forced to make during the analysis, such as defining the weights used to combine labor and capital and the choice of indices used to capture price trends in the nonextractive sector. Different calculations based on other reasonable judgments yielded the same conclusions.

What interpretation can be placed on these results?[13] Barnett and Morse offer four explanations for the absence of any evidence of scarcity in the face of increasing demand and a finite resource base: (a) historically when higher-grade resources were exhausted, lower-grade resources became available in even greater abundance; (b) as the possibility for scarcity emerged, resource users began to switch to other less scarce resources; (c) as prices rose, exploration for new sources was encouraged and this exploration was remarkably successful; and (d) technological change reduced the costs of extraction and expanded the universe of recoverable resources. They suggest that, historically, the combined effect of these mitigating factors was so strong that they eliminated evidence of current or future scarcity, except for forest products.

This generally optimistic view of the past was complemented by an equally optimistic view of the future. They suggested:

> That man will face a series of particular scarcities as the result of growth is a forgone conclusion; that these will impose general scarcity—increasing cost—is not a legitimate corollary. The twentieth century's discovery of the uniformity of energy and matter has increased the possibilities of substitution to an unimaginable degree and placed at man's disposal an indefinitely large number of alternatives from which to choose. To suppose that these alternatives must eventually become so restricted, relative to man's wants, that increasing cost will be inescapable, is not justified by the evidence. An absolute limit to the possibilities of escape may exist, but it cannot be defined or specified. The finite limits of the globe, so real in their unqueried simplicity, lose definition under examination. [pp. 244–245].

---

[13]An excellent technical evaluation of this study and others with a similar focus can be found in V. Kerry Smith, "The Evaluation of Natural Resource Adequacy: Elusive Quest or Frontier of Economics Analysis," *Land Economics* Vol. 56 (August, 1980): 257–298.

There are a number of reasons to be skeptical toward a sweeping conclusion like this one. One of these, the inadequacy of extraction costs as an indicator of scarcity, has been dealt with in the preceding section. Other reasons include the time frame of the analysis (the Barnett-Morse data end in 1957) and a singular focus on the United States. Would studies using later data, a wider geographic frame of reference, and a richer set of indicators tend to support the Barnett-Morse conclusions?

Such studies have provided some support for at least the historical interpretation of the Barnett-Morse data. Johnson, Bell, and Bennett [1980] extended the analysis on American unit extraction costs by incorporating data through 1970 (1966 in a few cases). By performing traditional hypothesis tests, they found:

1. The Barnett-Morse finding of increasing scarcity in forestry was reversed in the 1958–70 period.

2. Of the fifteen agricultural commodity groups studied, *all* had declining unit extraction cost during the 1958–72 period. Of these, only three—food grains, oil crops, and vegetables—had smaller declines during this period than the earlier period studied by Barnett and Morse.

3. Of the eleven mineral and fuel commodity groups studied, *all* had declining unit extraction costs during the 1958–72 period. Of these, only copper registered a smaller decline during the later period.

4. Since 1962, unit extraction costs have risen in commercial fishing. This was the only documented case of increasing scarcity that these three authors found and, after reading Chapter 12, this particular scarcity should surprise no one.

Harold Barnett [1979], one of the authors of *Scarcity and Growth*, has also recently expanded upon his earlier analysis by using more recent data covering the global resource situation, rather than merely that in the United States. After analyzing a wide variety of data, he found:

1. Unit extraction cost, measured as labor per unit output, declined over all time periods, all countries, and all commodities.

2. Of twenty cases examined, the unit extraction cost, measured as labor per unit output, declined more slowly in mineral industries than it did in manufacturing for only three cases.

Thus even when examination of extraction costs is expanded to include other countries and other time periods, the conclusion of declining extraction costs seems to be borne out. Extraction costs are not forward looking, however, so if we are to assess future resource scarcity, we must examine the behavior of resource prices as well. Extraction costs are not enough.

Studies of Resource Price Trends.   If resource scarcity is increasing in some sense, we should be able to discover that natural resource prices are rising more rapidly than prices in general. In the Harold Barnett [1979] study mentioned earlier, prices of commodities were examined, as well as unit extraction costs. His price findings were:

1. Of 53 cases examined, agricultural prices rose faster than a general wholesale price index in 23 cases.
2. In West Germany over the period 1950 to 1971, prices of minerals and raw materials rose faster than prices in general in three out of the six cases studied.

This provides some evidence that prices are rising more rapidly in the natural-resource sectors than in others, a finding which is compatible with projections of future increases in resource scarcity.

Recent work by V. Kerry Smith [1978 and 1979] complements this study by examining more recent relative price data for the United States. Using more sophisticated statistical analyses than used in other previous studies, Smith found that conclusions concerning the rise or fall of natural-resource prices were very sensitive to the choice of time periods used in the analysis. Different periods yielded different results. Even so, there seemed to be a general tendency for the historical decline in relative resource prices to be smaller in more recent periods with some reversals (and, hence, increases in prices) evident for some resources. He concluded:

FIGURE 13.4 History of Deflated Prices and Fitted Linear and Quadratic Trends for Nickel

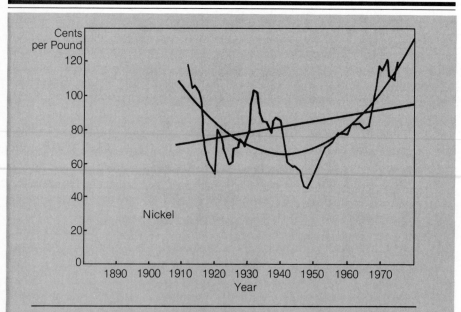

Source: Margaret E. Slade, "Trends in Natural Resource Commodity Prices: An Analysis of the Time Domain," *Journal of Environmental Economics and Management* 9 (1982), p. 132, Figure 6.

The analysis in this paper has raised questions as to whether the conclusions drawn from the empirical data considered by Barnett and Morse were warranted, both in terms of the inherent limitations in the use of the outcome measure and the data themselves. Our analysis with updated data indicates that this evidence alone is not sufficient to arrive at what is [*sic*] commonly accepted interpretation of Barnett and Morse—namely, there is no evidence of natural-resource scarcity. [1978, p. 165]

The work described above relies upon linear functions which do not allow for relative prices to initially decline and then increase. Yet our description of the role of technological progress in Chapter 6 would lead us to expect precisely this kind of pattern. Can the presence of this nonlinear price pattern be refuted or confirmed?

Margaret Slade [1982] has specifically investigated this question for a variety of types of resources. Using statistical techniques, she fitted a quadratic equation of the form:

$$P_{it} = b_{0i} + b_{1i}t + b_{2i}t^2 + V_{it}$$

where P_{it} is the deflated price of the *i*th commodity at time *t*,

   t is time measured in years (1800 = 0), and

   V_{it} is a random error term.

The virtues of this simple approach are the use of a function that can first decline and then rise,[14] the existence of this pattern can be statistically verified,[15] and if the relationship appears valid, the parameters can be used to determine the year in which the decline stopped and the increase began.[16]

Slade estimated this relationship for eleven commodities. The results for two commodities (silver and nickel) are shown in Figures 13.4 and 13.5. The actual data are plotted along with the linear and quadratic approximations. As can be seen from these figures, the quadratic form does seem quite appropriate for these two minerals.

In fact, Slade found that the quadratic function fit the data better than the linear function for all but one of the resources examined (lead), implying that the minimum point on the U-shaped curve had already been passed. For these resources, at least, the pattern of falling, followed rising relative prices seems to be the rule rather than the exception, and the turning point seems to have passed.

Slade sums up this evidence with:

Therefore, if scarcity is measured by relative prices, the evidence indicates that nonrenewable natural-resource commodities are becoming scarce. [p. 136]

---

[14]This pattern results when $b_0 > 0$, $b_1 < 0$ and $b_2 > 0$.

[15]If $b_2 = 0$ then the equation is linear. Thus the test is to see whether $b_2 = 0$ or $b_2 > 0$.

[16]The bottom of the price decline can be found using calculus to be when $t = \dfrac{-b_1}{2b_2}$. Since $b_1 < 0$ this will be a positive number.

FIGURE 13.5   History of Deflated Prices and Fitted Linear and Quadratic Trends for Silver

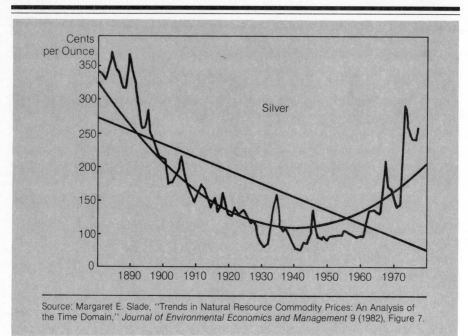

Source: Margaret E. Slade, "Trends in Natural Resource Commodity Prices: An Analysis of the Time Domain," *Journal of Environmental Economics and Management* 9 (1982), Figure 7.

Discovery Cost.   In closing our review of the empirical evidence, let's consider what information can be gleaned from an examination of discovery costs. Table 13.3 compares price information with average discovery costs in the United States for oil and gas for the years 1950–71. All figures are expressed in constant 1947–49 dollars. Because the preferred indicator, marginal discovery cost, was not available, average discovery cost was used instead.[17]

This table shows that over the period no real increase in crude oil prices occurred. According to that indicator, no scarcity was apparent. Yet a somewhat different picture is painted by the discovery cost data. Though the pattern is somewhat erratic, a distinct increase in discovery costs seems to characterize the later years. The message seems clear; the discovery costs were picking up an impending scarcity by the early 1970s that price information had missed. Thus, some evidence of resource scarcity on the horizon has been detected by the discovery cost indicator, as well as the relative price indicators reviewed by Slade.

---

[17]When marginal discovery costs are rising (as in Table 13.3), average costs will understate marginal discovery costs.

TABLE 13.3   Constant Dollar Prices and Average Discovery Costs for Oil, 1950–71

Year	Price per barrel* of crude oil	Average discovery cost for** oil and gas
1950	2.43	0.497
1951	2.20	0.748
1952	2.27	0.827
1953	2.43	0.692
1954	2.52	0.628
1955	2.50	1.036
1956	2.44	0.789
1957	2.63	0.653
1958	2.52	0.950
1959	2.42	1.449
1960	2.41	1.213
1961	2.42	1.509
1962	2.42	0.98
1963	2.42	1.35
1964	2.41	1.26
1965	2.35	0.98
1966	2.29	1.65
1967	2.32	1.39
1968	2.28	0.14
1969	2.30	1.78
1970	2.28	1.24
1971	2.32	1.38

*Prices in average 1947–49 dollars.

**Dollars per equivalent barrel of oil discovered (average 1947–49 dollars). To combine oil and gas discoveries, physical units were aggregated on the basis of market values.

Source: Anthony C. Fisher, *Resource and Environmental Economics* (New York: Cambridge University Press, 1981), pp. 109 & 110, Tables 4.6 and 4.7.

SUMMARY

In view of the rapidly developing state of the art in the assessment of resource scarcity, is there anything concrete that can be said? There are, indeed, several conclusions to be drawn.

1. The problem is not whether or not we shall run out of resources. As the work of Goeller and Weinberg makes clear, the air, water, and crust of the earth provide a storehouse of the very resources we use. For most resources, this storehouse would not be exhausted for literally millions of years. The problem is not their existence but whether or not we are willing to pay the price to extract and use those resources.

2. The evidence suggests the likelihood that localized (as opposed to generalized) scarcity will be experienced by some resources. For certain types of fish and for some minerals, we may, within the next 50 years, encounter extraction costs which shall cause the rate of consumption of those resources to decline.

3. Although the evidence on resource scarcity is mixed, there is mounting evidence suggesting that for several major minerals and fuels we have now passed the point where the prices of resources are rising more slowly than the prices of other commodities. While this evidence is not strong enough to be used to forecast generalized shortages, it does suggest that we are entering an age of increasing relative resource cost.

4. Our ability to detect resource scarcity is currently limited by the nonexistence of an indicator which is forward looking, comprehensive, and computable. While there are several indicators currently being used, none is appropriate for all resources and all market situations.

5. One of the most serious deficiencies in both our detection system and our ability to respond to scarcity is the failure of the market system to incorporate the various environmental costs of increasing resource use, be they radiation hazards, the loss of genetic diversity or aesthetics, the pollution of the air we breathe and the water we drink, or modification of the climate. Without including these costs, our detection indicators give falsely optimistic signals and the market makes choices that put society inefficiently at risk.

To complete our examination of the *Limits to Growth*, we must determine whether or not these environmental costs can be included in the indicators as well as in the incentives of those who will, by their choice, define what the future holds for this generation and those which follow. The next few chapters will examine this question for air pollution, water pollution, and toxic substances.

FURTHER READING

Barnett, Harold, and Chandler Morse. *Scarcity and Growth: The Economics of Natural Resource Availability* (Baltimore: The Johns Hopkins University Press for Resources for the Future, Inc., 1963). The pioneering book that initiated research on the use of economic indicators for assessing resource scarcity.

Leontief, Wassily, et al. *The Future of the World Economy* (New York: Oxford University Press, 1977). A monumental effort led by a Nobel Laureate to quantify (on a regional basis) the effects on the environment (including the natural-resource base) of the world economy to the year 2000. The study also looks at how the natural resource base would affect the degree to which goals established by the United Nations for the developing nations could be met.

Portney, Paul R., ed. *Current Issues in Natural Resource Policy* (Washington, D.C.: Resources for the Future, 1982). An excellent collection of essays on public lands, mineral endangered species, marine fisheries, the global climate, water supplies, agricultural land, and private forests. Highly recommended.

Ridker, Ronald G., and William D. Watson. *To Choose a Future: Resource and Environmental Consequences of Alternative Growth Paths.* (Baltimore: The Johns Hopkins University Press for Resources for the Future, Inc., 1980). This study examines, using computer simulations, various economic growth scenarios for the United States over the period 1975–2025. It concludes that although problems will arise in the future under any of the scenarios, "the

United States has the physical, technological, and management capabilities to resolve them without serious losses in welfare."

Smith, V. Kerry, ed. *Scarcity and Growth Reconsidered* (Baltimore: The Johns Hopkins University Press for Resources for the Future, Inc., 1979). A systematic assessment of the methodology and conclusions of the Barnett-Morse book by twelve different authors aided by some sixteen years of hindsight. The authors bring diverse backgrounds and viewpoints to their assessment. Most of the book is accessible to those with minimal mathematics training.

ADDITIONAL REFERENCES

Barnett, Harold J. "Scarcity and Growth Revisited," in *Scarcity and Growth Reconsidered*, V. Kerry Smith, ed. (Baltimore: Johns Hopkins Press for Resources for the Future, 1979): 163–217.

Berndt, Ernst R., and Barry C. Field, eds., *Modeling and Measuring Natural Resource Substitution* (Cambridge, Mass.: The MIT Press, 1981).

Brown, Gardiner, Jr., and Barry Field. "The Adequacy of Measures for Signalling the Scarcity of Natural Resources," in V. Kerry Smith, ed., *Scarcity and Growth Reconsidered* (Baltimore: The Johns Hopkins University Press, 1979).

Devarajan, S., and A. C. Fisher. "Exploration and Scarcity," *Journal of Political Economy.* Vol. 90 (December, 1980): 1279–1290.

Devarajan, Shantayanan, and Anthony C. Fisher. "Measures of Resource Scarcity under Uncertainty," V. Kerry Smith and John V. Krutilla, eds. *Explorations in Natural Resource Economics* (Baltimore: The Johns Hopkins University Press for Resources for the Future, Inc., 1982): 330–343.

Goeller, H. E. and A. M. Weinberg. "The Age of Substitutability," *The American Economic Review*, Vol. 68 (December, 1978): 1–11.

Irland, L. C. "Is Timber Scarce: The Economics of a Renewable Resource," Bulletin No. 83 (New Haven, Yale School of Forestry and Environmental Studies, 1974).

Johnson, Manual H., W. Frederick, and James T. Bennett, "Natural Resource Scarcity: Empirical Evidence and Public Policy," *Journal of Environmental Economics and Management* 7 (September 1980): 256–271.

Manthy, Robert S. *Natural Resource Commodities – A Century of Statistics* (Baltimore: The Johns Hopkins University Press for Resources for the Future, 1978).

Skinner, B. J. "A Second Iron Age Ahead?" *American Scientist* 64 (1976): 258–269.

Slade, Margaret E. "Trends in Natural Resource Commodity Prices: An Analysis of the Time Domain," *Journal of Environmental Economics and Management*, Vol. 9 (June, 1982): 122–137.

Smith, V. Kerry. "The Evaluation of Natural Resource Adequacy: Elusive Quest or Frontier of Economic Analysis?" *Land Economics* Vo. 56 (August, 1980): 257–298.

Smith, V. Kerry, and John V. Krutilla, eds. *Explorations in Natural Resource Economics* (Baltimore: The Johns Hopkins University Press for Resources for the Future, 1982).

Smith, V. Kerry. "Measuring Natural Resource Scarcity: Theory and Practice," *Journal of Environmental Economics and Management* 5 (June 1978): 150–171.

Smith, V. Kerry. "Natural Resource Scarcity: A Statistical Analysis," *Review of Economics and Statistics*, Vol. 61 (August, 1979): 423–427.

CHAPTER FOURTEEN

Economics of Pollution Control: An Overview

Democracy is not a matter of sentiment, but of foresight. Any system that doesn't take the long run into account will burn itself out in the short run.
CHARLES YOST, *The Age of Triumph and Frustration*

INTRODUCTION

In Chapter 2 we introduced a schematic describing the relationship between the natural and the economic systems. One side depicted the flow of mass and energy to the economic system, while the other depicted the flow of waste products back to the environment. In the last few chapters we have dealt extensively with achieving a balanced set of mass and energy flows; it now remains to discuss how a balance can be achieved in the reverse flow of waste products back to the environment.

There are two questions with which we must deal: (1) What is the appropriate level of flow? (2) How should the responsibility for achieving this flow level be allocated among the various sources of the pollutant when reductions are needed?

In this chapter we shall lay the foundation for understanding the policy approach to controlling the flow of these waste products by developing a general framework for analyzing pollution control. This framework allows us to define efficient and cost-effective allocations for a variety of pollutant types, to compare these allocations to market allocations, and to demonstrate how efficiency and cost effectiveness can be used to design desirable policy responses. This overview is then followed by a series of chapters that apply these principles by examining the policy approaches which have been taken in the United States and in the rest of the world to establish control over waste flows.

A POLLUTANT TAXONOMY

When waste products are transmitted to the environment, the damage caused depends crucially on the ability of the environment to assimilate them (Figure 14.1).

The amount of waste products emitted determines the load upon the environment. The damage done by this load depends on the capacity of the environment to assimilate the waste products. We shall refer to this ability of the environment to absorb pollutants as its *absorptive capacity*. If the emissions load exceeds the absorptive capacity, then the pollutant accumulates in the environment.

Pollutants for which the environment has little or no absorptive capacity are called *stock pollutants*. Stock pollutants accumulate over time as emissions enter the environment. Examples of stock pollutants include nonbiodegradable bottles tossed by the roadside; heavy metals, such as lead, which accumulate in the soils near the emission source; and persistent synthetic chemicals such as dioxin and PCBs (polychlorinated biphenyls).

Pollutants for which the environment has some absorptive capacity are called *fund pollutants*. For these pollutants, as long as the emission rate does not exceed the absorptive capacity of the environment, the pollutants do not accumulate. Examples of fund pollutants are easy to find. Many organic pollutants injected into an oxygen-rich stream will be transformed by the resident bacteria into less-harmful inorganic matter. Carbon dioxide is absorbed by plant life and the oceans.

The point is *not* that the mass is destroyed; the law of conservation of mass suggests this can't be the case. Rather, when fund pollutants are injected into the air or water, they may be transformed into substances that are not considered harmful to people or to the ecological system, or they may be so diluted or dispersed that the resulting concentrations are not harmful.

Pollutants can also be classified by their zone of influence, defined both horizontally and vertically. The horizontal dimension deals with the domain over which dam-

FIGURE 14.1 The Relationship Between Emissions and Pollution Damage

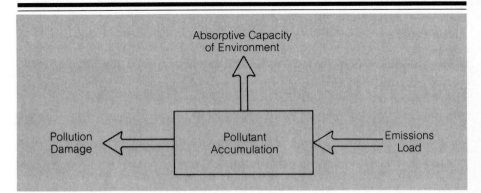

age from an emitted pollutant is experienced. The damage caused by *local* pollutants is experienced near the source of emission, while the damage from *regional* pollutants can be experienced at great distances from the source of emission. The local and regional categories are not mutually exclusive; it is possible for a pollutant to be both. Sulfur oxides and nitrogen oxides, for example, are both local and regional pollutants.

The vertical zone of influence describes whether the damage is caused mainly by ground-level concentrations of an air pollutant or by concentrations in the upper atmosphere. When the damage caused by a pollutant is determined mainly by concentrations of the pollutant near the earth's surface, it is called a *surface pollutant*. When its damage is related more to its concentration in the upper atmosphere, the substance is called a *global pollutant*.

Water pollutants are obviously surface pollutants, but air pollutants can be surface pollutants, global pollutants, or both. One common global pollutant, carbon dioxide, injected into the atmosphere as a product of fossil-fuel combustion, has been implicated in rising world temperatures via the "greenhouse effect." In addition, chlorofluorocarbon emissions are currently suspected of playing a role in the destruction of the ozone level which protects the earth's surface from harmful solar radiation. As we shall see, the appropriate policy responses for global and surface pollutants are quite different.

This taxonomy will prove useful in designing policy responses to these various types of pollution problems. Each type of pollutant requires a unique policy response. The failure to recognize these distinctions leads to counterproductive policy.

DEFINING THE EFFICIENT ALLOCATION OF POLLUTION

Pollutants are the residuals of production and consumption. These residuals must eventually be returned to the environment in one form or another. Since their presence in the environment may depreciate the service flows received, an efficient allocation of resources must take this cost into account. What is meant by the efficient allocation of pollution depends on the nature of the pollutant.

Stock Pollutants

The efficient allocation of a stock pollutant must take into account the fact that the pollutant accumulates in the environment over time and that the damage caused by its presence increases and persists as the pollutant accumulates. By their very nature, stock pollutants create an interdependency between the present and the future, since the damage imposed in the future depends on current actions.

It is not hard to establish what is meant by an efficient allocation in these circumstances.[1] Suppose, for example, that we consider the allocation of a commodity

---

[1]The mathematically adept reader can find a formal analysis of this issue in Vernon L. Smith, "Dynamics of Waste Accumulation versus Recycling," *Quarterly Journal of Economics*, LXXXVI (November 1972): 600–616.

which we shall refer to as X. Suppose further that the production of X involves the generation of a proportional amount of a stock pollutant. The amount of this pollution can be reduced, but that takes resources away from the production of X. The damage caused by the presence of this pollutant in the environment is further assumed to be proportional to the size of the accumulated stock. As long as the stock of pollutants remains in the environment, the damage persists.

The efficient allocation, by definition, is the one which maximizes the present value of the net benefit. In this case the net benefit at any point in time t is equal to the benefit received from the consumption of X minus the cost of the damage caused by the presence of the stock pollutant in the environment.

This damage is a cost that society must bear, and in terms of its effect on the efficient allocation, this cost is not unlike that of extracting minerals or fuels. While for minerals the extraction cost rises with the cumulative amount of the depletable resource extracted, the damage cost associated with a stock pollutant rises with the cumulative amount deposited in the environment. The accretion of this stock pollutant is proportional to the production of X, which creates the same kind of linkage between the production of X and this pollution cost as exists between the extraction cost and the production of a mineral. They both rise over time with the cumulative amount produced. The one major difference is that the extraction cost is borne only at the time of extraction, while damage is borne as long as the stock exists in the environment.

We can exploit this similarity to infer the efficient allocation of a stock pollutant from our knowledge of the efficient allocation of a depletable resource with rising extraction cost. As discussed in Chapter 6, when extraction cost rises, the efficient quantity of a depletable resource extracted and consumed declines over time.

Exactly the same pattern would emerge for a commodity which is produced jointly with a stock pollutant. The efficient quantity of X (and therefore, the addition to the accumulation of this pollutant in the environment) would decline over time as the marginal cost of the damage rises. The price of X would rise over time reflecting the rising social cost of production. To cope with the increasing marginal damage, the amount of resources committed to controlling the pollutant would increase over time. Ultimately, a steady state would be reached where additions to the amount of the pollutant in the environment would cease and the size of the stock would stabilize. At this point all further emission of the pollutant created by the production of X would be controlled (through recycling). The price of X and the quantity consumed would remain constant. The damage caused by the stock pollutant would persist.

As was the case with rising extraction cost, technological progress could modify this efficient allocation. Specifically, technological progress could reduce the amount of pollutant generated per unit of X produced, it could create ways to recycle the stock pollutant rather than injecting it into the environment, or it could develop ways of rendering the pollutant less harmful. All of these responses would lower the marginal damage cost associated with a given level of production of X. Therefore, more of X could be produced with technological progress than without it.

Stock pollutants are, in a sense, the other side of the intergenerationalequity coin from depletable resources. With depletable resources it is possible for current generations to create a burden for future generations by using up resources, thereby diminishing the remaining endowmment. Stock pollutants can create a burden for future generations by passing on a damage cost which persists well after the benefits received from incurring that damage cost have been forgotten. Though neither of these situations automatically violates our sustainability criterion, they clearly require further scrutiny. We shall exmaine the relationship between stock pollutants and sustainability as well as depletable resources and sustainability in Chapter 21.

Fund Pollutants

To the extent that the emission of fund pollutants exceeds the assimilative capacity of the environment, they accumulate and share some of the characteristics of stock pollutants. When the emission rate is low enough, however, the emission can be assimilated by the environment with the result that the link between present emissions and future damage may be broken.

When this happens, current emissions affect current damage and future emissions affect future damage, but the level of future damage is independent of current emissions. This independence of allocations among time periods allows us to explore the efficient allocation of fund pollutants using the concept of static, rather than dynamic, efficiency. Because the static concept is simpler, this affords us the opportunity to incorporate more dimensions of the problem without unnecessarily complicating the analysis.

The normal starting point for the analysis would be to maximize the net benefit from the waste flows. However, pollution is more easily understood if we deal with an equivalent formulation involving the minimization of two rather different types of costs: damage costs and control, or avoidance, costs.

In order to examine the efficient allocation graphically, we need to know something about how control costs vary with the degree of control and how the damages vary with the amount of pollution emitted. Though our knowledge in these areas is far from complete, there seems to be general agreement on the shapes of these relationships.

Generally the marginal damage caused by a unit of pollution increases with the amount emitted. When small amounts of the pollutant are emitted, the marginal damage is quite small. However, when large amounts are emitted, the marginal unit can cause signficantly more damage. It is not hard to understand why. Small amounts of pollution are easily diluted in the environment, and the body can tolerate small quantities of substances. However, as the amount in the atmosphere increases, dilution is less effective and the body is less tolerant.

Marginal control costs commonly increase with the amount controlled. For example, suppose a source of pollution tries to cut down on its particulate emissions by purchasing an electrostatic precipitator which captures 80 percent of the particulates as they flow past in the stack. If the source wants further control, it can purchase another precipitator and place it in the stack above the first one. This second precipitator captures 80 percent of the remaining 20 percent or 16 percent of the uncontrolled emissions. Thus, the first precipitator would achieve an 80-percent reduction from uncontrolled emissions, while the second precipitator, which costs the same as the first, would achieve only a further 16-percent reduction. Obviously each unit of emission reduction costs more for the second precipitator than for the first.

In Figure 14.2 we use these two pieces of information on the shapes of the relevant curves to derive the efficient allocation. A movement from right to left refers to greater control and less pollution emitted. The efficient allocation is represented by Q^*, the point at which the damage caused by the marginal unit of pollution is exactly equal to the marginal cost of avoiding it.[2]

Greater degrees of control (points to the left of Q^*) are inefficient because the further increase in avoidance costs would exceed the reduction in damages. Hence, total costs would rise. Similarly, levels of control lower than Q^* would result in a lower cost of control, but the increase in damage costs would be even larger, yielding an increase in total cost. Either increasing or decreasing the amount controlled causes an increase in total costs. Hence, Q^* must be efficient.

The diagram suggests that, under the conditions presented, the optimal level of pollution is not zero. If you find this disturbing, remember that we confront this principle every day. Take the damage caused by automobile accidents, for example. Obviously, a considerable amount of damage is caused by automobile accidents. Yet we do not reduce that damage to zero, because the cost of doing so would be too high.

The point is *not* that we don't know how to stop automobile accidents. All we would have to do is eliminate automobiles! Rather, the point is since we value the benefits of automobiles, we take steps to reduce accidents (using speed limits) only to the extent that the costs of accident reduction are commensurate with the damage reduction achieved; the efficient level of automobile accidents is not zero.

The second point to be made is that in some circumstances the optimal level of pollution *may* be zero or close to it. This situation occurs when the damage caused by even the first unit of pollution is so severe that it is higher than the marginal cost of controlling the last unit of pollution. This would be reflected in Figure 14.2 as a leftward shift of the damage cost curve of sufficient magnitude that its intersection with the vertical axis would lie above the point where the marginal cost curve intersects the vertical axis. This circumstance seems to characterize the treatment of highly dangerous radioactive pollutants such as plutonium.

Insights besides the one that a zero level of pollution is not normally efficient are easily derived from our characterization of the efficient allocation. For example, it should be clear from Figure 14.2 that the optimal level of pollution generally is not the same for all parts of the country. Areas which have higher population levels or are particularly sensitive to pollution should have lower levels, while areas which have lower population levels or are less sensitive should have more.

Examples of ecological sensitivity are not hard to find. For instance, some parts of the country are less sensitive to acid rain than others because the local geological strata neutralize moderate amounts of the acid. Thus, the marginal damage caused by

---

[2]At this point we can see why this formulation is equivalent to the net-benefit formulation. Since the benefit is damage reduction, another way of stating this proposition is to state that marginal benefit must equal marginal cost. That is, of course, the familiar proposition derived by maximizing net benefits.

FIGURE 14.2 The Efficient Allocation of a Fund Pollutant

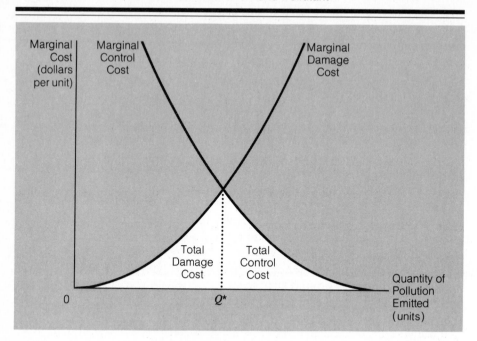

a unit of acid rain is lower in those fortunate regions than in others less tolerant. It can also be argued that pollutants affecting visibility are more damaging in national parks and other areas where visibility is an important part of the aesthetic experience than in other, more industrial, areas.

MARKET ALLOCATION OF POLLUTION

Since air and water are treated in our legal system as common-property resources, at this point in the book it should surprise no one that the market misallocates them. Our general conclusion that common-property resources are overexploited certainly applies here. Air and water resources have been overexploited as waste repositories. However, this conclusion only scratches the surface; there is much more to be learned about market allocations of pollution.

When firms create products, rarely does the process of converting raw materials into outputs use 100 percent of the mass. Some of the mass, called a *residual*, is left over. If the residual is valuable, it is simply reused. However, if it is not valuable, the firm has an incentive to deal with it in the cheapest manner possible.

The typical firm has several alternatives. It can control the amount of the residual by using inputs more completely so that less is left over. It can also produce less output, so that smaller amounts of the residual are generated. Recycling the residual is sometimes a viable option, as is removing the most damaging components of the waste stream and disposing of the rest.

Because damage costs are externalities but control costs are not, what is cheapest for the firm is not always cheapest for society as a whole. When pollutants are injected into water courses or the atmosphere, they cause damages to those firms and consumers downstream or downwind of the source. These costs are *not* borne by the emitting source and, hence, not considered by it, although they certainly are borne by society at large.[3] As with other services which are systematically undervalued, the disposal of wastes into the air or water becomes inefficiently attractive. As we saw in Chapter 3, inefficient pollution-control choices lead to further inefficiencies in product and input markets. markets.

In the case of stock pollutants, the problem is particularly severe. Uncontrolled markets would lead to an excessive production of *X*, too few resources committed to pollution control, and an inefficiently large amount of the stock pollutant in the environment. Thus the burden on future generations caused by the presence of this pollutant would be inefficiently large.

There are important differences between this case and the previously discussed inefficiencies associated with the extraction or production of mineral, energy, and food. For private-property resources, the market forces provide automatic signals of impending scarcity. These forces may be understated (as when the vulnerability of imports is ignored), but they operate in the correct direction. Even when some resources are treated as common property (fisheries), the possibility for a private-property alternative (fish farming) is enhanced. As we saw with Example 12.1 when private-property and common-property resources sell in the same market, the private-property owner tends to ameliorate the excesses of those who exploit common properties. Efficient firms are rewarded with higher profits.

With pollution there is no automatic amelioration.[4] Because this cost is borne partially by consumers, rather than producers, it does not find its way into product prices. Firms which attempt to unilaterally control their pollution are placed at a competitive disadvantage; their costs of production are higher than those of their less conscientious competitors due to the added expense. Not only does the unimpeded market fail to generate the efficient level of pollution control, it penalizes those firms which might attempt to control an efficient amount. Hence the case for some sort of government intervention is particularly strong for pollution control.

---

[3] Actually, the source certainly considers some of the costs if only to avoid adverse public relations. The point, however, is that this consideration is likely to be incomplete; the source is unlikely to internalize all of the damage cost.

[4] There is an incentive for affected parties to negotiate among themselves, a topic covered in Chapter 3. As pointed out in that chapter, however, that approach only works in cases where the number of affected parties is small.

COST-EFFECTIVE POLICIES FOR
UNIFORMLY MIXED FUND POLLUTANTS

Defining a Cost-Effective Allocation

Our use of the efficiency criterion has helped in demonstrating why markets fail to produce an efficient level of pollution control and in tracing out the effects of this less-than-optimal degree of control on the markets for related commodities. However, the criterion is less helpful in defining the exact response to be undertaken because the amount of information needed to define the efficient level of pollution is very large and existing estimates lack reliability.

In the following chapters we will discuss how control authorities in the United States choose the specific legal levels of pollution. Once they have made this choice, they have resolved only one-half of the problem. The other half deals with deciding how to allocate the responsibility for meeting that predetermined pollution level among the large number of emitters.

This is precisely where the cost-effectiveness criterion comes in. Once the objective is stated in terms of meeting the predetermined pollution level at minimum cost, it is possible to derive the conditions that any cost-effective allocation of the responsibility must satisfy. These conditions can then be used as a basis for choosing among various kinds of policy instruments.

We begin our analysis with uniformly mixed, fund pollutants, which analytically are the easiest to deal with. The damage caused by these pollutants depends on the amount entering the atmosphere. In contrast to nonuniformly mixed pollutants, the damage caused by uniformly mixed pollutants is relatively insensitive to where the emissions are injected into the atmosphere. Thus, the policy can focus simply on controlling the total weight of emissions in a manner that minimizes the cost of control. What can we say about the cost-effective allocation of control responsibility for uniformly mixed fund pollutants?

Consider a simple example. Assume that there are two emission sources currently emitting a total 30 units of emissions. Assume further that the control authority determines that the environment can assimilate 15 units so that a reduction of 15 units is necessary. How should this 15-unit reduction be allocated between the two sources in order to minimize the total cost of the reduction?

With the aid of Figure 14.3 we can demonstrate the answer. Figure 14.3 is drawn by measuring the marginal cost of control for the first source from the left-hand axis (MC_1) and the marginal cost of control for the second source from the right-hand axis (MC_2). Notice that a total of 15 units in reduction is achieved for every point on this graph, where each point represents some different combination of reduction by the two sources. Drawn in this manner, the diagram represents all possible allocations of the 15-unit reduction between the two sources. The left-hand axis, for example, represents an allocation of the entire reduction to the second source, while the right-hand axis represents a situation in which the first source bears the entire responsibility. All points

FIGURE 14.3 Cost Effective Allocation of a Uniformly Mixed Pollutant

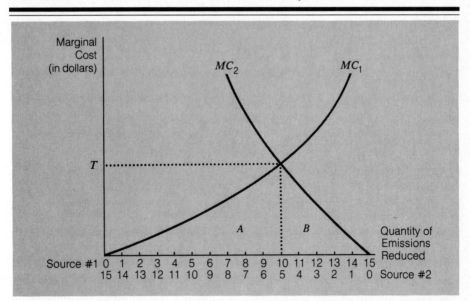

in between represent different degrees of shared responsibility. What allocation minimizes the cost of control?

In the cost-effective allocation, the first source cleans up 10 units, while the second source cleans up 5 units. The total variable cost of control of this particular assignment of the responsibility for the reduction is represented by area *A* plus area *B*. Area *A* is the cost of control for the first source, area *B* the cost of control for the second. Any other allocation would result in a higher total control cost. (Convince yourself that this is true.)

Figure 14.3 also demonstrates one of the most important propositions in the economics of pollution control. *The cost of achieving a given reduction in emissions will be minimized if and only if the marginal costs of control are equalized for all emitters.*[5] This is demonstrated by the fact that the marginal cost curves cross at the cost-effective allocation.

Cost-Effective Pollution-Control Policies

This proposition can be used as a basis for choosing among the various policy instruments which the control authority might use to achieve this allocation. In the previous section we listed a few of the large number of ways that sources can control the amount of pollution they inject into the environment. The cheapest method of control will differ

---

[5]This statement is true when marginal cost increases with the amount of emissions reduced (Figure 14.3). Suppose that for some pollutants the marginal cost were to decrease with the amount of emissions reduced. What would be the cost-effective allocation in that admittedly unusual situation?

widely, not only among industries, but also among plants in the same industry. The selection of the cheapest method requires detailed information on the possible control techniques and their associated costs.

Generally, plant managers are able to acquire this information for their plants when it is in their interest to do so. However, the government authorities responsible for meeting pollution targets are not likely to have this information. Since the degree to which these plants would be regulated depends on cost information, it is unrealistic to expect these plant managers to transfer unbiased information to the government. There would be a strong incentive for plant managers to overstate control costs in hopes of reducing their ultimate burden.

This situation poses a difficult dilemma for control authorities. The cost of incorrectly assigning the control responsibility among various polluters is likely to be large. Yet the control authorities do not have the information at their disposal to make a correct allocation. Those who have the information – the plant managers – are not inclined to share it. Can the cost-effective allocation be found? The answer depends on the particular approach taken by the control authority.

Emission Standards

We start our investigation of this question by supposing that the control authority pursues a traditional legal approach by imposing a separate emission standard on each source. In the economics literature this approach is referred to as the "command-and-control" approach. An *emission standard* is a legal limit on the amount of the pollutant an individual source is allowed to emit. In our example it is clear that the two standards should add up to the allowable 15 units, but it is not clear how, in the absence of information on control costs, these 15 units are to be allocated between the two sources. The easiest method of resolving this dilemma – and the one chosen in the earliest days of pollution control – would be simply to allocate each source an equal reduction. As is clear from Figure 14.3, this strategy would not be cost effective. While the first source would have lower costs, this cost reduction would be substantially smaller than the increase faced by the second source; total costs would increase if both sources were forced to clean up the same amount.

When emission standards are used there is no reason to believe that the authority will assign the responsibility for emission reduction in a cost-minimizing way. This is probably not surprising. Who would have believed otherwise?

Surprisingly enough, however, there are policy instruments that allow the authority to allocate the emission reduction in a cost-effective manner even when it has no information on the magnitude of control costs. These policy approaches rely on economic incentives to produce the desired outcome. The two most common approaches are known as emission charges and transferable emission permits.

Emission Charges

An *emission charge* is a fee, collected by the government, levied on each unit of pollutant emitted into the air or water. The total payment any source would make to the government could be found by multiplying the fee times the amount of pollution emit-

FIGURE 14.4 Cost-Minimizing Control of Pollution with an Emission Charge

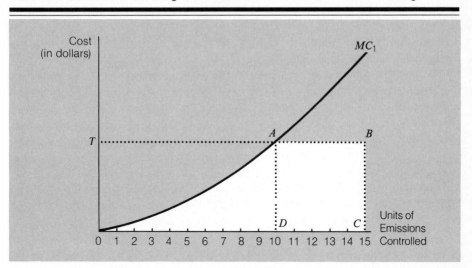

ted. Emission charges reduce pollution because pollution costs the firm money. To save money the source seeks ways to reduce its pollution.

How much pollution control would the firm choose to purchase? A profit-maximizing firm would control, rather than emit, pollution whenever it proved cheaper to do so. We can illustrate the firm's decision with Figure 14.4. The level of uncontrolled emissions is 15 units and the emission charge is T. Thus, if the firm were to decide against controlling any emissions, it would have to pay T times 15, represented by area $OTBC$.

Is this the best the firm can do? Obviously not, since it can control some pollution at a lower cost than paying the emission charge. It would pay the firm to reduce emissions until the marginal cost of reduction is equal to the emission charge. The firm would minimize its cost by choosing to clean up 10 units of pollution and emitting 5 units. At this allocation the firm would pay control costs equal to area OAD and total emission charge payments equal to area $ABCD$ for a total cost of $OABC$. This is clearly less than $OTBC$, the amount the firm would pay if it chose not to clean up any unit of pollution.

Let's carry this one step further. Suppose that we levied the same emission charge on both sources discussed in Figure 14.3. Each source would then control its emissions until its marginal control cost equalled the emission charge. (Faced with an emission charge T, the second source would clean up 5 units.) Since they both are facing the same emission charge, they will *independently* choose levels of control consistent with equal marginal control costs. This is precisely the condition that yields a cost-minimizing allocation.

This is a rather remarkable finding. We have shown that as long as the control authority imposes the same emission charge on all sources, the resulting reduction allocation *automatically* minimizes the costs of control. This is true in spite of the fact that the control authority may not have any knowledge of control costs.

However, we have not yet dealt with the issue of how the appropriate level of the emission charge is determined. Each level of a charge will result in *some* level of emission reduction. Furthermore, the responsibility for meeting that reduction will be allocated in a manner that minimizes control costs. How high should the charge be set to ensure that the resulting emission reduction is the *desired* level of emission reduction?

Without knowing the costs of control, the control authority cannot establish the correct tax rate on the first try. It is possible, however, to develop an iterative, trial-and-error process to find the appropriate charge rate. This process is initiated by choosing an arbitrary charge rate and observing the amount of reduction that occurs when that charge is imposed. If the observed reduction is larger than desired, it means the charge should be lowered; if the reduction is smaller, the charge should be raised. The new reduction which results from the adjusted charge can then be observed and compared with the desired reduction. Further adjustments in the charge can be made as needed. This process can be repeated until the actual and desired reductions are equal. At that point the correct emission charge would have been found.

The charge system not only causes sources to choose a cost-effective allocation of the control responsibility, it also stimulates the development of newer, cheaper means of controlling emissions as well as promoting technological progress. This is illustrated in Figure 14.5.

The reason for this is rather straightforward. Control authorities base the emission standards on specific technologies. As new technologies are discovered by the control authority, the standards are tightened. These more strict standards force firms to bear higher costs. Therefore with emissions standards firms have an incentive to hide technological changes from the control authority.

FIGURE 14.5 Cost Savings from Technological Change: Charges vs. Standards

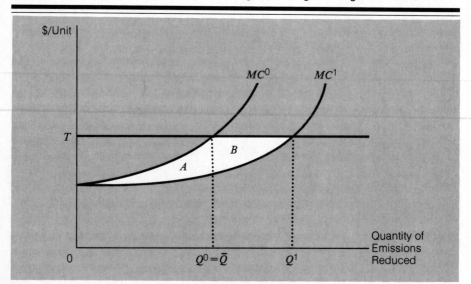

With an emissions charge system the firm saves money by adopting cheaper new technologies. As long as the firm can reduce its pollution at a marginal cost lower than T, it pays to adopt the new technology. In Figure 14.5 the firm saves A and B by adopting the new technology and voluntarily reduces its emissions from Q^0 to Q^1.

With an emissions charge, the minimum cost allocation of meeting a predetermined emission reduction can be found by a control authority even when it has no information on control costs. An emission charge also stimulates technological advances in emission reduction. Unfortunately, the process for finding the appropriate rate would take some experimenting. During the trial-and-error period of finding the appropriate rate, sources would be faced with a volatile emission charge. This would make planning for the future difficult. Investments that would make sense under a high emission charge might not make sense when it falls. From either a policymaker's or business manager's perspective, this process leaves much to be desired.

Transferable Emission Permits

Is it possible for the control authority to find the cost-minimizing allocation without going through a trial-and-error process? It is possible if a *transferable emission permit system* is used to control pollution. Under this system, all sources are required to have permits to emit. Each permit specifies exactly how much the firm is allowed to emit. The permits are freely transferable. The control authority issues exactly the number of permits needed to produce the desired emission level. Any emissions by a source in excess of those allowed by its permit would cause the source to face severe monetary sanctions.

Why this system automatically leads to a cost-effective allocation can be seen in Figure 14.6 on page 320, which treats the same set of circumstances as Figure 14.3. Suppose that somehow the first source found itself with 7 permits. Since it has 15 units of uncontrolled emissions, this would mean it must control 8 units. Similarly, suppose that the second source has the remaining 8 permits, meaning that it would have to clean up 7 units. Notice that both firms have an incentive to trade. The marginal cost of control for the second source (C) is substantially higher than that for the first (A). The second source could lower its cost if it could buy a permit from the first source at a price lower than C. The first source, meanwhile, would be better off if it could sell a permit for a price higher than A. Since C is greater than A, there are certainly grounds for trade.

A transfer of permits would take place until the first source had only five permits left (and is controlling 10 units), while the second source had 10 permits (and was controlling 5 units). At this point, the permit price would equal B, since that is the marginal value of that permit to both sources, and neither source would have any incentive to trade further. The permit market would be in equilibrium.

Notice that the market equilibrium for an emission-permit system is the cost-effective allocation! Simply by issuing the appropriate number of permits (15) and letting the market do the rest, the control authority can achieve a cost-effective allocation without having even the slightest knowledge about control costs. This system allows the govern-

FIGURE 14.6   Cost Effectiveness and the Emission Permit System

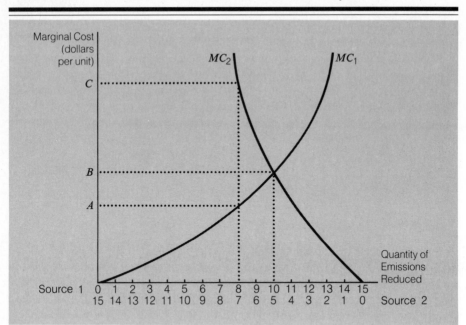

ment to meet its policy objective while allowing greater flexibility in how that objective is met.

The incentives created by this system ensure that sources use this flexibility to achieve the objective at the lowest possible cost. As we shall see in the next two chapters, this remarkable property has been responsible for the prominence of this type of approach in current attempts to reform the regulatory process.

COST-EFFECTIVE POLICIES FOR NONUNIFORMLY MIXED SURFACE POLLUTANTS

The problem becomes more complicated when dealing with nonuniformly mixed surface pollutants rather than uniformly mixed pollutants. For these pollutants the policy must be concerned not only with the weight of emissions entering the atmosphere, but also with the location of emissions. For nonuniformly mixed pollutants it is the concentration in the air, soil, or water that counts. The concentration is measured as the amount of pollutant found in a given volume of air, soil, or water at a given location at a given point in time.

It is easy to see why pollutant concentrations are sensitive to the location of emissions. Suppose that three emission sources are clustered together and emit the same amount as three separate, but otherwise identical, sources. The emissions from the clustered sources generally cause higher pollution levels because they are all entering the same volume of air or water. Because the two sets of emission do not share a common receiving volume, those from the dispersed sources result in lower concentrations. This is the main reason why cities generally face more severe pollution problems than do rural areas; urban sources tend to be more densely clustered.

Since the damage caused by nonuniformly mixed surface pollutants is related to their concentration levels in the air, soil, or water, it is natural that our search for cost-effective policies for controlling these pollutants focus on the attainment of ambient standards. *Ambient standards* are legal ceilings placed on the concentration level of specified pollutants in the air, soil, or water. They represent the target concentration levels which are not to be exceeded. A cost-effective policy results in the lowest cost allocation of control responsibility consistent with meeting that the predetermined ambient standards are met at specified locations called receptor sites.

The Single-Receptor Case

We can begin the analysis by considering a simple case in which we desire to control pollution at one, and only one, receptor location. We know that all units of emissions from sources do not have the same impact on pollution measured at that receptor. Consider, for example, Figure 14.7.

Suppose that we hypothetically allow each of the four sources individually, at different points in time, to inject 10 units of emission into the stream. Suppose further that we measured the pollutant concentration resulting from each of these injections at receptor *R*. In general, we would find that the emissions from *A* or *B* would cause a larger rise in the recorded concentration than would those from *C* and *D*, even though the same amount was emitted from each source. The reason for this, of course, is that the emissions from *C* and *D* would be substantially diluted by the time they arrived at *R*, while those from *A* and *B* would arrive in a more concentrated form.

FIGURE 14.7 The Effect of Location on Local Pollutant Concentration at a Particular Receptor

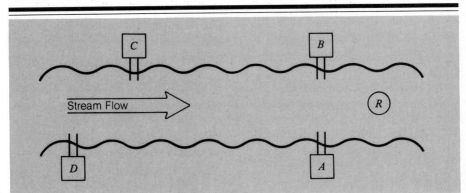

Since emissions are what can be controlled, but the concentrations at R are the policy target, our first task must be to relate the two. This can be accomplished by using a transfer coefficient. A *transfer coefficient*, a_i, captures the constant amount the concentration at the receptor will rise if source i emits one more unit of pollution. By using this definition and the knowledge that the a_i's are constant, we can relate the concentration level at R to emissions from all sources:

$$K_R = \sum_{i=1}^{I} a_i E_i + B \qquad (14.1)$$

where K_R is the concentration at the receptor; E_i is the emission level of the ith source; I is the total number of sources in the region; and B is the background concentration level (resulting from natural sources or sources outside the control region).

We are now in a position to define the cost-effective allocation of responsibility. A numerical example involving two sources is presented in Table 14.1. In that example the two sources are assumed to have the same marginal cost curves for cleaning up emissions. This assumption is reflected in the fact that the first two corresponding columns of the table for each of the two sources are identical.[6] The main difference between the two sources is their location *vis-à-vis* the receptor. The first source is closer to the receptor, so it has a larger transfer coefficient than the second (1.0 as opposed to 0.5).

The objective is to meet a given concentration target at minimum cost. Column 3 of the table translates emission reductions into concentration reductions for each source, while column 4 records the marginal cost of each unit of concentration reduced. The former is merely the emission reduction times the transfer coefficient, while the latter is the marginal cost of the emission reduction divided by the transfer coefficient (which translates the marginal cost of *emission* reduction into a marginal cost of *concentration* reduction).

Suppose the concentration at the receptor has to be reduced by 7.5 units in order to comply with the ambient standard. The cost-effective allocation would be achieved when the marginal costs of concentration reduction (*not* emission reduction) are equalized for all sources. In Table 14.1 this occurs when the first source reduces 6 units of emissions (and 6 units of concentration) and the second source reduces 3 units of emissions (and 1.5 units of concentration). At this allocation the marginal cost of concentration reduction is equal to $6 for both sources. By adding up all marginal costs for each unit reduced, we can calculate that the total variable cost of this allocation is $27. From the definition of cost effectiveness, no other allocation resulting in 7.5 units of concentration reduction would be cheaper.

---

[6]This assumption has no bearing on the results we shall achieve. It serves mainly to illustrate the role location plays by eliminating control cost differences as a factor.

TABLE 14.1 Cost Effectiveness for Nonuniformly Mixed Pollutants: A Hypothetical Example

		Source 1 ($a_1 = 1.0$)		
Emissions Units Reduced	*Marginal Cost of Emission Reduction (Dollars per Unit)*	*Concentration Units Reduced**	*Marginal Cost of Concentration Reduction** (Dollars per Unit)*
1	1	1.0	1
2	2	2.0	2
3	3	3.0	3
4	4	4.0	4
5	5	5.0	5
6	6	6.0	6
7	7	7.0	7

		Source 2 ($a_2 = 0.5$)		
Emissions Units Reduced	*Marginal Cost of Emission Reduction (Dollars per Unit)*	*Concentration Units Reduced**	*Marginal Cost of Concentration Reduction** (Dollars per Unit)*
1	1	0.5	2
2	2	1.0	4
3	3	1.5	6
4	4	2.0	8
5	5	2.5	10
6	6	3.0	12
7	7	3.5	14

*Computed by multiplying the emission reduction in column 1 by the transfer coefficient (a_i).
**Computed by dividing the marginal cost of emission reduction (column 2) by the transfer coefficient (a_i).

Policy Approaches.   This framework can now be used to evaluate various policy approaches that the control authority might use. We begin with the *ambient charge*, the charge used to produce a cost-effective allocation of a nonuniformly mixed pollutant. This charge takes the form:

$$t_i = a_i \times F \qquad (14.2)$$

where t_i is the per-unit charge paid by the ith source on each unit emitted, a_i is the ith source's transfer coefficient, and F is the marginal cost of a unit of concentration reduction, which is the same for all sources. In our example F is \$6, so the first source would pay a per-unit emission charge of \$6, while the second source would pay \$3. Note that sources will, in general, pay different charges when the objective is to meet an ambient standard at minimum cost because their transfer coefficients differ. This stands in contrast to the uniformly mixed pollutant case in which a cost-effective allocation required that all sources pay the same charge.

How can the cost-effective t_i be found by a control authority with no information on control costs? The transfer coefficients can be calculated using knowledge of hydrology and meteorology, but what about F? Here there is a striking similarity to the uniformly mixed case. Any level of F would yield a cost-effective allocation of control responsibility for achieving *some* level of concentration reduction at the receptor. That level might not, however, be compatible with the ambient standard.

We could ensure compatibility by changing F in an iterative process until the desired concentration is achieved. If the actual pollutant concentration is below the standard, the tax could be lowered; if it is above, the tax could be raised. The correct level of F would be reached when the resulting pollution concentration is equal to the desired level. That equlibrium allocation would be the one that meets the ambient standard at minimum cost.

Table 14.1 allows us to consider another issue of significance. The cost-effective allocation of control responsibility for achieving surface-concentration targets places a larger information burden on control authorities; they have to calculate the transfer coefficients. What is lost if the simpler emission charge system (where each source faces the same charge) is used to pursue a surface concentration target? Can location be safely ignored?

In Table 14.1 a uniform emission charge equal to $5 would achieve the desired 7.5 units of reduction (5 from the first source and 2.5 from the second). Yet the total variable cost of this allocation (calculated as the sum of the marginal costs) would be $30 ($15 paid by each source). This is $3 higher than the allocation resulting from the use of the ambient charge discussed earlier. In subsequent chapters we shall present empirical estimates of the size of this cost increase in actual air- and water-pollution situations. In general, they show the cost increases to be large; location matters.

Table 14.1 also helps us to understand why location matters. Notice that with a uniform emissions charge, 10 units of emissions are cleaned up, while with the ambient charge, only 8 units are cleaned up. Both achieve the concentration target, but the uniform-emission charge results in fewer emissions. The ambient charge results in a lower cost allocation than the emission charge because it results in less emission control. Those sources having only a small effect on the recorded concentration at the receptor location are forced to control less than they would with a uniform charge.

With the ambient charge, we have the same problem that we encountered with emission charges in the uniformly mixed pollutant case—the cost-effective level can only be determined by an iterative process. Can a permit system get around this problem when dealing with nonuniformly mixed pollutants?

It can by designing the permits in the correct way. An ambient permit entitles the owner to cause the concentration to rise at the receptor by a specified amount, rather than allowing the same amount of emissions to each owner. Using ΔK_R to represent this permitted rise and E to indicate the units of emissions allowed by each permit held by the ith source, we can see that from equation 14.1 that

$$\frac{\Delta K_R}{a_i} = \Delta E_i. \tag{14.3}$$

The larger the transfer coefficient (that is, the closer the source is to the receptor), the smaller is the amount of emissions legitimized by a permit. Proximate sources must purchase more permits than distant sources to legitimize a given level of emissions.

In this case the sources pay the same price for each permit, but the amount of emissions allowed by each permit varies from location to location. The market automatically determines this common price, and the resulting allocation of permits is cost effective. With respect to Table 14.1, the ambient permit price would be $6. This cost-effective system is called an *ambient permit system* to differentiate it from the *emission permit system*, which is used to achieve a cost-effective allocation of control responsibility for uniformly mixed pollutants.

We can reinforce our understanding of what is going on with the ambient permit system by examining a specific trade. Suppose our two sources in Table 14.1 want to trade permits with the first source buying from the second. In order to maintain the same concentration level before and after the trade, we must ensure that

$$a_1 \Delta E_1 = a_2 \Delta E_2$$

where the subscripts refer to the first and second source. Solving this for the allowable increase in emission by the buyer yields

$$\Delta E_1 = \frac{a_2}{a_1} \Delta E_2. \tag{14.4}$$

Using $a_2 = 0.5$ and $a_1 = 1.0$, this equation suggests that for each permit traded, the buyer (the first source) is allowed to emit only one-half the amount of emissions allowed by that same permit when it was used by the seller. After this trade, the total amount of emissions by both sources goes down.[7] This could not happen in an emissions permit system, since the design of those permits causes all trades to leave emissions (but not concentrations!) unchanged.

The Many-Receptors Case

How does this analysis generalize to the many-receptors case? Easily. The cost-effective ambient charge paid by any source would in this case be

$$T_i = \sum_{j=1}^{J} a_{ij} \cdot F_j$$

where T_i is the charge paid by the ith source for each unit of emissions, a_{ij} is the transfer coefficient that translates emissions by source i into concentration increases at the jth receptor, J is the number of receptors, and F_j is the monetary fee associated with the jth receptor. Thus, the source has to pay a charge that incorporates its effect on all

---

[7] Emissions could rise with ambient permit trades as well. This would occur whenever the transfer coefficient of the seller was larger than that of the buyer.

receptors. The control authority could manipulate F_j for each receptor location until the desired concentration level is achieved at that receptor.[8]

The extension of the ambient permit system to the many-receptor case requires that a separate permit market be created *for each receptor*. The price prevailing in each of these markets would reflect the difficulty of meeting the ambient standard at that receptor. All other things being equal, permit markets associated with receptors in heavily congested areas could be expected to sustain higher prices than those affected by a relatively few emitters.

Since both the ambient permit system and the ambient charge system take location into account, when these policies are chosen, the marginal cost of emission control varies from location to location. Sources located in heavily populated portions of the region pay higher marginal costs, since their emissions have a greater impact on the receptors of interest. This variation of costs depending on location provides incentives for new sources when they are deciding where to locate. Since heavily polluted areas have high control costs, there is some incentive to locate elsewhere, even though pollution-control expenditures are only part of the costs a firm considers when deciding where to locate. For nonuniformly mixed pollution problems, *where* the emissions occur is important. Therefore, it is also important that the location component of the cost be internalized by relocating sources. With the ambient permit and charge systems, this is precisely what occurs.

OTHER POLICY DIMENSIONS

We have seen that there are two main pollution-control policy instruments that rely on economic incentives—charges and transferable permits. Both of these allow the control authority to distribute the responsibility for control in a cost-effective manner. The major difference between them discussed so far is that the appropriate charge can be determined only by an iterative trial-and-error process over time, while the permit price can be determined immediately by the market. Are there other differences?

One major additional difference concerns the manner in which these two systems react to changes in external circumstances in the absence of further decisions by the control authority. This is an important consideration, because bureaucratic procedures are notoriously sluggish, and changes in policies are usually rendered rather slowly.[9]

---

[8]Because any higher F_j reduces concentrations at several locations, not just at the *j*th receptor, not all selections of F_j which result in the ambient standards being met will result in cost-effective allocations. In the single receptor case the charge equilibrium is unique and equal to the cost-effective allocation. In the many receptor case there are many equilibria and they are not all cost effective. This is a further burden on the control authority of using an emission charge system as opposed to the permit system where the equilibrium is unique and cost effective. The permit system equilibrium is unique because all equilibria other than the cost-effective one involve higher costs and, therefore, further opportunities for trade.

[9]This is probably particularly true when the modification involves a change in the rate at which firms are charged for their emissions.

We shall consider three such circumstances—growth in the number of sources, inflation, and technological progress.

If the number of sources were to increase in a permit market, the demand for permits would shift to the right. Given a fixed supply of permits, the price would rise, as would the control costs, but the amount of emissions or pollution concentrations (in the case of the ambient permit system) would remain the same. If charges were being used, in the absence of additional action by the control authority the charge level would remain the same. This implies that the existing sources would control only what they would control in the absence of growth. Therefore, the arrival of new sources would cause a deterioration of air or water quality in the region. The costs of abatement would rise, since the costs of control paid by the new sources must be considered, but by a lesser amount than in a permit market, because of the lower amount of pollution being controlled.

With a permit system inflation in the costs of control would automatically result in higher permit prices, but with a charge system it would result in lower control. Essentially the real charge (the nominal charge adjusted for inflation) declines with inflation if the nominal charge remains the same.

We should not, however, conclude that, over time, charges always result in less control than permits. Suppose, for example, technological progress in designing pollution control equipment were to cause the marginal cost of abatement to fall. In a permit system this would result in lower prices and lower abatement costs but the same aggregate degree of control. With a charge system the amount controlled would actually increase and would, therefore, result in more control than a permit system which, prior to the fall in costs, controlled the same amount.

If the control authority were to adjust the charge in each of the above cases appropriately, the outcome would be identical to that achieved by a permit market. The permit market reacts automatically to these changes in circumstances, while the charge system requires a conscious administrative act to achieve the same result.

The second major difference between permits and charges involves the cost of being wrong. Suppose that we have very imprecise information on damages caused and avoidance costs incurred by various levels of pollution and yet we have to choose either a charge level or a permit level and live with it. What can be said about the relative merits of permits versus charges in the face of this uncertainty?

The answer depends upon the circumstances.[10] Permits offer a great deal of certainty about the quantity of emissions, while charges confer more certainty about the marginal cost of control. Therefore, permits are the only system which allow an ambient standard or an aggregate emission standard to be met with certainty. In other cases, however, when the objective is to minimize total costs (the sum of damage costs and control costs), permits would be preferred when the costs of being wrong are more

[10]A more formal and mathematical treatment of this issue can be found in M. Weitzman, "Prices vs. Quantities," *Review of Economic Studies,* XLI (1974): 447–91. A specific application to pollution control is presented in Z. Adar and J. M. Griffin "Uncertainty and Choice in Pollution Control Instruments," *Journal of Environmental Economics and Management,* Vol. III (1976): 178–88.

sensitive to changes in the quantity of emissions than to changes in the marginal cost of control. Charges would be preferred when control costs were more important. When would that be the case?

When the marginal damage curve is steeply sloped and the marginal cost curve is rather flat, certainty about emissions is more important than certainty over control costs. Smaller deviations of actual emissions from expected emissions can cause rather large deviations in damage costs, whereas control costs would be relatively insensitive to the degree of control. Permits would prevent large fluctuations in these damage costs and would, therefore, yield a lower cost of being wrong than charges.

Suppose, however, that the marginal control cost curve was steeply sloped, but the marginal damage curve was flat. Small changes in the degree of control would have a large effect on abatement costs but wouldn't affect damages very much. In this case it makes sense to rely on charges to give more precise control over control costs accepting the less dire consequences from possible fluctuations in damage costs.

These cases suggest that a preference either for permits or for charges in the face of uncertainty is not universal; it depends on the circumstances. Theory is not strong enough to dictate a choice. Empirical studies are necessary to establish a preference for particular situations. Example 14.1 discusses one such empirical study.

SUMMARY

In this chapter we have developed the conceptual framework needed to evaluate current approaches to pollution control policy. We have seen that there are many different types of pollutants, and different policy approaches are appropriate for each one.

Stock pollutants pose the most serious intertemporal problems. The efficient production of a commodity that generates a stock pollutant could be expected to decline over time. Eventually, a point would be reached when all of the pollutant would be recycled. After this point the amount of the pollutant in the environment would not increase. The amount already accumulated, however, would continue to cause damage perpetually, unless some natural process could reduce the amount of the pollutant over time.

The efficient amount of a fund pollutant was defined as the amount which minimizes the sum of damage and control costs. Using this definition we were able to derive two propositions of interest: (1) the efficient level of pollution would vary from region to region; and (2) the efficient level of pollution would not generally be zero, though in some particular circumstances it might.

Since pollution is a classic externality, markets will generally produce more than the efficient amount of both fund pollutants and stock pollutants. For both pollutants this will imply higher-than-efficient damages and lower-than-efficient control costs. For stock pollutants an excessive amount of pollution would build up in the environment, imposing a detrimental externality on future generations as well as on current generations.

The market would not provide any automatic ameliorating response to the accumulation of pollution as it would in the case of natural-resource scarcity. Firms attempting

EXAMPLE 14.1

Energy-Demand Uncertainty and the Cost of Being Wrong: Permits vs. Charges

The Four Corners area (where Utah, Arizona, New Mexico, and Colorado intersect) poses a classic confrontation between energy development and preserving the environment. Though sparsely populated, it is near several unique parks and wilderness areas and serves as the base for several large electrical generating stations which provide power to a large number of southwestern and western states.

One of the uncertainties affecting the air quality of the region is the amount that electricity demand will grow over the next several years. The higher the growth in demand, the more uncontrolled emissions. The higher the level of uncontrolled emissions, the more control that has to be placed on each source in order to preserve air quality. If, in incorrect anticipation of too high growth, the regulators impose too stringent a degree of control, then control costs will be excessively high. If controls are established at too low a level, damage costs would be too high. There are costs associated with each type of mistake.

In a doctoral dissertation submitted at Stanford, Charles Kolstad [1982] used this setting to investigate whether regulators would be better off using a permit system or an emission charge system to protect air quality in the face of this uncertainty. Capturing the control cost and damage functions[1] in a computer simulation model, he calculated the cost of being wrong if regulators chose permits or if they chose charges. His findings were completely in accord with our analysis:

> For constant or declining marginal damage, emission [charges] yield total costs (including damage) 5–10% lower than for [permits]. However, for even slightly upward sloping marginal damage, [permits] yield roughly 20% lower costs than emission [charges] [p. 206].

Since the increasing marginal cost case is probably the most likely for sulfur oxide emissions, the use of permits in the Four Corners would seem preferable.[2]

[1]To get around this inability to obtain a precise damage function, Kolstad used several different ones to see how sensitive the results were to various specifications of this function.

[2]See Ronald Krumm and Ralph Graves, "Morbidity and Pollution: Model Specification Analysis for Time-Series Data on Hospital Admissions," *Journal of Environmental Economics and Management,* 9 (December 1982): 311–327.

Source: Charles Kolstad, *Economic and Regulatory Efficiency* (Los Alamos, N.M.: Los Alamos National Laboratory, 1982), Report # LA-9458-T (Thesis).

to unilaterally control their pollution are placed at a competitive disadvantage. Hence the case for some sort of government intervention is particularly strong for pollution control.

Although the damage estimates are not sufficiently precise to base pollution-control policy completely on them, we can use economic analysis to define the most cost-effective ways of meeting predetermined pollution targets.

In the case of uniformly mixed-fund pollutants, uniform emission charges or an emission-permit system could be used to attain the cost-effective allocation even when the control authority has no information whatsoever on control costs. Uniform emission standards would not, except by coincidence, be cost effective. In addition, either permits or charges would stimulate more technological progress in pollution control than would emission standards.

Policies to control nonuniformly mixed pollutants must take the location of the emissions into account as well as the amount. This can be accomplished with either an appropriately designed ambient permit system or ambient charge; either one can result in a cost-effective allocation of the control responsibility even when the control authority has no information on control costs. A policy based on emission standards cannot.

Policies ignoring these distinctions are not cost effective. An excessively narrow focus on local pollution can make the regional pollution problem worse. Similarly, the use of a uniform emission charge or an emission permit system (which are appropriate for uniformly mixed pollutants!) to allocate the responsibility for controlling a local or regional nonuniformly mixed surface pollutant will *not* be cost effective whenever transfer coefficients differ.

There are differences between the permit approach and a charge approach. They respond differently to growth in the number of sources, to inflation, to technological change, and to uncertainty. As we shall see in the next few chapters, some countries (primarily in Europe) have chosen to rely on emission charges while others (primarily the United States) have chosen to rely on permits. We can now use this framework to evaluate the rather different policy approaches that have been taken toward the major sources of pollution.

FURTHER READING

Baumol, W. J., and W. E. Oates. *Economics, Environmental Policy and the Quality of Life* (Englewood Cliffs, N.J.: Prentice-Hall, 1979). An excellent undergraduate text dealing mainly with pollution control.

Baumol, W. J., and W. E. Oates. *The Theory of Environmental Policy* (Englewood Cliffs, N.J.: Prentice-Hall, 1975). A classic on the economic analysis of externalities. Accessible only to those with a thorough familiarity with multivariate calculus.

Burrows, Paul. *The Economic Theory of Pollution Control* (Cambridge, Mass.: MIT Press, 1980). This summary of the economic theory of pollution control is compact, tightly written, but quite comprehensive. Suitable for those who have had only a principles course in microeconomics, as well as those with more economics experience.

Organization for Economic Co-operation and Development. *Pollution Charges in Practice* (Paris: OECD, 1980). A comprehensive survey of the application of pollution charges for air and water pollution control primarily, but not exclusively, in Western Europe.

Tietenberg, T. H., *Emissions Trading: An Exercise in Reforming Pollution Policy* (Washington: Resources for the Future, Inc., 1985). An examination of the use of marketable permits to control pollution in principle and in practice.

ADDITIONAL REFERENCES

Anderson, Frederick R., et al. *Environmental Improvement Through Economic Incentives* (Baltimore: Johns Hopkins University Press for Resources for the Future, Inc., 1977).

Barnett, Andy H., and Bruce Yandle, Jr. "Allocating Environmental Resources," *Public Finance,* Vol. 28 (1973): 11–19.

Collinge, R. A., and W. E. Oates. "Efficiency in Pollution Control in the Short and Long Runs: A System of Rental Emission Permits," *Canadian Journal of Economics,* Vol. 15 (May, 1982): 347–54.

Dales, J. H. *Pollution, Property and Prices* (Toronto: University Press, 1968).

Hahn, Robert W., and Robert G. Noll. "Designing a Market for Tradable Emissions Permits" in Wesley A. Magat, ed., *Reform of Environmental Regulation* (Cambridge, Mass.: Ballinger Publishing Company, 1982).

Kneese, Allen V., and Charles L. Schultze. *Pollution, Prices, and Public Policy* (Washington, D.C.: The Brookings Institution, 1975).

Lyon, R. M., "Auctions and Alternative Procedures for Allocating Pollution Rights," *Land Economics,* Vol. 58 (February, 1982): 16–32.

Montgomery, David W. "Markets in Licenses and Efficient Pollution Control Programs," *Journal of Economic Theory,* Vol. 5 (December, 1972): 395–418.

Orr, Lloyd. "Incentive for Innovation as the Basis for Effluent Charge Strategy," *The American Economic Review,* Vol. 66 (May, 1976): 441–47.

Plourde, C.G. "A Model of Waste Accumulation and Disposal," *Canadian Journal of Economics,* Vol. V (February, 1982): 119–25.

Weitzman, M. "Prices vs. Quantities," *Review of Economic Studies,* XLI (1974): 447–91.

DISCUSSION QUESTIONS

1. In his book *What Price Incentives?* Steven Kelman suggests that from an ethical point of view, the use of economic incentives (such as emission charges or transferable discharge permits) in environmental policy is undesirable. He argues that transforming our mental image of the environment from a sanctified preserve to a marketable commodity has detrimental effects not only on our use of the environment but also on our attitude toward it. His point is that applying economic incentives to environmental policy weakens and cheapens our traditional values toward the environment.

(a) Consider the effects of economic-incentive systems on prices paid by the poor, on employment, and on the speed of compliance with pollution-control laws—as well as the Kelman arguments. Are economic-incentive systems more or less ethically justifiable than the traditional regulatory approach?

(b) Kelman seems to feel that because transferable emission permits automatically prevent environmental degradation, they are more ethically desirable than emission charges. Do you agree? Why or why not?

PROBLEMS

1. Two firms can control emissions at the following marginal costs: $MC_1 = \$200q_1$, $MC_2 = \$100q_2$, where q_1 and q_2 are, respectively, the amount of emissions reduced by the first and second firms. Assume that with no control at all, each firm would be emitting 20 units of emissions or a total of 40 units for both firms.

(a) Compute the cost-effective allocation of control responsibility if a total reduction of 21 units of emissions is necessary.

(b) Compute the cost-effective allocation of control responsibility if the ambient standard is 27 ppm, and the transfer coefficients which translate a unit of emissions into a ppm concentration at the receptor are, respectively, $a_1 = 2.0$ and $a_2 = 1.0$.

2. Assume that the control authority wanted to reach its objective in 1(a) above using an emission charge system.

(a) What per-unit charge should be imposed?

(b) How much revenue would the control authority collect?

CHAPTER FIFTEEN

Control of Stationary-Source Local Air Pollution

*When choosing between two evils, I always like to try the one
I've never tried before.*
MAE WEST, Actress

INTRODUCTION

Attaining and maintaining clean air is an exceedingly difficult policy task. There are an estimated 27,000 major stationary sources of air pollution in the United States. These sources involve many distinct production processes that emit many different types of pollutants. The resulting damages range from minimal effects on plants and vegetation to the possible modification of the earth's climate.

Congress enacted the first legislation to grapple with these problems in 1955. Called the Air Pollution Control Act of 1955, that law mainly subsidized research into air-pollution problems. The following fourteen years ushered in a period of vigorous legislative activity.

Yet, the amount of legislation is a misleading indicator of what was actually accomplished. It was not until 1967 that the federal government began to play much of a role other than subsidizing research, and even the 1967 law was mainly an attempt to cajole the states into action. The common thread woven by the statutes during this period was a reliance on cooperation from the states.

By 1970 the national government had discovered that this reliance was misplaced; state cooperation was not forthcoming. Fearing that the imposition of strict controls on industrial sources would place them at a competitive disadvantage in their quest for increases in employment and taxable industrial property, states were unwilling to take the lead in air pollution control policy.

In this atmosphere of frustration, the Clean Air Act Amendments of 1970 were passed. They set a bold new direction which has been retained and refined by subsequent acts. By virtue of that act, the federal government assumed a much larger and much more vigorous direct role. The U.S. Environmental Protection Agency (EPA) was created to implement and oversee this massive attempt to control the injection of substances into our air. Individually tailored strategies were created to deal with mobile and stationary sources. These strategies depend in part on whether the type of pollutant being controlled is a "criteria" pollutant or a "hazardous" pollutant.

CRITERIA POLLUTANTS

The characteristics shared by criteria pollutants are that they are relatively common substances, are found in almost all parts of the country, and are presumed to be dangerous only in high concentrations. They are listed, along with their chief associated damages and sources, in Table 15.1. These pollutants are called *criteria pollutants* because the act requires EPA to produce "criteria documents" to be used in setting acceptable standards for these pollutants. These documents summarize and evaluate all of the existing research on the various health and environmental effects associated with these pollutants. The central focus of the Clean Air Act during the 1970s was on criteria pollutants.

The Command-and-Control Policy Framework

In Chapter 14 several possible approaches to controlling pollution were described and analyzed in theoretical terms. The historical approach to air pollution control has been based primarily on emission standards. It has been a traditional command-and-control (CAC) approach. In this section we shall outline the specific nature of this approach, analyze it from an efficiency and cost-effectiveness perspective, and show how a series of recent reforms based on economic incentives has worked to rectify some of these deficiencies.

For each of the criteria pollutants, EPA has established ambient air-quality standards. These standards set legal ceilings on the allowable concentration of the pollutant in the outdoor air averaged over a specified time period. Many pollutants have the standard defined in terms of a long-term average (defined normally as an annual average) and a short-term average (such as a three-hour average). These short-term averages can usually be exceeded no more than once a year. These standards have to be met everywhere, though as a practical matter they are monitored at a large number of specific locations. As Example 4.4 pointed out, control costs can be quite sensitive to the level of these short-term averages.

The *primary standard* is designed to protect human health. This is the first standard to be determined, and it has the earliest deadlines for compliance. All pollutants have a primary standard. The *secondary standard* is designed to protect other aspects of human welfare from those pollutants having separate effects. Currently, only sulfur oxides and particulates have separate secondary standards. Protection is afforded by the secondary standard for aesthetics (particularly visibility), physical objects (houses, monuments, and so on), and vegetation.

When a separate secondary standard exists, it is more stringent than the primary standard. Once the deadline for compliance with the secondary standard has been reached, it, rather than the primary standard, governs the degree of required control. The existing primary and secondary standards are given in Table 15.2.

The ambient standards are required by statute to be determined without any consideration given to the costs of meeting them. They are supposed to be set at a level sufficient to protect even the most sensitive members of the population.

While EPA is responsible for defining the ambient standards, the primary responsibility for ensuring that the ambient air-quality standards are met falls on the state control agencies. They exercise this responsibility by developing and executing an acceptable state implementation plan (SIP), which must be approved by EPA. This plan divides the state up into separate air-quality control regions. (There are special procedures for handling regions that cross state borders, such as Metropolitan New York.)

The SIP spells out for each control region the procedures and timetables for meeting local ambient standards and for abatement of the effects of locally emitted pollutants on other states. The degree of control required depends on the severity of the pollution problem in each of the control regions.

By 1975 it had become apparent that, despite some major gains in air quality, many areas had not met and would not meet the ambient standards by the statutory deadlines. Therefore, in the 1977 Amendments to the Clean Air Act, Congress extended the deadline for attainment of all primary (health-related) ambient standards to 1982 with further extensions to 1987 possible for ozone and carbon monoxide. The amendments also required EPA to designate all areas not meeting the original deadlines as *nonattainment regions*.

The areas receiving this designation were subjected to particularly stringent controls. After the 1977 Amendments were passed, all portions of state implementation plans applying to nonattainment regions had to be revised by the state control authorities to ensure compliance with the new deadlines. To prod the states into action, Congress gave EPA the power to halt the construction of major new or modified pollution sources and to deny federal sewage and transportation grants for any state not submitting a plan showing precisely how and when attainment would be reached.

State implementation plans in nonattainment regions must include a permit program for newly constructed large sources or large sources that have undergone some major modification. Permits cannot be granted to these sources unless the state can demonstrate that emissions resulting from commencing or expanding operations would not jeopardize the region's progress toward attainment. The state can satisfy this requirement by controlling existing sources to a suffciently high degree that progress can be demonstrated even with the new sources in operation.

A second condition for the permit to be issued stipulates that all major new or modified sources in nonattainment areas must also control their own emissions to the *lowest achievable emission rate* (LAER). The LAER is defined as the lowest emission rate achieved by any similar source anywhere in the country or the lowest emission rate included in any state implementation plan *whether or not any source is currently achieving that rate*. This part of the law was designed to ensure that only the most stringent controls would be used by any source locating in a nonattainment area. It

TABLE 15.1 Criteria Pollutants

Pollutant	Health effects	Welfare effects
Sulfur Dioxide (SO₂) —*a gas*	Aggravates symptoms of heart and lung disease, obstructs breathing (particularly in combination with other pollutants); increases incidence of acute respiratory diseases including coughs and colds, asthma, bronchitis and emphysema.	Toxic to plants; can destroy paint pigments, erode statues, corrode metals, harm textiles; impairs visibility; precursor to acid rain.
Total Suspended Particulates (TSP) — *solid particles or liquid droplets*	Can carry heavy metals and cancer-causing organic compounds into the deepest, most sensitive parts of the lung; with SO₂, can increase incidence and severity of respiratory diseases.	Obscure visibility; dirty materials and buildings; corrode metals.
Carbon Monoxide — *a gas*	Interferes with blood's ability to absorb oxygen, thus impairing perception and thinking, slowing reflexes and causing drowsiness, unconsciousness and death. CO inhaled by pregnant women may threaten the unborn child's growth and mental development. Long-term exposure is suspected of aggravating arteriosclerosis and vascular disease.	
Nitrogen Oxides (NOₓ) —*a gas*	High concentrations can be fatal; at lower levels, can increase susceptibility to viral infections such as influenza, irritate the lungs, and cause bronchitis and pneumonia.	Toxic to vegetation, reducing plant growth and seed fertility when present in high concentrations; causes brown discoloration of the atmosphere; is a precursor to acid rain and ozone.
Ozone—*a gas*	Irritates mucous membranes of respiratory system, causing coughing, choking, impaired lung function, reduced resistance to colds and serious diseases such as pneumonia; can aggravate chronic heart disease, asthma, bronchitis, emphysema.	Corrodes materials such as rubber and paint; can injure and kill many crops, trees, shrubs.

Major sources	Controls
Electricity generating stations, smelters, petroleum refineries, industrial boilers.	Switching to low sulfur fuel, flue gas scrubbers.
Industrial processes and combustion; about 7% from natural, largely uncontrollable, sources (windblown dust, forest fires, volcanoes).	Most common method: electrostatic precipitators in utility boilers, to trap particulates by charging them with electricity so they will adhere to retaining magnets. Other methods: cyclone collectors, bag-houses, wet scrubbers.
Motor vehicles.	Engine modifications to achieve more complete combustion; use of catalytic converters.
Electric utility boilers and motor vehicles	Most difficult pollutant to control. "Low NO_x burners" are one method for reducing emissions from new and existing industrial boilers. They use a *staged combustion* process that varies the fuel-air mixture. Other techniques under investigation: *fuel denitrogenation* to produce cleaner fuel prior to burning; *catalytic combustion* in industrial boilers; industrial *flue gas treatment; three-way catalytic converters* for automobiles change exhaust gases into molecular nitrogen, CO_2 and water vapor.
Formed by chemical reactions in the atmosphere from two other airborne pollutants—NO_x and HC.	Strategies are directed at controlling NO_x and HC.

(continued)

TABLE 15.1 Criteria Pollutants *(Continued)*

Pollutant	Health effects	Welfare effects
Lead—*a metal*	Affects blood-forming, reproductive, nervous and kidney systems; can accumulate in bone and other tissues, posing a health hazard even after exposure has ended. Children are particularly susceptible, and behavioral abnormalities including hyperactivity and decreased learning ability have recently been demonstrated.	

Source: League of Women Voters, *Current Focus: Blueprint for Clean Air*, Pub. 222 (Washington, D.C.: League of Women Voters Education Fund, 1981).

TABLE 15.2 National Primary and Secondary Ambient Air Quality Standards

Pollutant	Primary Standard*	Secondary Standard
Sulfur Oxides	a. 80 $\mu g/m^3$ (0.03 p.p.m.) annual arithmetic mean b. 365 $\mu g/m^3$ (0.14 p.p.m.) maximum 24-hour concentration not to be exceeded more than once a year	1,300 $\mu g/m^3$ (0.5 p.p.m.) 3-hour concentration
Particular Matter	a. 75 $\mu g/m^3$—annual geometric mean b. 260 $\mu g/m^3$—maximum 24-hour concentration not to be exceeded more than once per year	a. 60 $\mu g/m^3$ annual geometric mean b. 150 $\mu g/m^3$—maximum 24-hour concentration not to be exceeded more than once per year
Carbon Monoxide	a. 10 mg/m^3 (9 p.p.m.) maximum 8-hour concentration not to be exceeded more than once per year b. 40 mg/m^3 (35 p.p.m.) maximum 1-hour concentration not to be exceeded more than once per year	No separate secondary standard
Ozone	235 $\mu g/m^3$ (0.12 p.p.m.) maximum average hourly concentration not to be exceeded more than once a year	No separate secondary standard
Nitrogen Dioxide	100 $\mu g/m^3$ (0.05 p.p.m.) annual arithmetic mean	No separate secondary standard
Lead	1.5 $\mu g/m^3$ arithmetic mean averaged over a calendar quarter	No separate secondary standard

*Guide to measurements: $\mu g/m^3$ is micrograms per cubic meter; mg/m^3 is milligrams per cubic meter; and p.p.m. is parts per million.

Source: *Code of Federal Regulations,* Volume 40, Parts 50.4, 50.6, 50.7, 50.8, 50.9, 50.11 and 50.12 (1985).

Major sources	Controls
Motor vehicle exhaust; lead smelting and processing plants.	Major strategy: to phase out use of leaded gasoline.

is controversial because it implies that new sources could be forced to use technologies which have never been commercially tested.

Regions with air quality at least as high as the standards by the original deadline were subject to another set of controls known collectively as the PSD policy. This policy derives its name from its objective, namely the *Prevention of Significant Deterioration* of the air in cleaner regions. The origin of this policy is found in the preamble to the 1970 Clean Air Act, which stated as an objective: "to protect and enhance the quality of the nation's air."

In 1972 EPA was successfully sued by the Sierra Club for promulgating regulations that did not ensure that this objective would be met. The system of ambient standards prevented the deterioration of the air *beyond* the standard, but air significantly cleaner than the standard would normally have deteriorated until it reached the standard. Following the court's decision, EPA adopted a PSD program in 1974, and the 1977 Amendments to the Clean Air Act continued a modified version of that program.

The PSD regulations specify the maximum allowable increases or increments in pollution concentration beyond some baseline. To allow some variability in the size of these increments, Congress specified that PSD regions be subdivided into three types of areas with each type allowed a different increment. Class I areas include national parks and wilderness areas. The increments for these regions are the smallest. Practically any degradation in these areas is considered significant and is disallowed.

All other areas were initially designated as Class II regions, where a modest increment is allowed. States may redesignate any Class II region as a Class I region (thus allowing less future deterioration) or as a Class III region (allowing more). Class III regions are allowed the largest increment. In no case, however, can pollutant concentrations in any PSD region rise above the governing ambient standard.

New sources seeking to locate in PSD regions must secure permits. As a condition of securing their permits, these sources must install the *best available control technology* (BACT). The specific technologies that satisfy this requirement are determined by states on a case-by-case basis. Each new source permitted consumes a portion of the allowable increment. Once the increment has been completely consumed, no further deterioration of the air is allowed in that area even if the air is cleaner than required by the prevailing ambient standard. Thus, where the PSD increments are binding, for all practical purposes they define a tertiary standard varying in magnitude from region to region.

In addition to defining the ambient standards and requiring states to define BACT and LAER emission standards, the EPA, itself, has established national uniform emission standards for new sources of criteria pollutants or major modifications of existing sources.

The progress in defining those standards has been very slow. The standards governing new and modified sources of criteria pollutants are called the *New Source Performance Standards* (NSPS), and they were designed to merely serve as a floor for BACT and LAER determinations by the states. Congress wanted to ensure that all sources would have to meet a minimum standard regardless of where it was located. This was seen as a way to prevent states from caving in as industry attempted to play one state off against another in its attempt to seek the lowest possible emission standards. Neither LAER nor BACT can be lower than the new-source performance standards.

Simply stating the regulations is not enough. They must be enforced with appropriate sanctions whenever noncompliance occurs. Prior to the 1977 amendments, noncompliance was a significant problem, with delays of up to six years common. Because of this situation, in 1977 Congress established the *noncompliance penalty* as a means of reducing the profitability in delaying compliance.

Without sanctions, the source benefits from delaying compliance. The equipment purchases necessary to ensure compliance are expensive and add nothing to profits. In addition, court action is slow and sometimes sympathetic toward business. The noncompliance penalty is designed to harmonize these private incentives with the social objectives pursued by the act.

Patterned after a system first used in Connecticut, the magnitude of noncompliance penalty is determined by the economic value of delay to the source. Any economic gains received by the source as a result of noncompliance are included in the penalty and are transferred to the EPA; they no longer accrue to the source. The initial indications are that the existence of this penalty has cut delays by 30 to 40 percent.[1]

The final characteristic of the Clean Air Act that we shall discuss is that it rules out tailoring the degree of control to the prevailing meteorological conditions. All strategies must achieve better air quality through emission reductions stringent enough to ensure compliance even in quite adverse conditions.

The Efficiency of the Command-and-Control Approach

Efficiency presumes that the ambient standards are set at efficient levels. To ascertain whether or not the current standards are efficient, it is necessary to inquire into four aspects of the standard-setting process: (1) the threshold concept on which the stan-

---

[1]See Sue Anne Batey Blackman and William J. Baumol, "Modified Fiscal Incentives in Environmental Policy," *Land Economics* 56 (November 1980): 419.

dards are based, (2) the level of the standard, (3) the choice of uniform standards over standards more tailored to the regions involved, and (4) the timing of emission flows.

The Threshold Concept.   Some basis is needed for setting the ambient standard. Since the Clean Air Act prohibits the balancing of costs and benefits, some alternative criterion must be used. For the primary (health-related) standard, this criterion is known as the *health threshold.* The standard is to be defined with a margin of safety sufficiently high that no adverse health effects would be suffered by any member of the population as long as the air quality was at least as good as the standards. This approach presumes the existence of a threshold such that concentrations above that level produce adverse health affects, but concentrations below it produce none.

If the threshold concept were valid, the marginal damage function would be zero until the threshold was reached and would be positive at higher concentrations. The belief that the actual damage function has this shape is not consistent with the evidence, because we are now learning that adverse health effects can occur at pollution levels lower than the ambient standards.[2] The standard that produces no adverse health effects among the general population (which, of course, includes especially susceptible groups) is probably zero or close to it. It is certainly lower than the established ambient standards. There is a difference between what the standards purport to accomplish and what they actually accomplish.

The Level of the Standard.   The fact that no threshold exists complicates the analysis. Some other basis must be used for establishing the level at which the standard should be established. Efficiency would dictate setting the standard in order to maximize the net benefit, which includes a consideration of costs as well as benefits.

The current policy explicitly excludes costs from consideration in setting the ambient standards. Costs are allowed to enter the process only when the policy instruments used to meet ambient standards are being defined. It is difficult to imagine that the process of setting the ambient standard would yield an efficient outcome when it is prohibited from considering one of the key elements of that outcome!

Unfortunately, for reasons which were discussed in some detail in Chapter 4, our current benefit measurements are not sufficiently reliable as to permit the identification of the efficient level with any confidence. Freeman [1982] for example, in his extensive survey of the evidence concludes that the benefits (in 1978 dollars) derived from controlling stationary sources lie somewhere in the interval from $4.8 billion to $49.4 billion per year with a most likely point estimate of $21.4 billion per year. This can be compared to a cost of stationary-source control of around $9.0 billion per year. These figures suggest that a high degree of confidence can be attached to the belief that government intervention is justified, but they provide no evidence whatsoever on whether current policy is efficient. A similar fate met a recent attempt to use benefit/cost analysis to ascertain the efficiency of the particulate standard (Example 15.1).

---

[2]See, for example, the research by Lave and Seskin which discovered a positive association between pollution and mortality even in those cities meeting the primary standards. Lester B. Lave and Eugene P. Seskin, *Air Pollution and Human Health* (Baltimore: Johns Hopkins University Press, 1977).

EXAMPLE 15.1

Net Benefit Analysis of the Particulate Ambient Standard

Although EPA is precluded from considering benefit/cost analysis in setting ambient standards, it is not precluded from having the studies done. One such study was done as part of the process of considering whether to change the stringency or the form of the particulate ambient standard.

The purpose of the study was to aggregate on a national basis estimates of various forms of damage that would be done by particulate emissions, including health effects, soiling and materials damage, and visibility effects, under various regulatory regimes. The aggregation brought together a number of different studies, each relying on different data and different valuation techniques. These aggregate benefit estimates were then combined with cost information to produce net benefit information for each of the considered options.

Aggregating these rather different studies posed some problems. First, they were not all of equal quality. Some had gone through extensive peer review while others hadn't. Second, it was not clear whether the studies could legitimately be added together without double accounting some of the benefits. For example, the property and wage studies may indirectly be valuing the health effects that are more directly valued by epidemiological studies.

To grapple with these problems Mathtech, Inc., the contractor on the study, did the net benefit analysis on a variety of regulatory options separately for each

---

Uniformity. The same primary and secondary standards apply to all parts of the country. No account is taken of the number of people exposed, the sensitivity of the local ecology, or the costs of compliance in various areas. All of these would have some effect on the efficient standard and efficiency would, therefore, dictate different standards for different regions. In general, the evidence suggests that the inefficiencies associated with unformity are greatest in the rural areas, but we shall leave a full description and interpretation of that evidence for Chapter 20.

The PSD program does introduce some variability by establishing more stringent standards for regions with the cleanest air. If national parks and other Class I areas are especially sensitive to pollution, that portion of the program could represent a move toward efficiency. Since states have some flexibility in choosing which portions of their area would be designated as Class II and Class III regions, it is conceivable, but by no means obvious, that they would make efficient choices.

Furthermore, it remains true that there are no provisions for any area to be allowed to experience air-quality levels worse than the primary and secondary standards.

of six aggregation procedures. Unfortunately they discovered that the ranking of standards in terms of economic efficiency was very sensitive to the different benefit estimation procedures employed. For the most restrictive accounting of benefits all changes would lead to lower net benefits than merely continuing the current policy. For less restrictive benefit aggregation procedures, net benefits were highest for much more stringent standards.

The study also compared the net benefits from some of the more restrictive ambient standards depending upon whether the implementation deadline was 7 years or 9 years. For this aspect the results were conclusive—the 9-year implementation period produced higher net benefits.

Two insights on the use of benefit/cost analysis can be carried away from this specific example. First the application of benefit/cost techniques to discover the efficient set of ambient standards is subject to a large number of uncertainties; the notion that analysts can derive a single, generally agreed-upon net benefit calculation for a specific regulatory option is naive. Second, despite these uncertainties, a great deal can be learned from the analysis even if it doesn't produce a single definitive answer. In this specific case, not only was the evidence on the implementation deadline unambiguous, but the analysis found that some regulatory options were dominated by others; armed with this evidence serious consideration can be focused on the undominated options.

Source: MATHTECH, INC., "Benefit and Net Benefit Analysis of Alternative National Ambient Air Quality Standards for Particulate Matter," Volume I of a report prepared for the Benefits Analysis Program of the U.S. Environmental Protection Agency (March, 1983).

Timing of Emission Flows. Because concentrations are important for criteria pollutants, the timing of emissions is an important policy concern. Emissions clustered in time are as troublesome as emissions clustered in space. How do we handle those relatively rare but devastating occasions when thermal inversions prevent the normal dispersion and dilution of the pollutants? From an economic efficiency point of view, the most obvious approach is to tailor the degree of control to the circumstances. Stringent control would be exercised when meteorological conditions were relatively stagnant and less control would be applied under normal circumstances. The strong stand against intermittent controls in the Clean Air Act, however, rules this out.

It turns out that a reliance on a constant degree of control, rather than allowing intermittent controls, raises compliance costs substantially, particularly when the required degree of control is high. In perhaps the earliest empirical study soundly based on economic theory, Teller [1970] examined the costs of controlling sulfur dioxide in Nashville, Tennessee, through fuel substitution. He specifically examined two strategies: constant abatement, which requires the same degree of control over time; and forecasted abatement, which allows the degree of control to be tailored to forecasted weather conditions.

Both strategies achieve compliance with the ambient standards, but forecasted control requires less total emission reduction. His results indicate that constant abatement would be five times more expensive than forecasted abatement.

Cost-Effectiveness of the Command-and-Control Approach

Though there are reasons for believing that the current levels of the ambient standards are not efficient, the evidence on which this conclusion is based is plagued by uncertainties. It is not possible to definitively state just how inefficient they are.

Cost-effectiveness is based on somewhat more solid evidence. Though it does not allow us to shed any light on whether a particular ambient standard is efficient or not, cost-effectiveness studies do allow us to see whether the command-and-control policy described above has resulted in the ambient standards being met in the least costly manner possible.

The theory covered in Chapter 14 makes it clear that the CAC strategy cannot be cost-effective. What it does not make clear, however, is the degree to which this strategy diverges from the least-cost ideal. If the divergence is small, the proponents of reform would not likely be able to overcome the inertia of the status quo. If the divergence is large, the case for reform is stronger.

The cost-effectiveness of the CAC approach depends on local circumstances such as prevailing meteorology, the locational configuration of sources, stack heights, and how costs vary with the amount controlled. Several simulation models capable of dealing with these complexities have now been constructed for a number of different pollutants in a variety of airsheds (Table 15.3).

Since for a number of reasons the estimated costs cannot be directly compared across studies, it is appropriate to develop a means of comparing them that minimizes the comparability problems. One such technique, the one we have chosen, involves calculating the ratio of the CAC allocation costs to the lowest cost of meeting the same objective for each study. A ratio equal to 1.0 implies that the CAC allocation is cost-effective. By subtracting 1.0 from the ratio in the table, it is possible to interpret the remainder as the percentage increase in cost from the least cost ideal due to relying on the CAC system.

Of the nine reported comparisons, eight find that the CAC policy costs at least 78 percent more than the least-cost allocation. If we omit the Hahn and Noll (1982) study (for reasons discussed in the next two paragraphs), the study involving the *smallest* cost savings (sulfur dioxide control in the Lower Delaware Valley) finds that the CAC allocation results in abatement costs that are 78 percent higher than necessary to meet the standards. In the Chicago study, the CAC costs are estimated to be 14 times as expensive as necessary, while in the Lower Delaware Valley they are estimated to be 22 times more expensive than necessary.

The one study (Hahn and Noll, 1982) finding that the CAC strategy was close to being cost-effective was somewhat unique in a couple of respects. Because we can learn something from this study about the conditions under which CAC policies may not be far off the mark, it is worth a bit of time to subject it to close scrutiny.

The city studied by Hahn and Noll, Los Angeles, has a large sulfate problem, necessitating a very high degree of control. In effect, virtually every source is forced to control as much as is economically feasible. Because the menu of options in essence consists of a single feasible allocation, all policies must ultimately arrive at this allocation.[3]

Does the degree of cost excess associated with the CAC approach depend on the stringency of the ambient standard being met? The evidence seems to suggest that it does depend on the stringency, but in rather well defined ways. Atkinson and Lewis (1974, p. 245) find, for example, that within a middle range of possible ambient standards the divergence between the CAC allocation and the least-cost allocation becomes larger as the ambient standard target becomes harder to meet. Concentrating on the most stringent range of control (as opposed to the middle ranges of control examined by Atkinson and Lewis), however, two authors have found the relative divergence between the CAC and least-cost allocations declines as the ambient standard becomes tougher to meet. Spofford (1984, pp. 57, 66, and 77) finds this to be the case for both particulates and sulfur oxides, while Maloney and Yandle (1984, Table V) find it to be true for hydrocarbon control. This evidence suggests that the CAC air pollution policy approximates the least-cost allocation only at sufficiently high degrees of control that any control flexibility is effectively eliminated.

THE EMISSIONS TRADING PROGRAM[4]

Stripped to its bare essentials, the Clean Air Act's approach toward stationary sources involves the specification of emission standards (legal ceilings) on all major emission sources. These standards are imposed on a large number of specific emission points such as stacks, vents, or storage tanks.

The emissions trading program attempts to inject more flexibility into the manner in which the objectives of the Clean Air Act are met. Sources are encouraged to change the mix of control technologies envisioned in the standards as long as air quality is improved or at least not adversely affected by the change. The program is implemented by means of four separate policies, linked by a common element known as the emis-

[3]Hahn and Noll also suggest that the California Air Resources Board has specifically used its multi-million dollar budget in part to promulgate cost-effective emission standards. Therefore this board may be atypically cost-effective in its approach to a CAC strategy due to both the amount of resources at its disposal and its inclination to use them to pursue cost-effective allocations of control responsibility.

[4]This section relies heavily on T. H. Tietenberg, *Emissions Trading: An Exercise in Reforming Pollution Policy* (Washington: Resources for the Future, Inc., 1985).

TABLE 15.3 Empirical Studies of Air Pollution Control

Study and year	Pollutants covered	Geographic area
Atkinson and Lewis (1974)	Particulates	St. Louis Metro. Area
Roach, et al. (1981)	Sulfur dioxide	Four Corners in Utah, Colorado, Arizona, and New Mexico
Hahn and Noll (1982)	Sulfates	Los Angeles
Krupnick (1983)	Nitrogen dioxide	Baltimore
Seskin, Anderson, and Reid (1983)	Nitrogen dioxide	Chicago
McGartland (1984)	Particulates	Baltimore
Spofford (1984)	Sulfur dioxide	Lower Delaware Valley
	Particulates	Lower Delaware Valley
Maloney and Yandle (1984)	Hydrocarbons	All domestic DuPont plants

Definitions: CAC = Command and control, the traditional regulatory approach.
   SIP = State implementation plan.
   RACT = Reasonably available control technologies, a set of standards imposed on existing sources in nonattainment areas.

References: See references at the end of the chapter.

Source: T.H. Tietenberg, *Emissions Trading: An Exercise in Reforming Pollution Policy* (Washington: Resources for the Future, 1985) 42–43.

sion reduction credit. The emission reduction credit is the currency used in trading among emission points, while the offset, bubble, emissions banking, and netting policies govern how the currency can be spent.

The Components of the Program

The Emission Reduction Credit.   Should any source decide to control any emission point to a higher degree than necessary to fulfill its legal obligations, it can apply to the control authority for certification of the excess control as an emission reduction credit. Certified credits can be banked or used in the bubble, offset, or netting programs. To receive certification, the emission reduction must be: (1) surplus, (2) enforceable, (3) permanent, and (4) quantifiable.

The Offset Policy.   The offset policy was established to resolve a conflict between economic growth and progress toward meeting the ambient standards in nonattainment areas. The dilemma posed by this conflict involved how new or expanded sources could

CAC benchmark	Assumed pollutant type	Ratio of CAC cost to least cost
SIP regulations	Nonuniformly mixed	6.00
SIP regulations	Nonuniformly mixed	4.25
California emission standards	Nonuniformly mixed	1.07
Proposed RACT regulations	Nonuniformly mixed	5.96
Proposed RACT regulations	Nonuniformly mixed	14.4
SIP regulations	Nonuniformly mixed	4.18
Uniform percentage reduction	Nonuniformly mixed	1.78
Uniform percentage reduction	Nonuniformly mixed	22.0
Uniform percentage reduction	Uniformly mixed	4.15

be accommodated while meeting the statutory requirement that the ambient standards be met as expeditiously as possible. Since these sources would add emissions to the region, some means of offsetting them had to be found.

The offset policy allows qualified new or expanding sources to commence operations in a nonattainment area provided they acquire sufficient emission reduction credits from existing sources. By buying the credits, new sources, in effect, finance emission controls undertaken by existing sources. This approach was designed to ensure that regional emissions would be lower after the source began operations (counting the acquired emission reduction credits) than before. Major new or modified sources are qualified to participate in this program only if they control their own emissions to the degree required by the LAER standard and all existing major sources owned or operated by the applicant in the same state as the proposed source are in compliance with their legal control responsibilities.

The Bubble Policy. The bubble policy allows existing sources to use emission reduction credits to satisfy their SIP control responsibilities. For example, existing sources in nonattainment areas can meet their assigned RACT standards either by adopting the control technology used to define the standard or by adopting some technology that emits the pollutant at a somewhat higher rate, making up the difference with acquired emission reduction credits. The sum of emission reduction credits plus actual reductions must equal the assigned reduction.

This policy derives its unusual name from its treatment of multiple emission points as if they were contained within an imaginary bubble, regulating only the amount leaving the bubble. These bubbles can be extended to include not only emission points within the same plant, but emission points in plants owned by other firms as well (Example 15.2).

Netting.   Netting allows sources undergoing modification or expansion to escape the burden of new source review requirements so long as any net increase (counting the emission reduction credits) in plant wide emissions is insignificant. Traditionally, the test of whether a source was subject to the new source review process or not was applied by calculating the expected increases in emission occurring after modernization or expansion. When these increases passed predetermined thresholds, the source was subject to review. Netting allows emission reduction credits earned elsewhere in the plant to offset the increases expected from the expanded or modernized portion in order to determine whether the threshold had been exceeded. By "netting out" of review, the facility may be exempted from the need to acquire preconstruction permits as well as from meeting the associated requirements, such as modeling or monitoring the impact of the new source on air quality, installing BACT or LAER control technology, or meeting the offset requirement; it may also avoid any applicable bans on new construction. Those facilities satisfying the significant increase threshold must still meet emission limits established by the NSPS. Emission reduction credits cannot be used to avoid this national standard.

Banking.   The banking component of the emissions trading program establishes procedures that allow firms to store emission reduction credits for subsequent use in the bubble, offset, or netting programs. States are authorized to design their own banking programs as long as the rules specify the ownership rights over the banked credits; the sources eligible to bank emission reduction credits; and the conditions governing the certification, holding, and use of these credits.

The Effectiveness of the Reforms

As the particular trades described in Example 15.2 illustrate, these reforms have reduced costs, substantially in some cases. By the simple device of allowing sources to trade their control responsibility as long as air quality was not degraded in the process, EPA has been able to reduce the pressure on the control system and the political backlash against it. This has been a nonetheless cautious venture into permit markets and there are a number of ways in which it has not yet become fully cost effective.

The Spatial Dimension.   In Chapter 14 we pointed out that the cost-effective pursuit of ambient air-quality standards (as established for criteria pollutants) required the use of ambient permit systems rather than emission permit systems. The current trades under the bubble and offset policies involve emission trades rather than ambient air-quality trades and, therefore, are not cost effective.

Empirically, several studies have found that, compared to the ambient permit system, the use of an emissions system (defined solely in terms of emissions) to achieve a surface pollutant ambient standard causes a *significant* increase in compliance costs.

Atkinson and Lewis [1974] found that for particulate control in St. Louis, the use of an equal marginal cost rule for allocating the control responsibility causes the compliance costs to be twice what they would be in a minimum cost allocation.

Similar results were obtained for a different pollutant (nitrogen dioxide) in a different city (Chicago) by Anderson et al. [1979]. Though not all studies involving different locations and pollutants find that the spatial dimension is an empirically important component of cost reduction (such as Noll [1982]), most do. For the preponderance of locations and pollutants where the location of the source matters, the current system is not cost effective.

The use of an unrestricted emission permit system can also give rise to what has become known as the hot spot problem. The *hot spot problem* refers to the fact that while emissions trades hold emissions constant, they do not hold the ambient air quality constant. An emissions trade, for example, involving the sale of permits by a source located far from the receptor to a source located near the receptor would certainly make air quality at that receptor worse in spite of the fact that total emissions remain constant. The practical consequence of the hot spot problem is that even when a region is in complete compliance with the ambient standards prior to a trade, an emission trade can result in a violation at one or more receptors.

Potential Imperfect Competition.   One problem that has worried some observers about the introduction of this permit system concerns whether or not competition will prevail. The fear is that the fixed supply of permits will allow some source to use the transferable permit market as a means of gaining power in other markets. The results of microeconomic theory are quite clear that market power on either the buyer or seller side of the market can cause inefficiencies that could spill over from the permit market into other markets. Because of the fixed supply of permits, market power could cause the cost of compliance to be higher than necessary, but it would not lead to lower air quality.

The effects of this behavior on permit markets can be illustrated through the use of a simple numerical example. Not only does this example lend a certain concreteness to the argument, it turns out that many of the conclusions derived from it persist in more realistic situations.

Suppose a particular auction market was established by the government to auction off permits. The revenue from the sale of these permits is presumed to be retained by the government. For simplicity assume that only two sources are bidding for these permits. The first source is presumed to use its purchasing behavior to control the price while the second source is presumed to be a price taker. The first source adjusts its permit demands so as to minimize its financial burden, taking into account the reactions of the second source. In particular, it knows that the second source, being a cost minimizer, will choose that number of permits equating its marginal control cost to the price. The lower the price, the more permits it would acquire.

Let the marginal costs of control for each of the two sources be $MC_1 = Q_1$ and $MC_2 = 2Q_2$ where Q_1 and Q_2 are, respectively, the emissions reduced by the first and second source. In the absence of any control, these two sources are assumed to emit five units of emissions each (for a total of ten). Since the control authority is presumed

EXAMPLE 15.2

The Bubble and Offset Policies in Action

At the end of 1981, EPA had been approached about 93 different bubble trades, and the number was growing daily. A number of these presented the prospect of saving the purchaser substantial sums of money:

1. The Narraganset Electric Company has two generating stations in Providence, Rhode Island. Under the bubble policy they were allowed to use high-sulfur oil (2.2 percent sulfur) at one plant when the second plant was burning natural gas or was not operating, instead of being required to burn 1 percent sulfur oil at both plants. This action resulted in a savings of $3 million annually, reduced the use of imported oil by 600,000 barrels per year, and reduced sulfur emissions by 30 percent.

2. The DuPont Corporation was allowed to control five major sources of volatile organic compounds to more than 97 percent efficiency in exchange for relaxed controls on more than 200 difficult-to-control sources of fugitive emissions. The expected savings include $12 million in capital costs plus several million dollars in recurring operating costs.

3. Manufacturers of cans were allowed to comply with existing regulations for each individual can-coating line by averaging emissions of volatile organic compounds on a daily basis so long as the source did not exceed the total allowable plant-wide emissions per day. This is expected to save the industry $107 million in capital expenditures, $28 million per year in operating costs, and 4 trillion BTUs of natural gas per year, chiefly because expensive add-on pollution-control equipment which would have been energy-consuming is no longer necessary.

to allow only four units, six units must be reduced. By auctioning off four permits, each worth one unit of emissions, the control authority could fulfill this objective.

By definition, the financial burden of the first (price-setting) source is the sum of its permit expenditures and control costs. Symbolically this source's decision to minimize its financial burden can be characterized as

$$\min_{Q_1} P(5 - Q_1) + Q_1^2/2 \tag{1}$$

where the first term is permit expenditures (permit price times the number of permits needed to legitimize remaining emissions) and the second term is control cost.[5]

---

[5]The total control cost can be found by integrating marginal cost. Since the marginal cost is Q_1, the total cost is $Q_1^2/2$ plus a constant (the fixed cost). In this example the fixed cost is assumed to be zero for simplicity.

The exact number of offset transactions that have occurred is not known with any certainty. One search, however, uncovered hundreds.* Some examples serve to illustrate the flexibility this system provides.

1. A cement company in Texas entered into an agreement with another local company providing for that company to install dust collectors. The cement company paid for the equipment, while the other company agreed to accept the maintenance costs, which were negligible.
2. The emissions from a 90-megawatt refuse-burning powerplant to be operated by the city of Columbus, Ohio, were offset at the city's expense by installing pollution controls at two privately owned asphalt plants and by increasing the height of a smokestack at a third company.
3. A company wanting to build an oil terminal to handle 40,000 barrels a day in Contra Costa County, California, was granted a permit when it acquired, for $250,000, an offset created when a local chemical company shut down.
4. In the mid-1970s the state of Pennsylvania created an offset by altering its road-paving practices—which served to reduce hydrocarbon emissions—and used this offset to successfully induce the Volkswagen Corporation to locate its first American production facility in a depressed region in that state.

*Jorge A. del Calvo y Gonzales, "Markets in Air: Problems and Prospects of Controlled Trading," *Harvard Environmental Law Review* 5 (1981): 401.

Source: These examples were taken from National Commission of Air Quality, *To Breathe Clean Air* (Washington, D.C.: U.S. Government Printing Office, 1981) pp. 136–37; and Richard A. Liroff, *Air Pollution Offsets: Trading, Selling and Banking* (Washington, D.C.: The Conservation Foundation, 1980), p. 13.

Permit price would be a function of the behavior of both sources. Since the second source, by assumption, is a price taker, it will seek additional permits until its marginal cost of control is equal to the permit price. This implies $P = 2Q_2$. Furthermore, we know that six units of reduction are needed, so $Q_1 + Q_2 = 6$. Putting these facts together allows us to explain price solely in terms of the first source's behavior.

$$P = 2(6 - Q_1) \tag{2}$$

Substituting this into (1) yields

$$\min_{Q_1} 2(6 - Q_1)(5 - Q_1) + Q_1^2/2 \tag{3}$$

Since this equation is expressed solely in terms of the choice variable, (Q_1), it is a simple matter to derive the necessary and sufficient condition for Q_1 to minimize financial burden:

$$4Q_1 - 22 + Q_1 = 0$$
$$Q_1 = 4.4 \qquad\qquad (4)$$

The price-setting source would minimize its financial burden by choosing 4.4 units of control, implying (from equation 2) a price of 3.2. This immediately implies that the second source would control 1.6 units (from $2Q_2 = P = 3.2$).

Before examining the nature of this solution, let us be clear about what is going on. Equation (4) expresses the cost-minimizing choice as the one which equates the marginal expenditure on permits, *taking the effect of further purchases on price into account*, to the marginal cost of control. Every additional permit purchased by the first source would drive the price higher, not merely for the additional permits, but for all permits. Therefore to hold price down, the price-setting source must purchase fewer than normal permits, implying that its control costs would be higher than normal. These impressions are confirmed in Table 15.4 where the values of key variables for the two sources are compared for a competitive and noncompetitive auction market.[6]

Several key insights can be gained from this simple numerical example which can serve to focus our inquiry in more realistic situations:

1. Permit prices are lower in the noncompetitive than in the competitive market.

2. The price-setting firm controls more emissions than it would if it were merely acting as a price-taker. Because total emissions from all sources would be the same in competitive and noncompetitive markets by the design of the permit system, the price-taking source would have to control fewer emissions in competitive than noncompetitive markets.

3. The noncompetitive auction market allocation of control responsibility is not cost effective; control costs are higher in noncompetitive markets.

4. In terms of percentage change, the impact of noncompetitive behavior on permit prices is quite a bit greater than the impact on total control cost. Though the price-setting source was able to reduce the permit price by 20 percent, control costs rose by only 2 percent.

5. In terms of reduced financial burden, the price-taking source benefits more than the price-setting source. The financial burden for the price-setting source is reduced by 3.3 percent in noncompetitive markets while that for the price-taking source is reduced 16 percent.

To those envisioning the price-setting source as inflicting significant harm on other less aggressive sources, these findings may appear surprising. Control costs do rise when one source becomes a price-setter, but no harm is inflicted on other sources. The higher control costs are due to the price-setting firm assuming more of the control respon-

---

[6] The derivation of the competitive results are straightforward since the market will be cost effective. This implies $MC_1 = MC_2$, which further implies $Q_1 = 2Q_2$. Using $Q_1 + Q_2 = 6$ yields $Q_1 = 4$ and $Q_2 = 2$.

TABLE 15.4　Competitive and Noncompetitive Auction Markets: A Numerical Example

Variable	Competitive auction	Noncompetitive auction
Emissions controlled		
Source 1	4	4.4
Source 2	2	1.6
Permits purchased		
Source 1	1	0.6
Source 2	3	3.4
Permit price	4	3.2
Permit expenditures		
Source 1	4	1.92
Source 2	12	10.88
Control costs		
Source 1	8	9.68
Source 2	4	2.56
Total financial burden		
Source 1	12	11.60
Source 2	16	13.44

Source: Calculations by the author based on parameters described in the text.

sibility for itself; the greatest benefits are derived by the price-taking, not the price-setting source.

Hahn (1984) has extended this analysis by examining the case where permits are allocated to emitters without charge (as is done in the Emissions Trading Program) rather than allocating them by an auction. His most important finding was that this initial allocation could have an effect on both the final (post-trade) allocation of permits and the permit price in the presence of market power. This finding is in direct contrast to what would happen in competitive markets (as described in Chapter 14), where the market equlibrium would be independent of the initial allocation.

It is not hard to obtain an intuitive understanding of why the initial allocation might have an effect on the potential for price-setting behavior. Whenever a single price-setting source receives an initial allocation that is either higher than or lower than its cost-effective allocation, an incentive for trading would be created. When a price-setting source receives in an initial allocation fewer permits than its cost-effective allocation, it would exercise power on the buyer's side of the market. If it received more, it would exercise power on the seller's side of the market. The farther the initial allocation diverges from the cost-effective allocation, the greater the potential for the price-setter to exercise power over the market.

Is the potential for price manipulation a serious potential flaw in permit markets? The simulation studies that have been accomplished suggest that it is not. Hahn (1984, p. 762) found in simulating the sulfate market in Los Angeles that the total cost function was rather flat with respect to the initial allocation unless the price-settig firm receives a sufficiently large number of permits that it was able to become virtually a monopoly seller.

In another set of published data from the Du Pont Corporation involving some 52 plants and 548 sources of hydrocarbons, Maloney and Yandle (in 1984) investigated the effects of cartelization of plants on the permit market. Assuming that all sources receive a proportional initial distribution of the permits based on their uncontrolled emissions, they calculate the effects on control costs if plants collude. Their analysis allows collusion to take place separately among buyers and sellers and allows the number of colluding plants to vary from 10 to 90 percent of the total number of plants buying or selling.

In general, these data support the notion that high degrees of cartelization are necessary before control costs are affected to any appreciable degree and that even high degrees of cartelization do not significantly erode the large savings to be achieved from permit markets. At the 90 percent credit monopoly (achieved when the cartel controls 90 percent of all credits sold), for example, yielding a 41 percent increase in control costs, Maloney and Yandle point out that the cost savings from this severe market power situation, compared with command-and-control regulation, is still 66 (instead of 76) percent. The presence of market power does not seem to diminish the potential for cost savings very much. Even with market power, transferable permit systems seem to result in lower control costs than the command-and-control allocation.

Property Rights and Permit Banking.   A final problem arises because the property rights to the emission reductions which are to be banked are not always vested in the supplier, a necessary condition if cost effectiveness is to be achieved. In both San Francisco and Los Angeles there has been considerable resistance in the community against vesting ownership of these deposits in the sources.[7] This resistance stems from a feeling that these deposits should, at least to some extent, be appropriated by the community at large to be used for public purposes. In San Francisco, for example, deposits made by corporations in the emissions reduction bank could subsequently be confiscated if the control authority found a need to impose more stringent standards.

The purpose of establishing an emission banking system was to stimulate extra reduction by sources purchasing control equipment, making the achievement of air-quality goals easier. The incentive for firms to voluntarily undertake a higher degree of control than required is the profits to be gained from the sale of the excess permits. If the source does not have a clear title to those permits, the possibility for profit is diminished with a corresponding reduction in the willingness of firms to do more than required. Thus, however laudable it may be on other grounds, treating these excess permits as community, rather than private property, will result in less flexibility and higher control costs.

In summary the current regulatory reforms embodying transferable permits represent a large, but incomplete, step toward cost effectiveness. By focusing on emission trades, rather than ambient air-quality trades, and by prohibiting intermittent control as a complement to constant control, significant opportunities for cost reduction have been ignored. Furthermore, some restrictions on the market, such as the lack of clearly

---

[7]For a description of these problems, see U.S. General Accounting Office, *A Market Approach to Air Pollution Control Could Reduce Compliance Costs Without Jeopardizing Clean Air Goals,* PAD-82-15 (March 23, 1982).

defined property rights, restrict the volume of trade and also increase the possibility of noncompetitive markets.

Hazardous Pollutants

Hazardous pollutants are those that pose a localized risk of severe harm to human health. They are distinguished from criteria pollutants both by the degree of harm they pose to those exposed and by the fact that emissions usually occur only at a few key locations. In recognition of these unique characteristics, the Clean Air Act sets up a special process for dealing with hazardous pollutants.

The first step in the control process involves identifying those substances which are designated as hazardous substances and therefore must receive this special treatment. The Act requires the Administrator of EPA to make and periodically update a list of hazardous pollutants. It allows a great deal of discretion in the choice of criteria to be used in distinguishing hazardous and criteria pollutants and in the length of time necessary to decide whether a particular substance should be listed.

Once a substance is listed, EPA must move with great speed (180 days) either to regulate emissions of the substance or to remove it from the list after finding that the evidence failed to support the tentative hazardous-substance designation. The decision to regulate a substance imposes on EPA a requirement to establish a national emission standard or workplace standard for each regulated substance. These standards must be designed to protect human health with an adequate margin of safety.

The somewhat ambiguous language in this section of the Act has led to a great deal of controversy as well as litigation concerning the meaning of this mandate. It is generally conceded that there is no safe threshold level for airborne carcinogens. Therefore environmentalists maintain that protecting the public with an adequate margin of safety requires eliminating all exposure to listed substances. Completely eliminating emissions would at a minimum be very expensive and as a practical matter in some cases may not be possible without shutting down the operation.

EPA has reacted to this dilemma in two ways: (1) it has moved slowly in listing pollutants, and (2) it has chosen to balance costs and risks in deciding whether to list a substance or not. By 1980, EPA had listed only seven pollutants: asbestos (1971), beryllium (1971), mercury (1971), vinyl chloride (1975), benzene (1977), radionuclides (1979), and inorganic arsenic (1980). Despite the 180-day deadline, only four had been regulated: asbestos, beryllium, mercury, and vinyl chloride. As a result of court action, by 1984 EPA had proposed standards for radionuclides, benzene, and arsenic.

In addition to moving very slowly in listing pollutants, the agency began to incorporate risk assessment and benefit/cost analysis into their decisions. The first step in this process is to decide whether the risk posed by the substance is "significant." Substances which are not found to be posing significant risks are not listed. The second step, taken only for listed pollutants, involves identifying the level of control that will be required. This entails comparing the costs of various control possibilities with the damages to health prevented by adopting the controls.

Based on this analysis EPA has since listed coke oven emissions (1984) as a hazardous substance and announced its intention to list additional substances.[8] By announcing its "intention to list" the substances, rather than simply listing them, EPA has bought time to do the analysis before it is subject to the 180-day deadline.

Based on the work of Haigh, Harrison, and Nichols (1983), it is possible to see how this kind of economic analysis can be applied to hazardous pollution regulation. In their study, the authors applied benefit/cost analysis to three hazardous pollutants: benzene, coke oven emissions, and acrylonitrile. Benzene is a major industrial chemical, ranking among the top 15 in terms of production volume. Coke, produced by distilling coal in ovens, is essential to the production of steel. Acrylonitrile is an important industrial chemical used in the manufacture of a wide range of consumer products, including rugs, clothing, plastic pipe, and automobile hoses.

The analysis involved several steps. The amount and location of emissions had to be identified for each substance. The number of people exposed to this risk and the amount of health risk they would experience had to be calculated. Finally a dollar value had to be put on this risk so it could be directly compared with the control costs. All of these steps had to be repeated for each considered regulatory option.

Three regulatory strategies were considered for each pollutant. The first strategy was a rather stringent set of uniformly applied emission standards designed to require the use of the "best available technology." (For benzene, the controls were applied to maleic anhydride plants, the largest source of emissions.) The second considered strategy involved a somewhat more relaxed version of the first strategy. While the standards were still applied uniformly in this second case, the level of required control was lower. The final strategy involved differential controls based on exposure. The notion of uniform controls was dropped in this case in favor of placing heavier controls on those sources posing the greatest health risk.

The authors present their results in two main forms. The first calculates the value of human life that would be needed to justify that particular regulatory option. This form of presentation allows the reader to make the decision of whether the regulatory option is a good idea or not by supplying his or her own sense of what the value of human life should be. The second uses a $1 million value of human life and calculates the net benefits of each option based on that assumption.

Using the $1 million figure for a human life, the results (Table 15.5) indicate that for all three pollutants the standard best available technology (BAT) strategy would yield negative net benefits. The combination of uniform standards with a very stringent level of control produces a situation where the costs exceed the benefits. A relaxed uniform standard reduces, but does not eliminate, the negative net benefits. Although lowering the uniform degree of control represents an improvement in the sense that costs are more commensurate with benefits, it still fails to target the reductions in the areas where they result in the most reduction in risk.

By configuring the controls in such a way as to target the costs on those emitters posing the greatest risk to human health (the differential strategy), a dramatic improve-

---

[8]The seven substances were either chromium or hexavalent chromium, carbon tetrachloride, chloroform, ethylene oxide, 1,3 butadiene, ethylene dichloride, and cadmium.

TABLE 15.5 Net Benefits ($Millions/Year) of Alternative Strategies for a Value of Life Saved of $1 Million

Regulatory Strategy	Maleic Anhydrite	Coke Oven Emissions	Acrylonitrile
Best Available Technology	−2.2	−8.7	−28.8
Relaxed Uniform	−1.1	−3.2	−8.0
Differential	−0.6	2.3	−4.9

Source: Haigh, Harrison and Nichols (1983, Table 2.16)

ment in net benefits is achieved for all three pollutants. For only one, however, coke oven emissions, are the net benefits positive. For the rest even the differential strategy falls short of being justified by the benefits.

The significance of these data lie less in what they tell us about the correct regulatory option to choose for these specific pollutants than in the clues they provide concerning directions for policy to move in achieving greater efficiency in regulating hazardous pollutants in general. First, tailoring the strategy to the specific circumstances can produce significant reductions in cost while achieving the same risk or can achieve much larger risk reductions for the same cost. Uniformity, in short, imposes a large cost penalty. Second, the policies being pursued in regulating hazardous pollutants imply values for human life which differ by a factor of more than 100. This finding implies that by allocating more resources to the control of those substances which can be justified with even a low value of life and less to those which can be justified only with a high value for life, more lives could be saved with the same expenditure of money.

How can these lessons be translated into policy? One answer is to consider the adoption of a charge levied not on emissions, but rather on exposure (Example 15.3). By forcing those emitters exposing large numbers of people to a health risk to exert greater cleanup efforts than those emitters exposing fewer people to the same health risk, more lives can be saved with the same expenditure of resources. In this context uniform exposure charges have much to recommend them.

SUMMARY

The Clean Air Amendments of 1970 charted a bold new approach to air-pollution control. These amendments created a federal partnership in which the national government established ambient air-quality standards and national emission standards for selected sources, while the states were given primary responsibility for ensuring that the ambient standards were met. Though the Clean Air Act recognized two types of pollutants—criteria pollutants and hazardous pollutants—most government attention has been focused on the former.

EXAMPLE 15.3

Efficient Regulation of Hazardous Pollutants: The Benzene Case

Regulatory approaches tend to emphasize uniform standards. As was clear from the discussion in the text, this can cause a particularly large deviation from efficiency when hazardous pollutants are involved, because both the control costs and damages are so localized.

Eight maleic anhydride plants in the United States emit more than half of the benzene from chemical manufacturing. From Table 15.5 we know that BAT uniform standards yield negative net benefits. Is there a more efficient approach?

The damage caused by these emissions (primarily an increase in the risk of leukemia) is a function both of the concentration level and the exposed population. The highest economic marginal damage estimate found by a government agency was $1 for each person exposed continuously to a concentration of one part per billion (ppb) of benzene for one year. This corresponds to a risk of 3.4 extra leukemia deaths from exposing 10 million people to a concentration of 1 part per billion for one year and a value of $360,000 placed on each life lost.

The efficient solution would be to impose an emission charge of $1 per ppb person-year exposed since this is the (high) estimate of marginal damage. Firms would respond by choosing that level of control where their marginal cost was equal to $1 per ppb person-year exposed. Since this would guarantee the equivalence of marginal cost and marginal benefit, efficiency would be achieved.

The costs of the uniform standard weren't justified by the benefits. The major problem with the proposed standard was that it didn't take into account either the rather large differences in control costs or number of people exposed among the plants. Some plants in isolated areas exposed very few people while others in more densely populated areas clearly put more people at risk. The $1 uniform *exposure* charge solves both of these problems simultaneously. A uniform *emission* charge would take into account the differences in costs, but not the differences in exposure. Uniform emission standards take neither costs nor exposure into account and, therefore, are doubly cursed.

Source: This example is based on Albert L. Nichols, "The Importance of Exposure in Evaluating and Designing Environmental Regulations: A Case Study," *The American Economic Review* 72 (May 1982): 214–219.

The historical approach to air pollution control has been a traditional command-and-control approach. It has been neither efficient, nor cost-effective.

The command-and-control policy has not been efficient in part because it has been based on a legal fiction, a threshold below which no health damages are inflicted on any member of the population. In fact damages occur at levels lower than the ambient standards to especially sensitive members of the population, such as those with respiratory problems. This attempt to formulate standards without reference to control costs has been thwarted by the absence of a scientifically defensible health-based threshold. In addition the policy fails to adequately consider the timing of emission flows. By failing to target the greatest amount of control on the period when the greatest damage is inflicted, the current policy encourages too little control in high-damage periods and excessive control during low-damage periods. Unfortunately because the existing benefit estimates have large confidence intervals, the size of the inefficiency associated with these aspects of the policy has not been measured with any precision.

The policy is not cost-effective either. The allocation of responsibility among emitters for reducing pollution has resulted in control costs which are typically several times higher than necessary to achieve the air quality objective. This has been shown to be true for a variety of pollutants in a variety of geographic settings.

Recently, EPA has initiated the Emissions Trading Program, based on economic incentives that is designed to provide more flexibility in meeting the air quality goals while reducing the cost and the conflict between economic growth and the preservation of air quality. These reforms, known as the bubble, offset, netting and emissions banking programs, also promise to stimulate more rapid development of new control technologies than was possible under the traditional system.

The program to control hazardous pollutants is inefficient in both the speed with which the process is operating and quality of the decisions being rendered. Faced with unrealistically short deadlines for publishing standards once a hazardous substance is listed, EPA has reacted by taking an excessively cautious approach to listing hazardous substances. Past decisions have resulted in the application of stringent standards that are uniformly applied to emitters. The evidence suggests that strategies tailored more closely to the risk posed (with emissions posing the greatest risk being reduced more) produce substantially lower risks for the same expenditure as uniformly applied standards. One reform proposal based on this analysis would impose an exposure (as opposed to an emissions) charge on emitters which would take into account not only the concentration of the emission (and the resulting health risk to each exposed person), but also the number of people exposed.

FURTHER READING

Freeman, A. Myrick, III. *Air and Water Pollution Control: A Benefit-Cost Assessment* (New York: John Wiley & Sons, 1982). A detailed survey and critical evaluation of the literature on benefit-cost analysis as it applies to air and water pollution control. Contains chapters on defining and measuring benefits associated with health of humans, vegetation, and aesthetics as well as on water recreation. Calculates a range of estimates as well as the "most likely" point estimate.

Joeres, Erhard F., and Martin H. David, eds. *Buying a Better Environment: Cost Effective Regulation through Permit Trading.* (Madison, Wis.: The University of Wisconsin Press, 1983). An excellent collection of essays on aspects of permit trading including permit design, distributional matters, and dealing with uncertainty.

Lave, L. B., and Omenn, G. S. *Clearing the Air: Reforming the Clean Air Act* (Washington, D.C.: The Brookings Institution, 1981). Written to influence Congress in the revision of the Clean Air Act, this book concludes that some innovative restructuring of the law is necessary. Suggests that most of the improvement in air quality during the last decade resulted from a lagging economy and the continuing substitution of clean fuels (natural gas and oil) for more heavily polluting fuels (coal), rather than from the Clean Air Act.

Nichols, Albert L., *Targeting Economic Incentives for Environmental Protection* (Cambridge, MA: The MIT Press, 1984). An excellent review of the use of economic incentives to control pollution with a detailed treatment of the use of exposure charges to control airborne carcinogens.

Tietenberg, T. H., *Emissions Trading: An Exercise in Reforming Pollution Policy* (Washington, D.C.: Resources for the Future, Inc., 1985). A detailed examination of EPA's Emissions Trading Program and how effectively it has coped with implementation complexities.

ADDITIONAL REFERENCES

Anderson, Robert J., Jr. et al., "An Analysis of Alternative Policies for Attaining and Maintaining a Short-Term NO_2 Standard," a report prepared by MATHTECH, Inc. for the Council on Environmental Quality (17 September 1979).

Atkinson, Scott E., and Donald H. Lewis, "A Cost-Effective Analysis of Alternative Air Quality Control Strategies," *Journal of Environmental Economics and Management*, I (Nov., 1974): 237–250.

Blackman, Sue Anne Batey, and William J. Baumol, "Modified Fiscal Incentives in Environmental Policy," *Land Economics,* Vol. 56 (November, 1980): 417–431.

Hahn, Robert W., and Roger G. Noll, "Designing a Market for Tradeable Emissions Permits," in *Reform of Environmental Regulation,* Wesley A. Magat, ed. (Cambridge, Mass.: Ballinger Publishing Company, 1982).

Hahn, Robert W., "Market Power and Transferable Property Rights," *Quarterly Journal of Economics*, Vol. 99, No. 4 (November, 1984): 753–765.

Haigh, John A., David Harrison, Jr. and Albert L. Nichols, "Benefits Assessment and Environmental Regulation: Case Studies of Hazardous Air Pollutants," John F. Kennedy School of Government Energy and Environment Policy Center Discussion Paper E–83–07 (August, 1983).

Krupnick, Alan J., "Costs of Alternative Policies for the Control of NO_2 in the Baltimore Region" (unpublished Resources for the Future Working Paper, 1983).

McGartland, Albert M., "Marketable Permit Systems for Air Pollution Control: An Empirical Study" (Ph.D. dissertation, University of Maryland, 1984).

Maloney, Michael T., and Bruce Yandle, "Estimation of the Cost of Air Pollution Control Regulation," *Journal of Environmental Economics and Management,* Vol. 11, No. 3 (September, 1984): 244–263.

Roach, Fred, Charles Kolstad, Allen V. Kneese, Richard Tobin, and Michael Williams, "Alternative Air Quality Policy Options in the Four Corners Region," *Southwest Review*, Vol. 1, No. 2 (Summer, 1981): 29–58.

Seskin, Eugene P., Robert J. Anderson, Jr., and Robert O. Reid, "An Empirical Analysis of Economic Strategies for Controlling Air Pollution," *Journal of Environmental Economics and Management*, Vol. 10, No. 2 (June, 1983): 112–124.

Spofford, Walter O., Jr., "Efficiency Properties of Alternative Source Control Policies for Meeting Ambient Air Quality Standards: An Empirical Application to the Lower Delaware Valley," unpublished, Resources for the Future Discussion Paper D-118, February, 1984.

Schelling, Thomas C., ed. *Incentives for Environmental Protection* (Cambridge, Mass.: The MIT Press, 1983).

Teller, Azriel. "Air Pollution Abatement: Economic Rationality and Reality," in Roger Revelle and Hans H. Landsberg, eds., *America's Changing Environment* (Boston: Beacon Press, 1970).

U.S. General Accounting Office. *A Market Approach to Air Pollution Control Could Reduce Compliance Costs Without Jeopardizing Clean Air Goals,* PAD-82-15 (23 March 1982): 70–71.

DISCUSSION QUESTIONS

1. As shown in Example 15.3, the efficient regulation of hazardous pollutants should take exposure into account—the more persons exposed to a given pollutant concentration, the larger is the damage caused by it and therefore the smaller is the efficient concentration level, all other things being equal. An alternative point of view would simply insure that concentrations would be held below a uniform threshold regardless of the number of people exposed. For this point of view, the public policy goal is to expose any and all people to the same concentration level—exposure is not used to establish different concentrations for different settings.

   What are the advantages and disadvantages of each approach? Which do you think represents the best approach? Why?

2. European countries have relied to a much greater extent on emission charges than has the United States, which seems to be moving toward a greater reliance on transferable emission permits. From an efficiency point of view, should the United States follow Europe's lead and shift the emphasis toward emission charges? Why or why not?

PROBLEMS

1. The marginal control cost curves for two air pollutant sources affecting a single receptor are $MC_1 = \$0.3q_1$ and $MC_2 = \$0.5q_2$ where q_1 and q_2 are controlled emissions. Their respective transfer coefficients are $a_1 = 1.5$ and $a_1 = 1.0$. With no control they would emit 20 units of emission apiece. The ambient standard is 12 ppm.

   (a) If an ambient permit system were established, how many permits would be issued and what price would prevail?

   (b) How much would each source spend on permits if they were auctioned off? How much would each source ultimately spend on permits if each source was initially given, free-of-charge, half of the permits?

CHAPTER SIXTEEN

Regional and Global Air Pollutants: Acid Rain and Atmospheric Modification

The interdependencies among peoples and nations, over time and space, are far greater than commonly imagined: actions taken at one time in one part of the world have far-reaching consequences that are often difficult to anticipate intuitively and are probably impossible to predict (totally, precisely, perhaps at all) even with computer models.

U.S. CONGRESS, OFFICE OF TECHNOLOGY ASSESSMENT,
Global Models, World Futures, and Public Policy (1982)

INTRODUCTION

As the zone of influence of pollutants extends beyond local boundaries, the political difficulties of implementing comprehensive, cost-effective control measures are compounded. Pollutants crossing boundaries impose external costs; neither emitters nor the nations within which they emit have the proper incentives for controlling them.

Compounding the problem of improper incentives is the scientific uncertainty which limits our understanding of most of these problems. As the opening quote to this chapter indicates, our knowledge about the various relationships which form the basis for our understanding of the magnitude of the problems and the effectiveness of various strategies to control them is far from complete. Unfortunately, the problems are so important and the potential consequences of inaction so drastic, procrastination is not usually an optimal strategy. To avoid having to act in the future under emergency conditions when the remaining choices are few in number, strategies which have desirable properties must be formulated now on the basis of the available information, as limited as it may be. Options must be preserved.

The costs of inaction are not limited to the damages caused. International cooperation among such traditional allies such as the United States, Mexico, and Canada and the countries of Europe has been undermined by disputes over the proper control of acid rain.

In this chapter we shall survey the scientific evidence on the severity of global and regional pollution and the potential effectiveness of policy strategies designed to alleviate these problems. We shall also consider difficulties confronted by the government in implementing solutions and the role of economic analysis in understanding and circumventing these difficulties.

REGIONAL POLLUTANTS

The primary difference between regional pollutants and local pollutants is the distance they are transported in the air. While the damage caused by local pollutants occurs in the vicinity of emission, for regional pollutants the damage can occur at significant distances from the point at which they were emitted into the air.

The same substances can be both local pollutants and regional pollutants. Sulfur oxides, nitrogen oxides and ozone, for example, have already been discussed as local pollutants, but they are regional pollutants as well. For example, sulfur emissions, the focal point for most acid-rain legislation, have been known to travel some 200 to 600 miles from the point of emission before returning to the earth. As the substances are being transported by the winds, they undergo a complex series of chemical reactions. Under the right conditions both sulfur and nitrogen oxides are transformed into sulfuric and nitric acids. Nitrogen oxides and hydrocarbons can combine in the presence of sunlight to produce ozone.

Acid Rain

Acid rain, the popular term for atmospheric deposition of acidic substances, is actually a misnomer. Acidic substances are deposited not only by rain and other forms of moist air, but are deposited as dry particles as well. In some parts of the world, such as the Southwestern United States, dry deposition is a more important source of acidity than wet deposition.

Precipitation is normally mildly acidic, with a global background pH of 5.0 (pH is the common measurement for acidity; the lower the number, the more acidic the substance, with 7.0 being the border between acidity and alkalinity). Industrialized areas commonly receive precipitation well in excess of the global background. Rainfall in Eastern North America, for example, has a typical pH of 4.4. Wheeling, West Virginia once experienced a rainstorm with a pH of 1.5. The fact that battery acid has a pH of 1.0 may help put this event into perspective.

Though there are natural sources of acid deposition, the evidence is quite clear that anthropogenic (human-made) sources have dominated deposition in recent years. An analysis of ice cores from Greenland, for example, covering the period from 1869–1984, indicates that anthropogenic sulfate has dominated sulfur deposition since the early twentieth century and anthropogenic nitrate has dominated nitrogen deposition since about 1960.[1]

---

[1]P.A. Mayewski, et. al., *A Detailed (1869–1984) Record of Sulfate and Nitrate Concentrations from South Greenland* (forthcoming) as cited in World Resources Institute and International Institute for Environment and Development, *World Resources: 1986* (New York: Basic Books, 1986): 169.

Of the many forms of damage inflicted by acid rain, the acidification of aquatic ecosystems is perhaps the best documented. The most studied acidified waters are in the Northeastern United States, Canada, and Western Europe, but evidence is accumulating that the problem is much more widespread than that.

When lake surface waters reach a pH of 5.0 or lower, fish populations are adversely affected. (Example 16.1) Fish reproduction and health are impaired not only by the direct effects of the acidity, but by the toxicity of metals released by the acids as well. Aluminum poisoning is one example, since as the pH decreases the toxicity of aluminum to fish increases.

The Office of Technology Assessment in the U.S. Congress has estimated that there are about 3,000 lakes and 20,000 miles of streams, scattered throughout the Eastern United States, that are extremely vulnerable to acid deposition or are already acidic.[2] Other studies have documented that Sweden has some 4,000 lakes that are highly acidified; in Southern Norway lakes with a total surface area of 13,000 square kilometers support no fish at all; similar reports have been received from Germany, Scotland and Canada.[3]

Aquatic life is not the only casualty of acid deposition. Another significant form of damage results from the degrading effects of airborne pollutants on both natural and human-made materials. Discoloration of paint, corrosion of metals and deterioration of surface stone are some of the main effects of acid deposition. Acid deposition has been implicated, for example, in the deterioration of such architectural treasures as the Parthenon in Greece and the Taj Mahal in India.

Other effects of acid deposition include visibility reduction and some dimunition of forest growth. Sulfate particulates are the single greatest factor in reducing visibility in the Eastern United States, responsible for about half of the decrease in visibility annually and even more during the summer.[4] Furthermore as made clear by Example 11.1 acid deposition is one of the pollution sources implicated in the massive forest death taking place in Europe.

In many countries with a federal form of government, such as the United States, the policy focus in the past has been on treating all pollutants as if they were local pollutants, overlooking the adverse regional consequences in the process. By giving local jurisdictions a large amount of responsibility for achieving the desired air quality and by measuring progress at local monitors, the stage was set for making regional pollution worse rather than better.

In the early days of pollution control local areas adopted the motto "dilution is the solution." As implemented, this approach suggested that the way to control local pollutants was to emit from tall stacks. By the time the pollutants hit the ground, the

---

[2]Office of Technology Assessment, U.S. Congress, *Acid Rain and Transported Air Pollutants: Implications for Public Policy* (Washington: U.S. Government Printing Office, 1984).

[3]See the review in World Resources Institute and International Institute for Environment and Development, *World Resources: 1986* (New York: Basic Books, 1986): 169–70.

[4]See the discussion of sulfates and the visibility problem in Office of Technology Assessment, U.S. Congress, *Acid Rain and Transported Air Pollutants: Implications for Public Policy* (Washington: U.S. Government Printing Office, 1984).

EXAMPLE 16.1

Adirondack Acidification

About 180 lakes in the Adirondack Mountains of New York State, mostly at higher altitudes, which had supported natural or stocked brook trout populations in the 1930s, no longer supported these populations by the 1970s. In some cases entire communities of six or more fish species had disappeared.

The location of these lakes, some distance east of any local emission sources, makes it quite clear that most of the acid deposition is coming from outside of the region. These lakes have relatively little capacity to neutralize deposited acid because they are in areas with little or no limestone or other forms of basic rock that might serve to buffer the acid.

This is a prime recreational area, particularly for fishing. Most of the sites are within the boundary of the six million acre Adirondack Park, the last substantially undeveloped area of its size in the northeastern United States. Its remoteness, mountainous terrain and multitude of lakes provide an accessible outdoor recreation experience for the 55 million people who live within a day's traveling distance.

There is little doubt that acidification has substantially reduced the recreational value of the area. Using a version of the travel cost method discussed in Chapter 4, Mullen and Menz (1985) conclude that the annual losses to New York resident anglers is in the neighborhood of at least $1 million in 1976 dollars.

One possibility for restoring these lakes would be to add lime (calcium carbonate) to buffer the effects of the acid. Would liming be efficient? In their investigation Menz and Driscoll (1983) have found that a 5-year lake neutralization program would cost in the neighborhood of $2–$4 million. Given the $1 million estimate of *annual* losses to recreational fishing, there seems little doubt that some neutralization would be efficient. The exact number of lakes to be limed would have to be determined by comparing the marginal cost of liming each lake with the marginal gain to recreation that would result. The authors are quick to point out that while liming may be used to restore damaged lakes, it is not a substitute for controlling emissions.

Sources: Government Accounting Office, *An Analysis of Issues Concerning "Acid Rain,"* Report #GAO/RCED-85-13, December 11, 1984: p. 13; John K. Mullen and Frederic C. Menz, "The Effect of Acidification Damages on the Economic Value of the Adirondack Fishery to New York Anglers," *American Journal of Agricultural Economics,* Vol. 67, No. 1 (February, 1985): 112–119; Fredric C. Menz and Charles T. Driscol, "An Estimate of the Costs of Liming to Neutralize Acidic Adirondack Surface Waters," *Water Resources Research,* Vol. 19, No. 5 (October, 1983): 1139–49.

concentrations would be diluted, making it easier to meet the ambient standards at nearby monitors.

This approach had several effects. First, it lowered the amount of emission reduction necessary to achieve ambient standards; with tall stacks any given amount of emission would produce lower nearby ground level concentrations than an equivalent level of emission from a shorter-stack source. Second, the ambient standards could be met at a lower cost. Using Cleveland as a case study, Atkinson (1983) has shown that control costs would be approximately 30 percent lower, but emissions would be two and one half times higher if a local, rather than a regional, strategy were followed in a marketable permit system. In essence, local areas would be able to lower their own cost by exporting emissions to other areas. By focusing its attention on local pollution, the Clean Air Act actually made the regional pollution problem worse.

It has become painfully clear in the United States that the Clean Air Act is ill-suited to solve regional pollution problems. Therefore a lot of attention has been focused on revamping the legislation to do a better job of dealing with regional pollutants such as acid rain.

Politically, that is a tall order. By virtue of the fact that these pollutants are transported long distances, the set of geographic areas receiving the damage is typically not the same as the set of geographic areas responsible for most of the emissions causing the damage. In many cases the recipients and the emitters are even in different countries! In this political milieu, it should not be surprising that those bearing damages should call for a large, rapid reduction in emissions, while those responsible for bearing the costs of that cleanup should want to proceed more slowly and with greater caution.

Economic analysis can be and has been helpful in finding a feasible path through this political thicket. In particular, a recent Congressional Budget Office (CBO) study helps to set the parameters of the debate by quantifying the consequences of various courses of action. The basic strategy of the U.S. Congress has been to seek reductions of SO_2 emissions from utilities anywhere from 8 to 12 million tons below the emissions levels from those plants in 1980. To analyze the economic and political consequences of various strategies designed to achieve these targets, the Congressional Budget Office used a computer-based simulation model that relates utility emissions, utility costs, and coal-market supply and demand levels to the strategies under consideration. The model, called the National Coal Model, is maintained by the Department of Energy.

The results of this modeling exercise will be presented in two segments. In the first segment we shall examine the basic available strategies including both a traditional command-and-control strategy which simply allocates reductions on the basis of a specific formula and an emissions charge strategy. This analysis will serve to show how sensitive costs are to various levels of emission reduction and to highlight some of the political consequences of implementing these strategies. The second segment of analysis then considers various strategies designed to mitigate the adverse political effects of the basic strategies as a means of ascertaining what is gained and lost by adopting these compromises.

In the command-and-control strategies, the emission reductions are allocated to states on the basis of what is known as the "excess emissions" formula. For each plant, this formula subtracts from actual emissions the amount of emissions the plant would have been allowed to emit if it were forced to meet the 1979 NSPS sulfur standard for utilities. (Since that is a new source standard, plants built before that date do not automatically need to meet it.) The amount left, the excess emissions, are then summed over all the excess emission plants within each state and, finally, across states to get

TABLE 16.1 Costs Associated with Basic Strategies to Reduce Sulfur Emissions

Strategy	Total Program Cost[1] (Billions of $)	Annual Cost to Utilities[2] (Billions of $)	Key State Employment Change[3] (# of Jobs Lost)	Cost Effectiveness[4] ($ per ton)
8 Million Ton Rollback	$20.4	$1.9	14,100	$270
10 Million Ton Rollback	$34.5	$3.2	21,900	$360
12 Million Ton Rollback	$93.6	$8.8	13,400	$779
Emission Charge	$37.5	$7.7	17,900	$327

Notes: [1]The present value (in 1985 dollars) of additional discounted utility costs incurred (over a current policy benchmark) from 1986–2015, using a real discount rate of 0.03. Any emission charges paid are not included.

[2]The additional cost to utilities of this strategy over the current policy benchmark in 1995 expressed in 1985 dollars. This value includes any emissions charges paid.

[3]The additional coal mining job losses expected if this strategy were implemented over the current policy benchmark in the states of Indiana, Illinois, Ohio, and Pennsylvania.

[4]The discounted program cost divided by the annual discounted SO_2 reduction measured over the 1986–2015 period.

Source: Congress of the United States, Congressional Budget Office, *Curbing Acid Rain: Cost, Budget, and Coal-Market Effects* (Washington: U.S. Government Printing Office, 1986) pp. xx, xxii, 23 and 80.

a national total. Each state is then required to meet the same share of the stipulated reduction (8, 10, or 12 million tons) that it has of the total excess emissions.

With the emission charge each utility is faced with a $600 per ton charge for all uncontrolled SO_2 emissions. The model assumes that utilities minimize costs by cleaning up their emissions until the marginal cost of further cleanup is equal to $600 dollars. This results in a degree of emission reduction which is roughly comparable to the 10-million ton command-and-control reduction.

The first implication of the analysis is that the marginal cost of additional control rises rapidly, particularly after 10 million tons have been reduced (Table 16.1). The cost of reducing a ton of SO_2 rises from $270 for an 8-million ton reduction to $360 for a 10-million ton reduction, while it rises to a rather dramatic $779 per ton for a 12-million ton reduction. Costs would rise much more steeply as the amount of required reduction is increased because switching to low sulfur coal—a relatively low-cost strategy—would be insufficient, by itself, to achieve the larger reductions. At stricter standards reliance on the more expensive scrubbers would become necessary. (Scrubbers involve a chemical process to extract or "scrub" sulphur gases before they escape into the atmosphere.)

The second insight, one that should be no surprise to readers of this book, is that the emissions charge would be more cost-effective than the comparable command-and-control strategy. Whereas the command-and-control strategy could secure a 10-million ton reduction at about $360 a ton, the emission charge could do it for $327 a ton. The superiority of the emissions charge is due to the fact that it results in equalized marginal costs, a required condition for cost-effectiveness.[5]

A third insight is that the magnitude of the cost-effectiveness superiority of the emissions charge is not very large, especially when compared with the numbers presented in the previous chapter. In essence it appears that the "excess emissions" formula is not a particularly costly way to allocate emission reductions in this particular context.

It may seem a bit of a paradox that program costs are not minimized by an emissions charge, since it is the most cost-effective strategy. The resolution of this paradox lies in the timing of the emission reductions achieved by an emissions charge strategy. Because the authors of this study chose in their analysis to impose the charge earlier than the command-and-control regulations, the utilities secure the reductions earlier with an emissions charge than with the command-and-control approach. Earlier reductions can only be achieved with earlier financial outlays, which, since all costs are discounted, causes higher program costs for the emissions charge. Unlike the program cost calculation, which gives no credit for early emission reduction, the construction of the particular cost-effectiveness measure chosen by the Congressional Budget Office takes the timing of the emission reduction into account.

One of the difficulties in enacting acid-rain legislation in the United States is its effect on the coal industries in certain key states. To the extent that coal switching becomes the utility strategy of choice, those areas producing high sulfur coal will be hard hit, as they lose business to the low-sulfur coal producing states. To the extent that scrubbers are adopted, however, the use of high-sulfur coal can be continued with lower impacts on employment in those states.

The high-sulfur coal industry is especially important in the states of Illinois, Indiana, Ohio, and Pennsylvania (noted as key states in Table 16.1). In the absence of special acid rain legislation, coal production in these states is expected to be stable over time. With acid rain legislation it could be expected to decline. The size of the decline depends on the strategy chosen.

Job losses in the key high-sulfur coal states increase rather dramatically from 14,100 to 21,900 as the amount of required reduction is increased from 8 to 10 million tons. With a 12-million ton reduction, they drop to 13,400. This reversal is due to the necessity of using scrubbers if this highest level of reduction is to be achieved. Once scrubbers are installed, high-sulfur coal can continue to be used and the impact on the industry is reduced.

Coal mining job losses are a local, not a national, problem. On a nationwide basis coal-mining employment losses would be negligible. Losses in these four key states would be counterbalanced by gains in low-sulfur coal producing areas.

This favorable impact of higher control levels on coal-mining employment in these four key states is counterbalanced by the fact that installing scrubbers is very expensive, as can be easily seen in the program cost, annual cost to utilities and cost-

---

[5]Why, the alert reader might ask, isn't location of the emissions taken into account? Since the objective was stated as securing a reduction in emissions, not achieving an ambient standard, the cost-effective allocation is achieved when marginal control costs are equalized.

effectiveness columns (Table 16.1). One implication is that the cost to the utilities, and, hence, their customers in the form of higher electricity bills would be higher if scrubbers were installed.

The largest electricity rate increases would occur primarily in the midwestern and Appalachian states because that area is responsible for the largest share of excess emissions. These are precisely the states, however, that have traditionally enjoyed lower than average rates, in part because they have not spent what the rest of the country has on reducing emissions. According to the CBO study the higher electricity prices these areas might experience from almost all of the acid rain legislation being considered would still remain below the national average.

Though the emission-charge approach may be the most cost-effective policy, it is not the most popular, particularly in states with a lot of excess emissions. With an emission charge approach utilities not only have to pay the higher equipment and operating costs associated with the reductions, they also have to pay a charge on all uncontrolled emissions. As Table 16.1 indicates, the additional financial burden associated with controlling acid rain by means of an emission charge would be significant. Instead of paying the $3.2 billion for reducing 10 million tons under a command-and-control approach, utilities would be saddled with a $7.7 billion financial burden with an emissions charge. The savings from lower equipment and operating costs achieved because the emission-charge approach is more cost-effective would be more than outweighed by the additional expense of paying the emission charges. What is least cost to society is not, in this case, least cost for the utilities.

These results have triggered a search for approaches to mitigate the adverse consequences of the basic strategies, while obtaining the desired control at as low a cost as possible. We shall subject three of these to more careful scrutiny. All have been actively considered in Congress.

The first mitigating strategy, designed to reduce the adverse impacts on the high-sulfur coal mining states, involves restricting fuel-switching by requiring that 80 percent of the coal purchased by utilities in 1995 be of the same type as purchased in 1985. This rather direct strategy turns out to be a very expensive way to accomplish the objective (Table 16.2). Although it could be expected to save some 9,100 jobs, program costs would rise some $16.3 billion and the cost per ton would rise $168.

The second strategy involves modifying the emissions charge approach by using the revenue to subsidize the installation and operation of scrubbers. Specifically this approach would offer a 90 percent capital subsidy and a 50 percent operating subsidy to utilities purchasing scrubbers. Although, compared to the pure emissions charge approach, this would raise the cost of the program (from $327 to $384 per ton), it would encourage additional emission reductions, lower the costs borne by utilities and customers (from $7.7 billion to $6.4 billion), and maintain the use of high-sulfur coal (saving some 9,400 jobs). Because utilities still have to pay the charge, however, this strategy results in higher annual utility costs than most of the other strategies and, hence, higher electric bills for utility customers.

The third strategy is similar to the second strategy in that it provides the same capital and operating subsidies to utilities installing scrubbers. Instead of financing these subsidies with a tax on emissions, however, it finances them with a tax on electricity

TABLE 16.2 Costs Associated with Strategies to Reduce Sulfur Emissions While Mitigating Adverse Consequences

Strategy	Total Program Cost[1] (Billions of $)	Annual Cost to Utilities[2] (Billions of $)	Key State Employment Change[3] (# of Jobs Lost)	Cost Effectiveness[4] ($ per ton)
10 Million Ton Rollback	$34.5	$3.2	21,900	$360
Rollback with Coal-Switching Restrictions	$50.8	$4.7	12,800	$528
Emissions Charge	$37.5	$7.7	17,900	$327
Modified Emissions Charge	$45.9	$6.4	8,500	$384
Electricity Tax Plus Subsidy	$41.5	$4.8	11,200	$431

Notes: [1]The present value (in 1985 dollars) of additional discounted utility costs incurred (over a current policy benchmark) from 1986–2015, using a real discount rate of 0.03. Any emission charges paid are not included.

[2]The additional cost to utilities of this strategy over the current policy benchmark in 1995 expressed in 1985 dollars. This value includes any emissions charges paid and subtracts any subsidies received.

[3]The additional coal mining job losses expected if this strategy were implemented over the current policy benchmark in the states of Indiana, Illinois, Ohio, and Pennsylvania.

[4]The discounted program cost divided by the annual discounted SO_2 reduction measured over the 1986–2015 period.

Source: Congress of the United States, Congressional Budget Office, *Curbing Acid Rain: Cost, Budget, and Coal-Market Effects* (Washington: U.S. Government Printing Office, 1986) pp. xx, xxii, 23, 53, and 80.

generated by fossil-fuel plants. The tax would be 1 mill (one-tenth of a cent) per kilowatt-hour with collection beginning in 1986 and ending in 1995. Though this particular approach could disperse the cost of emission reduction among all fossil-fuel utilities, rather than concentrating the costs on those utilities responsible for the most emissions, a cost-effectiveness penalty would be paid. The cost per ton of this approach would be $431 as opposed to the $384 associated with the modified emission charge.

What are the major conclusions to be drawn from this analysis? The cost of reducing emissions increases as efforts are made to protect jobs in the high-sulfur coal industries. The electricity rate increases that would be experienced from introduction of even the basic strategies would in general be small and those states experiencing the greatest increases could, even after the increases, be expected to have electricity prices below the national average. These results tend to diminish the case for special treatment of these states based on fairness grounds.

With this in mind, if any effort to ameliorate the political consequences of the basic strategies is necessary, the modified emission charge becomes very attractive. It saves many jobs while paying a small cost-effectiveness penalty. Its one drawback—the higher cost to utilities due to the fees paid on emissions—is not particularly serious because the effects on electricity prices are perceived to be small and concentrated in those states with below-average electricity rates.

Using a tax on emissions as a revenue source rather than a tax on fossil fuel electricity makes sense both on fairness and efficiency grounds. It would be fair because those utilities causing the problem bear the cost. The more emissions injected into the air, the higher the payments would be. This approach would be more efficient as well because the charge would serve as a constant reminder that emissions cause damage and should be reduced whenever reduction is cost-justified. Other schemes relying merely on installing scrubbers would not exert this continual pressure for improvement.

The cost to utilities could be further reduced, while retaining the cost-effectiveness properties of the straight emissions charge, by instituting a sulfur-reduction emissions permit system. In such a system the excess emissions formula would be used to allocate the initial control responsibility. Utilities would then be able to create emission reduction credits for exceeding their assigned control; other utilities could purchase these emission reduction credits to help them meet their assigned control responsibilities. Compared to an emission charge approach, this would cut the cost to utilities almost in half by eliminating the charge on uncontrolled emissions. The drawback, of course, is that this approach generates no revenue for subsidizing the installation of scrubbers, so the employment effects would be the same as the unmodified emissions charge.

GLOBAL POLLUTANTS

Chlorofluorocarbons and Ozone Depletion

In the troposphere, the portion of the atmosphere closest to the earth, ozone (O_3) is a pollutant, and its presence has been linked to agricultural damage as well as to some adverse effects on human health. More will be said about this form of tropospheric pollution in the next chapter.

However, in the stratosphere, the portion of the atmosphere lying just above the troposphere, the rather small amounts of ozone present have a crucial positive role to play in determining the quality of life on the planet. In particular, by absorbing the ultraviolet wavelengths, stratospheric ozone shields people, plants and animals from harmful radiation and, by absorbing infrared radiation, it is a factor in determining the earth's climate.

Chlorofluorocarbons (CFCs) have been implicated in depleting this stratospheric ozone shield as a result of a complicated series of chemical reactions. These highly stable chemical compounds are used as aerosol propellants and in cushioning foams, packaging and insulating foams, industrial cleaning of metals and electronics components, food freezing, medical instrument sterilization, refrigeration for homes and food stores, and air conditioning of automobiles and commercial buildings.

The major known effect of the increased ultraviolet radiation resulting from ozone depletion is an increase in non-melanoma skin cancer. Other potential effects, such as an increase in the more serious melanoma form of skin cancer, suppression of human

TABLE 16.3   Worldwide Cumulative Release of Two Chlorofluorocarbons, Selected Years (Thousands of tons)

Year	CFC-11	CFC-12
1940	0.3	7.3
1950	14.8	148.9
1960	254.4	706.3
1970	1470.2	2691.1
1980	4375.2	6685.1
1983[1]	5164.0	7849.6

Notes: [1]The 1983 data are OECD Secretariat estimates.

Source: Organization for European Co-operation and Development, *OECD Environmental Data* (Paris: OECD, 1985): 41.

immunological systems, damage to plants, eye cancer in cattle and an acceleration of degradation in certain polymer materials, are suspected, but are not as well established.

On June 30, 1978 the U.S. Environmental Protection Agency promulgated a regulation banning the manufacture, processing, and distribution of any "fully halogenated chlorofluoroalkane" for those aerosol propellant uses that are subject to the Toxic Substances Control Act (which is almost all aerosol uses).[6] This ban has reduced the U.S. share from about one half to about one third of worldwide production. Nonetheless worldwide release of the two principal chlorofluorocarbons – CFC-11 and CFC-12 – continues to grow (Table 16.3).

Since further progress on this issue is going to require instituting new controls on non-aerosol uses, a group of economists from the Rand Corporation was commissioned by the USEPA to model the regulatory options. The Palmer, Mooz, Quinn and Wolf (1980) study collected detailed information on the costs of controlling non-aerosol applications of these gases in the United States and constructed a 10-year simulation model to capture the effects of various regulatory approaches. Because chlorofluorocarbons accumulate in the atmosphere (they are expected to remain in the atmosphere for approximately a century), the desired reductions were defined in cumulative terms over the 10-year period.

Three specific policies were considered in the analysis: (1) a system of emission standards for producers or users of these gases, which would force them to adopt specific technologies, (2) a constant emissions charge of $0.50 (in real terms) per pound emitted over the 10 years, and (3) a marketable permit system. In the simulation model all of the approaches were constrained to yield roughly the same cumulative level of emission reduction (Table 16.4).

Because this is an accumulating pollutant, the permits in this case would be designed to allow a one-time release, not a continuing flow as would be the case with permit systems designed to control more conventional pollutants. The holder of a permit would be entitled to emit a fixed quantity of CFCs any time during the ten-year period. By

---

[6]This regulation can be found in 45 FR 43721.

TABLE 16.4 Comparisons of Alternative Policies Having Similar Cumulative Emissions Reductions

	Emissions Reduction (millions of permit pounds)			Total Compliance Costs (millions of 1976 dollars)		
Policy Design	1980	1990	Cumulative 1980–90	1980	1990	Cumulative 1980–90*
Mandatory controls	54.4	102.5	812.3	20.9	37.0	185.3
Economic incentives						
Constant Charge**	54.8	96.9	816.9	12.3	21.8	107.8
Permit System***	36.6	119.4	806.1	5.2	35.0	94.7

*Present value of annual compliance costs, discounted at 11 percent.

**Based on a constant tax rate of $0.50 from 1980 through 1990 (in 1976 dollars).

***Based on permit price or emissions charge rising from $0.25 in 1980 to $0.71 in 1990.

Source: Palmer, Mooz, Quinn and Wolf (p. 225, Table 4.7).

controlling the number of permits issued, the cumulative emission of CFC's would be controlled.

In this type of permit system, the price could be expected to rise over time as the remaining number of unused permits declined. Permit use would typically be high in the early years, while substitution options were being worked out, declining to zero at the end of the ten-year period.

Theory tells us that the constant-emission charge modeled in this study will not be fully cost effective for this problem because it cannot fulfill the condition that price rise over time. A constant real-emission charge will cause marginal costs to be equated within each period, a part of a cost-effective strategy, but it will fail to signal the increasing scarcity of the allowable CFCs over time, leading to a distorted temporal pattern of permit use. To be specific, since the constant charge has to yield approximately the same cumulative level of emissions reduction as the permit system, the charge must be higher than the cost-effective charge in the earlier years and lower than the cost-effective charge in the later years. This, in turn, implies that the constant charge system will allow too little emission in the earlier years and too much in the later years.

The magnitude of the superiority of the permit system in this case can be seen in Table 16.4. It could produce approximately the same amount of reduction as the mandatory controls at about one-half the cost. The relationship of the constant charge to the permit system is exactly as theory would have us expect. Costs are higher for the charge in the earlier years (since less emission is allowed) and lower in the latter years. Over the 10-year period the constant charge system results in a higher present value of costs due to this intertemporal distortion, though the increase is only on the order of 14 percent.

The Rand study also looked at the issue of transfer costs (the payments made to the government by the emitters for each unit of uncontrolled emissions). If an emission charge were used, firms would be faced not only with the cost of purchasing the control equipment or changing the production process, they would have to pay the charges as well. Thus, depending on the relative magnitude of the cost savings from inducing cost-effective behavior and the additional cost imposed by the charges, firms may or may not be better off under this type of economic incentive system than they are under mandatory controls. This can only be determined by discovering the magnitude of the transfer costs.

The Rand study is quite clear that for this particular problem transfer costs are huge. On average, charge payments are some 15 times as large as the expenditures incurred in controlling emissions. Furthermore, they would be rather unequally distributed among the various industries responsible for reducing CFC emissions (Figure 16.1).

One of the aspects of this figure that is particularly noteworthy in Figure 16.1 is the "other" category. This category contains some product areas (rigid insulating foams, liquid fast freezing, and sterilants) where the authors found that no control methods would be introduced, even in the face of an emission charge. For these product areas, the *only* expense is the emission charge and it represents a huge outlay. The manufacturers of these product lines could be expected to be unusually vociferous in their support for a policy of no action or, if action is inevitable, of the traditional regulatory approach which, in all likelihood, would place no controls on them at all.

On October 7, 1980, the USEPA issued an Advance Notice of Proposed Rulemaking announcing that it was considering controlling non-aerosol uses of CFCs, but by mid-1986 no rules implementing this control had been promulgated. Opposition remains strong.

Some European countries have also taken unilateral action. Sweden, a nonproducer of CFCs, was the first country to ban aerosols using CFCs as propellants. West Germany reached an agreement with its industry to reduce CFC usage in aerosols by one-third by 1981. Both the United Kingdom and France have agreed to follow the recommendations of the European Economic Community for a 30 percent reduction in aerosol uses of CFCs.[7]

Coordinated action at the international level beyond the easy reductions in aerosol use has been no more decisive than in the United States. At the urging of the United States, a group of experts prepared a world plan of action in 1977. The United Nations Environmental Program has established a coordinating committee to produce a yearly assessment of ozone layer depletion and its impact. Aside from these actions, little coordinated effort to control the nonaerosol aspect of this important problem has been forthcoming.[8]

The failure to adopt more stringent policies may not be the serious problem it first appears to be. According to a study by Bailey (1982) of CFC control in the U.S., re-

---

[7]For a summary of these policies and a comparative analysis of their severity and timing see Thomas E. Downing and Robert W. Kates, "The International Response to the Threat of Chlorofluorocarbons to Atmospheric Ozone," *The American Economic Review*, Vol. 72, no. 2 (May, 1982): 267–272.

[8]For a description of the international attempts to deal with this issue in a coordinated fashion see James E. Harf and B. Thomas Trout, *The Politics of Global Resources: Energy, Environment, Population, and Food* (Durham: Duke University Press, 1986): 218–19.

FIGURE 16.1 Cumulative Industry Expenses Under Mandatory Controls and Uncompensated Economic Incentives

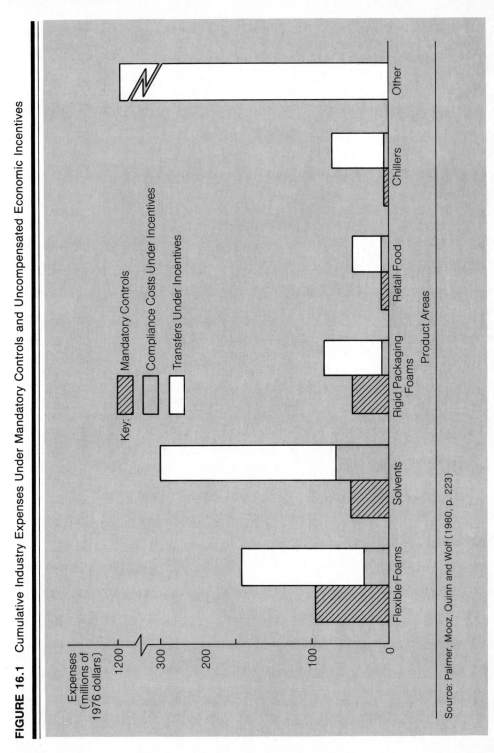

Source: Palmer, Mooz, Quinn and Wolf (1980, p. 223)

stricting aerosol uses seems to be cost-justified on the basis of currently known information about both the potential costs and benefits of CFC regulation, but the same cannot be said about nonaerosol uses. The costs of control arise so rapidly for this type of control that only the highest plausible estimates of damage would justify the expenditure. In this kind of environment the strategy recommended by Bailey is to wait and see. (As Example 16.2 points out, wait and see is not a viable strategy for all global pollution problems; the damage from nuclear winter would be much more immediate.) If better knowledge in the future demonstrates the need for further control, it could still be implemented then without serious consequences.

The Greenhouse Effect

One class of global pollutants, the so-called greenhouse gases, absorb the long-wavelength (infrared) radiation from the earth's surface and atmosphere, trapping heat that would otherwise radiate out into space. The mix and distribution of these gases within the atmosphere is in no small part responsible for both the hospitable climate on the earth and the rather inhospitable climate on other planets. Changing the mix of these gases can affect climate.

Though carbon dioxide is the most abundant and the most studied of these greenhouse gases, there are many others that have similar thermal radiation properties. These include the chlorofluorocarbons, nitrous oxide, methane, and tropospheric ozone. New evidence suggests that these gases may in the future be even more important in modifying climate than the more abundant CO_2.[9]

The current concern over the effect of this class of pollutants on climate arises because emissions of these gases are increasing over time, changing their mix in the atmosphere. Evidence is mounting that by burning fossil fuels, leveling tropical forests, and injecting more of the other greenhouse gases into the atmosphere, humans are creating a thermal blanket capable of trapping enough heat to raise the temperature of the earth's surface. A recent National Research Council report (1983, p.2) concludes that it is likely that atmospheric CO_2 will double during the third quarter of the next century. It further suggests that this doubling of CO_2 concentrations could result in a surface air warming of between 1.5° C and 4.5° C. A 1.5° C increase in the temperature within a century would produce the warmest climate in 6000 years.

The report goes on to suggest the likely consequences of this trend. For the United States as a whole, the effect on agriculture is expected to be small, as positive and negative effects largely cancel each other out. For arid parts of the country which depend on irrigation from scarce water supplies, the picture is more grim. Rising temperatures are expected to reduce the quantity and quality of available water in arid regions.

The sea-level is also expected to rise. If global warming in the 3° to 4° range were to take place over the next hundred years, the authors conclude that a global sea-level

---

[9]See the description of this evidence in Michael Shepard, "The Greenhouse Effect: Earth's Climate in Transition," *EPRI Journal*, Vol. 11, No. 4 (June, 1986): 4–15.

EXAMPLE 16.2

Nuclear Winter

In 1982, a landmark paper suggested that the amount of carbon injected into the atmosphere by a large nuclear war could precipitate rather dramatic and rapid changes in the climate of the earth.[1] The thrust of this concept, dubbed the nuclear winter hypothesis, is that the onset of a nuclear war involving a commitment of weapons well within the current capability of the superpowers would inflict not only the blast and radiation damage, but due to the lingering clouds of particles, would precipitate a third form of heretofore unrecognized damage as well, the dramatic cooling of the earth's surface. By blocking the sunlight, while allowing the infrared radiation to escape, the resulting clouds of particles would lead to a substantial decline in the surface temperature.

The original work supporting the nuclear winter hypothesis was based on a simple model that was somewhat naive, even by the standards of a few years later. Yet subsequent, more complex and realistic models have validated the general thrust of the nuclear winter theory, if not all of its details.

The nuclear winter concept is very important because it changes the role of nuclear war as a strategic option in international politics. No longer can it be assumed that a nation launching a nuclear first strike would survive with only minimal damage. Wind patterns tend to disperse the clouds of particles widely, so the cooling trend would blanket the Northern Hemisphere and, to a somewhat reduced extent, the Southern Hemisphere. No nation would completely escape.

From an economic point of view there is no small amount of irony in the nuclear winter concept. War, in a sense, is the ultimate externality. Indeed the damage imposed on another nation during a war is an intentional means of making the invaded nation subservient to the will of the invader. It has been frequently, and in many cases successfully, used as a means of furthering the aims of aggressor nations. The irony in the nuclear winter concept lies in its suggestion that if the externality is large enough, a substantial portion of the damages will be borne by the aggressor nation; externalities of this magnitude may internalize themselves, at least to some degree.

[1]Crutzen, P.J. and J.W. Birks, "The Atmosphere After a Nuclear War: Twilight at Noon," *Ambio*, Vol. 11 (1982): 114–125.

rise of about 70 centimeters would be likely. This compares with a rise of only 15 centimeters over the last century. Much larger increases (on the order of 15–20 feet) could be expected if the warming caused the West Antarctic Ice Sheet to disintegrate, a low-probability event.

The effects of climate change are expected to fall unequally on the world's people. Regions with a characteristically cold climate, such as large portions of the Soviet Union, may actually benefit from this warming trend, while others that are naturally somewhat

EXAMPLE 16.3

Ethics, Risk-Aversion, and the Greenhouse Effect

Can benefit/cost analysis be trusted to reach an optimal decision about strategies to control the greenhouse effect? There are two sources of concern: (1) the long time period before the damage would be felt, and (2) the uncertainty about the ultimate size of the damage.

A complete loss of the world GNP that is expected 100 years from now, at current interest rates would have a present value of about $1 million. This is trivial in comparison to the present value of potential costs of controlling the greenhouse effect because they would be spent in the near future. Due to discounting, events that happen so far in the future have little weight in decisions where costs are born in the present. Although maximizing the present value of net benefits guarantees that the pie to be shared among generations is as large as possible, it does not automatically guarantee that the slices of pie are actually shared equitably among generations. The logical conclusion of this form of argument is that future generations may be inadequately protected from an ethical point of view by benefit/cost analysis.

A second concern deals with risk-aversion. As pointed out in Chapter 4, conventional benefit/cost analysis assumes risk-neutrality. Is risk-neutrality a credible assumption in the face of a potential catastrophe? Common sense suggests that most people react to uncertainty by acting in a cautious, risk-averse manner. Should our governments act any differently?

Concluding that conventional benefit/cost analysis is ethically flawed when applied to the greenhouse problem, d'Arge, Schulze, and Brookshire (1980, 1982) have proposed a modest alternative. In particular, they proposed to establish whether the current generation would be willing to pay some amount of money to avoid climate modification. Relying on three samples of college students as a pilot study, they did find a willingness to spend current income to avoid an environmental catastrophe even if it would ocur in all likelihood after the respondent's death. Though these samples can hardly be called representative of the population at large, the amounts per person were sufficiently large that they would justify a much larger commitment of current resources to control the problem than would be justified by a conventional benefit/cost analysis.

Sources: Ralph d'Arge, William Schultze, and David Brookshire, "Benefit-Cost Valuation of Long Term Effects: The Case of CO_2," a paper prepared for the "Workshop on the Methodology for Economic Impact Analysis," April 24–25, 1980, Fort Lauderdale, Florida; and Ralph C. d'Arge, William D. Schultze and David S. Brookshire, "Carbon Dioxide and Intergenerational Choice," *The American Economic Review,* Vol. 72, No. 2 (May, 1982): 251–256.

arid may see marginal agricultural land become unproductive desert, triggering a diminished capacity to raise food. These differences could prove quite divisive in the search for solutions.

The greenhouse effect poses a particularly difficult problem for our economic and political institutions to handle. The troposphere is a public good. Its scarcity is not reflected in rising prices; it is not automatically rationed only to the highest valued uses. The damage caused by greenhouse pollutants is an externality in both space and time. Emitters impose costs not only on residents of other countries, but on subsequent generations as well. Market allocations can certainly be expected to violate the efficiency criterion and may well violate the sustainability criterion as well (Example 16.3).

The first step in attempting to chart a course for the public sector is to discover just how serious the problem is and to ascertain the costs of being wrong, either by acting too hastily or by procrastination. Due to the rampant uncertainties in virtually every logical link in the chain from human activities to subsequent consequences, no one at this juncture can state unequivocally how serious the damage will be. We can, however, begin to elaborate the range of possibilities and see how sensitive the outcomes are to choices before us.

One of the major uncertainties which we must deal with is associated with forecasting what emissions of CO_2 will be for sustained periods into the future. That will depend on the level of economic and population growth, the amount of energy needed to support this growth and the form of energy chosen to satisfy this need. Nordhaus and Yohe (1983) have put together a very interesting global energy model to assist in the process of tracing out the implications of what we know and don't know about the problem.

The Nordhaus-Yohe (N–Y) model is a highly aggregative representation of the world economy and energy sector. It relates growth in the Gross World Product (GWP) to the use of labor, and both fossil fuel and non-fossil fuel energy. The model explicitly incorporates the degree to which nonenergy inputs (such as insulation or radial tires) can be substituted for energy inputs and the substitution possibilities between fossil and nonfossil forms of energy. Prices play a crucial role in the model both in stimulating greater efficiency of energy use and in dictating the form of energy used.

In contrast to other models forecasting carbon dioxide buildup, the N–Y model explicitly incorporates uncertainty in a rather ingenious way. Rather than use "best guess" estimates for all of the parameters and variables subject to some uncertainty, leading to a single forecast, this model generates a range of paths which reflect the underlying uncertainties. By associating subjective probability distributions with each of the values assumed for the parameters and variables and running a large number of scenarios, it is possible to gain not only an appreciation for the possible range of outcomes, but also their likelihood (Figure 16.2). The numbers on the right-hand side indicate the mean concentration for the year 2100 and the extreme high and low outcomes. In essence, the model translates subjective probability estimates for variables and parameters into probability estimates for CO_2 outcomes.

One chief conclusion of the N–Y model is that there is a 1-in-4 probability that doubling of the carbon dioxide concentration will occur before 2050 and a 1-in-20 possibility that doubling will occur before 2035. The median estimate of the year in which doubling will occur is 2065. Notice that the effect of the uncertainty is to raise the question of when doubling will occur, not whether it will occur.

Nordhaus and Yohe also conducted a series of sensitivity analyses to establish which uncertainties seemed to make the most difference in determining the projected outcome. By far the most important factor was the ease of substitution between fossil and nonfossil fuels. The greater the ease of substitution, the lower the projected rate of carbon

FIGURE 16.2   Atmospheric Concentration (Parts per Million) of Carbon Dioxide for 100 Randomly Drawn Emission Runs.

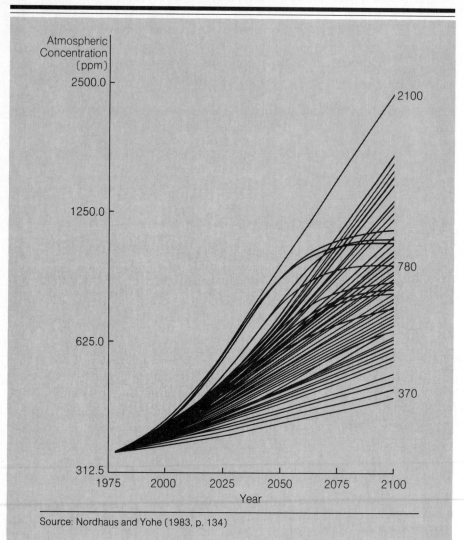

Source: Nordhaus and Yohe (1983, p. 134)

dioxide increase. This finding is particularly important for establishing energy research budgets; to the extent that future evidence suggests a need to restrict fossil fuel use, it will be important to assure that it will be relatively easy to substitute nonfossil for fossil fuels. We can provide that assurance by conducting research now on ways to ease the transition. Other particularly important factors uncovered by the study included general productivity growth and trends in the real cost of producing energy. The least important factor was the total amount of fossil fuels available.

How about the effectiveness of alternative policies? Very little analysis has been conducted in this area. Nordhaus and Yohe do present some tentative estimates of the effect of a $10 per ton coal-equivalent tax on all fossil fuels. Their conclusion is that since such a tax would produce only a modest reduction in CO_2 concentrations, to reduce concentrations significantly would require very stringent policies.

Unilateral solutions will not solve this problem. Nations acting on their own to reduce emissions while others take no action will incur costs while receiving very little benefit. Successful negotiation of an agreement among nations seems to be the only way a worldwide, long-term commitment of the magnitude needed could be achieved.

Unfortunately, the prognosis for agreements of this sort is not good. Not only is our historical track record on negotiated international agreements rather dismal, in this case the objectives of the major participants do not coincide. For example it is commonly believed that both Canada and the Soviet Union, two major emitters of carbon dioxide, may actually benefit from global warming due to their colder climates. If this turns out to be an accurate representation, their enthusiasm for adopting stringent controls will be limited. Meanwhile, many of the countries which stand to lose a great deal from global warming are not major contributors of CO_2 emissions.

SUMMARY

Regional pollutants differ from local pollutants chiefly in the distance they are transported in the air. Whereas local pollutants damage the environment near the emission site, regional pollutants can cause damage far from the site of emission. Some substances, such as sulfur oxides, nitrogen oxides and ozone, are both local and regional pollutants.

As the zone of influence of pollutants extends beyond local boundaries, the political difficulties of implementing comprehensive, cost-effective control measures increase. Pollutants crossing political boundaries impose external costs; neither emitters nor the nations within which they emit have the proper incentives to institute efficient control measures.

Acid rain is a case in point. Sulfate and nitrate deposition has caused problems both among regions within countries and between countries. In the United States the Clean Air Act has had a distinctly local focus. To control local pollution problems, state governments required the installation of tall stacks to dilute the pollution before it hit ground level. In the process a high proportion of the emissions were exported to other areas, reaching the ground hundreds of miles from the point of injection. A focus on local control made the regional problem worse.

Finding solutions to the acid rain problem has been very difficult because those bearing the costs of further control are usually different parties than those who will benefit from the control. In the United States, for example, Congress has been focusing on securing an additional 8–12 million ton reduction of sulfur oxide emissions, but has not yet been able to work out the details due to opposition from the midwestern and Appalachian states that would bear the brunt of the costs. Stumbling blocks include the higher electricity prices that would result from the control and the employment impacts on those states which would suffer losses of jobs in the high-sulfur coal mining industry.

Economic analysis of the policy options indicates that the cost of reducing emissions rises dramatically as the amount of reduction is increased from 10 million tons to 12 million tons. Economic incentive approaches, as expected from Chapter 14, would be the most cost-effective, but their superiority is not overwhelming. The command-and-control strategy, which allocates responsibility based on an excess emissions formula, is only mildly less cost-effective. All attempts to reduce the adverse impacts of control on the midwestern and Appalachian states exact a cost-effectiveness penalty. This penalty is highest for restricting coal-switching and lowest for a modified version of an approach based on a charge on uncontrolled sulfur emissions coupled with capital and operating subsidies for the installation and operation of scrubbers. The rise in electricity prices that could be anticipated from the enactment of acid rain legislation is estimated to be small; furthermore, the greatest increases would be concentrated in those states having lower-than-average prices.

Chlorofluorocarbons, the first of the discussed global pollutants, are a problem because they have been implicated in the destruction of the stratospheric ozone shield that protects the earth's surface from harmful ultraviolet radiation. Since this is an accumulating pollutant, an efficient response to this problem would involve declining use over time. This could be accomplished either by an emission charge on CFCs that rises over time or a permit system allowing a fixed amount of emissions. Studies of nonaerosol uses of CFCs indicate that economic incentive approaches such as these could achieve the emissions target at about one-half the cost of regulatory standards. These studies also indicate, however, that an emissions charge would impose a large additional financial burden on the emitters. (The emission charge payments on uncontrolled emissions would be 15 times as large as the payments for controlling the pollution.) This financial burden could be avoided with a grandfathered permit system.

Nuclear winter is a somewhat unique global pollutant both because of the source of the pollution (war as opposed to commercial or residential emission) and the fact that the damage is both global and immediate. For this global pollutant the emitter is separated by neither space nor time from the consequences of the nuclear incident. This internalization of the costs of nuclear winter may ultimately provide the basis for international agreements limiting the size of the nuclear arsenal.

The greenhouse effect, or global warming due to changing the composition of atmospheric gases, is a different story. For this pollutant the emitters are separated in time from the consequence of their emission. A doubling of carbon dioxide emissions is expected to occur well into the next century when virtually all of the current decision makers will have passed away. The current generation bears the cost of control while future generations would reap the benefits. Furthermore, international agreements are made more difficult by the fact that some countries may be benefited, not harmed, by global warming, diminishing even further their incentive to control.

Economic analysis of this problem suggests that the most important uncertainty in establishing the potential severity of the problem is the ease with which fossil and nonfossil fuels can be substituted in the future. While the analysis suggests that drastic action is not called for yet, the next few years should be used fruitfully to gain more knowledge about the problem and do everything possible to assure that substitution will be easy if the time for action comes. During the waiting period, options must not only be preserved, they must be enhanced.

Responding in a timely and effective fashion to global and regional pollution problems will not be easy. Our political institutions are not configured in such a way as to make decision-making on a global scale easy. International organizations exist at the pleasure of the nations they serve. Only time will tell if the mechanism of international agreements will prove equal to the task.

ADDITIONAL REFERENCES

Bailey, Martin J., "Risks, Costs, and Benefits of Fluorocarbon Regulation," *The American Economic Review,* Vol. 72, No. 2 (May, 1982): 247–250.

Croker, Thomas D., ed., *Economic Perspectives on Acid Deposition Control* (Boston: Butterworth Publishers, 1984).

Cumberland, John H., *Economics of Managing Chlorofluorocarbons: Stratospheric Ozone and Climate Issues* (Baltimore: Johns Hopkins University Press, 1982).

National Research Council, *Changing Climate: Report of the Carbon Dioxide Assessment Committee* (Washington: National Academy Press, 1983).

Nordhaus, William, "How Fast Should We Graze the Global Commons?" *The American Economic Review,* Vol. 72, No. 2, (May, 1982): 242–246.

Nordhaus, William D., and Gary W. Yohe, "Future Paths of Energy and Carbon Dioxide Emissions" in National Research Council, *Changing Climate: Report of the Carbon Dioxide Assessment Committee* (Washington: National Academy Press, 1983): 87–153.

PROBLEMS

1. Explain why an acid rain policy using emission charge revenue to provide capital and operating subsidies for scrubbers is less cost-effective than an emission charge policy alone.

2. The transfer costs associated with an emission charge approach to controlling chlorofluorocarbon pollution are unusually large in comparison to other pollutants. What circumstances would be favorable to high transfer costs?

CHAPTER SEVENTEEN

Control of Mobile-Source Air Pollution

*There are two things you shouldn't watch being made, sausage
and law.*
ANONYMOUS

INTRODUCTION

Though they emit many of the same pollutants as stationary sources, mobile sources
of pollution require a different policy approach. These differences arise from the mobility
of the source, the number of vehicles involved, and the role of the automobile in the
American lifestyle.

Mobility has two major impacts on policy. On the one hand, pollution is partly
caused by the temporary location of the source — a case of being in the wrong place
at the wrong time. This occurs, for example, during rush hour in metropolitan areas.
Since the cars have to be where the people are, relocating them — as might be done
with electric power plants — is not a viable strategy. On the other hand, it is more difficult
to tailor vehicle emission rates to local pollution patterns, since any particular vehicle
may end up in many different urban and rural areas during the course of its useful life.

Mobile sources are also more numerous than stationary sources. While there are
approximately 27,000 major stationary sources, there are well over 100 million vehicles
on American roadways. Enforcement is obviously more difficult the larger the number
of sources being controlled.

Whereas stationary sources generally are large and run by professional managers,
automobiles are small and run by amateurs. Their small size makes it more difficult
to control emissions without affecting performance, while their amateur ownership makes
it more likely that emission control will deteriorate over time due to a lack of depen-
dable maintenance and care.

These complications might lead us to conclude that perhaps we should ignore mobile sources and concentrate our control efforts solely on stationary sources. Unfortunately, that is not possible because, as Table 17.1 indicates, though each individual vehicle represents a minuscule part of the problem, mobile sources collectively represent a significant proportion of three criteria pollutants—ozone, carbon monoxide, and nitrogen dioxide. (Hydrocarbons and nitrogen dioxide are precursors of ozone.)

For two of these—ozone and nitrogen dioxide—the process of reaching attainment has been particularly slow. With the increased use of diesel engines, mobile sources are becoming responsible for a rising proportion of particulate emissions and, though not reflected in Table 17.1, vehicles which burn leaded gasoline are a major source of airborne lead.

Since it is necessary to control mobile sources, what other policy options exist? What points of control exist and what are the advantages and disadvantages of each? In exercising control over these sources, the government must first specify the agent charged with the responsibility for the reduction. The obvious candidates are the manufacturer and the owner-driver. The balancing of this responsibility should depend on a comparative analysis of costs and benefits, with particular reference to such factors as (1) the number of agents to be regulated; (2) the rate of deterioration while in use; (3) the life expectancy of automobiles; and (4) the availability, effectiveness, and cost of programs to reduce emissions at the point of production and at the point of use.

Although automobiles are numerous and ubiquitous, they are manufactured by a small number of firms. Since it is easier and less expensive to administer a system that controls relatively few sources, regulation at the point of production has considerable appeal.

There are, however, problems associated with limiting controls solely to the point of production. If the factory-controlled emission rate of the automobile deteriorates

TABLE 17.1 Mobile Source Contributions to Nationwide Pollutant Emission Levels in 1977

Vehicle Type	Contribution to Total Pollutant Levels (in %)			
	Particulates	Carbon Monoxide	Hydrocarbons	Nitrogen Oxides
Automobiles	3.85	50.73(68)[a]	23.65(69)[a]	16.03(55)[a]
Light trucks	0.74	10.75(14)[a]	5.64(16)[a]	3.85(13)[a]
Heavy trucks	1.62	13.93(18)[a]	4.97(15)[a]	9.07(32)[a]
Motorcycles	0	0.64	0.74	0
Off-Highway	0.79	5.88	1.99	5.57
Rail	0.47	0.26	0.64	3.06
Air	0.54	0.73	0.78	0.48
Vessels	0.24	1.48	1.59	0.63
Total	8.38	83.52	39.86	38.7

[a]Figures in parentheses are relative percentages of total automobiles, light trucks, and heavy trucks.

Source: National Commission on Air Quality, *To Breathe Clean Air* (Washington, D.C.: U.S. Government Printing Office, 1981), p. 192, Table 16.

during normal usage, control at the point of production may buy only temporary emission reduction. Though this problem of emission-control durability can be combatted with warranty and recall provisions, the costs of these supporting programs have to be balanced against the costs of local control.

Since automobiles are durable, *new* vehicles make up only a relatively small percentage of the total fleet of vehicles. Therefore, control at the point of production, which affects only new equipment, takes longer to produce a given reduction in aggregate emissions since newer, controlled cars replace old vehicles very slowly. Thus control at the point of production would produce emission reductions more slowly than a program that could reduce emissions from used vehicles as well as new vehicles.

Some possible means of reducing mobile-source pollution cannot be accomplished by regulating emissions at the point of production because they involve choices made by the owner-driver. The point of production strategy is oriented toward reducing the amount of emissions *per mile driven* in a particular type of car, but only the owner can decide what kind of car to drive, as well as when and where to drive it.

These are not trivial concerns. Diesel automobiles, buses, trucks, and motorcycles emit rather different amounts of pollutants than do gasoline-powered automobiles. By changing the mix of vehicles on the road, the amount and type of emissions can be affected even if passenger miles are not changed.

Where and when the car is driven is also important. Since clustered emissions cause higher concentration levels than dispersed emissions, driving in urban areas causes more environmental damage than driving in rural areas. Local control strategies could internalize these location costs, while a uniform national strategy focusing solely on the point of production could not.

Timing of emissions is particularly important because conventional commuting patterns lead to a clustering of emissions during the morning and evening rush hours. Indeed, plots of pollutant concentrations in urban areas during an average day typically produce a graph with two peaks corresponding to the two rush hours.[1] Since high concentrations are more dangerous than low concentrations, some spreading over the twenty-four hour period could also prove beneficial.

FEDERAL POLICY TOWARD MOBILE SOURCES

Legislative History

Concern about mobile-source pollution originated in Southern California in the early 1950s following a path-breaking study by Dr. A.J. Haagen-Smit of the California Institute of Technology. The study by Dr. Haagen-Smit identified motor-vehicle emissions as a key culprit in forming the photochemical smog for which Southern California was becoming infamous.

---

[1]The exception is ozone formed by a chemical reaction between hydrocarbons and nitrogen oxides in the presence of sunlight. Since, for the evening rush-hour emissions, there are too few hours of sunlight remaining for the chemical reactions to be completed, ozone frequently exhibits a single peaked graph.

During the early 1960s while Congress held hearings, required reports, and appointed committees, California passed legislation requiring that exhaust control devices be installed on all new cars sold in California one year after the state had certified that at least two acceptable devices were available at reasonable cost. By 1964 the state had certified four devices and exhaust-control devices became mandatory for the 1966 model year.

The Clean Air Act Amendments of 1965 set national standards for hydrocarbon and carbon-monoxide emissions from automobiles to take effect during 1968. Interestingly, the impetus for this act came not only from the scientific data on the effects of automobile pollution, but also from the automobile industry itself. The industry saw uniform federal standards as a way to avoid a situation in which every state passed its own set of standards. Producing fifty different cars for fifty different states was something the auto industry wanted to avoid. This pressure was successful in that the law prohibits all states except California from setting their own standards.

By 1970 there was general dissatisfaction with the slow progress being made on air-pollution control in general and automobile pollution in particular. In a "get tough" mood as it developed the Clean Air Act Amendments of 1970, Congress required new emissions standards which would reduce emissions by 90 percent below their uncontrolled levels. This reduction was to have been achieved by 1975 for hydrocarbon and carbon-monoxide emissions and by 1976 for nitrogen dioxide. It was generally agreed at the time the Act was passed, the technology to meet the standards did not exist. By passing this tough Act, Congress hoped to force the development of an appropriate technology.

It did not work out that way. The following years ushered in a series of extensions of the deadlines. In 1972 the automobile manufacturers requested a one-year delay in the implementation of the standards. The Administrator of EPA denied the request and was taken to court. At the conclusion of the litigation in April 1973, the administrator granted a one-year delay in the 1975 deadline for the hydrocarbon and carbon monoxide standards. Subsequently, in July, 1973, a one-year delay was granted for nitrogen oxides as well.[2]

About this time two additional factors intervened. First, the OPEC embargo occurred, resulting in substantially higher crude oil prices. Second, Congress became aware of the trade-off between emissions control and fuel efficiency that characterized the control devices at that time. In June 1974, an additional one-year delay in the enforcement of all emissions standards was granted by Congress as part of an energy bill, the Energy Supply and Coordination Act.

Meanwhile, for cars sold in California, the manufacturers had begun installing catalytic converters to meet that state's stricter standards. The administrator of EPA, acting on some preliminary research, feared that widespread introduction of catalytic converters would increase sulfur-oxide emissions. As a result, he granted a further one-

---

[2] The only legal basis for granting an extension was technological infeasibility. Only shortly before the extension was granted, the Japanese Honda CVCC engine was certified as meeting the original standards. We can wonder what the outcome would have been if the company meeting the standards was American rather than Japanese.

year delay for the attainment of the hydrocarbon and carbon-monoxide emission standards. Though EPA subsequently concluded that the sulfur oxide problem from catalytic converters was not serious, by the time that conclusion was reached, the standards had been delayed three times and the original 1975–76 standards were scheduled for 1978. Even that schedule was not adhered to. In the Clean Air Act Amendments of 1977, Congress granted further extensions of two years while tightening the standards.

Structure of the Federal Approach

The current approach to mobile-source air pollution represents a blend of controlling emissions at the point of manufacture with controlling emissions from vehicles in use. The emission standards at the factory are administered through a certification program and an associated enforcement program.

Certification Program.   The certification program tests prototypes of car models for conformity to federal standards. During the test a prototype vehicle from each engine family is driven 50,000 miles on a test track or a dynamometer, following a mandated strict pattern of fast and slow driving, idling, and hot-and-cold starts. The manufacturers run the tests and record emission levels at 5000 mile intervals. If the vehicle satisfies the standards over the entire 50,000 miles, it passes the deterioration portion of the certification test.

The second step in the certification process is to apply less demanding (and less expensive) tests to three additional prototypes in the same engine family. Emission readings are taken at the 0 and 4000 mile points and then, using the deterioration rate established in the first portion of the test, are projected to the 50,000 mile point. If those projected emission levels meet the standards, then that engine family is given a certificate of conformity. Only engine families with a certificate of conformity are allowed to be sold.

Associated Enforcement Programs.   The certification program is complemented by an associated enforcement program which contains assembly-line testing, as well as recall and anti-tampering procedures and warranty provisions. To ensure that the prototype vehicles are representative, EPA tests a statistically representative sample of assembly-line vehicles. If these tests reveal that more than 40 percent of the cars do not conform with federal standards, the certificate may be suspended or revoked.

EPA has also been given the power to require manufacturers to recall and remedy manufacturing defects that cause emissions to exceed federal standards. If EPA uncovers a defect, it usually requests the manufacturer to recall vehicles for corrective action. If the manufacturer refuses, EPA can order a recall. As of May 10, 1978, EPA had negotiated the voluntary recall of about 9.3 million cars and had ordered the recall of about 2.7 million more.[3]

---

[3]Arnold W. Reitze, Jr., "Controlling Automotive Air Pollution through Inspection and Maintenance Programs," *The George Washington Law Review* 47 (May 1979): 705–739.

The Clean Air Act also requires two separate types of warranty provisions. These warranty provisions are designed to ensure that a manufacturer will have an incentive to produce a vehicle which, if properly maintained, will meet emission standards over its useful life. The first of these provisions requires the vehicle to be free of defects that could cause the vehicle to fail to meet the standards. Any defects discovered by consumers would be fixed at the manufacturer's expense under this provision.

The second warranty provision requires the manufacturer to bring any car which fails an inspection and maintenance test (described below) during its first 24 months or 24,000 miles (whichever occurs first) into conformance with the standards. After the 24 months or 24,000 miles, the warranty is limited solely to the replacement of devices specifically designed for emission control, such as catalytic converters. This further protection lasts sixty months.

The earliest control devices used to control pollution had two characteristics that rendered them susceptible to tampering: they adversely affected vehicle performance, and they were relatively easy to circumvent. As a result, the Clean Air Act Amendments of 1970 prohibited anyone from tampering with an emission-control system prior to the sale of an automobile, but, curiously, prohibited only dealers and manufacturers from tampering after the sale. The 1977 amendments extended the coverage of the post sale tampering prohibition to motor-vehicle repair facilities and fleet operators.

Lead. Section 211 of the Clean Air Act provides EPA with the authority to regulate lead and any other fuel additives used in gasoline. Under this provision gasoline suppliers are required to make unleaded gasoline available. By ensuring the availability of unleaded gasoline, this regulation sought to reduce the amount of airborne lead, as well as to protect the effectiveness of the catalytic converter, which is poisoned by lead.[4] Penalties are assessed on distributors (but not individual owners) for supplying catalyst-equipped vehicles with leaded gasoline.

On March 7, 1985, EPA issued a regulation imposing strict new standards on the allowable lead content in refined gasoline. This regulation required further reductions from the then existing 1.10 grams per leaded gallon (gplg) to 0.50 gplg in July 1985 and to 0.10 gplg in January 1986. These actions followed a highly publicized series of research findings by doctors on the rather severe medical consequences, particularly to small children, of even rather low levels of atmospheric lead.

Local Responsibilities. The Clean Air Act Amendments of 1977 recognized the existence of nonattainment areas. Special requirements were placed on control authorities to bring nonattainment areas into attainment. Since many of the nonattainment areas received that designation for pollutants generated by mobile sources, local authorities in those areas were required to take further actions to reduce emissions from mobile sources.

---

[4]Three tankfuls of leaded gasoline used in a car equipped with a catalytic converter will produce a 50 percent reduction in the effectiveness of the catalytic converter.

Measures that local authorities are authorized to use include requiring new cars registered in that area to satisfy the more stringent California standard (with EPA approval) and the development of comprehensive transportation plans. These plans could include measures such as on-street parking controls, road charges, and measures to reduce the number of vehicle-miles traveled.

In nonattainment regions that could not meet the primary standard for photochemical oxidants, carbon monoxide, or both by December 31, 1982, control authorities could delay attainment until December 31, 1987, provided they agreed to a number of additional restrictions. For the purposes of this chapter, the most important of these is the requirement that each region gaining this extension must establish a vehicle inspection and maintenance (I&M) program for emissions.

By mid-1980, 29 states were required to establish an I&M program. Arizona, California, Colorado, Georgia, New Jersey, New York, Oregon, Rhode Island, Virginia, and Washington already had operating programs in nonattainment areas.

The objective of the inspection and maintenance program is to identify vehicles that are violating the standards and to bring them into compliance, to deter tampering, and to encourage regular routine maintenance. Because the federal test procedure used in the certification process is much too expensive to use on a large number of vehicles, shorter, less expensive tests were developed specially for the I&M programs. Because of the expense and questionable effectiveness of these programs, they are one of the most controversial components of the policy package used to control mobile-source emissions.

AN ECONOMIC AND POLITICAL ASSESSMENT

The Timing of Attainment

Perhaps the most glaring deficiency in the 1970 amendments occurred when an infeasible compliance schedule for meeting the ambient standards was established for mobile-source pollutants. The chief instruments to be used by local areas in meeting these standards were the new-car emission standards. Because these applied only to new cars, and because new cars make up such a small proportion of the total fleet, significant emission reductions were not experienced until well after the deadline for meeting the ambient standards. This created a very difficult situation for local areas, since they were forced to meet the ambient standards prior to the time that the emission standards (the chief sources of reduction) were having much of an impact.

The only strategy open to them was the development of local strategies to make up the difference. Recognizing the difficulties the states faced, EPA granted an extension in the deadline for submitting the transportation plans that would spell out the manner in which the standards would be reached. This extension was challenged in court by the Natural Resources Defense Council[5], who successfully argued that EPA did not

---

[5]475 F. 2d 968 (1973).

have the authority to grant the extension. Faced with the court's decision, EPA was forced to reject the state implementation plans submitted by most states as inadequate, because those plans could not ensure attainment by the deadlines. Because the law clearly states that EPA must substitute its own plan for an inadequate plan, EPA found itself thrust into the unfamiliar and unpleasant role of defining transportation-control plans for states with rejected SIP's.

There were two main problems with this development: EPA was not administratively equipped either in terms of staff or resources to design and implement these plans; and because of the severity of the mismatch between deadline and implementation, there was very little that EPA could have done, even if the staff and resources had been available.

EPA made a valiant but futile attempt to meet its statutory responsibilities. It concluded that the best way to resolve its dilemma was to work backwards from the needs to the transportation plans and, once the plans were defined, to require states to implement and enforce them. To ensure state cooperation, they set up a system of civil penalties to be applied against states that failed to cooperate.

The resulting plans were virtually unenforceable because they were so severe. For example, in order to meet the ambient standard in Los Angeles by the deadline, the plan designed by EPA called for an 82-percent reduction in gasoline consumption in the Los Angeles basin. The reduction was to be achieved through gasoline rationing during the six months of the year when the smog problem is most severe. In publishing the plan, EPA Administrator William Ruckelshaus acknowledged that it was infeasible and would effectively destroy the economy of the state if implemented, but argued that he had no other choice under the law.

The states raised a number of legal challenges to this approach.[6] These were never really resolved in the courts by the time Congress revised the Act in 1977. The Clean Air Act Amendments of 1977 remedied the situation by extending the deadlines.

The lesson from this episode seems to be that tougher laws do not necessarily result in more rapid compliance. By creating a statutory requirement that could not be met, virtually nothing was accomplished as the various parties attempted to fashion a resolution through the courts.

Technology Forcing and Sanctions

This lesson was underscored by EPA's experience in gaining compliance with the national emission standards by the automobile manufacturers. The industry was able to obtain a number of delays in meeting those standards. The law was so tough that it was difficult to enforce within the time schedule envisioned by Congress.

This problem was intensified by the sanctions established by the act to ensure compliance. They were so brutal that EPA was unwilling to use them; they did not represent a credible threat. For example, when an engine family failed the certification test,

---

[6]These are described in Robert Wigington, "The Implementation of Transportation Controls Under the 1977 Clean Air Act Amendments," *University of Colorado Law Review* 50 (1979): 251–258.

EXAMPLE 17.1

Setting the National Automobile Emission Standards

A set of national emission standards provide the backbone of the 1970 Clean Air Act Amendments. It is natural to imagine that these standards were set after a careful weighing of the benefits and costs of various levels, but the manner in which they were established was quite different. The analysis used to justify the standards could have been accomplished on the back of an envelope.

The basic approach was developed by D. Barth. His calculations relied on a rollback model that simply assumes that a linear relationship exists between emission reductions and reductions in pollutant concentrations. To initiate the analysis, he needed to pick a year in which the standards would be met—1990 was chosen. He then needed to calculate how much emissions would grow in the absence of controls and in the presence of more cars, more miles traveled, and so on. He assumed emissions would grow 2.18 times between 1967 and 1990. Finally, he needed to choose an actual air-quality level in 1967 and, for that, he chose the highest ambient pollution-concentration reading during the year in any city. These pieces of information he then combined in a formula:

$$DER = [1.00 - \frac{(2.18 \times 1967\ Max) - DL}{(2.18 \times 1967\ Max) - BL}] \times 1967\ Rate$$

where DER is the desired emissions rate (in grams per mile), 1967 Max is the maximum ambient concentration, DL is the desired ambient concentration, BL is the background concentration level, and 1967 rate is the actual emission rate (in grams per mile) that prevailed in 1967.

These calculations have been widely criticized, not only for ignoring costs, but also because the numbers which went into the formula seem excessively conservative. The use of the worst concentration level, for example, does set the standard at a level sufficiently stringent to solve the problem in the most polluted city.

Furthermore, since the most polluted cities are heavily congested, it is unlikely that traffic (and emissions) could grow 2.18 times! To a limited extent these errors were counterbalanced by the implicit assumption that emission rates achieved would not deteriorate with use, an assumption which historically has not been valid.

Source: This example was based on D. S. Barth, "Federal Motor Vehicle Emission Goals for CO, HC and NO$_x$. Based on Desired Air Quality Levels," in *Air Pollution 1970, Part 5*, U.S. Senate Committee on Public Works (Washington, D.C., 1970); and Eugene P. Seskin, "Automobile Air Pollution Policy," in *Current Issues in U.S. Environmental Policy*, Paul R. Portney, ed. (Baltimore: Johns Hopkins University Press, 1978): 68–104.

the law is quite specific in stating that vehicle classes not certified as conforming with the standards cannot be sold! Given the importance of the automobile industry in the American economy, this sanction was not likely to be applied. As a result there were considerable pressures on EPA to avoid the sanctions by defining more easily satisfied procedures for certification and by setting sufficiently flexible deadlines that no manufacturer would fail to meet them.

Differentiated Regulation

In controlling the emissions of both mobile sources and stationary sources, the brunt of the reduction effort is borne by new sources. This raises the cost of new sources, and from the purchaser's point of view, increases the attractiveness of used cars relative to new ones. The benefit from increased control is a public good and therefore is not able to be appropriated exclusively by the new-car purchasers. One result of a strategy focusing on new sources would be to depress the demand for new cars while enhancing that for used cars.

Apparently this is precisely what happened in the United States.[7] In response to the higher cost of new cars, people held onto old automobiles longer. This has produced several unfortunate side effects. Since new cars are substantially cleaner than older cars, emission reductions have been delayed. In effect, this shift in composition is equivalent to a setback of three to four years in the timetable for reducing emissions.[8] Also, since older cars get worse gas mileage, gasoline consumption is higher than it would otherwise be. The focus on new sources is, to some extent, inevitable; the lesson to be drawn is that by ignoring these behavioral responses to differentiated regulation, the policy maker is likely to expect results sooner than is likely to occur.

Uniformity of Control

With the exception of the California standards, which are more stringent, the Clean Air Act requires the same emission standards on all cars. Example 17.1 shows how these standards were established. The required levels of control were set at sufficiently stringent levels to meet the special pollution problems existing in Los Angeles or in high-altitude cities such as Denver.[9] As a result, many of the costs borne by people in other parts of the country—particularly rural areas—do not yield much in the way of benefits.

This sounds like an inefficient policy and, indeed, most of the studies which have been accomplished indicate that this is so. One such study was accomplished by the U.S. Ad Hoc Committee on the Cumulative Regulatory Effects on the Cost of Automobile Transportation (known popularly as the RECAT report). The committee estimated annual benefits from the original 1975–76 standards to be in the interval $3.5 to $9.1 billion, while the costs were estimated as $10.1 billion per year. A later report

---

[7]See Howard K. Gruenspecht, "Differentiated Regulation: The Case of Auto Emission Standards," *The American Economic Review* 72 (May 1982): 328–331.

[8]Crandall, et. al. (1986, p. 96).

[9]There is now considerable evidence that in-use emission rates are substantially higher in high altitudes. See National Commission for Air Quality, *To Breathe Clean Air* (Washington, D.C.: U.S. Government Printing Office, 1981): 203–206.

published by the National Academy of Sciences and the National Academy of Engineer-ing estimated the discounted present value of benefits and costs over the period 1975–2101. They estimated the costs at $126 billion and the benefits at $137 billion. Thus, the first study found negative net benefits, while the latter found positive but small net benefits.

Positive net benefits, of course, are not synonymous with efficiency, although negative net benefits do imply inefficiency. One study by Schwing, Southworth, Busick, and Jackson [1980], researchers at the General Motors Research Laboratories, attempt-ed to use cost/benefits analysis to find the efficient levels of control. Their analysis suggested:

> One clear conclusion that emerges from the forgoing is that optimal levels, from an economic standpoint, are well below the statutory values of the amended Clean Air Act: 0.94, 0.97, 0.98 for NO_x, CO and HC respectively. The highest level that emerges would put NO_x, CO and HC at 0.73, 0.31 and 0.82 of the 1960 values, respectively. . . . These optimal levels are relatively insensitive to the social discount rate and gasoline costs. . . . The calculated values of net benefits are dependent on the nonmarket benefits of reduced pollu-tion levels, but the control levels are relatively insensitive. [pp. 57–58]

The conclusion that the costs of control exceed the benefits for automobile pollution control seems to be generally shared.[10] There are, of course, large uncertainties in the benefit estimations, a theme we have explored in several previous chapters. It is nonetheless interesting that because the current policy forces manufacturers to operate on a very steep portion of the marginal control cost function, this benefit uncertainty does not seem to affect the conclusion that the current standards are inefficiently strict.

The Deterioration of New Car Emission Rates

As part of its investigation of the Clean Air Act, the National Commission on Air Quality [1981] investigated the emissions of vehicles in use and compared these emission levels to the standards. Their estimates were a blend of actual measured emissions for model years already in the fleet plus forecasts for future model years based on a knowledge of the technologies to be used. The results are presented in Table 17.2. Particularly for hydrocarbons and carbon monoxide, the deterioration of emission rates in use seems pronounced.

The Commission also investigated the factors contributing to poor in-use emis-sions performance. It found that the principal reason for the poor performance was improper maintenance. Carburetor and ignition-timing misadjustment were key fac-tors. Component failure and tampering were also found to affect emission levels, though to a lesser degree.

---

[10]See the discussion in Crandall, et. al. (1986, pp. 109–116).

TABLE 17.2   Average Lifetime (100,000 miles) Emissions of Gasoline Automobiles

Pollutant	Year Model	Standard (gm/ml)	Average Emissions (gm/ml)	Ratio of Emissions to Standard
Hydro-carbons	Pre-1968	None		
	1975–1976	1.5	2.41	1.6
	1977–1978	1.5	2.55	1.7
	1979	1.5	1.83	1.2
	1980	0.41	0.94	2.3
	1981	0.41	0.87	2.1
	1982	0.41	0.82	2.0
	1983	0.41	0.76	2.1
	1984+	0.41	0.79	1.9
Carbon monoxide	Pre-1968	None		
	1975–1976	15.0	29.8	2.0
	1977–1978	15.0	32.9	2.2
	1979	15.0	22.6	1.5
	1980	7.0	16.9	2.4
	1981	3.4	16.9	5.0
	1982	3.4	14.7	4.3
	1983	3.4	11.7	3.4
	1984+	3.4	12.4	3.6
Nitrogen oxides	Pre-1968	None		
	1975–1976	3.1	2.55	0.8
	1977–1979	2.0	2.10	1.1
	1980	2.0	2.10	1.0
	1981	1.0	1.34	1.3
	1982+	1.0	1.44	1.4

Source: National Commission on Air Quality, *To Breathe Clean Air* (Washington, D.C.: U.S. Government Printing Office, 1981), p. 199, Table 22.

Inspection and Maintenance Programs. The policy response to emission rate deterioration was to require inspection and maintenance programs in nonattainment regions seeking extensions in the deadlines for reaching the ambient standards. There are reasons for concern, however, as to whether this is a cost-effective response.

The first concern arises out of the change taking place in emission-control equipment. The new devices are becoming much more sophisticated. While they will be more difficult to tamper with than earlier devices, their malfunctions will not be picked up as easily by the tests used during the inspection.[11] In addition, the costs of repair may turn out to be quite high. No longer will the turn of a carburetor screw do the trick!

A second concern arises over the timing of the program. All nonattainment regions must put these programs in place when seeking an extension of their ambient standards

---

[11]Reitze, for example, points out that Ford relied on a fully electronic three-way catalyst system. The short emission tests used by most inspection and maintenance systems did not detect many of the major problems with this system. In Arnold W. Reitze, Jr., "Controlling Automotive Air Pollution Through Inspection and Maintenance Programs," *The George Washington Law Review* 47 (May 1979): 726.

to 1987, *whether the program is necessary in meeting the standards in 1987 or not.* Washington, D.C., for example, is a city which did comply with the 1982 deadline, but it will meet the 1987 deadline, whether an inspection and maintenance program is in place or not.[12] Thus, for this area and others like it, the inspection and maintenance program represents an unnecessary expense.

An additional concern over this program questions whether this form of reduction is the cheapest way to reach the ambient standard. Reitze [1979, p. 735] compares the cost per ton of reducing hydrocarbon emissions through an inspection and maintenance program with a comparable cost-per-ton reduction from stationary sources. According to his estimates, the cost per ton from inspection and maintenance programs turns out to be two to three times higher than that for securing an equivalent reduction from stationary sources. Inspection and maintenance programs do have merit, since they reduce other pollutants, but the current system provides little flexibility in how the program's objectives are met.

Do vehicle inspection programs yield positive net benefits? The evidence is mixed. A comparison of EPA studies on the costs of the program ($645/ton) with other EPA studies of the benefits for automotive pollutants ($260 to $721/ton) reveals that for some geographic areas, but not all, the programs are justified. A recent study of the Maryland inspection program, however, suggests that the EPA cost estimates may be understated by a large amount because they do not include the costs of driver time and mileage to complete the inspection and to comply with the findings. Including these costs yields a benefit/cost ratio in the neighborhood of 0.125 for Maryland.[13]

It is easy to see why inspection and maintenance programs are controversial. There are reasons for believing that requiring all nonattainment areas requesting an extension in the deadline to implement those standards is costly overkill. In areas such as Washington, D.C., the programs are simply not needed for attainment, and the associated costs are unnecessary. In other areas the desired reductions could well be obtained more cheaply from stationary sources.

Other Local Strategies.   Another possible way to counter the effects of deterioration rates of new-car emissions involves the implementation of local transportation controls, such as stimulating mass-transit usage. This approach allows the highly polluted areas to tailor the degree of control to their needs. The question of interest is whether or not these strategies are cost-effective.

To examine this question and others, the National Science Foundation funded a multidisciplinary, multiuniversity study to examine the emissions payoff and costs of implementing various local strategies. The analysis was based on an economic model which was designed to simulate the transportation system of Boston, Massachusetts, and how that system would respond to various policies available to local authorities.

---

[12]See Arnold W. Reitze, Jr., "Controlling Automotive Air Pollution Through Inspection and Maintenance Programs," *The George Washington Law Review* 47 (May 1979): 730–731.

[13]Virginia D. McConnell, "A Social Cost/Benefit Study of the Maryland Vehicle Emissions Inspection Program," Maryland Institute for Policy Analysis and Research (1986): 41.

The model was based on a large amount of data on the origins and destinations of trips in the Boston area. It contained equations that simulated the choice of mode (such as bus or auto) as a function of such factors as travel time, cost, and so on. Once the travel patterns were simulated, the model projected the effects of these travel patterns on aggregate emissions and finally on the concentrations of pollutants expected in each of 123 different receptor locations in the city. With this model it was therefore possible to keep track, not only of the size of the emission reductions, but also of where pollutant concentrations were reduced. This latter piece of information is important because some parts of the city are more heavily polluted than others, and reductions in those areas would make a particularly valuable contribution to meeting the ambient air-quality standards.

As is generally true with simulation models of this sort, an enormous amount of information was generated. A small portion of this output is presented in Table 17.3. The benchmark column represents the transportation and air-quality situation in the Boston Air-Quality Control Region in 1970. For all other simulations the population, income, and automobile fleet are assumed the same as for the benchmark case.

The fare reduction column portrays the effect of a 10 percent reduction in mass-transit fares, while the transit extension column gives the effect of a vigorous program of extending subway lines further into the suburbs. The 1980 emission-standard column reflects the effect of having the degree of emission control on automobiles which should have been achieved by 1980.

The fare reduction clearly dominates the system extension on grounds of cost effectiveness, since it costs less and reduces pollution more, though neither strategy makes much of a difference. It is impossible, however, to compare the other strategies, since the 1980 emission standards are both much more expensive and much more effective (in terms of reducing pollutants).

TABLE 17.3 Automobile Pollution Simulation

Statistic	Benchmark	Fare Reduction	Transit Extension	1980 Emission Standard
Annual vehicle miles traveled	19,818,000	19,510,000	19,799,000	19,818,000
Percent of trips originating on transit	10.37	10.78	11.92	10.37
Average length of auto trip (miles)	9.91	9.80	10.06	9.91
Aggregate auto emissions (grams/second)				
CO	19,609	19,343	19,497	4,022
HC	2,755	2,716	2,744	485
NO$_x$	934	919	933	401
Annual passenger miles traveled on transit by auto users who switch to transit during trip	410,400	494,300	451,500	410,400
Annual dollar resource cost (thousands of dollars)	0	$11,517	$95,083	$120,000

Source: Frank P. Grad et al., *The Automobile and the Regulation of Its Impact on the Environment* (Norman: The University of Oklahoma Press, 1975), Tables 5-4, 5-5 and 5-11.

Most of the local strategies considered (omitting national-emission standards) are expensive and do not have a profound impact on air quality. Therefore, heavy reliance on local strategies like those covered in this study as a substitute for control over new car emission rates would seem misguided. Local strategies represent more of a last resort and a way to respond to special local needs.

Lead Banking

In the month prior to the issuance of the new, more stringent regulations on lead in gasoline, EPA announced the results of a cost/benefit analysis of their expected impact. The analysis concluded that the 0.10 gplg standard would result in $49 million in benefits (from reduced adverse health effects) at an estimated cost to the refining industry of $3.5 billion.

A main concern of EPA in issuing these regulations was the rigidity of the intermediate deadlines used to implement the phasedown. While some refineries could meet them with ease, others could do so only at a significant increase in cost. Recognizing that meeting the environmental goal did not require every refiner to meet every deadline (as long as the excess reductions of those complying early would be at least as large as the amount of excess lead introduced by those complying late), EPA initiated the lead banking program to provide additional flexibility in meeting the regulations.

While not formally part of the emissions trading program discussed in the previous chapter, the lead banking program does have some design similarities to it. Under this progam, refiners reducing lead more than required by the applicable standard in each quarter of the year can bank the credits for use or sale in some subsequent quarter. Banked credits are transferable among refiners.

The lead banking program, though plagued by less-than-perfect implementation procedures, has eased the transition to the more stringent regulatory regime.[14] Refiners have an incentive to respond quickly because lead reductions undertaken prior to the deadlines become valuable under this new program. The availability of these credits makes it possible for other refiners to comply with the deadlines even in the face of equipment failures or Acts of God rather than fight the deadlines in court. Designed only as a means of facilitating the transition, the lead rights program is scheduled to end by December 31, 1987.

POSSIBLE REFORMS

We have seen that the current approach has some salient weaknesses. Reliance on controlling emissions at the point of production has produced major improvements in cars leaving the assembly line, but there is considerable evidence that the emission rates deteriorate with use. The use of uniform standards has resulted in more control than

---

[14]For some of the details of the program as well as a description of some of the implementation difficulties, see United States General Accounting Office, *Vehicle Emissions: EPA Program to Assist Leaded-Gasoline Producers Needs Prompt Improvement* (GAO/RCED–86–182, August, 1986).

necessary in rural areas and perhaps less than necessary in our most heavily polluted areas.

Manufacturers have been able to delay implementation deadlines because the sanctions for noncompliance are so severe that EPA is reluctant to deny a certificate of conformity. Automobile users have little incentive to drive or maintain their cars in a manner that minimizes emissions. Is there a way that automobile emissions policy could be reformed to make headway on these important deficiencies?

Emission Charges

A most interesting and quite detailed proposal has been suggested by Mills and White [1978]. In their proposal emission standards are replaced by emission charges designed to provide the appropriate incentives for both manufacturers and drivers.

The chief elements of the proposal include:

1. A uniform charge levied on all new cars and paid at the time the cars are sold to dealers. The size of the charge would depend on the amounts of the three major pollutants emitted by the engine class during the regular EPA test. The lower the emissions are, the smaller the tax to be paid.

2. Particularly polluted areas would be permitted to augment this basic charge with another charge to reflect the greater need for clean cars in those areas. This would induce consumers in those areas to choose cleaner cars in order to avoid paying the higher fees assessed on dirty ones. Drivers in rural areas, meanwhile, would face lower emission charges in general (because no supplemental fee would be imposed), so they would not have to buy the cars with significant control overkill as they do under current policy.

3. Manufacturers would no longer be issued a certificate of conformity. All cars could be sold. Dirtier cars would pay higher emission fees. This would eliminate the current problem with the sanctions so severe that they do not represent a credible threat, but it would provide a clear incentive for manufacturers to reduce emissions in order to hold their costs (including the charge) down.

4. An additional emission charge would be paid by drivers at their annual inspection. This fee would take into account grams per mile (as determined by the inspection) and miles driven since the last inspection. Thus a driver could reduce this fee by maintaining the car to emit less, using retrofit devices, if available, and by driving fewer miles. The incentives to keep a car clean would persist over the lifetime of the automobile and the current incentive to hold older, dirtier cars longer would no longer persist.

In Chapter 14 we developed a theorem stating that properly designed emission charges would allocate the control responsibility in a cost-minimizing way. The Mills and White proposal would appear to offer the opportunity to use this theorem as the basis for a reform of the current approach to air-pollution control of mobile sources.

The Two-Car Strategy

A main source of inefficiency in the current approach is the geographic uniformity of emission standards. National uniformity fails to yield enough control in the most polluted areas, and it exercises too much control in the relatively clean areas.

Recognition of this inequity has lead to a reform proposal which, although it is not nearly as comprehensive or sweeping as the emission charge proposal, does allow a more careful tailoring of the degree of control (and control costs) to the need. This proposal suggests that there be not one emission standard, but two. One of these would be very strict and would apply to cars destined for use in heavily polluted areas, and the other would be somewhat less strict and would apply to cars used in areas currently in compliance.

It has been estimated that only about 35 percent of the vehicle population needs to be made up of the low-emitting vehicles in order to meet the ambient standards for mobile-source pollutants. This means the remaining 65 percent are currently over controlled.[15]

The current system involves two emission rates—the California rate and the rate for the rest of the country. These two rates do not fill the bill, however, because they are both very strict. Rather, a two-car strategy might use the California standard as the strict standard and the 1968 standard (modified to control some moderate amount of nitrogen oxides) or something similar for the less-strict standard.

The chief question is the administrative costs involved in implementing this strategy. Presumably, the car registration process would be used; after a certain date, cars made in a specific model year or later could be registered in nonattainment areas only if they were low-emitting vehicles. If, however, all vehicles driving in the heavily polluted urban areas are to be low-emitting, all vehicles registered in the suburbs would have to be included as well.

Where to draw the boundary between areas that require low-emitting vehicles and those that do not is not a trivial exercise. Boundaries too close to the urban areas will encourage some movement beyond the boundaries with more miles traveled (and more emissions). Expansive boundaries, on the other hand, would encompass a substantially higher proportion of the population, including many who presumably rarely drive into the heavily polluted areas. Thus, the case for this reform is less convincing than that for emission charges, though it has the redeeming virtue of representing a somewhat less radical departure from current policy.

Retirement Strategies

A final reform possibility involves strategies to accelerate the retirement of older, polluting vehicles. This could be accomplished either by raising the cost of holding onto older vehicles (as with higher registration fees for vehicles that pollute more) or

---

[15]Frank P. Grad, et al., *The Automobile and the Regulation of Its Impact on the Environment* (Norman: University of Oklahoma Press, 1975), Chapter 5.

by providing a bounty of some sort to those retiring heavily-polluting vehicles early. Though probably more bureaucratically cumbersome, the subsidy approach would respond to the large number of poor households who own these older vehicles and who could ill-afford to pay higher registration fees.

This approach would tend to counteract the tendency for vehicles to be used longer as a result of the new-source focus of current automotive regulations. By eliminating these heavily-polluting vehicles from the fleet earlier than would otherwise be the case, greater emission reductions could be achieved at an earlier date. This approach could be applied selectively in those local areas for which it could make a significant difference.

SUMMARY

The current policy toward motor vehicle emissions blends point-of-production control with point-of-use control, but the existing blend seems quite removed from what efficiency or cost/effectiveness would dictate. The history of legislation in this area has been a turbulent one, moving from a low federal profile—concerned mainly with studying the problem and assisting states—to a high federal profile involving a preemptive responsibility for emission controls.

In a period of frustration, Congress wrote such a tough law that little was accomplished during the early years. The ambient standards could not be met by the deadlines. The sanctions used for noncompliance were so severe that EPA was reluctant to use them. Because they were not a credible threat, the sanctions did little to alter behavior.

The focus on new-source controls has caused the problem of people using older, more heavily polluting cars, delaying significant improvements in air quality. In addition, the technologies chosen by the manufacturers to meet their statutory responsibilities have failed to prevent a deterioration in operating vehicle-emission rates.

The national emission standards, which represent the core of the current approach, seem to be inefficient for two rather different reasons: (1) they are too stringent; and (2) with the exception of California, they are uniform. These two inefficiencies are somewhat related. The controls are too stringent primarily because they require cars not contributing to nonattainment to bear the same cost of control as those that do contribute. The current high standards cause these costs to be large. Thus, if uniform standards are to be retained, they probably should be lower.

Uniform emission standards, however, cannot be fully cost effective, whatever their level. Cost-effectiveness requires higher control costs in areas having real difficulty in meeting the ambient standards than in the rest of the country. Uniform emission standards are powerless to make this crucial distinction.

Likewise, local approaches relying on inspection or maintenance and encouraging the use of mass transit are not generally cost effective. Some areas are currently required to establish these programs, whether they facilitate attainment or not. Other areas could find stationary-source controls cheaper, but these areas, under current rules, are not allowed to substitute one for the other.

One promising proposed reform is to introduce economic incentives into mobile-source control, much as they were introduced into stationary-source control. In the case of mobile sources, however, the best strategy appears to be based on a carefully designed emission charge. This approach, if implemented, would appear to be more cost-effective and more flexible than the current approach while eliminating many of its deficiencies. Another less radical change would involve strategies to accelerate the retirement of older, polluting vehicles.

FURTHER READING

Crandall, Robert W., Howard K. Gruenspecht, Theodore E. Keeler, and Lester B. Lave, *Regulating the Automobile* (Washington, D.C.: The Brookings Institution, 1986). An examination of the effectiveness and efficiency of the federal regulation of automobile safety, emissions, and fuel economy in the United States.

Dewees, Donald N. *Economics and Public Policy: The Auto Pollution Case* (Cambridge, Mass.: MIT Press, 1974). An interesting, if somewhat dated, use of economic analysis to analyze automobile air pollution. Filled with technical detail about many of the issues covered in this chapter.

Grad, Frank P. et al. *The Automobile and the Regulation of Its Impact on the Environment* (Norman: The University of Oklahoma Press, 1975). A comprehensive multidisciplinary, multiuniversity study of automobile pollution financed by the National Science Foundation. Includes analyses by economists, engineers, and lawyers.

Mills, Edwin S., and Lawrence J. White. "Government Policies Toward Automobile Emissions Control" in Ann F. Friedlaender, ed. *Approaches to Control Air Pollution* (Cambridge, Mass.: MIT Press, 1978): 348–402. A detailed, highly readable article describing the emission charge reform in detail.

ADDITIONAL REFERENCES

Gruenspecht, Howard K. "Differentiated Regulation: The Case of Auto Emission Standards," *The American Economic Review,* Vol. 72 (May, 1982): 328–331.

Jacoby, Henry D., et al. *Clearing the Air: Federal Policy on Automotive Emission Control* (Cambridge, Mass.: Ballinger, 1978).

National Commission on Air Quality. *To Breathe Clean Air* (Washington, D.C.: U.S. Government Printing Office, 1981).

Reitze, Arnold W., Jr. "Controlling Automotive Air Pollution through Inspection and Maintenance Programs," *The George Washington Law Review* 47 (May 1979): 735.

Schwing, Richard C., et al. "Benefit-Cost Analysis of Automotive Emission Reductions," *Journal of Environmental Economics and Management,* Vol. 7 (1980): 44–64.

Seskin, Eugene P. "Automobile Air Pollution Policy," in Paul R. Portney, ed., *Current Issues in U.S. Environmental Policy.* (Baltimore: Johns Hopkins University Press, 1978): 68–104.

White, Lawrence J. "American Automotive Emissions Control Policy: A Review of the Reviews," *Journal of Environmental Economics and Management,* Vol. 2 (1974): 231–246.

White, Lawrence J. "U.S. Automotive Emissions Controls: How Well Are They Working?" *The American Economic Review,* Vol. 72 (May, 1982): 332–335.

DISCUSSION QUESTIONS

1. When a threshold concentration is used as the basis for pollution control as it is for air pollution, one possibility for meeting the threshold at minimum cost is to spread the emissions out over time. One way to accomplish this is to establish a peak hour pricing system in which emissions during peak periods are charged more. Singapore does this by disallowing all private vehicle traffic in the city during rush hour which does not conspicuously display a permit. The permits can be purchased by anyone, but they are very expensive.
   (a) Would this represent a movement toward efficiency? Why or why not?
   (b) What effects should this policy have on mass transit usage, gasoline sales, downtown shopping, and travel patterns?

2. The Mills and White [1978] emission charge discussed earlier in this chapter would, if implemented, represent quite a departure from existing policy. Discuss the desirability of implementing such a policy. What are the advantages and disadvantages of changing from the current approach to the Mills and White scheme?

CHAPTER EIGHTEEN

Control of Water Pollution

*It was the best of times, it was the worst of times, it was the
age of wisdom, it was the age of foolishness, it was the epoch
of belief, it was the epoch of incredulity. . . .*
CHARLES DICKENS, A Tale of Two Cities (1859)

INTRODUCTION

While various types of pollution share common attributes, there are important differences as well. These differences form the basis for the elements of policy unique to each pollutant. We have seen, for example, that although the types of pollutants emitted by mobile and stationary sources are often identical, the policy approaches differ considerably.

Water-pollution control has its own unique characteristics as well. Two stand out as having particular relevance for policy:

1. Whereas health benefits dominate all others for air pollution control, recreation benefits are quantitatively the most important for water-pollution control.[1]

2. Large economies of scale in treating sewage and other wastes create the possibility for large, centralized treatment plants as one control strategy, while for air pollution, on-site control is the standard approach.

These characteristics create a need for yet another policy approach. In this chapter we shall explore the problems and prospects for controlling this unique and important form of pollution.

---

[1]See Daniel Feenberg and Edwin S. Mills, *Measuring the Benefits of Water Pollution Abatement* (New York: Academic Press, 1980): 164.

NATURE OF WATER POLLUTION PROBLEMS

Types of Waste-Receiving Water

Two primary types of water are susceptible to contamination. The first, *surface water,* consists of the rivers, lakes, and oceans covering most of the earth's surface. Historically, policy makers have focused almost exclusively on preventing and cleaning up surface-water pollution.

Recently that has changed. Ground water, once considered a pristine resource, has been shown to be subject to considerable contamination from toxic chemicals. *Ground water* is subsurface water that occurs beneath a water table in soils or rocks, or in geologic formations that are fully saturated.

Ground water is a vast natural resource. It has been estimated that the volume of ground water is approximately fifty times the annual flow of surface water.[2] Though ground water currently supplies only 25 percent of the fresh water used for all purposes in the United States, its use is increasing more rapidly than the use of surface water.

Ground water is used primarily for irrigation and as a source of drinking water. Approximately 50 percent of the population relies on ground water as the primary source of water for drinking. The percentage is even higher for rural areas.

Surface water also serves as a significant source of drinking water, but it has many other uses as well. Recreational benefits such as swimming, fishing, and boating are important determinants of surface-water policy in areas where the water is not used for drinking.

Sources of Contamination

Contamination of ground water occurs when polluting substances leach into a water-saturated region. Many potential contaminants are removed by filtration and absorption as the water moves slowly through the rocks. Toxic organic chemicals are one major example of a pollutant which may not be filtered out during migration. Once these substances enter ground water, very little, if any, further cleansing takes place. Moreover, since the rate of replenishment for many groundwater sources, relative to the stock, is small, very little mixing and dilution of the contaminants occur (Example 18.1).

Whereas contamination has generally been accidental, the product of unintended and unexpected waste migration beneath the surface, a portion of the contamination of surface water was deliberate. Water courses were simply a convenient place to dump municipal or private sewage and industrial wastes. Thus, dotting the shoreline of lakes

---

[2]Council on Environmental Quality, *Environmental Quality—1980* (Washington, D.C.: U.S. Government Printing Office, 1980): 83.

EXAMPLE 18.1

Incidents of Ground-Water Pollution

Traditional federal policies have paid little attention to ground water, partly because of the high cost of testing and monitoring. Recent data, however, have shown that ground water in many locations is contaminated by toxic chemicals. This may be posing unacceptable health risks for the public, since ground water is widely used for drinking water. Currently, there are no federal health standards for most of the organic compounds found in drinking-water wells. Many of the chemicals now being discovered in drinking water are either known or suspected carcinogens or mutagens.

Recently discovered incidents of ground-water contamination by toxic organic substances include the following:

1. In 1979 a Massachusetts Legislative Commission on Water Supply found that at least ⅓ of the 351 communities in the Commonwealth were affected by chemical contamination of drinking-water, and wells were restricted or closed in 22 towns.

2. All wells in Groveland and Rowley (Mass.) were closed because of trichloroethylene (TCE) contamination, a known carcinogen in animals.

3. In North Reading, Massachusetts, TCE concentrations exceeded 90 ppb. in two wells supplying 30 percent of the town's water. The state maximum acceptable contamination level is 10 ppb.

4. In January, 1980, California public health officials closed 37 public wells that supplied water to 400,000 people in the San Gabriel Valley because of TCE contamination.

5. A New York Public Interest Research Group documented that all three major aquifers under Long Island were seriously contaminated with effluent from industrial wastes, municipal treatment plants, and runoff from highways. They also found evidence of mutagenic substances in twelve ground water sites.

Source: Council on Environmental Quality, *Environmental Quality—1980* (Washington, D.C.: U.S. Government Printing Office, 1980): 81–83.

or rivers, it was not and is not uncommon to find pipes dumping human or industrial wastes directly into the water.

For policy purposes it is useful to distinguish between two sources of contamination—point and nonpoint sources—even though the distinction is not always crystal clear. *Point sources* generally discharge into surface waters at a specific location through a pipe, outfall, or ditch, while *nonpoint sources* usually affect the water in a more indirect and diffuse way. From the policy point of view, nonpoint sources are more difficult to control and have received little legislative attention. The General Accounting Office has estimated that as a result of the gains made in controlling point sources, nonpoint sources now compose over half of the waste load borne by the nation's waters.[3]

Nonpoint Sources.   The most important nonpoint sources of pollution for surface waters are agricultural activity, urban storm-water runoff, silviculture, and individual disposal systems. Contamination from agriculture includes eroded topsoil and fertilizer. Urban storm-water runoff contains a number of pollutants, including, typically, high quantities of lead. Forestry, if not carefully done, can contribute to soil erosion and, by removing shade cover, could have a large impact on the temperature of normally shaded streams. Malfunctioning septic systems, more prevalent in rural areas, are estimated to be a major source of pollution for some 43 percent of the nation's river basins.

The contamination of groundwater supplies usually results from the migration of harmful substances from sites where high concentrations of chemicals can be found. These include industrial waste storage sites, landfills, and farms. Industrial wastes have been identified by EPA as the most important source of ground water contamination.[4]

Point Sources.   The primary point sources are industries and municipalities. As of 1980, EPA had identified some 59,907 point sources. Of these, 15,395 were municipal dischargers (mostly sewage treatment plants), while industrial sources made up most of the rest. Of the 7350 "major" dischargers responsible for well over half of all discharges, municipalities and industries were about equally represented.

Types of Pollutants

There are a large number of rather different types of water pollutants but for our purposes they can be usefully classified by means of the taxonomy we developed in Chapter 14.

Fund Pollutants.   Fund pollutants are those for which the environment has some assimilative capacity. Thus, the rate at which they accumulate in the medium is less than the rate of injection and, if the absorptive capacity is high enough, they may not accumulate at all. One type of fund water pollutant is called *degradable* because it degrades, or breaks into its component parts, within the water. Degradable wastes are normally organic residuals that are attacked and broken down by bacteria in the stream.

---

[3]U.S. Comptroller General, "National Water Quality Cannot Be Attained Without More Attention to Pollution from Diffused or Nonpoint Sources," CED–78–6 (Washington, D.C.: General Accounting Office, 1977): 1.

[4]Council on Environmental Quality, *Environmental Quality—1980* (Washington, D.C.: U.S. Government Printing Office, 1980): 116–120.

The process by which organic wastes are broken down into component parts consumes oxygen. The amount of oxygen consumed depends upon the magnitude of the waste load. All of the higher life forms in watercourses are *aerobic;* they require oxygen for survival. As a stream's oxygen levels fall, fish mortality increases, with the less tolerant fish becoming the first to succumb. The oxygen level can become low enough that even the aerobic bacteria die. When this happens, the stream becomes *anaerobic* and the ecology changes drastically. This is an extremely unpleasant circumstance because the stream takes on a dark hue, and the stream water stinks!

To control these waste loads, two different types of monitoring are needed: (1) monitoring the ambient conditions in the watercourse; and (2) monitoring the magnitude of emissions. The measure commonly used to keep track of ambient conditions for these conventional fund pollutants is *dissolved oxygen* (DO). The amount of dissolved oxygen in a body of water is a function of ambient conditions, such as temperature, stream flow, and the waste load.[5] The measure of the oxygen demand placed on a stream by any particular volume of effluent is called the *biochemical oxygen demand* (BOD).

Using modeling techniques, emissions (measured as BOD) at a certain point can be translated into DO measures at various receptor locations along a stream. This step is necessary in order to implement an ambient permit system or an ambient emission charge.

If we were to develop a profile of dissolved oxygen readings on a stream where organic effluent is being injected, that profile would typically exhibit one or more minimum points called oxygen sags. These *oxygen sags* represent locations along the stream where the dissolved oxygen content is lower than at other points. An ambient permit or ambient emission charge system would be designed to reach a desired DO level at those sag points, while an emission permit or emission charge system would simply try to hit a particular BOD reduction target. The former would take the location of the emitter into account, while the latter would not. Later in this chapter we will examine studies which model these systems on particular watercourses.

A second type of fund pollutant is thermal pollution, caused by the injection of heat into a watercourse. Typically, *thermal pollution* is caused when an industrial plant or electric utility uses surface water as a coolant, returning the heated water to the watercourse. This heat is dissipated in the receiving waters by evaporation. By raising the temperature of the water near the outfall, thermal pollution lowers the dissolved oxygen content and can result in dramatic ecological changes in that area.

Not all transformations of fund pollutants in streams and lakes are congenial. One example is provided by a class of pollutants, such as nitrogen and phosphorus, which are plant nutrients. These pollutants stimulate the growth of aquatic plant life, such as algae and water weeds. In excess these plants can produce odor, taste, and aesthetic problems. A lake with an excessive supply of nutrients is called *eutrophic*.

---

[5]The danger of anaerobic conditions is highest in the late summer and early fall, when temperatures are high and the stream flow is low.

The various types of fund pollutants could be ordered on a spectrum. On one end of the spectrum would be pollutants for which the environment had a very large absorptive capacity and on the other end pollutants for which the absorptive capacity is virtually nil. The limiting case, with no absorptive capacity, are stock pollutants.

Near the end of that spectrum a class of inorganic synthetic chemicals called persistent pollutants, having little absorptive capacity, could be found. These substances are called *persistent* because their complex molecular structures are not effectively broken down in the stream. Some degradation takes place, but so slowly that these pollutants can travel long distances in water in a virtually unchanged form.

These persistent pollutants accumulate, not only in the watercourses, but in the food chain as well. The concentration levels in the tissues of living organisms rise with the order of the species. Concentrations in lower life forms such as plankton may be relatively small, but, because small fish eat a lot of plankton and do not excrete the chemical, the concentrations in small fish would be higher. The magnification continues as large fish consume small fish; concentration levels in the larger fish would be even higher.

Because they accumulate in the food chains, persistent pollutants present an interesting monitoring challenge. The traditional approach would involve measurements of pollutant concentration in the water, but that is not the only variable of interest. The damage is related not only to its concentration in the water, but its concentration in the food chain as well. Although monitoring the environmental effects of these pollutants may be more compelling than monitoring other pollutants, it is also more difficult. Since effective monitoring is a prerequisite for successful policy, this suggests one major continuing role for EPA.

A final type of fund pollutant, infectious organisms such as bacteria and viruses, is carried into surface and ground water by domestic and animal wastes and by wastes from such industries as tanning and meat packing. These live organisms may either thrive and multiply in water or their population may decline over time, depending upon how hospitable or hostile the watercourse is for continued growth.

Stock Pollutants. The most troublesome cases of pollution result from *stock pollutants*, which merely accumulate in the environment. There is no natural process to remove or transform stock pollutants; the watercourse cannot cleanse itself of them.

Inorganic chemicals and minerals comprise the main examples of stock pollutants. Perhaps the most notorious members of this group are the heavy metals, such as lead, cadmium, and mercury. Extreme examples of poisoning by these metals have occurred in Japan. In a case referred to as the *Minamata Disease*, named for the location where it occurred, some 52 people died and 150 others suffered serious brain and nerve damage. Scientists puzzled for years over the source of the ailments until tracing them to an organic form of mercury that had accumulated in the tissues of fish eaten three times a day by local residents.

In another case in Japan, known as the *Itai Itai* (literally, ouch-ouch) *Disease*, scientists traced the source of a previously undiagnosed, extremely painful bone disease to the ingestion of cadmium. Nearby mines provided the source of the cadmium, which apparently was ingested by eating contaminated rice and soybeans.

As is typical with persistent pollutants, some of the stock pollutants are difficult to monitor. Those accumulated in the food chains give rise to the same problem as is presented by the persistent pollutants. Ambient sampling must be supplemented by sampling tissues from members of the food chain. To further complicate matters, the heavy metals may sink rapidly to the bottom, remaining in the sediment. Though these could be detected in sediment samples, merely drawing samples from the water itself would allow these pollutants to escape detection.

FEDERAL WATER POLLUTION CONTROL POLICY

Federal policy for water-pollution control antedates federal air-pollution control by a considerable amount of time. We might suppose that the policy for water pollution control is superior, since authorities had more time to profit from early mistakes. Unfortunately, that isn't the case.

Early Legislation

The first federal legislation dealing with discharge into the nation's waterways occurred when Congress passed the 1899 Refuse Act. Designed primarily to protect navigation, this act focused on preventing any discharge that would interfere with using rivers as transport links. All discharges into a river were prohibited unless approved by a permit from the Chief of the U.S. Engineers. Most permits were issued to contractors dredging the rivers and they dealt mainly with the disposal of the removed material. This act was virtually unenforced for other pollutants until 1970, when this permit program was rediscovered and used briefly (with little success) as the basis for federal enforcement actions.

The Water Pollution Control Act of 1948 represented the first attempt by the federal government to exercise some direct influence over what previously had been a state and local function. A hesitant move, since it reaffirmed that the primary responsibility for water-pollution control rested with the states, it did initiate the authority of the federal government to conduct investigations, research, and surveys.

The first hints of the current approach are found in the amendments to the Water Pollution Control Act, which were passed in 1956. There were two especially important provisions of this act: (1) federal financial support for the construction of waste-treatment plants and (2) direct federal regulation of waste discharges via a mechanism known as the *enforcement conference.*

The first of these provisions envisioned a control strategy based on subsidizing the construction of a particular control activity—waste treatment plants. Municipalities could receive federal grants to cover up to 55 percent of the construction of municipal sewage-treatment plants. This approach not only lowered the cost to the local government of constructing these facilities, it also lowered the cost to users. Since the federal government contribution was a grant, rather than a loan, the fees charged users did not reflect the federally subsidized construction portion of the cost. The user fees were set at a lower rate that was high enough to cover merely the unsubsidized portion of construction cost, as well as operating and maintenance cost.

The 1956 Amendments envisioned a relatively narrow federal role in the regulation of discharges. Initially, only polluters contributing to interstate pollution were included, but subsequent laws have broadened the coverage. By 1961 discharges into all navigable waters were covered.

The mechanism created by the Amendments of 1956 to enforce the regulation of discharges was the enforcement conference. Under this approach the designated federal control authority could call for a conference to deal with any interstate water-pollution problem or it could be requested to do so by the governor of an affected state. The fact that this authority was discretionary and not mandatory and that the control authority had very few means of enforcing any decisions reached meant that the conferences simply did not achieve the intended results.

The Water Quality Act of 1965 attempted to improve the process by establishing ambient water-quality standards for interstate water courses and by requiring states to file implementation plans. This sounds like the approach currently being used in air-pollution control, but there are important differences. The plans forthcoming from states in response to the 1965 act were vague and did not attempt to link specific effluent standards on discharges to the ambient standards. They generally took the easy way out and called for secondary treatment, which removes 80–95 percent of BOD and 85 percent of suspended solids. The fact that these standards bore no particular relationship to ambient quality made them difficult to enforce in the courts, since the legal authority for them was based on this relationship.

Subsequent Legislation

Point Sources.   As discussed in the preceding chapters, an air of frustration regarding pollution control pervaded Washington in the 1970s. As with air-pollution legislation, this frustration led to the enactment of a very tough water control law. The tone of the act is established immediately in the preamble which calls for the achievement of two goals: (1) ". . . that the discharge of pollutants into the navigable waters be eliminated by 1985"; and (2) ". . . that wherever attainable, an interim goal of water quality which provides for the protection and propagation of fish, shellfish, and wildlife and provides for recreation in and on the water be achieved by July 1, 1983." The stringency of these goals represented a major departure from past policy.

This act also introduced new procedures for implementing the law. Permits were required of all dischargers (replacing the 1899 Refuse Act which, because of its navigation focus, was difficult to enforce). The permits were issued by EPA, at least until the states met certain conditions. These permits would be granted only when the dischargers met certain technology-based effluent standards. The ambient standards were completely bypassed as these effluent standards were uniformly imposed and, hence, could not depend upon local water conditions.[6]

---

[6]Actually the ambient standards were not completely bypassed. If the uniform controls were not sufficient to meet the desired standard, the effluent limitations would have to be tightened accordingly. This provision has not yet been widely used.

According to the 1972 Amendments, the effluent standards were to be implemented in two stages. By 1977 industrial dischargers, as a condition of their permit, were required to meet effluent limitations based on the "best practicable control technology currently available" (BPT). In setting these national standards, EPA was required to consider the total costs of these technologies and their relation to the benefits received, but not to consider the conditions of the individual source or the particular waters into which it discharged. In addition, all publicly-owned treatment plants were to have achieved secondary treatment by 1977. By 1983 industrial discharges were required to meet effluent limitations based on the presumably more stringent "best available technology economically achievable" (BAT) while publicly owned treatment plants were required to meet effluent limitations which depended upon the "best practicable waste treatment technology."

The program of subsidizing municipal waste treatment plants, begun in 1956, was continued in a slightly modified form by the 1972 Act. Whereas the 1965 Act allowed the federal government to subsidize up to 55 percent of the cost of construction of waste treatment plants, the 1972 Act raised the ceiling to 75 percent. The 1972 act also increased the funds available for this program. In 1981 the federal share was reduced to 55 percent.

The 1977 Amendments continued this regulatory approach, but with some major modifications. This legislation drew a more careful distinction between conventional and toxic pollutants with more stringent requirements placed on the latter and it extended virtually all of the deadlines in the 1972 Act.

For conventional pollutants a new treatment standard was created to replace the BAT standards. The effluent limitations for these pollutants were to be based on the "best conventional technology" and the deadline for these standards was set at July 1, 1984. In setting these standards, EPA was required to consider whether the costs of adding the pollution-control equipment were reasonable when compared with the improvement in water quality. For unconventional pollutants and toxics (any pollutant not specifically included on the list of conventional pollutants), the BAT requirement was retained but the deadline was shifted to 1984.

Other deadlines were also extended. The date for municipalities to meet the secondary treatment deadline moved from 1977 to 1983. Industrial compliance with the BPT standards was delayed until 1983 whenever the contemplated system had the potential for application throughout the industry.

The final modification made by the 1977 Amendments involved the introduction of pretreatment standards for waste being sent to a publicly owned treatment system. These standards were designed to prevent the discharges that could inhibit the treatment process and to prevent the introduction of toxic pollutants that would not be treated by the waste-treatment facility. Existing facilities were required to meet the standards three years after the date they were published, while facilities constructed later would be required to meet the pretreatment regulations upon commencement of operations.

Nonpoint Sources.   In contrast to the control of point sources, EPA was given no specific authority to regulate nonpoint sources. This type of pollution was seen by Congress as a state responsibility.

Section 208 of the act authorized Federal grants for state-initiated planning that would provide implementable plans for areawide waste treatment management. Section 208 further specified that this areawide plan must identify significant nonpoint sources of pollution, as well as procedures and methods for controlling them. The reauthorization of the Clean Water Act, passed over President Reagan's veto during February 1987, authorized an additional $400 million for a new program to help states control runoff.

As of 1981 ten states had passed and five others had proposed programs under which the state would share with farmers the cost of controlling nonpoint pollution. In Illinois, for example, the General Assembly enacted a $500,000 program to encourage farmers to use farming techniques that would stem soil erosion. This program would pay farmers from $3 to $25 per acre, depending upon the methods chosen.

The Safe Drinking Water Act

The 1972 policy focused on achieving water quality sufficiently high for fishing and swimming. Because that quality is not high enough for drinking water, the Safe Drinking Water Act of 1974 issued more stringent standards for community water systems. These set maximum allowable concentration levels for bacteria, turbidity (muddiness), and chemical-radiological contaminants.

The 1986 Amendments require EPA to issue standards within three years for 83 contaminants and at least 25 more by 1991, to set standards based on "best available technology," and to monitor public water systems for both regulated and unregulated chemical contaminants. Civil and criminal penalties for any violations of the standards were also increased by the amendments.

EFFICIENCY AND COST-EFFECTIVENESS

Ambient Standards and the Zero Discharge Goal

The 1956 Amendments defined ambient standards as a means of quantifying the objectives being sought. A system of ambient standards allows the control authority to tailor the quality of a particular body of water to its use. Water used for drinking would be subject to the highest standards, swimming the next highest, and so on. Once the ambient standards are defined, the control responsibility could be allocated among sources. Greater efforts to control pollution would be expended where the gap between desired and actual water quality was the largest.

Unfortunately, the early experience with ambient standards for water was not reassuring. Rather than strengthening the legal basis for the effluent standards, while retaining their connection to the ambient standards, Congress chose to downgrade the importance of ambient standards by specifying a zero discharge goal. Additionally, the effluent standards were given their own legal status apart from any connection with ambient standards. The wrong inference was drawn from the early lack of legislative success.

In his own inimitable style, Mark Twain put the essential point rather well:

> We should be careful to get out of an experience only the wisdom that is in it—and stop there; lest we be like the cat that sits down on a hot stove lid. She will never sit down on a hot stove lid again—and that is well; but also she will never sit down on a cold one anymore.[7]

The most fundamental problem with the current approach is that it rests on the faulty assumption that the tougher the law, the more that is accomplished. The zero discharge goal provides one example of a case in which passing a tough standard, in the hopes of actually achieving a weaker one, can backfire. Kneese and Schultze [1975] point out that in the late 1960s the French experimented with a law that required zero discharge and imposed severe penalties for violations. The result was that the law was never enforced because it was universally viewed as unreasonable. Less control was accomplished under this law than would have been accomplished with a less stringent law that could have been enforced.

Is the United States case comparable? It appears to be. In 1972 EPA published an estimate of the costs of meeting a zero discharge goal, assuming that it is feasible. They concluded that over the decade from 1971–81, removing 85 to 90 percent of the pollutants from all industrial and municipal effluents would cost $62 billion. Removing all of the pollutants would cost $317 billion, more than five times as much, and this figure probably understates the true cost.[8]

Is this cost justified? Probably not for *all* pollutants, though for some it may be. Unfortunately, the zero discharge goal makes no distinction among pollutant types. For some fund pollutants it seems extreme. Perhaps the legislators realized this because when the legislation was drafted, there were no specific timetables or procedures established to ensure that the zero discharge goal would be met by 1985 or anytime.

National Effluent Standards

The first prong in the two-pronged Congressional attack on water pollution was the national effluent standards (the other being subsidies for the construction of publicly owned waste-treatment facilities). Deciding on the appropriate levels for these standards for each of the estimated 60,000 sources is not a trivial task. Not surprisingly, difficulties arose.

Enforcement Problems.   Soon after passage of the 1972 Amendments, EPA geared up to assume its awesome responsibility. Relying on a battery of consultants, it began

---

[7]From *Pudd'nhead Wilson*, by Mark Twain, 1897, p. 125.

[8]See the discussion in Allen V. Kneese and Charles L. Schultze, *Pollution, Prices and Public Policy* (Washington, D.C.: The Brookings Institution, 1975): 78.

to study the technologies of pollution control available to each industry in order to establish reasonable effluent limits. In establishing the guidelines, EPA is required to take into account "the age of the equipment and facilities involved, the process employed, the engineering aspects of the application of various types of control techniques, process changes, nonwater quality environmental impact (including energy requirements) and such factors as the Administrator deems appropriate. . . ."

It is not clear whether this provision means that individual standards should be specified for each source, or general standards for broad categories of sources. Cost effectiveness would require the former, but in a system relying on effluent standards (but not one relying on emission charges or permits), the transaction costs associated with that approach would be prohibitively high and the delay unacceptably long. Therefore, EPA chose the only feasible interpretation available and established general standards for broad categories of sources. While the standards could differ among categories, they were uniformly applied to the large number of sources within each category.

EPA inevitably fell behind the Congressional deadlines. In fact, not one effluent standard was published within the year deadline. As the standards were published, they were immediately challenged in the courts. By 1977 there were already some 250 cases pending, challenging the published standards.[9] Some of these challenges were successful, requiring EPA to revise the standards. All of this took time.

By 1977 it was clear that EPA was having so much trouble defining the BPT standards that the deadlines for the BAT standards were completely unreasonable. It was also becoming increasingly clear that, for conventional pollutants, not only the deadlines but the standards themselves were irrational. Many bodies of water would have met the ambient standards without the BAT standard, while for others the effluent standards were not sufficient, particularly in areas with large nonpoint pollution problems. In addition it was not clear that the technologies required by BPT would be compatible (or even necessary) once the BAT standards were in effect. The situation was in a shambles.

The 1977 Amendments changed both the timing of the BAT standards (delaying the deadlines) and their focus (toward toxic pollutants and away from conventional pollutants). As a result of these amendments, EPA was required to develop industry effluent standards based on the BAT guidelines for control of 65 classes of toxic priority pollutants. In a 1979 survey EPA discovered that all primary industries regularly discharge one or more of these toxic pollutants. As of 1980 EPA had proposed BAT effluent limitations for control of toxic priority pollutants for nine primary industries.

The 1977 Amendments certainly improved the situation. Because toxics represent a more serious problem, it makes sense to set stricter standards for those pollutants. Extension of the deadlines was absolutely necessary; there was no alternative.

These amendments have not, however, resulted in a cost-effectiveness strategy. In particular, they tend to retard technological progress and to assign the responsibility for control in an unnecessarily expensive manner.

---

[9] A. Myrick Freeman, III, "Air and Water Pollution Policy," in *Current Issues in U.S. Environmental Policy,* Paul R. Portney, ed. (Baltimore: Johns Hopkins University Press for Resources for the Future, 1978): 46.

Allocating Control Responsibility. Because the effluent standards established by EPA are based upon specific technologies, these technologies are known to the industries. Therefore, in spite of the fact that the industry can choose any technology that keeps emissions under the limitation stated in the standard, in practice, industries tend to choose the specific equipment cited by EPA when it established the standard. This, they reason, minimizes their risk. If anything goes wrong and they are hauled into court, they can simply argue they did precisely what EPA had in mind when it set the standard.

The problem with this reaction is that it focuses too narrowly on a particular technology rather than on the real objective, emission reduction. The focus should be less on the purchase of a specific technology and more on doing what is necessary to hold emissions down, such as maintenance, process changes, and so on. In a field undergoing rapid technological change, tying all control efforts to a particular technology (which may become obsolete well before the standards are revised) is a poor strategy. Unfortunately, technological stagnation has become a routine side effect of the current policy to the detriment of securing clean water.

In allocating the control responsibility among various sources, EPA was constrained by the inherent difficulty of making unique determinations for each source and by limitations in the act itself, such as the need to apply relatively uniform standards.[10] We know from Chapter 14 that uniform effluent standards are not cost-effective, but it remains an open question whether or not the resulting increases in cost are sufficiently large to recommend an alternative approach, such as effluent charges or permits. The fact that the cost increases are large in the control of stationary-source air pollution does not automatically imply that they are large for water-pollution control as well.

A number of empirical studies have investigated how closely the national effluent standards approximate the least-cost allocation (Table 18.1). These studies support the contention that the EPA standards are not cost-effective, though the degree of cost-ineffectiveness is typically smaller than that associated with the standards used to control air pollution.

Perhaps the most famous study examining the cost-effectiveness of uniform standards in contrast with emission and ambient charges and permits was conducted on the Delaware Estuary.[11] This river basin, though small by the standards of the Mississippi or other major basins, does drain an area serving a population in excess of six million people. It is a highly industrial, densely populated area.

In this study a simulation model was constructed to capture the effect on ambient dissolved oxygen content of a variety of pollutants discharged by a large number of polluters into the river at numerous locations. In addition, this model was capable of simulating the cost consequences of various methods used to allocate the responsibility for controlling effluent to meet dissolved oxygen standards.

---

[10]These limitations are spelled out in detail in C. James Koch and Robert A. Leone, "The Clean Water Act: Unexpected Impacts on Industry," *Harvard Environmental Law Review* 3 (1979): 96–104.

[11]This study is described in some detail in Allen V. Kneese and Blair T. Bower, *Managing Water Quality: Economics, Technology, Institutions* (Baltimore: Johns Hopkins Press, 1968), Chapter 11; and Allen V. Kneese, *Economics and the Environment* (New York: Penguin Books, 1977).

TABLE 18.1 Empirical Studies of Water Pollution Control

Study and year	Pollutants covered	Geographic area	CAC benchmark	DO target (mg/liter)	Ratio of CAC cost to least cost
Johnson (1967)	Biochemical oxygen demand	Delaware Estuary—86-mile reach	Equal proportional treatment	2.0 3.0 4.0	3.13 1.62 1.43
O'Neil (1980)	Biochemical oxygen demand	20-mile segment of Lower Fox River in Wisconsin	Equal proportional treatment	2.0 4.0 6.2 7.9	2.29 1.71 1.45 1.38
Eheart, Brill, and Lyon (1983)	Biochemical oxygen demand	Willamette River in Oregon	Equal proportional treatment	4.8 7.5	1.12 1.19
		Delaware Estuary in Penn., Delaware, and New Jersey	Equal proportional treatment	3.0 3.6	3.00 2.92
		Upper Hudson River in New York	Equal proportional treatment	5.1 5.9	1.54 1.62
		Mohawk River in New York	Equal proportional treatment	6.8	1.22

Definitions: CAC = Command and control, the traditional regulatory approach.

DO = Dissolved oxygen: Higher DO targets indicate higher water quality.

Source: T.H. Tietenberg, *Emissions Trading: An Exercise in Reforming Pollution Policy* (Washington, D.C.: Resources for the Future, Inc., 1985), Table 5, p. 46.

Four specific methods of allocating responsibility were considered. The first was the *least-cost* (LC) method, which would correspond to an ambient charge or ambient permit system. This method takes both locations of the emissions and control costs into account.

The second method was a *uniform treatment* (UT) strategy in which all dischargers were faced with an effluent standard requiring them to remove a given percentage of their waste before discharging the remainder into the river. This method mirrors, in a crude way, the current EPA strategy.

The third method simulated the allocation attained from the use of a *uniform emission charge* (UEC) or an emissions permit system. This method takes control costs but not emission locations into account. The final case simulates a *zoned effluent charge* (ZEC). For this case the river basin was subdivided into a series of zones. All dischargers within a zone would face the same emission charges, while dischargers in different zones could face different emission charges. This fourth simulation was an intermediate step between the first and third strategies. It allowed location to be more of a factor than in the third method but less of a factor than in the first method. The first simulation would be identical to the fourth if the zones were sufficiently small that each discharger was in its own unique zone; it would be identical to the third if there were only one zone containing all sources (Table 18.2).

For control of water pollution, the UT strategy does increase the cost substantially. For either dissolved-oxygen objective, the costs are roughly three times higher. Also of interest is the fact that the zonal system results in costs that are quite close to the minimum for the higher DO objective, while the UEC does not. Even rudimentary attempts to take location into account may make a big difference for water pollution just as it does for air pollution.

The desirability of economic incentives seems as evident for water pollution as it did for air pollution. Despite this evidence, the regulatory reform movement that played such an important role for air-pollution control has not had anywhere near the same impact in water-pollution control. As Example 18.2 demonstrates, there is movement in that direction which is promising.

The European Experience. Economic incentives have been important in water-pollution control in Europe, where effluent charges play a prominent role in a number of countries.[12] These charge systems take a number of forms. One common approach illustrated by Czechoslovakia uses charges to achieve predetermined ambient standards. Others, such as West Germany, use charges mainly to finance regional or local action toward meeting water-quality goals. A third group, illustrated by Hungary and East Germany, shows how charge systems can be combined with effluent standards to form a program more powerful than one relying on standards alone.

Czechoslovakia has used effluent charges to maintain water quality at predetermined levels for more than fifteen years. A basic charge is placed on BOD and suspended

---

[12]For a summary of this experience, see Frederick R. Anderson, *et al. Environmental Improvement Through Economic Incentives* (Baltimore: The Johns Hopkins University Press for Resources for the Future, 1977): pp. 59–68.

TABLE 18.2   Cost of Treatment under Alternative Programs: The Delaware Estuary

DO Objective (ppm)	Program			
	LC	UT	UEC	ZEC
		(million dollars per year)		
2	1.6	5.0	2.4	2.4
3–4	7.0	20.0	12.0	8.6

Source: Allen V. Kneese, *Economics and the Environment* (New York: Penguin Books, 1977), p. 164, Table 16.

EXAMPLE 18.2

Marketable Emission Permits on the Fox River

With the advent of the bubble and offset policies, marketable emission permits have become the centerpiece of the regulatory reform movement in air-pollution control. Though no comparable scale of reform exists for control of water pollution, action has been initiated in northern Wisconsin.

The Lower Fox River flows from Lake Winnebago to Green Bay, Wisconsin. Lining the banks of a key 22-mile segment of this river are ten pulp and paper mills and four municipalities that discharge effluent into the river. During the summer the desired dissolved oxygen targets are not reached at two critical sag points, even when the industrial polluters are in compliance with BPT standards and municipal polluters are providing secondary treatment.

The Wisconsin Department of Natural Resources was faced with meeting the standards in the face of industrial resistance. To assist in choosing a policy strategy, they funded a simulation model of the river to compare traditional regulatory rules with a marketable permit system.

This model revealed significant differences among dischargers, a precondition if the market approach is to save a significant amount of money. Transfer coefficients varied by a factor of three and, under traditional abatement rules, marginal abatement costs differed by a factor of four. The study concluded that the control costs would be some 40 percent higher if the department were to rely on traditional abatement rules. The potential annual savings realized from a permit approach were estimated at $6.7 million.

In March of 1981 the department approved regulations allowing dischargers on the Lower Fox River to transfer permits by approved contracts. By 1982 the first trade had already taken place.

Source: This example was drawn from William B. O'Neil, *Pollution Permits and Markets for Water Quality,* an unpublished Ph.D. dissertation completed at the University of Wisconsin—Madison, 1980, and subsequent conversations with the author.

solids and complemented by a surcharge ranging from 10 to 100 percent, depending upon the contribution of the individual discharge to ambient pollutant concentrations. The basic rates can be adjusted to reflect the quality of the receiving water. This system is conceptually very close to the ambient emission charge system known to be cost-effective.

The West German system, which is used in the Ruhr Valley, levies effluent charges primarily as a source of revenue. The level of charge generally reflects the difficulty of treatment and the toxicity of the substance. The accumulated revenue is used to finance regional waste-treatment facilities, as well as systems designed to increase the absorptive capacity of the river by reaeration or flow augmentation. Some rivers are essentially used as sewers to carry waste to the treatment plants, while others are kept clean for drinking water or recreation.

The final apporach, used in Hungary and East Germany, combines effluent charges with effluent standards. The charge is levied on discharges in excess of fixed effluent limits. In the Hungarian system the level of the charge is based on the condition of the receiving waters, among other factors. Initially, the Hungarian charges had little effect, but when the charge levels were raised, a flurry of waste-treatment activity resulted.

Though these European approaches are quite different and are not all cost effective, their existence suggests that effluent charge systems are possible and practical. In view of the huge cost reductions possible with their use, the United States may be ready for such action.

Municipal Waste-Treatment Subsidies

The second phase of the two-pronged water-pollution control program involves subsidies for waste-treatment plants. This program has run into problems as well, ranging from the less-than-blinding speed with which the program has been implemented to the lack of results achieved.

Speed of Implementation.   To help municipalities meet sewage-treatment goals, Congress made available a considerable amount of funds. From 1972 to 1981 appropriations totaled some $39.2 billion. Between 1972 and 1981 EPA funded over 22,000 planning, design, or construction projects. By September 1981, only an estimated 4000 projects were physically complete and operating. By 1983 another 6300 projects, including many larger ones, were expected to be on line.[13] The average time from initiation to completion is approaching a decade.[14]

---

[13]Council on Environmental Quality, *Environmental Quality—1980* (Washington, D.C.: U.S. Government Printing Office, 1980): 123.

[14]Council on Environmental Quality, *Environmental Quality—1980* (Washington, D.C.: U.S. Government Printing Office, 1980): 74.

The Allocation of Funds. The available funds were initially allocated on a first-come, first-served basis. Therefore, it is not surprising that the funds were not spent in areas having the greatest impact. It was not uncommon, for example, for completed treatment plants to dump effluent that was significantly cleaner than the receiving water. Also, federal funds have traditionally been concentrated on smaller, largely suburban, communities rather than the larger cities with the most serious pollution problems.[15]

The 1977 Amendments attempted to deal with this problem by requiring states to set priorities for funding treatment works while giving EPA the right, after holding public hearings, to not only veto a state's priority list but to request a revised list. This tendency to ensure that the funds are allocated to the highest priority projects was reinforced with the passage of the Municipal Wastewater Treatment Construction Grant Amendments of 1981. Under this act states are required to establish project priorities that will target funds to projects with the most significant water quality and public-health consequences.

Operation and Maintenance. The current approach subsidizes the *construction* of treatment facilities but provides no incentive to *operate* them effectively. The existence of a municipal waste treatment plant does not by itself guarantee cleaner water. EPA's annual inspection surveys of operating plants in 1976 and 1977 found only about half of the plants performing satisfactorily. More recent surveys have found that the general level of waste-treatment performance has remained substantially unchanged from previous years.

When sewage treatment plants chronically or critically malfunction, EPA may take a city to court to force compliance with either a direct order or a fine. Because of various constitutional legal barriers, it is very difficult to force a city to pay a fine to the federal treasury. Without an effective and credible sanction, EPA is in a difficult position to deal with municipalities. Therefore, the end of the treatment plant malfunction problem can not yet be pronounced with any assurance.

Pretreatment Standards

To deal with hazardous wastes entering municipal waste treatment plants that cannot be treated or removed by those plants EPA has defined pretreatment standards regulating the quality of the wastewater flowing into the plants. These standards suffer the same deficiencies as other effluent standards; they are not cost-effective (Example 18.3). The control over wastewater flows into treatment plants provide one more aspect of environmental policy where economic incentive approaches offer an opportunity to achieve equivalent results at a lower cost.

---

[15]An extended critical discussion of the manner in which these funds were allocated can be found in A. Myrick Freeman III and Robert H. Haveman, "Clean Rhetoric and Dirty Water," *The Public Interest* (Summer, 1972).

EXAMPLE 18.3

Cost-Effective Pretreatment Standards

The electroplating operations of the Rhode Island jewelry industry produce high concentrations of cyanide, copper, nickel, and zinc, which are routinely discharged into municipal sewer systems. Since the treatment plants are not designed to remove these hazardous substances, EPA has defined pretreatment standards to prohibit excessive concentrations of these metals from entering the plants. These standards are financially burdensome, with some estimates suggesting that some 30 to 60 percent of the small firms could go out of business if the standards were imposed.

An economic analysis by Opaluch and Kashmanian (1985) of the alternatives for meeting the EPA concentration objectives concludes that the EPA pretreatment standards achieve the objective at a cost almost 50 percent greater than the least-cost means of achieving the same concentration objectives. An emissions permit system with a permit price of $40 per pound would, after trading, achieve the target at a cost of $12.5 million. Compared to the $19.3 million the EPA proposal would cost, this represents a considerable savings.

If the permits were auctioned off, the government would collect some $5.0 million from the sale. Although the financial burden of this auction system for allocating permits would be lower on the jewelry industry as a whole than complying with the EPA proposal, even considering this $5.0 million transfer, not every segment of the industry would be better off with the auction. In particular, the permit fees paid by large firms would be sufficiently high that they would bear more financial burden under the auction scheme than with the EPA proposal. If the permits were grandfathered (allocated free-of-charge) rather than auctioned off, however, all existing firms would be better off under the permit system than the EPA proposal.

Source: James J. Opaluch and Richard M. Kashmanian, "Assessing the Viability of Marketable Permit Systems: An Application in Hazardous Waste Management," *Land Economics,* Vol. 61, No. 3 (August, 1985): 263–271.

Nonpoint Pollution

The current law does little to control nonpoint pollution, which in many areas is a significant part of the total problem. In some ways the government has tried to compensate for this uneven coverage by placing more intensive controls on point sources. Is this emphasis efficient?

It could conceivably be justified on two grounds. If the marginal damages caused by nonpoint sources are significantly smaller than those of point sources, then a lower level of control could well be justified. Since in many cases nonpoint-source pollutants are not the same as point-source pollutants, this is a distinct possibility. Or, if the costs of controlling nonpoint sources even to small degree are very high, this could justify benign neglect as well. Are either of these conditions met in practice?

Costs. Because research is in its infancy, cost information is scarce. Of the small amount of literature available, one study can give us a sense of the economic analysis. Palmini [1982] conducted an analysis of the potential effects of agricultural nonpoint policies on two small rural counties in Illinois. The specific policies he examined were designed to control nitrogen (which can cause eutrophication), sediment (soil erosion), and pesticides. His model relates these policies to the choice of various farming practices, the effects of these choices on costs, and the financial return to farmers after covering variable costs.

His results indicated that rather dramatic reductions (74 percent) in soil erosion could be achieved at a cost of less than 1 percent of the earnings after variable costs were covered. A ban on selected pesticides was predicted to cause a switch to other less damaging pesticides, which would reduce the return to farmers by 0.7 percent.

The major estimated economic impact came from policies designed to reduce nitrogen use. Palmini considered the effects of quantity restrictions (ceilings on amount used per acre) and the impact of taxes on nitrogen use. Quantity restrictions necessary to reduce pollution also substantially reduced revenues and production. Since the demand for nitrogen is price inelastic, if nitrogen taxes were used, very high rates would be needed to reduce nitrogen use very much.

The extra expense of nitrogen control would represent a large financial burden on farmers which they could only pass on in higher prices if all farmers were subjected to similar controls. This would make unilateral state control difficult because it would place the farmers in that state in jeopardy.

This study suggests that some nonpoint control can probably be reasonably undertaken, since the costs seem low. Yet it also suggests that the conclusion that all nonpoint sources can be cheaply controlled is not correct. As in other areas of environmental policy, the form and intensity of government intervention would have to be tailored to the specific problem.

The fact that point and nonpoint sources have received such different treatment from EPA suggests the possibility that costs could be lowered by a more careful balancing of these control options. One study of phosphorous control in the Dillon reservoir in Colorado by Industrial Economics, Inc. (1984) supports the validity of this suspicion.

In this reservoir, four municipalities constitute the only point sources of phosphorous, while there are numerous uncontrolled nonpoint sources in the area. The combined phosphorous load on the reservoir from point and nonpoint sources is projected to exceed its assimilative capacity.

The traditional way to reduce the projected phosphorous load wold be to impose even more stringent controls on the point sources. The study found, however, that by following a balanced program controlling both point and nonpoint sources, the desired phosphorous target could be achieved at a cost of approximately $1 million a year less than would be spent if only point sources were controlled more stringently. The more general point that should be carried away from this study is that as point sources are controlled to higher and higher degrees, rising marginal control costs will begin to make controlling nonpoint sources increasingly attractive.

Damages.   One way to tailor the policy is to focus, at least initially, on those pollutants causing the most damage. Unfortunately, there is very little hard information available on the damages caused by nonpoint pollution. This makes it difficult not only to set priorities for controlling various categories of nonpoint pollution, but also to secure the efficient balance between controlling point and nonpoint sources.

How should policy makers react to this uncertainty? Watson and Ridker [1982] set out to answer this question by quantifying the costs associated with various policy approaches. They specifically considered the cost of being wrong in the sense of making one policy choice (a strict focus on point sources) when another choice (a balanced program of controlling point and nonpoint sources) was appropriate.

Their results indicate that the cost of being wrong is so high that the government would benefit from investing time (by delaying implementation of the most stringent point source controls) and resources (by conducting research on the intensity of nonpoint pollution damages and costs) before making a specific policy choice that could prove to have been a serious mistake. Sometimes procrastination can be efficient!

An Overall Assessment

Though the benefit estimates from water-pollution control are subject to much uncertainty, they do exist. While being careful not to place too much reliance on them, we can see what information can be gleaned from the studies in existence.

Freeman [1982] has summarized these studies, focusing on 1985 as a target year. His survey of the field suggests that the 1985 benefit (in 1978 dollars) from conventional water-pollution control policy could be as low as $3.8 billion or as high as $18.4 billion with a most likely point estimate of $9.4 billion. This compares to estimated 1985 annual costs (in 1978 dollars) ranging from a low of $15 billion to a high of $20 billion. Thus Freeman estimates that the net benefit from conventional control is probably negative.

Using cost-effective policies rather than the current approach, it would be possible to reduce costs substantially without affecting the benefits. Cost-effectiveness would require the development of better strategies for point source control and for achieving a better balance between point and non-point source control. The resulting reduction in costs probably would cause net benefits to become positive. That result would not necessarily make the policy efficient, however, because the level of control might still be too high or too low. Unfortunately, the evidence is not rich enough to prove whether or not the overall level of control maximizes the net benefit.

In addition to promoting current cost-effectiveness, economic incentive approaches would stimulate and facilitate change better than a system of rigid, technology-based standards. Russell (1981) has attempted to assess the importance of the facilitating role by simulating the effects on the allocation of pollution control responsibility in response to regional economic growth, changing technology, and changing product mix. Focusing on the steel, paper, and petroleum-refining industries in the eleven-county Delaware Estuary Region, his study estimated the changes in permit use for three water pollutants (BOD, total suspended solids, and ammonia) that would have resulted if a marketable permit system were in place over the 1940–78 period. The calculations assume that the plants existing in 1940 would have been allocated permits to legitimize their emissions at that time, that new sources would have had to purchase permits, and that plant shutdowns or contractions would free up permits for others to purchase.

This study found that for almost every decade and pollutant a substantial number of permits would have been made available by plant closings, capacity contractions, product-mix changes, and/or by the availability of new technologies. In the absence of a marketable permit program, a control authority would not only have to keep abreast of all technological developments so emissions standards could be adjusted accordingly, but it would also have to assure an overall balance between effluent increases and decreases so as to preserve water quality. This tough assignment is handled completely by the market in a marketable permit system, thereby facilitating the evolution of the economy by responding flexibly and predictably to change.

Marketable permits encourage, as well as facilitate, this evolution. Since permits have value, in order to minimize costs firms must continually be looking for new opportunities to control emissions at lower cost. This search eventually results in the adoption of new technologies and in the initiation of changes in the product-mix which result in lower amounts of emissions. The pressure on sources to continually search for better ways to control pollution is a distinct advantage that economic incentive systems have over bureaucratically-defined standards.

SUMMARY

Historically, policies for controlling water pollution have been concerned with conventional pollutants discharged into surface waters. More recently, concerns have shifted toward toxic pollutants, which apparently are more prevalent than previously believed, and also toward ground water, which traditionally was thought to be an invulnerable pristine resource.

Early attempts at controlling water pollution followed a path similar to that of air-pollution control. Legislation prior to the 1970s had little impact on the problem. Frustration then led to the enactment of a tough federal law that was so ambitious and unrealistic that little progress resulted.

There the similarity ends. Whereas in air pollution a wave of recent reforms have improved the process by making it more cost-effective, no parallel exists for control of water pollution. Current policy is based upon the subsidization of municipal waste-treatment facilities and national effluent standards imposed on industrial sources.

The former approach has been hampered by delays, by problems in allocating funds, and by the fact that about half of the constructed plants are not performing satisfactorily. The latter approach has given rise to delays and to the need to defend the standards in a series of court suits. In addition, effluent standards have assigned the control responsibility among point sources in a way that excessively raises cost. Nonpoint pollution sources have, until recently, been virtually ignored. Technological progress is inhibited rather than stimulated by the current approach. Benefit-cost analyses focusing on 1985 show the net benefit from the current approach to be negative.

This lack of progress could have been avoided and did not result from a lack of toughness. Rather, it has resulted from a reliance on direct regulation rather than on emission charges or emission permits, which are more flexible and cost-effective in both the dynamic and static sense. In this respect we can perhaps take some lessons from the European experience and watch with interest to see whether the Fox River program catches on elsewhere.

FURTHER READING

Anderson, Frederick R., et al. *Environmental Improvement Through Economic Incentives* (Baltimore: Johns Hopkins University Press for Resources for the Future, 1977). This book sympathetically analyzes the political, legal, and technical problems that must be faced in a more widespread reliance on emission or effluent charges. An extensive survey of existing and proposed charge systems is included.

Freeman, A. Myrick, III. "Water Pollution Policy." In *Current Issues in U.S. Environmental Policy*, edited by Paul R. Portney, revised edition (Baltimore: Johns Hopkins University Press for Resources for the Future, forthcoming). An excellent, detailed analysis of control policy for water pollution, including the 1977 amendments.

Kneese, Allen V., and Blair T. Bower. *Managing Water Quality: Economics, Technology, Institutions* (Baltimore: Johns Hopkins University Press for Resources for the Future, 1968). Generally considered one of the classics in the field. Contains, among many others, chapters describing the Delaware Estuary Study and pollution-control policies in Europe.

Kneese, Allen V., and Charles L. Schultz. *Pollution, Prices, and Public Policy* (Washington, D.C.: The Brookings Institution, 1975). A highly readable analysis of water-pollution (as well as air-pollution) control policy by two highly respected economists. Does not include the 1977 air or water acts.

ADDITIONAL REFERENCES

Eheart, J. Wayland, E. Downey Brill, Jr., and Randolph M. Lyon, "Transferable Discharge Permits for Control of BOD: An Overview" in Erhard F. Joeres and Martin H. David, eds., *Buying a Better Environment: Cost-Effective Regulation Through Permit Trading* (Madison, WI: University of Wisconsin Press, 1983): 163–195.

Feenberg, Daniel, and Edwin S. Mills, *Measuring the Benefits of Water Pollution Abatement* (New York: Academic Press, 1980).

Freeman, A. Myrick, III. *Air and Water Pollution Control: A Benefit-Cost Assessment* (New York: John Wiley and Sons, 1982): 169–171.

Freeman, A. Myrick, III and Robert H. Haveman. "Clean Rhetoric and Dirty Water," *The Public Interest* (Summer, 1972).

Griffin, Ronald C. "Environmental Policy for Spatial and Persistent Pollutants," *Journal of Environmental Economics and Management,* Vol. 14, No. 1 (March, 1987): 41–53.

Industrial Economics, Inc., *Case Studies on the Trading of Effluent Loads: Dillion Reservoir Final Report* (Cambridge, MA: Industrial Economics, Inc., 1984).

Johnson, Edwin L. "A Study in the Economics of Water Quality Management," *Water Resources Research*, Vol. 3, No. 1 (Second Quarter, 1967): 291–305.

Koch, C. James, and Robert A. Leone. "The Clean Water Act: Unexpected Impacts on Industry," *Harvard Environmental Law Review*, Vol. 3 (1979): 84–111.

Leone, Robert A., and John E. Jackson. "The Political Economy of Federal Regulatory Activity: The Case of Water-Pollution Controls" in Gary Fromm, ed. *Studies in Public Regulation* (Cambridge, Mass.: MIT Press, 1981).

O'Neil, William B. "Pollution Permits and Markets for Water Quality," (Ph.D. dissertation, University of Wisconsin–Madison, 1980).

Palmini, Dennis J. "The Secondary Impact of Nonpoint Pollution Controls: A Linear Programming–Input/Output Analysis," *Journal of Environmental Economics and Management* 9 (September 1982): 263–278.

Peskin, Henry M., and Eugene P. Seskin. *Cost-Benefit Analysis and Water Pollution Control Policy* (Washington, D.C.: The Urban Institute, 1975).

Rothfelder, M. "Reducing the Cost of Water Pollution Control under the Clean Water Act," *Natural Resources Journal,* Vol. 22 (April, 1982): 407–21.

Russell, Clifford S. "Controlled Trading of Pollution Permits," *Environmental Science and Technology*, Vol. 15, No. 1 (January, 1981): 1–5.

Spurlock, S. R., and I. D. Clifton. "Efficiency and Equity Aspects of Nonpoint Source Pollution Controls," *Southern Journal of Agricultural Economics,* Vol. 14 (December, 1982): 123–29.

Walker, D. J. "A Damage Function to Evaluate Erosion Control Economics," *American Journal of Agricultural Economics,* Vol. 64 (November, 1982): 690–98.

Watson, William D., and Ronald G. Ridker. "Revising Water Pollution Standards in an Uncertain World," *Land Economics,* Vol. 57 (November, 1981): 485–506.

DISCUSSION QUESTIONS

1. "The only permanent solution to water pollution control will occur when *all* production by-products are routinely recycled. The zero discharge goal recognizes this reality and forces all dischargers to work steadily toward this solution. Less stringent policies are at best temporary palliatives." Discuss.

2. "In exercising its responsibility to protect the nation's drinking water, the government needs to intervene only in the case of public water supplies. Private water suppliers will be adequately protected without any government intervention." Discuss.

PROBLEMS

1. Consider the situation posed in Problem 1(a) in Chapter 12.

   (a) Compute the allocation which would result if 10 emission permits were given to the second source and 9 were given to the first source. What would be the market permit price? How many permits would each source end up with after trading? What would the net permit expenditure be for each source after trading?

   (b) Suppose a new source entered the area with a constant marginal cost of control equal to $1600 per unit of emission reduced. Assume further that it would add ten units in the absence of any control. What would be the resulting allocation of control responsibility? How much would each firm clean up? What would happen to the permit price? What trades would take place?

CHAPTER NINETEEN

Toxic Substances

*The fact that a problem will certainly take a long time to
solve, and that it will demand the attention of many minds for
several generations, is no justification for postponing the
study. . . . Our difficulties of the moment must always be dealt
with somehow, but our permanent difficulties are difficulties of
every moment.*

T. S. ELIOT, *Christianity and Culture* (1949)

INTRODUCTION

It is one of the ironies of history that the place which focused public attention in the
United States on toxic substances is called the Love Canal. *Love* is not a word any
impartial observer would choose to describe the relationships among the parties to that
incident.

The Love Canal typifies in many ways the dilemma posed by toxic substances.
Until 1953, Hooker Electrochemical (now Hooker Chemical, a subsidiary of Occidental Petroleum Corporation) dumped waste chemicals into an old abandoned waterway
known as the Love Canal, near Niagara Falls, New York.[1] At the time it seemed a
reasonable solution, since the chemicals were buried in what was then considered to
be impermeable clay.

In 1953, Hooker deeded the Love Canal property for one dollar to the Niagara
Falls Board of Education which then built an elementary school on the site. The deed
specifically excused Hooker from any damages that might be caused by the chemicals.
Residential development of the area around the school soon followed.

The site became the center of controversy when, in 1978, residents complained
of chemicals leaking to the surface. News reports emanating from the area included
stories of spontaneous fires and vapors in basements. Medical reports suggested that

---

[1]Hooker was acquired by Occidental Petroleum in 1968.

the residents had experienced abnormally high rates of miscarriage, birth defects, and diseases of the liver.

Similar experiences befell Europe and Asia. In 1976 an accident at a F. Hoffman–La Roche & Co. plant in Sevesco spewed dioxin over the Italian countryside. More recently, explosions in a Union Carbide plant in Bhopal, India spread deadly gases over nearby residential neighborhoods with significant loss of life, and water used to quell a warehouse fire at a Sandoz warehouse near Basel, Switzerland carried an estimated 30 tons of toxic chemicals into the Rhine River, a source of drinking water for a number of towns in the Federal Republic of Germany.

In previous chapters we touched on a few of the policy instruments used to combat toxic-substance problems. Emission standards govern the types and amounts of substances that can be injected into the air. Effluent standards regulate what can be discharged directly into water courses, and pretreatment standards control the flow of toxics into waste-treatment plants. Maximum concentration levels have been established for many substances in drinking water.

This impressive array of policies is not sufficient to resolve the Love Canal problem or others having similar characteristics. When violations of the standards for drinking water are detected, for example, the water is already contaminated. The standards do nothing to cope with the source of the problem. The various standards for air and water emission that do protect against *point* sources do little to prevent contamination by *nonpoint* sources. Furthermore, most water-borne toxic pollutants are stock pollutants, not fund pollutants; they cannot be absorbed by the receiving waters. Therefore, temporally constant controls on emissions (a traditional method used for fund pollutants) is inappropriate for these toxic substances since they would allow a steady rise in the concentration over time. Thus some additional form of control may be necessary to curb toxic-substance pollution.

In this chapter we shall describe and evaluate the pollution policies that deal specifically with toxic substances. There are many dimensions to be considered. What are appropriate ways to dispose of toxic substances? How can the government ensure that all waste is appropriately disposed of? How do we prevent surreptitious dumping? Who should clean up old sites? Should victims be compensated for damages caused by toxic substances under the control of someone else? If so, by whom? What are the appropriate roles for the legislature and the judiciary in creating the proper set of incentives?

NATURE OF TOXIC-SUBSTANCE POLLUTION

The main objective of the current legal system for controlling toxic substances is to protect human health, though protecting other forms of life is a secondary objective. The potential health danger depends upon the toxicity of a substance to humans and their exposure to the substance. *Toxicity* occurs when a living organism experiences detrimental effects when exposed to a substance. In normal concentrations most chemicals are not toxic. Others, such as pesticides, are toxic by design. Yet, in excess concentrations, even a benign substance such as table salt can be toxic.

There is a degree of risk when using any chemical substance. There are benefits as well. The task for public policy is to define an acceptable risk by balancing the costs and benefits of controlling the use of chemical substances.

Health Effects

The two main health concerns associated with toxic substances are risk of cancer and effects on reproduction.

Cancer.   Since the 1900s, mortality rates have fallen for most of the major causes of death. The most conspicuous exception is cancer. Even the mortality rate for heart disease, the number-one killer, has declined in recent decades. Meanwhile, the mortality rate for cancer, currently the second most-common cause of death, has increased steadily throughout this century.

This increased mortality rate for cancer may be related to increased exposure to carcinogens. Unfortunately, establishing the source of this rise in cancer is not easy; it is rendered more difficult by the fact that there can exist a considerable period of latency for cancer. *Latency* refers to the state of being concealed during the period between exposure to the carcinogen and the detection of cancer. Latency periods for cancer can run from 15 to 40 years in length, but have been known to run as long as 75 years.[2]

In the United States, part of the increase in cancer has been convincingly linked to smoking, particularly among women. The proportion of women who smoke has increased, and the incidence of lung cancer has increased as well. Smoking does not account for all of the increase in cancer, however. A smaller percentage of men smoke today than in earlier decades, and modern cigarettes contain less tar. Despite this, the incidence of lung cancer among men has increased.[3]

Though it is not entirely clear what other agents may be responsible, one cause that has been suggested is the rise in the manufacture and use of synthetic chemicals since World War II.[4] A number of these chemicals have been shown in the laboratory to be carcinogenic. That does not necessarily implicate them in the rise of cancer, however, because it does not take exposure into account. The laboratory can reveal, through animal tests, the relationship between dosage and resulting effects. To track down the significance of that chemical in causing cancer in the general population would require an estimate of how large a segment of the population was exposed to various doses. Currently, our data are not extensive enough to allow these kinds of calculations to be done with any confidence.

---

[2]Paul R. Portney, "Toxic Substance Policy and the Protection of Human Health," in *Current Issues in U.S. Environmental Policy,* Paul R. Portney, ed. (Baltimore: Johns Hopkins University Press, 1978): 100.

[3]Council on Environmental Quality, *Environmental Quality–1980* (Washington, D.C.: U.S. Government Printing Office, 1980): 194.

[4]See, for example, Davis and Magee who raise this possibility but who also conclude that, because of the latency period, it is too early to tell how much, if any, of the responsibility can be assigned to the increased exposure to synthetic chemicals. See Devra Lee Davis and Brian H. Magee, "Cancer and Industrial Chemical Production," *Science* 206 (21 December 1979): 1356–1358.

Reproductive Effects.[5]   Tracing the influence of environmental effects on human reproduction is still a new science. There is a growing body of scientific evidence, however, which suggests that exposure to smoking, alcohol, and chemicals may contribute to infertility, may affect the viability of the fetus and the health of the infant after birth, and may cause genetic defects which can be passed on for generations.

Problems exist for both men and women. In men, exposure to toxic substances has resulted in lower sperm counts, malformed sperm, and genetic damage. In women, exposure can also result in sterility or birth defects in their children.

Policy Issues

Many aspects of the toxic-substance problem make it difficult to resolve. Three important aspects are the numbers of substances involved, latency, and uncertainty.

Number of Substances.   Of the two million or so known chemical compounds, approximately 70,000 are actively used in commerce. More than 30,000 of these are in substantial use. Many exhibit little or no toxicity, and even a very toxic substance represents little risk as long as it is isolated. The trick is to identify the substances that present problems and to design appropriate policies as responses. The massive number of substances involved makes that a difficult assignment. The geographic location of the substances is given in Table 19.1.

Latency.   The period of latency that many of these relationships exhibit compounds the problem even more. Two kinds of toxicity are exhibited—acute and chronic. *Acute toxicity* is present when a short-term exposure to the substance produces a detrimental effect on the exposed organism. *Chronic toxicity* is present when the detrimental effect arises from exposure of a continued or prolonged nature.

The process of screening chemicals as potentially serious causes of chronic illness is even more complicated than that of screening for acute illness. The traditional technique for determining acute toxicity is the lethal dose determination, a relatively quick test on animals that calculates the dose which results in the death of 50 percent of the animal population. This test is less well suited for screening substances that exhibit chronic toxicity.

The appropriate tests for discovering chronic toxicity have typically involved subjecting animal populations to sustained low-level doses of the substance over an extended period of time. These tests are very expensive and time-consuming.[6] If all proposed chemicals were subjected to such long and detailed tests, the process itself

---

[5]For an excellent summary of the literature, see Council on Environmental Quality, *Environmental Quality— 1980* (Washington, D.C.: U.S. Government Printing Office, 1980): 199–205.

[6]A standard test could cost $750,000 and take three years or more, says Paul R. Portney, "Toxic Substance Policy and the Protection of Human Health," in *Current Issues in U.S. Environmental Policy,* Paul R. Portney, ed. (Baltimore: Johns Hopkins University Press, 1978): 136.

would preclude the introduction of many new chemicals. If EPA were to do the tests, given its limited resources, it could only test a few of the estimated 500 new chemicals introduced each year. If the industries were to do the tests, the expense could preclude the introduction of many potentially valuable new chemicals which have limited, specialized markets.

EPA has attempted to respond by developing a series of screening tests that can be accomplished in a shorter period of time and at less expense. The chemicals identified by those screening tests as posing an unacceptable risk can be subjected to the more expensive tests. As long as the short tests are sufficiently reliable as a sorting mechanism, the testing problem can be reduced to manageable proportions.

One particularly promising class of screening uses *in vitro* techniques; the screening is conducted in test tubes rather than in the bodies of animals. These tests involve adding a chemical substance to a bacteria culture no longer capable of growth. If the

TABLE 19.1 Estimated Generation of Industrial Hazardous Waste in 1983, by State (In thousands of metric tons)

State	Quantity	Percent of National Generation	State	Quantity	Percent of National Generation
Alabama	6,547	2.5	Montana	662	0.2
Alaska	52	*	Nebraska	739	0.3
Arizona	642	0.2	Nevada	379	0.1
Arkansas	3,729	1.4	New Hampshire	431	0.2
California	17,284	6.5	New Jersey	12,948	4.9
Colorado	1,902	0.7	New Mexico	619	0.2
Connecticut	4,238	1.6	New York	9,876	3.7
Delaware	894	0.3	North Carolina	3,954	1.5
Florida	2,981	1.1	North Dakota	269	0.1
Georgia	3,338	1.3	Ohio	19,692	7.4
Hawaii	202	0.1	Oklahoma	2,673	1.0
Idaho	1,160	0.4	Oregon	969	0.4
Illinois	14,810	5.6	Pennsylvania	18,260	6.9
Indiana	10,189	3.8	Rhode Island	1,745	0.7
Iowa	1,774	0.7	South Carolina	3,669	1.4
Kansas	2,564	1.0	South Dakota	159	0.1
Kentucky	4,647	1.7	Tennessee	12,159	4.6
Louisiana	13,801	5.2	Texas	34,866	13.1
Maine	337	0.1	Utah	1,139	0.4
Maryland	2,989	1.1	Virginia	4,038	1.5
Massachusetts	4,536	1.7	Vermont	226	0.1
Michigan	12,399	4.7	Washington	5,523	2.1
Minnesota	2,212	0.8	Wisconsin	3,297	1.2
Missouri	6,046	2.3	West Virginia	5,642	2.1
Mississippi	1,816	0.7	Wyoming	572	0.2
			Total	265,595	100.0

Notes: Projections for 1983 based on 1981 state employment shares found in Bureau of Census, U.S. Department of Commerce, *County Business Patterns 1981* (1981).

*Less than one-tenth of one percent.

Source: Congressional Budget Office, *Hazardous Waste Management: Recent Changes and Policy Alternatives* (May, 1985): 22.

substance is a mutagen, and therefore a likely carcinogen, the bacteria resume growth. As a convenient side benefit, the rate of growth seems to indicate the toxicity of the substance. In contrast to longer tests, these *in vitro* tests cost about $500 in 1978 dollars and take only about two weeks.[7]

Uncertainty. Another dilemma inhibiting policymakers is the uncertainty surrounding the scientific evidence on which regulation is based. Effects uncovered by laboratory studies on animals are not perfectly correlated with effects on humans. Large doses administered over a three-year period may not produce the same effects as an equivalent amount received over a twenty-year period. Some of the effects are *synergistic*—that is, their effects are compounded by other variable factors. They are either more serious or less serious in the presence of other substances or conditions than they would be in the absence of those substances or conditions.[8] Once cancer is detected, in most cases it does not bear the imprint of a particular source. Policymakers have to act in the face of limited information.

From an economic point of view, how the policy process reacts to this dilemma should depend on how well the market handles toxic-substance problems. To the extent that the market generates the correct information and provides the appropriate incentives, policy may not be needed. On the other hand, when the government can best generate information or create the appropriate incentives, intervention may be called for. As the following pages demonstrate, the nature of the most appropriate policy response may depend crucially on the type of relationship existing between the polluter and the affected party or parties.

MARKET ALLOCATIONS AND TOXIC SUBSTANCES

Toxic-substance contamination can arise in a variety of settings. In order to define the efficient policy response, we must examine what responses would be forthcoming in the normal operation of the market. Let's look at three possible relationships between the source of the contamination and the victim: employer-employee, producer-consumer, and producer-third party. The first two of these involve normal contractual relations among the parties, while the latter involves noncontracting parties whose connection is defined solely by the contamination.

Occupational Hazards

Many occupations involve risk, including, for some people, exposure to toxic substances. Do employers and employees have sufficient incentives to act in concert toward achieving safety in the workplace?

---

[7]Paul R. Portney, *Current Issues in U.S. Environmental Policy* (Baltimore: Johns Hopkins University Press, 1978): 136.

[8]For example, it has been shown that asbestos workers are 30 times more likely to get lung cancer if they smoke than are their nonsmoking fellow workers.

The caricature of the market used by the most ardent proponents of regulation suggests not. In this view the employer's desire to maximize profits precludes spending money on safety. Sick workers can simply be replaced. Therefore, the workers are powerless to do anything about it; if they complain, they are fired and replaced with others who are less vocal.

The most ardent opponents of regulation respond that this caricature omits significant market pressures and is not a particularly accurate guide. They argue that it fails to take into account employee incentives and the feedback effects of those incentives on employers.

If employees are to accept work in a potentially hazardous environment, they will do so only if appropriately compensated. Riskier occupations should call forth higher wages. The increase in wages should be sufficient to compensate them for the increased risk. These higher wages represent a real cost of the hazardous situation to the employer. They also produce an incentive to create a safer work environment, since greater safety would result in lower wages. One cost could be balanced against the other. What was spent on safety could be recovered in lower wages (Figure 19.1).

The first type of cost, the marginal increase in wages, is drawn to reflect the fact that the lower the level of precaution, the higher the wage bill. Two such curves are drawn to reflect high-exposure and low-exposure situations. The higher exposure case refers to a situation in which larger numbers of workers are exposed, while in the low-

FIGURE 19.1   The Market Provision of Occupational Safety

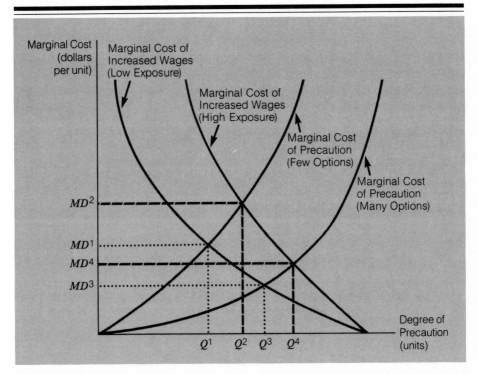

exposure case, few are exposed. The low-exposure cost curve rises more slowly because the situation is less dangerous at the margin. In the high-exposure case the sensitivity of wages to precaution is much higher because the damage caused at the margin is much larger.

The second type of curve, the marginal cost of providing precaution, is drawn to reflect increasing marginal cost. The two different curves depict different production situations. A firm with a few expensive precautionary options will face a steeply sloped marginal-cost curve, while a firm with many cheaper options will face a lower marginal cost at every comparable degree of precaution chosen.

The graph depicts four possible outcomes—one for each possible combination of these four marginal-cost curves. Notice that very different choices will be made, depending upon the circumstances. Also notice that there is not a perfect correlation between the level of risk chosen (as indicated by the marginal damage, labeled *MD*) and the degree of precaution. The highest marginal risk is MD^2, but the associated level of precaution (Q^2) is not the largest. The reason, of course, is that the cost of taking precautions matters, and sometimes it is cheaper to accept the risk and compensate for it than it is to prevent it.

Because the marginal increased-wages curve accurately reflects marginal damages (since the higher wages are demanded by workers to compensate them for damages), these market equilibria are also efficient. Thus, the efficient resolution of the occupational-hazards problem varies not only from substance to substance, but from plant to plant as well. As long as this stylized view of the world is correct, the market will tailor the appropriate degree of precaution to the situation.

Proponents point out that this allocation would also allow more choices for workers than would, for example, a system requiring all workplaces to be equally safe. With varying occupational risk, those occupations with more risk (such as working with radioactive materials) would attract people who were less averse to risk. These workers would receive higher than average wages (to compensate them for the increased risk), but paying these higher wages would be cheaper to the firm (and, hence, consumers) than producing a workplace safe enough for the average worker. The risk-average workers would be free to choose less risky occupations.[9]

Which view is correct? Is there no role for the public sector in controlling contamination in the workplace when market allocations are efficient? Not necessarily. There are reasons for believing that this stylized version of occupational hazards also misses some key points.

One point raised by the court system is whether or not market solutions are always ethical. For example, if the employee is a pregnant woman and the occupational hazard involves potential damage to the fetus, does the expectant mother have the right to risk the unborn child, or is some added protection for the fetus needed? Furthermore, if

---

[9]In a survey of wages, Portney found that wage differentials reflecting risk were common, though those arising from exposure to toxic substances seem to reflect more concern about acute effects than chronic effects. See Paul R. Portney, *Current Issues in U.S. Environmental Policy* (Baltimore: Johns Hopkins University Press, 1978): 114–5.

the lowest cost solution is to ban pregnant—or even fertile—women from a workplace that poses a risk to a fetus, is that an acceptable solution, or is it unfair discrimination against women? As Example 19.1 suggests, these are not idle concerns.

Ethical concerns are not the only challenges for market solutions. The ability of the worker to respond to a hazardous situation depends upon his or her knowledge of the seriousness of the danger. With toxic substances, that knowledge is likely to be incomplete. Consequently, the marginal increased-wages curve may be artificially rotated toward the origin with the result that the employer chooses too little precaution. The employer may be in the best position to assess the degree of risk posed, since it would presumably have access to the health records of all employees, but the employer also has an incentive to suppress that information. To publicize risk would mean demands for higher compensatory wages and possible lawsuits.

Information on the dangers posed by exposure to a particular toxic substance is a public good to employees; each employee has an incentive to be a *free rider* on the

---

EXAMPLE 19.1

Susceptible Populations in the Hazardous Workplace

Some employees are especially susceptible to occupational hazards. Two particularly vulnerable groups are pregnant women and women in the childbearing years. When an employer presides over a work situation that poses a hazardous threat, the employer can either separate the susceptible population from the hazard or control the hazard to a sufficient level that its risk is acceptable to even the most susceptible employees.

The economic aspects of this choice are easily deduced from Figure 19.1. Suppose that the firm has few control options and is on the uppermost of the two marginal cost-of-precaution curves. By removing the susceptible population, it could face the law-exposure curve. Removal of the susceptible population results in lower marginal risk to the workers, lower costs to the firm, and less precaution taken. But is it fair to those who are removed from their jobs?

This issue came to a head in 1978 when American Cyanamid decided to respond to an occupational risk by banning all fertile women from jobs in the section manufacturing lead chromate pigment at Willow Island, West Virginia. After reviewing this decision, the Occupational Safety and Health Administration (OSHA) cited the company under the general duty clause of the Occupational Safety and Health Act, which requires an employer to provide a workplace free of hazards, and fined it $10,000. That was not the last of it. In early 1980, the Oil, Chemical, and Atomic Workers Union sued the company under the 1964 Civil Rights Act on the ground that the company had discriminated unfairly against women.

Source: This example was taken from Council on Environmental Quality, *Environmental Quality—1980* (Washington, D.C.: U.S. Government Printing Office, 1980), 205.

discoveries of others. Individual employees do not have an incentive to bear the cost of doing the necessary research to uncover the degree of risk either. Thus, it seems neither employers nor employees can be expected to produce the efficient amount of information on the magnitude of risk.

As a result, there may be a substantial role for government in setting the boundaries on ethical responses, in stimulating research on the nature of hazards, and in providing for the dissemination of information to affected parties. It does not necessarily follow, however, that the government should be responsible for determining the level of safety in the workplace once this information is available and the ethical boundaries are determined.

Our analysis suggesting that the market will not provide an efficient level of information on occupational risk is consistent with recent activity in state legislatures. As of 1982, New York, California, Michigan, and five other states had already enacted "Right to Know" laws, while similar measures were pending in about 20 state legislatures.[10] These laws require businesses to disclose to their employees and to the public any potential health hazards associated with toxic substances used on the job.

Product Safety

Exposure to a hazardous or potentially hazardous substance can also occur as a result of using a product, as when eating food containing chemical additives or when using pesticides. Does the market efficiently supply safe products?

One view holds that the market pressures on both parties are sufficient to yield an efficient level of safety. Safer products are generally more expensive to produce and carry a higher price tag. If consumers feel that the additional safety justifies the cost, they will purchase the safer product. Otherwise they won't. Producers supplying excessively risky products will find their market drying up, because consumers will switch to competing brands that are more expensive, but safer. Similarly, producers selling excessively safe products (meaning they eliminate, at great cost, risks consumers are perfectly willing to take in return for a lower purchase price) find their markets drying up as well. Consumers will choose the cheaper, riskier product.

This theory also suggests that the market will not (and should not) yield a uniform level of safety for all products. Different consumers will have different degrees of risk aversion. While some consumers might purchase riskier, but cheaper, products, others might prefer safer, but more expensive, products.[11]

Thus, it would be common to find products with various safety levels supplied simultaneously, reflecting and satisfying different consumer preferences for risk. Forc-

---

[10]These laws are described in Frank Allen "Battle Building Over 'Right to Know' Laws Regarding Toxic Items Used by Workers," *Wall Street Journal* (4 January 1983): 31. Significantly, proponents of these laws suggest that the targets are not the large chemical companies, which generally have excellent disclosure programs, but the smaller, largely nonunion plants.

[11]A classic example is provided by the manner in which Americans choose their automobiles. It is quite clear that many of the larger domestic cars are safer and more expensive than smaller, cheaper foreign cars. Some consumers are willing to pay for the safety and others aren't.

ing all similar products to conform to a single level of risk would not be efficient. Uniform product safety is no more efficient than uniform occupation safety.

If this view of the market were completely accurate, there would be no efficiency case for government intervention to protect consumers. By the force of their collective buying habits, consumers would protect themselves.

The problem with the market's ability to provide such self-regulation is the availability of information on product safety. The consumer acquires his or her information on a product generally from personal experience. With toxic substances the latency period may be so long as to preclude any effective market reaction. Even when some damage results, it is difficult for the consumer to associate it with a particular source. While an examination of the relationships between purchasing patterns of a large number of consumers and their subsequent health might well reveal some suggestive correlations, it would be difficult for any individual consumer to deduce this correlation.

While there may well be a need for government to provide information to consumers about the safety of products, the need to dictate a prevailing level of safety is much more nebulous, particularly if the dictated level is uniformly applied. In situations where adequate information is available to them on the risks, consumers should have a substantial role in choosing the acceptable level of risk through their purchases.

Third Parties

The final case to consider is one involving *third parties,* victims who have no contractual relationship to the source. This would be the situation, for example, when ground water is contaminated by a neighboring waste-treatment facility, by surreptitious dumping of toxic wastes, or by the improper applications of a pesticide. In any of these situations, there is no direct market pressure the affected party can bring to bear on the source. Since these are nonpoint sources and are generally not controlled by the air and water regulations, the case for additional government intervention is strongest for third-party situations.

This does not necessarily imply, however, that executive or legislative remedies are appropriate. As discussed in Chapter 3, the most appropriate response may well come from the court system.

Liability law provides one judicial avenue for internalizing the external costs in third-party situations. If the court finds that damage occurred, that it was caused by a toxic substance, and that a particular source was responsible for the presence of the substance, the source can be forced to compensate the victim for the damages caused. Unlike regulations that are uniformly (and, hence, inefficiently) applied, a court decision can be tailored to the exact circumstances involved in the suit. Furthermore, the impact of any particular liability assignment can go well beyond the parties to that case. A decision for the plaintiff can remind other sources that they should take the efficient level of precaution to avoid paying damages.

In short, when liability law is functioning appropriately, it can force sources, including nonpoint sources, to choose efficient levels of precaution. Unlike regulation, liability law can provide compensation to the victims. Example 19.2 shows how a judicial response to one spill has caused an increase in environmental precaution.

CURRENT POLICY

Common Law

The common-law system is an extremely complicated approach to regulation. When a victim seeks recourse through the court system, a number of legal grounds can be used to pursue a claim. Not all of these may be available to every plaintiff (the person

EXAMPLE 19.2

Judicial Remedies in Toxic-Substance Control: The Kepone Case

Kepone is a highly toxic substance used in the manufacture of pesticides. Kepone was produced at Hopewell, Virginia, by Life Science Products Company, a company started by former employees of Allied Chemical Corporation. The kepone produced by Life Science was sold to Allied Chemical.

Conditions at the plant and spills into the James River resulted in high contamination levels which affected workers and people eating fish taken from the river. Allied Chemical Corporation was indicted by a grand jury on criminal charges during May 1976, and was subsequently sued by various injured parties. Eventually, it paid more than $20 million in compensation, penalties, and legal fees.

As a result of the suit, Allied and a number of other companies have begun to dramatically increase expenditures on prevention. In 1977 Allied hired Arthur D. Little, a consulting firm, to develop a broad program to anticipate and prevent further accidents. By 1981 Allied had over 400 employees concerned with environmental control.

Interestingly, the staff has discovered that pollution control sometimes yields unexpected benefits. In the past Allied treated its waste, including calcium chloride, from its Baton Rouge plant and discharged it into the river. New regulations from EPA would have raised the costs of treating the waste. Allied decided to look for a market for the calcium chloride and found one, turning a liability into an asset.

The kepone suit changed this corporation's behavior, as well as the behavior of other chemical companies. They have found that anticipating can be much less costly than reacting.

Source: This example is based upon Georgette Jasen, "Like Other New-Breed Environmental Managers, Hillman of Allied Isn't Merely a Trouble Shooter," *The Wall Street Journal* (30 July, 1981): 50.

initiating the suit), since which doctrines can be used depends partially on the legal tradition in the state where the suit is filed. Not all states allow a plaintiff to file on all grounds. Two of the more common legal grounds are negligence and strict liability.

Negligence.   Probably the most common legal theory used by plaintiffs to pursue claims is negligence. This body of law suggests that the defendant (the party allegedly responsible for the contamination) owes a duty to the plaintiff (the affected party) to exercise due care. If that duty has been breached, the defendant is found negligent and is forced to compensate the victim for damages caused. If the defendant is found to have exercised due care and to have performed that duty to the plaintiff, no liability is assessed. Under negligence law the victim bears the liability unless it can be proven that the defendant was negligent.

Interestingly, the test conventionally applied by the courts in deciding whether or not the defendant has exercised due care, the *Learned Hand Formula,* is fundamentally an economic one. Named after the judge (*yes,* Learned Hand!) who initially formulated it, this test suggests that the defendant is guilty of negligence if the loss caused by the contamination, multiplied by the probability of contamination, exceeds the cost of preventing the contamination.[12] When correctly applied, this is simply a version of the expected net-benefit formula developed in Chapter 4.[13] The maximization of expected net benefits is efficient as long as society is risk-neutral. Therefore, the common-law approach embodied in negligence law in principle is compatible with efficiency.

There are other means the plaintiff can use to prove negligence on the part of the defendant, such as showing that the defendant violated a statute. In many states, any related statutory violation is taken as sufficient evidence of negligence.

Strict Liability.   Strict liability can be used by plaintiffs in some states and in some circumstances. Under this doctrine the plaintiff does not have to prove negligence. As long as the activity causes damage, the defendant is declared liable even if the activity is completely legal and complies with all relevant laws.

Strict liability is usually applied in circumstances where the activity in question is inherently hazardous. Since the disposal of toxic substances is frequently considered such an activity, states are increasingly allowing toxic-substance suits to be brought under this doctrine. In contrast to negligence, this strict liability transfers liability for damages to the source whether or not the source has exercised much care.

Strict liability can also be compatible with efficiency. The agent dealing with toxic wastes must balance the costs of taking precautions with the likelihood of, and expected costs of, lawsuits. In cases where the precautionary expenditures are particularly high and the damages low, only limited precaution is likely to be taken. However, for truly dangerous substances it is advantageous to take extraordinary precautions and avoid large damages.

---

[12]For a detailed discussion of this formula, see Richard A. Posner, "A Theory of Negligence," *Journal of Legal Studies* 1 (1972): 29–96.

[13]For a description of necessary conditions for the formula to be applied, see J. P. Brown [1973].

Criminal Law

Strict liability and negligence are civil-law doctrines. They involve one private party suing another. Increasingly in environmental policy, the civil-law approach is being complemented by the use of criminal law, in which the government serves as prosecutor, presumably acting as an agent of the people. The Kepone Case, described in Example 19.2, involved both civil and criminal law.

The remedies under criminal law are different from those under civil law. Jail sentences may be handed out to those found breaking the law. Corporate executives, for example, could spend up to five years in jail for particularly onerous violations of the law. Fines could also be levied against guilty parties.

There are several important differences between the civil and criminal judicial approaches to pollution control. Criminal charges can be brought against only those charged with breaking one or more specific laws, while civil suits can be brought against those causing damage, whether or not a law has been violated. The burden of proof is higher in a criminal trial. To convict a person, the state must prove he or she is guilty "beyond a reasonable doubt," whereas, in civil trials, the decision is based merely upon the "preponderance of evidence." The presumption of innocence, which plays such an important part in criminal trials, has no counterpart in civil trials. In civil trials, there is no presumption in favor of either party.

The final major difference between civil liability law and criminal law is that *civil liability law compensates victims directly while criminal law doesn't.* Criminal law focuses more on punishing the perpetrator than on compensating the victim.[14] Though the severity of punishment can be tailored to the amount of damage caused, the correspondence between the length of a jail sentence and the damage caused is much less direct than forcing the defendant to pay the exact monetary damages. By breaking the link between the monetary damage caused and the punishment received—the cornerstone of liability law—criminal law would be less likely to result in efficient resolutions of toxic-chemical contamination problems than civil law. Efficiency could result, but it would be more of a coincidence than an inherent characteristic of the process.

Statutory Law

These civil and criminal common-law remedies have been accompanied by a host of legislative remedies. The statutes have evolved over time in response to particular toxic-substance problems. Each time a new problem surfaced and people were able to get legislators aroused, a new law was passed to deal with it. The result is a collage of laws on the books, each with its own unique focus. We shall cover only the main ones here.

---

[14]Criminal law remedies forcing restitution do compensate the victim, but they are the exception rather than the rule. With restitution the guilty party is forced to pay a stipulated amount of money to the victim as part of the punishment.

Federal Food, Drug, and Cosmetic Act. The first concerns with toxic substances arose with *food additives,* since these are ingested and potentially pose a serious and immediate threat to health. Food and drug additives are regulated under the Federal Food, Drug, and Cosmetic Act of 1938, as amended in 1958. The organization administering this act is the Food and Drug Administration (FDA).

The 1938 act contained a general safety provision authorizing FDA to prohibit the sale of any food which "contains any poisonous or deleterious substance which may render it injurious to health." This provision was complemented in 1958 by a provision known as the Delaney Clause after its legislative sponsor. This provision states that no additive should be deemed safe if it was found to induce cancer in humans or animals. Coupled with the first provision, this addition prohibits any food additive determined by FDA to be a carcinogen in any dosage.

Manufacturers wishing to introduce new food additives or drugs must demonstrate the safety of their products through premarket testing. For cosmetics no premarket testing is required. For the FDA to take any action on cosmetics it must bear the burden of proof to demonstrate the product is unsafe. The burden is on the manufacturer to prove the safety of food additives and drugs.

Occupational Safety and Health Act. This 1970 act created the Occupational Safety and Health Administration (OSHA) and charged the agency with the regulatory responsibility for protecting workers from hazards in the workplace. The act also created the National Institute for Occupational Safety and Health (NIOSH), which, among other responsibilities, must make recommendations for the OSHA regulatory standards.

In 1974 OSHA promulgated the first regulation establishing levels of pollutants that would be acceptable in the workplace atmosphere. The statute required the standards to be established at a level sufficiently stringent so that no employee would suffer material impairment of health, even if that employee were exposed to the substance on a regular basis throughout his or her working life. In addition, occupational standards requiring special precautions and/or protective devices have been adopted or proposed for a number of workplace contaminants.

Carcinogens are handled more severely. Once any substance is confirmed as a carcinogen, ambient workplace standards are set, rapidly followed by the imposition of special handling requirements, protective devices, and minimum contact regulations.

The approach taken by OSHA was to specify, often in excruciating detail, acceptable contaminant levels, as well as the approaches to be taken by employers to ensure the attainment of those containment levels.[15] In response to adverse public opinion about silly regulations, in 1978 OSHA revoked 928 previously promulgated regulations as unnecessary.

Federal Environmental Pesticide Control Act. This 1972 act amended the Federal Insecticide, Fungicide, and Rodenticide Act (Congress has a flair for titles!). The thrust

---

[15]The humor in the situation was nicely illustrated by an ad for a political candidate opposed to OSHA. A cowboy is pictured riding off to the prairie. On the back of his horse is strapped a plastic toilet required by an OSHA regulation setting the maximum distance any employee could be from a comfort station.

of the legislation is to provide for the registration of all pesticides, the certification of individuals applying these pesticides, and the premarket testing of all new pesticides.

All pesticide registrations automatically expire every five years. To secure a new registration, the manufacturer must prove that the benefits derived from that pesticide will outweigh its social costs. When the evidence permits, EPA has the power to prohibit the sale of a pesticide or to restrict its use to specific applications. EPA has used this power to dramatically decrease the use of a number of pesticides, with DDT being the earliest and most publicized example.

Certification procedures for individuals applying the pesticides represent a recognition that the danger posed is to a large extent dependent on how the substances are applied. With this procedure EPA can ensure proper training for commercial applicators, and by threatening the withdrawal of certification (and the livelihood of the applicators), EPA can influence their behavior.

Resource Conservation and Recovery Act.   To counteract the unsafe dumping of toxic wastes, Congress passed Subtitle C of the Resource Conservation and Recovery Act of 1976. This act imposes standards for handling, shipping, and disposing of toxic wastes.

The regulations implementing this act define hazardous wastes and establish a cradle-to-grave management system, including standards for generators of hazardous wastes, standards for transporters, and standards and permit requirements for owners and operators of facilities that treat, store, or dispose of hazardous wastes.

The centerpiece of this rather large regulatory system is a manifest system for keeping track of the fate of the substances from their creation to their disposal. Waste generators are required to prepare a manifest for all controlled substances. If the substance is on the EPA list, it must be properly packaged and labeled, and must be delivered only to a permitted waste disposal site. Through this recording system, EPA hopes to monitor all hazardous substances and detect any surreptitious dumping. Failure to comply with the act is punishable by civil penalties and, in certain cases, by fines and imprisonment.

In 1984 this act was amended by the Hazardous and Solid Waste Amendments of 1984. The 1984 amendments contain three major categories of changes: (1) they expanded the amount of waste covered by the regulations, (2) they limited, or in some cases, banned the use of land disposal for certain kinds of waste, and (3) they brought under regulation some activities not previously controlled, such as underground storage tanks for certain chemicals.

Toxic Substances Control Act.   This 1976 act was passed as a complement to the Resource Conservation and Recovery Act. Whereas the Resource Conservation and Recovery Act was designed to ensure safe handling and disposal of existing substances, the Toxic Substances Control Act was designed to provide a firmer basis for deciding which of the chemical substances not controlled by the above acts should be allowed to be commercially produced.

This act requires EPA to inventory the approximately 55,000 chemical substances in commerce; to require premanufacture notice to EPA of all new chemical substances;

and to enforce recordkeeping, testing, and reporting requirements so that EPA can assess and regulate the relative risks of chemicals. At least 90 days before manufacturing or importing a new chemical, a firm must submit test results or other information to EPA showing that the chemical will not present "an unreasonable risk" to human health or the environment.

On the basis of the information in the premanufacture notification, EPA may limit the manufacture, use, or disposal of the substance. The act is significant in that it represents one of the few instances where the burden of proof is on the manufacturer to prove that the product should be marketed, rather than forcing EPA to show it shouldn't be marketed.

Comprehensive Environmental Response, Compensation, and Liability Act. Known popularly as the "Superfund Act," the Comprehensive Environmental Response, Compensation, and Liability Act of 1980 created a $1.6 billion fund to be used over a five-year period to clean up existing toxic waste sites. The revenue was derived mainly from taxes on chemical industries. It offers compensation for the loss or destruction of natural resources controlled by the state or federal government, but it does not provide any compensation for injured individuals. A $9 billion reauthorization bill was passed in 1986 significantly increasing the amount of money dedicated to the cleanup of these sites.

This act, as amended, authorized federal and state governments to respond quickly to incidents such as occurred in Times Beach, Missouri. Times Beach, a town of 2800 residents located about 30 miles southwest of St. Louis, had been contaminated by dioxin. Dioxin is a waste by-product created during the production of certain chemicals. One such chemical is Agent Orange, the defoliant used during the Vietnam War. The contamination occurred when a waste-oil hauler bought about 55 pounds of dioxin in 1971 from a now-defunct manufacturer, mixed it with oil, and under contract with the local government, spread it on unpaved roads as a dust control measure. On December 23, 1982, after soil tests revealed dangerous levels of dioxin, the Center for Disease Control recommended total evacuation of the town.

By February 22, 1983, the federal government had authorized a transfer of some $33 million from the Superfund to cover the cost of buying out all businesses and residents and relocating them. By June of 1983, all but 40 families had been relocated and a separate multimillion dollar cleanup, also funded by Superfund, was set to begin following the complete evacuation of the town.

The existence of the fund allows the governments involved to move rapidly. They are not forced to wait until the outcome of court suits against those responsible to raise the money or to face the uncertainty associated with whether the suits would ultimately be successful. For its part the State of Missouri has agreed to pay ten percent of the cost—$3.3 million—into the Superfund, and fund representatives are free to attempt to recover damages from the responsible parties. Though the words are not mentioned in the act, the doctrine of strict liability usually is imposed, because any defense related to the exercise of due care by the defendant is disallowed.[16]

---

[16]A further discussion of the liability provision can be found in 11 ELR 10103.

This is a formidable list of statutory and common-law remedies embodying a variety of approaches to the resolution of toxic-substance problems. The question is whether or not these approaches are efficient or cost-effective.

AN ASSESSMENT OF THE LEGAL REMEDIES

The Common Law

Judicial-Legislative Complementarity.   Common law provides a useful complement to statutory law for occupational, consumer-product, and third-party hazards. For all three types of toxic-substance problems, the market may create pressures preventing the flow of information about the dangers of these substances. The parties (employers or producers) in the best position to transmit the information to parties who can best assess the risk (the employees, consumers, or third-parties) are not always willing to seek or relay the information. In a market where damages are not placed on the source, there is very little reason for sources to uncover potential problems. Uncovering health problems will only lower sales or increase wages.

Legislative remedies such as the "Right to Know" laws described earlier are not sufficient if there is too little information to be shared. Because court actions that subject sources to liability for their damages make health-damage information useful to the firm, they create incentives to keep good records and to analyze the results. The failure to accurately perceive a health risk could cause an enormous financial burden on the company.[17] Therefore, it is cheaper to anticipate and prevent damages before the cost becomes prohibitive.

Even premarket testing of consumer products by the government is not an adequate substitute for the judicial approach. Government has neither the staff nor the financial resources to serve as the sole source of health-damage information. Some substances inevitably slip through the safety net provided by government testing. It is essential that the prime responsibility for testing fall on the producer, with the costs being passed on to the consumer as part of the price of the product. The government would then bear the responsibility for ensuring the validity of the testing process.

Judicial remedies are especially important in handling third-party contamination. Without liability there would be an insufficient incentive to exercise due care by the manufacturers, transporters, users, and disposers of these substances. The use of the court system to control the third-party problem was enhanced by the passage of the Resource Conservation and Recovery Act of 1976.

---

[17]During 1982, for example, the Manville Corporation faced up to $5 billion in lawsuits resulting from worker exposure to asbestos. During that same year, Monsanto was fighting a $4.7 billion class-action suit for alleged prolonged worker exposure to a hazardous substance in a West Virginia plant.

Because of the manifest system created by this act, good information is available to the courts on the types and quantities of substances involved. It also assists in tracing responsibility so that the sources can be identified and confronted with the evidence. This recordkeeping system is immensely costly, however, and may turn out, in the glare of hindsight, to be excessively ambitious. With experience, the system will hopefully evolve toward a harmonious balance between the gains from this monitoring system and the administrative burden it imposes.

There are two additional features of judicial remedies that make them a useful complement to legislative remedies. First, liability law usually provides the only way the victim of a toxic-substance accident can get compensated.[18] Even the "Superfund" bill does not compensate individuals for health-related damages. It only compensates for property damage.

The second attractive feature of judicial remedies is the degree to which they can be tailored to individual circumstances. We have seen in the chapters on air and water pollution the strong tendency for legislative remedies to be applied uniformly. We have also seen that uniform remedies are rarely efficient and that often the resulting loss of net benefit is substantial. When the courts impose the damage correctly, an efficient allocation of precaution is automatically tailored to the specific circumstances involved.

Limitations of Judicial Remedies.   The common law is not a panacea, however. It does not cope with the largest or most complex problems, such as the emission of hazardous substances by large numbers of sources affecting large numbers of people. This was illustrated nicely in *Roger J. Diamond* v. *General Motors*, a California case in which the judge ruled that the court system was not the appropriate forum to resolve the Los Angeles problem of air pollution.[19] The problem was so complex and it involved so many parties that it had to be resolved by the legislature.[20] Court remedies are administratively expensive and can be used efficiently only when they are used sparingly.

The common law also currently places a large burden of proof on the plaintiff that is difficult to meet. Generally, a plaintiff must be able to (1) identify the harmful substances; (2) demonstrate that the defendant was the source of this substance; (3) and prove that identifiable damages occurred as a result of the presence of that substance. The last two steps may be difficult to establish in practice.

---

[18]Normally workers' compensation insurance provides for occupational hazards. However, a study conducted by the Labor Department during 1981 found that of the two million Americans who were partially or severely disabled as a result of an occupational disease, only 5 percent received workers' compensation. Many states have disallowed claims against workers' compensation for maladies that can take 30 years to show up.

[19]97 Cal. Rept. 639.

[20]Even when the number of sources is small, the courts can be overwhelmed as long as the number of plaintiffs is large. It has been estimated that asbestos suits against the Manville Corporation were being filed at the rate of 500 per month during 1982. (See "Manville May Drive Congress to Action," *Business Week*, September 13, 1982, p. 35.)

Suppose, for example, that a well owner who discovered a harmful substance in the well simultaneously experienced a series of illnesses for which he or she had no medical history. The owner might have discovered a source emitting the same chemical nearby, but that is not enough evidence to win a lawsuit. The court would have to be convinced that the substance traveled from the source to the well. Furthermore, the plaintiff would have to prove that the illnesses were caused by the substance and not by unrelated causes. The frequent failure to establish these links can undermine the incentive properties of common law.[21]

Japan's court system has reacted to this problem by shifting the burden of proof from the injured plaintiff to the industry. The plaintiffs in those cases have to establish the nature and cause of their diseases and the mechanism by which they were affected. To establish the link to the defendant, they were able to introduce a high statistical correlation between the defendant's activity and the incidence of the disease. Once these elements have been established, a rebuttable presumption is created that shifts the burden of proof to the defendant. The defendant is then liable unless he or she can prove that the activities are not responsible for the damage.

If the American court system were to move in this direction, it would represent a radical departure from current practice.[22] The statistical approach lacks the rigor usually required by American courts because establishing a positive correlation between activity levels and the incidence of the disease does not establish causation. Other factors correlated with the activities of the defendant may be responsible.

The Japanese system does, however, effectively raise the question of who should bear the burden of proof. If the source were to bear it, nuisance suits could arise. Nuisance suits are filed mainly to harass defendants by making them spend a lot of money on defense. Such suits are without merit. As we have seen, however, if the plaintiff bears it, the burden is particularly difficult, because the defendant generally knows so much more about the contaminating activities.

The Japanese approach gets around this problem by placing a sequential burden of proof on each party. The plaintiff is required to bear a burden sufficiently large that nuisance cases are eliminated. On the other hand, for serious cases where the plaintiff has been able to bear the burden of proof, the defendant (who presumably is the most knowledgeable about the subject) must then gather the information at his or her disposal.

Although we can quibble about whether the initial burden on the plaintiff is too low or too high under the Japanese system, with its inherent shared responsibility, this

---

[21]If it becomes too easy to prove these links, the defendant will be forced to pay liability even when the substance produced by the defendant did not cause the plaintiff's problem. In this case efficiency would be lost because too much precaution would be taken.

[22]Some movement in this direction is now evident. A plaintiff with asbestosis, for example, may be required to prove only that he or she has a disease more probably than not caused by any of several asbestos manufacturers. Having met this burden of proof, the plaintiff shifts the burden to the individual manufacturer to prove, if it can, that it did not cause the plaintiff's disease. See Abel v. Eli Lilly & Co., 343 N. W. 2d 164 (1984).

system reduces the likelihood of nuisance suits while providing incentive for the most knowledgeable party to supply the necessary information to reach a decision.

One final concern should be noted about judicial remedies. Sometimes the source of the toxic-substance problem is "judgment proof" in the sense that it has no assets (or too few assets) to pay the damages. The marginal cost of additional damages to the source is zero, and profit-maximizing behavior leads the source to exercise too little precaution.

This problem is more serious for toxic substances than for conventional pollutants, because the latency of the effects means the suits must be filed much later than other kinds of suits. By this time, the source may have gone out of business or have been transformed into a quite different corporate entity somewhat immune from past transgressions.

The Statutory Law

A commendable virtue of common law is that remedies can be tailored to the unique circumstances the parties find themselves in. The disadvantage is that common law remedies are expensive to tailor in time and money, and they are ill-suited to solving widespread problems affecting large numbers of people. Thus, the statutory law has a role to play as well.

Balancing the Costs.   Statutory law, as currently structured, does not efficiently fulfill its potential as a complement to the common law. The main reason for this is the failure of many of the current laws to allow any balancing of compliance cost with the damages being protected against.

The Delaney Clause is the most flagrant example. It precludes any balancing of costs whatsoever. A substance that has been shown to be carcinogenic in any dose cannot be used as a food additive even if the risk is counterbalanced by a considerable compensating benefit. As Example 19.3 illustrates, a rule this stringent can lead to considerable political mischief as attempts are made to circumvent it.

The Delaney Clause is not the only culprit; other laws also fail to balance costs. The Resource Conservation and Recovery Act requires the standards imposed on waste generators, transporters, and disposal site operators to be high enough to protect human health and the environment. No mention is made of costs.

These are extreme examples, but even in less extreme cases, policymakers must face the question of how to balance costs. The Occupational Safety and Health Act, for example, requires standards that ensure "to the extent feasible that no employee will suffer material impairment of health or functional capacity. . . ." In changing the standard for the occupational exposure to benzene from 10 ppm. to 1 ppm., EPA had presented no data to show that even a 10 ppm. standard causes leukemia. Rather, EPA based its decision on a series of assumptions indicating that some leukemia might result from 10 ppm., so even fewer cases might result from 1 ppm.

EXAMPLE 19.3

Weighing the Risks: Saccharin

Saccharin is an artificial sweetener that had been used since the early part of the twentieth century. Used in diet foods, particularly soft drinks, by the 1970s it had become the staple of the diet-food industry.

In the late 1960s a researcher at the University of Wisconsin reported that combinations of cholesterol and saccharin injected in the urinary bladders of mice resulted in a high incidence of bladder cancer. A special research group of the National Academy of Sciences convened to investigate the safety of saccharin and a year later declared it safe.

In January of 1972, however, the FDA removed saccharin from its list of additives "generally recognized as safe." This action forced food processors to list saccharin on the ingredient label and to conform to maximum recommended dosages. Following some additional Canadian tests showing a link between bladder cancer and saccharin, in 1977 the FDA proposed a ban on the use of saccharin in all foods and beverages, citing the Delaney Clause.

Since saccharin was the only approved artificial sweetener at that time, reaction was swift and vehement. Diabetics attacked the move as denying them access to any sweetener. Groups concerned with weight gain charged that this decision increased the risk of heart attacks. In April of 1977 the FDA modified its proposed ban to the extent of allowing saccharin to be labeled as an over-the-counter drug (thus escaping the Delaney Clause) and sold in tablets, powder, or liquid form. It still proposed to ban saccharin from commercially prepared foods and beverages.

Since then a number of studies have appeared, some upholding the link to cancer and others disputing it. Congress reacted by passing a series of moratoriums on the banning of saccharin, thus preventing the Delaney Clause from having its intended effect.

These actions strongly suggest that zero risk is usually not an appropriate policy goal. The objective should be to balance the risks. Provisions that prevent the balancing process, such as the Delaney Clause, are simply bad policy.

In a case receiving a great deal of attention, the Supreme Court set aside the new benzene standard largely on the grounds that it was based on inadequate evidence.[23] In rendering their opinion the justices stated:

> . . . the Secretary must make a finding that the workplaces in question are not safe. But "safe" is not the equivalent of "risk-free." A workplace can hardly be considered "unsafe" unless it threatens the workers with a significant risk of harm. (100 S. Ct. 2847)

---

[23]Industrial Union Department, AFL-CIO V. American Petroleum Institute, *et al.*, 100 S. Ct. 2844 (1980).

In a concurring opinion that did not bind future decisions because it did not have sufficient support among the remaining justices, Justice Powell went even further:

> . . . the statute also requires the agency to determine that the economic effects of its standard bear a reasonable relationship to the expected benefits. (100 S. Ct. 2848)

It seems clear that the notion of a risk-free environment has been repudiated by the high court, as it should have been. But what is meant by an *acceptable risk?* Efficiency clearly dictates that an acceptable risk is one that maximizes the net benefit. Thus the efficiency criterion would support Justice Powell in his approach to the benzene standard.

It is important to allay a possible source of confusion. The fact that it is difficult to set a precise standard using cost-benefit analysis because of the imprecision of the underlying data does not imply that some balancing of costs and benefits cannot, and should not, take place. It can and it should. While cost-benefit analysis may not be sufficiently precise and reliable to suggest, for example, that a standard of 8 p.p.m. is efficient, it usually is reliable enough to indicate clearly that 1 p.p.m. and 15 p.p.m. are inefficient. By failing to consider compliance cost in defining acceptable risk, statutes are probably attempting more and achieving less than we might hope for.

Degree and Form of Intervention.   The second criticism of the current statutory approach concerns both the degree of intervention and the form that intervention should take. The former issue relates to how deeply the government controls go, while the latter relates to the manner in which the regulations work.

The analysis in the second section of this chapter suggested that, in consumer products and labor markets, there was less need for government intervention than in the third-party case. The main problem in those two areas was seen as the lack of sufficient information to allow producers, consumers, employees, and employers to make informed choices. With the Delaney Clause as an obvious exception, most consumer-product safety statutes deal mainly with research and labeling. They are broadly consistent with the results of our analysis.

This is not, however, the case with occupational exposure. Government regulations have had a major and not always beneficial effect on the workplace. By covering such a large number of potential problems, OSHA has spread itself too thin and has had too little impact on problems that really count. Selective intervention, targeted at those areas where OSHA efforts could really make a difference, would get more results.

The form the OSHA regulations have taken also causes inflexibility. Not content merely to specify exposure limits, the regulations also specify the exact precautions to be taken. The contrast between this approach and the marketable permit approach in air pollution is striking.

Under the bubble policy, EPA specifies the emission limit but allows the source great flexibility in meeting that limit. OSHA regulations, by dictating the specific activities to be engaged in or to be avoided, deny this flexibility. In the face of rapid technological change, this can grow to be an inefficient approach even if the specified activities were efficient when they were first required. Furthermore, having so many detailed regulations makes enforcement more difficult and probably less effective.

A serious flaw in the current approach to controlling hazardous wastes is the insufficient emphasis placed on reducing the generation and recycling of these wastes. In order to provide revenue to fund the cleanup, for example, the 1980 Superfund bill imposed a tax on petroleum and chemical feedstocks. Because this tax is imposed on the front end of the production process and is not calibrated by toxicity, it does not provide the appropriate incentives to switch to less hazardous substances or to recycle the wastes.

An alternative, which is widely regarded as a superior means of raising revenue, involves the imposition of variable unit taxes (called "waste-end" taxes) on waste generated or disposed of. Waste-end taxes would not only spur industry to switch to less toxic substances and to reduce the quantity of these substances used, it would also encourage consumers to switch away from products using large amounts of hazardous materials in the production process because higher production costs would be translated into higher prices. As of 1985, some 20 states had already adopted some form of waste-end taxation. Unfortunately the Superfund Amendments and Reauthorization Act of 1986 chose to replenish the Superfund with broad-based taxes rather than taxes specifically designed to reduce the generation of toxic waste.

Scale.   The size of the hazardous waste problem dwarfs the size of the EPA staff and budget assigned to control it. The Superfund process for cleaning up existing hazardous waste sites is a good case in point. While EPA estimates that about 2000 sites (out of a total 19,000 sites considered) will be placed on the National Priorities List for permanent cleanup, the Office of Technology Assessment (a research arm of Congress) has estimated that 10,000 sites or more will ultimately be deemed dangerous enough to be placed on the list. All agree that it is not technologically and economically feasible to permanently clean up even 2000 sites over the next few decades even with the replenishment of the Superfund voted by the U.S. Congress in 1986.

The huge scale of this undertaking has important implications for both the bureaucracy and the citizens it serves. Priorities must be established and the most serious problems attacked first. It is a fact of life that an exclusive reliance on the bureaucracy to provide complete safety is infeasible. Citizens should not abdicate their own responsibilities after being lulled into a false sense of security by the mistaken impression that the bureaucracy can and should provide adequate protection.

SUMMARY

The potential for contamination of the environmental asset by toxic substances is one of the most complex environmental problems. The number of potential substances that could prove toxic number literally in the millions. Some 55,000 of these are in active use.

The market provides a considerable amount of pressure toward resolving toxic-substance problems as they affect employees and consumers. With reliable information at their disposal, all parties have an incentive to reduce hazards to acceptable levels. This pressure is absent, however, in cases involving third parties. Here the problem frequently takes the form of an external cost imposed on innocent bystanders.

The efficient role of government can range from assuring the provision of sufficient information (so that participants in the market can make informed choices) to setting exposure limits on hazardous substances. Unfortunately, the scientific basis for decision-making is weak. Only limited information on the effects of these substances is available, and the cost of acquiring complete information is prohibitive. Therefore, priorities must be established and tests developed to screen substances so that efforts can be concentrated on those that seem most dangerous. The *in vitro* tests currently under further development seem to be a promising avenue.

In contrast to air and water pollution, the toxic-substance problem is one in which the courts may play a particularly important role. The screening tests will probably never be foolproof and therefore some substances may slip through. Liability law not only creates a market pressure for more and better information on potential damages associated with chemical substances, it also provides incentives to manufacturers of substances, the generators of waste, the transporters of waste, and those who dispose of it to exercise efficient precaution. It also allows the level of precaution to vary with the occupational circumstances and provides a means by which victims can be compensated.

Judicial remedies are not sufficient, however. They are expensive and ill-suited for dealing with problems affecting large numbers of people. The burdens of proof under the current American system are difficult to surmount, though in Japan some radical new approaches have been developed to deal with this problem.

The statutory response, though clearly a positive step, seems to have gone too far in regulating behavior. The exposure standards in many cases seem excessively stringent, having been set without balancing the costs involved. Furthermore, OSHA and EPA have gone well beyond the setting of exposure limits by dictating specific activities that should be engaged in or avoided. The enforcement of these standards has proved to be very difficult and has probably spread the available resources too thin.

Reinhold Niebuhr once said, "Democracy is finding proximate solutions to insoluble problems." That seems an apt description of the institutional response to the toxic-substance problem. Our political institutions have created a staggering array of legislative and judicial responses to this problem that are neither efficient nor complete. They do, however, represent a positive first step in what must be an evolutionary process.

FURTHER READING

Crandall, Robert W., and Lester B. Lave. *The Scientific Basis of Health and Safety Regulation* (Washington, D.C.: The Brookings Institute, 1981). For each of five health and safety regulatory actions this book juxtaposes the views of a scientist, an economist, and a regulator on the scientific basis for the regulation and the desirability of the resulting decision. Cases considered are passive restraints in automobiles, cotton dust, saccharin, waterborne carcinogens, and sulfur dioxide.

Kneese, Allen V., and William Schulze. "Environment, Health, and Economics: The Case of Cancer." *American Economic Review,* LXVII (Feb. 1977): 326–32. Provides an example of how economic analysis can be used to measure the size of the health damage caused by toxic substances. Case study of exposure to nitrogenous compounds.

Lave, Lester B. *The Strategy of Social Regulation: Decision Frameworks for Policy* (Washington, D.C.: The Brookings Institution, 1981). An inquiry into the ways in which the scientific foundations of regulation could be improved. Contains chapters on food additives and health, safety, and environmental regulations.

Portney, Paul R. "Toxic Substance Policy and the Protection of Human Health," in *Current Issues in U.S. Environmental Policy,* edited by Paul R. Portney, pp. 105–43 (Baltimore: Johns Hopkins University Press, for Resources for the Future, 1978). A comprehensive analysis of the pre-1978 statutes and implementation procedures used to combat toxic-substance pollution.

ADDITIONAL REFERENCES

Amabile, Phyllis E. "Reinterpretation of the Delaney Clause," *Northwestern University Law Review,* Vol. 73 (1979): 1090–1118.

Brown, J. P. "Toward an Economic Theory of Liability," *Journal of Legal Studies* 2 (June 1973): 323–49.

Doniger, David D. *The Law and Policy of Toxic Substance Control: A Case Study of Vinyl Chloride* (Baltimore: Johns Hopkins University Press, for Resources for the Future, 1978).

Lave, Lester B., ed. *Quantitative Risk Assessment in Regulation* (Washington, D.C.: The Brookings Institution, 1982).

Nichols, Albert L. "The Importance of Exposure in Evaluating and Designing Environmental Regulations: A Case Study," *The American Economic Review,* Vol. 72 (May 1982): 214–19.

Rea, Raymond A. "Hazardous Waste Pollution: The Need for a Different Statutory Approach," *Environmental Law,* Vol. 12 (1982): 443–67.

Singer, Steven T. "Analysis of Common Law and Statutory Remedies for Hazardous Waste Injuries," *Rutgers Law Journal,* Vol. 12 (1980): 117–50.

Trauberman, Jeffrey. "Compensating Victims of Toxic Substances Pollution: An Analysis of Existing Federal Statutes," *Harvard Environmental Law Review,* Vol. 5 (1981): 1–29.

Viscusi, W. Kip, *Regulating by Choice: Regulating Health and Safety in the Workplace* (Cambridge, MA: Harvard University Press, 1983).

Wang, Charleston C. K. "Toxic Agents, Carcinogens, Worker Health, Cost-Benefit Analysis, and the Clamor for Reasonable OSHA Regulations: A Survey of Judicial and Other Answers to a Complex Socio-technological Controversy," *Northern Kentucky Law Review,* Vol. 8 (1981): 589–629.

Weinstein, Milton C. "Decision Making for Toxic Substance Control: Cost-Effective Information Development for the Control of Environmental Carcinogens," *Public Policy,* Vol. 27 (Summer 1979): 333–83.

DISCUSSION QUESTIONS

1. How should the courts resolve the dilemma posed in Example 19.1? Why?

2. Over the last several decades in product liability law, there has been a movement in the court system from *caveat emptor* ("buyer beware") to *caveat venditor* ("seller beware"). The liability for using and consuming risky products has been shifted from buyers to sellers. Does this shift represent a movement toward a more efficient allocation of risk or away from an efficient allocation of risk? Why?

CHAPTER TWENTY

Pollution-Control Policy: Distributional Effects

There are many in this old world of ours who hold that things break about even for all of us. I have observed for example that we all get the same amount of ice. The rich get it in the summertime and the poor get it in the winter.

BAT MASTERSON, GUNFIGHTER/NEWSPAPER REPORTER

INTRODUCTION

Environmental policy has been attacked from *both* the political left and right as being unfair. In his attack on the motives of environmentalists, William Tucker (in *Progress and Privilege,* 1982) portrays the environmental movement as an extension of the self-interests of the rich. Having achieved financial security, the rich protect the serenity of their surroundings to the detriment of less fortunate people. By erecting a highly bureaucratic structure to preserve and protect their privileged position under the guise of environmental policy, the rich confer benefits on themselves while imposing costs on the poor. The restitution of fairness, he believes, requires less government, and thus less environmental regulation.

This conservative critique is similar to the radical critique. Left-wing radicals believe that the government is controlled by capitalists and used to pursue their own ends. Though this left-wing view would suggest there is too little control (as capitalists protect their profits from regulatory erosion) rather than the excessive control decried by the conservatives, it shares with the conservative view the notion that whatever environmental control takes place primarily benefits the capitalists who are the wealthiest members of society.[1]

---

[1]Gellen, for example, states, "Thus pollution control programs illustrate the ways in which government promotes the welfare of business at the expense of the taxpaying public. The non-taxpaying poor will also suffer." See Martin Gellen, "The Making of a Pollution-Industrial Complex," *Ramparts* 8 (May 1970): 27.

Taken at face value, these views suggest not only that pollution-control policy may be unfairly implemented, but also that, given the policy-making process, this lack of fairness may be inevitable. Previous chapters have suggested that, though existing policies have not been efficient, the net benefits have, in general, been positive. While a positive net benefit implies that the gains from environmental policy have exceeded the losses for society as a whole, this may not be true for all members of society. Who are the gainers and losers? Are the net benefits fairly distributed, or is the policy biased in one way or another?

There are two reasons for paying attention to the benefits and costs of the policy process—one ethical and the other pragmatic. The ethical dimension concerns the distribution of benefits in accordance with the norms of social justice. The desire for just policies is a conventional complement to the desire for efficient policies. The pragmatic dimension concerns the relationship between the distributional burden, and both the likelihood that environmental legislation will pass and its ultimate form. The ability to enact legislation depends on the existence of majority support for it. Altering the form of the legislation to suit reluctant supporters is a traditional way to build majority coalitions. Knowing something about the distributional burden of environmental legislation therefore sheds some light on one aspect of the political process which enacts it.

In economics, as in other disciplines, the norms of social justice are not well defined in the sense that no norm is beyond reproach. Nonetheless, some conventional approaches have arisen which can serve to guide our inquiry. These involve two concepts known as horizontal and vertical equity.

Horizontal equity occurs when people with equal income are treated equally. (The conventional definition of "equals" in economics is based upon income levels.) With respect to pollution control, the principle of horizontal equity is satisfied if all persons with the same income level receive the same net benefit. This principle can be used to assess the geographic fairness of policy. If people with comparable income levels in different parts of the country receive different net benefits, then the horizontal equity principle is violated.

Vertical equity deals with the treatment of unequals, or—using income as a basis—with the treatment of those with different income levels. The first step in assessing whether or not a particular policy satisfies vertical equity is to calculate how the net benefit is distributed among income groups: *progressively, regressively,* or *proportionally.*

The distribution is said to be *proportional* if the net benefit received is proportional to income. It is said to be *regressive* if the net benefit represents a larger proportion of the income of the rich than of the poor and is *progressive* if, as a proportion of their income, the poor receive a larger share than the rich.[2] One implication of this definition is that a policy that confers a larger *net benefit* on the rich than the poor is

---

[2]It is also possible to use these concepts to refer to the distribution of benefits or costs. Benefits are regressive if the *rich* get a larger proportional share, while costs are said to be regressive if the *poor* get a larger proportional share. The easiest way to keep these straight is to remember that progressive means beneficial to the poor.

not necessarily regressive. A regressive allocation occurs only if the *ratio of net benefit to income* is significantly larger for the rich than the poor.

According to conventional practice, regressive policies violate the vertical equity principle. This practice is in line with the evident societal concern for the poor which is manifested in the health, housing, and income-transfer programs that exist solely to improve their economic status. It suggests that when policies are equitable the poor get at least their share of the benefits. If environmental policies primarily benefit the rich, as argued by the two views discussed at the beginning of this chapter, then we should find that the distribution of net benefits is strongly regressive.

THE INCIDENCE OF POLLUTION-CONTROL COSTS: INDIVIDUAL INDUSTRIES

The initial incidence of much of the current policy falls on industry. In order to comply with air, water, and solid-waste regulations, industries have had to invest a considerable amount of capital in equipment (Table 20.1).

The data in Table 20.1 suggest that the proportion of new-plant and equipment expenditures going to pollution control in the average industry is large, though it has diminished since the middle 1970s. These data also suggest that, according to this way of measuring it, the distribution of the cost burden among industries is quite uneven.

The fact that the costs of pollution control may fall initially on the source of pollution does not mean that the entire burden ultimately resides there, however. In general, the ultimate incidence of pollution control costs is determined by the nature of the market. Depending on such factors as barriers to entry and elasticity of demand, these costs can be passed forward to consumers in the form of higher prices, backward to laborers in the form of lower employment and/or wages, or directly to the owners in the form of lower returns on their capital investment (or any combination of the three).

A Competitive Industry

Incidence.   In order to understand the conditions under which the costs can be passed forward or backward, it is necessary to be fairly specific about how an industry reacts to a change in its cost structure. To get at the essence of the problem without unnecessary detail, consider a perfectly competitive industry which is composed of identical firms. Assume that this industry is initially in long-run equilibrium (Figure 20.1). Faced with the market determined price of P^0, the representative firm maximizes its profits by producing q^0, where marginal cost equals price. Since the price is also equal to average cost at q^0, economic profits are zero. There is no incentive for firms to enter or exit the industry.

Suppose now that this equilibrium is disturbed by an EPA regulation forcing each firm to reduce its pollution. Assume that the effect of this regulation on the industry can be reflected as a uniform upward shift in the marginal and average cost curves by a vertical distance d. Because the market supply curve is the sum of the marginal

TABLE 20.1 Percent of New Plant and Equipment Expenditures by Nonfarm Business on Pollution Control

	1975[a]	1980[b]	1981[b]	1984[c]
Total Nonfarm Business	5.8	3.1	2.8	2.1
Manufacturing	9.3	4.8	4.3	3.3
Durable Goods	8.1	3.9	3.2	2.6
Primary Metals*	17.2	12.7	9.6	9.5
Blast furnaces, steel works	13.5	18.5	15.5	11.3
Nonferrous metals	24.1	8.7	6.6	9.9
Fabricated metals	NA	2.4	2.4	1.7
Electrical machinery	5.8	1.7	1.7	1.2
Machinery, except electrical	1.8	1.3	1.1	1.2
Transportation equipment	3.4	2.9	2.5	2.1
Motor vehicles	3.9	4.3	3.5	2.7
Aircraft	2.8	1.4	1.6	1.1
Stone, clay, and glass	14.3	6.5	5.1	4.2
Other durables**	5.3	2.8	2.8	1.7
Nondurable Goods	10.3	5.7	5.3	3.9
Food including beverage	5.2	3.7	3.6	2.9
Textiles	4.6	4.3	3.2	2.1
Paper	16.8	5.7	5.7	7.5
Chemicals	10.9	5.8	6.5	3.8
Petroleum	11.8	8.3	6.6	5.0
Rubber	4.0	1.7	2.3	2.3
Other nondurables***	2.8	0.7	0.6	0.7
Nonmanufacturing	3.2	2.1	1.8	1.5
Mining	1.9	3.6	2.7	2.2
Transportation	NA	0.9	0.7	0.4
Railroad	1.4	0.9	0.9	0.7
Air	0.6	0.2	0.3	<0.1
Other	1.4	1.8	1.3	0.3
Public Utilities	8.4	8.1	7.3	6.8
Electric	9.7	10.0	9.1	8.6
Gas and other	1.5	1.0	1.0	0.8
Trade and services	NA	0.2	0.1	0.2
Communication and other****	0.6	0.1	0.1	<0.1

[a]*Survey of Current Business* Vol. 58 (June 1978): 34.

[b]*Survey of Current Business* Vol. 62 (June 1982): 18. Percentage was derived by dividing total pollution abatement expenditure by total new-plant and equipment expenditures.

[c]*Survey of Current Business* Vol. 66 (February 1986): 41.

*Includes industries not shown separately.

**Consists of lumber, furniture, instruments, and miscellaneous.

***Consists of apparel, tobacco, leather, and printing-publishing.

****Consists of communication; construction; social services and membership organizations; and forestry, fisheries, and agricultural services.

cost curves of the individual firms (all of which have shifted up by d), it will shift up by d as well. Therefore, the market price will rise from P^0 to P^1, an increase less than d. In the short run, price does not rise the full amount of the increase in marginal cost.

The effect on the individual firm can now be seen. The firm will now maximize profits by producing the smaller amount q^1 because that is where the new marginal

FIGURE 20.1   Market Reactions to Pollution-Control Costs

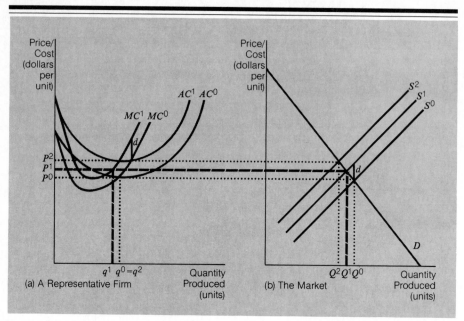

(a) A Representative Firm — Quantity Produced (units)

(b) The Market — Quantity Produced (units)

cost curve (MC^1) equals the new price (P^1). Notice, however, that P^1 is lower than AC^1 when q^1 is produced so that economic profits are negative. Therefore, some firms will exit the industry until zero economic profits are restored.

This departure is reflected in market supply as a further shift leftward. The magnitude of the shift is determined by the amount of exit needed to restore the equality of price and average cost. This occurs at price P^2, which is exactly d greater than P^0. The market produces the smaller amount Q^2, but each remaining firm produces the same amount it did before the increase in cost.

In the short run, in response to a uniform increase in marginal cost of d, price would rise by less than d, all firms would reduce production, and negative profits would be earned. In the long run, zero profits would be restored by firms leaving the industry, but all remaining firms would produce the same amount as before the cost rise. The price would rise by the exact amount of the rise in marginal cost. Notice that in this case consumers and laborers would both bear part of the burden. Consumers would pay higher prices for a smaller level of production, while the lower production levels would imply a lower demand for labor and, hence, lower employment and wages.

The respective burdens borne by these two segments of the population are determined to a large extent by the elasticity of demand for the product. Imagine, for example, that the demand curve for the product was perfectly inelastic (a vertical line) at Q^0. In this case the short-run price increase would be equal to d and short-run economic profits would be zero. There would be no effect on the level of production and no resulting effect on the demand for labor. The consumers would bear the entire burden.

At this point it should be easy to see that the more elastic the demand curve, the larger the impact on production and, hence, labor. This relationship suggests that the impact of pollution control depends not only on the degree of labor intensiveness of the industry, which determines how severely labor would be affected by declines in production, but also by the elasticity of demand, which determines how large the declines in production would be. For example, industries facing severe competition from imports not subject to the same controls would face greater threats of employment declines than those producing products with no effective substitute, domestic or foreign.

Scale Effects. In our analysis, the fact that the regulations did not affect the size distribution of firms arises from our assumptions that the cost curves shift up uniformly by d, that all firms in the industry were identical, and that the regulations affected the cost structure of every firm in the industry in exactly the same way. If the cost curves were not uniformly shifted upward, the firm would not produce the same amount after the regulation as before, because economies of scale would have been affected. In addition, because industries are not really populated by identical firms and the regulations have not been uniformly applied, both the number of firms in an industry and the size of the average firm can be affected by the regulations.

Some recent empirical studies have suggested that the air and water pollution control regulations have not been neutral with respect to the size distribution of firms, but the evidence is incomplete and not conclusive. With respect to the uniform application of regulations, Evans (1986) has found that pollution abatement costs per employee are typically smaller for small firms operated by single-plant companies than for large plants operated by multi-plant companies. He attributes this to "regulatory tiering", a strategy designed in part to offer special protection to small business.

Based on this evidence alone, it would be reasonable to expect that the regulatory structure might have reduced the market shares of larger firms by raising costs more for them than their smaller competitors, but that does not appear to have been the case. Pashigian (1984), for example, has found that after controlling for changes in fuel costs, market size, and other regulatory programs, industries with relatively high environmental regulatory burdens had become more capital intensive, had larger increases in mean plant size and had larger decreases in the number of plants in the industry during the regulatory period than industries with low regulatory burdens. Pittman (1981) also found for water pollution control that the regulations tended to increase the economies of scale in complying plants, resulting in an increase in the operating capacity of the optimally sized plant.

On the surface the Evans evidence seems to contradict the Pashigian and Pittman evidence, but that need not be the case. First, the Pittman results deal with scale effects on complying plants, not the relationships among large and small plants *per se*. Second, while the regulations may well favor *existing* small plants, they may discourage potential new small plants from entering an industry. Finally, although the movement of market shares may well coincide with the peak of regulatory activity, correlation does not necessarily imply causation; the changes in the size distribution of firms could have occurred for reasons other than environmental regulations. More research may shed more light on these relationships and help us to clear away the remaining ambiguity.

New Source Bias.   The current system of controls has another feature we have not yet considered in the analysis. Under the current regulatory approach, new sources face more stringent control requirements than existing sources, resulting in higher compliance costs than for old sources. Under the conditions of stable demand over time, no new firms would be entering so no firms would be bearing the higher new source costs. Differentiated regulation wouldn't make any difference when demand is stable. However, if demand were increasing over time, then new firms would enter the market. When an industry is growing, the imposition of higher control costs on new firms, but not on old ones, would delay the entrance of new firms and would reduce their market share relative to what their share would be with regulations affecting old and new plants to the same degree.

In a study of capital turnover in the electric power industry, Maloney and Brady (1986) find that the new source bias embodied in the regulatory system has had a significant independent effect on increasing the amount of time existing facilities are operated before retirement. By imposing a disproportionate share of the pollution control burden on new facilities, the desirability of investing in new plants has been undermined. Since the older plants pollute more, this reduction in the rate of capital turnover results in a delay in the amount of emission reduction achieved by any particular date.

Old plants can actually benefit from this new source bias in the regulation, and could end up making positive profits. These profits would not generally be bid to zero because the normal mechanism for accomplishing that result (competition from new low-cost firms) is not allowed to work.

Since the new firms are higher cost producers, because of higher control costs, their profits would be bid to zero. Meanwhile, existing firms receive a form of Ricardian rent. As Example 20.1 illustrates, the tissue industry has experienced precisely this kind of circumstance. This differential regulation effect makes the burden of labor in existing plants smaller than it would be if the regulations raised the costs of new and existing sources by the same amount.

Other studies have confirmed the fact that existing regulations have increased, rather than reduced, the value of existing firms by limiting competition from potential entrants. Maloney and McCormick [1982], for example, found evidence of this in several different industries.[3]

When OSHA imposed a standard limiting the amount of cotton dust workers in textile plants could be exposed to, new and old firms faced very different compliance costs. An examination of stock prices revealed that a number of textile firms affected by the standard registered an increase in value at the same time that OSHA announced its proposed standards. Moreover, the value increases were positively related to the fraction of cotton used by the firms in their production. This finding suggests that the value of existing plants was increased, not reduced, by the regulation.

---

[3]A portion of this evidence has been challenged by Hughes, Magat, and Ricks (1986).

EXAMPLE 20.1

The Effects of Environmental Controls on the Tissue Industry

The tissue industry is made up of plants that manufacture, either from raw wood or pulp, bulk tissue for such products as facial and bathroom tissue, disposable diapers, and paper napkins. As a water polluter, it was forced to install pollution control equipment. The standards were more stringent for new sources than old.

The results of a major study to estimate the impact of these controls on the tissue industry were reported in Koch and Leone [1979]. They found:

In the tissue industry, the imposition of water pollution controls suggested near-term price increases that would be exceeded by near-term compliance costs, thus creating substantial reductions in profits or actual losses. In the long run, however, the high costs of compliance for new facilities suggested an eventual price increase that exceeded the increases in average costs. [p. 92]

In the long run, existing plants were actually *more* profitable than they would have been without the regulation, because the regulation served to diminish competition from new sources.

Koch and Leone also point out that the demand for tissue is relatively price inelastic, implying that the effect of cost increases on reductions in production would be small, and therefore the employment impact would be small. They suggest that this is likely to be true for most industries. Hence, the theory that a large number of plant closings result from environmental regulation is suspect. In the tissue industry they expect pollution controls to *reduce* the number of plant closings by conferring a competitive advantage on existing plants.

Source: James C. Koch and Robert A. Leone, "The Clean Water Act: Unexpected Impacts on Industry," *Harvard Environmental Law Review* 3 (1979): 92.

Maloney and McCormick also found that an increase in stock prices of companies owning smelters occurred immediately following a 1973 Supreme Court decision to uphold the Prevention of Significant Deterioration program. This decision had the effect of limiting competition from new smelters that otherwise would have located in PSD regions, increasing the value of existing firms. Clearly, environmental regulations have rather complicated effects on industries, but the notion that these regulations force many firms out of business seems clearly overstated.

Other evidence seems to confirm that few plants have been forced to close because of environmental regulations. The "Economic Dislocation Early Warning System" was set up by EPA to monitor plant closings and associated job losses where pollution control was alleged to be a factor in the closing. The data collected by this monitoring system from January 1971 through September 1982 suggest that a total of 154 plants were closed, involving a total of 32,749 jobs. Twenty-three percent of the plant closings and thirty-four percent of the jobs lost were in the primary metals industries. An additional fourteen percent of the closings and twenty percent of the jobs were lost in the chemicals and allied products industries. From Table 20.1 it can be deduced that both of these industries are among the leaders in terms of the percent of new plant and equipment expenditures going toward pollution control. In addition, steel, one of the primary metals industries, has faced heavy import competition, making the demand for its product more price elastic.

The adverse employment impacts have been geographically concentrated as well as sectionally concentrated. About sixty-two percent of the plant closings and sixty-six percent of the associated job losses were concentrated in the Northeast and the Midwest. Over one half of these were in the Midwest.

Monopoly

The effect of pollution control expenditures on any industry also depends on the market structure of that industry. In a monopoly, the entry of new firms would not occur with or without environmental controls. The absence of this pressure changes the way in which a typical firm would react to regulations.

The effect of an increase in control costs on a monopoly is shown in Figure 20.2. Initially, the monopoly is shown in a profit-maximizing equilibrium, where it produces at Q^0 and charges price P^0. If an environmental regulation forced its marginal cost to rise uniformly from MC_1 to MC_2, the firm would no longer maximize output by producing at Q^0. It must adjust its output level. At Q^0 marginal cost exceeds marginal revenue, so profits would be increased by reducing output until marginal cost once again was equal to marginal revenue. That would occur at output level Q^1. The price corresponding to this is P^1.

There are some interesting differences between the effect of a similar rise in control cost on a monopoly and on a competitive firm. The price, for example, does not rise as much in a monopolized industry as it would in a competitive industry. In the competitive industry, if the marginal cost curve shifts up by an amount d, the price eventually shifts up by the same amount. In a monopoly the price shifts up by less than that amount. This result runs contrary to a commonly preconceived notion that a monopoly would automatically pass on all costs. It would not, because it would lose profits if it did. The monopoly would not pass on all costs, because to do so would cause demand to be reduced excessively. It pays the monopolist to absorb part of the cost.

As long as the competitive industry and the monopoly face identical market-demand curves, the monopoly would reduce production by a smaller amount than would the competitive industry. The effect on employment would be smaller in a monopoly than in a comparable competitive industry. To some extent, a monopolist insulates its workers from cost shocks.

FIGURE 20.2 The Effect of Pollution-Control Costs on a Monopoly

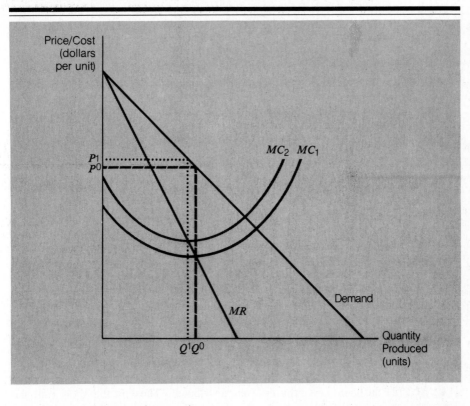

THE INCIDENCE ON HOUSEHOLDS

An increase in the environmental cost affects households in a number of ways. Increases in the prices of products purchased by households cause a decline in the purchasing power of a fixed income. Declines in wages or employment lead to lower incomes, as do the reduced dividends being derived from the lower earnings of industries with some market power.

These are not the only channels, however, by which households end up bearing the costs of pollution control. The money paid to municipalities to subsidize the construction of waste-treatment plants is derived from tax revenues. The ultimate incidence of control costs depends not only on the nature of demand and market structure of the industries; it depends on the tax structure as well.

A number of studies have been accomplished within the last few years that trace the expenditures back through these channels of influence for the purpose of estimating the ultimate incidence of control expenditures. Because of the complexity of these relationships, the estimates are necessarily crude, but some clear insights do emerge.

Air Pollution

Households receive rather different net benefits from stationary-source and mobile air-pollution control because of the rather different ways in which their respective cost burdens are shared. Therefore, we need to consider each of these separately in order to assess the effects as a whole.

Automobile Control. In the early 1970s, the EPA [1973] put out a study suggesting that the costs of automobile air-pollution control were probably progressively distributed. In essence, the argument was that since the poor had lower rates of auto ownership, and the control policy was focused on new cars, the largest burdens would fall on the middle- and upper-income groups.

Subsequent studies have not supported that conclusion. Rather, they suggest that the problem is more complex than realized by the early EPA study. In particular, the increase in the cost of emission controls on new cars affects used-car prices.

These secondary effects create a fairly complicated incidence pattern. While new-car buyers clearly face higher prices, the owners of used cards receive a gain in the form of a higher resale value for their cars. This gain, however, is transitory. All future purchasers of automobiles will pay higher prices regardless of whether they buy new cars or used cars.

Studies by Dorfman [1975], Harrison [1975], and Freeman [1977] attempt to trace these effects. Only Freeman attempts to capture the short-term effects. He derives two rather interesting results: (1) the gain to used-car owners within each income group (caused by the increased resale value of the used car) is on balance larger than the loss (caused by the cost of the emission controls) to new-car owners in that same income group and (2) the gains are progressively distributed. Thus, in the short run, the automobile pollution control costs are more than offset by used-car capital gains, and the largest capital gains are received by lower income groups.

As interesting as this result is, we should not make too much of it. The offsetting capital gain is a one-time benefit, not to be repeated. Furthermore, it can only be realized when the automobile is sold. And as soon as another car is purchased, the higher cost associated with the emission controls would have to be paid regardless of whether a new or used car were purchased.

For these reasons the most interesting aspect of automobile air-pollution control cost incidence concerns the long run when all cars cost more. Once again, there will be several factors to consider: (1) the increase in cost to new-car purchasers, (2) the increase in cost to used-car purchasers, and (3) the number of new-car and used-car purchasers in each income group.

All three studies have found that automobile pollution control costs are regressively distributed. Harrison has the most complete description of the incidence. He finds, for example, that costs are higher in the suburbs than in the central city, and are higher in smaller cities than in larger cities. He also finds the degree of regressivity higher in the suburbs and generally in smaller cities (Los Angeles is an exception, being a large city with a highly regressive incidence).

This evidence addresses only part of the story. In order to determine the ultimate incidence, it is necessary to complement these estimates of cost incidence with some estimate of the benefits. To complement his analysis of the distribution of the cost burden, Harrison also conducted a detailed study of the incidence of the benefits of automobile pollution control policy. Because of the difficulties of estimating a generally accepted monetary value for benefits, he measured benefits solely in terms of improvements in the concentrations of three automobile pollutants (CO, NO_x, and O_x). These improvements were calculated for each geographic area and, using data on the income levels of people in those areas, he calculated the degree of reduced exposure experienced by each of these groups.

He found that the benefits from improvement in air quality were progressive *for those living in urban areas*. Furthermore, they were most progressively distributed in the very largest cities. This results from the disproportionate representation of the poor in the most heavily polluted areas in our largest cities.

When he puts his cost and benefit estimates together for other parts of the country, Harrison concludes:

> Households living in suburban areas, small urban areas, and nonurban areas—which make up two-thirds of United States households—do poorly under the current scheme. Households in these areas gain quite modest air-quality benefits while paying large costs. Lower income groups in these areas fare particularly poorly since the costs fall quite heavily upon them under the current scheme. [p. 109]

In a general sense the Harrison study suggests that the automobile air-pollution control policy, so carefully designed to be uniformly applied, has led to a highly unbalanced distribution of the benefits. The imbalance appears both in the distribution of net benefits among geographic areas and among socioeconomic groups. Those living in rural areas, particularly the poor, seem to be relatively more burdened than other segments of society.

Stationary-Source Control.   Are these results unique to automobile control? Because the programs are quite different, we cannot assume similarity without performing the analysis. Stationary-source controls also result in higher prices, but the commodities affected are not the same. Furthermore, while rates of automobile ownership are quite low among the poor, particularly the urban poor, the exposure to increases in other commodity prices might well reach more of the poor.

Most studies assume that increased costs of stationary-source controls are passed forward to consumers in the form of higher prices. Therefore, they affect households in proportion to what each household spends on that commodity. In general, the poor spend a higher proportion of their income on these commodities, meaning they save less. Therefore, it is not surprising that those who have derived estimates (such as Gianessi, Peskin, and Wolff [1979] and Dorfman [1975]) have found them to be regressively distributed.

Studies of the benefits of air-pollution control tell a rather different story. A study by Asch and Seneca [1978] examined how the exposure to air pollution was distributed in the United States. They wanted to know if exposure was systematically related to the economic and social characteristics of the population.

To answer this question, they constructed two different samples of data. The first sample consisted of observations on the annual geometric mean concentrations of particulates taken from 284 cities. Socioeconomic variables, such as income levels, age composition, and education levels, were collected for these cities. Doing separate computations for each state, the particulate pollution levels were correlated with these socioeconomic characteristics. Their results indicated that in virtually all states, high pollutant concentrations were found in cities with higher percentages of lower-income people, higher percentages of the aged, and higher percentages of nonwhites.

They complemented this analysis with another sample which examined the intracity variation in air quality. For this second sample the exposure to three air pollutants — sulfur dioxide, nitrogen dioxide, and particulates — was correlated with socioeconomic characteristics within three cities: Chicago, Cleveland, and Nashville. Measuring pollution levels and socioeconomic characteristics at a number of sites within each city allowed for a much more precise link between local pollution levels and the immediately affected pollution to be established.

The income distribution measures consistently confirmed that the poorest portions of these cities experienced higher pollution levels. Similar patterns were associated with property values. Higher pollution levels were generally found in neighborhoods with lower property values. The results for racial exposure were mixed. In Chicago higher pollution levels were found in neighborhoods with a high percentage of nonwhites, but in Cleveland the opposite was true — higher concentrations of nitrogen dioxide were found in neighborhoods containing relatively high proportions of whites.

Asch and Seneca also examined whether the improvements in air quality achieved in the early 1970s were progressively, proportionally, or regressively distributed. They found that the physical improvements were progressively distributed — the lower-income portions of the cities received the greatest reductions in pollutant concentrations. They found that many high-income areas actually became more polluted during the period. Similar results were obtained by Zupan [1973] who studied the New York region.

A Combined Assessment.   The Asch/Seneca and Zupan studies deal with exposure rather than economic benefits. The two are not the same because the concept of economic benefits deals with the worth of reducing exposure, not merely the exposure reduction. Gianessi, Peskin, and Wolff [1979] attempted to bridge this gap by distributing to local areas the national damage estimates computed by the EPA and then prorating the benefits among socioeconomic groups on the basis of exposure.

Their first finding was that the variability of benefit per family estimates across regions and income groups was several times larger than the variability in costs. While the average family in large urban areas received many times the benefits from the program than did the average suburban or rural family, their costs differed by a much smaller amount. Therefore, it is not surprising that the heavily industrialized, highly populated areas of the eastern United States lead the list of the largest gainers, while the rural and agricultural areas are at the bottom of the list.

Gianessi, Peskin, and Wolff also considered the specific areas in which net benefits are positive or negative. For automobile air pollution, they found only four areas of the country (Jersey City, New York, Patterson, and Newark) enjoyed positive net benefits. For stationary-source air pollution, they found 61 (out of 274) areas receiving positive net benefits. When the mobile and stationary-source net benefits were combined, they found 24 areas experiencing positive net benefits. These 24 areas contain approximately 28 percent of the population. The majority of the areas (and population) are paying costs for air-pollution control that are higher than the benefits received.

Analyzing the distribution of net benefits among income classes, the Gianessi, Peskin, and Wolff study found the net benefit from stationary-source pollution to be progressively distributed, and the net benefit from mobile-source control to be regressively distributed. The combination of policies yields ambiguous results with no clear pattern emerging. Generally, the poor and lower-middle class seem somewhat harder hit, although the poorest of the poor end up with the smallest net burden.

We probably should not make too much of any listing of areas which are net beneficiaries or net losers, such as the one described above, because the magnitude of the net benefit is subject to a great deal of uncertainty, particularly in the calculation of benefits. It does seem clear, however, that automobile air-pollution control policy and, to a lesser extent, stationary-source air-pollution control policy, violate both the horizontal and vertical equity dimensions. Equals in different parts of the country are not treated equally, and the net benefits of air-pollution control policy are distributed in a mildly regressive manner.

Water Pollution

Water pollution presents an interesting contrast. The program of control erected to combat water pollution includes not only industrial effluent standards similar to the industrial emission standards used to combat air pollution, but it also includes federal subsidies to waste-treatment plants. Since these subsidies are financed through the tax system, their impact could conceivably be quite different from measures financed chiefly by higher product prices.

Point Sources. Three separate studies—Dorfman [1975], Gianessi and Peskin [1980], and Lake, Hanneman, and Oster [1979]—sought the distribution of costs of federal water-pollution control policy for point sources. All three studies came to similar conclusions.

In general, they found that the distribution of the costs was regressive. The industrial effluent standards imposed a large regressive burden, while the burden of subsidies for municipal treatment plants was progressive. Industrial standards were found to be regressive because they result in higher consumer prices. Because the poor spend a larger percentage of income and save less, they are affected proportionately more. Progressiveness of the municipal waste-treatment subsidies results from their major source of financing—the progressive federal tax system.

To place these results into perspective, Gianessi and Peskin compared the incidence of water-pollution costs to the incidence of air-pollution costs. They found the cost of water-pollution control incidence less regressive, partly because of the manner in which municipal treatment plant subsidies are financed and partly because of the lack of any component in the water-pollution policy resembling the highly regressive automobile policy.

The conclusion that the municipal waste-treatment subsidies are progressive has not gone unchallenged. In an examination of the incidence of these subsidies in EPA region VII (Iowa, Missouri, Kansas, and Nebraska), Collins [1977] found that they tended to redistribute income from the middle-income classes primarily to the very rich. This conclusion depends critically on one particular assumption in the analysis and characteristics that may be somewhat unique to the region studied.

This study assumes that the subsidies received by industrial users of the waste-treatment plants are not passed forward to consumers in lower prices, but rather are retained by the owners. Since the owners of capital, in general, tend to be in the upper portion of the income distribution, this assumption results in a major gain by that group. If this assumption were changed to distribute the subsidy to industrial customers rather than owners, the burden of the municipal waste-treatment subsidy would be quite progressive.

Assuming that the owners of capital retain the subsidy turns out to be particularly important in the Collins study, because over one-half of the subsidies in the region studied accrue to industrial users. Using exactly the same methodology as Collins to estimate the distributional burden of waste-treatment subsidies within the Boston metropolitan area, Ostro [1981] found the burden to be quite progressively distributed. This rather different finding results from the fact that in Boston the industrial share of the subsidy was only 7.85 percent, making the results less sensitive to the assumption about the incidence of the industrial subsidy.

The literature on the distribution of the benefits of water-pollution control is very thin. In one study, Winston Harrington [1981] investigated the distribution of water-based recreation benefits resulting from the implementation of the BPT portion of the 1972 Water Pollution Control Amendments. Using the RFF Water Network Model to simulate the effects of the policy on water quality and an econometric model to estimate the change in recreational demand resulting from the improvement in water quality, Harrington found the benefits to be very unequally distributed. In particular, he found whites favored relative to nonwhites, middle-income families favored relative to the poor, city-dwellers favored relative to those living in the country, and Northeast residents favored relative to those residing in other regions.

Nonpoint Sources.   The studies described above deal with pollution caused by point sources. It is now becoming clear in the United States that as point sources are becoming increasingly controlled, nonpoint sources are becoming relatively more important. The RFF Water Network Model has also been used by Gianessi and Peskin [1981] to analyze the geographic distribution of the benefits of agricultural sediment control.

The basic approach was to simulate water quality under a variety of point and non-point control strategies. The main conclusion derived from this exercise was that only approximately one-third of the nation's river points would experience significantly improved water quality with the adoption of cropland sediment control policy as a supplement to point-source control policy. For this reason the authors suggested that nonpoint control policies should be focused on those agricultural regions where they would make a difference. The simulations also indicated, however, that approximately one-half of the nation's rivers would still experience violations of the total phosphorus and total nitrogen standards unless more stringent controls were established for other nonpoint sources such as pastureland, rangeland, and urban runoff.

IMPLICATIONS FOR POLICY

These results suggest unambiguously that net benefits have historically been distributed in such a way as to violate both the horizontal- and vertical-equity criteria. The vertical-equity criterion was violated because the net benefits have been disproportionately received by well-to-do people. The horizontal criterion was violated for air pollution, in part, because positive net benefits flow mainly to residents of large urban areas. Rural residents with similar incomes receive substantially smaller and possibly negative net benefits.

We must not place too much faith in these estimates. The data on which they are based are imprecise, and every step in the analysis requires some assumption capable of affecting the outcome. The estimated effects are also quite small. The most adversely affected groups are estimated to spend no more than two percent of their income to cover the costs of pollution control.[4] The degree of regressiveness of the distribution of the cost burden is roughly equal to that of a sales tax.[5] When net benefits are considered, both the degree of regressiveness and the percentage of income represented are smaller than is the case when only costs are considered.

Was this distribution inevitable or could the policies have been implemented in such a way that the horizontal and vertical equity criteria could have been satisfied without sacrificing efficiency? It was not inevitable because it is possible to pursue policies that are more efficient and more equitable. This can be illustrated by suggesting alternative approaches that could accomplish both objectives.

In the case of automobiles, generally acknowledged to be the most serious offender, Harrison [1975] estimated the distribution of the burden that would result if the current policies were modified in specific ways. One of the modifications he considered was the two-car strategy (explained in Chapter 17).

With respect to horizontal equity, he found the two-car strategy to be superior to the current policy. This result is easy to understand, since the two-car strategy allows

---

[4]See, for example, the graphs in N. S. Dorfman, "Who Will Pay for Pollution Control? The Distribution by Income of the Burden of the National Environmental Protection Program, 1972–1980," *National Tax Journal* 28 (March 1975): 101–115; and in Robert Dorfman, "Incidence of the Benefits and Costs of Environmental Programs," *The American Economic Review* 67 (February 1977): 334–340.

[5]For a comparison of the regressiveness of a general sales tax with that of the costs of pollution control, see N. S. Dorfman, "Who Will Pay for Pollution Control? The Distribution by Income of the Burden of the National Environmental Protection Program, 1972–1980," *National Tax Journal* 28 (March 1975): 114.

lower costs in less polluted areas and brings the net benefits in rural areas more in line with those in urban areas. With a two-car strategy, households with comparable incomes in different geographic areas receive comparable net benefits, instead of the current situation where net benefits are disproportionately reaped in highly polluted urban areas.

Harrison also finds that vertical equity would be improved by the adoption of a two-car strategy. By reducing control costs in medium and small cities, as well as rural areas, the burden on low-income groups is diminished more than that for higher-income groups. In contrast to large urban areas where the poor have very low rates of car ownership (presumably because of mass transit), much larger proportions of the poor own cars in smaller urban areas and rural areas. Therefore, a two-car strategy would not only be more efficient, it would also be more equitable.

The next most regressive portion of the control package involved the controls placed on stationary sources. The cost of these controls are regressive because they raise the cost of goods. Since the poor spend a larger proportion of income on goods than do the rich, they are hit harder by price increases.

The magnitude of the price increases can be influenced by policy. In the second section of this chapter we demonstrated that, in the long run, the magnitude of the price increase is determined by the height of the minimum point on the long-run average cost curve. Changes in policy affecting average cost also affect prices; the larger the amount average cost is raised, the larger the impact on prices.

The transferable permit system embodied in the bubble and offset policies provides an example of how air-quality objectives can be met with smaller increases in average cost than were possible prior to the adoption of these reforms. We have shown that these reforms substantially reduce compliance costs, both average and marginal, for existing sources and therefore cause smaller increases in prices. Since none of the studies described above take those reforms into account, they overstate the regressive effects of current policy.

It is also noteworthy that markets in which the permits are allocated free of charge experience smaller price increases than either an emission charge system or an auction market, where permits are purchased by sources from the government. Both the emission charge and the auction market entail an extra expense to the source that can be avoided by existing sources. It is premature, however, to label the system where the permits are given away as less regressive than the other economic incentive systems until we determine definitively what is to be done with the revenue derived from the auction or the charge. If this revenue were somehow transferred to the poor, it is conceivable that other systems would be less regressive in spite of the fact that they cause larger increases in industrial prices.[6]

The general point, however, is that the movement toward these economic-incentive systems from the more traditional pure regulation systems can increase equity as well

---

[6]It is also true that *new* sources would face the same costs under any of the three economic incentive systems. Even if the permits were given away to existing sources, new sources would have to buy them. In the long run the regressiveness of the three systems is identical. Only in the short run do they differ.

as efficiency. The distribution of the burden should not represent a major stumbling block to the adoption of sensible environmental policy.

Is there any evidence that the popular support for environmental policy has been weakened by the distributional patterns? The polls that have been taken suggest not. A *Business Week*/Harris National Poll, early in 1983,[7] asked the question, "Given the costs involved in cleaning up the environment, do you think Congress should make the Clean Air and Clean Water Acts stricter than they are now, keep them about the same, or ease them?" Sixty percent said they would prefer a stricter approach to water-pollution control and forty-seven percent said they preferred stricter controls for air pollution. Significantly less than 10 percent wanted to make either law less strict. Since this poll appears to be typical, it seems clear that the political support for environmental policy has not been undermined by the deficiencies in the current approaches.

Is there any evidence that regional self-interest has shaped environmental policy? Such evidence does exist and it comes in many forms. On a qualitative level, for example, it seems quite clear that the concerns of Midwestern states and some of the coal-producing regions of the East have had a major effect on delaying acid rain legislation as well as on the shape of the emerging legislation.

On a quantitative level, several studies have demonstrated strong correlations between regional voting patterns in the U.S. Congress and projected regional impacts of proposed legislation. Leone and Jackson (1977) found this to be the case for water pollution control legislation, while Crandall (1983) has suggested that votes on air quality issues are better explained by projected effects on the growth rate in income in the region than by predicted air quality effects.

A particularly interesting study was recently published by Pashigian (1985). Relying on an econometric analysis of voting patterns on legislation establishing the PSD policy, he found that regional economic self-interest had a strong, but not exclusive, explanatory power. In particular he interprets his results as suggesting that a strong demand for improved air quality in the Northeast was complemented by an equally strong desire to prevent a large scale exodus of firms from the nonattainment regions as they attempted to escape the increasingly stringent controls. According to this interpretation the PSD policy was an attempt to assuage the fears of the Northeast, a powerful voting coalition, while continuing to give U.S. voters the improvements in air quality they so clearly wanted.

SUMMARY

A highly debated issue is whether environmental policy is used by the rich to promote their own interests at the expense of the poor. To determine whether the net benefits are equitably distributed, two principles of equity are useful: the vertical principle and the horizontal principle.

---

[7]"A Call for Tougher—not Weaker—Antipollution Laws," *Business Week,* 24 (January 1983): 87.

Applying these principles requires a knowledge of how the costs and benefits are initially distributed and how these burdens can be shifted by market reactions. Beginning with the initial incidence of control costs on industries, we discovered a high degree of variability among industries. The ability of these industries to shift this burden to consumers or employees depends upon such factors as the market demand for the product, labor intensiveness of the production process, and market structure. Some industries are hit much harder than others.

The empirical evidence on the ultimate incidence suggests that the costs are regressively distributed in general for air pollution, while the benefits are progressively distributed. The evidence further suggests that net benefits from stationary-source controls are progressively distributed and regressively distributed for mobile sources.

For air-pollution control as a whole, net benefits are mildly regressively distributed because of the dominance of automobile pollution control. Environmental policy does not live up to the vertical equity criterion, though the degree by which it fails is small.

Current policy violates the horizontal equity principle as well. Net benefits are substantially higher for residents of large urban areas than they are for suburban or rural residents.

Less evidence is available on the distribution of water-pollution control net benefits, though the evidence we have suggests they violate both the horizontal and vertical equity criteria as well. Though the costs of water-pollution control are less regressive than their air-pollution control counterparts, the benefits seem to be regressively distributed with a high degree of geographic variability.

While these results strongly suggest that current distribution of benefits is not as equitable as it might be, they provide little evidence of the intentional exploitation of the poor. Many parts of the control policy involve progressively distributed net benefits, particularly for the urban poor. The regressive nature of the entire package is milder than would be the case if the rich were out to exploit the poor.

These deficiencies have not apparently diminished the popular support for environmental policy to any appreciable degree. According to polls, it remains high. Regional self-interest has been a factor, however, in determining the form of environmental legislation.

Policy changes could improve the situation. Specifically, a two-car strategy for automobile pollution and transferable discharge permits for the control of stationary sources could be the basis for policies that are more efficient and equitable than those relying on pure uniform regulation.

FURTHER READING

Christiansen, G. B., and T. H. Tietenberg. "Distributional and Macroeconomic Aspects of Environmental Policy," in Allen V. Kneese and James L. Sweeney, eds. *Handbook of Natural Resource and Energy Economics* (Amsterdam: North-Holland, 1985). A more detailed and more technical survey of the material covered in this chapter.

Gordon, David, ed. "Environment," in *Problems in Political Economy: An Urban Perspective*, 1st ed. (Lexington, Mass.: D.C. Health and Company, 1971). An interesting treatment of the radical, conservative, and liberal points of view on the distribution of benefits from pollution-control policy. Unfortunately this discussion was dropped in the second edition so it is available only in the first edition.

Peskin, Henry. "Environmental Policy and the Distribution of Benefits and Costs," in Paul R. Portney, ed. *Current Issues in U.S. Environmental Policy* (Baltimore: Johns Hopkins University Press, for Resources for the Future, 1978). A more policy-oriented discussion of the distribution of the benefits and costs of the Clean Air Act Amendments of 1970 than the readings discussed in this text.

ADDITIONAL REFERENCES

Asch, Peter, and Joseph J. Seneca. "Some Evidence on the Distribution of Air Quality," *Land Economics,* Vol. 54 (August 1978): 278-97.

Collins, Robert A. "The Distributive Effects of Public Law 92-500," *Journal of Environmental Economics and Management,* Vol. 4 (December 1977): 344-54.

Crandall, Robert W. *Controlling Industrial Pollution* (Washington, D.C.: The Brookings Institution, 1983).

Dorfman, N. S. "Who Will Pay for Pollution Control? The Distribution by Income of the Burden of the National Environmental Protection Program, 1972-1980," *National Tax Journal,* Vol. 28 (March 1975): 101-15.

Dorfman, Robert. "Incidence of the Benefits and Costs of Environmental Programs," *The American Economic Review,* Vol. 67 (February 1977): 333-40.

Evans, David S. "The Differential Effect of Regulation Across Plant Size: Comment on Pashigian," *The Journal of Law and Economics,* Vol. 29, No. 1 (April 1986): 187-200.

Freeman, A. Myrick III. "The Incidence of the Cost of Controlling Automotive Air Pollution," in F. T. Juster, ed., *The Distribution of Economic Well-Being* (Cambridge, Mass.: Ballinger, 1977).

Gianessi, L. P., H. M. Peskin, and Edward Wolff. "The Distributional Effects of Uniform Air Pollution Policy in the United States," *Quarterly Journal of Economics,* Vol. 93 (May 1979): 281-301.

Gianessi, Leonard P., and Henry M. Peskin. "Analysis of National Water Pollution Control Policies, 2: Agricultural Sediment Control," *Water Resources Research,* Vol. 17 (1981): 803-21.

Gianessi, Leonard P., and Henry M. Peskin. "The Distribution of the Costs of Federal Water Pollution Control Policy," *Land Economics,* Vol. 56 (February 1980): 85-102.

Harrington, Winston. "The Distribution of Recreational Benefits from Improved Water Quality: A Micro Simulation," Discussion Paper D-80, Quality of the Environment Division, Resources for the Future (Washington, D.C., 1981).

Harrison, David, Jr. *Who Pays for Clean Air: The Cost and Benefit Distribution of Automobile Emission Standards* (Cambridge, Mass.: Ballinger, 1975).

Hughes, John S., Wesley A. Magat, and William A. Ricks. "The Economic Consequences of the OSHA Cotton Dust Standards: An Analysis of Stock Price Behavior," *The Journal of Law and Economics,* Vol. 29, No. 1 (April 1986): 29-59.

Lake, Elizabeth, William M. Hanneman, and Sharon M. Oster. *Who Pays for Clean Water? The Distribution of Water Pollution Control Costs* (Boulder, Colo.: Westview, 1979).

Leone, Robert A. and John J. Jackson. "The Political Economy of Federal Regulatory Activity" in Gary Fromm, ed. *Studies in Public Regulation,* (Cambridge, Mass.: The MIT Press, 1977): 231–71.

Maloney, Michael T., and Gordon L. Brady. "Capital Turnover and Marketable Pollution Rights," a revised paper originally prepared for "Emissions Trading: The Implications for Western Coal Policy," a conference sponsored by the Department of Interior and the President's Council on Environmental Quality, July 16 and 17, 1984, Clemson University (August 1986).

Maloney, Michael T., and Robert E. McCormick. "A Positive Theory of Environmental Quality Regulation," *The Journal of Law and Economics* XXV (April 1982): 99–123.

Ostro, Bart D. "The Distributional Effects of Public Law 92–500," *Journal of Environmental Economics and Management,* Vol. 8 (June 1981): 196–98.

Pashigian, B. Peter. "The Effects of Environmental Regulation on Optimal Plant Size and Factor Shares," *The Journal of Law and Economics,* Vol. 28, No. 1 (April 1984): 1–28.

Pashigian, B. Peter. "Environmental Regulation: Whose Self-Interests Are Being Protected?", *Economic Inquiry,* Vol. 23 (October 1985): 551–84.

Pittman, Russell W. "Issues in Pollution Control: Interplant Cost Differences and Economies of Scale," *Land Economics,* Vol. 57 (February 1981): 1–17.

U.S. Environmental Protection Agency, *The Economics of Clean Air—1972* (Washington, D.C.: Environmental Protection Agency, 1973).

U.S. Environmental Protection Agency, *Third Quarter Report of the Economic Dislocation Early Warning System* (Washington, D.C.: Environmental Protection Agency, 1982).

Zupan, Jeffrey M. *The Distribution of Air Quality in the New York Region* (Washington, D.C.: Resources for the Future, 1973).

DISCUSSION QUESTIONS

1. "There is an inevitable conflict between the goals of environmental policy and our concern for the poor. The burden of any attempt to improve the environment necessarily falls disproportionately on the poor." Discuss.

2. "Environmental policy in the United States has been extremely fair in that it has been uniformly applied. This is evident, for example, in the uniform ambient air-quality standards, uniform new-source performance standards, uniform hazardous-pollutant standards, uniform new-car emission standards, and uniform discharge standards for water pollution." Does uniformity in these policies guarantee "fairness"? Defining "fairness," explain why or why not.

CHAPTER TWENTY-ONE

Growth in a Finite Environment

*If there is any period one would desire to be born in, is it not
the age of revolution when the old and the new stand side by
side and admit of being compared? When the energies of all
men are searched by fear, and by hope? When the historic
glories of the old can be compensated by the rich possibilities
of the new era? This time, like all times, is a very good one, if
we but know what to do with it.*

RALPH WALDO EMERSON, *The American Scholar* (1873)

INTRODUCTION

In previous chapters we have invested much time and effort investigating individual
environmental and natural-resource problems and the policy responses that have been,
and could have been, taken to solve them. In general, these problems are soluble, and
our economic and political institutions, with some exceptions, seem to be muddling
through toward solutions.

Our next step must be a consideration of the growth process itself. How will all
these policy initiatives affect the growth process? Are these individual initiatives sufficient to restore a healthy balance between the economic system and the environmental
assets, while protecting the interests of future generations, or is some additional control of the growth process needed?

The two visions in Chapter 1 suggest two different answers to these questions. The
Limits to Growth view holds that exponential growth will continue unabated until the
physical limits are reached. At that time society will overshoot its resource base and
collapse. In this view the only rational policy is to exercise direct control over the growth
process itself. No other course, including the collection of individual policies discussed
in the preceding chapters, would avoid the collapse.

Kahn and his associates, however, envision an automatic transition to a steady-
state economy where eventually growth would cease, but all future households would
be significantly better off than current households. Thus, they foresee the prospect for
continued growth which slowly declines to zero over time. Far from being detrimental, economic growth provides the vehicle for improving the welfare of future genera-

tions. As Kahn sees it, to deny that growth would consign the members of poor Third World countries to perpetual poverty. Which view of the future is correct?

To help in making our decision, we need to answer two questions. In the absence of direct government controls, what is the likely future for economic growth? In light of this future, should direct controls be placed on the growth process?

The first question can be answered with descriptive (as opposed to normative) economics and will be the primary concern of this chapter. We will begin by defining how growth takes place and how the growth process is affected by increasing resource scarcity and rising environmental costs. We will then address the sustainability of market-oriented growth and the likely future of economic growth in the United States.

In the next chapter we shall concentrate on the second question, which requires normative judgment.

THE GROWTH PROCESS

Nature of the Process

How does growth occur? It occurs in two main ways: through increases in inputs such as capital, labor, energy, and other resources, or through increases in the productivity of those resources as a result of technological progress. The former source of growth involves increasingly greater outputs, given the state of the art in production, while the latter source involves improvements in the state of the art.

Increases in Inputs. The amount of growth occurring from increases in inputs is governed by two important economic concepts: economies of scale and the law of diminishing returns. The term, *economies of scale,* refers to the amount of increase in output obtained when all inputs are increased in the same proportion. The *law of diminishing returns* governs the relationship between inputs and output when some inputs are increased and others are held fixed.

We can add precision to these definitions by introducing a concept known as the production function. A *production function* expresses mathematically the relationship between inputs and outputs. A common general production function is expressed as

$$O = f(K, L, E, M) \tag{21.1}$$

where O = output, K = capital, L = labor, E = energy, and M = materials or, more generally, other resources. This equation simply states that output is functionally related to these inputs by the production function f. To know something about the growth process we have to know more about f.

Suppose that we were to multiply the inputs by a constant (λ) and observe that output grew by another constant (θ). Thus

$$\theta O = f(\lambda K, \lambda L, \lambda E, \lambda M). \tag{21.2}$$

If $\lambda = \theta$, then f is said to exhibit constant returns to scale. If $\lambda < \theta$, f exhibits increasing returns to scale (a λ change in all factors leads to a change in output which is greater than λ).

The law of diminishing returns governs what happens when some, but not all, of the inputs are increased. Suppose, for example, that all the inputs are held fixed, except for capital, which increases. As constant and successive increments of capital are added to the other fixed resources, the law of diminishing returns implies that eventually a point will be reached where each increment will produce smaller and smaller increments of output.

Technological Progress.   The final source of growth, technological progress, involves the implementation of better, less wasteful ways of doing things. With technological progress growth can occur even in the absence of increases in inputs simply because the inputs available are used more effectively. For example, with a new production technique, less energy might be wasted or fewer resources used to make a particular product.

Example 21.1 provides one example of a commonly used production function. It shows how these concepts of economies of scale, law of diminishing returns, and technological progress can be given specific definitions so that their importance in the growth process can be assessed.

Potential Sources of Reduced Growth

Historically, increases in factor inputs and technological progress were both important sources of growth. This does not automatically mean that they will continue to provide growth at historic levels in the future, however. There are a number of reasons for being suspicious of extrapolating historically valid arguments into the future.

Reduced Input Flows.   Not all input flows are continuing at historic levels. Population growth has slowed considerably in most countries, which causes the growth in the labor force to slow and possibly stop. The growth fed by increasing labor is diminishing and will continue to diminish in the future.

The cost of energy and of raw materials seems to be rising, even in real terms. Producers respond by cutting back on the use of these inputs, which diminishes their contribution to the growth process.

Capital formation has played a pivotal role in the past and is likely to continue doing so. As workers were given more sophisticated capital equipment to work with, their productivity increased. Capital has broken down the barriers imposed by human limitations. Earthmoving, once limited by the strength and endurance of workers, with the advent of bulldozers, is limited no more.

Size of the market, once limited by the time and effort required to transport commodities in a horse and buggy, expanded with the advent of the railroad, the truck, and the airplane. Limits on coporate controllability imposed by the size and competence of recordkeeping staffs—as they attempted to stay on top of the information and paper

EXAMPLE 21.1

The Generalized Cobb-Douglas Production Function

In attempting to understand the effect of changes in input streams on the growth process, the notion of a production function becomes important. Several production functions have been used by economists, but perhaps one of the most powerful and yet simplest to understand is the Generalized Cobb-Douglas (GCD) Production Function. It is useful to know this function, both to make general constructs, such as economies of scale, more concrete, and to pave the way for structuring the evidence on how the growth process could be expected to be affected by such things as slower growth in the labor force.

The GCD function is expressed as the power function:

$$Q_t = Ae^{rt}K_t^{a_1} \cdot L_t^{a_2}E_t^{a_3}M_t^{a_4},$$

where K, L, E, and M are capital, labor, energy, and materials; A, a_1, a_2, a_3, a_4 and r are constants; and t refers to the year in question. Using econometrics, the branch of economics used to derive empirical estimates, actual data can be used to derive values for all constants.

Several properties in this function can be easily derived. Constant returns to scale will prevail whenever the sum of the "a" exponents is equal to 1.0. Most analysts find it difficult to reject the conclusion that constant returns to scale prevail for the U.S. economy as a whole.

It can also be shown that the laws of diminishing returns will apply to any factor when its associated exponent (a) is less than 1.0. Given the above values, the law seems to apply to all four factors.

We can convert this equation into a rate of growth equation as follows:

$$\frac{\dot{Q}}{Q} = r + a_1\frac{\dot{K}}{K} + a_2\frac{\dot{L}}{L} + a_3\frac{\dot{M}}{M} + a_4\frac{\dot{E}}{E},$$

where the rate of growth of any variable X is denoted as $\dot{X}/X$. Thus the rate of growth of output is a weighted sum of the individual rates plus r, which is interpreted as the rate of technological progress. Notice that as long as $r > 0$ growth can continue, even in the absence of any growth in inputs.

Source: Ronald L. Cooper, "The Energy-Economic-Connection: 1974–1979 and Beyond," *Business Economics* 15 (September 1980): 6; E. R. Berndt and D. Wood, "Technology, Prices and the Derived Demand for Energy," *Review of Economics and Statistics* 57 (August 1975): 264.

flows—have fallen in the face of computers providing instant access to important information compiled in the most useful format.

Although capital is a reproducible asset, there may be some indirect limits on its role in the future because of limitations on its ability to substitute for other factors, on the productivity of future investment, and on the incentive to invest. We shall consider each of these in turn.

The ability of capital to promote historical growth rates lies in part in its ability to substitute for those factor inputs which are experiencing limits. In Chapter 13 we introduced the concept known as the elasticity of substitution and noted that when this concept takes on a value of one or greater, substitution is easy and growth should not be inhibited. Therefore, we need only to refresh our memory concerning those results and to draw out their implications.[1]

The first substitution possibility to be considered is between capital and labor. As population growth dwindles, the growth rate in the supply of labor diminishes as well. Historically, the economic growth rate has exceeded the growth rate of labor supply, as capital was continually substituted for labor. Most studies of production have found capital and labor to be quite strong substitutes. When we think about the modern manufacturing sector, this seems quite reasonable. Therefore, dwindling population, by itself, doesn't seem a particularly large barrier.

Describing the substitution possibilities for other resources, however, becomes more complex. For example, while Brown and Field [1979] found capital-resource substitution elasticities to be greater than 1.0 in all four of the industries they examined, Humphrey and Moroney [1975] found capital-resource elasticities less than 1.0 in three other industries. It seems clear that no general consensus has emerged concerning the degree of substitutability existing between capital and resources. This substitutability seems to depend upon the industry being considered.

The relationship between capital and energy is even more puzzling. Studies of the capital-energy relationship over time in the United States—such as that made by Berndt and Wood [1975]—find that capital and energy are complements, rather than substitutes. Thus, capital and energy have together substituted for labor and other resources but not for each other. If one thinks of the tractor, the bulldozer, and the airplane, this seems like a natural finding.

The question of interest is whether capital and energy would remain complements in the future or whether substitution of capital for energy might be possible. In some energy uses substitution is clearly feasible because energy-saving equipment, such as computer-controlled heating and cooling, already exists. Furthermore, some capital

---

[1] For the more advanced students it should be noted that the generalized Cobb-Douglas function implies substitution elasticities equal to 1.0. Therefore, the estimation of those elasticities has relied on more general functional forms that permit the elasticities between each factor input to differ.

investments will clearly hasten the transition to passive solar energy, which conserves energy by making better use of what is available.

In other sectors such as transportation, the substitution possibilities are not quite as obvious, but that does not mean they do not exist. Bicycles are an obvious substitute for personal transportation, as are cars powered by solar energy. To some extent communication can even substitute for transportation, as more people use home-based computer terminals and phone lines to do their jobs without leaving home. While our historical experience would suggest limited substitution possibilities, it is not at all clear that experience is relevant for the future. Nonetheless, it would be premature to feel confident that the future elasticity of substitution between capital and energy will be uniformly greater than 1.0. Though it is likely that the elasticity of substitution between energy and labor is quite high, this does not offer much promise for growth in an era of declining growth in the labor force. Some drag on economic growth from higher energy prices appears likely.

The second possible source of growth drag relates to the future productivity of capital. As pollution rises, the amount of resources committed to combating it also rises. As we saw in the preceding chapter, a substantial proportion of new plant and equipment expenditures is being allocated to pollution control. Unlike conventional investments, however, these investments do not cause more goods to be produced; they produce a cleaner environment. Because the value of this cleaner environment is not usually recorded in the conventional measures of economic output, conventionally measured output should rise more slowly as a larger proportion of inputs is diverted from productivity enhancement to environment enhancement.

The final source of drag concerns the incentive to invest. The amount of capital investment should depend upon the rate of return on that investment. The more profitable the investment is, the larger the amount undertaken. Yet we have already identified two related factors that reduce the rate of return on investments – the regulatory bias against new sources and the composition of investment. By focusing on new sources, the regulatory system diminishes the relative profitability of new investment while enhancing the profitability of existing capital stock. This new source bias diminishes the incentive to invest in new capital. Meanwhile, the large proportion of new-plant and equipment expenditures going for pollution control tends to diminish the profitability of those expenditures being made, since improvements in the environment do not, in general, add to profits.

In sum, it appears that expecting increases in capital to completely compensate for reduced flows of other inputs would be risky. There are some important transitions going on. While they do not imply a cessation of growth catastrophically or otherwise in the near future, these transitions certainly suggest some diminution in the rate of economic growth resulting from reduced factor input flows.

Limits on Technological Progress.   Can technological progess take up the slack? As is clear from Example 21.1, if technological progress is to compensate for declining input flows, an increase in the rate of technological progress must occur. Is that likely?

Some observers are beginning to suggest that there may be limits to the degree to which technological progress can continue to play its historic role as a growth stimulant. Some of the these limits are perceived as institutional and a matter of choice, while others are perceived as natural and inexorable.

The new-source regulatory bias in pollution-control policy provides one example of an institutional limit. Because most technological progress bears fruit when it is embodied in new or modified production facilities, by reducing the number of these facilities, this new-source bias inhibits technological progress.

Another institutional barrier is the decreasing commitment of resources to basic research, particularly by the public sector. Since basic research is frequently a precursor for technological progress, this trend could also diminish the rate of technological progress.

A second set of concerns has arisen over the existence of natural limits to technological progress. A most interesting and provocative formulation of this argument is put forth by Ayres and Miller [1980]. Their model of the growth process specifically assumes that technological progress is embodied in new capital, and that the construction and use of this capital necessarily requires energy. Therefore, in their model, the role of capital in economic growth is ultimately limited by the availability of energy. The availability of energy, in turn, is limited by the second law of thermodynamics.[2] When this model is solved for the resulting allocation of resources over time, the optimal path of production and consumption leads inevitably and gradually toward a stationary state in which economic growth is zero and technological progress ceases.

Having examined the conceptual arguments on future prospects for growth, it seems reasonable to suspect that some diminution in growth will eventually occur as limits constrain the traditional sources of growth. The next step is to survey evidence relating to the magnitude and timing of these impacts.

There is no doubt that during the 1970s economic growth fell below that in earlier periods (Table 21.1). The average rates of growth in manufacturing output were down

TABLE 21.1   Growth Rates of Output, Labor Productivity, and Technological Progress 1958–77

Time Period	Gross Manufacturing Output	Labor Productivity	Technological Progress*
1958–65	5.411	3.152	1.495
1965–73	3.827	2.777	0.707
1973–77	1.030	1.745	0.340

Source: Ernst R. Berndt, "Energy Price Increases and the Productivity Slowdown in United States Manufacturing," a paper presented at the Federal Reserve Bank of Boston Conference on Productivity (June 1980), Tables 2 and 3.

*Measured as growth in output minus growth in aggregate input, where aggregate input is the cost share weighted growth of individual inputs. This is also known in the literature as the rate of growth of *total factor productivity* and would correspond to *r* in Example 21.1.

---

[2]This concept was defined in Chapter 2.

markedly, as are growth rates in labor productivity (output divided by labor input) and technological progress. Does this dramatic decline reflect the beginning of a new era?

A number of economists have tried to isolate the sources of this decline—an assignment made difficult because so many interacting variables are involved. Nonetheless, some progress has been made and is worthy of our attention. We begin with an analysis of the effects of environmental policy on growth.

Environmental Policy

We have seen that pollution control laws impose large compliance costs on industry. These should have some effect on inflation (by boosting output prices), employment, as well as on growth. The question of interest is how large those impacts have been, and could be expected to be, in the future.

One estimate by Data Resources, Inc. [1979] is rather typical. Though there are other estimates, they do not convey a significantly different impression. The impact of environmental policy on the rate of inflation (measured using the urban consumer price index) is very small, less than one half of a percentage point.

The effect on employment is particularly interesting. We suggested in the previous chapter that one effect of the new-source bias would be to diminish the adverse employment impacts on existing pollution sources. Any adverse employment impacts that occur are further offset to some degree by the gains in employment experienced by firms producing the pollution-control equipment. The sales and employment in these industries would have increased as a direct result of the environmental regulations. The Data Resources results suggest that the gains to those producing the equipment more than offset the losses to those installing the equipment, resulting in more, not less, employment in the economy as a whole.

Economist Robert Haveman [1978] has surveyed the results of a range of studies conducted around the world on the effect of pollution-control expenditures on employment. These studies go beyond aggregate employment effects and delve into the types of workers affected as well as into the effects of alternative ways of financing investments in pollution control. He concludes:

1. The employment demands of public sector spending for pollution control are greater than equivalent government spending for alternative purposes. About 60,000 to 70,000 jobs are created for each $1 billion dollars of pollution control spending. For purposes of comparison, each $1 billion of GNP generates approximately 50,000 jobs on the average.

2. Changes in the composition of employment triggered by environmental policy are likely to adversely affect low-skill low-wage workers relative to high-skill high-wage workers.

3. In a limited number of countries, environmental policy has been employed as a demand-inducing antirecession instrument, apparently with some success. This result is in part due to the deficit public financing of the expenditures or subsidies.

4. Available evidence suggests that the adverse employment effects from plant closings   attributable   to   environmental   policy   are   very   limited.

However, this generally positive prognosis for the impact of environmental policy
on employment should not obscure the problems that exist. Gains in employment
generally benefit a different set of workers than losses do. New jobs are rarely in the
same location as those lost and, as Haveman points out, rarely involve the same skill
levels. Even when overall employment effects are positive, the rising costs of environmental control could cause severe localized problems.

According to the DRI simulation, the dampening effect on growth doesn't really
begin to emerge consistently until the period following 1982. After 1982 the effect remains small (less than 1 percent of GNP), but the simulations suggest that the reduction in GNP grows over time. If these simulations are at all accurate, environmental
policy does not bear much responsibility for much of the decline in the economic growth
rate in the late 1970s.

Christainsen and Haveman [1981] have pushed this analysis further by studying
the effect of environmental policy on labor productivity, a major determinant of growth.
Their analytical approach captures, albeit crudely, the direct and indirect effects of environmental regulations., It includes whatever inhibiting effects environmental regulations may have had on capital investment and on capital-labor ratios. They conclude:

> . . . little evidence exists to suggest that as much as 15 percent of the slowdown can be
> attributed to them. A reasonable estimate would attribute, say, 8 percent–12 percent of the
> slowdown in productivity growth to these regulations. [p. 388]

If these estimates are accurate, environmental policy cannot escape responsibility for
some portion of the decline in labor productivity, but at least the degree is small.

The final item of interest in the DRI simulations concerns the effect of environmental
policy on the balance of trade. To the extent that pollution-control expenditures cause
prices of domestic products to rise more rapidly than prices of foreign products, some
decline in exports accompanies a rise in imports. This is precisely what the DRI simulations suggests, though this effect is also small.

Energy

A second possible source of growth drag considered in the previous section was energy.
Since large price increases occurred during 1973–74, this period provides a unique
opportunity to study the magnitude of the growth-inhibiting effects of energy.

What should we expect to find? Since energy and capital historically have been
complements, we should find that price increases would slow down capital formation.
At the same time the fact that energy and labor are substitutes would suggest that the
use of labor should be rising, which, in turn, would cause the average productivity
of labor to fall.

On a general level the evidence is consistent with this set of expectations. Investment is lower and the average productivity of labor has fallen. Work by Jorgenson [1981] and others, such as Uri and Hassanein [1981], confirms this impression.

Focusing on 1973–76, a period characterized by rapidly increasing energy prices, Jorgenson first examined the question of whether the decline in growth was due to declines in input growth or to declines in productivity. He found that input declines were much less significant than declines in productivity. He then attempted to discover the sources of this productivity decline by looking at the specific experience of 35 different industries.

Though a decline in productivity could conceivably be caused either by a shift in resources from high-productivity industries to low-productivity industries or by a decline in the productivity in each industry, Jorgenson found the latter to be far more important than the former. His analysis of the causes of these declines revealed that in 29 of the 35 sectors examined, technical change was biased toward the use of energy. This result suggests that in 1973–76, productivity growth resulting from technical progress declined as energy prices rose. If this is an accurate depiction of the future, as well as the past, then this evidence provides some, albeit weak, empirical confirmation of the Ayers-Miller model.

One puzzle to be explained by those who believe energy prices have already played a significant role in productivity declines is how that could be so when the energy cost share is so small. Factors with small cost shares should in general have rather small effects on output.

Recent work by Berndt and Wood (Forthcoming) suggests a resolution to this puzzle that seems consistent with the evidence. Their view suggests that in the short run the capital services provided by the capital stock are largely fixed, as are its operating characteristics. Once the capital stock is in place, the ratio of energy to capital services actually utilized is therefore fixed. Dramatic changes in energy prices therefore affect the degree to which this capital is used, with the most energy-inefficient vintages being used least. By lowering the utilization of the existing capital stock, higher energy prices reduce total factor productivity.

In this story the lower productivity does not necessarily persist. As long as new capital can be purchased which uses less energy, utilization rates rise and productivity is restored as these new machines are installed. Once the stock of capital adjusts to the new regime of higher energy prices, productivity growth rebounds.

The key to thinking about the long run is to keep straight the differences between *ex post* and *ex ante* substitution possibilities. *Ex ante* refers to the time period prior to investment, while *ex post* refers to the time period after the equipment is installed. Limited *ex post* substitution possibilities, which seem to have played a significant role in the slowdown of productivity growth after the major energy price increases in the 1970s and early in the 1980s, do not automatically indicate that *ex ante* substitution possibilities will be small. It is the *ex ante* substitution possibilities which will determine the future of economic growth over the long run.

Our experience with higher energy prices is quite limited. Transformations of the kind envisioned by these growth models take time to unfold. Old machines are not replaced instantaneously. Therefore, the estimates must be judged for what they are— an attempt to extract as much information as possible from a limited set of data.

OUTLOOK FOR THE NEAR FUTURE

Some of the future portends for the United States and other developed countries is becoming clear. Because we are in a period of transition, some striking differences between our experiences in the recent past and what we will encounter in the near future are emerging. Though a detailed examination would be beyond the scope of our study, we will highlight some of the emerging changes in the following discussion.

Population Impacts

The dramatic fall in fertility rates experienced by most countries of the world will have a profound impact. Inevitably, the average age of the population will rise, putting pressure on social-security systems. Since the United States relies on an unfunded social security system, current payments to retirees are financed out of current payments by workers. As long as the population is growing, the ratio of workers to retirees remains high enough to provide adequate benefit levels for retirees without putting excessive strain on current workers. When population growth declines, however, as is now happening, the ratio of workers to retirees declines as well. To keep the system solvent, benefit growth has to decline and/or worker payments have to increase.

Some studies by economists and demographers suggest that labor-market implications of declining population growth will be significant.[3] One very positive effect will be a reduction in the unemployment rates of young adults. Because fewer young inexperienced workers will be entering the labor market, it will be easier to absorb those that do.

As a result of declines in population growth, the labor force will not grow as much as it has historically, creating some upward pressure on wages. These higher wages should reinforce and support the rising participation rates for women and should entice older workers to stay in the work force longer. These enhanced job opportunities for women should keep the fertility rate low, reinforcing the tendency for low rates of population growth.

The work by Lindert [1978], studied in Chapter 5, suggested that periods of tight labor markets have an equalizing effect on the income distribution. If this model is accurate, and if there are no countervailing tendencies, we should witness a trend toward greater income equality in the future as the rewards to labor rise relative to other factors.

The Information Economy

The importance of capital and resources in the American economy is a product of the Industrial Revolution. The Industrial Revolution ushered in an era of mass production where manufacturing replaced agriculture as the dominant source of employment and

---

[3]William P. Butz, et al. *Demographic Challenges in America's Future.* Report # R-2911-RC, The Rand Corporation (May 1982); Joseph M. Anderson. "An Economic-Demographic Model of the United States Labor Market," in *Research in Population Economics* Vol. 4, Julian L. Simon and Peter H. Lindert (Greenwich, Conn.: JAI Press, 1982).

earnings. This transformation depended upon massive amounts of capital investment and the scale of operations it brought about consumed large amounts of resources.

It now seems clear that the economy is in the midst of an equally important transformation from an industrial society to what Daniel Bell has labeled the *post industrial society*.[4] The key elements of this transformation are a change from a goods-producing to a service economy, a rise in the importance of theoretical knowledge as a source of growth, and an increasing reliance on information processing.

In 1977 the Department of Commerce released a nine volume study which tracked the progress of this transformation.[5] Until 1905 agricultural workers outnumbered industrial, service, and information workers. (Porac defines an *information worker* as one whose income originates primarily in the manipulation of symbols or information.) Industrial workers became the dominant force for the next 50 years. By 1955 information workers made up the largest category.

This transformation has profound implications for our society.[6] Computer-controlled robots will step in to fill the slots vacated by lower population growth in a direct substitution of capital for labor. Working at home will become possible for larger numbers of people as computer communication provides a substitute for transportation. Such changes will boost productivity while reducing pollution and our dependence on raw materials and energy. Intelligence will replace oil as the prime mover of the system.

This vision suggests that the demand for skilled labor will rise in the future more rapidly than the demand for unskilled labor. Education will, therefore, grow in importance, not only as the means of providing that skilled labor, but as the wellspring of ideas that fuel the new growth.

SUSTAINABILITY OF GROWTH

Our review of the evidence suggests that the economic system is reacting—in some cases dramatically—to changes in input flows and prices. The growth process is being transformed. Where this transformation will ultimately lead cannot be stated with any certainty.

Yet there are reasons to suspect that the rate of economic growth, as well as the type of economic growth, will be affected by this transformation. The Jorgenson evidence [1981] that technological change in many industries is biased toward the use of energy, coupled with the Ayers and Miller model of growth [1980], which incorporates the second law of thermodynamics, provides a plausible basis for the belief that economic

---

[4]Daniel Bell. *The Coming of the Post-Industrial Society: A Venture in Social Forecasting* (New York: Basic Books, 1973).

[5]Marc Porat. *The Information Economy: Definition and Measurement* (Washington, D.C.: U.S. Department of Commerce, Office of Telecommunications, 1977).

[6]For a more detailed explanation, see Robert D. Hamrin. *Managing Growth in the 1980s: Toward a New Economics* (New York: Praeger, 1980).

growth must eventually diminish to zero. The interesting question is whether the enhanced levels of welfare received from economic growth in the interim are sustainable or whether current growth is, in some sense, at the expense of future generations (Figure 21.1).

Four Possible Outcomes

Suppose we were to map out possible future trends in the long-term welfare of the average citizen. Using a time scale measured in centuries on the horizontal axis (Figure 21.1) four basic future trends emerge, labeled *A, B, C,* and *D,* with t_0 representing the present. *D* portrays sustainable exponential growth in which the future becomes a simple repetition of the past. Our concern for intergenerational justice would lead us to favor current generations, since they would be the poorest. There would be no need to worry about future generations. We have seen, however, that there are reasons for being skeptical about the likelihood of this scenario.

The second scenario (*C*) envisions slowly diminished growth culminating in a steady state where growth diminishes to zero. The welfare of each future generation is at least as well off as all previous generations. Since the level of welfare of each generation is sustainable, there is no reason to artificially constrain growth. To do so would injure all subsequent generations. This is the scenario supported by Kahn.

The third scenario (*B*) is similar in that it envisions initial growth followed by a

FIGURE 21.1   Possible Alternative Futures

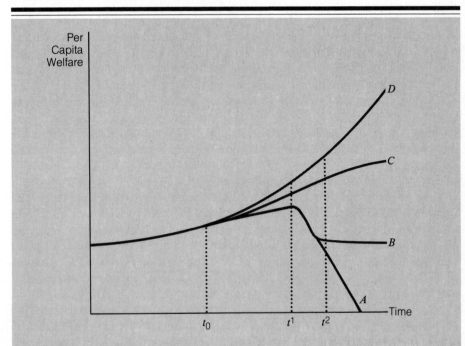

steady state, but there is also an important difference—those generations between t^1 and t^2 are worse off than the generations preceding them. This is the type of scenario anticipated by Meadows and his colleagues. Neither growth nor welfare levels are sustainable at current levels and the sustainability criterion would call for an immediate transition to sustainable welfare levels.

The final scenario (*A*) denies the existence of sustainable per-capita welfare levels, suggesting that the only possible sustainable level is zero. All consumption by the current generation serves simply to hasten the end of civilization.

These scenarios suggest that three dimensions of the sustainability issue are important: (1) the existence of a positive sustainable level of welfare; (2) the magnitude of the ultimate sustainable level of welfare *vis a vis* current welfare levels; and (3) the sensitivity of the future level of welfare to actions by previous generations. The first dimension is important because if positive sustainable levels of welfare are possible, scenario *A*, which in some ways is the most philosophically difficult, is ruled out. The second is important because, if the ultimately sustainable welfare level is higher than current level, radical surgery to cut current living standards is not necessry. The final dimension raises the issue of whether the ultimate sustainable level of welfare can be increased or reduced by the actions of current generations. If so, the sustainability criterion would suggest taking these impacts into account, lest future generations be unnecessarily impoverished by involuntary wealth transfers to previous generations.

The first dimension is relatively easy to dispense with. The existence of positive sustainable welfare levels is guaranteed by the existence of renewable resources, particularly solar energy, as well as by nature's ability to assimilate a certain amount of waste. Therefore we can rule out scenario *A*.

No one knows exactly what level of economic activity can ultimately be sustained, but the prediction of early societal collapse certainly seems grossly exaggerated. Since growth is slowing as a natural process, and the most serious excesses of unregulated growth (such as pollution) are being mitigated, and there is an abundance of solar energy, scenario *C* seems likely, though no one can completely rule out *B*.

Current generations can affect the sustainable welfare levels of future generations both positively and negatively. We could use our resources to accumulate a capital stock, providing future generations with shelter, productivity, and transportation, but our decaying inner cities illustrate that machines and buildings do not last forever. Even capital that physically stands the test of time may become economically obsolete by being ill-suited to the needs of subsequent generations.

Our most lasting contribution to future generations would probably come from what economists call human capital—investments in people. Though the people who receive education and training are mortal, the ideas they bring forth are not. Knowledge endures.

We could also reduce future welfare levels, however. The combustion of fossil fuels could modify the climate to the detriment of future agriculture. Current chlorofluorocarbon emissions might, by depleting the atmosphere's ozone, raise the incidence of skin cancer. The storage of radioactive wastes could increase the likelihood of genetic damage in the future. The reduction of genetic diversity in the stock of plants and animals could well reduce the possibilities for future crossbreeding. Even though high levels of sustainable welfare may be feasible, current actions may prevent the achievement of the maximum possible levels.

Suppose that high levels of sustainable welfare are feasible. Would our economic system automatically choose a growth path that produces sustainable welfare levels, or could it choose one that improverishes future generations?

We shall attack this general question by answering two specific ones. Would an *efficient* market always yield sustainable growth paths? Would an *actual* market (whether or not it is efficient) always yield sustainable growth paths?

Efficiency and Sustainability

From Chapter 6 it is easy to see that even an efficient market does not always yield sustainable welfare levels. Imagine a simple economy where the only activity is the extraction and consumption of a single depletable resource. Even when the population is constant and the demand curves are stable, the efficient quantity profiles show declining consumption over time. In this hypothetical world, later generations would be unambiguously worse off. The existence of a renewable resource would not solve the problem; even in this more congenial set of circumstances, the quantity profile of the depletable resource would still involve declining consumption until the backstop was reached.

Dasgupta and Heal [1979] find a similar result for a slightly more realistic model. They assume an economy where a single consumption good is produced (using a Cobb-Douglas type of production function) by combining capital with a depletable resource. The finite supply of the depletable resource can be used to produce capital as well as be used in combination with capital to produce the consumption good. The more capital produced, the higher is the marginal product of the remaining depletable resource.

They prove that a sustainable constant consumption level exists in this model. The rising capital stock (implying a rising marginal product for the depletable resource) would compensate for the declining availability of the depletable resource. They also prove, however, that the use of any positive discount rate would necessarily result in declining efficient consumption levels. Efficiency in this more realistic case violates sustainability as well.

What would have to be done to achieve a sustainable growth path in this kind of model? Hartwick [1977] shows that the achievement of a constant per capital consumption path results when all scarcity rent is invested in capital. None of it should be consumed by current generations. With a positive discount rate some of the scarcity rent is consumed, violating the Hartwick rule. Though this is too simple a model to be used to draw precise policy conclusions, it does suggest one path for approaching sustainability – using the scarcity rent from the sale of depletable resources to compensate future generations. We shall explore this idea later in this chapter.

We must be careful to distinguish between what has been said and what has not been said. We have shown that efficient markets would not always achieve sustainable growth paths. This does not mean that they wouldn't normally result in sustainable allocations! Indeed, the historical record suggests that the incompatibility of the efficiency criterion and the sustainability criterion is very much the exception, not the rule. Capital accumulation and technological progress have expanded the ways in which resources could be used and have increased subsequent welfare levels in spite of a declining resource base. Nonetheless, the two criteria are not inevitably compatible.

As we look to the future, automatically achieving a balance between positive and negative transfers to future generations is not a certainty. The scale of activity has increased so substantially that negative transfers such as climate modification are on the rise. Furthermore, these problems take so long to unfold that the use of a positive discount rate diminishes their importance in current decisions and makes any guarantee of sustainability less likely.

Some have responded to this problem by suggesting that a discount rate of zero be used in defining the efficient allocation. This is a very crude and unsatisfactory way of dealing with the imperfections inherent in discounting. The use of a zero discount rate would be equivalent to a comparison of undiscounted benefits and costs. Yet, because of the return on capital, benefits now *are* worth more than benefits later, since current returns can be invested for even larger future gains. Ignoring this fact could lead to substantially smaller benefits being received for all generations taken as a whole.

Perhaps the most serious problem with the government using a zero discount rate is its distortion in the role of the public and private sectors in allocating resources. The use of a positive rate requires the public sector to consider the opportunity cost of capital in the private sector. If the government were to use a zero discount rate, it would undertake more investment projects than would be justified, since the apparent cost of capital would be so low. The public sector would play a much larger role than it does now. As we have seen in our examination of energy policy, that does not automatically mean increased benefits for future generations.

The present-value criterion should be seen as a useful, if incomplete, part of economic analysis. Rather than eliminating the discount rate, the present-value criterion should be complemented by other criteria, such as sustainability. These criteria can serve as a constraint in making final choices. For example, we might choose to maximize present value subject to the constraint that future generations are not made worse off.

This formulation of the intergenerational justice problem relies heavily on some sort of compensation principle to restore the balance between present and future generations in those cases where this constraint might otherwise be violated. If a particular project being considered maximizes the present value, but confers some unacceptably low or negative net benefits on future generations, then some of the current gains could be set aside as a trust fund to compensate for the negative net benefits. This fund would earn interest until it was needed and would serve to balance the distribution of the net benefits among generations without undermining the inherent desirability of the project. A variant of this approach is currently being used for toxic-substance control. Agents are required to post a bond to compensate victims for any damage which might subsequently occur.

Compensation paid future generations does not necessarily have to be monetary; it could be in the form of spending more on researching better ways to use renewable resources or on education. Whatever its form, the compensation mechanism provides a way of sharing maximum net benefits among generations without resorting to a policy that wastes net benefits in a misguided search for intergenerational fairness.

Market Allocations

How about actual market allocations? When inefficiencies occur, do they tend to exacerbate or to mitigate the occasional tendency for efficient allocations to lead to unsustainable consumption paths? It depends on the source of the inefficiency. The existence of common-property resources makes the tendency toward unsustainable allocations worse. Common-property resources are overexploited by current generations. As we saw with fisheries, extinction of species could occur even when extinction would violate both the efficiency and sustainability criteria.

The general conclusion that markets exacerbate the problem of unsustainability, however, would not be correct. For example, the existence of an oil cartel holding up prices serves to retard demand and conserve more for future generations than would otherwise be the case.

Markets can sometimes provide a safety valve to ensure sustainability when the supply of a renewable resource is threatened. Fish farming is one example where declining supplies of a renewable resource trigger the availability of an alternative renewable substitute. Even when the government intervenes detrimentally in a way that benefits current generations at the expense of future generations, as it did with natural gas, the market can limit the damage. The market for solar energy still exists as a substitute for natural gas, so the effect of the government regulation was to make the transition significantly less smooth than it might have been, rather than preventing the transition.

The notion that left to their own devices markets would automatically provide for the future is overstated. Yet, they have done a rather good job of providing for generations in the past. When market (or even government) allocations threaten future generations, procedures exist to identify those circumstances, and institutions can be developed or modified to restore intergenerational harmony.

SUMMARY

In this chapter we have examined how a market-driven growth process constrained by public policy could be expected to react to the existence of limits on inputs.

There are two main engines of growth—increases in inputs and technological progress. Historically, both were important. In the future some factors of production, such as labor, will not increase as rapidly as they have in the past. The effect of this decline on growth depends on the interplay among the law of diminishing marginal productivity, substitution possibilities, and technological progress. The law of diminishing marginal productivity suggests slower growth rates, while technological progress and the availability of substitution possibilities counteract this drag. One view suggests that there are limits to technological progress imposed by the second law of thermodynamics, implying that the growth process must culminate in a steady or stationary state where growth diminishes to zero.

An examination of evidence suggests the impacts of these limits on growth are not currently large for the economy as a whole, although certain industries have been hit quite hard. Environmental policy has caused only a small rise in the rate of inflation and a mild reduction in growth. Environmental policy has apparently contributed more jobs than it has cost.

The situation is similar for energy. Though rather large increases in energy prices have occurred, the portion of the slowdown in economic growth during the 1970s attributed to these increases is not large. Some diminution of growth has certainly occurred, but it seems premature to suggest that rising energy prices have already forced a transition to a period of substantially lower growth rates.

This is not to say, however, that the economy is not being transformed. It is. Two particularly important aspects of this transformation are the decline in population growth and the rise in importance of information as a driving economic force. Both aspects tend to reduce the degree that physical limits constrain economic growth and increase the degree to which current welfare levels are sustainable.

The welfare levels achieved from continued growth in the near future appear to be sustainable. Welfare levels from market-driven growth on most occasions are sustainable, but not always. Even efficient markets do not always ensure a growth path that satisfies the sustainability criterion. Thus while the market can be relied upon to a substantial extent, the choices made by the market cannot go unmonitored. While the maximization of the present value of net benefits guarantees that sufficient compensation *could* be paid to future generations to make them as well off as current generations, there is no guarantee that this compensation *would* be paid. Some adjustments of market choices, such as for fisheries and pollution control, may be necessary.

FURTHER READING

Berndt, Ernst R., and Barry C. Field, eds. *Modeling and Measuring Natural Resource Substitution* (Cambridge, Mass.: The MIT Press, 1981). A highly technical but insightful collection of twelve essays on the state of the art in measuring factor substitution and technical change.

Cleveland, Harlan, ed. *The Management of Sustainable Growth* (New York: Pergamon Press, 1981) and Coomer, James C., ed. *Quest for a Sustainable Society* (New York: Pergamon Press, 1981). The two volumes contain a wide ranging multidisciplinary series of essays coming out of the third in a series of five biennial conferences dedicated to a rethinking of growth policy.

Hamrin, Robert D. *Managing Growth in the 1980s: Toward a New Economics* (New York: Praeger Publishers, 1980). Hamrin suggests that the traditional sources of economic growth can no longer support growth. He suggests new actions and policies shaped by a selective growth ethic.

Peskin, Henry M., Paul R. Portney, and Allen Kneese. *Environmental Regulation and the U.S. Economy* (Baltimore: Johns Hopkins University Press for Resources for the Future, 1981). Six essays on the effect of environmental regulations on the economy combined with an excellent introduction to the issues and summary of the implications of the evidence presented.

ADDITIONAL REFERENCES

Ayers, R.U., and S.M. Miller. "The Role of Technological Change," *Journal of Environmental Economics and Management,* Vol. 7 (December, 1980): 353–371.

Berndt, Ernst R. "Energy Price Increases and the Productivity Slowdown in United States Manufacturing," a paper presented at the Federal Reserve Bank of Boston Conference on Productivity (June 1980).

Berndt, E.R., and D. Wood. "Technology, Prices, and the Derived Demand for Energy," *Review of Economics and Statistics,* Vol. 57 (August, 1975): 259–268.

Berndt, Ernst R., and David O. Wood. "Energy Price Shocks and Productivity Growth: A Survey" an essay to be included in a Festschrift in honor of Morris A. Adelman (forthcoming).

Brown, Gardiner, Jr., and Barry Field. "The Adequacy of Measures for Signalling the Scarcity of Natural Resources," in *Scarcity and Growth Considered,* V. Kerry Smith, ed. (Baltimore: Johns Hopkins University Press, 1979).

Christainsen, Gregory B., and Robert H. Haveman. "The Contribution of Environmental Regulations to the Slowdown in Productivity Growth," *Journal of Environmental Economics and Management,* Vol. 8 (December 1981): 381–390.

Council on Environmental Quality and Department of State, *The Global 2000 Report to the President of the U.S.: Entering the 21st Century Vol. 1: The Summary Report* (New York: Pergamon Press, 1980).

Dasgupta, P.S., and G. M. Heal. *Economic Theory and Exhaustible Resources* (Cambridge, England: Cambridge University Press, 1979): 299.

Data Resources Inc. "The Macroeconomic Impact of Federal Pollution Control Programs, 1978 Assessment" submitted to the Environmental Protection Agency and the Council on Environmental Quality (Washington, D.C., January 29, 1979).

Dennison, Edward, *Accounting for United States Economic Growth, 1929–1969* (Washington, D.C.: The Brookings Institution, 1974).

Hartwick, J. M. "Intergenerational Equity and the Investing of Rents from Exhaustible Resources," *American Economic Review,* Vol. 67 (December, 1977): 972–974.

Haveman, Robert H. "The Results and the Significance of the Employment Studies" in Organization for Economic Co-operation and Development, *Employment and Environment* (Paris: Organization for Economic Cooperation and Development, 1978): 48–53.

Hirsh, Fred. *Social Limits to Growth* (Cambridge, Mass.: Harvard University Press, 1976).

Hudson, Edward A., and Dale W. Jorgenson. "Energy Policy and U.S. Economic Growth," *The American Review,* Vol. 68 (May, 1978): 118–123.

Hueckel, Glenn, "A Historical Approach to Future Economic Growth," *Science,* Vol. 191 (14 March 1975): 925–31.

Humphrey, David B., and J. R. Moroney. "Substitution Among Capital, Labor, and Natural Resource Products in American Manufacturing," *Journal of Political Economy* 83 (February 1975): 57–82.

Jorgenson, Dale W., "Energy and the Future U.S. Economy," *The Wharton Magazine,* Vol. 3 (Summer, 1979): 15–21.

Jorgenson, D. W., "Energy Prices and Productivity Growth," *Scandinavian Journal of Economics,* Vol 83 (1981): 165–179.

Lindert, Peter. *Fertility and Scarcity in America* (Princeton: Princeton University Press, 1978).

Ridker, Ronald G., and William D. Watson. *To Choose a Future: Resource and Environmental Consequences of Alternative Growth Paths* (Baltimore: Johns Hopkins University Press for Resources for the Future, 1980).

Uri, Noel D. and Saad A. Hassanein, "Energy Prices, Labour Productivity, and Causality: An Empirical Examination," *Energy Economics* Vol. 4 (April 1982): 98–104.

DISCUSSION QUESTIONS

1. "Every molecule of a nonrenewable resource used today precludes its use by future generations. Therefore, the only morally defensible policy for any generation is to use only renewable resources." Discuss.

2. "Future generations can cast neither votes in current elections nor dollars in current market decisions. Therefore, it should not come as a surprise to anyone that the interests of future generations are ignored in a market economy." Discuss.

CHAPTER TWENTY-TWO

Further Economic Growth?

> *It must have been seen, more or less distinctly by political economists, that the increase in wealth is not boundless; that at the end of what they term the progressive state lies the stationary state, that all progress in wealth is but a postponement of this, and that each step in advance is an approach to it.*
> JOHN STUART MILL, *Principles of Political Economy* (1857)

INTRODUCTION

In the last chapter it was suggested that economic growth for the world economic system as a whole is likely to slow down in the future, and to a limited extent, the slowdown has already begun. There are several sources of this decline. Population growth has slowed considerably. Rising costs of extracting minerals, increasing energy prices, and rising amounts of resources being commited to pollution control all exert a drag on growth. If the characterization of the growth process by Ayers and Miller is accurate, the economy would in the long run move to a steady state.

Taken as a whole, these arguments suggest that growth in the future is likely to be of a different magnitude and a different character than that of the past. This reformed growth doesn't pose the same kind or same intensity of problems envisioned in *The Limits to Growth*. It is likely that the increased welfare levels brought about by growth could, with appropriate institutional safeguards, be sustained and could satisfy the fairness criterion for current and future generations.

There remains the question, however, of whether or not an immediate forced transition to a steady state might be preferable, even if it is not necessary. In this chapter we shall examine the issues surrounding the desirability of a forced immediate transition to a steady state. In particular we will study the modifications to our existing social institutions needed to ensure this transition, as well as the consequences of instituting these modifications. Then we shall examine the desirability of the alternative strategy—

continued economic growth. Particular attention shall be paid to the concern raised by Kahn and his associates that an immediate transition to the steady state is unjust because it most adversely affects the poor.

FORCED TRANSITION

The most concrete proposals for a forced transition to the steady state come from an economist by the name of Herman Daly [1977]. Daly is very sympathetic with the goal of a rapid transition to the steady state and has spent a good deal of his professional life looking into the best way to achieve that objective. We will focus on his proposals in examining how an economy might be forced to the steady state more rapidly than would normally be the case.

Defining the Target

Daly begins by attempting to define what is meant by a steady state and how we know when it is achieved. His definition is couched in physical, rather than value, terms. For Daly the *steady state economy* is characterized by constant stocks of people and physical wealth maintained at some chosen, desirable level by a low rate of throughput. This throughput—involving flows of resources and energy—provides direct consumption benefits (such as food and shelter) and investment, insofar as necessary to counteract depreciation of the capital stock.

Conceiving of the steady state in physical rather than value terms is significant because it forms an important difference between Daly and others who see the steady state as simply the absence of any economic growth. Daly recognizes that some growth would and should occur even in the steady state in spite of a constant stock of people and physical wealth. For example, as society learns more efficient ways to use energy, the value derived from the flow of energy may increase, even when the flow itself doesn't. Due to technological progress, the value of the services received can grow, even if the physical stocks and flows are unchanging. *The steady state and zero economic growth are not necessarily the same thing.*

Institutional Structure

Daly sees three institutional modifications as necessary for the rapid attainment of the steady state:

1. an institution for stabilizing population,
2. an institution for stabilizing the stock of physical wealth and throughput, and
3. an institution to ensure that the stocks and flows are allocated fairly among the population.

Population Stabilization. According to the Daly proposals, population would be stabilized over the long run using an idea first put forth by Kenneth Boulding [1964]. In this scheme each individual would be given the inalienable right to produce one (and only one!) child. Because this scheme over a generation allows each member of the current population to replace himself or herself, births would necessarily equal deaths and population stability would be achieved.

This scheme would award each person a certificate entitling him or her to have one child. Couples could pool their certificates to have two. Every time a child was born a certificate would be surrendered. Failure to produce a certificate would cause the child to be put up for adoption.

These certificates would be fully transferable. Families who placed a particularly high value on children could purchase extra certificates, while those who viewed parenting with something less than enthusiasm could sell certificates. As one of its virtues, this system would ensure that the overall objective of population stability would be achieved, but no family would be required to maintain a particular family size. Though every couple would be guaranteed the right to have two children, they could choose to have fewer or more than two.

Stock and Throughput Stabilization. Daly suggests that *throughput* (the flow of resources) should be held at some minimum level using depletion quotas for all depletable resources. These quotas would define the amount of the resource which could be extracted and used. Any extraction and use in excess of this quota would be illegal.

The size of these quotas would be determined by bureaucrats, but according to Daly, these bureaucrats would follow a specific rule. The quotas would be set at a level sufficiently stringent that the price of the resource in question would equal the price of the closest renewable substitute. When no close renewable substitute was available, the bureaucrats would be empowered to decide the most ethical level. Because the quotas would be auctioned off by the government, the government would extract all of the scarcity rent associated with the depletable resources. The quota prices would equal the scarcity rent of the covered resources.

Daly envisions no separate means of controlling pollution. Arguing that most pollution is caused by the excessive use of resources, he sees the control of resource use as a more direct approach to the problem.

Ensuring Distributional Fairness. Daly also sees a need to override the normal channels for distributing income in the steady-state economy. In a growth economy, tensions between the rich and poor can be ameliorated by the opportunities for social and economic mobility that a growth economy provides. In a steady-state economy those opportunities are diminished as the number of new jobs created is smaller.

To alleviate these tensions Daly proposes the establishment of a maximum- and minimum-income level, as well as a maximum limit on wealth. The minimum-income level would be financed in part by progressive taxes with 100 percent marginal rates above the maximum income and wealth limits. Since these 100 percent tax rates would presumably yield very little revenue (the incentive to earn more having been eliminated), most of the revenue would come from the sale of depletion quotas and from lower tax rates on income levels between the minimum and maximum.

A Critical Appraisal

The Daly arguments provide an excellent example of how a good idea can be misapplied. The use of transferable permits to control pollution has been a worthwhile reform, but to use this same notion to control all resources, including births, carries the concept well beyond its useful domain.

There are important distinctions to be drawn among these possible applications. Because there is no natural market force limiting pollution, some countervailing government power is necessary. Since government intervention is essential, the permit approach is a relatively flexible way to impose that power. In contrast, natural market forces foster the transition to renewable resources and cause depletable resource prices to rise. While there are observable weaknesses in this process, these are selective and require a selective response. To respond with quotas on all depletable resources is to unleash a bureaucratic nightmare. While this extreme respose might be justified in a crisis situation (resource rationing has been used during periods of war), it seems like an overreaction to those deficiencies which currently exist.

The Daly system would be expensive to implement. Large bureaucratic staffs would be needed to define the quotas, run the auctions, and ensure compliance. In an age where public sentiment seems to be for decreasing rather than increasing bureaucracy, this proposal would buck the trend without good reason.

This quota system would also have detrimental effects on the incentive to explore for new sources of minerals and energy. The existence of scarcity rent is a powerful incentive to find new sources of these substances. By appropriating all of this scarcity rent for the government, Daly is designing a system which removes this incentive.

The incentive to find cheaper ways to extract and use resources would also be destroyed. Whenever a new breakthrough occurred lowering costs, the Daly system would respond by lowering the quota in order to keep the price from falling. All of the profit to be gained from this breakthrough would be appropriated by the government, and the incentive for innovation would be undermined.

In summary, a universal quota system for depletable and renewable resources, in addition to being excessively expensive and bureaucratically cumbersome, holds the potential to disrupt a smoothly operating institutional structure. It is not only unnecessary; it is counterproductive.

Since they are also administratively cumbersome and unnecessary, the same arguments can be levied against child certificates. In addition, child certificates raise moral questions. For example, this system tends to preserve the existing racial status quo. To minority roups with above-average birth rates and below-average incomes, this looks like a policy to limit their proportion in the population. Even though that is clearly not the intended result, the suspicions raised create unnecessary tensions.

All of these institutional modifications impose heavy costs in the form of greater bureaucratic control. They also impose opportunity costs by denying the members of the population the fruits that growth could bring. How large are these fruits? Has growth really made the average person better off? Would the lowest income members of the United States and the world fare better with economic growth or without it?

MEASURING GROWTH BENEFITS

These are difficult questions to answer but we must start with what we mean by growth. Much of the disenchantment with growth can be traced to the way that growth is measured. It is not so much that all growth is bad, but rather that increases in conventional indicators of growth are not always good. Some of the enthusiasm for zero economic growth stems from the fact that economic growth, as currently measured, can be shown to have several undesirable characteristics. This raises the question of whether or not appropriately measured economic growth is desirable.

Conventional Measures

The most desirable measure would be one in which any increase would mean that we, as a nation or as a world, were better off and any decrease would mean that we were worse off. Such a measure is called a *welfare measure* and no conventional existing measure is designed to be a welfare measure.

What we currently have are *output measures,* which attempt to indicate how many goods and services have been produced, not how well off we are. Measuring ouput sounds fairly simple, but in fact it isn't. The measure of economic growth with which most are familiar is based upon the GNP, or gross national product. This number represents the sum of the outputs of goods and services in any year produced by the economy. Prices are used to weigh the importance of these goods and services in GNP. Conceptually, this is accomplished by adding up the value added by each sector of the production process until the product is sold.

Why weight by prices? Some means of comparing the value of extremely dissimilar commodities is needed. Prices provide one readily available system of weights that takes into account the value of those commodities to consumers. From early chapters we know that prices should reflect both the marginal benefit to the consumer and the marginal cost to the producer.

GNP is not a measure of welfare and is not meant to be one. One limitation of this indicator as a measure of welfare is that it includes the value of new machines that are replacing worn out ones rather than increasing the size of the capital stock. To compensate for the fact that some investment merely replaces old machines and does not add to the size of capital stock, a new concept known as net national product (NNP) was introduced. *NNP* is defined as the gross national product minus depreciation.

NNP and GNP share the deficiency that they are both influenced by inflation. If the flow of all goods and services were to remain the same while prices doubled, both NNP and GNP would also double. Since neither welfare nor output would have increased, an accurate indicator should reflect that fact.

To resolve this problem, national-income accountants present data on *constant-dollar GNP* and *constant-dollar NNP*. These numbers are derived by "cleansing" the actual GNP and NNP data to take out the effects of price rises. Conceptually, this is accomplished by defining a market basket of goods that stays the same over time. Each year this same basket is repriced. If the cost of the goods in the basket went up 10 percent, then because the quantities are held constant, we know that prices went up by 10 percent. This information is used to remove the effects of prices on the indicators; remaining increases should be due to an increased production of goods and services.

This correction doesn't solve all problems. For one thing not all components of GNP contribute equally to welfare. Probably the closest component we could use in the existing system of accounts would be *consumption,* the amount of goods and services consumed by households. It leaves out government expenditures, investments, exports, and imports.

The final correction which could easily be made to the existing accounts would involve dividing real consumption by the population to get *real consumption per capita.* This correction allows us to differentiate between rises in output needed to maintain the standard of living for an increasing population and rises indicating more goods and services consumed by the average member of that population.

Real consumption per capita is about as close as we can get to a welfare-oriented output measure using readily available data. Yet it is a far cry from being an ideal welfare indicator.

An Alternative Welfare Measure

William Nordhaus and James Tobin [1972] have attempted to adjust real consumption per capita figures to come up with a measure that is closer to being a welfare measure. Their first adjustment involves an attempt to account for the amount of welfare-reducing environmental damage being inflicted by pollution. Reasoning that part of the increased wages of urban workers represents compensation for having been exposed to the higher pollution concentrations, they used a portion of the income differential between urban and rural families as their measure of the monetary value of the damage caused. This estimate is then subtracted from the real consumption data.

They then adjust the data to treat consumer durables in a different way. In conventional accounts, consumer durables are incorporated by adding in their full cost at the time of purchase, in spite of the fact that services from that durable good are received throughout its useful life. Nordhaus and Tobin subtract these durable good *purchases* and add back in an estimate of the annual *services* they provide.

The final subtraction from the conventional accounts involves excluding consumer expenditures which do not seem to raise welfare. The major expenditures they excluded were the costs of commuting to and from work. These are necessary expenditures, but they do not themselves raise welfare.

Nordhaus and Tobin also correct for omissions that tend to bias the conventional accounts downward when interpreted in welfare terms. These include the value of leisure time and household production, neither of which is valued in conventional accounts. One benefit of growth is that productivity increases have resulted in a decline in the average workweek. This increased leisure is valued by Nordhaus and Tobin at the market wage rate that could have been earned if the time were spent working rather than in leisure activities. Household production involves the many services performed around the house by a spouse or relative. Because these are not market activities, unless there are hired servants, they do not enter the conventional accounts.

The problem with the conventional approach is nicely illustrated by an example. When a single person marries his or her housekeeper, GNP goes down, because an activity which was formerly a market activity is no longer that. Yet we presume, since marriage is a voluntary arrangement, that welfare was increased. The change in the indicator sends the wrong signal. Nordhaus and Tobin correct this conventional approach by adding in an imputed value for nonmarketed household production.

Their final correction involves adding into personal consumption expenditures a value for the government services provided. Traditionally, the government sector is treated separately in the GNP and its output is valued at cost. By including this measure, Nordhaus and Tobin are correcting two problems: (1) the omission of government services from the personal consumption expenditures; and (2) valuing these services as received rather than (in the case of government durables, such as roads) at the time of purchase.

After making all these adjustments, they arrive at an indicator they call the *Measure of Economic Welfare* (MEW). The MEW per capita rose by about 42 percent between 1929 and 1965. This increase was only about one-half of the 87.5 percent increase in real NNP per capita over the same period. According to Nordhaus and Tobin, real NNP per capita does overstate growth in economic well-being, but their estimates leave no doubt that they believe correctly measured economic well-being has increased substantially since 1929.

Others have attempted to make different adjustments, but the general conclusion that growth increases economic well-being seems to characterize all of these attempts. In particular, Usher [1980] has adjusted the conventional accounts to incorporate the value of increased life expectancy and finds that this adjustment boosts the growth rate of the adjusted measure above the conventional measure.

Another author performed a similar but somewhat more detailed set of calculations for the particular purpose of discovering whether there had been a decline in the benefits of growth over time [Zolotas, 1981]. The trends in his measure of welfare suggest that the additional benefits of growth are becoming smaller and smaller as growth continues. If this evidence is valid, the benefits of growth are positive but declining over time.

A Critical Appraisal

As the authors of the above studies would readily concede, there are reasons to be skeptical about the specific magnitude of these estimates. The procedures provide only crude approximations to those required to produce a true measure of welfare. Furthermore, these estimates leave a lot out.

The most glaring omission involves the failure to consider the distribution of the welfare among the population. The calculation of these trends in terms of average welfare obscures a great deal what may be happening in a society. Two societies may have the same per capita growth, but if the fruits of this growth are shared uniformly in one and unequally in the second, it seems overly simplistic to argue that the increase in welfare levels would be the same in the two countries. As Example 22.1 indicates, relative income levels seem to make a difference in how well-off people feel.

These measures also do not distinguish between increases in welfare which come at the expense of future generations and those which don't. It would be possible to construct a situation in which the MEW would increase but the source of the increase was a consumption binge that could only leave future generations impoverished. Though this is probably not an empirically significant flaw, it is a conceptual difficulty that could become important as circumstances change.

What can be said about the desirability of economic growth? Even given the crudity of the estimates we can see that economic growth has improved the welfare of the average American citizen and is likely to continue to do so in the near future, albeit at a slower rate. That realization, however, should not be translated into a naive belief in maximizing the growth in GNP or any other indicator in the conventional accounts. Some portion of the growth in GNP is desirable; other portions are not. It would be a mistake, however, to conclude that growth is undesirable because all increases in GNP do not make people better off. Some increases in GNP unambiguously reflect increases in the quality of life.

ECONOMIC GROWTH AND POVERTY

The evidence suggests that growth has improved the lot of the average citizen. To determine whether the poorest citizens also benefit, we must dig deeper into the nature of the growth process. We will consider separately two different groups of low-income persons because their fates are not necessarily the same: (1) the relatively small proportion of residents in the developed countries who are poor; and (2) the larger proportion of residents of the developing nations who are poor.

The Poor in Developed Nations

There are reasons for believing that growth can help the poor, though history suggests that these beneficial effects are not inevitable. It is generally believed that it is easier to transfer income when the amount to be shared is growing. The donors can give up some of their gains and still be better off, while in a no-growth situation any sharing must come from a reduction in the real income of the donor.

On the surface many observers believe that growth has not, in fact, lived up to its billing as a means of alleviating poverty. Lee Rainwater [1977], a Harvard sociologist, in his survey of the situation found:

EXAMPLE 22.1

Does Money Buy Happiness?

In a highly subjective but interesting study, economist Richard Easterlin [1973] collected data from 30 surveys conducted in 19 developed and less developed countries that analyze the relationship between happiness and income. In every one of these surveys, the respondents were asked to rate how happy they were feeling on a scale: "very happy," "mildly happy," "mildly unhappy," and "very unhappy." Information on respondent income levels was also collected.

In analyzing these data he found:

1. At a point in time a larger portion of high-income people are happier than low-income people—for all countries and all years.

2. The proportion of happy and unhappy in each group remained relatively constant over time in spite of generally rising incomes. For example, in the United States, roughly the same percentage of wealthy people and poor people said they were very happy in 1940 as in 1970.

The first finding suggests that higher income is positively correlated with happiness, while the second suggests that despite large increases in income, the percentage saying they were very happy did not increase. How are these apparently contradictory findings to be explained?

Easterlin explains them by suggesting that one of the components of happiness for people is their relative income. Thus, a person at the top of the heap in any particular country may be happier than he or she would be if that same income were earned in a richer country where lots of people earned that income. If this hypothesis is correct, it suggests that the average level of welfare in an economic system is an inadequate indicator of the total welfare in the society. The distribution of the fruits of economic growth makes a difference.

Source: Richard A. Easterlin, "Does Money Buy Happiness," *The Public Interest* (Winter, 1973): 3–10.

It seems well established that income and wealth inequality have not declined significantly over the past half century, and probably have not declined at all in the past quarter century. [p. 263]

This finding does not, as it might appear, imply that growth has not benefited the poor. In the first place many of the published studies do not take into account the significant transfers to the poor that are rendered in kind (such as food stamps and Medicaid) rather than in cash. Therefore, published income levels may understate the positive effects on the poor. In addition, stating the problem in this relative form ignores the increases in absolute welfare that all persons, including the poor, derive.

With respect to the first point, it seems abundantly clear that transfers to the poor have been significant recently and have made a difference. One way to demonstrate this is to examine what has happened during recent periods of growth to the number of persons in the United States living below the poverty threshold. This threshold, which is adjusted upward each year to hold purchasing power constant in the face of rising inflation, represents the minimum income necessary to provide a person or family with the basic necessities of life.

Table 22.1 shows what has happened to the proportion of persons living below the poverty threshold with and without transfers. *Market income* shows what would have happened to the proportion if no transfers had taken place. *Census income* shows these proportions after adjusting for the major cash transfer programs, and the *adjusted income* column shows the proportion after adjusting for both cash and in-kind transfers.

Several characteristics of these data should be noticed. First, the difference between the census income and adjusted income suggests that in-kind transfer programs have had a significant impact on the poor. Studies such as those accomplished by Rainwater which don't include these in-kind transfers tend to underestimate the positive impact experienced by the poor during a growth period.

The second conclusion is that the transfers have made the difference, not growth itself. The market-income column shows that economic growth, in the absence of transfers, would not have lifted many persons from below to above the poverty threshold. The linkage between growth and the poor depends more upon its affect on the willingness to transfer than on direct market effects.

TABLE 22.1 Persons Living below Absolute Income Thresholds, 1965–80 (Percentages)

	Census Income (percent)	Adjusted Income (percent)	Market Income (percent)
1965	15.6	12.1*	21.3
1968	12.8	10.1	18.2
1970	12.6	9.4	18.8
1972	11.9	6.2	19.2
1974	11.6	7.8	20.3
1976	11.8	6.7	21.0
1978	11.4	n.a.	20.2
1980	13.0	6.1	20.0
Percentage change	−16.7	−49.59	−6.10

Sources: S. Danziger and R. Plotnick, "The War on Income Poverty: Achievements and Failures," in *Welfare Reform in America,* ed. P. Sommers (Hingham, Mass.: Martinus Nijhoff, 1982). Adjusted income for 1968–74 is from T. Smeeding, "Measuring the Economic Welfare of Low-Income Households and the Antipoverty Effectiveness of Cash and Noncash Transfer Programs," (Ph.D. diss., Department of Economics, University of Wisconsin-Madison, 1975); and T. Smeeding, "The Antipoverty Effectiveness of In-Kind Transfers," *Journal of Human Resources,* 12 (1977): 360–78. Adjusted income for 1976 and 1980 are from Smeeding, "The Antipoverty Effect of In-Kind Transfers: A 'Good Idea' Gone Too Far?" *Policy Studies Journal,* forthcoming.

*Cited in Eugene Smolensky, "Poverty in the United States: Where Do We Stand?" *University of Wisconsin-Madison Institute for Research on Poverty Focus* 5 (Winter, 1981–82): Table 1, p. 3.

By focusing on relative incomes, Rainwater is seeking to discover whether the poor are becoming better off more rapidly than the rich. His answer is no. By using an absolute standard such as the poverty threshold, however, Table 22.1 focuses on the well-being of the poor *per se,* without considering the rich at all. That focus suggests that the poor were made better off in terms of meeting basic needs during the 15-year period studied, even if their rate of progress did not exceed that of the rich.

To lend concreteness to the arguments that the poor are better equipped during growth periods to meet basic needs, consider what has happened to one aspect of the quality of life for the poor—the desirability of their housing.

The U.S. Bureau of the Census maintains records on two indicators of poor housing quality. The *overcrowding* indicator measures the percentage of dwelling units having an average of 1.01 or more persons per room. The *substandard* indicator records the percentage of dwelling units that are considered dilapidated or are lacking complete plumbing facilities. As Table 22.2 indicates, the decline in these indicators has been strong and pervasive. The effects were felt in urban and rural areas and by both blacks and whites.

Although growth cannot be seen as a vehicle that inevitably creates equality of income among the rich and poor, the evidence shows that, in the United States at least, the quality of life for the poor has been improved by it. This improvement has come both from a general rising standard of living and the rise in transfers from the rich to the poor.

Table 22.2 Trends in the Condition of Urban and Rural Housing by Race of Occupant, 1950–80*

	ALL RACES		WHITE**		BLACK***	
	Urban	Rural	Urban	Rural	Urban	Rural
Overcrowded Housing (Percentage of units occupied by 1.01 or more persons per room)						
1950	13.3	20.6	–	–	–	–
1960	10.2	15.1	8.5	12.9	24.7	40.8
1970	7.6	10.1	7.0	7.5	18.1	30.1
1980	4.5	4.7	2.7	3.6	10.3	16.8
Substandard Housing (Percentage of dilapidated or lacking complete plumbing facilities)						
1950	22.0	62.4	15.9	56.2	57.2	92.7
1960	10.5	36.0	7.4	30.3	31.8	85.6
1970	3.4	16.9	3.5	16.5	8.5	62.3
1980	1.4	4.6	1.1	3.3	3.0	22.7

*Data refer to combined totals for owner-occupied and renters.

**In 1950, 1960, and 1980 includes only whites, in 1970 includes whites and other races except blacks.

***In 1950 and 1960 includes all non-whites; in 1970 and 1980 includes only blacks.

Sources: All information for the various years was drawn from the appropriate Census of Housing, General Housing Characteristics, United States Summary. This document is issued by the U.S. Department of Commerce, Bureau of Census.

The Poor in Less-Developed Nations

Identifying the effect of growth on the poor in less-developed countries (LDCs) is even more complicated, since we must consider the international repercussions of policies undertaken by the developed countries (DCs). These policies have effects on the *volume of trade,* the *composition of trade,* and the *terms of trade.*

To start our analysis it seems reasonable to suppose that environmental controls will be less stringent for some time in LDCs than they are in DCs. This supposition is supported by two observations about LDCs: (1) production levels are generally lower, so potential residuals generation is lower; and (2) income levels are lower, so there is a lower demand for environmental quality. The former observation suggests that there is a lower need for control, while the latter suggests there is a lower commitment to using funds for this purpose.

If this supposition is correct, it has several important implications. Costs of production will rise more rapidly in the developed world than in the developing world. This would tend to have a dampening effect on the LDC demand for DC products and a stimulating effect on the DC demand for LDC products, so activity levels should be boosted in developing countries as they respond to this increase in demand.

Multinational corporations could be expected to accelerate this movement, since they are the best equipped to take advantage of the shift in comparative advantage. They would find it profitable to locate new facilities in developing countries to take advantage of the lower cost.

The industries most likely to shift would be those for which pollution costs are an important part of total costs and for which transport costs are small enough that they could relocate without losing access to their markets. Some industries facing heavy pollution control costs, such as electric utilities, will not relocate because the cost of transporting electricity is so high. Even there, however, it is noteworthy that electricity imports to the United States from Canada's gigantic hydroelectric projects are growing. Thus, in terms of the composition of trade, developing countries should benefit from more stringent environmental controls in the developed countries.

The effect on the terms of trade is less clear. The terms of trade refer to the amount of imports that can be purchased with a given amount of exports. If the price of a country's exports is rising faster than the price of its imports, there is a favorable trend in that country's terms of trade. With increasingly favorable terms of trade, the international purchasing power of a country's exports increases.

During the late 1970s, the dominant factor in the terms of trade for most developing countries was the cost of energy. With the notable exception of a relatively few oil-rich nations, most developing countries import a great deal of energy. Because their demand is relatively price inelastic, their expenditures on imports have risen tremendously without similar compensating increases in receipts from the sale of exports. For those countries importing significant quantities of energy, this terms-of-trade effect dominates the composition effect, leaving them worse off. This drain on foreign exchange has pushed international debt levels to an all-time high, putting a severe strain on the international monetary system. It has also served to constrain import-driven growth in those developing countries.

The situation is reversed in many of the oil-exporting countries, which are commanding abnormally high prices for their oil. They have favorable terms of trade, though that has not totally insulated all of them from financial difficulties.[1]

One common stereotype of the difference between developed and less-developed countries involves their respective supplies of minerals. According to this stereotype, less-developed countries control most of the world's mineral resources, while the developed world creates the demand for them. If accurate, this view would suggest that rising mineral prices would eventually create favorable terms of trade for most developing countries.

Unfortunately, upon closer inspection this stereotype represents at best an oversimplification. While exports of minerals have increased from less developed to developed countries, not all developing countries share these higher export levels. A few have large reserves of petroleum or nonfuel minerals, but most don't. The benefits from increasing mineral prices tends to by-pass most LDCs.

The final effect to be considered involves the international volume of trade – the total amounts of goods and services crossing national borders. The volume of trade is determined mainly by the degree of specialization in the world economy, while the degree of specialization is determined by differences in local factor endowments, economies of scale, and transportation costs.

One of the main shifts in factor endowments that can be forecasted with some certainty is labor. The sharp decline in population growth in developed countries will create an even larger relative abundance of labor in the developing countries. If the educational systems in developing countries keep pace with population growth, developing nations could serve as a major future source of productive labor. The substitution of labor for energy could work to the advantage of developing countries and increase the volume of world trade.[2]

However, there is another factor working in the opposite direction – energy. Since transportation is an energy-intensive service, when relative energy prices rise, transportation costs rise as well. Rising transport costs could have a dampening effect on the volume of international trade if they were to become a significant proportion of total costs.

As transport costs rise, delivered prices also rise. The farther the buyer is from the point of production, the higher the delivered cost. In countries distant from the main manufacturing centers, local producers may be able to compete more effectively for the local market. Even when their costs of production are higher than those of the foreign producer, they may be able to undersell that foreign producer because of lower shipping cost. Rising transport costs could cause some increase in the domestic production of commodities formerly imported by the developing countries.

---

[1] In 1982, for example, Mexico – an oil-exporting country – nationalized its banks as one of the many fairly radical steps taken to gain control over its external debt.

[2] This is not to say that very high population growth rates in the developing countries are desirable because most of these countries already have an abundance of labor. High population-growth rates create redundant labor.

The evidence suggests that while growth is by no means a panacea for the problems of the developing world, it is probably better than no growth. However, it is a mistake to treat all developing nations homogeneously. Some have vast reserves of fuels and nonfuel minerals and will benefit as relative prices rise. Other nations, however, are not so fortunate. As importers they are adversely affected by energy and mineral price increases and the growth in demand by the rest of the world is inimical to their interests.

SUMMARY

In this chapter we have examined the concept known as steady state, as well as the consequences of forcing a more rapid transition to the steady state than would be achieved by a reformed growth approach. We began by defining the steady state as a situation in which constant stocks of people and physical wealth are maintained at some chosen desirable level by a low rate of throughput.

To examine how a rapid transition to this state could be initiated by the government we considered the proposals of the sympathetic economist, Herman Daly. He sees three institutional modifications as necessary: (1) a new mechanism to control the distribution of income and wealth; (2) a system of annual quotas to govern the rate of consumption of both depletable and renewable resources; and (3) a plan to control population.

The plan to control births involves transferable certificates conveying the right to have children. In the developed world at least, fertility rates are below replacement levels, so the plan seems unnecessary for those countries. In the developing countries, other less intrusive and less morally objectionable policies seem to be working. Therefore, such an extreme response seems unwarranted.

The depletion quotas would be administratively expensive and difficult to implement. If they were placed on all resources, the cost in time and effort would be prohibitive. If the government extracted all the scarcity rent from these resources by holding auctions for the right to extract them, the incentive to find new sources would diminish.

The institutional modifications suggested by Daly would be implemented at a very high cost. Whether this modification is worth it depends upon whether the alternative, reformed growth, is beneficial or detrimental, both to the average citizen and the poorest citizen of the world economy.

An examination of the conventional methods of measuring growth reveals that not all measured growth is desirable. Some activities recorded as increases in conventional measures of economic growth are desirable; some are not. The existing measures are not—and were not meant to be—welfare indicators. To treat them as if they were (as some people do in espousing that we maximize the growth rate in GNP or real consumption per capita) misses this essential point.

Some crude attempts have been made to assess whether or not growth has historically made people better off. Results of these studies suggest that because growth has ultimately generated more leisure, longer life expectancy, and more goods and services, it has been beneficial. These indicators do not, however, shed light on how these benefits have been distributed among the citizens.

Our examination of the evidence suggests that the naive notion that all of the world's people are automatically benefited by economic growth is overstated. Growth has benefited the poor in the developed countries, mainly through transfers from more well-off members of society, a source that most observers assume would be diminished by a rapid transition to the steady state.

The outlook for the developing world is at best mixed. There are natural tendencies in the reformed growth process for developing nations to experience relative, as well as absolute, gains in future economic growth. These tendencies, however, do not benefit all developing countries equally. Those importers of petroleum and nonfuel minerals will find their terms of trade deteriorating rather than improving.

Growth is not all things to all people. Yet, it seems clear that some continued economic growth is desirable. Even the Club of Rome, the group that sponsored *The Limits to Growth* study, seems to have backed off from its initial call for zero economic growth. In their sequel to *The Limits to Growth,* Mesarovic and Pestel [1974] call for reformed growth rather than zero economic growth. On this point, at least, opinions have converged.

FURTHER READING

Pirages, Dennis Clark, ed. *The Sustainable Society* (New York: Praeger Publishers, 1977). A multidisciplinary series of essays on the transition to a steady state.

Renshaw, Edward F. *The End of Progress: Adjusting to a No-Growth Economy* (North Scituate, Mass.: Duxbury Press, 1976). Argues that the economy is already adjusting to a steady state much more rapidly than previously believed even in the absence of any additional controls.

Walter, Ingo. *International Economics of Pollution* (Toronto: John Wiley & Sons, 1975). A comprehensive evaluation of the effects of environmental policy on international trade. Includes a chapter that discusses the secondary effects of stringent policies in developed countries on less-developed countries.

Usher, Dan. *The Measurement of Economic Growth* (New York: Columbia University Press, 1980). An attempt to assess systematically what should be accomplished by measures of economic growth. Recommends changes in the conventional accounts and shows how significant these are in Canada. Particularly good on incorporating changes in life expectancy.

ADDITIONAL REFERENCES

Brown, Lester R. *Building a Sustainable Society* (New York: W. W. Norton & Company, 1981).

Boulding, Kenneth E. *The Meaning of the Twentieth Century* (New York: Harper and Row, 1964).

Daly, Herman E. *Steady-State Economics* (San Francisco: W.H. Freeman and Company, 1977).

Mesarovic, Michaklo, and Edward Pestel. *Mankind at the Turning Point: The Second Report to the Club of Rome* (New York: The New American Library, 1974).

Nordhaus, William D., and James Tobin. "Is Growth Obsolete?" in National Bureau of Economic Research, *Economic Growth, Fiftieth Anniversary Colloquium,* Vol. 5 (New York: National Bureau of Economic Research, 1972): 4–17.

Rainwater, Lee. "Equity, Income Inequality, and the Steady State," in Dennis Clark Pirages, ed. *The Sustainable Society* (New York: Praeger Publishers, 1977): 262–273.

Weintraub, Andrew, et al. eds., *The Economic Growth Controversy* (New York: International Arts and Sciences Press, 1973).

Zolotas, Xenophon. *Economic Growth and Declining Social Welfare* (New York: New York University, 1981).

DISCUSSION QUESTIONS

1. "Economic growth has historically provided a valuable vehicle for raising the standard of living. Now that the standard of living is so high, however, further economic growth is unnecessary. When the undesirable side-effects are considered, it is probably counterproductive. Economic growth is a process that has outlived its usefulness." Discuss.

2. Discuss the mechanism favored by Daly to control population growth. What are its advantages and disadvantages? Would it be appropriate to implement this policy now in the United States? For those who believe that it would, what are the crucial reasons? For those who believe it isn't appropriate, are there any circumstances in any countries where it might be appropriate? Why or why not?

CHAPTER TWENTY-THREE

Visions of the Future Revisited

Mankind was destined to live on the edge of perpetual disaster.
We are mankind because we survive. We do it in a half-assed
way, but we do it.

PAUL ADAMSON, A FICTIONAL CHARACTER IN
JAMES A. MICHENER'S *Chesapeake* (1978)

We have now come full circle. We began our study with two lofty visions of the future. Following the overview, we examined the details of the various components of these visions — population, the management of depletable and renewable resources, pollution, and the growth process itself. During these inquiries a number of individual insights were gained. Now it is time to step back and to bring together those insights into a systematic assessment of the two visions.

ADDRESSING THE ISSUES

In Chapter 1 we posed a number of questions to serve as our focus for the overarching issue of growth in a finite environment. Those questions addressed three major issues: (1) How is the problem correctly conceptualized? (2) Can our economic and political institutions respond in a timely and democratic fashion to the challenges presented? (3) What is and what should be the likely future for economic growth? The next three portions of this section summarize the evidence uncovered.

Conceptualizing the Problem

At the beginning of this book we suggested that if the *Limits to Growth* team had correctly conceptualized the problem, theirs was the only conclusion that could be drawn. An exponential growth in demand coupled with a finite supply of resources implies that the resources must eventually be exhausted. If those resources are essential, society will collapse when the resources are exhausted.

We have seen that this is an excessively harsh characterization. The growth in the demand for resources is not insensitive to their scarcity. Though the rise in energy prices was triggered more by politics than by scarcity, it is possible to use higher energy prices as an example of how the economic system reacts.

The growth in demand following the increase in prices fell dramatically, with petroleum experiencing the largest reductions. In the United States, for example, total energy consumption in 1981 (73.8 quadrillion BTUs) was lower than it was in 1973 (74.6 quadrillion BTUs), despite increases in income and population. Petroleum consumption went from 34.8 quadrillion BTUs in 1973 to 32.0 quadrillion BTUs in 1981. Though some of this reduction was caused by sluggishness of the economy, price certainly played a major role.

Price is not the only factor which retards demand growth. Declines in population growth also play a significant role. Since the developed nations appropriate a disproportionate share of the world's resources, the dramatic declines in population growth in those countries should have a disproportionate effect on slowing the demand for resources.

There are also problems with the second portion of the model—characterizing the resource base as finite: (1) this characterization ignores the existence of a substantial renewable resource base that is not finite; (2) it focuses attention on the wrong issue; and (3) it supports ill-conceived attempts to measure the size of the resource base. We will consider each problem in turn.

In a very real sense the resource base is not finite. There are plentiful supplies of renewable resources including, significantly, energy. The normal reaction to increasing scarcity of depletable resources is to switch to renewable resources. That is clearly happening. The most dramatic examples can be found in the transition to solar energy in its various forms.

Labeling the resource base as finite is also misleading because it suggests that our concern should be "running out." In fact we shall never run out. There are millions of years of finite resources left at current consumption rates. Concern should be with the rising cost of extracting and using those resources rather than with the threat of exhausting them. The limits on our uses of these resources are not determined by their scarcity in the crust of the earth, but rather by what we would have to sacrifice to extract and process the ores. The work by Skinner and others suggests that we may not be willing to pay the price required to extract some of the lower-grade sources of those minerals.

Ignorance of this basic point has led to a number of ill-fated attempts to measure the size of this finite resource base. The timing of the societal collapse in the *Limits to Growth* forecast was quite sensitive to the techniques they used to forecast resource exhaustion. Conventional physical indicators, such as the static reserve index and the exponential reserve index, are excessively pessimistic because they fail to take into account possibilities for expanding current reserves. Historically, no forecast based on these techniques has stood the test of time. There is no reason to expect any similar forecast to do so in the future. They are convenient in that they can be readily calculated and easily interpreted, but they are also usually dead wrong.

There are, in fact, many ways in which current reserves can be expanded. These include finding new sources of conventional materials, as well as discovering new uses for unconventional materials, including what was previously considered waste. We can also stretch the useful life of these reserves by reducing the amount of materials needed to produce the products. A striking example is provided by the degree to which the size of a typical computer system needed to process a given amount of information has shrunk over time.

Not all errors in resource-base measurement have been committed by those having a tendency to understate the adequacy of the resource base. Errors in the other direction are committed by those who point to the abundance in the earth's crust and atmosphere of almost all substances on which we depend. While the existence of those substances may be supported by the evidence, there are good reasons for believing that the amounts we actually use will fall far short of the amounts available.

Although our ability to assess what is happening to cost is far from perfect, two things seem clear. Historically, there has been very little, if any, evidence of impending scarcity. Our ability to develop lower-cost technologies for processing resources dominated the necessity to extract lower-grade sources. As a result, in real terms, extraction costs have fallen, rather than risen over time. The most recent evidence suggests, however, that for a number of minerals a turning point has been reached in the last few years. For those resources evidence of scarcity – in the form of rising relative prices and increased exploration activity – has appeared.

Correct conceptualization of the cost problem suggests that both extremely pessimistic and extremely optimistic views are wrong. There are not impenetrable physical limits of resource availability, but neither is there an infinity of resources that could support continued economic growth at current rates forever. Plenty of resources are available if we are willing to pay the price, but that price is now rising. Transitions to renewable resources and less costly depletable resources have already begun.

Institutional Responses

One of the keys to understanding how society will cope with increasing resource scarcity lies in understanding how social institutions will react. Are market systems, with their emphasis on decentralized decision making, and democratic political systems, with their commitment to public participation and majority rule, equal to the challenge?

Our examination of the record seems to suggest that our economic and political systems have, on balance, done rather well. No fatal flaw is evident. Yet they are far from infallible and some rather glaring deficiencies have become evident.

On the positive side, markets have responded swiftly and automatically to deal with those resources experiencing higher prices. Demand has been reduced and substitution encouraged. Markets for recycling are growing and consumer habits are changing. No one has had to oversee these responses to make sure they occur. As long as property rights are well defined, the market system provides incentives for consumers and producers to respond to scarcity in a variety of useful ways. This characteristically rapid and smooth response illustrates none of the overshoot and collapse behavior anticipated by the *Limits to Growth* team.

As compelling as the evidence is for this point of view, it does not support the conclusion that, left to itself, the market would automatically choose a dynamically efficient or a sustainable path for the future. The most serious limitations of the market become evident in the manner in which it treats common-property resources, such as the fish we eat, the air we breathe, and the water we drink. Left to its own devices, a market will overexploit common-property resources, substantially lowering the net benefits received by future generations. Such overexploitation could, if serious enough, result in a violation of the sustainability criterion.

Even in this area of market weakness, the market provides some self-correction. The decline of common-property fish catches, for example, has led to the rise of private-property fish farming. The artificial scarcity created by imperfectly defined property rights gives rise to incentives for the development of a private-property substitute.

This capacity of the market for self-healing, while comforting, is not always an adequate response. In some cases there are cheaper ways of solving the problem. Preventative medicine is frequently superior to corrective surgery. In other cases, such as when our air is polluted, there are no good private substitutes available. To provide an adequate response, it is sometimes necessary to complement market decisions with political ones.

The need for government intervention is particularly acute in controlling pollution. Uncontrolled markets not only produce too much pollution, but they also tend to underprice commodities that contribute to pollution either when produced or consumed. Firms which unilaterally attempt to control their pollution run the risk of pricing themselves out of the market. The government is needed to ensure that firms which neglect environmental damage in their operating decisions do not thereby gain a competitive edge.

Significant progress has been made in reducing the amount of pollution, particularly air pollution. Recent regulatory innovations, such as the bubble and offset policies, represent major steps toward the development of a flexible but potent framework for controlling air pollution. By making it less costly to achieve environmental goals, these reforms have limited the potential for a backlash against the policy. They have brought perceived costs more in line with perceived benefits. On a smaller scale there are similar developments for water pollution.

It would be a great mistake, however, to assume that government intervention in resolving environmental problems has been uniformly benign. The acid-rain problem was almost certainly made worse by a policy structure that focused on local rather than regional pollution problems. The requiring of scrubbers for all new coal-fired electrical generating stations was done for purely political reasons and served to raise the cost of compliance unnecessarily.

One aspect of the policy process that does not seem to have been handled well is the speed with which improvement is sought. Public opinion polls have unambiguously shown that the general public supports environmental protection even when it raises costs and lowers employment. Policy makers have reacted to this resolve by writing very tough legislation designed to force rapid technological development.

Paradoxically, it has had the opposite effect. Unreasonably tough regulations are virtually impossible to enforce. Recognizing this, polluters have repeatedly sought and received delays in compliance. It has frequently been better, from the polluter's point of view, to spend resources to change the regulations than to comply with them. This would not have been the case with less stringent regulations, since the firms would have had no legally supportable grounds for delay.

Perhaps the most flagrant examples of counterproductive government intervention are to be found in treatment of energy and water resources. By imposing price ceilings on natural gas and oil, the government removed much of the normal resiliency of the economic system. With price controls the incentives for expanding the supply are reduced and the time profile of consumption is tilted toward the present. As was the case with natural gas, these controls can even cause biases that interfere with the transition to renewable resources. By holding water prices below the marginal cost of supply, water authorities have subsidized excess use. Resources which in a normal market would have been conserved for future generations are, with price controls, consumed by the current generation. When price controls are placed on normal market transactions, the overshoot syndrome anticipated by the *Limits to Growth* team can occur. The smooth transition to renewable resourcs that characterizes the normal market allocation is eliminated by price controls; shortages can arise.

Price controls are also playing a key role in the world hunger problem. By controlling the price of food, many developing countries have found that they have undervalued domestic agriculture. The long-run effect of these controls has been to increase their reliance on food imports at a time when foreign exchange to pay for those imports is becoming increasingly scarce. Whereas developed countries have gone substantially down the road to price decontrol, less developed countries have not yet been able to extricate themselves to a similar degree.

In summary, the record compiled by our economic and political institutions has been mixed. It seems clear the simple prescriptions such as "leave it to the market" or "more government intervention" simply do not bear up under a close scrutiny of the record. The relationship between the economic and political sectors has to be one of selective engagement, complemented in some areas by selective disengagement. Each problem has to be treated on a case-by-case basis. As we have seen in our examination of a variety of environmental and natural-resource problems, the efficiency and sustainability criteria allow such distinctions to be drawn and serve as a basis for policy reform.

The Growth Process

It seems likely that economic growth in the future will be slower and of a different character than that experienced in the past, even in the absence of direct controls on the growth process. There are several sources of growth drag. Government controls on pollution cause investment to be directed away from productivity-enhancing projects and toward projects that improve the environment. Since the former boosts measured growth and the latter does not, measured growth is likely to decline as a result.

The cost of energy is a second source of growth drag. Much of our high rate of growth was attained as labor was replaced with energy-using machines such as tractors, bulldozers, and trucks. As the decline in population growth leads to declines in the growth of the labor force, even more substitution of labor for energy will be necessary if historic growth rates are to be maintained. Yet with the high cost of energy, those substitutions can no longer be accomplished as cheaply as in the past when real energy prices were declining.

One characterization of the growth process based on the energy-using nature of technological progress suggests that growth will inevitably slow down until a steady state is reached. This ultimate steady state would be supported primarily by renewable resources and could offer future generations even higher welfare levels than that currently experienced. The transition to this steady state would be dictated by the entropy law, not by any intrusive direct controls on growth by the government.

This congenial view on the existence of a sustainable transition to the steady state must be tempered by the evidence that our social institutions will not always choose the sustainable path. The economic system provides both positive and negative transfers to future generations. While the positive transfers have normally exceeded the negative ones, nothing automatically guarantees that result. The likelihood for negative transfers in the form of climate modification and radioactive waste storage has increased with the scale of activity.

Markets may also tend to bias allocations toward the present when the resources being allocated are treated as common property. For these resources the natural market tendency to conserve is destroyed; even renewable resources which, with appropriate management, could provide a perpetual flow of services, become susceptible to exhaustion.

The existence of circumstances in which the sustainability criterion might be violated does not necessarily mean that the scale of operations has to be drastically reduced or growth stopped. It does mean that in circumstances when violations could occur the distribution of net benefits among generations has to be altered in such a way as to be more just. This can be accomplished by adopting means by which some of the net benefits can be transferred into the future to compensate for the costs they bear.

This approach is already being used in toxic-substance control policy where waste disposers are required to post bond to handle any financial liabilities that could arise in the future. The cost of posting bond will be borne by current users and will prevent a shifting of the burden to future generations. Other more imaginative transfers, such as spending more money on research and development, or on education, are also possible.

Physical limits do not seem to constrain the ability of the poor to break the bonds of poverty. In the United States, growth has improved the lot of the poor by moving large numbers of individuals above the poverty threshold and by substantially reducing the number of poor who live in substandard housing.

Developing countries should experience a boost in their growth rates as a result of the more stringent environmental controls being implemented in the developed countries. This boost will not have a large or immediate effect on most oil-importing developing countries, however. High energy prices have caused a serious deterioration in their terms of trade which, until they can be brought under control, will tend to reduce current consumption. Although higher prices will thereby save more oil for subsequent generations, those generations are to a large extent being enriched at the expense of the poor currently living in the oil-importing countries of the Third World.

UNRESOLVED ISSUES

There are still a number of issues for which the jury is out. The evidence is not yet strong enough for us to discern whether or how these issues will be resolved. Though there are others, these are of particular importance.

Global and Regional Pollutants

Global air pollutants are those entering, and remaining, in the atmosphere for sustained periods of time. They are not cleansed by gravity or rain. Their presence in the atmosphere alters its chemical composition. This altered chemistry can modify the climate, as may be the case with carbon dioxide, or it can attack the shield of ozone that protects us from harmful radiation from the sun, as may be the case with chlorofluorocarbons.

Regional pollutants are generally removed from the atmosphere, but usually not until they have traveled long distances. As a result, they share with global pollutants a propensity to cross political borders.

We have seen that solving pollution problems requires a creative partnership between the government and the economic system, and the success of this partnership depends on whether the boundaries of the problem match those of the government's jurisdiction. When the damage caused by pollution is confined to a relatively small geographic area around the source, the geographic jurisdiction of the government coincides with the boundaries of the problem. Both the sources of the pollution and those affected by it fall under a single government's purview. Achieving a balance between these conflicting interests has not always been easy, but it has been possible.

As the damage from pollution becomes more regional or global in scope, it becomes more difficult for governments to handle. Pollution that crosses state or national boundaries creates the potential for political externalities. A government concerned with balancing the benefits and costs within its jurisdiction may pay insufficient attention to costs and benefits received by those outside its borders.

Acid rain provides a good example of the problems created by a trans-boundary regional pollutant. Canada and the United States are currently grappling with this issue, as are a number of European countries.

Though the resolution of these disputes will prove much harder than resolving disputes that fall within the confines of a single nation's borders, the prerequisites for a successful resolution seem present. The parties to the dispute are readily identified. Though there are unresolved scientific issues, the research currently underway should help clear up these issues. Finally, and perhaps most important, the number of countries involved is not sufficiently large to preclude bilateral or multilateral negotiations.

The case for successful resolution of the global pollutant problem seems less clear. Virtually all nations are parties to the control of global pollutants, so multilateral negotiations seem hopelessly complex. One obvious solution, a world government, does not exist. The United Nations does not have sufficient power at this point to carry out a successful program of control. Whether any of our existing social institutions will prove equal to the challenge remains an open question.

Scientific Uncertainty

The ability of the policy process to reach decisions about the appropriate level of use of the environmental asset presumes the existence of solid scientific information. Only when the physical consequences of various courses of action are understood can the task of weighing the costs and benefits begin. In many significant areas we simply do not have solid scientific information on which to base decisions. Making a wrong choice based on incomplete or misleading information could prove very costly.

Reflecting back on the previous chapters, it is not difficult to identify a number of areas of environmental concern where better scientific evidence is needed. What is happening to stratospheric ozone and why? What are the dynamics of the greenhouse effect? To what extent will climate ultimately be modified? What are the exact causes of forest death in Germany? Can a simple, accurate, inexpensive test be developed to predict which new substances will prove toxic? Will fusion energy live up to the potential foreseen by its supporters?

Though far from complete, this list is sufficient to suggest that the reduction of uncertainty should play an important role in any long-range plan to assure harmony between the economic and ecological systems. Furthermore the scientific findings have to be presented in such a way that those in a position to implement policy can understand both the nature of the evidence and its policy implications. Although the increasing complexity of the problems at hand makes this a tall order, expanding the frontiers of knowledge and integrating the new findings into the policy process will be essential.

Siting Hazardous Waste Facilities

As the furor over the siting of waste disposal facilities has demonstrated, another key unresolved issue is how to site hazardous waste facilities. Simply put, the "not in my backyard, you don't!" philosophy is able to mobilize a substantial amount of local sentiment in opposition to facilities which from some larger geographic perspective may make good sense. Unfortunately virtually every potential site is in someone's backyard.

The solution to this issue may at first seem rather simple—don't produce hazardous wastes! Certainly we can do more in this regard and in the preceding chapters we have discussed some possible means of reducing the quantity of hazardous waste. Yet this view neglects the fact that many hazardous substances are involved in some valuable social functions (medical uses, for example) that would exact a very high cost if ceased. The conclusion that some hazardous substances will continue to be produced seems inescapable.

Better processes for identifying suitable sites and for securing the acquiescense of local residents must be developed. Economists naturally feel that compensation provides the key to solving the acquiescense issue, but implementing this abstract idea is far from trivial. How much compensation is to be awarded? Who is entitled to receive it? How much should each recipient receive? Establishing a framework for answering these questions and a process for implementing this framework remains a pressing need.

Controlling Toxic Substances

Regulating the amount and type of toxic substances introduced into the economic system is another of the most difficult issues to confront our social institutions. As if the latency of the damage caused by toxic substances and the scientific uncertainty about the relationships involved were not enough, the number of potential toxic substances involved is staggering.

Our society is currently evolving a complementary relationship among the economic system, the court system, and the legislative and executive branches of government which holds promise. We are, however, not yet out of the woods. More reliable, inexpensive screening devices need to be developed. Courts must develop procedures for handling liability in cases where the damage-causing activities took place many years earlier and where the causal chain from activity to damage is less than completely proven. Significantly, the public must learn that part of the risk is theirs. The government cannot and should not provide a risk-free environment.

The toxic-substance problem provides an excellent opportunity to reassess the contrast between the role of values and the role of process in environmental decision making. By this point it should be clear that process bears a major share of the responsibility for our environmental problems. Persons who yearn for efficient allocations may find themselves in circumstances where, as individuals, they are powerless to achieve the desired outcome. Allocations can occur that virtually no one would find desirable.

Yet it would be a mistake to say that all values are equally acceptable, leaving it up to the government to produce harmony. The plain fact of the matter is that not all behavior can be regulated. It costs too much to catch every offender. Our law enforcement system works because most people obey the law, whether anyone is watching or not. A high degree of voluntary compliance is essential if the system is to work smoothly.

The best resolution of the toxic-substance problem is undoubtedly for all makers of potentially toxic substances to be genuinely concerned about the safety of their products and to bite the bullet whenever their research raises questions. The ultimate responsibility for developing an acceptable level of risk must rest on the integrity of those who make, use, transport, and dispose of the substances. The government can assist by penalizing and controlling those few who fail to exhibit this integrity, but it can never substitute for integrity on a large scale. We cannot and should not depend purely upon altruism to solve these problems, but we shouldn't underestimate its importance either.

The notion that we are at the end of an era may well be true. But we are also at the beginning of a new one. What the future holds is not the decline of civilization, but its transformation. As the opening quote to this chapter suggests, the road may be strewn with obstacles and our social institutions may deal with those obstacles with less grace and less finesse than we might hope for, but there seems little question that we are making progress.

PROBLEM SET ANSWERS

Chapter 2

1. (a) Net benefits are maximized where the demand curve intersects the marginal-cost curve. Therefore, the efficient q would occur when $80 - 1q = 1q$. Thus the efficient $q = 40$ units.
   (b) Draw the diagram. Draw a horizontal line from the place where the demand curve intersects the marginal-cost curve to the vertical axis. This intersection will take place at a price of $40. The net benefits can now be computed as the sum of the upper right triangle (the area under the demand curve and over this line) and the lower right triangle (the area under the price line and over the marginal-cost line). The area of a right triangle is $1/2 \times$ base $\times$ height. Therefore, the net benefits are $1/2 \times \$40 \times 40 + 1/2 \times \$40 \times 40 = \$1600$.

2. (a) Ten units would be allocated to each period.
   (b) $P = \$8 - 0.4q = \$8 - \$4 = \$4$
   (c) User cost $= P - MC = \$4 - \$2 = \$2$

3. Because in this example the static allocations to the two periods (those which ignore the effects on the other period) are feasible within the 20 units available, the marginal user cost would be zero. With a marginal cost of $4.00, the net benefits in each period would independently be maximized by allocating 10 units to each period. In this example there is no intertemporal scarcity so price would equal $4.00 marginal cost.

Chapter 3

1. (a) This is a public good, so add the 100 demand curves vertically. This yields $P = 1000 - 100q$. This demand curve would intersect the marginal cost curve when $P = 500$, which occurs when $q = 5$ miles.
   (b) The net benefits are represented by a right triangle where the height of the triangle is $500 ($1000, the point where the demand curve crosses the vertical axis, minus $500, the marginal cost) and the base is five miles. The area of a right triangle is $1/2 \times$ base $\times$ height $= 1/2 \times \$500 \times 5 = \$1250$.

2. (a) Consumer surplus $= \$800$. Producer surplus $= \$800$. Consumer plus producer surplus $= \$1600 =$ net benefits.
   (b) The marginal-revenue curve has twice the slope of the demand curve, so $MR = 80 - 2q$. Setting $MR = MC$ yields $q = 80/3$ and $P = 160/3$. Using Figure 3.8 producer surplus is the area under the price line (FE) and over the marginal-cost line (DH). This can be computed as the sum of a rectangle (formed by FED and a horizontal line drawn from D to the vertical axis) and a triangle (formed by DH and the point created by the intersection of the horizontal line drawn from D with the vertical axis).

   The area of any rectangle is base $\times$ height. The base $= 80/3$ and the

$$\text{height} = P - MC = \frac{160}{3} - \frac{80}{3} = \frac{80}{3}.$$

Therefore, the area of the rectangle is 6400/9. The area of the right triangle is

$$1/2 \times \frac{80}{3} \times \frac{80}{3} = \frac{3200}{9}.$$

$$\text{Producer surplus} = \frac{3200}{9} + \frac{6400}{9} = \frac{\$9600}{9}.$$

$$\text{Consumer surplus} = 1/2 \times \frac{80}{3} \times \frac{80}{3} = \frac{\$32000}{9}.$$

(c)   1. $\frac{\$9600}{9} > \$800$ 2. $\frac{\$3200}{9} < \$800$ 3. $\frac{\$12800}{9} < \$1600$

Chapter 4

1. In order to maximize net benefits, Coast Guard oil spill prevention enforcement activity should be increased until the marginal benefit of the last unit equals the marginal cost of providing that unit. Efficiency requires that the level of the activity be chosen so as to equate marginal benefit with marginal cost. When marginal benefit exceeds marginal cost (as in this example), the activity should be expanded.
2. (a) According to the figures given, the per-life cost of kidney transplants lies well under the implied value of life estimates given in the chapter, while per-life cost implied by the proposed standard for acrylonitrile lies well over those estimates. In benefit/cost terms the allocation of resources to kidney transplants should be increased, while the acrylonitrile standard should be relaxed somewhat to bring the costs back into line with the benefits.
   (b) Efficiency requires that the marginal benefit of a life saved in government programs (as determined by the implied value of a human life in that context) should be equal to the marginal cost of saving that life. Since the data given in the problem indicate that the marginal costs are much further apart than the marginal benefits, some equalization of marginal costs would be beneficial. Should all marginal costs be equal? Only if the marginal benefits are equal and, as we saw in the chapter, risk valuations (and hence the implied value of human life) depend on the risk context, so it is unlikely they are equal across all government programs.

Chapter 5

1. According to the microeconomic theory of fertility, the impact would be greater for tuition-funded education. With tuition funding, the cost of education for an additional child would be the present value of all tuitions paid. With property tax funding, the cost of education for an additional child would be miniscule; the amount the family would pay would depend on the value of their property, not on the number of children in the family. Hence the marginal cost of an additional child is higher with tuition funding, so the impact on the desired number of children would be larger.
2. It is a positive feedback loop. The rich typically have low fertility rates, while the poor typically have high fertility rates. High fertility rates among the por tend to widen the gap between rich and poor by increasing the supply of labor (placing downward pressure on wages, particularly unskilled wages) and by reducing the amount of resources committed to each child (thereby limiting future earning capacity).

Chapter 6

1. (a) With a demand curve shifting out over time, the marginal net benefits from a given future allocation increase over time. This raises the marginal-user cost (since it is the opportunity cost of using the resource now) and, hence, the total marginal cost. Thus the initial user cost would be higher.

   (b) Less of the resource would be consumed in the present; more would be saved for the future.

2. (a) This turns out to have the same effect as the environmental cost pictured in Figures 6.6a and 6.6b. The tax serves to raise the total marginal cost and, hence, the price. This tends to lower the amount consumed in all periods compared to a competitive allocation.

   (b) The tax also serves to reduce the cumulative amount extracted because it raises the marginal cost of each unit extracted. Some resources which would have been extracted without the tax would not be extracted with the tax; their after-tax cost to the producer exceeds the cost of the substitute. The price would be higher with the tax in all periods prior to the without-tax switch point. After that time the price would be equal to the price of the substitute with or without the tax.

Chapter 7

1. During a recession the demand curve shifts inward. If price is held constant, then the quantity demanded is reduced. Since the burden of holding the price up falls on the cartel, while the competitive fringe can keep on producing, the demand reduction causes production to fall most heavily in OPEC nations. This causes the cartel market share to fall. To protect their individual market shares, members start cutting prices. In growing markets cartel market shares can be protected without cutting price.

2. (a) Producer surplus $= \dfrac{\$3200}{9}$ $P = MC = \dfrac{\$80}{3}$

   Consumer surplus $= \dfrac{\$9600}{9}$ $q = \dfrac{80}{3}$

   (b) This is the mirror image of the monopoly allocation. The net benefits are identical in the two allocations, but they are distributed among producers and consumers rather differently. With this form of price control, the consumer surplus is larger and the producer surplus is smaller than the corresponding concepts when the allocation is governed by a monopoly. Essentially, the rectangle discussed in the answer to part (b) the second problem in Chapter 3 goes to consumers with price ceilings and to producers in a monopoly.

3. The paper company. The high-cost energy is appropriately assigned to the five paper machines because that is the energy cost that would be eliminated if the machines were shut down. The company would not shut down all energy sources in proportion; it would shut down the most expensive sources. In making a shutdown decision, therefore, it is essential that the machines in question cover the cost of the energy which would be saved if the machines were shut down; otherwise the company is losing money.

4. Peaking plants run only a small percentage of the time, so the capital expenditures remain unused most of the time. Operating costs are incurred only when they are needed. It makes sense therefore for utilities to design peaking plants so as to keep capital cost as low as possible, even if it means incurring higher operating cost. Base load plants on the other hand run almost continuously so the capital costs are prorated over a very large number of kilowatt-hours and therefore are less of a burden.

Chapter 8

1. (a) Assume that only virgin ores are used. In this case $P = MC_1$, so $10 - 0.5q_1 = 0.5q_1$ or $q_1 = 10$. This implies $MC_1 = 5$. The marginal cost of producing any units using recycled products is clearly higher than five, so none will be used. Therefore, ten units would be produced and all of them would be produced using virgin ores.

   (b) With the higher demand curve the price will be high enough to stimulate the producer to make some of the product with recycled materials. The key to solving this problem is provided by Figure 8.4, where it can be seen that the producer will equate the marginal costs of products made with recycled materials and those made with virgin ores. Using this fact we can set $0.5q_1 = 5 + 0.1q_2$ or $q_1 = 10 + 0.2q_2$. Substituting this into the demand function yields $P = 20 - 0.5(10 + 0.2q_2 + q_2)$ or $P = 15 - 0.6q_2$. Solving for $P = MC$ yields $15 - 0.6q_2 = 5 + 0.1q_2$ or $q_2 = \dfrac{100}{7}$ and

$$q_1 = 10 + 0.2 \left(\frac{100}{7}\right) = \frac{90}{7}.$$

   This solution can be verified by showing $P = MC_1 = MC_2 = \dfrac{45}{7}$.

2. (a) They will not have the same effect. Because the royalty is a per-ton fee, it raises the marginal cost of extraction to the firm, but the bonus bid, which does not affect the marginal cost of extraction, does not. If the mineral has an increasing marginal cost of extraction, less will be extracted with a royalty system than with a bonus bid system because the marginal cost of extraction (including the royalty payment) will hit the backstop price at a smaller cumulative amount extracted.

   (b) The bonus bid is consistent with efficiency because it does not distort the allocation over time. The allocation which maximized firm profits before the bonus bid will still maximize it after the bonus bid. While the government shares the profits, it does it without distorting incentives. By raising the marginal cost of extraction, royalty schemes distort incentives.

   (c) With a bonus bid scheme the firm bears the risk. The government gets a fixed payment. The firm can either win big or lose big, depending on how valuable the deposit turns out to be. With the royalty scheme, the risk is shared. If the mine turns out to be very valuable, profits and government fees both go up. If the deposit turns out not to be very valuable, the firm gains little but so does the government.

Chapter 9

1. Since the amount of capacity needed would depend on the maximum flow during the year, the extra cost of expanding capacity during this high-flow period should be reflected in higher prices charged to users during these periods.

Chapter 10

1. Norland has the comparative advantage in producing A. For every unit of A it produces Norland gives up *two* units of B. This is a lower opportunity cost than incurred by Souland which

gives up *three* units of *B* for each unit of *A* produced. Souland has a comparative advantage in producing *B*.

2. Food stamp programs give the poor more money to spend on food, thus shifting their demand curve for food to the right. Only if supply is perfectly inelastic would this shift in demand increase prices without increasing quantity sold. On the other hand, prices would normally rise somewhat unless the supply curve was perfeclty elastic. In general the more elastic the supply curve is, the larger would be the increase in quantity sold and the smaller would be the increase in prices for a given shift in demand.

Chapter 11

1. The plot being turned into a housing development would have the shortest rotation period because the cost of delaying the harvest would be greatest in this case. It would include an additional cost – the cost of delaying the construction of the housing development – that would have to be factored in, causing net benefits to be maximized at an earlier harvest age.
2. The cost trend is the result of two offsetting trends. Harvesting cost is a function of the volume of wood so it increases as the volume of wood increases. Since these costs are discounted, however, costs further in the future are discounted more. When the tree growth gets small enough, the discounting effect dominates the growth effect and the present values of the costs decline.

Chapter 12

1. (a) The maximum sustainable yield is obtained when the marginal benefit of an additional reduction in the population size is zero: $20P - 400 = 0$ or $P = 20$ thousand tons. The maximum sustainable yield can then be calculated using the g equation: $g = 4(20) - 0.1(20)^2 = 40$ tons.
   (b) The efficient sustained yield can be found by setting marginal cost equal to marginal benefit: $20P - 400 = 2(160 - P)$; therefore, $P = 32.7$, which is a larger population than that which would produce the maximum sustainable yield.
2. (a) No, despite the fact that this approach yields the efficient sustainable yield, this is not an efficient solution. Net benefits would not be maximized because costs would be too high. Everyone would have an incentive to capture as large a share of the quota for themselves as quickly as possible. This would lead to excessively large boats and would not guarantee that the fishermen who could catch the fish most cheaply would do the harvesting. The net benefits would be smaller than possible.
   (b) Yes, this would be efficient. This quota system creates exclusive property rights and, therefore, eliminates the need to catch as much as possible as soon as possible. Each fisherman can proceed on the most individually appropriate schedule because his or her share of the catch is guaranteed. Since the need to rush harvesting is eliminated, the need for excessively large boats is also eliminated. Fishermen with high harvesting costs would find it in their interest to sell their quotas to fishermen with low harvesting costs in order to maximize their return from their quota. These transfers guarantee that the fish are caught by those with the lowest harvesting costs so net benefits are maximized.

Chapter 14

1. (a) In a cost-effective allocation of emission reduction, the marginal control costs should be equal. So $200 q_1 = $100 q_2. Furthermore, the total reduction is 21 units so $q_1 + q_2 = 21$. Solving the first of these equations for q_1 yields $q_1 = 0.5q_2$. Substituting this into the second yields $0.5q_2 + q_2 = 21$. Solving this for q_2 results in $q_2 = 14$ and $q_1 = 7$.

   (b) From the text we know that in a cost-effective allocation with a single receptor
   $$\frac{MC_1}{a_1} = \frac{MC_2}{a_2}.$$

   Therefore, $\dfrac{\$200q_1}{2} = \dfrac{\$100q_2}{1}$. Furthermore, $a_1 (20 - q_1) + a_2 (20 - q_2) = 27$ or $2(20 - q_1) + (20 - q_2) = 27$. From the first equation it is clear that in a cost-effective allocation $q_1 = q_2$. It remains to derive the total amount of control using the second equation: $2(20 - q_1) + (20 - q_1) = 27$ so $q_1 = 11$ and $q_2 = 11$.

2. (a) From the text we know $T = MC_1 = MC_2$. From Problem 1(a) we know $MC_1 = MC_2 = \$1400$. Therefore $T = \$1400$.

   (b) Revenue $= T(20 - q_1) + T(20 - q_2) = \$1400(13) + \$1400(6) = \$26,600$.

Chapter 15

1. (a) There would be twelve permits issued, each worth 1 ppm. The price of the permit will be that price which will clear the market, i.e. $\dfrac{MC_1}{a_1} = \dfrac{MC_2}{a_2} = P$. We know that in equilibrium

   $$\frac{0.3q_1}{1.5} = \frac{0.5q_2}{1.0} \text{ or } q_1 = 2.5q_2$$

   Further, $a_1(20 - q_1) + a_2(20 - q_2) = 12$ or $1.5(20 - 2.5q_2) + 1.0(20 - q_2) = 12$. Solving this equation yields $q_2 = 8$ and $q_1 = 20$.

   $$\text{So } P = \frac{0.3(20)}{1.5} = \frac{0.5(8)}{1.0} = \$4 \text{ per ppm.}$$

   (b) Permits auctioned off

   $$\text{First source} = P(20 - q_1)a_1 = \$4(20 - 20)1.5 = \$0$$
   $$\text{Second source} = P(20 - q_2)a_2 = \$4(20 - 8)1.0 = \$48.$$

   The six permits are worth $24, so the first source would sell all its permits for a gain of $24. The second source would keep its initial allocation of six permits and would buy six more at a cost of $24. The cost to the second source exactly balances the gain to the first.

Chapter 16

1. The emission charge equalizes marginal cost, a required condition for cost-effectiveness. The subsidies incude utilities to choose options with a higher marginal cost. By equalizing their

after-subsidy marginal costs, utilities will minimize their outlays. This will not minimize total costs of control since a greater reliance on scrubbers will result than would be cost-effective.

2. High transfer costs in this context arise from a combination of high charges and large amounts of uncontrolled emissions. This circumstance arises when the marginal cost of control function rises steeply at relatively low levels of control. Since the charge is equal to the marginal cost of control, high marginal control costs imply a high charge rate. Furthermore, if the function rises steeply at relatively low levels of control, then there are large amount of emissions to which this high rate of charge is applied. Multiplying a high charge times a large amount of uncontrolled emissions yields high transfers costs.

Chapter 18

1. (a) This allocation would be similar to that in Problem 2(a) in Chapter 14. The price would be $1400. In the final allocation the first source would control seven units and would hold thirteen permits, where the second source would control fourteen units and hold six permits. The first source would have to purchase four permits—the thirteen it needs to minimize cost minus the nine it was initially given—at a total cost of $5600. The second source would sell four permits, thereby moving from the ten held initially to the six it needs to minimize costs, so it would gain $5600 from the sale.

   (b) We know that in the final equilibrium the marginal control costs will be equal. Since for the third source the marginal control cost is constant at $1600, this will determine the final marginal control cost. The final permit price will be $1600. The control allocation can be found for the first and second sources by choosing that level of control which yields a marginal control cost equal to $1600. Thus $1600 = $200q_1$ so $q_1 = 8$ and $1600 = $100q_2$, so $q_2 = 16$.

   The third source will have to clean up sufficient additional emissions to meet the target. Uncontrolled emissions were stated to be equal to 50. The first two sources would clean up 24 units, leaving 26 units uncontrolled. Since the target emission level is stated as 19 units, the third source would have to clean up the remaining seven units ($q_3 = 7$). The third source would have to purchase three permits, since it received no initial allocation. Two would be purchased from the second source and one would be purchased from the first.

NAME INDEX

Mill, John Stuart, 497n
Miller, G. Tyler, Jr., 2n
Miller, S. M., 483, 486, 488, 497
Mills, Edwin S., 404n
Molton, Lawrence S., 79n
Moore, Thomas Gale, 187n
Moroney, J. R., 294, 294n, 481
Morse, Chandler, 290, 291
Muir, John, 251
Mullen, John K., 365
Mulligan, Patricia J., 71n
Mushkin, Selma, 181n
Myers, Norman, 50n

Nichols, Albert L., 155n, 358, 360
Nixon, President Richard M., 84, 90, 156, 176
Noll, Roger G., 344, 345, 345n, 349
Nordhaus, William D., 379, 381, 502, 503
Norman, Colin, 150

O'Neil, William B., 71n, 419
Opaluch, James J., 422
Oster, Sharon M., 469

Packard, Vance, 188, 189n
Paddock, Paul, 215
Paddock, William, 215
Page, Talbot, 181n, 184n, 187
Palmini, Dennis J., 423
Pareto, Vilfredo, 25
Park, Rolla Edward, 165n
Pashigian, B. Peter, 461, 473
Pearse, Peter H., 275n
Pereira, Sir Charles, 228n
Peskin, Henry M., 74n, 467, 468, 469, 470
Pinchot, Gifford, 251, 280
Pindyck, Robert S., 148, 149, 294n
Pittman, Russell W., 461
Plotnick, R., 506
Pontecovo, G., 269n
Porat, Marc, 488n

Portney, Paul R., 392, 431, 432n, 434n, 436n
Posner, Richard A., 204, 441n
Powell, D., 40
Proxmire, Senator William, 80n

Rainwater, Lee, 504, 506, 507
Rawls, John, 32
Reagan, President Ronald, 64, 156n, 176
Reid, Robert O., 85
Reitze, Arnold W., Jr., 388n, 395n, 396, 396n
Repetto, Robert, 109
Ricardo, David, 43
Ricci, Paolo F., 79n
Ridker, Ronald G., 106n, 424
Roosevelt, President Theodore, 280
Rosenberg, Nathan, 286
Rubinoff, Ira, 253
Ruckelshaus, William, 391
Rucker, Randal R., 204n
Russell, Clifford S., 424
Russell, Milton, 159
Ryther, John H., 268n

Sabloff, Jeremy A., 2n
Salant, S. W., 150
Schaefer, M. B., 258
Schelling, Thomas C., 16
Schultz, Theodore W., 228n, 230
Schultze, Charles L., 414, 414n
Schulz, William, 378
Schulze, William D., 72n
Schumacher, E. F., 57
Seneca, Joseph J., 468
Seskin, Eugene P., 71n, 74n, 85, 341n, 392
Shepard, Lansing R., 253
Shepard, Michael, 376n
Sheridan, David, 198n
Simon, Cheryl, 175n
Simon, Julian L., 90, 101, 104, 487n
Skinner, B. J., 295–97
Slade, Margaret E., 300, 302
Smeeding, Timothy, 73n, 506

SUBJECT INDEX

Absorptive capacity, 307, 407, 409
Acceptable risk, 450–51
Acid rain, 157, 311–12, 362, 363–71, 519
Acrylonitrile, 356
Acute toxicity, 432
Adirondack acidification, 365
Adjusted income, 506
Aerobic process, 408
Aerosol propellants, 371, 372
Age structure effect, 95–97
Agent Orange, 445
Agricultural Trade Development and
 Assistance Act, 175
Agriculture
 economy and population growth, 106
 energy costs, 222
 and environmental costs, 222–23
 government intervention in, 230–31
 land allocation and global scarcity,
  221–22
 as a nonpoint source of pollution, 407
 pollution, 208, 423
 and price controls, 517
 and the price responsiveness of supply,
  229
 and sediment control, 470
 technological progress, 220
 undervaluation bias of, 228
Air pollution, 157, 308
Air pollution control
 global, 368, 377–81, 519
 mobile source, 384–86
  economic assessment of, 390–98
  federal policy toward, 386–90
  household costs of, 466–69
  political assessment of, 390–98
  reforms, 398–401
 regional, 368–71
 stationary source, 333–34
  acid rain, 157, 311–12, 362, 363–71
  banking, 348
  bubble policy, 346, 347–48
  criteria pollutants, 334–45

emission banking, 346
emission reduction credit, 346, 347
emission trading program, 345–57
household costs, 466–69
netting, 346, 348
offset policy, 346–47
Air Pollution Control Act of 1955, 333
Air-quality control regions, 335
Air-quality standards. See Ambient air-
 quality standards
Air resources
 market allocation of, 312–13
 and surface pollutants, 321
Airborne carcinogens, 355
Algeria, and OPEC, 145
Allocation. See Market allocation, Resource allocation
Aluminum, resource availability of, 292
Aluminum industry, old vs. new scrap,
 178
Aluminum poisoning, 364
Ambient air-quality standards, 334, 335,
 339, 340
 cost effectiveness of, 344–45
 and efficiency, 340–42
 offset policy, 346–47
 and tall stacks, 365–66
Ambient charge, 323, 324, 326–28
 and the least-cost method of allocating
  responsibility, 418
 many-receptors case, 325–26
 single-receptor case, 324
 and oxygen sags, 408
Ambient conditions, and water pollution
 control, 408
Ambient permit system, 324–28
 vs. emissions system, 348–49
 and the least-cost method of allocating
  responsibility, 418
 many-receptors case, 325–26
 single-receptor case, 324
 and oxygen sags, 408
Ambient standards, 321, 322, 413–14

Acknowledgments

p. 6 From *The Limits to Growth: A Report for The Club of Rome's Project on the Predicament of Mankind,* by Donella H. Meadows, Dennis L. Meadows, Jørgen Randers, William W. Behrens, III. A Potomac Associates book published by Universe Books, NY, 1972. Graphics by Potomac Associates. Reprinted by permission.

p. 10 "The Great Transition" from *The Next 200 Years* by Herman Kahn, William Brown, Leon Martl. Copyright © 1976 by Hudson Institute. Reprinted by permission of William Morrow & Company and Associated Business Press.

p. 99 From "Economic Effects of Chilean Fertility Decline" by Bruce H. Herrick in *Population, Public Policy, and Economic Development* by Michael C. Keeley. Copyright © 1976 by Praeger Publishers, Inc. Reprinted by permission.

p. 149 From "Gains to Producers from the Cartelization of Exhaustible Resources" by Robert S. Pindyck in *The Review of Economics and Statistics,* Vol. LX (May 1978): 238–251. Copyright © 1978 by the President and Fellows of Harvard College. Reprinted by permission of North-Holland Publishing Company.

p. 177 From "Assessing U.S. Vulnerability to Raw Material Supply Disruptions: An Application to Nonfuel Minerals" by Michael Hazilla and Raymond Kopp, *Southern Economic Journal,* Vol. 52, No. 2, p. 351 (October, 1984). Reprinted by permission.

p. 292 From *The Limits to Growth: A Report for The Club of Rome's Project on the Predicament of Mankind,* by Donella H. Meadows, Dennis L. Meadows, Jørgen Randers, William W. Behrens, III. A Potomac Associates book published by Universe Books, NY, 1972. Graphics by Potomac Associates. Reprinted by permission.

p. 297 From "The Assessment of Long-term Supplies of Minerals" by DeVerle P. Harris and Brian J. Skinner in *Explorations in Natural Resource Economics,* edited by V. Kerry Smith and John V. Krutilla. Copyright © 1982 by Resources for the Future, Inc. Published for Resources for the Future by The Johns Hopkins University Press. Reprinted by permission.

pp. 296–97 From "A Second Iron Age Ahead?" by B. J. Skinner in *American Scientist,* Vol. 64, 1976, pp. 263, 267. Reprinted by permission.

p. 303 From *Resource and Environmental Economics* by Anthony C. Fisher. Copyright © 1981 by Cambridge University Press. Reprinted by permission.

pp. 300, 302 From "Trends in Natural-Resource Commodity Prices: An Analysis of the Time Domain" by Margaret E. Slade from *Journal of Environmental Economics and Management* 9, 122–137 (1982). Copyright © 1982 by Academic Press, Inc. Reprinted by permission.

pp. 336, 345, 346 From *Emissions Trading: An Exercise in Reforming Pollution Policy* by T. H. Tietenberg. Copyright © 1985, Resources for the Future, Washington, DC. Reprinted by permission.

p. 380 From *Changing Climate: Report of the Carbon Dioxide Assessment Committee,* by William D. Nordhaus and Gary W. Yohe. Copyright © 1983 by National Academy of Sciences. Reprinted by permission.

p. 397 From *The Automobile and the Regulation of Its Impact on the Environment* by Frank P. Grad *et al.* Copyright © 1975 by the Trustees of Columbia University in the City of New York. Reprinted by permission of Frank P. Grad.

p. 419 From *Economics and the Environment* by Allen V. Kneese. Copyright © 1977 by Allen V. Kneese. Reprinted by permission of Penguin Books Ltd. and the author.

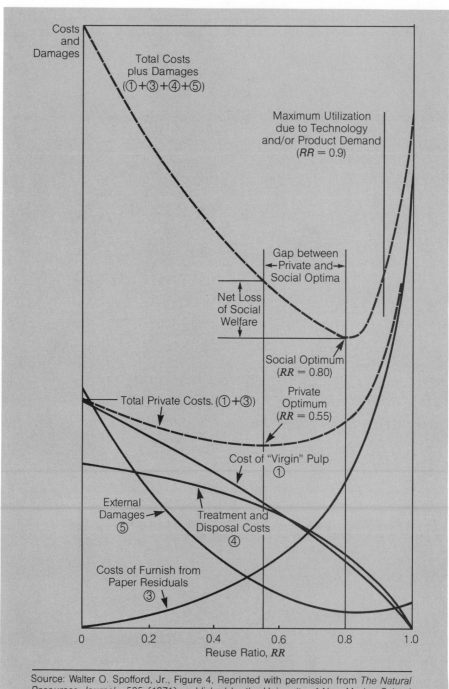

Costs and Damages

Total Costs plus Damages
(①+③+④+⑤)

Maximum Utilization due to Technology and/or Product Demand ($RR = 0.9$)

Gap between
←Private and→
Social Optima

Net Loss of Social Welfare

Social Optimum
($RR = 0.80$)

Private Optimum
($RR = 0.55$)

Total Private Costs. (①+③)

Cost of "Virgin" Pulp
①

External Damages
⑤

Treatment and Disposal Costs
④

Costs of Furnish from Paper Residuals
③

0   0.2   0.4   0.6   0.8   1.0

Reuse Ratio, RR

Source: Walter O. Spofford, Jr., Figure 4, Reprinted with permission from *The Natural Resources Journal*, 585 (1971), published by the University of New Mexico School of Law, Albuquerque, N.M.